A new chapter on intercultural communication.

Integrated coverage throughout the text and a new intercultural chapter (Chapter 3) drive home the effects that this dynamic area of study have on our interactions. Topics for study and discussion include cultural variations, social identity, group affiliation, intercultural communication challenges, and strategies for improving intercultural communication.

New, cutting-edge scholarship on mediated communication examines how we communicate *now*. ▶

The second edition incorporates exciting research and practical advice on communicating with technology. Special attention is paid to relevant topics like social networking, technology and privacy, and cyberbullying — as well as flaming and trolling.

texting for a specified period. Another remedy is to be mindful and considerate of others. You may think it's not a big deal to send text messages during a classmate's presentation in your human communication course, but if the roles were reversed, you might worry your speech was boring or that your skills as a speaker were truly lacking (Mello, 2009; Stephens & Davis, 2009). This point goes for interpersonal interactions as well—if you're texting Rodney or playing Words with Friends with Denise while you're engaged in a face-to-face conversation with Alex, you might be sending Alex an unintended message about how much (or how little) you value his company.

Sample Student Persuasive Speech 16.1

UNA CHUA
Tufts University

Preventing Cyberbullying

Appropriate attire and a sincere facial expression suit Una's serious topic.

On the evening of September 22, 2010, Rutgers University freshman Tyler Clementi updated his Facebook status: "Jumping off the gw [George Washington] Bridge sorry." A few hours later, he did just that. But what would cause Clementi, recognized as a bright student and talented musician with a promising future, to take his own life? The answer, unhappily, involves two bullies and a webcam.

According to a *New York Times* report, Clementi's roommate and a female acquaintance stand accused of invasion of privacy. The charge? Using a webcam to view and transmit private images of Clementi in an intimate encounter with another

---

◀ A new public speaking unit covers the essential skills, offers practical advice, and presents the best models for successful speeches.

New coverage offers more help with key challenges like researching, organizing and outlining, and informative vs. persuasive speaking. **New visually annotated student speeches** *show* delivery in action.

Real Communication

An Introduction

Real Communication

An Introduction

SECOND EDITION

DAN O'HAIR
University of Kentucky

MARY WIEMANN
Emeritus, Santa Barbara City College

With

DOROTHY IMRICH MULLIN
University of California, Santa Barbara

JASON J. TEVEN
California State University, Fullerton

Bedford/St. Martin's
Boston • New York

For Bedford/St. Martin's

Publisher for Communication: Erika Gutierrez
Senior Developmental Editor: Karen Schultz Moore
Contributing Editor: Ann Kirby-Payne
Senior New Media Editor: Tom Kane
Editorial Assistant: Mollie Laffin-Rose
Production Editor: Jessica Skrocki Gould
Senior Production Supervisor: Nancy Myers
Senior Market Development Manager: Sally Constable
Marketing Managers: Adrienne Petsick and Stacey Propps
Market Development Assistant: Diana Landes
Marketing Assistants: Alexis Smith and Allyson Russell
Copy Editor: Wendy Annibell
Indexer: Melanie Belkin
Photo Researcher: Susan McDermott Barlow
Permissions Manager: Kalina K. Ingham
Art Director: Lucy Krikorian
Text Design: Jerilyn Bockorick
Cover Design: Billy Boardman
Cover Photos: Getty Images
Composition: Cenveo Publisher Services/Nesbitt Graphics, Inc.
Printing and Binding: RR Donnelley and Sons

President: Joan E. Feinberg
Editorial Director: Denise B. Wydra
Director of Development: Erica T. Appel
Director of Marketing: Karen R. Soeltz
Director of Production: Susan W. Brown
Associate Director, Editorial Production: Elise S. Kaiser
Managing Editor: Shuli Traub

Library of Congress Control Number: 2011934519

6 5 4 3 2
f e d c b

For information, write: Bedford/St. Martin's, 75 Arlington Street, Boston, MA 02116
   (617-399-4000)

ISBN: 978-0-312-64420-8
ISBN: 978-1-4576-0279-5

preface

Now is a fascinating time to teach human communication. The field of interpersonal communication is evolving as new channels for communication develop; mediated communication is redefining the term *group*, making organizations flatter and generating new challenges for leadership and conflict management; public speaking is becoming a more crucial communication tool in too many professions to list; and the discipline as a whole is evolving at what seems like light speed, especially as scholars work to keep up with the profound changes wrought by technology. Our goal for *Real Communication* is to capture the dynamic and evolving nature of our discipline in a way that truly engages students while encouraging them to assess their own communication experiences and to consider the communication concepts at work in the world around them.

As scholars, we see communication concepts at work every day—in our interactions with others, in the screenplays of the films and TV shows we watch, in the carefully choreographed language of political campaigns, and in the subtle and blatant messages of advertising and marketing. But as instructors, we know that making these connections clear to students can be a challenge, especially in a course that requires us to cover diverse areas of the field (some of which may be outside of our area of expertise or research interest) all in approximately fourteen weeks. Perhaps the most disheartening comment we hear from students and from colleagues—who find themselves pressed for time and depending on their textbook to cover the basics—is that the course materials don't reflect real life or the real world. As one student told us some years ago, "I just don't see myself or anyone like me in the book we used. It's filled with examples about fake people. It's not real."

We developed *Real Communication* in response to those challenges. With this text, we wanted to reimagine the human communication course and what an effective textbook for it might look like. The answer came in addressing the course challenges: we have to make it real, make it relevant, and help students make sense of the course. This was the birth of *Real Communication: An Introduction,* inspired by our colleagues and students who reminded us that a truly effective book would give a cohesive view of human communication—and the discipline that studies it—and that it would feel, well, *real.* Books about hypothetical people will never drive home the point that effective, appropriate, and ethical communication can truly change our personal and professional lives.

The content of the book itself is the result of years of interactions, of communicating with students and colleagues, all in the service of creating the best possible introductory text. We include the strongest and most relevant scholarship—classic and cutting-edge. To create a truly innovative and effective learning tool for the introductory course, we applied the content and scholarship to real and compelling people. We talked to students, instructors, and professionals from around the country, seeking personal stories about how they used what they learned in the classroom. We searched countless media sources and real-world locations for inventive and intriguing ways to illustrate communication concepts at work. That is, the ways in which we see communication playing out in the world around us, whether in scenarios from reality television programs or examples taken from mainstream movies, the national political scene, or even visits to the grocery store. We involved instructors from all over the United States in reviews and discussion groups to get a true sense of what they want and need from a communication textbook. And as we followed up with students, both in our own classrooms and in focus groups around the country, we found them excited to engage with the scholarship and practice key skills in their own lives, making the discipline *relevant* in a whole new way. In response, we designed in-text pedagogical features and other learning tools to match. Finally, throughout the process, we looked for opportunities to draw more clear-cut connections between the various parts of our exceptionally broad discipline. On the one hand, we created unique pedagogical callouts that draw students' attention to important connections between different areas of communication; on the other, we carefully tailored coverage in the text itself to highlight the ways that fundamental principles help us understand widely divergent aspects of communication. Perception, for example, merits its own chapter, but we also show how it informs conflict management, public speaking, and interpersonal and organizational communication. By taking this approach, we encourage students to see that the value of these concepts goes well beyond their "assigned" chapter and applies to a variety of contexts students experience every day.

The overwhelming response to our first edition tells us that we were on to something. Over and over, we've heard from instructors and students that our approach—friendly, familiar, scholarly, and above all, *real*—provides a solid foundation for understanding and appreciating the nuances of modern communication in a way that is thought provoking, fun, and engaging. We are delighted to have heard from students who not only read our book, but keep thinking about what they've read long after they put it back on the shelf, applying the concepts they've learned to their own communication every day.

This positive response makes us even more excited about the new and improved second edition that you hold in your hand. We're confident that this text is an even better learning tool, from the cutting-edge scholarship, fresh examples, and new chapter on intercultural communication to the improved coverage of public speaking, expanded media program, and the new Mass Communication version of the text.

Features

The very *best* coverage of human communication. All of the coverage you expect from a human communication textbook is presented here in compelling fashion: self, perception, culture, language, nonverbal communication, listening, interpersonal relationships, interpersonal conflict, small group communication, and the fundamentals of public speaking. But we've also included topics and research relevant in today's fast-changing world, topics often underrepresented in competing texts: cyberbullying, organizational ethics, physical ability and public speaking, learning disabilities and listening, culture and language, nonverbal cues, mediated communication, and much more. And we consistently emphasize the concept of *competence* throughout, encouraging students to think about their verbal and nonverbal messages and the feedback they receive from their communication partners in the larger relational, situational, and cultural contexts.

***Real Communication* is, well, real**. It incorporates stories, tales, and interviews with former communication students plus insights and examples derived from communication scholars into each of the book's boxes, examples, and features. These rich materials ring true because they *are* true. And the book invites readers in with numerous self-examination features that allow them to consider their own experiences and evaluate their own communication skills.

Engaging examples—from pop culture and beyond—bring concepts to life and connect with students' lived experience. Today's students are interconnected as no generation has ever been. *Real Communication* harnesses this reality by illuminating communication concepts through students' shared experience of culture through novels, film, and TV; the viral language of the Internet; the borderless interactions of online social networking; and the influence of current events in an age of round-the-clock news. This perspective informs the examples, features, and overall voice with which we introduce the discipline.

Highlights *connections* among the different aspects of the course. On every page, *Real Communication* highlights ways that the different areas of our discipline support and inform one another. Along with relevant coverage in the main text and running examples that in some cases span several chapters, marginal CONNECT notes throughout the book help students truly make sense of the human communication course—and the discipline. These unique callouts draw *concrete links* between coverage areas in different parts of the text—for example, explaining that understanding interpersonal conflict can lead to improved leadership in a small group or that the steps students take to organize a speech can help them organize a group meeting.

Learning tools and apparatus that help students understand, internalize, and practice communication concepts and skills.

▶ **Attention-grabbing opening and closing vignettes.** Each chapter of *Real Communication* is bookended with a topic that we think will resonate with students, from viral sensation Susan Boyle (Chapter 2) to the unique relationship challenges faced by women and men whose spouses are on active military duty (Chapter 7). At the end of each chapter, we revisit the opening story to show students how the principles and theories they've learned apply to the opening example.

▶ **Critical thinking boxes on ethics, culture, and technology.** From the ethics of critiquing a speaker's physical ability to the struggle to create group cohesion on a multilingual baseball team to the wise use of presentation software, the boxes in *Real Communication* offer students the opportunity to think critically about the ways in which communication concepts play out in a variety of situations.

▶ **Unique features provide personal takes on communication.** In each chapter, Real Communicator boxes highlight how real people improved their lives by applying communication concepts. These interviews with real people explore the countless ways in which the application of communication concepts improves our lives, from novelist Matt Burgess struggling with publicity interviews to Anna Capps overcoming her hearing challenges to deliver a killer speech. And throughout the text, What About You? self-assessments and marginal And You? questions prompt students to build self-awareness and assess their own communication in light of research.

▶ **Powerful study tools for student success.** The Real Reference study tool at the end of each chapter contains a focused overview of the chapter's key concepts and terms, linked to specific pages in the chapter. Before each Real Reference, Things to Try activities encourage students to further explore the concepts and principles presented in the chapter.

What's New in the Second Edition?

Our goal for this second edition of *Real Communication* was not merely to keep up with our dynamic field, but to invite students to consider their own roles in creating and defining the rules of communication in the twenty-first century. To help us meet this challenge, we were delighted to bring on board two wonderful contributors, Dorothy ("Dolly") Imrich Mullin, of the University of California, Santa Barbara, and Jason J. Teven, of California State University, Fullerton. As noted scholars and course coordinators at their respective schools, Dolly and Jason were well prepared to help us remain on the cutting edge of both communication research and student experience. Dolly reviewed every chapter to add relevant scholarship and examples on mediated communication and wrote the Mass Communication chapter for the alternate edition of *Real Communication*. Her contributions to the new chapter on Intercultural Communication were vital to that chapter's development. Jason helped us to revitalize the Public Speaking unit, expanding the scholarship with relevant studies, adding enlightening new examples, and reorganizing coverage to better suit the way instructors teach public speaking today. We are indebted to both Jason and Dolly for their ideas, good humor, and excellent work. With their help, along with lots of great feedback from instructors and students who used the first edition, we made changes large and small to keep *Real Communication* fresh, relevant, engaging, and enlightening.

UPDATED scholarship throughout. We've pulled together the latest research on a host of topics to ensure that *Real Communication* is up-to-date and thorough. Fascinating new studies keep the book in tune with this dynamic discipline by offering insights and statistics on topics ranging from the relationship between language and listening to new findings about cell phone and broadband usage.

NEW Chapter 3, Communication and Culture. As in the first edition, we've endeavored to offer a detailed, relevant discussion of culture in every chapter. But in this second edition, we've also added a new chapter on this exciting and increasingly relevant topic. Thoughtful examination of concepts like social identity and salience are illustrated with fascinating, real-world examples like the It Gets Better Project and an examination of gender and online gaming. Examples from popular culture (*Glee, Slumdog Millionaire*) drive home the dynamic nature of intercultural encounters and offer opportunities to critique intercultural communication in a familiar way.

NEW enhanced coverage of mediated communication. Students often seem ahead of the curve on using new technologies to communicate, but as scholars, we want them to think more critically about how the nature of media channels affects their communication experience. Throughout the second edition, we've added scholarship and examples that help students understand the unique challenges and opportunities that mediated communication brings. Topics most interesting to students—social networking, technology and privacy, cyberbullying, flaming and trolling, and more—get special attention.

A BROADER RANGE of fresh examples from the real world and popular culture. Instructors and students have universally praised *Real Communication*'s use of real-life stories to drive home the importance of human communication. The second edition illuminates key concepts through hot topics (from the effects of the BP oil spill to perceptions of the Tea Party) and familiar faces (from Michelle Obama and John McCain to Neil deGrasse Tyson and Steve Jobs). And of course, the new edition is chock full of brand-new popular culture examples—from *Parks and Recreation* and *Jersey Shore* to *Inception* and *The Help*—that prompt students to compare the fictionalized universes of their favorite films, shows, and novels to the real, true principles of communication scholarship.

STRONGER and more practical coverage of public speaking. We've thoroughly revised the Public Speaking unit to offer more practical help with the issues and skills students find most challenging. The new edition offers new step-by-step guidelines on a host of key topics from researching, outlining, and developing presentation aids to incorporating verbal citations and avoiding plagiarism. New **visually annotated informative and persuasive student speeches** now *show* rather than just tell students how to achieve proper delivery skills like eye contact and body movements. And, as users have come to expect, both speeches offer helpful annotations on the speech text that point out organizational patterns, main points, transitions, and so on.

NEW Mass Communication edition available. For instructors who cover mass communication in their human communication course, we are happy to make available an alternate version of *Real Communication* with a **NEW** chapter devoted to the subject. This alternate edition offers students a solid and exciting overview of media convergence, mediated communication, media messages, and media effects, with all the features and real-world examples you've come to expect from *Real Communication*. To order this version of the text, use ISBN 978-0-312-60577-3.

EXPANDED ancillary and media package offers solutions for busy instructors and students. No matter how you teach your human communication class and no matter how much teaching experience you have, *Real Communication* offers you the best, most flexible support. In addition to our **updated** instructor's manual, test bank, free book companion site, and course management offerings, we also provide a large assortment of premium media solutions, including a variety of digital formats that can be used on a computer, tablet, or e-reader; hundreds of videos on *VideoCentral: Human Communication*; speech-building tools; the ability to upload and comment on video; and a **new** *HumanCommClass* (see page xi for more details).

Ancillaries

We are pleased to offer a complete set of media and print supplements to support instructors and students in the human communication course. For more information on these resources or to learn more about package options, please visit the online catalog at **bedfordstmartins.com/realcomm/catalog**.

Media Ancillaries

Book companion site for *Real Communication* at bedfordstmartins.com/realcomm, by Cassandra Carlson (University of Wisconsin, Madison). The student portion of the companion Web site offers a host of free resources and study tools to help students review concepts and prepare assignments. These include chapter outlines and review quizzes, activities, sample speeches and help with speech topic selection, RSS feeds of top news stories, and tools for researching and building a bibliography. Through the book companion site, instructors can also access a wealth of useful teaching tools, including chapter-by-chapter Power-Point slides and more. See the Resources for Instructors section on page xii for more information.

The book companion Web site is also the gateway to *Real Communication*'s premium media resources. Each resource has been carefully developed to support students' learning. Access to these tools can be packaged free or purchased on its own.

▶ *VideoCentral: Human Communication*. More than two hundred short video clips illustrating *Real Communication*'s most important terms and more than twenty videos of full-length speeches help students visualize, understand, and apply key concepts from the text.

▶ *The Bedford Speech Outliner* walks students through the process of building an outline, offering targeted help along the way.

▶ *The Audio Relaxation Download* helps students calm their nerves before giving a speech. This great feature can be downloaded onto students' computers or MP3 players.

***Real Communication e-Book* and digital options**. The Bedford e-book for *Real Communication* includes the same content as the print book and allows students to add their own notes and highlight important information. Instructors can customize the e-book by adding their own content and deleting or rearranging chapters. A variety of other digital versions of *Real Communication* are available that can be used on a computer, tablets like the iPad, or e-readers like the Nook. For more information, see **bedfordstmartins.com/ebooks**.

New *HumanCommClass for Real Communication* at yourhumancommclass .com. *HumanCommClass* is designed to support students in all aspects of the introduction to communication course. It's fully loaded with an e-book, hundreds of video clips and full sample speeches from *VideoCentral: Human Communication*, outlining and relaxation tools, learning modules, and multiple opportunities for students to assess their learning. Even better, new functionality makes it easy to upload and annotate video, embed YouTube™ clips, and create video assignments for the individual student, for groups, and for the whole class. *HumanCommClass* is a fully customizable course space that lets you mix and match our premium content and tools with your own to create the best experience for your students.

Content for course management systems and professional speeches on DVD and VHS are also available for instructors. See the Resources for Instructors section on page xii for more information.

Student Ancillaries

For more information on the student resources or to learn more about package options, please visit the online catalog at **bedfordstmartins.com/realcomm/ catalog**.

The Essential Guide to Intercultural Communication by Jennifer Willis-Rivera (University of Wisconsin, River Falls). This useful guide offers an overview of key communication areas, including perception, verbal and nonverbal communication, interpersonal relationships, and organizations, from a uniquely intercultural perspective. Enhancing the discussion are contemporary and fun examples drawn from real life as well as an entire chapter devoted to intercultural communication in popular culture.

The Essential Guide to Rhetoric by William M. Keith (University of Wisconsin, Milwaukee) and Christian O. Lundberg (University of North Carolina, Chapel Hill). This handy guide is a powerful addition to the public speaking portion of the human communication course, providing an accessible and balanced overview of key historical and contemporary rhetorical theories. Written by two leaders in the field, this brief introduction uses concrete, relevant examples and jargon-free language to bring concepts to life.

The Essential Guide to Presentation Software by Allison Ainsworth (Gainesville State College) and Rob Patterson (University of Virginia). This guide shows students how presentation software can be used to support but not overtake their speeches. Sample screens and practical advice make this an indispensable resource for students preparing electronic visual aids.

Outlining and Organizing Your Speech by Merry Buchanan (University of Central Oklahoma). This student workbook provides step-by-step guidance for preparing informative, persuasive, and professional presentations and gives students the opportunity to practice the critical skills of conducting audience analysis, dealing with communication apprehension, selecting a speech topic and purpose, researching support materials, organizing and outlining, developing introductions and conclusions, enhancing language and delivery, and preparing and using presentation aids.

Media Career Guide: Preparing for Jobs in the 21st Century, **8th edition,** by Sherri Hope Culver (Temple University) and James Seguin (Robert Morris University). Practical and student-friendly, this guide includes a comprehensive directory of media jobs, practical tips, and career guidance for students considering a major in communication studies and mass media.

Research and Documentation in the Electronic Age, **5th edition,** by Diana Hacker (Prince George's Community College) and Barbara Fister (Gustavus Adolphus College). This handy booklet covers everything students need for college research assignments at the library and on the Internet, including advice for finding and evaluating Internet sources.

Resources for Instructors

For more information or to order or download the Instructor Resources, please visit the online catalog at **bedfordstmartins.com/realcomm/catalog.**

Instructor's Resource Manual by Jennifer Willis-Rivera (University of Wisconsin, River Falls) contains helpful tips and teaching assistance for new and seasoned instructors alike. Content includes learning objectives, lecture outlines, general classroom activities, advice for teaching from the boxed pedagogy and CONNECT features, review questions, and additional resource films, as well as suggestions for setting up a syllabus, tips on managing your classroom, and general notes on teaching the course.

Print and Electronic Test Bank by Al Golden (Joliet Junior College). *Real Communication* offers a complete testing program, available in print and also for the Windows and Macintosh environments. Each chapter includes multiple-choice, true-or-false, short-answer, and essay questions keyed to various levels of difficulty.

Content for course management systems. Adopters can access content specifically designed for *Real Communication* like quizzing, activities, and course management systems such as WebCT and Blackboard. Use our most popular content in your own course management system. Visit **bedfordstmartins.com/cms** for more information.

PowerPoint Slides by Jill Rembetski provide support for important concepts addressed in each chapter, including graphics of key figures and models for class discussion. The slides are available for download from the instructor area of the Web site at **bedfordstmartins.com/realcomm**.

ESL Students in the Public Speaking Classroom: A Guide for Teachers by Robbin Crabtree (Fairfield University) and Robert Weissberg (New Mexico State University). As the United States increasingly becomes a nation of nonnative speakers, instructors must find new pedagogical tools to aid students for whom English is a second language. This guide specifically addresses the needs of ESL students in the public speaking arena and offers instructors valuable advice for helping students deal successfully with the unique challenges they face. Free to adopters.

Professional and student speeches. Available in DVD and VHS formats, Volume 19 of the esteemed Great Speeches series offers dynamic professional speeches for today's classroom, featuring such compelling speakers as Bill Clinton, Christopher Reeve, and the Dalai Lama. Additional professional videos are available from the Bedford/St. Martin's Video Library. In addition, three videotapes of student speeches (featuring students of varying abilities from Texas Tech and the University of Oklahoma) provide models for study and analysis. These professional and student speech resources are free to qualified adopters. Please contact your sales representative for more information.

Coordinating the Communication Course: A Guidebook, by Deanna Fassett and John Warren, offers the most practical advice on every topic central to the coordinator/director role. Starting with setting a strong foundation, this professional resource continues on with thoughtful guidance, tips, and best practices on crucial topics such as creating community across multiple sections, orchestrating meaningful assessment, hiring and training instructors, and more. Model course materials, recommended readings, and insights from successful coordinators make this resource a must-have for anyone directing a course in communication.

Customize *Real Communication*. Add your own content or more of ours. Qualified adopters can create a version of *Real Communication* that exactly matches their specific needs. Learn more about custom options at **bedfordstmartins.com/Catalog/other/Custom_Solutions**.

Acknowledgments

First and foremost, we owe a great deal of gratitude to our families and friends who supported us and listened to us as we worked through ideas for the book, who made us laugh during bouts of writer's block, and who were understanding when we had to cancel plans to meet deadlines. So thank you, Mary John, Erica, and Jonathan, as well as John, Molly, Chad, William, Jackson, John, and Andrea. You will always remain our litmus tests for just how real our communication is across its many applications. In addition, we both wish to credit and thank Gus Friedrich and John Wiemann, whose contributions to this book and our discipline are far too many to list. Thanks also to John O'Loughlin of HR Capital Partners and vice-president of Global Human Resources at SkinIt, for consulting on and reviewing the Interviewing Appendix. And of course, we must thank our students—including Daniel Bernard, Cory Cunningham, Kim Potts, Vanessa

Gonzales, Cynthia Inda, and Michel Haigh, among countless others—who continue to inspire us as teachers. We're grateful for the frank discussions that have opened our eyes to many of the challenges of this course from your point of view, and we are grateful for your helpful and thoughtful suggestions on examples.

We are likewise grateful to several colleagues who contributed to the first edition of *Real Communication*: Marion Boyer of Kalamazoo Valley Community College; Charee Mooney of Arizona State University; Celeste Simons of the University of Texas at Austin; Michele Wendell-Senter of the Art Institute of Washington; and Bobette Wolesensky of Palm Beach Community College.

We would also like to thank everyone at Bedford/St. Martin's who helped make this book possible, including President Joan Feinberg, Editorial Director Denise Wydra, Director of Development Erica Appel, and Director of Production Sue Brown. We owe a particular debt of gratitude to our editorial colleagues at Bedford: Publisher Erika Gutierrez for her leadership and passion for education; Senior Development Editor Karen Schultz Moore for her creativity, tenacity, constructive advice, calmness, and vision to create a book that truly reaches students; Contributing Editor Ann Kirby-Payne for her talent, dedication, and sense of humor that can be felt on each page of the book; Editorial Assistant Mollie Laffin-Rose for her artistic eye in organizing and executing our stunning art program; and Media Editor Tom Kane for managing all of the video material with professionalism and grace. Without the production staff at Bedford, this manuscript would be nothing more than black words on white paper fresh from our printers (with quite a few typos to boot!). So we thank Managing Editor Shuli Traub for her leadership; Project Editor Jessica Gould for her calm dedication and superior organizational skills; Associate Director, Editorial Production Elise S. Kaiser; Production Manager Marilyn Doof; and Senior Production Supervisor Nancy Myers for making a seemingly impossible schedule actually happen. Also, we credit our copy editor, Wendy Annibell; our proofreaders, Elizabeth Gardner and Lori Lewis; Art Director Lucy Krikorian; cover designer Billy Boardman; the designer of this beautiful book, Jerilyn Bockorick of Nesbitt Graphics; our permissions specialists, Linda Winters and Eve Lehmann; and our capable photo researcher, Sue McDermott Barlow. Finally, we wish to thank Bedford's extraordinary marketing staff for their incredible commitment and excitement about our book—and their willingness to share that excitement with others: Director of Marketing Karen R. Soeltz, Senior Marketing Manager Adrienne Petsick, Marketing Manager Stacey Propps, Senior Market Development Manager Sally Constable, Marketing Assistants Alexis Smith and Allyson Russell, and Market Development Assistant Diana Landes. We also thank Designer Kim Cevoli for our gorgeous marketing brochure.

Finally, books simply do not happen without the feedback and suggestions of respected colleagues who read drafts of every chapter and tell us what works and what doesn't. Thank you for being part of this process: Ritta Abell, Morehead State; Gabriel Adkins, Arkansas Tech University; Allison Ainsworth, Gainesville State College; Ashley Alfaro, Tarrant County College; Susan D. Allen, University of Maryland; Patricia Amason, University of Arkansas; Cory Armstrong, University of Florida; Doreen K. Baringer, Shippensburg University; Heather Aldridge Bart, Augustana College; Joanna Bauer, Kaplan University; Daniel Bernard, University of Oklahoma; Peter J. Bicak, Rockhurst

University; Cin Bickel, Laredo Community College; Brett Billman, Bowling Green State University; Shereen Bingham, University of Nebraska at Omaha; Tonya Blivens, Tarrant County College; Karen S. Braselton, Southern Illinois University; Jin Brown, University of Alaska Fairbanks; Jo Anne Bryant, Troy State University; Leah Bryant, DePaul University; Greg Carlisle, Morehead State University; Cassandra Carlson, University of Wisconsin–Madison; Mindy Chang, Western New England College; Leeva Chung, University of San Diego; Tim Cline, College of Notre Dame of Maryland; Tim Cole, DePaul University; Angela Cooke-Jackson, Eastern Kentucky University; Quinton Dale Davis, University of Texas at San Antonio; Jean M. DeWitt, University of Houston–Downtown; William Donohue, Michigan State University; Scott D'Urso, Marquette University; Jennifer Fairchild, Eastern Kentucky University; Diane Ferraro-Paluzzi, Iona College; Steve Forshier, Pima Medical Institute; Jodi Gaete, SUNY Suffolk; John Galyean, Abraham Baldwin Agricultural College; Randa Garden, Wayne State College; Tamara Gebelt, Keiser University; John R. Gillette, Lake City Community College; Al Golden, Joliet Junior College; LaKresha Graham, Rockhurst University; Jo Anna Grant, California State University, San Bernardino; Darlene Graves, Liberty University; Kelby K. Halone, University of Tennessee; Kay Hammond, Lindenwood University; Carla Harrell, Old Dominion University; Mike Hemphill, University of Arkansas, Little Rock; Thaddeus Herron, James Madison University; Emily Holler, Kennesaw State University; Gwen Hullman, University of Nevada, Reno; Jody Jahn, University of California, Santa Barbara; Laura Janusik, Rockhurst University; Maria Jaskot-Inclan, Wright College; Tibe Jordan, Keiser University; Andrea Joseph, University of California, Santa Barbara; Pamela Kalbfleisch, University of North Dakota; Erik Kanter, Virginia Tech; Charles Korn, Northern Virginia Community College, Manassas; Darci Kowalski, California State University, Fullerton; Bailey Lathem Kral, Palo Alto College; Gary Kuhn, Chemeketa Community College; Betty Jane Lawrence, Bradley University; Amy Lenoce, Naugatuck Valley Community College; Lois Leubitz, Cedar Valley College; Shirlee A. Levin, College of Southern Maryland; Justin Lipp, University of California, Santa Barbara; Louis A. Lucca, LaGuardia Community College (CUNY); Gilberto Martinez, Jr., Laredo Community College; Shana M. Mason, Dona Ana Community College; Joseph McGlynn III, University of North Texas; Anne McIntosh, Central Piedmont Community College; Robert Mild, Jr., Fairmont State University; Carol Montgomery, LaGuardia Community College (CUNY); Michael R. Moore, Morehead State University; Scott Moore, Fresno State University; Thomas P. Morra, Northern Virginia Community College; Alfred Mueller, Pennsylvania State University at Mont Alto; W. Benjamin Myers, University of South Carolina Upstate; Donald Nobles, Auburn University at Montgomery; Jessica A. Nodulman, Bowling Green State University; David Novak, Clemson University; Kekeli Nuviadenu, Bethune-Cookman University; Liz O'Brien, Phoenix College; Penelope J. O'Connor, University of Northern Iowa; Naomi Bell O'Neil, Clarion University of Pennsylvania; Jim L. Parker, Volunteer State Community College; John Parrish, Texas Christian University; Daniel M. Paulnock, Saint Paul College; Lisa Pavia-Higel, East Central College; Andrea Pearman, Tidewater Community College; Sandra Pensoneau-Conway, Wayne State University; Keith Perry, Abraham Baldwin Agricultural College; Lisa Peterson,

Boise State University; Evelyn Plummer, Seton Hall University; Bill Pogue, University of Houston–Downtown; Marlene Preston, Virginia Tech; Randall Reese, College of Western Idaho; Dan Rogers, Cedar Valley College; Kristen Ruppert-Leach, St. Charles Community College; Ethan Russell, Keiser University; Karin Russell, Keiser University; Lori Forneris Schahrer, Joliet Junior College; Juliann Scholl, Texas Tech University; David C. Schrader, Oklahoma State University; Jesse Schroeder, Northwestern Oklahoma State; Celeste DC Simons, the University of Texas at Austin; Sarah Smitherman, James Madison University; Debbie Sonandre, Tacoma Community College; Terri K. Sparks, Mesa Community College; Mark Steiner, the College of Wooster; Jane Sullivan, Jefferson College; Carol Teaff, West Virginia Northern Community College; Stephen Thompson, College of DuPage; Hank Tkachuk, Concordia College; Mary Anne Trasciatti, Hofstra University; Kristen P. Treinen, Minnesota State University; Judy Truitt, Volunteer State Community College; Becca Turner, Abraham Baldwin Agricultural College; Matthew Turner, Radford University; Tasha Van Horn, Citrus College; Jayne L. Violette, Eastern Kentucky University; Scott M. Vitz, Purdue University, Fort Wayne; Daniel Warren, Bellevue University; Kay Weeks, Abraham Baldwin Agricultural College; Michele Wendell, Northern Virginia Community College; Bruce Wickelgren, Suffolk University; Jennifer Willis-Rivera, University of Wisconsin–River Falls; Jim Wilson, Shelton State Community College; Michelle Witherspoon, Keiser University; Bobette Wolesensky, Palm Beach Community College; Catherine Wright, George Mason University; Alan Yabui, Bellevue Community College; Gustav Yep, San Francisco State University; Joe Zubrick, University of Maine at Fort Kent; and David Zuckerman, California State University, Sacramento.

We also offer a special thanks to our student reviewers who suggested examples, offered honest feedback about chapters, and unknowingly provided a great deal of encouragement. We may not know you personally, but we hope you feel personally invested in this project: Jazmine Brown, Virginia State University; Keegan Carroll, Cedar Valley College; Jennifer Colona, Hunter College; Chris D'Aprix, Palm Beach Community College; Graham Egan, University of Virginia; Cathy Guevara, Fordham University; Carla Parisi, University of Northern Iowa; Patrick Puckett, Eastern Kentucky University; Crystal Rubio, University of Houston; Lazya Silva, University of Houston; Victoria Skrip, Eastern Kentucky University; Jill Sweeney, University of Northern Iowa; Emily Van Gaasbeek, St. Olaf College; Bill West, Palm Beach Community College; Dov Zamore, New York University; Bart Zeligier, Farmingdale State College; and Philip L. Griffith, Meghan Hill, Tracy Mayfield, David Preston, and Alejandro Ramirez, from Gainesville State College.

about the authors

Dan O'Hair is dean of the University of Kentucky College of Communications and Information Studies. He is past presidential professor in the Department of Communication at the University of Oklahoma and past president of the National Communication Association. He is coauthor or coeditor of fifteen communication texts and scholarly volumes and has published more than eighty research articles and chapters in dozens of communication, psychology, and health journals and books. He is a frequent presenter at national and international communication conferences, is on the editorial boards of various journals, and has served on numerous committees and task forces for regional and national communication associations.

Mary Wiemann is professor emeritus in the Department of Communication at Santa Barbara City College in California. Her books, book chapters, journal articles, student and instructor manuals, and online instructional materials all reflect her commitment to making effective communication real and accessible for students. A recipient of awards for outstanding teaching, she is also a communication laboratory innovator and has directed classroom research projects in the community college setting. She serves on the editorial board of the *Journal of Literacy and Technology,* is a frequent presenter at the National Communication Association convention, and has held a number of offices in the Human Communication and Technology Division of that organization.

Dorothy "Dolly" Imrich Mullin is a continuing lecturer in the Department of Communication at the University of California, Santa Barbara. Her published research is in the area of media policy and effects. Her current focus is on teaching communication to undergraduates. She specializes in large introductory communication courses, including research methods and theory, and has been recognized for her efforts with a Distinguished Teaching Award. She also trains and supervises the graduate student teaching assistants, working to develop and promote excellent teaching skills among the professors of the future.

Jason J. Teven, an award-winning scholar and teacher, is professor of Human Communication Studies and the basic course coordinator at California State University, Fullerton. He has published widely in academic journals and is devoted to programmatic research and the social scientific approach to human communication, with research relating to credibility, caring, and social influence within instructional, interpersonal, and organizational communication contexts. His most recent scholarly activities include the examination of superior-subordinate relationships within organizations; communication competence; and the impact of personality traits on communication within the workplace and interpersonal relationships.

brief contents

contents

PART TWO

Interpersonal Communication *185*

PART THREE

Group and Organizational Communication 249

PART FOUR

Public Speaking *337*

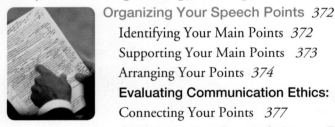

Real Communication

An Introduction

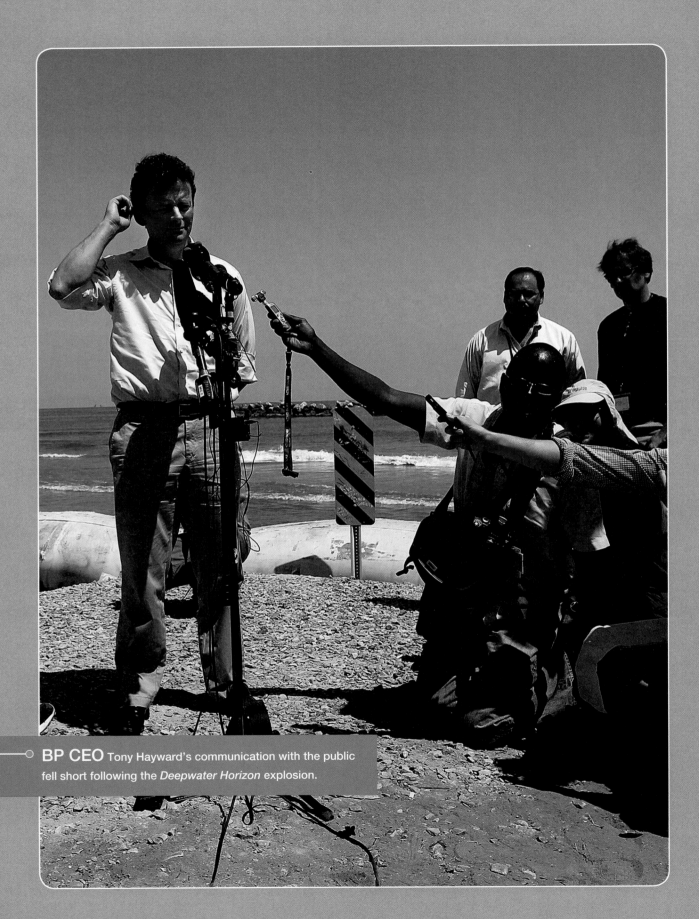

BP CEO Tony Hayward's communication with the public fell short following the *Deepwater Horizon* explosion.

Communication: Essential Human Behavior

It was, by any account, the very definition of a catastrophe: eleven men were killed on April 20, 2010, when an explosion rocked the BP drilling rig *Deepwater Horizon*, sparking a fire that was visible for more than thirty miles and burned for two days before the entire rig sank to the bottom of the Gulf of Mexico. In the aftermath of the initial disaster, the nation watched as millions of gallons of oil gushing from the blown-out rig began to assault wildlife, beaches, and the livelihoods of Gulf Coast residents still reeling from the Hurricane Katrina disaster five years earlier. As attempt after attempt to stop the leak failed, Americans, mourning the eleven lives and concerned about the immensity of the environmental disaster, were horrified when, on May 31, BP Chief Executive Tony Hayward told reporters, "We're sorry for the massive disruption it's caused. . . . There's no one who wants this over more than I do. I would like my life back" (Mouawad & Krauss, 2010, p. A1). When the embattled CEO spent a day watching his yacht compete in a big race the following month—with oil still spilling into the Gulf of Mexico at an alarming rate—one Alabama senator commented on Hayward's activity as the "height of arrogance," while a BP spokesperson said Hayward was just having some private time with his son (Robbins, 2010).

Outrage was focused not only on BP, but also on the U.S. government. Fingers were pointed in many directions. Some blamed BP; BP blamed Transocean (the company from which it rented the rig); others blamed the government agencies that had failed to enforce safety regulations (Barstow, Dodd, Glanz, Saul, & Urbina, 2010). Amid all the accusations and finger-pointing, a generation of Gulf Coast residents braced themselves for an even more uncertain future.

After you have finished
reading this chapter,
you will be able to

- Define the communica-
tion process

- Describe the functions
of communication

- Assess the quality
(communicative value)
of communication
by examining its six
characteristics

- Define what
communication
scholars consider
to be competent
communication

- Describe the visual
representations,
or models, of
communication

- Describe why
communication is vital
to everyone

Before we can analyze how communication affects our lives, we must be clear that **communication** is the process by which individuals use symbols, signs, and behaviors to exchange information. That process is real—and vitally important—so much so that communication is described as "the process through which the social fabric of relationships, groups, organizations, societies, and world order—and disorder—is created and maintained" (Ruben, 2005, pp. 294–295). Successful communication allows us to satisfy our most basic human needs, from finding food and shelter to functioning in our communities and developing meaningful relationships with others. Because communication is such a natural part of our daily lives, we often take it for granted and dismiss theories of communication as little more than common sense. Yet every day, communication failures lead to failed plans, isolation, misunderstandings, and hurt feelings. If communication were just common sense, then communication mishaps and failures wouldn't be so common or so potentially devastating, as the story of the BP disaster illustrates.

Communication challenges exist in every profession and every personal relationship. For example, communication professor (and reserve police officer) Howard Giles claims that 97 percent of law enforcement practices involve communication skills (Giles et al., 2006). But police academies usually spend little time teaching those skills and most citizens lack these crucial skills as well. One professor who teaches college-level communication classes to prisoners notes "the vast majority of my imprisoned students have been caged, in large part, because of their communicative illiteracy" (Hartnett, 2010, p. 68). Clearly, effective communication is essential in all aspects of life, but we seldom get the guidance needed to develop the necessary skills associated with it.

Throughout this chapter—and this book—we want you to take advantage of what you already know: your personal theories of how communication works. But we also want you to question and evaluate your theories against what social science tells us about the very complex communication process. In this way, you'll make the theories real for yourself and apply the best of what they have to offer to your personal communication situations. By doing this, you'll be better able to predict how your communication choices will affect *others* and why *their* communication choices affect *you* as they do. So let's get started by looking at why we communicate, how we communicate, and what it means to communicate well. Then we look at a few helpful models that assist in visualizing the communication process and provide an overview of the history of this very rich discipline.

We Must Communicate: The Functional Perspective

We communicate from the moment we're born. A baby's cry lets everyone within earshot know that something isn't right: there's an empty stomach or a missing blanket or an impending ear infection that needs to be taken care of. Throughout our lives, we'll dedicate a huge amount of time to the essential task of communicating with others in order to make sure that our needs are met—albeit in more sophisticated ways than we did as infants. We talk, listen,

BOX 1.1

COMMUNICATION IS *NOT* JUST COMMON SENSE

Everyone has ideas about what constitutes good communication. But just how correct are those ideas? Do your personal theories of communication match what social science tells us about the way we communicate? Consider the following questions:

▶ *Does talking equal effective communication?* Have you ever sat through a lecture only to find that your instructor was boring, unclear, disorganized, or even offensive? Talking is one way of giving information, but it isn't always effective on its own. To communicate effectively, we need to be thoughtful and to use silence, listening skills, and symbols other than words. When we do speak, we need to ensure that our words are effective.

▶ *Do body movements (often called "body language") constitute a language?* As you will learn in Chapter 5, nonverbal communication is important and useful, but there is no direct translation for what body movements mean. Because nonverbal communication can be interpreted in many different ways, it is not a true language.

▶ *Is more control necessarily better in communication?* While we admire people who can articulate their point of view, if we think they are trying to trick us or force us, we often resist what they are saying. Your father may stay on topic and clearly state his case against your choice of a major, for example, but he still can't make you do what he wants no matter how refined his intellectual skills may be.

▶ *Are most communication behaviors inborn and entirely natural?* No. Although we are certainly born with some ability to communicate, most of the skills we need in order to communicate must be learned—otherwise, we'd go through life crying whenever we needed something. We begin learning how to communicate during the first days of our life, and the best communicators never stop learning.

▶ *Is speaking well more important than listening?* An old conundrum asks, "If a tree falls in the woods and no one is there to hear it, does it make a sound?" Similarly, if you talk and nobody listens, has communication taken place? Communication is a two-way street, and listening is a crucial part of the process.

smile, and nod; we write up résumés and go on dates. In these ways, we ensure that we can learn, express ourselves, form relationships, and gain employment. This illustrates the **functional perspective** of communication, which examines how communication behaviors work (or don't work) to accomplish our goals in personal, group, organizational, or public situations. All communication "works" (or not) within the process of relationship formation. **Relationships** are the interconnections, or interdependence, between two or more people that function to achieve some goal. As the definition states, our relationships involve **interdependence**, meaning that what we do affects others and what others do affects us. For example, Jamie flips burgers to get a paycheck to help pay for college—that's her goal. Her boss depends on Jamie to do her job well and keep the business profitable. And the customers, who just want an inexpensive and quick lunch, depend on both of them. Jamie, the boss, and the lunch customers

● **ALL COMMUNICATION RELATIONSHIPS,** whether fleeting like a fund-raiser's exchange with a donor or more lasting like a familial relationship, involve interdependence.

are interdependent. Along the same lines, a communication relationship is one in which the interdependence is specifically based on the exchange or sharing of symbolic information.

A long line of research conducted in a variety of contexts—including work groups, families, and friendships—has found that virtually all communication behavior serves one or more primary functions, such as expressing affiliation, achieving goals, or influencing others (Wiemann & Krueger, 1980). Let's take a closer look at each of these functions of communication, keeping in mind that they are often intertwined.

Expressing Affiliation

Affiliation is the affect, or feelings, you have for others. You show how much you want to be connected to or associated with someone by expressing liking, love, or respect—or, alternatively, dislike, hatred, or disrespect (Wiemann, 2009). This love-hate continuum functions to establish and maintain relationships happily (or unhappily).

Affiliation serves a number of beneficial functions. For one, it simply feels good to be loved, liked, and respected. But affiliation may also meet practical needs, as when you marry someone you believe can offer a stable and secure life. Other times your expression of affiliation fulfills emotional needs, offering companionship or intellectual stimulation (or both).

Affiliation can be expressed in many different ways, both verbal ("I love you") and nonverbal (a big hug), and through face-to-face or mediated channels (like sending text messages or using social networking sites). In fact, we are increasingly using media technologies as ways to develop and maintain a positive affiliation with each other (Walther & Ramirez, 2009), especially when

AND YOU?

Have you ever been in a relationship in which you liked someone, but disliked some things about the person? How did you balance your expressions of liking, love, and respect with the more negative expressions?

people are far away physically. A "U can do it!" text message from Mom can be just the thing her daughter needs right before her midterm, and a simple click of the "Like" thumbs-up icon on Facebook can show that you enjoy something a friend posted.

Achieving Goals

If you've ever watched a show like *Hell's Kitchen* or *Top Chef,* you know that becoming a successful chef involves far more than just cooking skills: your risotto may indeed be perfect, but if you don't get it to the table at the same moment that the pan-seared foie gras is done, the meal will be a flop. Completing such tasks relies on communication. Without communication, such things as becoming educated, getting a job, and completing a variety of tasks, from simple business transactions to huge group-oriented projects (like preparing meals to order for large groups of people), would be impossible. We rely on communication in order to accomplish particular objectives, a function we call **goal achievement**.

● **CONTESTANTS IN DEMANDING COMPETITIONS** such as *Hell's Kitchen* know that it would be impossible to achieve goals without cooperation and clear communication.

   Communication that is highly goal- or task-oriented focuses on being practical and getting the job done. There are usually multiple goals at play in any given situation. For example, you may want to host Thanksgiving this year to illustrate your adult status in the family, but your mother-in-law may insist on keeping the holiday at her home out of tradition. If both relational partners are interdependent, they will likely try to accomplish their goal without losing the affection of their relational partner. In addition, goals may change over the course of the communication encounter; you may think you want to host Thanksgiving, but then realize you don't want that responsibility. Goals may be achieved in a variety of ways, too; you might make straightforward requests to accomplish goals, you might try to bully your way to the end you want, or you might be indirect, hinting at what you want or giving others a "guilt trip" in which you manipulate them to get your goals accomplished.

Influencing Others

One of the most important functions of communication is the ability to influence people. Virtually every communication is influential in one way or another: a politician's behavior during a press conference influences the way voters perceive her; Michael's lack of eye contact and quiet voice influence his professor's opinion of him during their interaction after class. You don't need to *decide* to influence someone; influence can be completely unintentional.

   The ability of one person, group, or organization to influence others, and the manner in which their relationships are conducted, is called **control**. Unlike affection, which you can give and receive infinitely, control is finite: the more

AND YOU?

Consider a communication situation that you were in today. What was your communication goal? Were you upfront and honest about your goal or did you keep your goal largely to yourself? For example, if you wanted to get your roommate to clean the mess in the kitchen, did you state this fact or did you complain about the mess without making a request?

what about you?

Assessing Your Control Needs

Answer these questions to understand how you negotiate control in certain situations.

1. You are unhappy with your roommate because you feel that he does not do his share of the cleanup in the kitchen. You
   A. continuously point out when it is his turn to clean up.
   B. tell him to forget it and do it yourself.
   C. give him the silent treatment until he realizes that you're upset.
   D. ask why he doesn't do the chores and consider reassigning tasks.

2. Your family is planning a summer reunion. You
   A. push to have it when and where you want.
   B. take over the planning yourself.
   C. leave it to other family members to haggle over all those annoying details.
   D. participate in the decision process, volunteering to do your share.

3. You're assigned to a group project in class. You
   A. take leadership early, telling others what to do to get an A.
   B. give up trying to get everyone to cooperate and just do the work yourself.
   C. sit back and let others take leadership roles.
   D. help distribute tasks and work on a time line with others.

4. You are in charge of reviewing an employee's performance. You
   A. speak to the employee about strengths and weaknesses and outline a plan to meet goals.
   B. deliver a written evaluation without a face-to-face meeting.
   C. avoid any formal evaluation and hope the employee figures things out.
   D. ask the employee for a self-evaluation and respond to it.

If you responded "a" to most items: You are comfortable exerting a lot of control, though you should express affiliation (respect, liking) so that others will realize you care about and respect them.

If you responded "b" to most items: You have a tendency to take control because you don't have much confidence in others. Instead, try having confidence in your ability to influence others so that you don't place all responsibility on yourself.

If you responded "c" to most items: You have a low control need. This often helps you avoid confrontation, but you're probably not getting your needs met in a number of areas.

If you responded "d" to most items: You are more willing to share control in relationships, making you more likely to accomplish goals with the cooperation of others.

control one person has in a relationship, the less the other persons have. The exact distribution of control in relationships is worked out between the relational partners through communication—by the way they talk with each other, the content and structure of the conversations, and the timing and frequency of their interactions. While this negotiation of control may at times seem like a power struggle,[1] it is a necessary aspect of every type of relationship: family, friends, romantic partners, colleagues, doctors and patients, teachers and students, and advertisers and consumers.

● **FOR MOST LEARNING** environments to be successful, teachers should have more control than students in the classroom.

The amount of control you have over others or that they have over you varies; it is based on situation and status, allowing control to shift from one party to another as necessary. For example, as a new bank employee, Manny looks to his manager, Alexis, for direction and advice about how to do his job well. The unequal control distribution is appropriate and meets both Manny's and Alexis's expectations of their job responsibilities. But as Manny becomes more comfortable in his new job, he will likely take more control, and Alexis will allow him to work more independently. This kind of redistribution of control is not so much a struggle as it is a natural process.

How We Communicate

Consider this simple scenario: It's 8:45 A.M. in New York City. A woman walks up to a street vendor's cart, smiles and nods quickly at the vendor, and says, "Regular." Without hesitation, the man prepares her a small coffee with milk and two sugars. He hands her the coffee; she hands him a dollar, says, "Thanks," and continues on her way.

With only two words spoken, an entire business transaction has been carried out to the satisfaction of both parties. But what exactly occurred? The characteristics of communication can explain.

Characteristics of Communication

Communication is best illustrated by examining it in terms of six characteristics: the extent to which the message is *symbolic*, the extent to which the *code is shared*, the degree to which the message is *culturally bound*, the perceived *intentionality*

---

[1] Some scholars use *dominance* as a synonym for *control*. See, for example, Dillard, Solomon, and Palmer (1999).

of the sender, the presence of a *channel*, and the degree to which the process of encoding and decoding messages is *transactional*. That's quite a mouthful, so let us explain further.

Communication Is Symbolic

Communication relies on the use of **symbols**—arbitrary constructions (usually in the form of language or behaviors) that refer to people, things, and concepts. The stronger the connection between symbol and object, the clearer the intended meaning, and vice versa. For example, our customer greeted the street vendor not with a hello but with a smile and a nod. In this encounter, her actions clearly indicated a greeting to the vendor.

People create and negotiate meanings in the course of their interaction. A symbol can take on a new meaning if at least two people agree that it will have that meaning for them. A romantic couple, for example, may create a symbol for their affection—perhaps a certain look, gesture, or joke—that no one else shares. Social groups, such as fraternities and sororities or sports teams, use this technique to establish their uniqueness and to create boundaries between themselves and the outside world; they might use a handshake or a password or clothing that sets them apart from others. We clarify both verbal and nonverbal symbols in Chapters 4 and 5.

Communication Requires a Shared Code

Symbolic behaviors are grouped into patterns to create a **code**, a set of symbols that are joined to create a meaningful message. For communication to take place, the participants must share the code used to encode and decode messages. **Encoding** is the process of mentally constructing a message for production, and **decoding** is the process of receiving a message by interpreting and assigning meaning to it. If the relational partners are using the same code, they are more likely to encode and decode messages more accurately and establish the shared meaning they are seeking to communicate.

Speaking a common language is the most obvious example of sharing a communication code, though it is certainly not the only one. Baseball teams, for example, develop elaborate codes for various pitches and plays, which are communicated through hand gestures and body movements that range from subtle (removing a baseball cap) to obvious (holding up three fingers and shaking them twice). Similarly, different groups share meanings for specific gestures, graphics, and other symbols. Consider the emoticons and texting and chat room shorthand we all make use of—especially when we're in a hurry.

Communication Is Linked to Culture

If you've ever traveled abroad, or even through the different neighborhoods of a large city, you know that communication is difficult to separate from culture. *Culture* refers to the shared beliefs, values, and practices of a group of people. A group's culture includes the language (or languages) and other symbols used by group members as well as the norms and rules about how behavior can appropriately be displayed and understood.

CONNECT

As we discuss in Chapter 4, the most symbolic behavior is language. There is no particular reason why the letters *t-r-e-e* should represent a very large plant form, but they do. And in Chapter 5, you learn that gestures serve a similar purpose. Holding up your thumb while clenching your other fingers stands for "good job" in U.S. culture, though you likely don't need to have this fact explained.

● **A SUBTLE TAP** on the nose, a slight raise of a baseball cap: these are some of the signals baseball players use to indicate pitches or plays to their teammates.

Cultural groups vary in scale, and most people are members of several co-cultures simultaneously. *Co-cultures* are smaller groups of people within a culture who are distinguished by features such as race, religion, age, generation, political affiliation, gender, sexual orientation, economic status, educational level, occupation, and a host of other factors. Consider Anna, who identifies with a number of co-cultures: she is an American, an African American, a midwesterner, a married lawyer with two children, a person with an income over $100,000 a year, a Democrat, and a Baptist. Each of these co-cultures carries different meanings for Anna and affects her communication, not only in terms of the languages she speaks, but also in how she presents herself to others and how she interprets others' behavior (Chen & Starosta, 1996). Cultural identities can even form around interests and hobbies. For example, a music critic at *Blender* magazine might make distinctions among rock, soul, and hip-hop and might even break those styles down further, using terms like *old-school, freestyle, classic, punk, techno,* and *R&B.* For someone less involved or less interested in the music scene, such distinctions might seem unimportant—it's all just popular music.

Communication Need Not Be Intentional

One communication system is characterized by behavior that is primarily *symbolic* and *intentional,* such as IMing a friend to let her know you will be away from your computer using a mutually understood code (BRB! ☺). But there is also a second system, based largely on the expression of emotions and body movements. This widely shared code has few cultural boundaries, is *spontaneous,* and is therefore unintentional (Buck, 1988; Motley, 1990). For example, you communicate a message when you blush, even though blushing is an involuntary action. The distinction between the two systems can be seen as the difference between *giving* information and *giving off* information (Goffman, 1967).

These distinctions are important: we tend to see involuntary messages as more honest and reliable because the person giving off the information doesn't have the opportunity to censor it. It is useful to note, however, that while some spontaneous messages (for example, emotional outbursts of grief and anger) are highly reliable and readily interpreted, most are ambiguous: Are you blushing because you're embarrassed? Or because you're angry? Or because you've had a hot cup of tea? Or because you just ran up six flights of stairs? Generally, information given off is interpreted by paying attention to many other surrounding cues, but even then, the final assessment is still questionable. The most successful communicators are sensitive to the fact that both intended and unintended messages have an impact on the people around them.

Communication Occurs Through Various Channels

Once, the only means of communication was face-to-face contact. But as society became more sophisticated, other types of communication emerged; smoke signals, handwritten correspondence, telegraph, telephone, e-mail, and text messaging are all examples of communication channels. A **channel** is simply the method through which communication occurs. We must have a channel in order to communicate.

CONNECT

As you learn in Chapter 5, nonverbal communication is wrapped up in culture. In Mediterranean cultures, for instance, men stand close together and frequently touch during conversation. But in North American cultures, the appropriate conversational distance is generally about three feet, and men seldom touch each other during social interaction, except when they shake hands in greeting.

AND YOU?

Have you ever given off an unintentional message that was improperly decoded (for example, blushing during an argument because you're angry, while your romantic partner assumes it means that you're lying)? What did you do to clarify that message? Was it effective?

Considering the appropriate channel for a specific message is important, particularly when conflict is involved. As you learn in Chapter 8, breaking up with someone via Facebook status rather than through a more personal channel (like face to face) can worsen an already difficult situation. Such channels don't allow for nonverbal communication (tone of voice, eye contact, etc.), which helps you present difficult news clearly and sensitively.

Relationships can be maintained through a variety of channels. The information superhighway, which electronically connects an ever-growing number of people to one another, has facilitated an increase in long-distance relationships, including those between parents and children, siblings, close friends, and even romantic partners. Professional relationships can thrive over great distances as well; telecommuters around the globe remain connected by computer and audio and video media channels. The book that you are holding, for example, was produced by a team of authors, editors, proofreaders, designers, artists, and indexers working in offices and homes all over the United States.

Most people in technologically advanced societies use many channels to communicate, though they are not always proficient at adapting communication for the channel being used. Do you have a friend who leaves five-minute voice mail messages on your cell phone as though speaking directly with you? Or do you have a cousin who shares deeply private information with all of her six hundred Facebook "friends"? We all need to identify the channel that will work best for certain messages, at certain points in our relationships with certain people, and then adapt our messages to that medium.

Communication Is a Transactional Process

You may recall the 2009 MTV Video Music Awards for one reason: rapper Kanye West jumped on stage during Taylor Swift's acceptance speech for best female music video to declare that Beyoncé had been robbed of that award. West later expressed regrets about his behavior and offered apologies on talk shows like *The View* and *The Tonight Show with Jay Leno*. Yet no amount of apologizing could change what Kanye had done, how Swift had reacted, or how the incident had been perceived by audiences worldwide. That's because communication is a **transactional** process: it involves two or more people acting in both *sender* and *receiver* roles, and their messages are dependent on and influenced by those of their partner (that is, their messages are interdependent). Once a communication transaction has been completed—once a message has been sent (intentionally or not) and received—it *cannot* be reversed, nor can it be repeated in precisely the same way. This ongoing process can be immediate (as in a real-time conversation) or delayed (as in the case of a text message exchange).

● **APOLOGIZE AS HE MIGHT,** Kanye West could not undo the widespread reproach that resulted from his takeover of Taylor Swift's acceptance speech at the MTV Video Music Awards.

As we illustrate throughout this book, when you engage others in communication, you are attempting to influence them in some way. Equally important, but perhaps not so obvious, is the fact that you are opening yourself to be influenced *by* others. For example, when you are working on an assignment in a class group, your classmates' comments and suggestions influence you and your comments and suggestions, and vice versa. All parties in an interaction are responsible for the outcome of communication, and they all have a hand in whether or not goals are met (such as the completion of the assignment). The burden of responsibility, however, is distributed according to the communication situation. In some situations, such as close friendships or romantic relationships, responsibility is often shared equally. In other situations, like public speaking scenarios, the speaker tends

Characteristic	Behavior
Communication is symbolic.	Both parties speak English.
Communication requires a shared code.	Both parties understand the meaning of "regular." Both parties understand the smile and nod greeting.
Communication is linked to culture.	Both parties are New Yorkers.
Communication need not be intentional.	The woman knows the meanings of her words and gestures; they are not ambiguous to the street vendor.
Communication occurs through various channels.	This example uses the spoken word, gestures, and eye contact.
Communication is transactional.	The woman understands the message she is giving, and the man understands the message he is receiving.

TABLE 1.1

COMMUNICATION CHARACTERISTICS: ANATOMY OF A COFFEE SALE
Approaching the study of communication through its characteristics will help you evaluate behaviors you encounter in terms of their communicative value. As you can see, the simple coffee sale described in the text is clearly communicative, meeting all six criteria.

to assume most of the responsibility and is seen as the person attempting to influence the audience.

Assessing Communicative Value

To understand communication more fully, you assess the quality, or communicative value, of your communication. You do this by examining communication as it relates to the six characteristics discussed earlier. If it is definitely symbolic, with a shared code, and definitely intentional, it has three characteristics that give it high communicative value; communication breakdowns are less likely.

For example, recall the coffee sale described at the beginning of this section. The woman and the street vendor share a clear, if unwritten, code: in New York City, "regular" coffee means coffee with milk and two sugars. The code is not universal; it has a cultural meaning that is unique to New York, and even within the city, it is somewhat specialized, limited to street vendors and delicatessens. Had she said the same word to the counterperson at a Seattle's Best coffee shop on the West Coast—or even at the Starbucks just down the street—she might have gotten little more than a perplexed stare in reply. See Table 1.1 for a more detailed breakdown of this transaction.

Communicating Competently

Most people can identify situations in which they wish they could communicate better. Communicating is inherently complex because people and situations vary. For example, the classic film *Walk the Line* depicts the singer-songwriter Johnny Cash as thoroughly at ease in front of an audience but

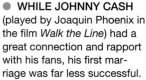

● **WHILE JOHNNY CASH** (played by Joaquin Phoenix in the film *Walk the Line*) had a great connection and rapport with his fans, his first marriage was far less successful.

falling apart entirely when communicating on the home front. Cash's relationship with his wife, Vivian, seems to be marked by a lack of understanding, dishonesty, and an inability to connect on a personal level. The Academy Award–winning film reveals that Johnny Cash has a set of useful and unique skills and talents but that he must adapt those skills to suit the needs of different people and situations—as he does in his second, successful marriage to June Carter Cash.

In studying communication, our goal is to become competent communicators. We do not mean merely adequate, average, or "OK"; communication scholars use the term **competent** to describe communication that is effective and appropriate for a given situation, in which the communicators evaluate and reassess their own communication process (Wiemann & Backlund, 1980). We examine each of these aspects of competent communication in the following sections.

Competent Communication Is Process-Oriented

An old sports adage says, "It's not whether you win or lose; it's how you play the game." Essentially, this means that the *process* (how you play) is more important than the *outcome* (who wins and who loses). In communication, an **outcome** has to do with the product of an interchange: in a negotiation, for example, the outcome may be getting a good deal on a product or getting a contract signed. In many contexts, the discussion of outcomes reveals little concern about the means to achieve those outcomes. Competent communication, by contrast, is more concerned with **process**, which measures the success of communication by considering the methods by which an outcome is accomplished. Although outcomes obviously still play a role in a process analysis, *what* is said and *how* it is said take on greater significance. From the process perspective, it is better to optimize outcomes for both partners than to fulfill the specific goals of either one: mutual satisfaction is used as the gauge of success (Wiemann, 1977). A study of fathers and daughters, for example, finds that the most satisfactory relationships involved a matching of needs and a balancing of control (Punyanunt-Carter, 2005). Asif, for example, hoped his daughter Laila would attend his alma mater. Over the summer before senior year, they traveled together to visit the university as well as several others. They worked together on her college applications and debated the merits of each school. Both Asif and Laila describe their relationship as satisfying and note that the process of searching for the right school made them even closer, even though Laila ultimately chose another school.

● **JON STEWART AND STEPHEN COLBERT'S** *Rally to Restore Sanity* was described by the organizers as a "call to reasonableness" in a time of polarized, vitriolic, and often unethical exchanges between Democrats and Republicans (Rally, 2010).

Ethical considerations are a crucial part of this process. **Ethics** is the study of morals, specifically the moral choices individuals make in their relationships with others. Your personal values, along with your culture's values, provide guidance on how to construct your messages appropriately as well as how to analyze messages directed toward you (Casmir, 1997; Christians & Traber, 1997). Ethical concerns arise whenever standards of right and wrong exert a significant impact on communication behavior (Johannesen, 1996). For example, the communication of a political spokesperson who lies or twists the truth to garner a jump in the polls for a candidate is not competent but unethical, manipulative, and exploitive.

BOX 1.2

NATIONAL COMMUNICATION ASSOCIATION CREDO FOR ETHICAL COMMUNICATION

Questions of right and wrong arise whenever people communicate. Ethical communication is fundamental to responsible thinking, decision-making, and the development of relationships and communities within and across contexts, cultures, channels, and media. Moreover, ethical communication enhances human worth and dignity by fostering truthfulness, fairness, responsibility, personal integrity, and respect for self and others. We believe that unethical communication threatens the quality of all communication and consequently the well-being of individuals and the society in which we live. Therefore we, the members of the National Communication Association, endorse and are committed to practicing the following principles of ethical communication:

▶ We advocate truthfulness, accuracy, honesty, and reason as essential to the integrity of communication.

▶ We endorse freedom of expression, diversity of perspective, and tolerance of dissent to achieve the informed and responsible decision-making fundamental to a civil society.

▶ We strive to understand and respect other communicators before evaluating and responding to their messages.

▶ We promote access to communication resources and opportunities as necessary to fulfill human potential and contribute to the well-being of families, communities, and society.

▶ We promote communication climates of caring and mutual understanding that respect the unique needs and characteristics of individual communicators.

▶ We condemn communication that degrades individuals and humanity through distortion, intimidation, coercion, and violence, and through the expression of intolerance and hatred.

▶ We are committed to the courageous expression of personal convictions in pursuit of fairness and justice.

▶ We advocate sharing information, opinions, and feelings when facing significant choices while also respecting privacy and confidentiality.

▶ We accept responsibility for the short- and long-term consequences for our own communication and expect the same of others.

● ON *BONES*, Dr. Temperance Brennan's commitment to scientific objectivity isn't always appropriate or effective communication.

Competent Communication Is Appropriate and Effective

The fictional doctor Temperance Brennan on the television show *Bones* believes in communicating clearly, without nuance, sarcasm, or self-censorship. Her commitment to absolute scientific objectivity means that she will describe a sexual encounter with the same precision that she might describe a body she is examining, and with the same detached language that someone else might use to describe a block of wood. Her communication, though clear, is largely inappropriate; it is also ineffective, because, while meant to inform her colleagues with as little ambiguity as possible, it tends to amuse or embarrass them instead.

If you've ever laughed or cringed at an inappropriate outburst, you already understand that for communication to be competent it needs to be both effective and appropriate. You would not speak to your grandmother in the same way you talk to your friends; nor would a lawyer ask her husband to complete a task the same way she would ask her office receptionist. Competent, successful communicators adjust their behavior to suit particular individuals and situations. To communicate well, we must ensure that our communication is both appropriate and effective.

Appropriate Behavior

When Congressman Joe Wilson (R-S.C.) shouted, "You lie!" during the 2009 State of the Union Address, few people were amused. While a good many Americans may have been dissatisfied with President Barack Obama's policies, and most Americans cherish their right to free speech, Wilson's outburst was widely regarded as inappropriate. Wilson's fellow Republicans condemned his behavior: Senator John McCain (R-Ariz.) called the outburst "totally disrespectful," noting that Wilson "should apologize immediately" (Reaction, 2009).

Communication is appropriate when it meets the demands of the situation, as well as the expectations of one's specific communication partner and any other people present. In almost all situations, cultural norms and rules set the standards for expectations. Had Wilson called the president a liar in a newspaper interview or even during debate on the House floor, the incident would have received less press. But the State of the Union is a nationally televised address, and a very formal affair, during which members of Congress traditionally defer to a code of etiquette that demands a certain degree of respect for the presidency and all that it represents, regardless of who holds office at the time. Wilson's outburst was considered inappropriate because of the particular circumstances in which he said it.

Cultural norms affect individual behaviors in a similar way. For example, research shows that women tend to feel more comfortable expressing emotional caring to one another, often outright (using words of sympathy and comforting gestures), while men often feel limited by cultural expectations that insist they show caring in less open ways (Burleson,

● THE SHOUT HEARD 'ROUND THE WORLD: "You lie!" Congressman Joe Wilson's outburst, directed at president Barack Obama, was roundly condemned as inappropriate and disrespectful.

Holmstrom, & Gilstrap, 2005). Thus, when comforting their friend Joe after the loss of his partner, Eva sat and held Joe's hand, while Dave got on the phone to help Joe manage details for the funeral.

A successful communicator needs to develop the ability to determine what is appropriate and what is not in a variety of cultures and situations. Your ability to have a number of behaviors at your disposal and your willingness to use different communication behaviors in different situations is known as your **behavioral flexibility**. So while you might love to talk about politics or your grades when you're with your friends, you might decide that it's just not appropriate at Passover dinner at your Aunt Myra's house.

Effective Behavior

Behaving appropriately is not enough to ensure success in communication. Competent communication must also be effective—it must help you meet your goals. This might sound obvious, but in practice it is not always easy to know what messages will work best—and it gets even more complicated when you have more than one goal (Canary, Cody, & Smith, 1994). For example, Travis is in a conflict with his fiancée, Leah, over whose family they will visit at Thanksgiving. Travis wants to meet competing—even conflicting—goals: he wants to see his family, but he also wants Leah to be happy, to join him with his family, and to see him as reasonable.

CONNECT

One skill that can help you communicate appropriately is *self-monitoring*. As you learn in Chapter 2, the ability to monitor yourself and your environment for clues on how to behave is quite powerful. At a party, you can assess how formal or informal a situation is, what types of messages are considered acceptable or off-limits, and so on. Such knowledge allows you to tailor your communication to be competent in your environment.

EVALUATINGCOMMUNICATIONETHICS

THINK ABOUT THIS

Gina's Confrontational Style

You and Gina have been friends since your first year of college. You both majored in marketing, you worked together often throughout college, and now the two of you are hunting for advertising jobs in Denver. You've always found Gina's authenticity refreshing and fun—she has a bold style of dress, a boisterous laugh, and a big and unbridled personality.

But lately you are noticing that Gina's brand of "authenticity" is becoming harsh and somewhat confrontational. When the two of you go shopping for interview clothes, Gina gravitates toward very short skirts and sweaters that are perhaps a little too casual for the workplace. When the saleswoman comments that she might want to appear a bit more conservative, Gina responds abruptly, "That is a matter of opinion."

You can see that people are not responding well to Gina's communication style, both in her way of speaking and in her manner of dress, but you're not sure if Gina is aware that it is a problem. You are sure that Gina could be more polished if she wanted to be, but you are hesitant to make suggestions. After all, what right do you have to tell your friend to change? Is it really Gina's problem anyway, or is it other people's problem for not appreciating Gina for the person she is? And who is to say whether your conservative manner is more likely to land you a job than Gina's brash attitude?

❶ What do you think is at issue here? List the multiple dynamics that could be involved in this ethical communication dilemma.

❷ Using your list, consider a fictional conversation with Gina. What are the ethical considerations you must keep in mind when confronting her?

❸ Imagine you are Gina. Would you want to know if others respond negatively to your communication style? What ethical considerations would you want for someone to keep in mind when raising a sensitive issue like this?

WIREDFORCOMMUNICATION

E-Mail Etiquette: How *Not* to Communicate with Your Professor

From: student@college.edu
Sent: Friday, September 9, 2011 11:42 A.M.
To: professor@college.edu
Subject: hey
hey, sorry i missed class today . . . i had a little too much fun last nite had a rough time waking up ;)
can you E-mail me your teaching notes ASAP? Tnx.

• • •

E-mails, when used effectively, are a valuable educational tool. They allow college students to ask questions outside of class and let professors provide instant feedback, making instructors more accessible than ever before. And while that's a great thing, many professors are complaining that some student e-mails are inappropriate.

Informal

Overly casual messages bother instructors and affect their perceptions of students' credibility (Stevens, Houser, & Cowan, 2009). Your message should be formal. It should open with a salutation ("Dear Professor Smith"), continue with a person/class identifier ("I'm Vera Yun in your 9:30 T/R conflict class"), and close with a proper signature ("Thanks in advance, Vera"). The rules of grammar, spelling, and capitalization all apply. There should be a clear subject line that should be appropriate to the content of the e-mail (otherwise, your professor may reject your e-mail as spam).

Inappropriate

The e-mail shown here is wholly inappropriate for student-professor correspondence. There's a halfhearted attempt at an apology and a thinly veiled reference to being hung over on the day of class. Here, as with any communication, it's important to analyze your audience. There are some things you can say to your friends that you shouldn't say to your professor. Review your draft before you send it; if you think you've written something that you think *might* offend or be inappropriate, take it out!

Demanding

Many professors complain that student e-mails are becoming increasingly pushy in tone. Recipients of poor grades send nasty notes, absent students demand teaching notes, and many students send more than ten e-mails a day, expecting their professors to be available around the clock.

Some guidelines: don't clutter inboxes with a barrage of requests, and give recipients plenty of time to respond. Use the tools that your professor has provided, such as the course syllabus, assignment sheets, or notes posted on a Web site before you e-mail; you may find that you already have what you need. And if you skipped class, don't ask your professor what you missed; that's what classmates are for.

THINK ABOUT THIS

❶ What is the value of an effective and appropriate subject line in an e-mail message? In what ways might the subject line influence your instructor's impression of the message and its sender?

❷ Why might students tend to use e-mail when a phone call or an office visit would be more appropriate? In what ways does the choice of communication channel influence the content and style of the message?

❸ What are the advantages of e-mail over other channels of communication when contacting a professor? How might a student capitalize on those advantages?

If you have some knowledge of your partner's expectations, you have a great advantage in deciding which messages will be relatively more effective than others. If Travis knows that Leah would like to spend Thanksgiving with her family because she wants to see her elderly grandmother, he might suggest that they spend the four-day Thanksgiving weekend with his family but the longer Christmas–New Year holiday with hers. In addition, knowing that you have multiple goals and prioritizing them—a task that is not always easy—can help you construct effective messages. If Leah thinks that spending Thanksgiving with her family and visiting her grandmother is a more important goal than pleasing Travis, she can construct an effective message that lets him know that she's sorry to let him down but that she absolutely must return home.

What is effective in one context might not always be appropriate communication in others. For example, research shows that many students feel that their most effective teachers are those who are organized, logical, enthusiastic, and approachable (Kramer & Pier, 1999). But if your roommate handed you a detailed syllabus of a day-by-day schedule of what you should do for the next semester while in your apartment, you might be quite annoyed.

Competent Communication Involves Communication Skills

Successful people usually have a well-developed set of skills that allows them to do their work successfully, inspiring others in the process. But having exemplary skills in one area does not make an individual competent overall: your mechanic may work wonders on your car, but that doesn't mean he can fix your computer. The same idea is true for great communicators: a politician who delivers a great speech may falter during a debate, press conference, or interview; and a social worker who conveys instructions clearly to her staff my have trouble clarifying her points during a meeting with the hospital board.

Communication skills are behavioral routines based on social understandings; they are used by communicators to achieve particular goals (such as asking for a raise, maintaining a relationship, or working successfully as a team member in an organization). You may know people who have few communication skills and do not use them in a very sophisticated manner but who are nonetheless in mutually satisfying long-term relationships. Conversely, even the most highly skilled communicator may be involved in an unsatisfying relationship.

People who are judged to be incompetent in some situations are often unaware that they are unskilled; their inflated image of themselves seems to keep them from adjusting their behavior to use more effective skills (Dunning & Kruger, 1999). For example, you may believe that you are a great team player and that working in a class group is easy. Imagine your surprise when evaluation time comes around and group members describe you as "bossy" and complain that you "micromanage" them. You may be very good at leading a team but less adept at working alongside others as an equal; you may need to learn new communication skills in order to be a competent group member. Simply having communication skills does not guarantee communication competence, although having a number of skills does increase your behavioral options, thereby boosting your odds of success.

Competent Communication Involves Using Technology

Developing skills to communicate competently in face-to-face situations is certainly complex. You can imagine how adding technology to the mix can present even more interesting opportunities, as well as challenges (Cupach & Spitzberg, 2011). So consider this question: can you measure the effectiveness and appropriateness of communication when you are on the phone or using a social networking site in the same way as when you are face to face? Research indicates that the answer is yes . . . and no.

Competent communication must still meet the goals of the communicators and be effective and appropriate for the situation. But those goals can sometimes be enhanced by the simultaneous use of more than one technology. For example, online communicators will often surf the Web while involved in an online chat to express themselves better or to locate sources to back up their arguments (Walther, Van Der Heide, Ton, Carr, & Atkin, 2010). If these communicators were face-to-face with someone, they might be considered rude to take their attention away from the conversation to surf the Web.

The technologies you use can also change others' perceptions of your communication competence. Texting a "thank you" might be an appropriate way to thank a friend for a compliment, but probably won't impress your Uncle Fred after his generous graduation gift.

Finally, research shows that if you are particularly comfortable with a particular technology you will describe yourself as more competent with that technology, and use it to accomplish your goals more often, even in difficult situations (Keaten & Kelly, 2008). For example, you may feel comfortable applying for jobs online; you are familiar with the technologies involved and are willing to wait for an electronic response. You will be more likely to use these technologies to accomplish your goals and will likely describe yourself as competent (Bakke, 2010), whereas your parents may see your approach as ineffective if they are less familiar or competent with technology.

Modeling Communication

As we've stated at various points in this chapter, the communication process is infinitely complex. For this reason, scholars have generated different models, or visual representations, of the process so that we may have another helpful way to examine our communication. We begin with the most basic representation of communication, the linear model, before moving on to the interaction model and, finally, the competent communication model.

The Linear Model

The simplest communication is linear. In a simple **linear model** of communication (see Figure 1.1), a **sender** originates communication, with words or action; those words or actions constitute the **message**. The message must be carried through a specific *channel* (air and sound waves, written or visual, over telephone

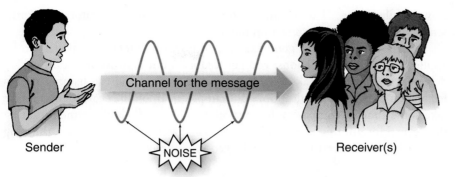

FIGURE 1.1
LINEAR MODEL

lines, cables, or electronic transmissions). Along the way, some interference, called **noise**, occurs, so that the message arrives (changed in some way from the original) at its target, the **receiver** (Shannon & Weaver, 1949).

The linear picture of communication is limited. There is no information on whether (or how) the message was received by anyone. This model may be useful for illustrating how television and radio transmit electronic signals to the public, but it does not show the receiver's active role in interpreting meaning. For this reason, linear models are no longer considered useful for most kinds of communication, particularly interactive forms. However, the basic terms of the linear model are important to the building of more complex pictures of communication.

The Interaction Model

An **interaction model** exhibits communication between sender and receiver that incorporates feedback (see Figure 1.2). **Feedback** is a message from the receiver to the sender that illustrates responses that occur when two or more people communicate. As with the linear model, noise occurs along the way.

Feedback can be a verbal message (your friend invites you to a party on Friday night, and you reply, "About nine?"), a nonverbal message (your roommate asks if you enjoyed the dinner, and you look up, smile, and nod), or both (you

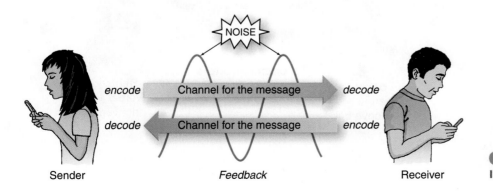

FIGURE 1.2
INTERACTION MODEL

frown while saying, "I don't think I understand"). Communicators take turns sending messages in the interaction model.

Instant messaging is a good example of how the interaction model can be applied in mediated situations; you get feedback, but it is not in "real time"—delays in transmission make the conversation less fluid and can hamper the effectiveness of the communication. For example, in an online chat, Melissa might take some time in composing her response to Howard's last comment; during the delay, Howard might have moved on to a new train of thought, or, thinking Melissa has lost interest in chatting, logged off entirely.

The Competent Communication Model

Though each of these models is helpful in illustrating the communication process, neither manages to capture the complex process of competent communication that we talked about in the preceding section (Wiemann & Backlund, 1980).

To illustrate this complex process, we developed a model of communication that shows effective and appropriate communication (see Figure 1.3). This **competent communication model** is *transactional:* the individuals (or groups or organizations) communicate *simultaneously,* sending and receiving messages (both verbal and nonverbal) at the same moment in time, within a relational context, a situational context, and a cultural context.[2]

The link between communication behaviors is shown in this model by the arrows representing the messages being sent and received. In face-to-face communication, the behaviors of both communicators influence each individual at the same

---

[2]The competent communication model is based on the research of John Wiemann (1977) and the Wiemann Competence Model (Wiemann & Wiemann, 1992).

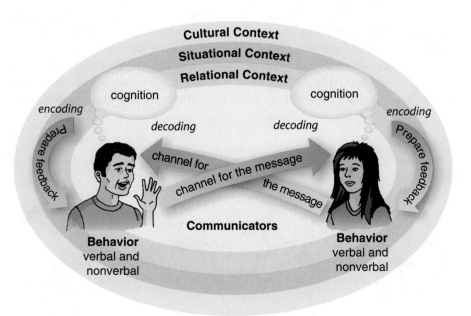

FIGURE 1.3

COMPETENT COMMUNICATION MODEL

time. For example, Cliff is smiling and nodding at Jalissa without saying anything as Jalissa talks about the meeting she hosted for her book club; Cliff is sending messages of encouragement while receiving her verbal messages. Jalissa is sending all sorts of messages about the book she chose for that week's discussion, as well as the foods she selected and the way she prepared for the get-together. But she is also receiving messages from Cliff that she interprets as positive interest. Both Cliff and Jalissa are simultaneously encoding (sending) and simultaneously decoding (receiving) communication behavior. This transaction changes slightly in different types of communication. For example, in a mediated form of communication—a Facebook wall posting or texting, for example—the sending and receiving of messages may not be simultaneous. In such cases, the communicators are more likely to take turns, or a delay in time may elapse between messages. In mass media contexts such as TV or radio, feedback may be even more limited and delayed—audience reactions are typically gauged only by the Nielsen ratings (how many people watched) or by the comments posted by fans on their blogs.

The competent communication model takes into account not only the transactional nature of communication but also the role of communicators themselves—their internal thoughts and influences as well as the various contexts in which they operate. There are four main spheres of influence at play in the competent communication model:

▶ The *communicators*. Two individuals are shown here, but many variations are possible: an individual speaking to a live audience, multiple individuals in a group communicating, and so on.

▶ The *relational context* in which the communication takes place.

▶ The *situational context* in which the communication occurs.

▶ The *cultural context* that frames the interaction.

Let's take a more in-depth look at each of these influences, as they are powerful and important considerations for effective and appropriate communication.

The Communicators

The most obvious parts of any communication situation are the communicators—the individuals who are engaged in communication. When sending and receiving messages, each communicator is influenced by **cognitions**, the thoughts that individuals have about themselves and others, including their understanding and awareness of who they are (smart, funny, compassionate, and so on), how well they like who they are, and how successful they think they are. We discuss this process in much more depth in Chapter 2, but for now, understand that your cognitions influence your behavior when you communicate. **Behavior** is observable communication, including both verbal messages (the words you use) and nonverbal messages (your facial expressions, body movements, clothing, and gestures). So your cognitions inform your behavior—the messages you encode and send—which are then received and decoded by your communication partner. Your communication partner's own personal cognitions influence how he or she interprets the message, prepares feedback, and encodes a new verbal or nonverbal message that is sent to you.

This constant cycle of communication can be seen in the following example. Devon knows that he's a good student, but he struggles with math, chemistry, and physics, and this embarrasses him because his mother is a medical doctor and his brother is an engineer. He rarely feels like he will succeed in these areas. He tells his friend Kayla that he can't figure out why he failed his recent physics test since he studied for days beforehand. When he says these words, his eyes are downcast and he looks angry. Kayla, who likes to think that she's a good listener and who prides herself on the fact that she rarely responds emotionally to delicate situations, receives and decodes Devon's message, prepares feedback, and encodes and sends a message of her own: she calmly asks whether or not Devon contacted his physics professor or an academic tutor for extra help. Devon receives and decodes Kayla's message in light of his own cognitions about being a poor science student and feeling like he's always struggling with physics. He notices that Kayla made very direct eye contact, that she didn't smile, and that her message didn't include any words of sympathy, and he assumes she must be accusing him of not working hard enough. He prepares feedback and sends off another message—his eyes are large and his arms are crossed and he loudly and sarcastically states, "Right, yeah, I guess I was just too dumb to think about that."

Because communication situations can vary so greatly, successful communicators usually have a high degree of cognitive complexity. That is, they are able to consider multiple scenarios, formulate multiple theories, and make multiple interpretations when encoding and decoding messages. In this case, Kayla might have considered that Devon really just needed some friendly reassurance rather than advice; Devon might have realized that Kayla was just trying to offer a helpful suggestion.

The Relational Context

All communication, from mundane business transactions to intimate discussions, occurs within the context of the relationship you have with the person or persons with whom you are interacting (represented by the inner sphere in the competent communication model). A kiss, for example, has a different meaning when bestowed on your mother than it does when shared with your spouse or romantic partner. When you make a new acquaintance, saying "Let's be friends" can be an exciting invitation to get to know someone new, but the same message shared with someone you've been dating for a year shuts down intimacy. The relationship itself is influenced by its past history as well as both parties' expectations for the current situation and for the future.

A relational history is the sum of the shared experiences of the individuals involved in the relationship. References to this common history (such as inside jokes) can be important in defining a relationship, both for the participants and for the participants' associates, because they indicate to you, your partner, and others that there is something special about this particular relationship. Your relational history may also affect what is appropriate in a particular circumstance. For example, you may give advice to a sibling or close friend without worrying about politeness, but you might be more hesitant or more indirect with an acquaintance you haven't known for very long. Relational history can complicate matters

● **THE MEANING** of a kiss changes depending on context. A kiss between mother and child doesn't have the same meaning as a kiss between romantic partners.

when communicating on social networking sites like Facebook. Your "friends" probably include those who are currently very close to you as well as those who are distant (for example, former high school classmates). Even if you direct your message to one friend in particular, all your friends can see it, so you might be letting those distant relationships in on a private joke (or making them feel left out).

Our communication is also shaped by our expectations and goals for the relationship. Expectations and goals can be quite different. For example, high school sweethearts may want their relationship to continue (a goal), but at the same time worry that going to college in different states may lead to a breakup (an expectation). With expectations and goals in mind, you formulate your behavior in the current conversation, and you interpret what your partner says in light of these same considerations. Clearly, our expectations and goals differ according to each relationship. They can and do change during the course of conversations, and they certainly change over the lifespan of a relationship.

The Situational Context

The situational context (represented by the middle sphere in the competent communication model) includes the social environment (a loud, boisterous party versus an intimate dinner for two), the physical place (at home in the kitchen versus at Chicago's O'Hare International Airport), specific events and situations (a wedding versus a funeral), and even a specific mediated place (a private message versus a Facebook status update). It also includes where you live and work, your home or office decorations, the time of day or night, and the current events in the particular environment at the time.

For example, if Kevin gets home from work and asks Rhiannon what's for dinner and Rhiannon shrieks, Kevin might conclude that she is mad at him. But if he considers the situational context, he might reinterpret her response. Looking around, he might see that his wife is still in her suit, meaning that she only just got home from a long day at work. He might notice that the kitchen sink is clogged, the dog has gotten sick on the living room rug, and the laundry (his chore) is still sitting, unfolded, on the couch because he didn't get around to finishing it. By considering the context, Kevin is able to ascertain that Rhiannon is upset because of these situational factors, rather than because of anything he has said or done.

AND YOU?

What relational, situational, and cultural contexts are influencing you as you read this book? Consider your gender, ethnicity, academic or socioeconomic background, and other factors. Have you studied communication or speech before? Have you taken a course with this professor before? What expectations and goals do you have for this book and this course?

The Cultural Context

Finally, we must discuss the fact that all communication takes place within the powerful context of the surrounding culture (represented by the outermost sphere of the competent communication model). Culture is the backdrop for the situational context, the relational context, and the communicators themselves. As discussed earlier, culture helps determine which messages are

COMMUNICATIONACROSSCULTURES

Judging Sex and Gender

Upon learning that she would be replaced on the U.S. Supreme Court by John Roberts, retiring Justice Sandra Day O'Connor was pleased, but not completely. "He's good in every way," she responded. "Except he's not a woman." (Balz & Fears, 2005). Appointed in 1981 by Ronald Reagan, O'Connor was the first woman ever to serve on the nation's highest court. Her disappointment that the court would once again include only one woman (O'Connor's colleague Ruth Bader Ginsberg, appointed in 1993 by Bill Clinton) would prove short lived: within six years, the court would be a full third female.[1]

If women make up roughly half of the U.S. population, it should logically follow that they will comprise a large portion of the courts as well. On the other hand, if justice is indeed blind, the sex (or race, ethnicity, religion, and so on) of individual justices should not matter. There is some argument over whether female justices rule differently than male justices—some research suggests that having three or more women on a panel can change the way the panel reaches decisions, even when the panel is predominantly male. Does gender affect the way justices come to decisions? There is some evidence that it does.

Consider the case of Savana Redding, a middle school student who, having been accused of supplying classmates with prescription strength ibuprofen, was stripped down to her underwear by two female school administrators, who searched through her underwear for the pills. None were found. Feeling that her Fourth Amendment protection from unreasonable search and seizure had been violated, Redding and her family sued the school district, and the case eventually found its way to the Supreme Court. Judging from the comments made by justices during arguments, Savana's case looked bleak, as justices didn't seem to understand why the situation was a big deal. "In my experience when I was 8 or 10 or 12 years old, you know, we did take our clothes off once a day, we changed for gym," noted Justice Stephen Breyer (Lithwick, 2009). But Justice Ginsberg, as a female, took a very different view, and spoke out both in the press and to her colleagues about how humiliating such an experience could be for a teenage girl. "They have never been a 13-year-old girl," she told one reporter. "It's a very sensitive age for a girl. I didn't think that my colleagues, some of them, quite understood" (quoted in Biskupic, 2009). The Court eventually ruled that Redding's rights had indeed been violated, in an 8–1 decision.

THINK ABOUT THIS

❶ Does it strike you as surprising that Ginsberg saw the case of Savana Redding differently than did her male colleagues? How might each justice's personal experiences— their specific relational and cultural context—influence their decisions?

❷ Why is it that sex and gender have become such issues in the past thirty years, particularly on the Supreme Court? Do you think gender might have influenced the decisions of the 101 men (all but one of them white) who preceded Sandra Day O'Connor to the bench during the court's first 190 years?

❸ Consider also the unique situational context of the Savana Redding case. Would justices have thought about it differently if she were a teenage boy? If she were older? Younger? If the drugs she was suspected of hiding were stronger than ibuprofen?

[1]Justice Sonia Sotomayor was appointed in 2009; Justice Elena Kagan was appointed in 2010.

● **WHEN IT COMES** to interacting with parents and older relatives, different cultures teach different values.

considered appropriate and effective, and it strongly affects our cognitions. For example, Hannah comes from a culture that shows respect for elders by not questioning their authority and by cherishing possessions that have been passed down in the family for generations. Cole, by contrast, was raised in a culture that encourages him to talk back to and question elders and that values new possessions over old ones. Both Hannah and Cole view their own behaviors as natural—their cognitions about elders and possessions have been influenced by their culture. But when each looks at the other's behavior, it might seem odd or unnatural. If Hannah and Cole are to become friends, colleagues, or romantic partners, each would benefit from becoming interculturally sensitive to the other.

Cultural identity—how individuals view themselves as a member of a specific culture—influences the communication choices they make and how they interpret the messages they receive from others (Lindsley, 1999). Cultural identity is reinforced by the messages people receive from those in similar cultures. In our example, both Hannah's and Cole's cognitions have been reinforced by their respective friends and family, who share their cultural identity.

The Study of Communication

If you've never studied communication before, right now you might feel like you know more about messages and relationships and communication contexts than you ever thought you'd need to know! But there is still so much more to study that can have a profound effect on your friendships, romantic relationships, group memberships, career, and overall success in life. You've seen that communicating well—communicating effectively, appropriately, and ethically—is not innate, nor is it common sense; it is a process that we can all improve on throughout our lives.

So what's behind this discipline? What do communication scholars (like us) do? Well, in democracies from ancient Greece to the United States, scholars realized early on that communication was crucial to helping people participate in the government. Public speaking, for example, was taught in America's first

CONNECT

Organizations also develop their own cultures, which have a huge impact on communication. You might work for a company that encourages casual dress, informal meetings, and the ability to openly share thoughts with management. Or you might work for an organization that is more formal and hierarchical. Your communication needs to be adjusted to be competent in a particular *organizational culture*, a point we address in Chapter 11.

universities, partly to reinforce the powerful effect that speaking out can have on society (Dues & Brown, 2004). A similar concern for the public's welfare was the reason for adding professional journalism courses to university curricula at the beginning of the twentieth century, when the sensationalistic excesses of the

real communicator

NAME: Vicky Sands
HOMETOWN: Queens, New York
OCCUPATION: Manager in the Analytics Department of Bloomberg
FUN FACT: I own a puffer fish named Shamu.

I came to college at the State University of New York at Oneonta wanting to get involved in student government. I was looking at courses my freshman year, and Introduction to Speech Communication looked like it might be helpful—there were sections on the syllabus devoted to group communication, listening, leadership, conflict, public speaking, things like that. Perfect.

The class changed my life. I know that sounds corny, but I loved it—I ended up majoring in communication. Before, I'd get into a group discussion and I'd just be participating. Since I took the class, it is like I'm in a different world, privy to all sorts of secrets and things that other people don't catch onto, from nonverbal cues to seating arrangements.

I ended up running for student government, and I won! My junior year, I was elected class president. And I never stopped using things I learned in that first communication course. Our executive board meetings—meetings with me, the vice president, the treasurer, and the secretary—were absolutely crazy. The VP had a lot of ideas, but he was terribly shy. The treasurer had a highly aggressive and dominating personality. And the secretary was so sensitive, she felt like the treasurer was always picking on her. Argue—that's all we did in those meetings.

But I started using some of the concepts I learned in class. I spoke to each of them individually. I knew not to surprise anyone in a group setting. Plus, I knew that people aren't going to listen to you unless they feel like you're on their side. So when I talked to the VP, I asked him a lot of probing questions—how do you think things are going, stuff like that. I wanted him to feel as if he had a voice, a real say in things. When I met with the treasurer, I was careful not to point any fingers because if I had his kind of personality, I'd shut right off if people came at me full of blame and anger. And I took the secretary out to lunch. I let each of them believe that I had a personal interest in hearing them out—and I did; I had a student government to run!

I didn't tell anyone that I was also meeting with everybody else. I wanted each of them to feel as if I was their ally. At the next meeting, I made sure to sit between the treasurer and the secretary and I began by asking the VP a question. Of course, the treasurer butted in immediately, but I told him to hear the VP out. The change was dramatic. The VP stiffened his back; he felt empowered. When he started talking, I looked at the treasurer, and the treasurer winked at me. I turned to the secretary, and she gave me a knowing nod. Everyone in that room thought we were in cahoots! It was our best meeting ever.

And it was just a matter of putting myself in other people's shoes. That's the class's best lesson. It takes you out of being self-absorbed. You have to pay attention to everyone and everything around you. And it works!

Area of Study	Focus of Study
Rhetorical theory and criticism	Analyzing speeches and other public messages
Argumentation and debate	Persuasion, reasoning, logic, and presentation
Interpersonal communication	Basic two-person (dyadic) processes
Intergroup communication	Ways in which communication within and between groups affects social relationships
Relational communication	Interpersonal communication in close relationships such as romances, families, and friendships
Small group communication	The function, dynamics, and performance of group members
Organizational communication	Communication efficiency and effectiveness in business and other organizations
Mass communication and media studies	The design and production of media messages and the identification and evaluation of media effects
Political communication	The study of politicians, voters, and audiences and their impact on one another
Public relations	The production of messages designed to improve the image of individuals and organizations
Intercultural communication	Communication rules and values across cultures and co-cultures
Family communication	Communication between parents and children and between generations
Health communication	The communication messages of health care providers and patients
Conflict management	Reducing adversarial messages in personal, organizational, and community contexts
Nonverbal communication	Nonlanguage codes that communicate
Communication technology and telecommunication studies	Development and application of new technologies in all communication situations

TABLE 1.2

COMMON AREAS OF SPECIALIZATION IN COMMUNICATION RESEARCH TODAY

"penny press" highlighted the need for newspeople who were trained in both the technical aspects of reporting and the ethical responsibilities of journalists in a free society.

Today, communication continues to be a dynamic and multifaceted discipline focused on improving interactions and relationships, including those between two individuals, between individuals of different cultures, between speakers and audiences, within small groups, in large organizations, and among nations and international organizations. (Table 1.2 illustrates some of the major areas of specialization and the focus of each.) The research in our field draws clear connections between these assorted types of relationships, and the principles of communication laid out in this chapter can be successfully applied to various communication situations and contexts. For example, as technology advances, communication becomes more complicated, expansive, and sometimes unclear. For most of human existence, an interpersonal relationship was limited to face-to-face interactions, later enhanced by mediated communication via the written word and the telephone. But today, individuals strike up personal and business relationships through e-mail, social networking groups, and phone contact across the globe, often without ever meeting in person.

Throughout this book, we'll draw connections (through our CONNECT feature) to show how communication skills, concepts, and theories apply to various communication situations and offer scholarship from four distinct areas of the discipline:

> ▶ *Basic Communication Processes.* All communication involves the basic processes of perception, intercultural interaction, verbal communication, nonverbal communication, and listening. Skills that we develop in these areas inform the way we handle communication in a variety of contexts, from talking with friends to making presentations in front of a class or a large public audience. In the remainder of Part 1 of the book, you will learn how these basic processes affect every communication situation.

> ▶ *Interpersonal Communication.* As social animals, human beings cannot avoid forming interpersonal relationships and interacting with other individuals. Interpersonal communication is the study of communication between **dyads**, or pairs of individuals. Most students find this study particularly relevant to their lives as they negotiate their friendships, romantic relationships, and family relationships. We investigate the exciting, nerve-racking, fun, confusing, tumultuous, and rewarding world of relationships and conflict in Part 2 of this book. An in-depth analysis of interviewing—one of the most daunting and important types of interpersonal communication—is offered in Appendix A at the back of the book.

> ▶ *Group and Organizational Communication.* If you've ever tried to run a professional meeting, manage a class or work group, or plan a day trip for a bunch of friends, you know that as the number of people involved in a conversation, activity, or project increases, communication becomes more complicated. By studying interactions in groups and organizations, communication scholars help create strategies for managing the flow of information and interactions among individuals in groups. We'll explore this in Part 3 of the book.

> ▶ *Public Speaking.* Don't panic! We're going to provide a lot of help and guidance to assist you as you become a competent public speaker. Even if you've never had to speak in front of a group before, in Part 4 you'll learn not only how to research and develop a presentation, but also how to connect with your audience on a personal level. We also offer tips on becoming

AND YOU?

Did you choose to take this course, or is it required? Regardless of why you're here, what do you hope to learn? What kind of communication most interests or intrigues you? What part of this book or course do you think will be most applicable to your life, future study, or professional career?

a more critical audience member whether you are engaged with a speaker in a lecture hall, a protest rally, or a professional conference.

We are confident that this book will provide you with an enjoyable reading experience as well as help you improve your communication (and thus your life, your work, your relationships, and your ability to speak out).

BACK TO The Gulf Oil Spill

At the beginning of this chapter, we talked about BP's failure to communicate competently in the wake of the *Deepwater Horizon* explosion. Let's consider the spill and reactions to it in light of what you've learned in this chapter.

▶ Communication disasters in the Gulf were many: public relations gaffes, lack of coordination, confusion over who was in control, and avoidance of responsibility. These communication failures had real economic consequences: fishing and tourism are crucial to the Gulf Coast economy, and many people lost their livelihoods as the oil spill killed marine life and fouled beaches. Deepwater drilling is also vital to the Gulf Coast economy; a Louisiana oil industry group estimated that each rig in the Gulf of Mexico represented monthly wages of at least $165 million (Zeller, 2010).

▶ BP executive Tony Hayward's comments and activity in the days and weeks that followed the spill showed that he failed to consider the situational context. Hayward's words and his behavior (enjoying the yacht race as oil gushed into the Gulf) failed to consider the needs and distress of the Gulf Coast community still suffering the economic and social effects of Hurricane Katrina.

▶ In the end, Hayward's apology largely fell flat because of the transactional nature of communication. He might be able to utter apologetic words for his statements and behavior, but nothing can ultimately erase listeners' memories. Once a communication transaction occurs, it cannot be reversed.

▶ Consider also the effectiveness of the corporate messages. While the media focused on the vastness of the devastation, offering insights from locals and showing detailed, twenty-four-hour coverage of the spill itself, messages from BP seemed more concerned with protecting the company than with conveying clear and accurate information. Thus, the messages were not appropriate for the situation, nor were they effective in helping the company's PR image.

THINGS TO TRY Activities

1. Think of someone (a family member, a celebrity, a politician, a friend, a professor) who exhibits competent communication in a particular context. What behaviors does this person exhibit that make him or her particularly effective? Would you want to model some of your own communication behavior after this person? Why or why not?

2. Keep a log of all the different channels (face-to-face, written, computer mediated, telephonic, others) you use to communicate during the course of one morning or afternoon. Do you regularly communicate with a particular person via a specific channel (for example, you talk with your mother mostly over the phone, your romantic partner through text messages, and your childhood best friend via Facebook postings)? What channels do you prefer to use when sending different types of messages (long and short messages, positive and negative messages, business and personal messages, and so on)?

3. Describe two communication situations, one in which the communication was appropriate but not effective, and one in which the communication was effective but not very appropriate. Analyze these situations, considering the situational and relational contexts involved.

4. Consider a scene from a favorite film or novel. Imagine how it would change if you had not seen the rest of the film or read the entire novel. Would you come away from it with the same meaning if you did not understand the relational context between the characters or the situational context within the larger story?

Now that you have finished reading this chapter, you can:

Define the communication process:

▶ **Communication** is the process by which individuals use symbols, signs, and behaviors to exchange information (p. 4).

▶ Communication is much more complex than "common sense" (p. 4).

Describe the functions of communication:

▶ The **functional perspective** examines how communication behaviors work (or don't work) to accomplish goals (p. 5).

▶ **Relationships** are the interconnections, or interdependence, between two or more people that function to achieve some goal (p. 5).

▶ Relationship **interdependence** means that what we do affects others, and vice versa (p. 5).

▶ A communication relationship is based on sharing symbolic information (p. 6).

▶ There are three primary functions in communication:
  • Expressing **affiliation**, or feelings for others (p. 6).
  • Relying on communication to accomplish particular objectives, or **goal achievement** (p. 7).
  • Negotiating **control**, the influence one individual, group, or organization has over others (p. 7).

Assess the quality (communicative value) of communication by examining its six characteristics:

▶ Communication relies on **symbols**, arbitrary constructions related to the people, things, or concepts to which they refer (p. 10).

▶ Communication requires a shared **code**, or a set of symbols that create a meaningful message; **encoding** is the process of producing and sending a message, while **decoding** is the process of receiving it and making sense of it (p. 10).

▶ Communication is linked to *culture*, the shared beliefs, values, and practices of a group of people, and *co-cultures*, smaller groups within a culture (pp. 10–11).

▶ Communication may be intentional or spontaneous (p. 11).

▶ Communication requires a **channel**, the method through which it occurs (p. 11).

▶ Communication is a **transactional** process: you influence others while they influence you (p. 12).

Define what communication scholars consider to be **competent** communication:

▶ Competent communication is more **process-** than **outcome-focused** (p. 14).

▶ **Ethics** is the study of morals (p. 15).

▶ Communication is appropriate when it meets the demands of the situation (p. 16).

▶ **Behavioral flexibility** involves knowing and using a number of different behaviors to achieve that appropriateness (p. 17).

▶ Communication is effective when it achieves desired goals (p. 17).
  • **Communication skills** are behaviors that help communicators achieve their goals (p. 19).

Describe the visual representations, or models, of communication:

▶ In the **linear model**, a **sender** originates the **message**, which is carried through a channel—perhaps interfered with by **noise**—to the **receiver** (pp. 20–21).

▶ The **interaction model** expands on the linear model by including **feedback** between the receiver and the sender (p. 21).

▶ The **competent communication model** is a transactional model incorporating three contextual spheres in which individuals communicate (pp. 22–23).
  • *Communicators:* **Cognitions**, thoughts communicators have about themselves, influence **behavior**, observable communication, and how the message is interpreted before preparing feedback (p. 23).
  • *Relational context:* Communication occurs within the context of a relationship and is influenced by the relational history (p. 24).
  • *Situational context:* The circumstances surrounding communication, including social environment and physical place, influence communication (p. 25).
  • *Cultural context:* Cultural identity, how individuals view themselves as a member of a specific culture, influences communication choices (p. 27).

Describe why communication is vital to everyone:

▶ The discipline of communication grew out of the need to have informed citizens aware of the power of speaking out (pp. 27–28).

▶ The discipline focuses on improving interactions and relationships between **dyads**, groups, organizations, and speakers and audiences (p. 30).

Susan Boyle's audience based its low—and highly mistaken—expectations of the singer on her less-than-glamorous image.

Perceiving the Self and Others

When Susan Boyle took the stage at *Britain's Got Talent* competition in 2009 and told the audience and judges that she wanted to be a professional singer, she was met mostly with eye rolls, barely muffled giggles, and at least one ironic cat-call. In a society that equates youth, beauty, and glamour with talent, they didn't expect much from a middle-aged, overweight, never-been-kissed cat lady from Scotland. As the music to "I Dreamed a Dream" from *Les Misérables* cued up over the sound systems, viewers steeled themselves for what they thought was certain to be a cringe-worthy performance.

But by the time Boyle belted out the first bar, those derisive expressions had melted away. Over the course of her pitch-perfect performance, cameras scanned through the audience, capturing tears welling up in the eyes that had been cynically rolling toward the ceiling just a few minutes prior. As she headed into the bridge of the song and audiences leapt to their feet, television presenter Anthony McPartlin joyfully chided viewers watching at home: "You didn't expect that, did you? Did you? No!" Judge Piers Morgan told Boyle, "Without a doubt, that was the biggest surprise I've had in three years of this show. . . . Everyone was laughing at you. No one is laughing now."

Within hours, footage of Boyle's performance was up on YouTube, snatching upwards of two million hits in less than three days; by the month's end it had been viewed more than 100 million times, and it remains today one of the most watched YouTube videos ever. Boyle would go on to live the dream she dreamed with a new look, a successful debut album and tour, and popularity that continues to this day.

chapter
outcomes

After you have finished reading this chapter, you will be able to

- Describe how our personal perspective on the world influences our communication

- Explain how we use and misuse schemas when communicating with others

- Define the attributions we use to explain behavior

- Describe cultural differences that influence perception

- Identify how our self-concept—who we think we are—influences communication

- Describe how our cognitions about ourselves and our behavior affect our communication with others

Certainly, most people know that one's ability to sing has little to do with one's appearance. So, why were audiences so stunned by Susan Boyle's performance on *Britain's Got Talent*? Why did that YouTube clip capture the public's imagination? One communication factor informs the answers to both of these questions: perception.

We all have a unique way of perceiving ourselves, others, and the world around us, and we communicate with others based on those perceptions. **Perception** is a cognitive process through which we interpret our experiences and come to our own unique understandings. Those thoughts and cognitions influence how and what we communicate to others and simultaneously influence the way that we interpret the behaviors and messages that others send to us. We perceive, and others around us perceive at the same time, though we may not perceive the same thing. As you can see, understanding the role that perception plays in the communication process is crucial to our success as communicators. In this chapter, we look at how we see ourselves, how we see others, and how culture affects both of these processes.

Perception: Making Sense of Your World

It's eight o'clock on a Wednesday night, and a roomful of singles are gathered at an Atlanta hot spot for an interesting event: over the next hour and a half, each woman will be introduced to no fewer than twenty eligible men. The problem: she'll have only three minutes with each of them. Each pair will divulge their first names, perhaps their occupations, where they're from, and why they're there.

Speed dating is a hot trend in many metropolitan areas.[1] Organized by upstart companies that promise to screen applicants and put together large groups of potentially compatible singles, the event is arranged so that each single person is introduced to anywhere from ten to twenty potential mates, with whom they spend a short interval of time (usually less than ten minutes) to see if there is any "chemistry." But how much can one person learn about another in three minutes? Or even ten minutes?

The truth is that for better or for worse, you glean quite a bit of information from first impressions. Irina might tell Adam that she's thirty-one, is a public relations executive, was born in Milwaukee but has lived in Atlanta for nine years, and has a passion for film noir. Adam might hear all this but also notice that Irina is quite tall and very attractive, that she meets his gaze with steady eye contact, and that she appears quite assertive in her mannerisms. This information might lead him to make certain conclusions about her: "She is probably more successful than I am," he thinks. Adam might also notice that Irina is what he considers a "funky" dresser—she wears lots of brightly colored bead jewelry along with her conservative business suit. This, and her mention of film noir, puts him off a bit—Adam wonders if she's an "artsy" type. His last girlfriend was into art and was always dragging him off to gallery openings that he found

---

[1]This speed-dating trend is found in the United States but is popular in England and India as well (Doshi, 2005, p. 60).

painfully boring and pretentious. He feels a little intimidated by Irina and decides that they probably aren't compatible.

Even during brief encounters—like Adam's meeting with Irina—you are barraged with information: the exact words of the message, the person's tone of voice, his or her facial expression, the level of eye contact. **Communication processing** is the means by which you gather, organize, and evaluate the information you receive. Although you receive information through your basic senses, this is just the beginning of the process. Whether you are looking at a painting, making a new acquaintance, or recounting the details of a specific event, your interpretation of what you see, hear, or touch will be unique to you, at least to some degree, because of the ways in which you select, organize, and interpret information.

● **WHEN OTHERS** approach you at a speed-dating event, you immediately start forming opinions about them. How they're dressed, the sound of their voice, and their smile all play into whether or not you feel a connection with these potential partners.

Selecting Information

If you've ever listened to testimony at a trial (or seen one on TV), you may have been struck by how one witness will remember the exact time of the accident or the color and make of the cars involved, while another witness will describe the scene and note the sequence of events. They both saw the same accident but selected different parts of it to remember. In any situation, we are faced with a great deal of information, which we must sift through to determine what is important. In our speed-dating example, Adam is taking in some of the information Irina provides: what she says, how she says it, what she looks like, and how she presents herself. But just as he has chosen to pay attention to some information, other information may have escaped his notice. For example, the next man Irina meets, Ben, might note that she has a warm smile and that she laughs really easily (at his bad jokes, no less). Of course, it is possible that Ben and Adam were exposed to different information: perhaps Irina was more comfortable with Ben. But often people can come to vastly different conclusions even in the exact same circumstances. This is because each individual organizes and adapts his or her perceptions into existing memory bases called *schemas*.

Schemas: Organizing Perceptions

As you receive information, you have to make sense of it. To do so, you rely not merely on the new information but also on how it fits with information you already have. For example, in evaluating Irina, speed dater Adam makes associations with his own experience and his own feelings. He compares Irina to his old girlfriend ("artsy") and to himself, guessing about her professional success. Adam, like all of us, is making sense of the endless inputs he receives through **schemas**, mental structures that put together related bits of information (Fiske & Taylor, 1991) (see Figure 2.1). Once put together, these chunks of information form patterns to create meaning at a more complex level.

AND YOU?

Think back to your first impressions of two different people, one whom you immediately liked and one who made a more negative impression. What role might your schemas have played in these first impressions? Did these individuals remind you of other people you like or dislike? Did they exhibit traits that you have found attractive or unattractive in others?

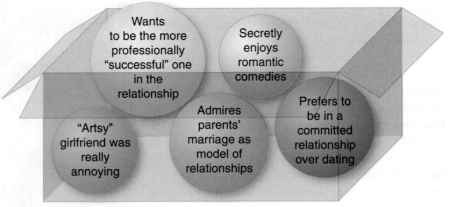

FIGURE 2.1

ADAM'S SCHEMA ABOUT DATING AND RELATIONSHIPS
Our schemas affect our communication and our relationships. Here is Adam's schema for dating and relationships, represented as a box containing pieces of information from various sources in his life.

Wants to be the more professionally "successful" one in the relationship

Secretly enjoys romantic comedies

"Artsy" girlfriend was really annoying

Admires parents' marriage as model of relationships

Prefers to be in a committed relationship over dating

The Function of Schemas

In essence, schemas help you understand how things work or anticipate how they should proceed. Communicators retrieve schemas from memory and interpret new information, people, and situations in accordance with those schemas. For example, imagine that during your walk across campus, a classmate approaches and says, "Hey, what's up?" An existing schema (memory of past encounters) tells you that you will exchange hellos and then, after some small talk, go your separate ways. When you recognize one component of a schema, the entire schema is activated and tells you what will most probably happen next.

As you go through life, you continually perceive new bits of information that help you structure and understand different situations. Your schemas adjust and enrich themselves through this process. Consider the popular *Harry Potter* books, in which author J. K. Rowling creates a world that continually challenges readers' (and Harry's) preconceived schemas. When young Harry first arrives at Hogwarts, he is both taken aback and delighted by his new environment: candles float, broomsticks fly, chess pieces move by themselves. Such magical objects and situations do not fit Harry's existing schemas of how things work. Yet as he moves through his seven years at Hogwarts, his schemas evolve: things that surprised him in year one no longer raise an eyebrow in year seven.

Challenges with Schemas and Perception

The schema process is a critical part of competent communication. To send and receive messages that are effective and appropriate, you must be able to process information in a way that makes sense to you but also has a high likelihood of being accurately perceived by others. Schemas can help you do all of these things. However, sometimes schemas can make you a less perceptive communicator; they may cloud your judgment or cause you to rely on stereotypes (which we discuss later in this chapter) or misinformation. Communication researchers note that schemas present three key challenges to competent communication: mindlessness, selective perception, and undue influence.

● **SEEING** "Mad-Eye Moody" use the Unforgivable Curses in Defense Against the Dark Arts in *Harry Potter and the Goblet of Fire* shocked Harry and made him feel uncomfortable. However, by the seventh book, hearing them no longer seems jarring.

Mindlessness.   To communicate competently, you must be focused on the task at hand, a process referred to as **mindfulness**. Schemas, however, may make you a less critical processor of information by producing a state of **mindlessness**, during which you process information passively. Mindlessness has its perks: it allows you to go through certain communication transactions automatically; you do not have to consciously think about how to place an order every time you go to a restaurant. But mindlessness can be problematic. Watch out for three signs of mindlessness in your interactions: reduced cognitive activity, inaccurate recall, and uncritical evaluation (Roloff, 1980). First, reduced cognitive activity means that when schemas take effect, you will simply think less or have fewer thoughts; it is much like you are fatigued and unstimulated. A second sign of mindlessness is the inaccurate recall of information. Your friend might ask for directions to a store you've shopped at, but you can't remember how, exactly, you got there: you were on "autopilot," following directions from your GPS, and can't recall the names of the roads you took. The third sign of mindlessness is the uncritical evaluation of what is processed. A mindless processor will not question the information that is being received and will react to the situation passively or lazily.

Selective perception.   A second and related perceptual challenge facing communicators is succumbing to the biased nature of perception, referred to as **selective perception**. Whereas mindlessness is passive, selective perception is usually active, critical thought. If a group of five people watches a televised debate between two political candidates, they will likely have five different interpretations of what took place and what was important. Based on their existing schemas, one person might focus on budget deficits; another might be most concerned with foreign affairs. Selective perception can be explained in part by the presence or absence of schemas. A person who is keenly interested in economics likely has a schema for ideas on balancing the federal budget and will pay attention to political opinions about it. By contrast, someone with no interest in economic matters may not pay attention to something a speaker says about balancing the budget.

Undue influence.   A third perceptual challenge that communicators deal with is resisting the **undue influence** of other people. Undue influence occurs when you give greater credibility or importance to something shown or said than

● **GRAPHIC NEWS STORIES** of muggings, murders, and brutal assaults might make you more likely to lock the doors and look repeatedly over your shoulder when you're out alone.

AND YOU?

Think of an individual whom you hold in very high regard, such as a parent, a favorite professor, a mentor, or a media pundit. How do this person's opinions influence your perceptions about specific matters? Is this an undue influence? Why or why not?

should be the case. For example, some people might have a tendency to give undue influence to male friends when discussing the topic of sports.

Even the media can be a source of undue influence. Research shows that people who watch talk shows develop perceptions that overestimate deviant behavior in society and develop less sensitive views of other people's suffering (Davis & Mares, 1998). Local media coverage of crimes also influences the perceptions that potential jurors have toward defendants. People who have been exposed to media reports are much more likely to perceive the defendants as guilty (Wright & Ross, 1997).

Attributions: Interpreting Your Perceptions

When perceiving others, we often try to explain why they say something or act in a certain way, especially if their behavior does not exactly fit our existing schema. Personal characteristics that are used to explain behavior are known as **attributions** (Jones, 1990). You make attributions to try to explain the causes of a behavior and to justify your perceptions, thus giving you greater control of the situation. Consider the following exchange:

EMMA   I'm heading over to Mark's place to help him study for our mid-term. He has really been struggling this semester.

CALEB   Well, he was never exactly a rocket scientist.

Emma can make some different kinds of attributions here. She might attribute Caleb's comment to his personality ("Caleb is such a mean person!") or to the situation ("Wow, something put Caleb in a bad mood."). When we attribute behavior to someone's personality (or something within the person's control), we call that an *internal* attribution, whereas situational attributions are *external* (outside the person's control). How do we decide? If Emma considers that Caleb is not usually so blunt or harsh about other people, she is likely to attribute his behavior to something outside his personality.

Attributions can be problematic, as the **fundamental attribution error** illustrates (McLeod, Detenber, & Eveland, 2001; Ross & Nisbett, 1991). Fundamental attribution error explains our tendency to overemphasize the internal and underestimate the external causes of behaviors we observe in others (for example, "Carla failed the midterm because she was too lazy to study"). When it comes to attributions about ourselves, however, the opposite effect is attributed. The **self-serving bias** holds that we usually attribute our own successes to internal factors ("I got an 'A' because I am smart") while we explain our failures by attributing them to situational or external effects ("I failed the midterm because my professor stinks").

We make attributions all the time, and once we do, it exerts a very powerful effect on our communication. That is not, however, to say that our attributions are set in stone. Unexpected events or simply time can change how people perceive others. For example, Mel Gibson (once considered a bona-fide megastar and *People* magazine's very first "Sexiest Man Alive") quickly morphed into box office poison after tapes of his violent, bigoted, and sexist rants became public.

Sandra Bullock, on the other hand, having held her head high during what could have been a humiliating breakup with her cheating husband, Jesse James, emerged from her very public divorce more popular—and powerful—than ever.

Interaction appearance theory helps explain how people change their attributions of someone, particularly their physical attractiveness, the more they interact (Albada, Knapp, & Theune, 2002). Audiences' perceptions of Gibson and Bullock adjusted as they witnessed more and more of their behavior. We go through a similar process in our own interpersonal relationships: people become more or less attractive to us as we get to know them better. This is an interdependent process, in which the social interaction and relational attraction feed each other. If you think back to past relationships, you may remember finding someone more attractive after you discovered, say, the person's quirky sense of humor. In this case, attributions work for the good of the relationship.

AND YOU?

Have you ever had an opinion of someone that was changed? How did that occur? Do you think something has to be major to change your opinion of someone?

Improving Your Perceptions

It is not always easy to make accurate perceptions. For example, in the classic basketball film *Hoosiers*, Gene Hackman plays Hickory High basketball coach Norman Dale. Dale's small-town players are intimidated by the cavernous arena where they are to play for the Indiana state championship. Though they are aware that the basketball court is supposed to be regulation size, it looks enormous to them. It isn't until Dale uses a tape measure in front of their eyes to measure the height of the basket and the distance from the foul line that they start to perceive that the distances are no different from those in their tiny gym. This corrects their selective perception and restores their confidence.

We all tend at one time or another to perceive selectively or to be mindless. The following suggestions can help you overcome these tendencies, improve your perception abilities, and thus become a better communicator.

▶ *Verify your perceptions.* It may be natural to jump to some conclusions—to depend to some degree on existing schemas—but it is crucial that you take the time to confirm (or debunk) your conclusions. At a park, you might see a parent yell at a small child and grab the child's arm. Your initial perception might be that the parent is extremely harsh and possibly even abusive. But look more closely—the child may have been about to reach for a sharp piece of a broken bottle on the ground.

▶ *Be thoughtful when you seek explanations.* Resist the natural tendency to fall back on the most obvious explanation for what you observe. For example, scuffles occasionally break out among players in college and professional sports. Your tendency may be to assume that the person who threw the first punch instigated the fight. Frequently, however, a fight starts when someone else says or does something that the fans cannot easily perceive: a hockey player might have thrown his stick high in the face of another player or may have uttered an offensive term. In these situations, you need to ask yourself whether some event or action might have preceded or provoked what you observed.

> *Look beyond first impressions.* A third way to improve the accuracy of your perceptions is not to rely completely on your very first impressions, which often lead to inaccurate conclusions. Consider Meghan, who frequently comes off as gregarious and loud when people first meet her. Meghan is actually quite thoughtful and kind—she just loves meeting new people and is exuberant when asking questions while getting to know them. Whenever possible, it is wise to delay reaction or judgment until further perceptions are made.

Perception in a Diverse World

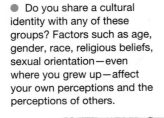

● Do you share a cultural identity with any of these groups? Factors such as age, gender, race, religious beliefs, sexual orientation—even where you grew up—affect your own perceptions and the perceptions of others.

A few generations ago, our great-grandparents may have gone months without coming into contact with someone from a different village or neighborhood; a wheelchair-bound child may have been unable to attend public schools; and in parts of this country, white and black Americans were not permitted to sit at the same lunch counter. In modern society, people from all walks of life learn, work, and play together. Through the use of technology, we are able to communicate with others across vast distances. A student in Louisville, Kentucky, can chat online with a student from Bangladesh; a salesperson in Omaha, Nebraska, may have steady working relationships with clients in Tokyo. Our perceptions are inextricably linked to the wide diversity we encounter in the world.

The Cultural Context

If you watch soccer—or football, as most of the world calls the game—chances are that you spent a good deal of time in 2010 following the World Cup. If so, you are quite familiar with the monotone buzzing sound that emanated loudly from the crowds, as tens of thousands of fans blew on long plastic horns called *vuvuzelas*. But how you perceived the noise depended a great deal on your particular culture. For American broadcasters, the buzzing

COMMUNICATIONACROSSCULTURES

Pregnancy, Perception, and Culture

Childbirth never seems to slow down Heidi Klum. Just a few weeks after giving birth to her fourth child, Klum was back at work, hosting the Victoria Secret runway show, doing modeling work, and gearing up for another season as producer, host, and judge on *Project Runway*. Klum's case isn't all that unusual in America. In the United States, many mothers remain active after pregnancy. They hit the gym, return to work, and go on with their lives.

But in China, a new mom is traditionally expected to spend the first forty days after pregnancy behind closed doors in an effort to enhance her milk-producing ability. It's feared that chills might be harmful to healthy breast milk, and so windows must remain closed and bathing is forbidden. This practice is known as *zuo yuezi* (Tao, 2000). In order for *zuo yuezi* to succeed, household members and friends wait on the new mother, taking care of both her home and her personal needs. They are also expected to watch over and wait on the newborn infant. It is understood that the practice of *zuo yuezi* brings the women of the family, particularly the mothers, closer together.

Imagine how perceptions of women can be influenced by these two very different practices, were the two cultures to intermingle. In the United States, a woman from China might be regarded as lazy, rude, weak, or even superstitious by her American hosts because she is not attending to her own baby's needs. But in China, an American woman might be perceived as selfishly endangering the baby's health by not protecting the quality of her milk.

According to Pam O'Sullivan, the director of the BC Women's Hospital Birthing Program, significant cultural intermingling is occurring in her hospital in Vancouver, where there is a high density of both Chinese and Caucasian women (Williams, 2005). But once a hospital understands *why* certain practices are in play, it can execute policies to balance cultural differences and safety regulations. O'Sullivan explains, "We will push beds to the far end of the rooms to accommodate extended families and supply boiled water to Asian mothers who like to drink it to avoid stress. Although hygiene is very important, we will allow sponge bathing for women who traditionally avoid bathing and showering around births" (quoted in Williams, 2005).

This kind of balance could not come about without first clarifying perceptions about a patient's culture.

THINK ABOUT THIS

❶ How might an American's perception of the *zuo yuezi* tradition lead to other perceptions about Chinese women and their home life, their friends, work, gender beliefs, and other matters? How might the reverse be true? How does one assumption often lead to others?

❷ Who has the responsibility to clarify perceptions?

❸ Are there instances in which making assumptions about another person's culture is helpful or necessary?

To ensure that *diversity* is respected in professional situations, organizations (as well as the U.S. government) enact policies and codes of behavior to protect employees from hurtful, antagonistic communication regarding their sex, race, religion, national origin, sexual orientation, age, and abilities. This type of derogatory communication, known as *harassment*, is discussed in Chapter 11.

was a nuisance and a technological hurdle; for some international players, it was a distraction and an aggravation. But for South African fans, it was part of the game. In the words of one commentator, the *vuvuzela* is the "recognised sound of football in South Africa . . . [and] absolutely essential for an authentic South African footballing experience" (Mungazi, 2009).

As you likely know from experience, culture is an incredibly powerful context of communication: it has a profound effect on the way we perceive ourselves and the people around us. It's why something perceived as delightful and fun by South African fans could seem inappropriate and irritating to fans from other cultures. Think back to the competent communication model in Chapter 1. The ring that comprises the cultural context is made up of variables that make our perceptions unique: race, ethnicity, religion, politics, gender, sexual orientation, age, education, role, occupation, abilities/disabilities, geography, and so on. These differences are known as *diversity* (Loden & Rosener, 1991). (Also see our discussion of co-cultural variation in Chapter 3.) To communicate effectively and appropriately in today's world, you must possess an understanding of and appreciation for people who perceive differently than you do. It's also important to understand the way your unique background affects your perceptions.

Perceptual Barriers

Karl Krayer is an independent communication consultant who does diversity training for corporations, schools, and other organizations. Based on his experience, Krayer notes that successful intercultural communication requires mindfulness, being respectful of others, and maintaining an accurate perception of the situation. "Resistance to cultural diversity usually boils down to ignorance," Krayer says. "Once people understand other cultural groups better, it doesn't take long to see the fruits of the labor— that is, people working cooperatively together for a common cause" (personal communication, May 19, 2004). In our diverse world, perceptual challenges can give rise to potential barriers to competent communication, including narrow perspectives and stereotyping.

A Narrow Perspective

When Hurricane Katrina devastated the city of New Orleans in 2005, leaving countless residents trapped on rooftops or huddled in the Superdome for shelter, many Americans wondered why New Orleans residents didn't just get into their cars and leave the city when the flood warnings were announced. Outsiders didn't understand the levee system or residents' strong allegiance to the city and its culture. For many upper- and middle-class Americans, the idea that a family might not own

● **MANY NEW ORLEANS RESIDENTS** who did not evacuate for Hurricane Katrina found themselves without food, water, or shelter. They perceived their government as abandoning them, while outsiders perceived the residents as crazy for not leaving.

a car, might not be able to afford to stay in a hotel out of town, or might fear that its abandoned home would be looted never crossed their minds. They were blinded by their own circumstances—their own socioeconomic or geographical experiences clouded their perception of other people's reality. Individuals who fail to consider other cultural perspectives in this manner are said to suffer from **cultural myopia**, a form of nearsightedness grounded in the belief that one's own culture is appropriate and relevant in all situations and to all people (Loden & Rosener, 1991). Cultural myopia is especially dangerous when members of the dominant group in a society are unaware of or are insensitive toward the needs and values of members of others in the same society.

Stereotyping and Prejudice

As you learned earlier in this chapter, we rely on schemas to organize information and create mental structures that suggest patterns and meaning. Yet schemas can be dangerous in a diverse society if we rely on them to make generalizations about people. **Stereotyping** is the act of fitting individuals into an existing schema without adjusting the schema appropriately; it involves organizing information about groups of people into categories so that you can generalize about their attitudes, behaviors, skills, morals, and habits. Stereotyping is an impression of a group of people that is fixed or set, so that when you meet an individual from this group, you apply your set of perceptions of the entire group to that individual.

Stereotypes may be positive, negative, or neutral; they may be about a group to which you belong or one that is different from your own. If you have a negative stereotype about corporate executives, for example, you may think that they are all greedy individuals participating in unethical, and perhaps illegal, financial activities, despite the fact that many, if not most, are hardworking men and women who have climbed the ranks of the corporate ladder. On the other hand, a positive stereotype might lead you to overlook bad behaviors that don't conform to your ideas.

Such stereotyping plays a role in the way we perceive individual behaviors. In a study of the effects of friends' posts on Facebook (Walther, Van Der Heide, Kim, Westerman, & Tong, 2008), researchers found that for men, negative posts about their excessive drunkenness and sexual exploits resulted in perceptions of greater attractiveness. But the same kinds of posts produced very negative judgments when posted about women. The researchers argue that these online reactions both reflect and reinforce the double standard about the acceptability of moral "misbehavior" among men versus women.

Stereotypes lead to what is perhaps the most severe barrier to intercultural communication: **prejudice**, a deep-seated feeling of unkindness and ill will toward particular groups, usually based on negative stereotypes and feelings of superiority over those groups. These attitudes make it easy to protect your own group's attitudes and behaviors while abusing those of other people. At its most extreme, prejudice can lead to a belief

CONNECT

As you learn in Chapter 3, stereotypes and prejudice can lead to *discrimination* in which your thoughts about an individual or group lead to specific behaviors. So if you believe that all sorority members are poor students (and you dislike them for this belief), you may discriminate against a Zeta Tau Alpha member in your study group, believing her incapable of handling the workload.

● **DESPITE THE NEGATIVE** stereotype of vampires as savage and dangerous creatures on *True Blood*, Sookie Stackhouse is able to look beyond deep-seated prejudices and find true love in vampire Bill Compton.

that the lives of some people are worth less than those of others; the entire institution of slavery in the United States flourished based on this belief. Even today, the cultural landscape of almost every nation is dotted with groups who advocate the notion of racial superiority.

Prejudice is not limited to groups, either. We might have preconceived ideas about an individual based on limited experience. If Shayla was feeling ill on the day that Clark met her, he might come to the conclusion that she is grumpy all the time. This snap judgment tends to prejudice Clark toward Shayla and may color his perception of her in future communication. Clark is committing the kind of fundamental attribution error we discussed earlier in this chapter. Sadly, making these errors based on judgments about race, culture, or ethnicity is a common trap. We'll discuss these perceptual barriers further—and detail ways of removing them—in Chapter 3.

Cognition: Perceiving Ourselves

Imagine spending the first nineteen years of your life without an official first name. That's what "Baby Boy" Pauson did. His father disappeared and his mother never got around to picking a name for his birth certificate. People referred to him as Max (after his mother, Maxine), yet his official records still noted his legal name as "Baby Boy." Tormented, teased, and bounced around for years, Pauson perceived himself as an outcast and escaped to comic books, animation, and fantasy. It wasn't until he entered San Francisco's School of the Arts that he discovered that his art and creativity were received positively and his nonconformity was valued. He finally found a lawyer who helped him create an official identity with the weighty name he had imagined for himself as a child— Maximus Julius Pauson (Eckholm, 2010).

For most of us, our name (or nickname) is an important part of the way we perceive ourselves. Many women who marry debate whether or not to change their last names: some worry that losing the last name they were born with might signify the loss of a personal identity; others look at adapting a new last name as a way to make their relationship status clear or to signify a new beginning as a joined "family." We introduce ourselves using the names we prefer (our full name, first or last name only, a nickname, or a moniker like "coach" or "doc"), based on the way we perceive ourselves and want others to perceive us. Though you may not have struggled with your name, you—like all people—have certainly struggled with the challenge of understanding and projecting your identity in order to become a more competent communicator. There are three important influences on our *cognitions*, or thoughts about ourselves: self-concept, self-esteem, and self-efficacy (see Figure 2.2 on p. 49).

Self-Concept: Who You Think You Are

Think for a moment about who you are. You may describe yourself to others as a college student, a Latino male, a white female, a heterosexual, a biology major, an uncle, a parent, or a friend. But who you are involves much more. As we discussed in Chapter 1, your awareness and understanding of who you are—as interpreted and influenced by your thoughts, actions, abilities, values, goals, and ideals—is your **self-concept**. You develop a self-concept by thinking about your strengths and weaknesses, observing your behavior in a wide variety of situations, witnessing your own reactions to situations, and watching others' reactions to you (Snyder, 1979). You have views about yourself as active and scattered, as conservative but funny, as plain and popular—the list goes on and on. These are your cognitions. Remember from the model in Chapter 1 that both cognition and behavior make a communicator. In Chapter 1, we focused on cognitions about other people, places, media, and so on. But cognitions about self matter, too.

The self-concept has incredible power to shape your communication with others. It can shape what you think of other people because your perception of others is related to how you view yourself (Edwards, 1990). If attributes like honesty and wit are important to you, you will consider them important traits in other people; if you think that using foul language makes you appear cheap and vulgar, you are likely to think the same of others when they use such language. When you interact, self-concept is in play as well. It can affect how apprehensive you get in certain communication situations (McCroskey, 1997), whether or not you are willing to interact with others (Cegala, 1981), and how you approach someone with a request (whether you are meek and timid or strong and confident). People whose self-concept includes pride in their ability to communicate well often place themselves in situations where they are able to use their skills most effectively—Barbara Walters and Conan O'Brien didn't become TV show hosts by accident! Similarly, people whose self-concept offers a less favorable view of their communication skills may shy away from opportunities (like seeking out a romantic partner or a new friendship) where such skills (or lack of them) would be in the spotlight.

So while your self-concept strongly influences how and when you communicate with others, the reverse is also true: when you interact with other people, you get impressions from them that reveal how they evaluate you as a person and as a communicator. This information gets reincorporated into your self-concept. In fact, many researchers believe that social interaction is key to developing one's self-concept because when you communicate with others, you receive evidence that you can then use to develop, confirm, or change your self-concept. *Direct evidence* comes in the form of compliments, insults, support, or negative remarks. For example, if a professor you admire tells you that you have great potential as a manager because you possess excellent leadership skills, you would probably make this information part of your self-concept. *Indirect evidence* that influences your self-concept might be revealed through innuendo, gossip, subtle nonverbal cues, or a lack of communication. For instance, if you ask a friend to evaluate your promise as a contestant on *American Idol* and he changes the subject, you might get the impression that you are

● **BARBARA WALTERS** and Conan O'Brien have honed their confident and charismatic personalities to build successful talk-show careers.

not such a great singer after all (not that such advice has stopped many terrible singers from trying out for this program!).

Other people with whom we have contact—be it direct contact with friends and acquaintances, or virtual contact through the mass media—also influence our self-concept. We tend to compare ourselves to others as we develop our ideas about ourselves. This is called **social comparison theory** (Bishop, 2000; Festinger, 1954), and it can influence how we think about ourselves and what we're willing to do to close the unavoidable gap created by this comparison. For example, if you are the least financially well-off among your friends, you may feel as though you are poor; given the same income and resources but a circle of less fortunate friends, you might consider yourself to be well-off. Images in the media—including concepts of beauty, wealth, and happiness—can affect self-concept in a similar way. Body image issues and eating disorders, for example, have been linked to individuals' perceptions of beauty and health, which in turn have been linked to images of perfection exhibited in the media (Bishop, 2000; Hendriks, 2002).

Clearly, the self-concept exerts a powerful influence on our lives, our relationships, and our communication. Struggles with self-concept—the way we see ourselves—are closely related to the way we feel about ourselves. Next, we examine how these feelings relate to communication.

Self-Esteem: How You Feel About Yourself

Self-esteem refers to how you feel about yourself, usually in a particular situation. Self-esteem is essentially a set of attitudes that people hold about their own emotions, thoughts, abilities, skills, behavior, and beliefs that fluctuate according to the situation or context. Self-concept and self-esteem are closely related: people need to know themselves in order to have attitudes about themselves. Consequently, many researchers believe that the self-concept forms first, and self-esteem emerges thereafter (Greenwalk, Bellezza, & Banaji, 1988).

You have probably noticed that people with high self-esteem have confidence in what they do, how they think, and how they perform. That's partly because these individuals are better able to incorporate their successes into their self-concept. This projection of confidence led the high-end Italian clothing company Canali to make Yankee baseball pitcher Mariano Rivera the first sports figure star in their advertising campaign history (Araton, 2010). Rivera's self-assurance and self-control add to the perception of Canali's elegant clothing.

Research shows that people with high self-esteem are more confident in their interpersonal relationships, too—perhaps because they are more likely to believe that being friendly will cause others to be friendly in return (Baldwin & Keelan, 1999). Research also shows that perceived commitment from a romantic partner enhances self-esteem (Rill, Balocchi, et al., 2009). So, individuals with high self-esteem may not feel a strong need for public displays of affection, whereas a man with low self-esteem might press his girlfriend to show affection in public in order to say, "Look! Someone loves me!"

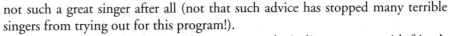

● **YANKEES PITCHER MARIANO** Rivera brings an essence of elegant self-assurance and self-control to an ad for Canali's high-end clothing.

Research suggests that some people have low self-esteem, or a poor view of themselves, because they either lack accurate information about themselves or mistrust the knowledge they do possess. For example, you may feel that you are a poor student because you have to study constantly to keep up your grades in German class. Your German professor, on the other hand, might find that your efforts and the improvement you've made over the semester reveal that you are a good, hardworking student. Low self-esteem may also result from an *inconsistent* view of oneself (Campbell, 1990). Some people who think they possess shortcomings or negative traits may prefer to ignore them so that these traits will not affect their more enduring self-esteem. A satirical example of this kind of denial is provided in the characters of the satire *It's Always Sunny in Philadelphia*. Siblings Dennis and Dee each exhibit some of the most unlikable characteristics imaginable. They are at once ignorant, smug, prejudiced, and childish. Yet each character remains convinced of his or her own superiority—believing themselves to be highly attractive and intellectually enlightened—and ignores any and all evidence that contradicts this view.

● **EACH MEMBER** of the *It's Always Sunny in Philadelphia* crew is so blinded by his or her own ego that butting heads is an almost constant occurrence among the pals.

Self-Efficacy: Assessing Your Own Abilities

The cosmetic industry typically relies on flawless models to sell its products. So how did Lauren Luke—a plain English woman—become a celebrity stylist? Luke began selling cosmetics for modest profit on eBay; instead of showing actual products, she used them on herself and took photos; soon she began posting videos on YouTube that she'd taped from her bedroom and was logging more than fifty million views. Luke may not have possessed the star quality of cosmetics spokeswomen like Queen Latifa and Eva Longoria, but she did have confidence in herself and her skills as a makeup artist. She was soon a celebrity in her own right, striking a deal with Sephora and being hailed by *Allure* magazine as a 2010 "Influencer" (La Ferla, 2009).

You have an overall view of all aspects of yourself (self-concept), as well as an evaluation of how you feel about yourself in a particular area at any given moment in time (self-esteem). Based on this information, you approach

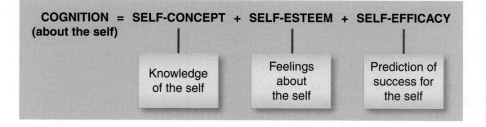

COGNITION = SELF-CONCEPT + SELF-ESTEEM + SELF-EFFICACY
(about the self)

| Knowledge of the self | Feelings about the self | Prediction of success for the self |

FIGURE 2.2

UNDERSTANDING COGNITION

a communication situation with an eye toward the *likelihood* of presenting yourself effectively. According to Albert Bandura (1982), this ability to predict actual success from self-concept and self-esteem is **self-efficacy**. Your perceptions of self-efficacy guide your ultimate choice of communication situations, making you much more likely to avoid situations where you believe your self-efficacy to be low. Indeed, many people who worry about their (in)ability to make a good impression choose computer mediated communication (CMC) over face-to-face interactions. Sugitani (2007) found that because CMC (such as e-mail) lacks the nonverbal cues that often reveal our nervousness, we can feel more confident in and have better control over how we present ourselves through text alone.

EVALUATINGCOMMUNICATIONETHICS

THINK ABOUT THIS

Ethics and the Self-Concept

You and your romantic partner, Peyton, have been together for three years and have supported each other through many ups and downs, particularly in your professional lives. Both of you have successful careers and have made sacrifices to help each other achieve personal and professional goals. Most recently, the two of you moved to Washington, D.C., from Saint Louis so that Peyton could accept a promotion with a large financial investment firm. Since you were thrilled for Peyton's career opportunity and since you are able to work from a home office, you consented to the move. But it has been difficult because Peyton works long hours and your entire family and most of your close friends are still in Saint Louis.

Peyton comes home early one afternoon to announce that the investment firm has offered another promotion to a position that would require travel from Monday to Friday two weeks out of the month. Peyton talks excitedly about the increase in status and in pay and the new opportunities that the position would afford you both. Your immediate reaction is one of anger. How could Peyton consider taking a position that required so much travel, especially since this would leave you alone in a city where you know few people and where you work alone out of your home? Hadn't you sacrificed enough by moving halfway across the country for Peyton's career?

You confront Peyton, who is first surprised and then angry. "I thought we were working for the same thing—a better opportunity for our future," Peyton said. "I am good to you, and I give you everything you want. I thought I could count on you to support me in this. It is not like it will be much different from the way it is now since I work so late. After all, I'll be home every weekend."

You are hurt. You value harmony in your home and your relationships, and you value time spent with your partner. You believe that you are a flexible, reasonable person who appreciates joint decision-making. You feel that you have been supportive and that you have made Peyton's career a priority in your home. Peyton's reaction, however, sends a much different message that makes you uneasy. You are upset by the different ways that you and Peyton perceive the situation and the ensuing communication difficulties.

❶ Consider the different elements that make up both your self-concept and your partner's. What do you each value? What are your goals and ideals? What are your thoughts and beliefs about work, relationships, and other important matters?

❷ How might your self-concept have affected the way that you perceived Peyton's message about the promotion? How might the message have affected your self-esteem?

❸ Now take Peyton's perspective. How might your partner's self-concept have affected the way that the news of the promotion was shared with you? How might your reaction have affected Peyton's self-esteem?

Even though a person's lack of effort is most often caused by perceptions of low efficacy, Bandura (1982) has observed that people with very high levels of self-efficacy sometimes become overconfident. Defending Olympic men's figure skating champion Evgeni Plushenko bragged to media that winning the Gold in 2010 would be easy; he even held up both index fingers when he finished, as if to say, "Was there any question?" But his overconfidence may have cost him the Gold to the U.S.'s Evan Lysacek. Bandura recommends that people maintain a high level of self-efficacy with just enough uncertainty to cause them to anticipate the situation accurately and prepare accordingly: a professional athlete might review footage of an opponent's best plays, for example, to keep a keen edge.

Interpreting Events

Self-efficacy also has an effect on your ability to cope with failure and stress. Feelings of low efficacy may cause you to dwell on your shortcomings. A snowball effect occurs when you already feel inadequate and then fail at something: the failure takes its toll on your self-esteem, causing you to experience stress and negative emotional reactions. These feelings then contribute to lower self-esteem, which in turn sends your self-efficacy level even lower. For example, Jessie is job-hunting but worries that she does not do well in interviews. Each job she doesn't get reinforces this assessment; with each failed interview, she lowers her expectations for herself, and her interview performance worsens as well. By contrast, individuals with high self-efficacy are less emotionally affected by failure because they usually chalk up their shortcoming to a "bad day" or some other external factor. When Erin doesn't get a job she interviewed for, for example, she concludes that she'd stumbled on her words this time because she wasn't as well prepared as she usually is. Rather than dwelling on the failure, she simply vows to be better prepared for the next interview.

Self-Fulfilling Prophecies

Inaccurate self-efficacy may lead to a **self-fulfilling prophecy**—a prediction that causes an individual to alter his or her behavior in a way that makes the prediction more likely to occur. If your friend Josh goes to a party believing that others don't enjoy his company, for example, he is more likely to stand in a corner, not talking to anyone and making no effort to be friendly. Thus, Josh's prophecy is fulfilled: others don't like him. Josh's problem began before he even reached the party. He had anticipated that the party might turn out poorly for him based on his understanding of his likeability. Self-efficacy and self-fulfilling prophecy are therefore related. When you cannot avoid situations where you experience low efficacy, you are less likely to make an effort to prepare or participate than you would for situations in which you are comfortable and perceive high efficacy. When you do not prepare for or participate in a situation (as Josh did not participate in the party), your behavior causes the prediction to come true, creating a self-fulfilling prophecy (see Figure 2.3).

● **OLYMPIC FIGURE SKATER** Evgeni Plushenko had no choice but to swallow his pride and settle for the silver medal in 2010 after bragging about how easily he would secure the Gold.

CONNECT

Self-fulfilling prophecies are deeply tied to verbal and nonverbal communication. If you believe you will ace a job interview because you are well prepared, you will likely stand tall and make confident eye contact with your interviewer (Chapter 5) and use appropriate and effective language (Chapter 4) to describe your skill set. Your confidence just may land you the position you want!

Self-Fulfilling Prophecy (SFP)

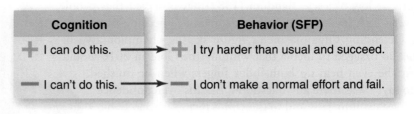

Self-fulfilling prophecy imposed on others:

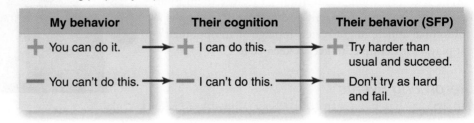

FIGURE 2.3
THE SELF-FULFILLING
PROPHECY

Self-fulfilling prophecies don't always produce negative results. If you announce you are going to improve your grades after a lackluster semester, and then work harder than usual to accomplish your goal, your prediction may result in an improved report card. But even the simple act of announcing your goals to others—for example, tweeting your intention to quit smoking or to finish a marathon—can create a commitment to making a positive self-fulfilling prophecy come true (Willard & Gramzow, 2008).

Assessing Our Perceptions of Self

As a communicator, you are constantly assessing your competence level for strengths and weaknesses. These assessments of self are important before, during, and after you have communicated, particularly when you've received feedback from other people. You evaluate your expectations, execution, and outcomes in three ways: self-actualization, self-adequacy, and self-denigration.

Self-Actualization

The most positive evaluation you can make about your competence level is referred to as **self-actualization**—the feelings and thoughts you get when you know that you have negotiated a communication situation as well as you possibly could. At times like these, you have a sense of fulfillment and satisfaction. For example, Shari, a school psychologist, was having problems with the third-grade teacher of one of the students she counsels. The teacher seemed to act uninterested in the student's performance, would not return Shari's phone calls or e-mails, and seemed curt and aloof when they did speak. Shari finally decided to confront the teacher. Although she was nervous at first about saying the right thing, she later felt very good about the experience. The teacher had seemed shocked at the criticism but offered an apology. At the end of the meeting, Shari was quite content that she had been honest and assertive, yet fair and understanding. This positive assessment of her behavior led to a higher level of self-esteem. When Shari needs to confront someone in the future, she will likely feel more confident.

Self-Adequacy

At times you may think that your communication performance was not stellar, but it was good enough. When you assess your communication competence as sufficient or acceptable, you are feeling a sense of **self-adequacy**, which is less positive than self-actualization. Feelings of self-adequacy can lead you in two directions—either to contentment or to a desire for self-improvement.

Suppose that Phil has been working very hard to improve his public speaking abilities and does a satisfactory job when he speaks to his fraternity about its goals for charitable work for the next year. He might feel very satisfied about his speech, but he realizes that with a little more effort and practice, he could become even more persuasive. In this case, Phil's reaction is one of *self-improvement*. He is telling himself that he wants to be more competent in his communication, regardless of his current level.

While self-improvement is a good motivation, in some circumstances being satisfied or content with your self-adequacy is sufficient. For example, Lilia has a long history of communication difficulties with her mother. Their relationship is characterized by sarcastic and unkind comments and interactions. But during her last visit home, Lilia avoided conflict and felt good about her communication with her mom. The two didn't become best friends or resolve all the old problems, but Lilia thought she communicated well under the circumstances. She was content with her self-adequacy.

Self-Denigration

The most negative assessment you can make about a communication experience is **self-denigration**. Self-denigration is criticizing or attacking yourself. It most often occurs when communicators place undue importance on their weaknesses or shortcomings ("I knew I'd end up fumbling over my own words and repeating myself—I am so inarticulate!"). Most self-denigration is unnecessary and unwarranted, and it prevents real improvement. Hunter, for example, thinks that he can't talk to his sister; he perceives her as stubborn and judgmental. Hunter says, "I know my sister won't listen. I can't do anything right in her eyes." Hunter needs to assess his communication behaviors: what specific words and nonverbal behaviors (like tone of voice) does he use with his sister? He must avoid self-denigration by focusing on times when he had positive communication with his sister; he can plan for communication improvement ("Next time, I will listen to my sister completely before I say anything back to her"). Thus our assessments of our competence run from self-actualization on the positive end to self-denigration on the negative end (see Figure 2.4 on the next page).

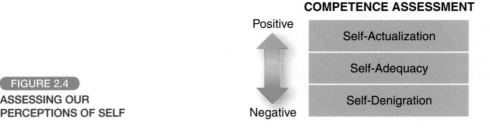

COMPETENCE ASSESSMENT

Positive

Self-Actualization

Self-Adequacy

Self-Denigration

Negative

FIGURE 2.4

ASSESSING OUR PERCEPTIONS OF SELF

Behavior: Managing Our Identities

As you've learned, you define yourself internally, through your self-concept and your ideas about self-esteem and self-efficacy. But you also make decisions about how to share your internal view with others; this is manifested in your behaviors, both verbal and nonverbal. Cognition and behavior play roles in the way you perceive others and the way that others perceive you.

We all have aspects of ourselves that we want to share and aspects that we would rather keep private. Many of the choices we make in our communication behavior, from the clothes we wear to the way we speak, are determined by the way we want others to perceive us. Here we'll look at how we let the world know just who we think we are and how our communication with others can shape the ways in which they view us.

Let's examine the process illustrated in Figure 2.5 for a moment. At the core of this process is the self. The self has cognitions (about the self) that con-

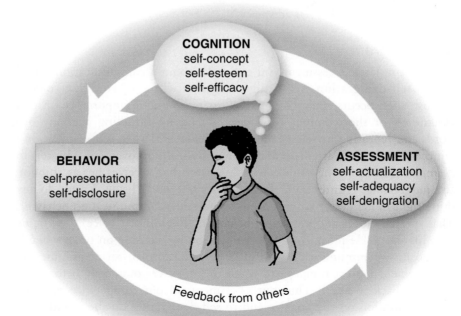

COGNITION
self-concept
self-esteem
self-efficacy

BEHAVIOR
self-presentation
self-disclosure

ASSESSMENT
self-actualization
self-adequacy
self-denigration

Feedback from others

FIGURE 2.5

THE SELF The self is composed of our cognitions, our behavior, and our self-assessments. These factors work together to affect our communication.

sist of self-concept (knowing and understanding the self), self-esteem (evaluating the self), and self-efficacy (predicting success), all of which we've discussed. These cognitions influence our verbal and nonverbal behavior, which are composed of self-presentation and self-disclosure, two terms we will explain next. Our behavior generates feedback from others, which leads to our assessments of self-actualization, self-adequacy, and self-denigration. These judgments of our performance then affect our cognition. As you read about self-presentation, self-disclosure, and feedback in the coming pages, refer to this illustration as a reminder of their roles in our continuously evolving interactions with others.

Self-Presentation

You let others know about yourself through **self-presentation**, intentional communication designed to show elements of self for strategic purposes. For example, if you want to create an impression among your coworkers that you are competent at your job as an editor, you might mention during conversations the names of popular authors you've worked with or tell stories about hilariously terrible errors you've found in various manuscripts you've worked on. You tend to focus on self-presentation more when your social identity is being evaluated (formally or informally) by others (Canary & Cody, 1993). This is why you'll usually act differently in a situation where you're trying to impress someone (for example, when you are meeting your significant other's parents for the first time) than you will in a situation where you feel entirely comfortable with the way others view you (hanging out with your own friends or family).

Self-presentation comes in many forms. You can present yourself through face-to-face conversation, through e-mail or text messaging, and on social networking sites like Twitter and Facebook. You may even have a preference for one of these channels of communication when self-presenting. For example, many people will use asynchronous channels (e-mail, text messages, cards) when they are unsure of the reaction they will get when they present themselves (O'Sullivan, 2000). For example, after a heated argument with her boyfriend Lance, Julie wanted to apologize. Because she was uncomfortable in making this self-presentation to Lance over the phone or in person, she chose to send him a text message when she knew that he would have his phone turned off. In fact, the most common reasons for choosing e-mail or texting over face-to-face interaction is the ability to carefully construct our messages and to "shield" ourselves from any immediate negative feedback that might come from the other person (Riordan & Kreutz, 2010).

Knowing how to present yourself in the best way usually involves paying attention to your behavior and that of others. **Self-monitoring** is your ability to watch your environment and others in it for cues as to how to present yourself in a particular situation (Snyder, 1974). High-self-monitoring individuals try to portray themselves as "the right person in the right place at the right time." These people watch others for hints on how to be successful in social situations and attempt to produce the verbal and nonverbal cues that seem most appropriate. You may know someone who is a high-self-monitoring communicator. During class, this person always sits in a certain strategic

AND YOU?

Like Julie, you have probably encountered situations in which you chose to engage in either face-to-face communication or mediated communication (text messaging, posting on a Facebook wall, e-mailing). Why did you choose a particular channel? If you chose a mediated channel, did you feel safer from an unknown reaction as the research suggests? Why or why not?

● **PLACES OF WORSHIP**
often have dress codes,
whether they are explicitly
stated or not. People may feel
that you are being disrespectful and inappropriate if you
ignore the rules and do things
your own way.

CONNECT

The process of choosing
what information to share
with others has long fas-
cinated researchers. In
Chapter 7, we examine the
Social Penetration Theory,
which uses an onion as a
metaphor to show how we
move from superficial con-
fessions to more intimate
ones. Your outer "layer"
might consist of disclosure
about where you are from,
but as you peel away the
layers, your disclosures
become more personal.

position, gets involved in discussions when others do
so, gestures in a similar manner to others, and when it
is time to let others talk, is very strategic with silence.
These "sufficiently skilled actors" are able to implement
situation-appropriate communication behaviors (Snyder,
1974).

Low-self-monitoring individuals are not nearly so sensitive to situational cues that prescribe communication behavior. They communicate according to their deep-seated
values or beliefs. They do not feel the need to adapt to situations or people; rather, they feel that people and situations must take them the way they are, at face value. If low
self-monitors anticipate a communication situation that is
different from their own self-presentation style, they will
either avoid the situation or accept the fact that their communication may not please all the parties involved.

Communicating successfully involves finding the appropriate level of self-
monitoring for the situation and the people involved. It might seem like high
self-monitors are the winners in social interaction, but this isn't always the case.
High self-monitors can drive themselves crazy by focusing on every little thing
that they say and do (Wright, Holloway, & Roloff, 2007). Competent communicators will monitor self-presentation just high enough to present themselves
effectively without forgetting that communication involves others. And of
course, don't forget that you cannot control what *others* do around you that may
affect your attempts to present yourself effectively, including what your friends
post on your Facebook wall!

Self-Disclosure

Angelica is a stylish dresser; has a lovely apartment in Austin, Texas; eats out
at nice restaurants regularly; and drives a new car. But she has a secret: she is
drowning in debt, barely keeping up with her minimum credit card payments.
She looks around at her friends, all the same age as she and living similar lifestyles. She wonders if they make more money than she does or if they too are
over their heads in debt. One night while out for coffee with her best friend,
Shawna, Angelica comes clean about her situation: she can't go on their upcoming trip to Cozumel, she tells Shawna, because her credit cards are maxed out.
Angelica has self-disclosed to Shawna.

When you reveal yourself to others by sharing information about yourself,
you engage in **self-disclosure**. To count as self-disclosure in a relationship, the
disclosure must be important; telling someone you like snacking on raw veg-
etables is not self-disclosure, but explaining to them the deeply held reasons why
you became a vegetarian is. The disclosure must be not easily known by others
and must also be voluntary.

Self-disclosure can be a tool for confirming our self-concept or improving
our self-esteem; it is often used as a tactic to obtain reassurance or comfort
from a trusted friend (Miller, Cooke, Tsang, & Morgan, 1992). For example,
Angelica might suspect that Shawna is also living on credit; if Shawna discloses

that she is, she might reassure Angelica that it's OK to buy things she can't afford on credit because everyone else is doing it too. However, if Shawna reveals that she makes more money than Angelica, or that she manages her money more wisely, Angelica's self-concept may be damaged. As you will recall from Chapter 1, information you receive about your self is termed feedback. The feedback Angelica receives from Shawna will be based on her self-disclosure; the same feedback—and how she interprets it—also influences Angelica's perception of herself.

what about you?

Self-Monitoring Test

To test your own perceived level of self-monitoring, complete the following items, being careful to answer them as accurately and truthfully as possible. Use a 5-point scale for your answers: 5 = strongly agree; 4 = agree; 3 = neither agree nor disagree; 2 = disagree; and 1 = strongly disagree.

_____ 1. I am concerned about acting appropriately in social situations.

_____ 2. I find it hard to imitate the behavior of others.

_____ 3. I have good self-control of my behavior. I can play many roles.

_____ 4. I am not very good at learning what is socially appropriate in new situations.

_____ 5. I often appear to lack deep emotions.

_____ 6. In a group of people, I am rarely the center of attention.

_____ 7. I may deceive people by being friendly when I really dislike them.

_____ 8. Even if I am not enjoying myself, I often pretend to be having a good time.

_____ 9. I have good self-control of my emotional expression. I can use it to create the impression I want.

_____ 10. I can argue only for ideas that I already believe in.

_____ 11. I openly express my true feelings, attitudes, and beliefs.

_____ 12. I'm not always the person I appear to be.

Add up your scores on items 1, 3, 5, 7, 8, 9, and 12. Now reverse the scoring on items 2, 4, 6, 10, and 11 (5 = 1, 4 = 2, 2 = 4, 1 = 5). Finally, add these scores to the sum you calculated from the first set of items. If you scored 43–60, you are a high self-monitor; if you scored 30–42, you are an average self-monitor; and if your score was 12–29, you are a low self-monitor.

Source: Adapted from Snyder (1974).

BEHAVIOR = SELF-PRESENTATION + SELF-DISCLOSURE
(verbal and nonverbal)

| Intentional communication to show elements of the self for strategic purposes | Revealing the self by sharing information about the self |

FIGURE 2.6
UNDERSTANDING BEHAVIOR

How you incorporate feedback into the self depends on several factors. One of the most important factors is your *sensitivity level* to feedback. Research demonstrates that some individuals are highly sensitive, whereas others are largely unaffected by the feedback they receive (Edwards, 1990). Presumably, people who are more sensitive to feedback are susceptible and receptive to information about their abilities, knowledge, and talents. Low-sensitive people would be less responsive to such information. For example, when Olympic short track skater Apolo Ohno bombed at the Olympic trials in 1998, he wasn't interested in hearing that his efforts weren't sufficient. He was demonstrating a low sensitivity level to the advice and feedback from his coach, friends, and family. Ohno's father sent him to a secluded cabin for eight days to contemplate his career. After that, Ohno decided that he was ready to receive the feedback that he needed to improve his game. He developed a higher sensitivity to feedback, and won eight Olympic medals at the 2010 Vancouver games (Bishop, 2010). Figure 2.6 illustrates how self-presentation and self-disclosure constitute the behavior segment of "The Self," seen in Figure 2.5.

Technology: Managing the Self and Perceptions

If you're wondering how your friend Ned is doing, all you need to do is check out his Facebook profile—right? There you see photographs of his recent trip to visit with his longtime girlfriend's family in Texas, you read funny status updates about his apartment hunt, and you see that others wrote on his wall to congratulate him on his recent promotion. Life is going well for Ned, so you send him a private message to let him know that you're glad for him. Would you be surprised if Ned responded to share that he is considering a breakup with his girlfriend, that he hates his job, and that he can't afford a decent apartment because his student loans are crushing him? How is this possible when Ned's profile seems to indicate that his life is fulfilling and happy?

In blogs, in chat rooms, and on dating and social networking sites, the presentation of self can be more controlled than in face-to-face encounters. When you manage the self online, you can potentially control self-disclosure, more easily choosing what to reveal and what to conceal. You can choose to reveal or not reveal your gender, ethnicity, and race, as well as your religious or political preferences. What's more, you can edit, revise, and organize the information you do disclose before the message goes out. In this way, you can present an image that is smart, charming, and eloquent, even if you tend to be nervous or timid in face-to-face communication. In Ned's case, he chose to present a self that is carefree and happy—even though his current situation is quite the opposite. Among adolescents in particular, the Internet presents an appealing opportunity to experiment with identity. Sherry Turkle, a technology researcher, notes

real communicator

NAME: Georgia Banks
HOMETOWN: Superior, Wisconsin
OCCUPATION: Master's degree candidate in social work
FUN FACT: I've lived in eight apartments and five states in the past three years.

I'm white. I grew up in a town in Wisconsin that you've probably never heard of. According to my East Coast friends, I talk funny.

I live in New York now and work in a predominantly black high school, mostly with kids who are dropout risks. It's my job to improve their attendance and keep them in school. Because I'm white, my students had some preconceived perceptions about me, some of which are true and some not.

They thought I was rich and that I go home to a luxury Manhattan apartment (wrong on both counts: I've got credit debt and live in Queens). They had this perception that because I am white, I must be constantly happy, never experiencing hardship, living one contented day after another. I can understand where this idea comes from. My kids live in this tough neighborhood where there aren't any white people, and when they do go to a nice neighborhood, all they see are white people. But their stereotypes made my job very difficult. To improve attendance, I need to find out why these kids aren't coming to school—what's going on at home, are they physically afraid of their ex-boyfriend, is their mom in the hospital? These are exceptionally personal, private things. When I first got here, my kids (adolescents who deal with racism every day of their lives) looked at me and said, No

way, I can't talk about that stuff with her. I was a white person coming into their world. I couldn't understand their world of gangs and violence and exceptional peer pressure. I couldn't relate.

I didn't disabuse them of their perceptions in a verbally aggressive way, angrily denying their assumptions. I engaged in self-monitoring, a concept I learned about in college. I took every opportunity to open channels of communication, remembering everyone's name, stopping kids in the hall to say hello and ask how they're doing. I was patient and looked for cues into their moods, their individual communication styles. When they wanted to talk, I listened. When they didn't, I was OK with that. There are plenty of things to do in my office—poetry kits, games—and kids can just come in, sit down, and hang out—no need to talk if they don't want to, no pressure to leave. I've built an environment of trust. I let my kids be who they need to be, and I don't judge them.

But they are right about some of their perceptions. There are things I'm never going to understand. I never went through the things they're going through. But I can be a sounding board for good judgment. My kids know that they can come to me and trust me; they know that I care and that I'll listen. I'm here to help them. And I do help them. I'm good at my job.

But who really knows? All of this is just my perception.

that the online environment offers young people a virtual "identity workshop" where they can try on different identities with little risk. "Things get too hot, you log off," Turkle notes, "while in time and space, you have consequences" (quoted in Wallis, 2006).

On the other hand, how *you* present yourself online may not be the only factor in how you come across to others. Statements made by your friends on Facebook, for example, can have a significant impact on people's impressions of *you*. A study by Walther, Van Der Heide, Kim, Westerman, and Tong (2008) found that when people post on their friend's wall positive statements about their friend's behavior, their friend's credibility and "social attractiveness" increase, compared to negative statements (for example, about excessive

WIREDFORCOMMUNICATION

Avatars: Virtual Faces

The face of Huey Freeman, the ten-year-old black activist at the heart of the comic strip (and popular Adult Swim cartoon) *The Boondocks*, stares out from the screen, his face set in his signature scowl, his left eyebrow cocked, his towering Afro extending above. This is the avatar, or virtual face, chosen by Trey, a regular contributor to an online political forum.

Logging into an Internet forum, chat room, or game typically involves creating an online identity. You choose a user name, create a one-line catch-phrase that you'll use as your signature, and carefully choose from among various avatars (commonly called "avs"). The avatars are typically little icons or pictures used to present a particular image of yourself. They can range from basic emoticons (smiley faces) to photos of beloved celebrities, cartoon characters, or images from nature and allow you to express your identity visually rather than through words alone. Avatars can be chosen for any number of reasons, including to draw attention to yourself, to give others a glimpse of your interests, or to capture some aspect of your personality (Suler, 2007).

The characteristics of selected avatars are important to both behavior and perception. Nick Yee and Jeremy Bailenson (2007) found that people's behavior was affected by the physical characteristics of the avatar assigned to them. For example, people who were assigned to more attractive avatars self-disclosed more and talked more intimately with others than those assigned less attractive avatars.

As graphic representations, avatars are open to a great deal of interpretation and thus rely heavily on the viewer's perceptions. For example, Trey's choice of Huey might be interpreted in several ways. Is Trey, like the fictional Huey, a militant black activist? Is he an aspiring cartoonist? Is he just angry, like Huey looks? The truth is that Trey loves the comic strip, and his friends joke that he and Huey must go to the same barber. On some level, Trey also identifies with Huey's activism, wit, and intelligence, but he would rather imply this association than say it out loud.

THINK ABOUT THIS

❶ How might the image of Huey be interpreted by someone who is unfamiliar with *The Boondocks*? Would a fan of the strip perceive Trey's online self differently?

❷ If Trey's postings clearly lean toward the political left or right, might readers' interpretations of his avatar change?

❸ If Trey is revealed to be black, would that influence the way the image of Huey is received? What if Trey is actually white? Buddhist? Female? A teenager? A senior citizen?

drunkenness or sexual behavior). Even the number and type of friends you appear to have on Facebook can have an influence too—too few friends appears to hurt your reputation, but too many are just as bad (Tong, Van Der Heide, Langwell, & Walther, 2008), and the attractiveness of your friends can affect perceptions of your own attractiveness (Walther, Van Der Heide, Kim, Westerman, & Tong, 2008).

AND YOU?

Randomly select five of your Facebook friends and visit their profiles. Consider their status updates, their friends' posts about them, the pages they like, and so on. What type of impression does their profile make on you? What words would you use to describe these individuals? Do you believe they present themselves accurately?

BACK TO ▶ *Britain's Got Talent!*

 At the beginning of this chapter, we asked why audiences were so stunned—and intrigued—by Susan Boyle's performance on *Britain's Got Talent.* Let's reconsider Boyle's performance—and people's reactions to it—in light of what we've learned about perception.

▶ When people looked at Susan Boyle, they quickly drummed up an assessment of her based on their own schemas. What they heard and saw from Boyle both surprised and delighted them because she was not what people expected—her voice and her poise did not conform to the perceptions they had about her, based on her age, appearance, and demeanor.

▶ Bear in mind that audiences' schemas were informed by more than just stereotypes—shows like *Britain's Got Talent* and *American Idol* often feature auditions from performers who lack any real musical gifts. Indeed, many who clicked on links to Boyle's clip on YouTube were probably expecting something more laughable (think of *American Idol*'s William Hung, whose performance of "She Bangs" ironically made him a star a few years back). The assumptions they had about Boyle were based on their experiences with these types of shows.

▶ Certainly, there have been a great many wonderful performances from a variety of singers on YouTube in the years prior and since. But none have had the same kind of buzz that Susan Boyle's first clip generated. That's because people were moved by the reactions of audience members as well as judges. As one writer noted, "Part of the joy of watching her performance was seeing the obnoxious, smarmy grimaces disappear from the faces of Simon Cowell and Piers Morgan, two of the show's judges, and seeing the audience shift, in an instant, from tittering condescension to open-mouthed admiration" (Lyall, 2009).

▶ Interaction appearance theory also plays a role here: as we get to know people better through positive interactions, we find them more socially attractive, which then leads to greater physical attraction. The more the audience heard Susan Boyle's amazing voice, the less dowdy she appeared to them. In fact, when Boyle underwent a makeover a few weeks later, some of her newfound fans were disappointed that she hadn't kept her original look.

▶ While the audience had a clear perception of Susan Boyle in their minds—assuming her to be a frumpy old lady who was about to make a fool of herself—she clearly had another, seeing herself as someone with the potential to be a professional singer. When it came to her own self-efficacy, Boyle's assessment of her own abilities was more accurate than anyone expected.

THINGS TO TRY Activities

1. Describe how you managed an impression of yourself in a face-to-face interaction and a mediated one. Describe your conscious preparations for this impression management, and then describe the outcome. What contributed to your successful or unsuccessful management of self? Were the impression-management strategies you employed in the face-to-face interaction different from the mediated situation?

2. Take a look at the text of a presidential speech online at www.whitehouse.gov. After reading the complete speech, consider how the speech is characterized in various sources (blogs, liberal and conservative news sources, late-night comedy and satires). How do perceptions of the speech change from one source to another? Does your perception of the speech change as you consider the points of view of these various sources?

3. Think about a co-culture (age, sexual orientation, socioeconomic status, race, religion, and so on) with which you identify. Then make a list of stereotypes that are associated with that group. In what ways do you conform to such stereotypes? In what ways do you not conform? Do you identify with more than one culture? If so, are there any stereotypes on your list that contradict each other? How might intersection of these cultures (for example, being a white, Christian, thirty-year-old stay-at-home dad or being a fifty-year-old Hispanic lesbian scientist) affect your perception of yourself as well as others' perceptions of you?

4. Watch some television programming or flip through a magazine that is typically geared toward a particular group. Pay close attention to the advertisements you see. Are they geared toward the groups that are expected to be watching the programming? If so, do you see instances in which the commercials allow for flexibility and mindfulness (for example, any advertising geared toward women during football games)? If you are a member of the group being targeted during such programming, do you find yourself more or less persuaded by the message based on stereotypes about your group?

Now that you have finished reading this chapter, you can:

Describe how our personal perspective on the world influences our communication:

▶ **Perception** is the cognitive process that helps us make sense of the world (p. 36).

▶ **Communication processing** is the means by which we gather, organize, and evaluate the information we receive (p. 37).

▶ Because we are constantly bombarded with information in any situation, we must sift through it all to determine what is important and what to remember (p. 37).

Explain how we use and misuse schemas when communicating with others:

▶ **Schemas** are mental structures we use to connect bits of information together (p. 37).

▶ Schemas help us understand how things work as well as decide how to act; they evolve as we encounter new information and situations (p. 38). **Mindfulness** helps us focus the communication process.

▶ Schemas present three challenges that derail good communication: **mindlessness**, a passive, automatic response that may be inaccurate; **selective perception**, allowing bias to influence thought; and **undue influence**, giving other sources too much say (pp. 39–40).

Define the attributions we use to explain behavior:

▶ When we need to explain why someone says or does something in a manner that does not fit into our schemas, we look to **attributions** to explain the cause of the behavior and justify our perceptions (p. 40).

▶ **Fundamental attribution error** explains our tendency to assume that another person's wrong behavior is due to an internal flaw, while the **self-serving bias** attributes our own failures to external causes (p. 40).

▶ **Interaction appearance theory** explains how people change their perception of someone's appearance as they spend more time together (p. 41).

Describe cultural differences that influence perception:

▶ Effective communication depends on understanding how diversity, the variables that make us unique, affects perception (p. 44).

▶ The failure to see beyond our own beliefs and circumstances, or **cultural myopia**, blinds us to alternative points of view (p. 45).

▶ **Stereotyping**, or generalizing about people, limits our ability to see the individual and can lead to **prejudice**, ill will toward a particular group, and a sense of one's own superiority (p. 45).

Identify how our **self-concept**—who we think we are—influences communication:

▶ We are more willing to interact in situations where we feel we have strengths, and our self-concept is confirmed or changed by responses from others (p. 47).

▶ We compare ourselves against idealized images in the media, according to **social comparison theory**, often to our own disadvantage (p. 48).

▶ **Self-esteem** relates to self-concept and is how we feel about ourselves in a particular situation (p. 48).

▶ **Self-efficacy** is the ability to predict, based on self-concept and self-esteem, one's effectiveness in a communication situation. Inaccurate self-efficacy may lead to a **self-fulfilling prophecy**, whereby behavior is altered to make the prediction more likely to come true (pp. 50–51).

▶ We assess our communication performances and rate ourselves through the lenses of **self-actualization** (high performance), **self-adequacy** (adequate performance), and **self-denigration** (poor performance) (pp. 52–53).

Describe how our cognitions about ourselves and our behavior affect our communication with others:

▶ **Self-presentation** is intentional communication designed to show elements of self for strategic purposes; it's how we let others know about ourselves (p. 55).

▶ The tendency to watch our environment and others in it for cues as to how to present ourselves in particular situations is called **self-monitoring** (p. 55).

▶ Sharing important information about ourselves, such as with a close friend, is **self-disclosure** (p. 56).

▶ The presentation of self can be more easily controlled when communicating online than in face-to-face encounters (pp. 58–60).

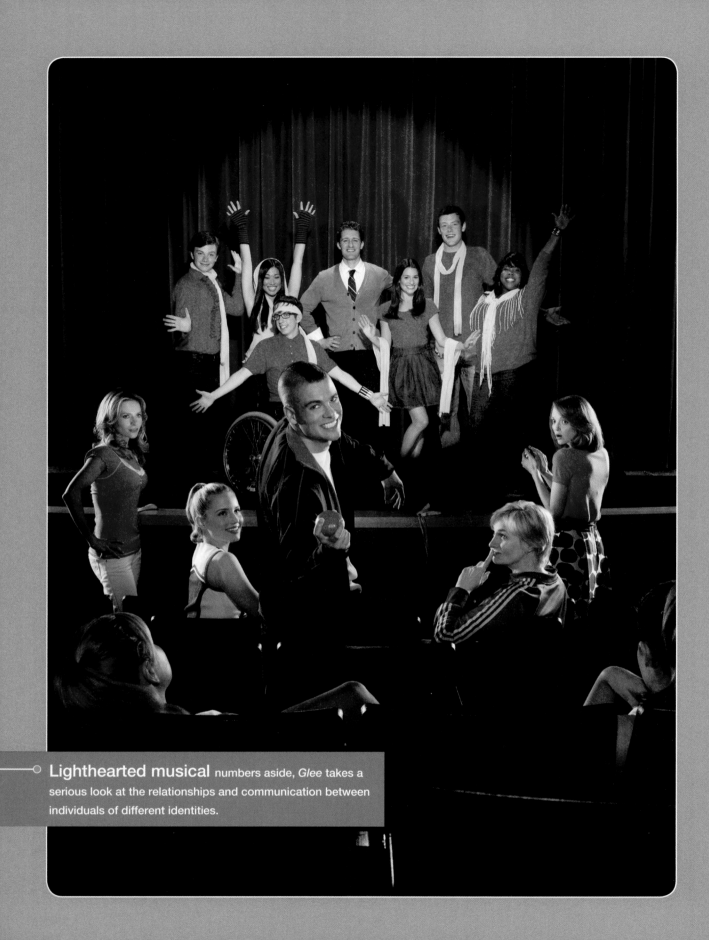

Lighthearted musical numbers aside, *Glee* takes a serious look at the relationships and communication between individuals of different identities.

Communication and Culture

If you were trying to imagine a group that clearly reflects the diversity of the United States, it might look a bit like the cast of *Glee*. And in case you don't catch the differences in race, ethnicity, religion, sexual preference, or physical abilities represented by the fictional William McKinley High School show choir, the politically incorrect cheerleading coach, Sue Sylvester, will be happy to point them out to you.

Glee debuted in May 2009 to rave reviews and an immediate audience following. It is at once a scathing satire of high school life and a joyful celebration of music. It is also a charming—and often troubling—exploration of intercultural and co-cultural communication and relationships. The diverse characters conform to stereotypes in many ways—Finn represents the not-so-intelligent jock; Rachel, the ambitious diva. But the show also deals with real communication issues and challenges in almost every episode, including bullying and teen pregnancy, as well as the way differences in religious beliefs, personal lifestyles, and social status affect group bonding.

There's no doubt that individuals from different co-cultures respond well to seeing people like them represented on television. But *Glee* is not a sweet take on multiculturalism: Sue Sylvester doesn't merely point out the differences between team members—she openly mocks them. Her mean-spiritedness not only provides the show with zinging laughs and a definable "bad guy," but also acknowledges the real struggles with which teens from just about every co-culture must deal. "That's real life," explains Kevin McHale, who plays Artie. "It's not like, oh, you need to be sensitive. High school is not always sensitive" (McLean, 2011).

While Sue Sylvester considers the glee club to be the lowest form of high school life, Jane Lynch (the actress who plays her) has a clear sense of why the show's celebration of outcasts and misfits has struck such a chord. "*Glee* presents this idealised [sic] world where no matter who you are or how different you are from the 'norm,' you're going to get supported in this glee club," says Lynch. "And you're going to be held up as unique, and you're going to be loved for it" (McLean, 2011).

After you have finished
reading this chapter,
you will be able to

● Define and explain
culture and its impact on
your communication.

● Delineate seven ways
that cultural variables
affect communication.

● Describe the
communicative power
of group affiliations.

● Explain key barriers to
competent intercultural
communication.

● Demonstrate behav-
iors that contribute to
intercultural competence.

As you witness on just about any episode of *Glee*, communication among individuals of different races, sexes, religions, and so on can be a messy experience—but it can also be exciting, challenging, enlightening, and enjoy-able. In order to be part of any team, or to be a good neighbor and an informed citizen, you need to understand this essential communication process. Whether you're looking to learn how to better communicate with your older relatives, understand the way your roommate's faith plays out in her communication, or contemplate current national debates surrounding issues like immigration and religious tolerance, this chapter aims to help you better understand cultural dif-ferences *and* similarities to increase your competence in intercultural encounters. We begin with an overview of culture, before exploring cultural variations and group affiliations as well as the challenges and opportunities that intercultural communication offers.

Understanding Culture

As you'll recall from the model of communication competence (Chapter 1), all of your encounters with others occur within overlapping situational, relational, and cultural contexts. **Culture** is a learned system of thought and behavior that belongs to and typifies a relatively large group of people; it is the composite of their shared beliefs, values, and practices. Although we might commonly think of culture as a person's nationality (for example, the "French culture"), it applies to any broadly shared group identity. In this section, we investigate how culture is learned, how it affects our communication, and why learning how to commu-nicate among different cultures is so important.

Culture Is Learned

Culture is not something you're born with, like blue eyes or black hair; culture is something you learn through communication. As children, you observe the behaviors of your parents, siblings, and extended family members. For example, they teach you how to greet guests in your home (with a bow, handshake, or hug, for example), whether to make direct eye contact with others, and what words are polite and appropriate rather than rude and inconsiderate. Later you observe the behaviors of your teachers and your peer groups. You learn what types of conversational topics are appropriate to discuss with peers rather than adults; you learn the nuances of interacting with members of the same and opposite sex. You also listen to and observe television, movies, and various forms of advertising that reflect what your culture values and admires.

Through these processes, you acquire a set of shared perceptions and develop models for appropriate behavior. This is the framework through which you interpret the world and the people in it—your **worldview** (Schelbert, 2009). Much of your worldview is not obvious. For example, many of your non-verbal behaviors (like gestures, facial expressions, eye contact, and tone of voice) occur at an unconscious level (Hall, 1976). You have learned these behaviors so well that you don't even notice them until someone else behaves in a manner that doesn't meet your expectations. For example, you may not realize that you

● **DO YOU EXTEND** a hand or bow to greet others? It probably depends on what you were taught by older relatives as a child.

routinely make eye contact during conversation until someone fails to meet your gaze. Your use of language carries more obvious cultural cues; speaking Italian in Italy enables you to fully participate in and understand the Italian way of life (Nicholas, 2009). And language can also be a big part of teaching you the rituals and traditions of your culture as evidenced by the prayers of your faith, the folk songs of your grandparents, or the patriotic oaths you make (such as the Pledge of Allegiance).

Culture Affects Communication

Just as we learn culture *through* communication, we also use communication to *express* our culture. Our worldview affects which topics we will discuss in personal and professional settings, as well as the way we communicate nonverbally. It also affects the way we perceive the communication of others.

In the United States, a popular worldview often equates thinness with feminine beauty; this perception is reflected in the mass media as well as personal messages we communicate. After actress and singer Jessica Simpson was mocked by the tabloids in 2009 for her supposed weight gain, she set off around the world with her two best friends to discover and share different notions of

You frequently communicate your worldview when you present yourself for strategic purposes (Chapter 2). For example, if you are meeting your significant other's parents for the first time or attending a job interview, you will likely present yourself in a manner that expresses key elements of your culture—perhaps bowing or shaking hands, using formal language, or dressing in a particular way.

beauty. They discovered that people in other cultures have different worldviews and, consequently, communicate different ideas about physical attractiveness. Their experiences in Japan, Thailand, France, Brazil, Uganda, Morocco, and India aired in 2010 as VH1's series *The Price of Beauty* (Hinckley, 2010). They were surprised to find that in Uganda, where larger women are considered desirable, women prepare for marriage in a "fattening hut," a marked difference from the way American brides-to-be get ready for the big day. While their findings are merely observations and lack the rigor of social science, they did expose an audience of young teens to the widely differing views of what is and isn't attractive, and the ways in which these views are expressed through cultural practices.

Intercultural Communication Matters

If you've watched the show *Outsourced*, you're familiar with Todd Dempsy, an American sales manager who finds himself, quite unexpectedly, relocated from Kansas City to India as the head of a call center. He's shocked not only by the simple cultural differences—he's never eaten Indian food before, for example—but also by the ways in which his new Indian staff perceive Americans and American culture. He can't understand why *they* can't understand why anyone would want to buy the novelty products they sell. And, if you think about it, trying to explain the cultural significance of a foam cheese head to someone who's never watched a Green Bay Packers game might be kind of difficult.

The fact remains that people from different cultures with different worldviews perceive the world quite differently. This can clearly lead to misunderstandings, anger, hurt feelings, and other challenges when individuals from various backgrounds interact. This is why communication scholars invest a great deal of time and effort to study and write about **intercultural communication**, the communication between people from different cultures who have different worldviews. Communication is considered intercultural when the differences between communicators are so substantial that they can potentially create different interpretations and expectations (Lustig & Koester, 1993).

Despite the potential challenges, the answer to addressing intercultural misunderstanding isn't to hide under a rock or only interact with those whom you perceive to be *exactly like you.* You live in a diverse and mobile society, and you study, play, and work with people who are different from you on a number of levels. Let's consider several reasons why studying intercultural communication matters so much.

● **WHEN *OUTSOURCED'S* TODD DEMPSY** finds himself relocated to India, he must explore all aspects of an unfamiliar culture in order to embrace his new home.

A Diverse Society

You probably meet people from different groups every day—in all the places your life takes you. The United States is a diverse country, with a population

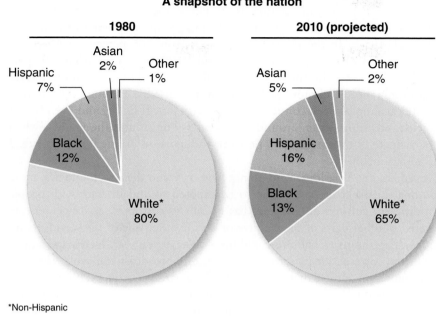

THEN & NOW
A snapshot of the nation

1980

Hispanic 7%
Asian 2%
Other 1%
Black 12%
White* 80%

2010 (projected)

Asian 5%
Other 2%
Hispanic 16%
Black 13%
White* 65%

*Non-Hispanic

FIGURE 3.1

U.S. CENSUS DATA INDICATING INCREASED DIVERSITY IN THE NATION
Source: U.S. Census Bureau; numbers have been rounded

that reflects a range of ethnic, racial, and religious backgrounds. Different regions of the country (and sometimes different neighborhoods in the same city) have distinct cultures as well (see Figure 3.1). You have a unique cultural background and communication style that are different in some ways from those of others. So, in order to function competently as a member of such a diverse society, you need to be able to communicate appropriately and effectively with a wide variety of individuals. Two key parts of this process are understanding your own cultural expectations for communication and respecting those of others. On *Outsourced*, Todd knows nothing about Diwali, a particularly sacred day for his Indian staff. After a few cultural fumbles, he discovers how important it is and agrees that the staff should have the day off.

Mobility

Outsourced's Todd Dempsy probably never thought he'd leave the Midwest. Likewise, Gupta, Manmeet, Asha, and the rest of his new staff probably never thought they'd spend their days dealing with an American supervisor or talking to American customers on the phone. More than six in ten adults have moved to a new community at least once in their lives, and more than one in five say the place they are living now is not "home" (Taylor, Morin, Cohn, & Wang, 2008). As such, you must be ready to address cultural differences—not just between nations but also between regions, states, and cities. Even if you don't plan on ever leaving your hometown, you will, almost without exception, communicate at some time or another with people from outside of it, both face to face and through a variety of media.

AND YOU?

How long have you lived in your current location? Are people in your community treated differently based on their status as a new or established member in the community? How might your response change based on your own level of involvement in the community?

Mediated Interaction

Clearly, mediated communication is changing the way we experience the world and broadening the range of people and groups with whom we interact on a regular basis. In the United States today, some 66 percent of American adults have broadband access at home (Smith, 2010a). In addition, 40 percent of adults access the Internet via mobile devices. Thus, we communicate electronically more and more each year (Smith, 2010b). Through the Internet and other technology, we connect not only with far-off family and friends, but also with individuals from around the country—or around the world—when we participate in online gaming, post our thoughts on online forums, or read others' personal blogs.

Even among Americans who do not have access to these technologies, more traditional media make it possible to be exposed to and interact with people from different cultures on a regular basis. Calls to customer service centers are answered in other parts of the country or on the other side of the world. Radio stations bring international music and news right to your car. Newspapers carry stories from correspondents across the globe. And broadcast and cable television offer glimpses of cultures that we might not be a part of—a typical night's television offerings might include world news on the evening network news, British situation comedies on PBS, soccer games broadcast from South America, and foreign films presented on the Independent Film Network. American programming has also become more multicultural, as the casts (and plots) of mainstream television shows have grown increasingly diverse, in recognition of the changing demographics of the country.

Diverse Organizations

The factors we've discussed so far point to the fact that any job you take—from salesperson to nurse to engineer—will involve some degree of intercultural communication. Any soldier returning from service in Afghanistan will tell you that speaking Farsi is not enough to communicate competently with locals there: you need to understand the culture of the people with whom you will be speaking in order to "win hearts and minds" (Moutot, 2010). Similar realities exist in business and in the public sphere. A teacher may have students whose families are from different parts of the country or are immigrants from outside of the United States; an entrepreneur will need to understand the ways different groups respond to her product and the way she markets it. Being aware of the way that culture impacts communication is especially crucial to business communication across borders (Busch, 2009). You may need to know how much to push a client to commit, when to be silent, or how to complete successful negotiations of a contract without offending the other party. On *Outsourced*, the staff learns to adapt to American styles of communication, suggesting additional products to increase sales.

As you can see, intercultural communication is important to you in your life as a student, as a citizen, and as a professional. The culture in which you live (or were raised) has particular ways of communicating in the world, which we illustrate now by examining seven essential cultural variations that have long intrigued scholars.

Communication and Cultural Variations

It is one thing to notice cultural differences; it is quite another to be able to *explain* them. *Why*, for example, might Germans seem very blunt and direct as they speak, while the Japanese may seem to never get to the point? Scholars have identified seven major communication variations[1] across cultures: high and low context, collectivist and individualist orientations, comfort with uncertainty, masculine and feminine orientations, approaches to power distance, time orientation, and value of emotional expression (Hall, 1976; Hofstede, 1984, 2001; Matsumoto, 1989). These variations describe the underlying cultural values that help us to better understand communication differences.

When you consider the seven variations we present here, it may seem as if they are opposites and that your culture must be one or the other (that, for example, the culture must be masculine or feminine). Contrary to that impression, these variations play out along a spectrum: your culture may be masculine in some ways and feminine in others. It's also important to recognize that within any culture, there is a great variance among different groups in terms of where they fall on the spectrum. And finally, it's imperative to keep individual differences in mind, as you will easily be able to find examples of people who reject the thinking and behaviors associated with their dominant culture. With these caveats in mind, let's take a look at each variation in closer detail.

High- and Low-Context Cultures

Research shows that our culture has a big impact on how direct we are in our use of language and how much we rely on other, nonverbal ways to communicate. For example, intercultural researcher William Gudykunst (2004) noted that some cultures use language that is very indirect; they are sensitive to situational factors, preferring to observe those factors rather than comment on each one. Individuals in **high-context cultures** (including Japan, Korea, China, and many Latin American and African countries) use contextual cues—such as time, place, relationship, and situation—to both interpret meaning and send subtle messages (Hall, 1976; Hall & Hall, 1990). A Chinese person who disagrees with someone, for example, may not say anything; the communication partner must look for clues of disagreement in the context. These clues may include the amount of time that passes before a response or the nonverbal behaviors that occur or don't occur. A person from a high-context culture is also likely to attribute a communication partner's behavior to factors related to the situation than to an individual's personality. In other words, people in high-context cultures would not assume that someone is rude for remaining silent; they would be more likely to think that the individual didn't respond because the situation called for restraint and politeness.

A **low-context culture**, by contrast, uses very direct language and relies less on situational factors to communicate. The United States, Canada,

CONNECT

If you are from a low-context culture, you may wonder how to decode communication from a high-context friend or colleague. The key lies in developing strong listening skills (Chapter 6). By participating in *active listening*, you can look for opportunities to select and attend to nonverbal messages or contextual clues that will help you understand the message your friend is encoding and sending.

---

[1]Geert Hofstede referred to these variations as cultural *dimensions*—largely psychological value constructs that affect the way people think about and perform communication behaviors.

TABLE 3.1

A COMPARISON OF HIGH- AND LOW-CONTEXT CULTURES

High-Context Cultures	Low-Context Cultures
• Rely on contextual cues for communication	• Rely on direct language for communication
• Avoid speaking in a way that causes individuals to stand out from others	• Value self-expression
• Avoid intruding on others	• Construct explicit messages
• Avoid saying no directly, preferring to talk around the point	• State opinions and desires directly
• Usually express opinions indirectly	• Persuade others by speaking clearly and eloquently
• Usually express disagreement by saying nothing	• Usually express disagreement clearly and directly
• Tend to find explanations for behaviors in the situation	• Tend to find explanations for behaviors in individuals
• Admire relationship harmony	• Admire verbal fluency

Australia, and most northern European countries tend to have a low-context style. In the United States, for example, it would seem normal for someone to say, "Alex, I need a list of twenty items for the Allan project from you by five o'clock today." Someone from a high-context culture would more likely say, "We are starting the project," and would assume that Alex would have the list ready on time because Alex understands the situation as the speaker does. If Alex did not get the list completed on time, a boss in a low-context culture would blame it on his laziness or incompetence, whereas a manager in a high-context culture would blame it on situational constraints, such as Alex having too many projects to work on. High- and low-context styles are compared in Table 3.1.

Collectivist and Individualist Orientations

An Arab proverb says that you must "smell the breath" of a man in order to know if he can be trusted. But in the United States, Americans get very uncomfortable when other people stand "too close" to them. Americans also tend to knock on a closed door before entering and usually ask the person inside if she would like to join the group for lunch. But in Lesotho (a tribal culture in South Africa), people's rooms often have no doors at all, and if someone sees you, they will grab you and expect you to have a meal with the group. Such differences in the value of personal space and independence versus belonging and group loyalty illustrate our second cultural value: collectivist and individualist orientations.

Individuals from **collectivist cultures** perceive themselves first and foremost as members of a group—and they communicate from that perspective (Triandis, 1986, 1988, 2000). Collectivist cultures (including many Arab and Latin American cultures as well as several Asian cultures, such as China and Japan) emphasize

AND YOU?

To what degree do you identify with individualist or collectivist cultures? How might the answer to this question be complicated if the family you grew up with identifies strongly with one dimension but the larger culture in which you were raised strongly identifies with the other?

cooperation and group harmony, group decision making, and long-term, stable friendships. Communication in such cultures is governed by a clear notion of status and hierarchy, and loyalty to the group and the honor of one's family are more important than individual needs or desires (Wang & Liu, 2010). In addition, collectivist communicators are generally concerned with relational support; they avoid hurting others' feelings, apologize, and make efforts to help others to maintain the group's reputation and position of respect (Han & Cai, 2010). For example, if an individual attending a business meeting discovers a financial error, she is not likely to mention who made the error nor will she call attention to her own success in discovering it. Instead she will emphasize the group's success in correcting the error before it became a problem for the company.

 **IS THIS A** single group or a group of individuals?

Conversely, people from **individualist cultures** value individuality; they place value on autonomy and privacy, with relatively little attention to status and hierarchy based on age or family connections. In individualist cultures, individual initiative and achievement are rewarded, and individual credit and blame are assigned. Thus, an individual who notes an error—even one by her superiors—is likely to be rewarded or respected for her keen observation (as long as she presents it sensitively). The United States is a highly individualist culture—American heroes are usually those celebrated for "pulling themselves up by their bootstraps" to achieve great things or change the world, be it in business and technology, athletics, or entertainment. Other western cultures, such as Great Britain, Australia, and Germany, are also at the high end of the individualism scale.

Comfort with Uncertainty

Cultures also differ in the degree of anxiety that individual members tend to feel about the unknown. All cultures, to some degree, adapt their behaviors in order to reduce uncertainty and risk, a process called **uncertainty avoidance**. Cultures that are more anxious about the unknown are said to be *high uncertainty avoidance cultures*—their behaviors are adapted to minimize risk and uncertainty. In high uncertainty avoidance cultures (such as Portugal, Greece, Peru, and Japan), communication is usually governed by very formal rules: there is a greater need for absolute truth, correct answers, and stability. Consensus is valued, and there is a low tolerance for differences of opinion. By following social rules, and minimizing dissent, they are able to reduce uncertainty and anxiety in prescribed communication situations (Gudykunst, 1993).

On the other hand, cultures with a higher tolerance for risk and ambiguity (like Sweden, Denmark, Ireland, and the United States) are considered *low uncertainty avoidance cultures* (Samovar, Porter, & McDaniel, 2009). Their lower level of anxiety about the unknown means that these cultures are comfortable with a variety of communication styles, are more tolerant of differences of opinion, and have fewer formal rules for behavior (Hoeken et al., 2003).

CONNECT

Just because people from cultures like those in the United States and Ireland have a greater acceptance for uncertainty than others doesn't mean that they are entirely comfortable with the unknown. In fact, members of low uncertainty avoidance cultures will engage in *passive*, *active*, and *interactive strategies* to reduce uncertainty when dealing with a new relational partner (Chapter 7); similarly, they will seek opportunities to learn about a new organizational culture so that they can *assimilate* competently (Chapter 11).

Masculine and Feminine Orientations

The masculinity or femininity of a culture refers to the way an entire culture (including both men and women within the culture) values and reflects characteristics that are traditionally—even stereotypically—associated with one sex or the other. Thus, a **masculine culture**—sometimes referred to as an *achievement culture*—places value on assertiveness, achievement, ambition, and competitiveness (Samovar, Porter, & McDaniel, 2009). Both men and women in such cultures also usually make clearer distinctions between the sexes, such as expecting more aggressiveness in men and more passiveness in women.

Highly **feminine cultures**, on the other hand—sometimes referred to as *nurturing cultures*—place value on relationships and quality of life. Such cultures place greater value on nurturance—the affection, friendliness, and social support between people; they are less concerned with assertiveness and more with understanding others. Scandinavian cultures (such as Sweden and Norway), as well as Chile and Portugal, tend to rank high in femininity, whereas Mexico, Japan, and Italy tend to be high in masculinity.

When discussing masculine and feminine orientation, it is particularly important to remember individual differences as men and women *within* each culture, not surprisingly, vary as to how much masculinity and femininity are valued (Tripathy, 2010). One of the principal researchers on this topic, Geert Hofstede (1984, 2001), noted that studies consistently find different scores for men and women within larger cultures. For example, Japan ranks as a highly masculine culture, yet in recent years many Japanese men have been embracing a less restrictive view of masculinity. Analysts note that these men may communicate in ways that are more gentle, shy, and sensitive (Faiola, 2005). Sugihara and Katsurada (2002) also made this point, noting that the Japanese men and women they studied expressed similar masculine and feminine characteristics.

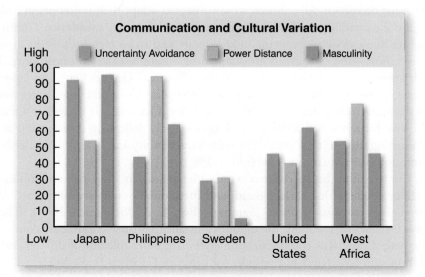

FIGURE 3.2

COMMUNICATION AND CULTURAL VARIATION
Source: Adapted from Hofstede, 1984, 2001.

Approaches to Power Distance

Perhaps you've seen the movie *Slumdog Millionaire* about Jamal, a Mumbai teen who grew up in the city slums and became a contestant on the Indian version of *Who Wants to Be a Millionaire?* Jamal is subjected to brutal police interrogation on suspicion of cheating because the show's producers cannot imagine that he could know so much coming from his lower class. This may seem shocking to readers in the United States, where upward mobility is a value and underdogs become folk heroes. Why?

It all has to do with the way in which a culture accepts and expects the division of power among individuals, a concept known as **power distance**. In India, social status is far more stratified than it is in the United States. The caste system—formally outlawed in 1950 but still lingering in India's culture—placed individuals, families, and entire groups into distinct social strata. That meant that the family that you were born into determined who you could associate with and marry, and what job you could hold. Those born into the lowest tier (the untouchables) were considered subhuman, even contagious, and were ignored by higher castes of people. At every level, individuals generally accepted their own place in the caste system. And today, more than half a century after it was officially dismantled, the idea that one's social status is set in stone lingers (Bayly, 1999).

Status differences in a culture result in some groups or individuals having more power than others. But a person's position in the cultural hierarchy can come from sources besides social class, including age, job title, or even birth order. In *high power distance cultures* (like India, China, and Japan), people with less power accept their lower position as a basic fact of life, and experience more anxiety when they communicate with those of higher status; they are likely to accept coercion as normal and are unlikely to challenge authority. People in *low power distance cultures* (such as the United States, Canada, Germany, and Australia), on the other hand, tolerate less difference in power between people and communicate with those higher in status with less anxiety. They are more likely to challenge the status quo, to consider multiple options or possibilities for action, and to resist coercion.

● **HYACINTH BUCKET** of the British sitcom *Keeping Up Appearances* epitomizes monochronic culture: she holds friends and neighbors to strict social appointments and tracks them down if they're so much as seconds past due.

Time Orientation

When you are invited to someone's home for dinner, when is it appropriate to arrive? At the exact time listed on the invitation or twenty minutes later? How about two hours later? Or not even show up at all? **Time orientation**, or the way that cultures communicate about and with time, is a very important—yet frequently overlooked—cultural dimension (Hall, 1959).

Many Western cultures (such as the United States and Great Britain) are extremely time-conscious. The English language is filled with expressions of time—*now, then, later, soon, early, late*, etc. And every portion of the day is oriented around time—including time for meals, bed, meetings, classes, and so on. Even sayings express the importance of time: *time is money, no time to lose, wasting time* (Mast, 2002). But in many Latin American and Asian cultures, time is fluid and the pace of life is slower.

In Chapters 14 and 16, we discuss the importance of emotionally connecting to your audience and appealing to their emotions (*pathos*). However, it's essential to understand your audience's comfort with emotional expression. A culture that favors understatement may be suspicious of a highly dramatic speaker. You would want to ensure that your verbal and nonverbal communication is logical, credible, and competent for the context while attempting to touch their hearts.

Arriving two hours late for an invitation is perfectly competent behavior. An American businessperson might get frustrated and give up after spending six months working on a deal with a Japanese company, when the Japanese may be wondering why the Americans quit so soon when they were all just getting to know each other!

A key cultural distinction operating here is whether cultures are monochronic or polychronic (Gudykunst & Ting-Toomey, 1988; Hall, 1976; Victor, 1992). **Monochronic cultures** treat time as a limited resource—a commodity that can be saved or wasted. Such cultures (including the United States, Germany, Canada, and the United Kingdom) use time to structure activities and focus on attending to one person or task at a time; they value concentration and stick to schedules. In monochronic cultures, people line up to wait their "turn"—to see a professor at office hours, to check out at the grocery store, to buy tickets for a concert. **Polychronic cultures**, on the other hand, are comfortable dealing with multiple people and tasks at the same time. Seven or eight people all crowding around a stall and shouting out their needs at a mercado in Mexico is expected, not rude. Polychronic cultures (such as in Mexico, India, and the Philippines) are also less concerned with making every moment count. They don't adhere as closely to schedules, are less likely to make or attend to appointments, and change plans often and easily.

Even Web-based communication can be affected by such differences in the perception of time. One study found that people from polychronic cultures (Egypt and Peru) were less bothered by download delays than were people from monochronic cultures (the United States and Finland), and they even perceived the wait times differently (Rose, Evaristo, & Straub, 2003).

Value of Emotional Expression

● DURING *FAMADIHANA,* the Malagasy people of Madagascar embrace their ancestor's bones, literally, and love for each other and their culture, figuratively.

In the central highlands of Madagascar, Rakotonarivo Henri is dancing with the bones of his grandfather. Accompanied by five brass bands, Henri and others on this island in the Indian Ocean emerge from family crypts with cheerful emotion. Amid joyful singing and dancing, they openly express their feelings to one another—and the dead—in a ritualistic ceremony called the *famadihana,* or the "turning of the bones." The ritual is meant to celebrate their ancestors, pass on the rituals and stories to the next generation, and publicly show how they love one another (Bearak, 2010).

One thing that people from all cultures share is their human ability to *experience* such emotion. But *expressing* emotions (including which emotions under which circumstances) varies greatly. You may find the thought of dancing with the bones of your family uncomfortable; you'd be more likely to make a little visit to your grandfather's grave, perhaps leave flowers or whisper a small prayer. You might believe that outward grieving shows you are too tied to worldly things (Stearns & Knapp, 1996). The value of emotional expression varies among cultures; in some, it is associated with

real communicator

NAME: Vanessa Gonzalez
HOMETOWN: Escalon, California
OCCUPATION: Marketing and public relations specialist
FUN FACT: I'm obsessed with Google.

If you had asked me who "I" am and what groups I belong to at the beginning of my college career, I could have answered you without a second thought: I'm Latina, I'm an American, I'm a first generation college student, I'm a serious student, and I love to travel. But my experiences studying global communication in college and intercultural communication while studying abroad in India really shook up these categories for me and taught me a great deal about my communication with others.

Have you ever stopped to consider how much you take your own view of the world to be normal or natural? I know I hadn't prior to my India studies. For example, I guess I always assumed that most people are middle class, like I am. Don't get me wrong—I was aware of very wealthy people as well as the very poor. But I never thought about what this means in terms of the way I communicate. I confess that I often complain that I have "nothing to wear," despite the fact that my closet is full of perfectly good clothes that have gone out of style. But in India, I came face to face with individuals who truly have "nothing to wear" because their socioeconomic status doesn't permit them to run to Old Navy and buy a new pair of jeans when an older pair becomes frayed. I'm now more aware of the fact that there are people in my own state and city—as well as at my university—that also face considerable financial hardships.

I also had to face two important cultural variations—high- versus low-context cultures and time orientation—during my time abroad. (And I openly confess that I found the process of addressing these cultural differences to be rather frustrating, at first). For example, the members of my group and I had trouble getting hot water for our showers at one of our hotels. I gladly took charge of the situation by calling down to the front desk. The hotel manager assured me that he would address

the issue, but an hour later we still didn't have hot water. A trip downstairs to see the manager in person reassured me, as the kindly gentleman shook his head and indicated that the hot water would be available soon. Three trips later, it dawned on me that his quiet gestures indicating "yes" actually meant "no": "No, there will not be any hot water today." It was up to me—the listener—to decode all of the contextual cues that pointed to this response, despite my own upbringing in a low-context culture (in which the manager would likely have said, "Our hot water heater is currently broken. We expect it to be fixed by 6 A.M. tomorrow.").

In addition, I learned the importance of respecting the different ways in which people communicate with and through time in India. I'm a schedule-oriented person and I show up to my job and my classes on time. I also think that I might be completely lost without my watch or the clock on my cell phone! But in India, time is more relaxed. People are less concerned about beginning a 10 A.M. class exactly at 10 A.M.; deadlines and appointment times are less rigid as well. Being mindful of this truth—and understanding that it's a cultural difference and not a lack of respect or concern on the part of our Indian professors and peers—allowed us to adjust with less frustration.

As you can see, my studies and my time in India had a deep impact on my life and my communication. I find that I'm simply more aware of the little ways in which my communication differs from others—and I always do my best to adjust, assimilate, and be considerate of others with different perspectives. This is true whether I'm communicating with an older relative (like my grandmother) or someone from a different race, religion, ethnicity, or even field of study. The fact is, there's something pretty freeing about losing the belief that your own ways of communicating and viewing the world are "normal."

strength (as with Henri above), while in others it is associated with weakness. Sometimes emotional expression is seen as chaos and other times as an identification of and processing of problems (Lutz, 1996).

How emotion is expressed verbally is an important cultural difference. Many collectivistic cultures (for example, Arab cultures) often use **hyperbole**—vivid, colorful language with great emotional intensity (and often exaggeration). Individualistic cultures (particularly English-speaking) tend toward **understatement**, language that downplays the emotional intensity or importance of events (often with euphemisms) (Wierzbicka, 2006). Consider, for example, the difference between describing a military battle by saying "the river ran red with the blood of the slaughtered" versus "there were a number of casualties." Indeed, in the United Kingdom and Ireland, three decades of

what about you?

Discovering Your Cultural Values

Consider each of the following statements and mark SA (strongly agree), A (agree), N (neither agree nor disagree), D (disagree), or SD (strongly disagree).

Value Statements	SA	A	N	D	SD
People who work hard are to be admired.					
People should take care of family before themselves.					
It is important to plan carefully for the future.					
It is important to show respect to your elders.					
Risk-taking is crazy; people should follow the rules.					
It is important to be on time to appointments.					
People should share their emotions with one another.					
People should say what they think clearly and directly.					
Competition is beneficial for society.					
Change is a necessary and good part of life.					

There is no official scale to help you grade this self-assessment; since cultural values occur on a continuum (and are not polar opposites), you will likely find that you will be discovering your cultural variation as you contemplate each question. Try to assess your answers according to the cultural value variations detailed in this chapter.

bombings and violence by paramilitary groups in northern Ireland is a period referred to simply as "the Troubles."

We've seen that communication in different cultures varies along continuums in seven key ways. Yet within these broadly defined cultures, we all vary our communication in many more specific ways based on the many groups to which we belong or with which we identify, as we see in the next section on group affiliation.

Understanding Group Affiliations

Ellen DeGeneres is many things. She is an American, a woman, and a baby boomer. She is white. She is a Californian, but also a southerner. She is a lesbian, a vegan, an animal rights activist, and an environmentalist. She is also a successful entertainer and is very wealthy. All of these characteristics—and many others—form DeGeneres's unique identity. These attributes also make her a member of various groups: some might be formal (as expressed by her affiliations with various animal rights groups), but most are informal, reflecting the more general ways in which we all group ourselves and others based on particular characteristics. Thus, Ellen is a member of the white community, the southern community, the wealthy community, the entertainment community, and so on.

As a complex human being, you too have multiple aspects to your identity, including the many groups to which you belong. And for better or worse, these group affiliations exert a powerful influence over your communication—and affect the ways in which others communicate with and about you. In this section we'll consider these facts by examining co-cultural communication as well as social identity theory and intergroup communication.

● **OF WHICH GROUPS** can Ellen DeGeneres claim membership?

Co-Cultural Communication

As we discussed in Chapter 1, **co-cultures** are groups whose members share at least some of the general culture's system of thought and behavior, but which have distinct characteristics or group attitudes that both unify them and distinguish them from the general culture. As you saw in our example about Ellen and as you can view in Figure 3.3, ethnic heritage, race (or races), gender, religion, socioeconomic status, and age form just a few of these co-cultures. But other factors come into play as well: some co-cultures are defined by interest, activities, opinions, or by membership in particular organizations (for example, "I am a Republican" or "I am a foodie").

Communication scholars have found that our communication is intrinsically tied to our co-cultural experience. For example, a **generation** is a group of people who were born into a specific time frame, along with its events and social changes that shape attitudes and behavior. Generations develop different worldviews and different ideas of how relationships work, thus affecting communication within and between generations (Howe & Strauss,

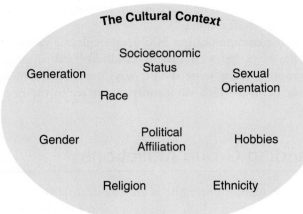

The Cultural Context

Generation

Socioeconomic
Status

Race

Sexual
Orientation

Gender

Political
Affiliation

Hobbies

Religion

Ethnicity

FIGURE 3.3

CO-CULTURES WITHIN
A LARGER CULTURE

1992). For example, Americans who lived through the Second World War are bound by that experience; they share common memories (the bombing of Pearl Harbor, the experience of war itself, or of home-front rationing and bond drives) that have shaped their worldviews in somewhat similar—though not identical—ways. This shared experience affects the ways in which they communicate, as you can see in Table 3.2.

Similarly, the interplay between our sex and our gender exerts a powerful co-cultural influence on our communication. *Sex* refers to the biological characteristics (that is, reproductive organs) that make us male or female, while **gender** refers to the behavioral and cultural traits assigned to our sex; it is determined by the way members of a particular culture define notions of masculinity and femininity (Wood, 2008, 2011). For example, according to well-known linguistics professor Deborah Tannen, men tend to develop a masculine "report" communication style that is assertive, focused on outcomes,

TABLE 3.2

GENERATIONS AS CO-CULTURE

Generation	Year Born	Characteristics Affecting Communication
Matures	Before 1946	Born before the Second World War, these are the generations that lived through the Great Depression and the war. They are largely conformist, with strong civic instincts.
Baby Boomers	1946–1964	The largest generation, products of an increase in births that began after the Second World War and ended with the introduction of the birth control pill. In their youths, they were antiestablishment and optimistic about the future, but recent surveys show they are more pessimistic today than any other age group.
Generation X	1965–1980	Savvy, entrepreneurial, and independent, this generation witnessed the fall of the Berlin Wall and the rise of home computing.
Millenials	1981–2000	The first generation of the new millennium, this group includes people under 30, the first generation to fully integrate computers into their everyday communication.

Source: Taylor & Keeter, 2010.

and competitive; men also tend to avoid many other nonverbal behaviors, including touching, gesturing, and vocalizations (fillers such as "uh-huh") when communicating with others (Tannen, 1992; Wood, 2009). On the other hand, Tannen noted that women often develop a "rapport" communication style that is collaborative and focused on others' feelings and needs. This feminine communication style also tends to include many nonverbal behaviors, such as touching communication partners and giving vocal, facial, and gestural indications that the partner is being heard (Tannen, 1992; Wood, 2009).[2]

---

[2]Scholars have long debated whether these communication differences are based on nature (inherent differences between men and women), nurture (the ways in which men and women are encouraged to have, and are rewarded for having, different styles), or some combination of the two. We cannot possibly do justice to the nuances of this debate in the confines of this chapter, but we will discuss these issues related to verbal and nonverbal communication in Chapters 4 and 5.

WIREDFORCOMMUNICATION

THINK ABOUT THIS

Online Gamers: Women Are Hardcore, Too

The stereotypical view of the gaming community—especially hardcore players—is that it is young and male. But industry reports note that more women own gaming consoles than men (Quenqua, 2007). In addition, more than 40 percent of online gamers are female (Entertainment Software Association, 2009). So what are women playing? And do they play differently than men?

Communication researchers studied more than seven thousand players involved in the Massively Multiplayer Online (MMO) game *Everquest II*, and found several distinct characteristics related to gender. Although they represented just under 20 percent of the players, female players proved to be more "hardcore"—they played more often and were less inclined to quit the game. Their motivations for playing were different too. Men were more motivated by achievement than were women, while women were slightly more motivated than men by social reasons (Williams, Consalvo, Caplan, & Yee, 2009). Interestingly, while both men and women tended to underreport the amount of time they spent playing, women were three times more likely than men to lie about how much they played.

However, the single biggest difference between the sexes in the study hinged on players' romantic relationships. More than 60 percent of the women in the study played with a romantic partner; less than 25 percent of the men did. Interestingly, male and female players who were in romantic relationships with other players perceived their relationships differently, with men noting less contentment and overall satisfaction with their partners, and women reporting higher levels of overall happiness and satisfaction (Williams, Consalvo, Caplan, & Yee, 2009).

1 Do you play live games online? Do you consider the gender of the players you compete against when you do? Do you choose to reveal your own gender when you play?

2 Do you or would you try online gaming with your romantic partner? Explain how you think your communication is (or might be) altered when you share games online.

3 Consider the discussion of gender as co-culture in this chapter. Why do you think women were so much more likely to underreport the amount of time they spent playing?

AND YOU?

Do you consider yourself more of a masculine or feminine individual? (Note that your choice may not align with your biological sex.) Do others communicate with you in ways that support or criticize this aspect of your communication?

So, are we destined to live our lives bound by the communication norms and expectations for our sex or gender, our generation, our profession, our hobbies, and our other co-cultures? Hardly. Recall the concept of *behavioral flexibility* discussed in Chapter 1, which notes that competent communicators adapt communication skills for use in a variety of life situations. There are contexts and relationships that call for individuals of both sexes to adhere to a more feminine mode of communication (for example, giving sufficient verbal and nonverbal feedback to a distraught family member), while other contexts and relationships require them to communicate in a more masculine way (for example, using direct and confident words and body movements when negotiating for a higher salary). Similarly, a teenager who feels most comfortable communicating with others via text messaging or Facebook might do well to send Grandma a handwritten thank-you note for his graduation gift—or even a physical card via snail mail for her birthday.

In addition, we would be remiss if we did not remind you of the great diversity of communication behaviors within co-cultures (as well as the diversity within larger cultures). For example, we would never want to leave you with the impression that your grandmother and your best friend's grandmother communicate in the exact same style simply because they were born in the same year or because they were both college graduates who became high school English teachers. Similarly, the group typically defined as African Americans includes Americans with a variety of cultural and national heritages, from those whose American story stretches back to colonial times, to more recent immigrants from Africa, the Caribbean, and elsewhere, and their descendants ("Census," 2010). Christians include a wealth of different denominations that practice various aspects of the larger faith differently. Christians also hail from different races and ethnicities, socioeconomic statuses, regions, political views, and so on. All of these intersecting factors affect communication within any given co-culture.

Social Identity and Intergroup Communication

In Chapter 2, you learn that the *self-serving bias* holds that we usually attribute our own successes to internal factors and our failures to external effects. Because we want to feel good about our group memberships as well, we tend to make the same attributions. So if your sorority sister gets an A on a difficult exam, you may attribute it to her intelligence; if she fails, you may assume that the exam was unfair.

Clearly our group memberships exert a powerful influence on our communication. This point is further illustrated and clarified by two powerful concepts: social identity theory and intergroup communication. According to **social identity theory** you have a *personal identity*, which is your sense of your unique individual personality, and you also have a *social identity*, the part of your self-concept that comes from your group memberships (Tajfel & Turner, 1986). We divide ourselves into "us" and "them" partly based on our affiliations with various co-cultures. The groups with which we identify and to which we feel we belong are our **ingroups**; those we define as "others" are **outgroups**. Social identity theory notes that, because we want to feel good about our affiliations—that is, because we want "us" to be distinct and better than "them"—we are continually comparing our co-cultures to others in the hope that we are part of the "winning" teams.

Studies in **intergroup communication**, a branch of the discipline that focuses on how communication within and between groups affects relationships, find that these comparisons have a tremendous impact on communication (Giles, Reid, & Harwood, 2010; Pagotto, Voci, & Maculan, 2010). For example, group members often use specialized language and nonverbal behaviors in order to reveal group membership status to others (Bourhis, 1985). So, a doctor might use a lot of technical medical terms among nurses in order to assert her authority as a doctor. The Chicago Bears fan proudly wears her team jersey on game day, while her husband and children proudly don their Dallas Cowboys T-shirts.

It is interesting to note that our identification and communication shift depending on which group membership is made **salient**—or brought to mind—at a given moment. For example, students often consider themselves ingroup members with other fellow students and outgroup members with nonstudents. However, a group of students at different schools might identify in smaller units—suddenly community college students consider themselves outgroups from students attending a four-year university, for example. But if all of these students find a common affiliation—if they discover that they're all rabid fans of the *Hunger Games* trilogy, for example, or that they all volunteered for Habitat for Humanity—they might see each other as ingroup members when they discuss these interests and experiences.

In addition, *you* may not identify equally with all of your group memberships (that is, they are not all equally salient for you at any given time), and your communication reflects this. In other words, you may be a Latina Catholic from a middle-class family and a straight-A student with a love of languages and a passion for outdoor adventure sports. However, when displaying who "you" are, you may emphasize your "studentness" (by wearing your college insignia) and sports enthusiasm (by participating actively in sporting events) while your race, religion, and socioeconomic status don't come to the forefront. But remember that your group memberships don't just influence your own communication—other people treat you based on the groups *they* think you belong to. So someone else might focus on other aspects of how you look or talk and see you primarily as "a woman," "a Catholic," or "a Latina."

The ways in which social identity is perceived by others influences communication on many levels. In the 1960s, Rock Hudson was a Hollywood heartthrob who kept his identity as a gay man a secret. It is unlikely that audiences at that time would have accepted him in heterosexual romantic roles if they knew that he was, in fact, not interested in women. Today, it remains unclear whether studios and audiences who are comfortable with straight actors taking on gay and lesbian roles (such as Heath Ledger and Jake Gyllenhall in *Brokeback Mountain)*, will fully accept gay and lesbian actors in straight roles. While the openly gay Neil Patrick Harris has no problem playing the womanizing Barney Stinson on *How I Met*

● **JOHN BOEHNER'S** tearful response upon becoming Speaker of the House in 2011 gained him much media airtime, perhaps because we are prone to criticize open displays of emotion from men.

Your Mother, actors like Rupert Everett and Richard Chamberlain have noted that coming out hurt their careers irreparably, and advised young gay actors to maintain their privacy in regard to their sexuality (Connelly, 2009; Voss, 2010).

COMMUNICATIONACROSSCULTURES

THINK ABOUT THIS

The It Gets Better Project

Columnist Dan Savage was stewing. He'd just heard about the suicide of an Indiana teenager, Billy Lucas, who had hanged himself in his grandmother's barn at the age of fifteen. Lucas, who may or may not have been gay, was perceived as gay by his classmates and bullied harshly because of it. Savage felt heartbroken and angry. Nine out of ten gay teenagers experience bullying and harassment, and like most other gay men and women, Savage had endured bullying during his teenage years. But in spite of it, he was now a happy adult with a fulfilling life. He was frustrated that Billy Lucas would miss out on those things. "I wish I could have talked to this kid for five minutes," Savage wrote in his column. "I wish I could have told Billy that *it gets better*. I wish I could have told him that, however bad things were, however isolated and alone he was, *it gets better*" (Savage, 2010).

It was too late to say those things to Billy Lucas. But Savage knew there were thousands more young people like Billy Lucas—teenagers who were gay or lesbian or simply unsure about their sexuality who had been targeted and tormented. He knew that gay teens are four times more likely to attempt suicide than others—and he believed that it wasn't too late to talk to them. So Savage and his partner sat down in front of their webcam and made a video. They talked about their own experiences at the mercy of bullies, about being isolated from their own parents when they came out. But they also talked about what comes later: about gaining acceptance, finding places where they weren't alone, and building families and careers. They posted the video to YouTube, and encouraged others to do the same. The It Gets Better Project was born.

By January 2011, more than five thousand videos had been posted—from straight and gay people, celebrities, and ordinary Americans—and the site had logged more than fifteen million views. Suddenly, isolated gay, lesbian, bisexual, transgendered, and questioning teens had a place to go to be assured that they were not alone, that they could survive the bullying, and that life would, indeed, get better.[1]

---

[1] The project does not offer any solutions for dealing with bullies or advise students to engage in conflict with those who abuse them. It simply offers them a peer experience, to show them that they're not alone, and tries to show them that life will go on after the bullying ends.

❶ Consider how the It Gets Better Project offers young people who are feeling isolated because of their sexuality the opportunity to envision their lives as part of a co-culture. Can the It Gets Better project help them to find peers and role models?

❷ Think about how technology allows individuals to connect with other people who share narrowly defined interests (graphic novels or vegan cooking) or face similar, but uncommon, challenges (a rare form of cancer or a specific physical disability). How can connecting with others who share these interests and challenges via the Internet enrich their lives?

❸ The It Gets Better Project is aimed at a very specific co-culture, but the videos posted there come from people of all walks of life. Is it important for gay teens to hear messages of encouragement from outside the co-culture? Do the messages posted on the It Gets Better Project have value for straight teens as well?

Intercultural Communication Challenges

With all of the existing cultural variations and the multitude of individual and overlapping co-cultures to which you (and every single person with whom you come into contact) belong, it is understandable that communication difficulties sometimes arise. Even with people you know well who are like you in many ways, you sometimes experience challenges and confusion with intercultural communication. Let's look at some of the more pressing intercultural challenges that communicators experience when interacting with others: anxiety, ethnocentrism, and discrimination.

Anxiety

"What if I say something offensive?" "What if I don't know how to behave?" "What if I embarrass myself?" These are just a few of the worries that sometimes accompany people as they approach intercultural communication encounters. Consider the experience of Allison Goodrich, an American student at Georgetown University about to set off on a semester abroad in China:

> Here I was, standing, in the check-out line of the Chinese market in Rockville, Maryland, listening to the cashier yell at me with an incomprehensible stream of syllables. This was after a rather harrowing attempt to find groceries in the overcrowded store. A year of Chinese wasn't helping me as I stood in front of an entire display of green vegetables, trying to figure out which sign would lead me to my desired product. During all of this, my accompanying friend turned to me and said, "This is how crowded it will be wherever you go in China." (Goodrich, 2007, para. 1)

You can probably imagine Allison's anxiety as she considered her upcoming adventure: if she felt uncomfortable navigating the market just a few miles from her dorm, how would she be able to communicate effectively several thousand miles away?

But like Allison, most of us who have traveled abroad forged friendships across cultural and co-cultural boundaries. Or we moved to a different geographical region of the United States to find that the more positive experiences we have with those who differ from us in salient ways, the less intimidated we feel. The less intimidated we feel, the more competent our communication becomes. In fact, a 2009 study found that American students who took the risk and studied abroad perceived themselves as being more proficient, approachable, and open to intercultural communication (Clarke, Flaherty, Wright, & McMillen, 2009). Even online interactions across cultures tend to ease anxiety and foster understanding. Users of Second Life, while physically isolated, engage in virtual

In Chapter 14 on speech delivery, we offer practical tips to help you build your confidence and face the natural anxiety that accompanies a speaking opportunity. Many of these tips are also useful for overcoming anxiety in intercultural encounters. For example, Allison might visualize her success in navigating a foreign city in order to boost her sense of efficacy.

● **THE IDEA OF STUDYING** abroad may initially cause you anxiety, but positive experiences in a foreign country can make you a more competent and interculturally sensitive communicator.

AND YOU?

Most people experience some degree of anxiety in new communication situations. What types of intercultural communication encounters make you anxious? Speaking with members of the opposite sex? Communicating outside of your native language? Why?

travels and interactions with other users around the world. These encounters encourage the use of multiple languages, cross-cultural encounters and friendships, greater awareness of inside cultural perspectives, and openness toward new viewpoints (Diehl & Prins, 2008).

While anxiety may be a natural part of any new experience or interaction, it would also be deeply unfortunate to allow it to prevent you from experiencing the clear benefits and enrichment gained in intercultural experiences.

Ethnocentrism

In the fashion world, the gowns worn by prominent trendsetters are always big news. So, when Michelle Obama wore a stunning Naeem Kahm sheath to a state dinner in 2009, newspapers and bloggers were bound to comment. But the buzz the following morning was not over what she wore, but on how to explain the color of the gown. The gown, described by its designer as "a sterling-silver sequin, abstract floral, nude strapless gown," was a color somewhere between peach and sand. The Associated Press initially described it as "flesh-colored," but changed it to "champagne" when one editor questioned: "Whose flesh? Not hers" (Phanor-Faury, 2010).

This is a simple and very common example of **ethnocentrism**, a belief in the superiority of your own culture or group and a tendency to view other cultures through the lens of your own. Ethnocentrism can make communication biased: we tend to communicate from the perspective of our own group without acknowledging other perspectives. The offense is unintended, which further reveals the fact that we sometimes behave in ways that "normalize" one group and marginalize another—without even realizing it. Describing a peachy-colored dress as "flesh" colored, for example, insinuates that light colored skin is the default standard, and that darker skin tones are therefore something "other" or different from the norm. It's also unclear. "While beige may be 'nude' for most white women," noted one commentator, " 'nude' for me would be brown" (Phanor-Faury, 2010).

It's important to bear in mind that ethnocentrism is not the same thing as ethnic or cultural pride. It's a wonderful and uniquely human experience to express feelings of patriotism, or to experience a deep respect for your religion or ethnic heritage. Ethnocentrism arises when you express a bias on behalf of your own co-cultures—when you treat others as inferior or inconsequential, or ignore them altogether. Carlos, for example, is a proud Catholic for whom the Christmas holidays have great religious meaning. And while he decorates his home with a nativity scene and sends Christmas cards to family and fellow Christians as December 25 draws near, he also sends a separate set of "Season's Greetings" cards to his friends who do not celebrate Christmas as a way of being respectful of their traditions while still sharing his wishes for peace and goodwill with them.

● **A BEAUTIFUL GOWN?** Yes. A flesh-colored gown? Not unless you're thinking ethnocentrically.

Discrimination

Ethnocentrism can lead to **discrimination**—behavior toward a person or group based solely on their membership in a particular group, class, or category—when attitudes about superiority of one culture lead to rules and behaviors that favor that group and harm another group.

Recall from Chapter 2 that *stereotypes* about and *prejudice* toward a particular cultural group may result in discrimination, preventing individuals from understanding and adapting to others (Cargile & Giles, 1996). Yet seemingly positive stereotypes can have similarly discriminatory effects. For example, consider the "model minority" stereotype of Asian Americans that characterizes them as quiet, hardworking, studious, and productive. As Suzuki (2002) points out, these beliefs lead some employers to dismiss Asian Americans' complaints about discrimination in the workplace and made government agencies and nonprofit organizations less inclined to support programs to assist lower income Asian Americans since Asian communities seemed largely self-sufficient.

Discrimination can be explained in part by research on intergroup communication. Studies show that we have a biased tendency to treat fellow ingroup members better than we treat members of outgroups (Giles, Reid, & Harwood, 2010). In fact, we even *interpret* ingroup behaviors more favorably than outgroup behaviors. For example, if you discovered that someone in your sorority was caught cheating on an exam, you would be likely to explain the behavior as an unusual situation brought on by challenging circumstances. On the other hand, if you heard about someone from another sorority (an outgroup) cheating, you would be more likely to attach a personal explanation, such as that the person is "dishonest" or "unethical."

On a related note, **behavioral affirmation** is seeing or hearing what you want to see or hear in the communication of assorted group members. In other words, if you think that teenagers are lazy, then regardless of how much effort your fourteen-year-old cousin puts forth, you don't see the effort and instead notice his eye-rolling or slumped shoulders, so you still perceive him to be unmotivated. **Behavioral confirmation** is when we act in a way that makes our expectations about a group come true (Snyder & Klein, 2005). Again, if you think your teenage cousin (like all teens) is lazy, you are more likely to give him tasks that do not require much effort. When he, in turn, fails to put in a great deal of effort, you confirm to yourself, "See? I knew he wouldn't try very hard."

Improving Intercultural Communication

Like many worthwhile things in life, intercultural communication can be improved with effort. Training programs help communicators become more mindful and considerate in their interactions across culture and lead to positive changes in people's thinking, feelings, and behavior (Landis, Bennett, & Bennett, 2004). Intercultural training generally focuses on three areas:

▶ **Changing thinking (or cognition).** Our thinking changes when we increase our knowledge about cultures and co-cultures and develop more complex (rather than simplistic) ways of thinking about a culture. This, in turn, reduces negative stereotypes and helps individuals appreciate other points of view.

▶ **Changing feelings (or affect).** Our feelings change when we experience greater enjoyment and less anxiety in our intercultural interactions, making us feel more comfortable and positive about intercultural exchanges.

▶ **Changing behavior.** When your thoughts and feelings are altered, behavioral changes occur as a result. Individuals develop better interpersonal relationships in work groups and perform their jobs better when they know what to say and not to say—do and not do—acting with greater ease and effectiveness in accomplishing goals.

You don't need to attend a special program or hire a professional intercultural trainer to improve your intercultural communication. You simply need to consider some important points as you communicate with people from other generations, faiths, ethnicities, and so on: be mindful, desire to learn, overcome intergroup biases, accommodate appropriately, and practice skills.

Be Mindful

As you learned in Chapter 2, being *mindful* means to be aware of your behavior and the behavior of others. In order to be mindful, you must be aware that many of your communication attitudes and behaviors are so rooted in your own culture that they are unconscious. When someone stands a bit too close to you, you might just sense "something funny." Or you might interpret someone's very direct eye contact as a sign of hostility rather than a cultural difference. Of course, not all uncomfortable interactions are the result of cultural differences, but being mindful of the possibility gives you a larger repertoire of effective ways way to respond.

You should also be mindful of your personal tendencies toward discrimination—you should question yourself to see if you are interpreting another's behaviors negatively or positively based on whether the individual shares your group memberships. Part of this mindfulness is practicing **intercultural sensitivity**, or mindfulness of behaviors that may offend others (Bennett & Bennett, 2004). When Caroline married Luke, his mother insisted that the family pictures be taken in front of the church altar or in front of religious statues in the garden outside, completely insensitive to the Jewish side of Caroline's family. Had she taken a bit of time to reflect on how she would have felt if her own religious beliefs had been disregarded in this manner, Luke's mother might have behaved very differently. Being sensitive doesn't mean giving up your own beliefs and practices, but it does involve not forcing them blindly on others.

Desire to Learn

Learning culture-specific information can be very useful as a starting point in intercultural communication; knowledge of general interaction patterns common for a particular group can increase your awareness of other ways of communicating and prepare you to adapt—or not adapt—as you consider the multitude of factors that influence an intercultural interaction.

But *how* do you go about learning about another culture or co-culture and its members' communication preferences? Is it okay to ask questions or to seek clarification? Do you have to visit a foreign country to learn about that nation's culture? Do you need a close friend within a given co-culture to understand aspects of that co-culture's communication? We encourage you to ask respectful and earnest questions and to experience other cultures

EVALUATING COMMUNICATION ETHICS

THINK ABOUT THIS

That's Not a Soy Substitute

You and your friend Greg signed a lease for an off-campus apartment—you both wanted the opportunity to cook for yourselves rather than eat in the dining hall every night. In fact, food is actually one of the main reasons that Greg brought up the idea of moving off campus in the first place.

Greg is a strict vegan and does not consume animal products, including meat, dairy, and even honey. You are not a vegan—in fact you're not even a vegetarian—but you've always admired and respected Greg's passion for animal rights, his affiliation with the American Society for the Prevention of Cruelty to Animals (ASPCA), and his hard work to become a veterinarian. Before you and Greg decided to move in together, you had a frank conversation during which he told you that he would be uncomfortable having animal products in the apartment and wondered if you would be willing to eat a vegan diet in your shared space. You thought Greg would make a great roommate and you wanted the situation to work out, so you agreed. Besides, you figured you could always grab a cheeseburger on campus.

The arrangement worked out rather well and you barely think about the food restrictions, except for when Greg's girlfriend Amanda visits. Amanda is well aware of Greg's desires and views but you suspect that she finds them to be ridiculous and insulting. Sometimes you even feel that she's trying to bait you into complaining about Greg's veganism so that the two of you can "gang up" on him in an effort to enact a change of behavior. You tried to stay out of it, but one evening you arrived home to find Amanda alone in your living room, eating a container of pork fried rice—and we're not talking about some sort of soy pork substitute. "Please don't tell Greg," she pleaded. "I told him I'd hang out here until he's done with class tonight and I got hungry. I cannot eat any of that tofu and wheat gluten stuff in your refrigerator so I ordered takeout. Besides, you must think that his restrictions on what we eat here are crazy . . . don't you?"

You feel annoyed by this conversation and want to mention it to Greg, but you also feel that Greg and Amanda's communication and discussions about personal practices and group affiliations are their business. What should you do?

① Would this situation be different if it took place in a freshman dorm and Greg was a randomly selected roommate? Would it be ethical for Greg to ask you to follow the same restrictions—and would it be unethical for you to refuse?

② What if Greg's reasons for having food restrictions encompassed additional co-cultural factors, such as religion? Would this be a more, less, or equally pressing reason for you to accommodate food restrictions in your home? Why or why not?

③ How might you structure an ethical response to Amanda or an ethical conversation with Greg based on the suggestions for improving intercultural communication provided in this chapter? How might you be mindful, be empathic, or desire to learn?

AND YOU?

Consider a time you felt competent in learning about another culture or co-culture. What was the situation? How did you gain knowledge about the culture? Did this knowledge cause you to change your behavior or thoughts?

in whatever way you are able—whether that means being open to trying foods outside of your own culture, studying the scriptures of another faith, or deciding to study abroad.

In fact, with all the technology available to you today, you can make contact through online communities and social networking groups, even if you can't personally travel around the world. For example, some students have taken to posting videos of themselves practicing a foreign language in order to elicit feedback from native speakers on the quality of their speech and accent. Such attempts to learn more about another culture's language or way of speaking can also be seen in YouTube videos in which American and British children attempt to swap accents and rate each other on how accurate they are.

Overcome Intergroup Biases

Learning about other cultures is a great start to improving intercultural communication, but many scholars believe that we also need to spend time with members of other cultures and co-cultures, virtually and face to face.

Intergroup contact theory is one prominent idea for addressing intercultural challenges (Allport, 1954). It holds that interaction between members of different social groups generates a possibility for more positive attitudes to emerge (Pettigrew & Tropp, 2006). In other words, if you have contact with people who are different from you, you realize that the expectations you had about them might be incorrect, and this helps you to better understand others. By getting to know others across the ocean or across the street, you will have *reduced uncertainty* by seeking information about what is likely to happen in encounters with them. You will become more confident, more knowledgeable about how to behave, more decisive, more able to predict behavior, and thus more likely to understand one another (Gudykunst, 2004).

Although contact theory has some support, researchers also find that mindlessly getting people from different groups together can actually backfire and reinforce cultural stereotypes (Paolini, Harwood, & Rubin, 2010). A very real consequence of this happened across many U.S. cities during the 1970s and 1980s, when there was a highly controversial effort to racially integrate schools by busing children to schools on faraway sides of their cities. Even staunch proponents of the plan admitted that the research findings showed that racial tensions became worse, not better (Frum, 2000).

So, how do we make successful intergroup interactions more likely? First, intergroup researchers argue that we must have *good quality contact* with outgroup members, because negative contact can increase the perception of differences (Paolini, Harwood, & Rubin, 2010). But good contact is not enough since it's easy for us to explain away such positive interactions as unique to the individual or the situation. For example, if you believe that fraternity brothers are simply party boys and you wind up in a study group with a particularly hardworking member of Phi Sigma Phi, you can mentally create excuses: "Ben is the exception to the rule." Instead, researchers also argue that we must have good contact with people that we think are "typical" of their group (Giles, Reid,

& Harwood, 2010). If you attended a few fraternity events and got to see Ben and several of his brothers more regularly in their fraternity setting, you might learn that many of them are serious students and that a few of them aren't even into the party scene. We all need to be aware of our *own* behaviors and biased perceptions when interacting with members of other cultures and groups, so that we do not simply confirm our existing expectations.

Accommodate Appropriately

Another way to improve intercultural communication is to adapt and adjust your language and nonverbal behaviors, a process called **accommodation**. On a very simple level, you do this when you talk to a child, squatting down to get eye contact and using a basic vocabulary; police officers also do this when they adopt the street slang or foreign phrases commonly used in the neighborhoods they patrol. When speakers shift their language or nonverbal behaviors *toward* each other's way of communicating, they are engaging in **convergence**. We typically converge to gain approval from others and to show solidarity (Gallois, Franklyn-Stokes, Giles, & Coupland, 1988). Convergence usually results in positive reactions, because if I speak like you, it is a way of saying "I am similar to you."

● **GOOD QUALITY** contact with members of a campus fraternity could serve to counter the bias that frat brothers are nothing more than jocks and partiers.

Accommodation is not an absolute, all-or-nothing goal: usually, it involves making small efforts to show that you respect others' cultural and communication behaviors, and appreciate their efforts to communicate with you. Ramon makes efforts to speak English when he greets his customers at the restaurant where he works, even though it is not his native language and he struggles with it at times. Conversely, many of his regular customers who do not speak Spanish will greet him with the Spanish words they do know ("Hola, Ramon! Buenos dias!") or when thanking him for their meal ("Gracias!").

However, it is important to be careful not to **overaccommodate**, which means going too far in changing your language or changing your language based on an incorrect or stereotypical notion of another group (Harwood & Giles, 2005). For example, senior citizens often find it patronizing and insulting when younger people speak "down" to them (slow down, increase volume, and use childish words) (Harwood, 2000). For Ramon, if his customers were to speak slowly and loudly, or in poorly mangled attempts to communicate in Spanish, Ramon might think they were making fun of him.

Practice Your Skills

Communicators need to use verbal and nonverbal behaviors effectively and appropriately to attain goals and get along in intercultural situations. Sometimes this literally means using the language of another culture well enough to communicate effectively. Sometimes it simply means communicating

● **WHILE SQUATTING** to speak at eye level with a child is an appropriate accommodation, a senior adult may perceive this behavior as patronizing. Sitting may be more respectful.

your interest and appreciation for another person's life experiences and point of view (Chen & Starosta, 1996). Communicators with fewer social skills have more difficulty managing the "different" interactions that intercultural situations demand, so it is important to develop the following skills (Arasaratnam, 2007).

▶ **Listen effectively.** You can't be mindful unless you listen to what people say (and what they don't say). For example, health practitioners first need to listen to what cultural groups say about themselves and their beliefs about what will make them healthy. Then health practitioners need to shape health messages for these specific audiences (Larkey & Hecht, 2010). Knowing when to talk and when to be quiet (so you can listen) is crucial to intercultural encounters.

▶ **Think before you speak or act.** Hold back—don't be the first to speak up or respond. When someone communicates in a way that seems strange to you—not meeting your gaze, for example, or speaking very directly—take a moment to think about whether his or her behavior is a cultural difference rather than evasion or hostility.

▶ **Be empathic.** By developing *empathy,* the ability to picture yourself in someone else's place in an attempt to understand that person's experience, you can change your perceptions and improve your understanding of the ways in which culture affects communication.

▶ **Do the right thing.** Be ethical. Stand up for someone who is being mocked for race, religion, or sexual orientation. Fight for those who don't have a voice. You don't need to be wealthy, established, or powerful to do this. When a friend makes a remark that you deem culturally insensitive, a simple reminder ("That's a rude statement" or "Oh, man, don't talk like that") can send a powerful message without chiding or berating.

BACK TO ▸ Glee

 At the beginning of the chapter, we talked about the hit musical comedy television show *Glee*, which depicts the complexity within and between co-cultures with a satirical take on high school life. Let's revisit *Glee*, and see how the show relates to and reflects some of the concepts described in this chapter.

▸ *Glee* reflects culture in the United States in terms of the diversity of the cast as well as in the overarching themes. The members of the McKinley glee club are underdogs not only at their school but also among the other show choirs with which they compete. As part of an individualist, low-power distance, and masculine culture, Americans tend to believe that with a level playing field and a lot of hard work, anyone can be successful. *Glee* taps into this sentiment, following a long tradition of underdog stories.

▸ *Glee* also explores the ways in which cultural differences can threaten, but not necessarily damage, relationships. Kurt and Mercedes may be best friends, but their different views about faith pose challenges that threaten their friendship: Mercedes is a devout Christian, while Kurt, a young gay man, has an extremely negative reaction to religion. Through exploration and discussion, the two learn to respect each other's views, even though they do not agree.

▸ Think about social identity. The first impression that most people get of Puck is that of a jock, but he also identifies closely with his Jewish heritage. Artie, who uses a wheelchair, is often seen as "different," but when popular cheerleader Brittany finds him attractive, others come to view him as a "normal" teen. In addition, the members of the football team and cheerleading squads who also participate in glee club try to balance expectations of them as athletes and "popular kids" with their participation in the traditionally outgroup glee club.

THINGS TO TRY ▸ Activities

1. On a blank piece of paper, begin listing all the co-cultures to which you belong. How many can you come up with? How do they overlap? If someone asked you to identify yourself by using only one of them, could you do it? Could you rank them in order of importance to you?

2. Make a list of all the places you have lived in or traveled to. (Remember, this does not just mean "travel to foreign countries." Think about trips to other neighborhoods in your city or areas of your state.) Create a bullet-point list

to describe the attitudes, customs, and behaviors of each place that seemed to typify the area. How was communication different in each area? How was it similar?

3. Many popular films in the United States are based on foreign language films from other cultures, such as *The Departed* (2006, based on the Hong Kong film *Infernal Affairs,* 2002), *The Tourist* (2010, based on the French film *Anthony Zimmer,* 2005), and *Let Me In* (2010, based on Sweden's *Let the Right One In,* 2008). Watch one such film, as well as the original foreign language film that inspired it. What cultural changes to the story can you detect? How do the nonverbal behaviors of the actors differ?

4. Do a little virtual shopping in the toy department of an online retailer, and use the search options to see what kinds of toys the retailer suggests for girls versus boys. What do these suggestions say about culture, gender, and the ways in which children play? Do these nonverbal messages influence culture, or are they more of a reflection of culture?

Now that you have finished reading this chapter, you can:

Define and explain culture and its impact on your communication:

▶ **Culture** is a learned system of thought and behavior that reflects a group's shared beliefs, values, and practices (p. 66).

▶ We learn culture through communication with others and, in turn, express our culture through communication (p. 66).

▶ Your **worldview** is the framework through which you interpret the world and the people in it (p. 66).

▶ **Intercultural communication** is the communication between people from different cultures who have different worldviews (p. 68).

Delineate seven ways that cultural variables affect communication:

▶ Individuals in **high-context cultures** use contextual cues to interpret meaning and send subtle messages; in **low-context cultures**, language is much more direct (pp. 71–72).

▶ In **collectivist cultures**, people perceive themselves primarily as members of a group and communicate from that perspective; in **individualist cultures**, people value individuality and communicate autonomy and privacy (pp. 72–73).

▶ Our comfort/discomfort with the unknown (**uncertainty avoidance**) varies with culture (p. 73).

▶ **Masculine cultures** tend to place value on assertiveness, achievement, ambition, and competitiveness; **feminine cultures** tend to value nurturance, relationships, and quality of life (p. 74).

▶ **Power distance** is the degree to which cultures accept the division of power among individuals (p. 75).

▶ **Time orientation** is the way that cultures communicate about and with time. In **monochronic cultures**, time is a valuable resource that is not to be wasted. **Polychronic cultures** have a more fluid approach to time (pp. 75–76).

▶ Cultures differ in their expression of emotion. Collectivist cultures often use **hyperbole**; individualist ones use more **understatement** (p. 78).

Describe the communicative power of group affiliations:

▶ **Co-cultures** are groups whose members share some of the general culture's system of thought and behavior, but have distinct characteristics (p. 79).

▶ A **generation** is a group of people born into a specific time frame (p. 79).

▶ **Gender** refers to the behavioral and cultural traits associated with biological sex (p. 80).

▶ **Social identity theory** notes that you have a *personal identity* as well as a *social identity*. Our social identity shifts depending on which group membership is most **salient** at a given moment (pp. 82–83).

▶ **Intergroup communication** finds that we communicate differently with people in **ingroups** versus **outgroups** (pp. 82–83).

Explain key barriers to competent intercultural communication:

▶ Anxiety may cause us to worry about embarrassing ourselves in an intercultural interaction (p. 85).

▶ **Ethnocentrism** is the belief in the superiority of your own culture or group (p. 86).

▶ **Discrimination** is behavior toward a person or group based on their membership in a group, class, or category. We often discriminate based on *stereotypes* and *prejudiced* views of other groups (p. 87).

▶ **Behavioral affirmation** is seeing or hearing what you want to see or hear in the communication of assorted group members (p. 87).

▶ **Behavioral confirmation** is when we act in a way that makes our expectations about a group come true (p. 87).

Demonstrate skills and behaviors that contribute to intercultural competence:

▶ You can improve intercultural communication by being mindful of cultural differences and developing **intercultural sensitivity**, an awareness of behaviors that might offend others (p. 88).

▶ **Intergroup contact theory** holds that interaction between members of different social groups generates more positive attitudes to emerge (p. 90).

▶ Research supports the importance of **accommodation**, adapting and adjusting your language and nonverbal behaviors. This can lead to **convergence**, adapting your communication to more like another individual's. If you **overaccommodate**, however, the interaction can be perceived negatively (p. 91).

Which of these pairs are partners?

Verbal Communication

Anne Kerry was walking to the bank in her San Francisco neighborhood when she suddenly ran into Scott, an old college friend, accompanied by another young man. "Anne," he said warmly, "I want you to meet my partner, Bryan." Anne was surprised—she hadn't realized that Scott was gay. She asked, "How long have you two been together?" Both men looked at her quizzically before they realized what she was thinking. "No," said Scott, "I became a police officer. Bryan and I work patrol together." "I was embarrassed," said Anne. "I didn't mean to misunderstand their relationship. I just figured that 'partner' meant love interest" (Anne Kerry, personal communication, March 7, 2008).

Like many words in the English language, *partner* has a variety of definitions: it can mean anything from "an associate" to "a dancing companion" to "a group of two or more symbiotically associated organisms." But like Anne, many of us immediately jump to another definition: "half of a couple who live together or who are habitual companions." Indeed, the term is widely used by gays and lesbians seeking a label for their loved one. Some heterosexual couples have also embraced the term to reveal their committed state, particularly when they feel that they've outgrown the term *boyfriend* or *girlfriend* or are unwilling to use the terms *husband* and *wife*.

The fact is, the labels we choose for our relationships have a huge impact on our communication. The term *partner* can give rise to ambiguity—is the person you introduce with this term a business colleague, someone you play tennis with, or your "significant other"? That ambiguity makes it difficult for others to grasp your intended meaning. Perhaps that's why some Massachusetts gays and lesbians who wed after the state ratified same-sex marriages avoid the term *partner*. Bob Buckley felt the power of such labels when his partner, Marty Scott, needed medical treatment. When hospital administrators asked his relationship to the patient, Buckley was able to say, simply, "husband," and was immediately allowed to stay with Scott, since spouses are afforded this privilege but partners are not (Jones, 2005).

After you have finished reading this chapter, you will be able to

○ Describe the power of language—the system of symbols we use to think about and communicate our experiences and feelings

○ Identify the ways language works to help people communicate—the five functional communication competencies

○ Label communication problems with language and discuss how to address them

○ Describe how language reflects, builds on, and determines context

Stop and think about the power of the words you use to describe your relationships. As you can see from our opening vignette, the name used to describe our connection with another person is significant and powerful. This goes beyond our romantic attachments. Calling your father "Dad" or "Father" can reveal a different level of formality in your relationship. In a stepfamily situation, calling your father's wife "Mom" or "Lisa" can indicate how close you and she feel. Choosing terms and using words can get pretty complicated. That's why we dedicate this chapter to studying verbal communication, the way we communicate with language. **Language** is the system of symbols (words) that we use to think about and communicate experiences and feelings. Language is also governed by grammatical rules and is influenced by various contexts.

Of course, communication is much more than pure language. Nonverbal behaviors that accompany the words we speak—pauses, tone of voice, and body movements—are an integral part of our communication. We look at nonverbal communication in Chapter 5, but for now just remember that language does not occur in isolation; it's always accompanied by a nonverbal component. We now examine the nature of language, the functions of language, some problems with language, and important contexts for language.

The Nature of Language

In 1970, a "wild child" was discovered in California. Thirteen-year-old "Genie" had been chained in a small room with no toys and little food for nearly her entire life. And what seems even crueler is that her abusive father did not allow her to experience human interaction—no hugs, no words of love or affirmation, and no conversation. As a result, Genie never developed language. Medical doctors, linguists, and psychologists worked intensely with Genie for over seven years, hoping to give the girl a chance at life in a community with others. But despite their efforts, Genie never learned more than a few hundred words and was never able to form sentences of more than two or three words (Pines, 1997; "Secret," 1997). Genie's sad story is of great interest to researchers who study how we acquire language, but it also highlights the complex nature of language. What Genie will never fully grasp is that language is symbolic, filled with multiple meanings, and informed by our thoughts. It is also ruled by grammar and bound by context. We examine these points in turn.

Language Is Symbolic

What comes to mind when you see the word *cat*? A furry childhood best friend? Fits of sneezing from allergies? Either way, the word evokes a response because *c-a-t* makes you think about your four-legged friend (or enemy). That's because a word is a type of *symbol,* a sign used to represent a person, idea, or thing. Symbols form the basis of language—there's no particular reason why *w-a-t-e-r* makes you think of the cool refreshing stuff that comes out of your faucet or that *b-o-o-k* makes you think of the physical object you are reading. They do because we speakers of English agree that they do, so we can use them to communicate ideas and thoughts dealing with those subjects. And using words as symbols is uniquely human (Wade, 2010).

● **THE WORD *SCHOOL*** has multiple denotative meanings: it is the place where students learn and a group of fish.

Words Have Multiple Meanings

As you saw in the opening vignette, a single word can have a lot of meanings. A dictionary can help you find the **denotative meaning** of a word—its basic, consistently accepted definition. But to be a competent communicator, you'll also need to consider the **connotative meaning** of a word, the emotional or attitudinal response people have to it. Consider the word *school,* which has several denotative meanings, including a building where education takes place and a large group of fish. But the word can also carry strong connotative meanings, based on one's attitudes toward and experience with school: it might bring back happy memories of class birthday parties in second grade, or it might make you feel anxious thinking about final exams.

Obviously, choosing words carefully is important. Not only must you make sure the denotative meaning is clear (using the word *ostentatious* with a bunch of six-year-olds isn't going to help you explain anything), but you also have to be aware of the possible connotative meanings of the words you use (Hample, 1987). Consider the terms *husband* and *wife.* For many people, these are simply words to describe a spouse who is either male or female. But for others, the words carry strong gender-role connotations: the term *wife* might imply a woman who does not work outside of the home, cooks all of her husband's meals, and does all of the household chores.

Thought Informs Language

Jamal Henderson is getting ready to apply to college. He keeps his father, Michael, involved in the process because he values his father's opinion. They both agree that Jamal should attend a "good college." But Michael feels hurt when Jamal starts talking seriously about urban universities in another state, thinking that his son has ruled out his own alma mater, the local campus of the state university system. The problem stems from Jamal and Michael's different concepts of what a "good college" is. Their language and their thoughts are related in their own minds, and each thinks he is using the term appropriately.

AND YOU?

What connotative meanings does each of the following words have for you: *religion, divorce, money, exercise, travel, dancing, parenthood*? Why do you have the reaction you do to each word?

CONNECT

As you learn in Chapter 13, it's important for speakers to choose clear and appropriate language when planning a speech. If your terms are confusing or inappropriate for the speaking occasion, your audience will quickly lose interest in what you're saying. This is true whether you are attempting to inform or persuade your listeners or even speaking in honor of a special occasion.

AND YOU?

Have you ever found yourself in a situation where you are entirely sure that you are using a term precisely ("a good restaurant," "a fun party," "an affordable car") only to have someone wholeheartedly disagree? How did you handle this language challenge?

Your **cognitive language** is the specific system of symbols that you use to describe people, things, and situations in your mind; it influences both language and message production (Giles & Wiemann, 1987); it is related to your thoughts, your attitudes, your co-cultures, and the society in which you live (Bradac & Giles, 2005). Michael may be thinking a good college is close to home, is involved in the local community, and offers small class sizes. Jamal may be thinking a good college involves the opportunity to live in a new city and the chance to study at an institution that has drawn an international student body.

Clearly, thinking affects the language you use, but language also affects thought. If you sum up a coworker as an "idiot" in your mind, it may influence things you will reveal to him (or not) and the kinds of messages you construct for him. Your evaluation of him may cause you to treat him abruptly, not give him a chance to respond, or avoid him altogether—perhaps even use the word *idiot* to his face. Even the words you use *with yourself* about others affect your experiences with them. For example, a study of women who stayed in violent romantic heterosexual relationships found that they often concocted dark romance narratives or fairy-tale accounts to explain why the violence was their fault or that the violence was somehow an expression of caring and concern ("He's in a great mood now—it must have been the alcohol. He really wants the best for me. I should try to please him more—not 'push his buttons'") (Boonzaier, 2008; Olson, 2004).

Language Is Ruled by Grammar

In Alice Walker's Pulitzer Prize–winning novel *The Color Purple* (1982), Celie, who is black, struggles with learning to read from a primer written for white children. Being corrected numerous times frustrates her, and she says, "Look like to me only a fool would want you to talk in a way that feel peculiar to your mind" (p. 184). Does good grammar equal good communication? Is it necessary for Celie to master standard grammatical English in order to communicate well?

The answer to these questions is yes, *to some extent.* As your third-grade teacher probably drilled into your head, **grammar**—the system of rules of a language that serves as a mechanism for the creation of words, phrases, and sentences—is absolutely important. Using the correct grammar of a particular language helps ensure communication clarity. For example, no one is going to legally stop you from pronouncing the word *tomato* "tommy-toe," but this doesn't mean that anyone will understand that you are referring to the red fruit that tastes really good on a hamburger. That's because grammar has *phonological rules,* or rules about how words should be pronounced.

Similarly, grammar has *syntactic rules,* or rules about the placement of words in a sentence. To prove this point, take any simple sentence, such as "I ran to the store to buy some milk," and place the words in a different order. Suddenly your sentence, and your message, becomes entirely unclear. The importance of grammar is also highlighted in our attempts to learn other languages. Native speakers of English, for example, must remember that the grammar of Romance languages (such as French and Spanish) requires a different syntax. For example, in

English, adjectives typically precede a noun ("I have an intelligent dog"), while in Spanish, they follow the noun (*"Tengo un perro intelegente,"* literally translated as "I have a dog intelligent"). But to communicate clearly in Spanish, an English speaker must adjust.

Nonetheless, excellent grammar will not automatically make you an outstanding communicator. Telling your professor in perfect English that her style of dress is a sorry flashback to the 1980s is still offensive and inappropriate. That's because competent communication considers the situational, relational, and cultural context.

Language Is Bound by Context

Imagine a scenario in which your cousin prattles on and on about her wild spring break in Miami—how much she drank, how many parties she went to, and so on. Now imagine that she's talking to your seventy-year-old grandmother . . . at your niece's fifth birthday party . . . in front of a group of conservative, devoutly religious family members. There are many responses to this particular scenario, which underscore one of the more complicated aspects of language: it is bound by contexts such as our relationship with the people we're with, the situation we're in, and the cultural factors at play. Does Grandma really want to hear about your cousin's behavior? Is it really OK to talk about this at a kid's party? And what about respecting the beliefs and sensibilities of your family members? We examine the relational, situational, and cultural context later on, but for now just know that communicating competently involves understanding context as much as it means understanding grammar.

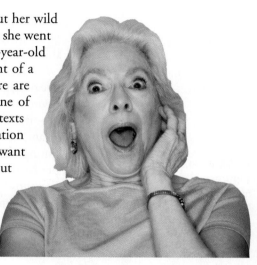

● **IT'S PROBABLY** a good idea to avoid regaling your grandmother with tales of your crazy spring-break shenanigans.

The Functions of Language

One of the very first phrases that little Josie learned to use was "thank you." Had this eighteen-month-old toddler already mastered the rules of etiquette? Was she just picking up a habit from her parents? Or was she learning that the use of certain phrases would help her get what she wants: a compliment, a smile, a cookie?

Effective language use is essential for successful communication. You learn isolated words and grammar as you acquire language. Little Josie, for example, probably picked up the expression "thank you" from her parents, her older brother, or her babysitter. But to be a competent communicator, she must learn to use symbols appropriately. If Josie uses "thank you" as a manner of greeting or as a name for her stuffed bear, she's not using it appropriately, so she's not communicating effectively. **Communication acquisition** requires that we not only learn individual words in a language but also learn to use that language *appropriately* and *effectively* in the context of the situation. And just as Josie gets a smile from her parents for saying "thank you," we must use language competently to achieve our goals.

Using language as an instrument of control is part of our *self-presentation*, discussed in Chapter 2. When you're on a job interview (see the Interviewing Appendix), you'll want to use clear, professional language that highlights your skills. Similarly, when delivering a speech (see Chapter 14), your language should let your audience know that you're engaged with and informed about your topic.

● **WE'VE ALL BEEN THERE:** a tourist asks you for directions and you mutter, "Um, yeah, you go a little bit up this way, and turn around that way . . ."

Five functional communication competencies have been identified (Wood, 1982) that focus on how language behaviors work or function for people. We all develop these when we're young by interacting with family and peers and observing television and other media (which give us a broader picture of the world). These competencies—controlling, informing, feeling, imagining, and ritualizing—remain important throughout our lives and are worth exploring in order to improve our communication.

Using Language as a Means of Control

Language is used as an instrument of *control,* to influence oneself, others, and the environment. Josie's use of the phrase "thank you" impresses her mother, who reassures her that using the term makes her a "good girl." Such appropriate use of language can make children seem cute, smart, or polite, giving them the ability to present themselves in a positive light. Recall from Chapter 1 that *control* is actually a neutral term; it is a crucial social skill whether used in a positive or negative way. As an adult, Josie will be able to use language to control her environment by persuading others to vote against land development in her community, negotiating a raise in salary, and bargaining with a car dealer. It is important, however, that Josie also learn to avoid negative control strategies such as whining, ridiculing, insulting, threatening, or belittling, as they are not signs of a productive, successful communicator.

For those who have been victims of humiliating and violent language and actions, speaking out—harnessing the power of language—can actually restore a sense of control. Tens of thousands of women have been brutally raped in the Congo and their shame has kept them silent. Cultural taboos about gender and sexual behavior have also prevented them from sharing their stories. However, local and international aid groups have recently organized open forums to help victims talk about the atrocities, connect with others, and regain control of their lives. The words are certainly hard to speak, but once out, they are empowering (Gettleman, 2008).

Using Language to Share Information

Have you ever asked a sick child to tell you "where it hurts," only to receive a vague and unhelpful answer? This is because young children are still developing the next functional competency, **informing**, or using language to both give and receive information. As an adult, if you've ever been asked for directions, you know very well that providing people with information that they can understand and in turn understanding the information others convey to you are equally important skills.

There are four important aspects of this informing competency: questioning, describing, reinforcing, and withholding.

► *Questioning* is a crucial step in communication that we learn at a young age and use throughout our lives. Young children hungry for information about their world quickly learn the power of the simple, one-word question "Why?"

► *Describing* helps us find out about the world and communicate our world to others. Parents and teachers may ask children to repeat directions to their school or their home or to detail the specifics of a story they've heard.

► *Reinforcing* information can be an important aspect of competent listening. We might take notes or simply repeat the information (to ourselves or to the other person) to confirm our comprehension.

► *Withholding* information or opinions may be the most useful thing to do in a number of situations. Knowing when to reveal information and when to withhold it requires a certain level of maturity—you may choose not to express your opposition to your manager's plan because you want to keep your job or not to reveal a piece of information that might embarrass a friend.

Together, these four skills form the basis of the informational competency that we use to communicate throughout our lives.

Using Language to Express Feelings

Poets, writers, and lyricists are celebrated for using language to capture and express emotions. But most expressions of feelings are less elaborately composed than a Shakespearean sonnet or an angry protest song. In everyday conversation and correspondence, we use language to send messages to others to express how we feel about ourselves, about them, or about the situation. Young children can say, "I'm sad," and cry or laugh to communicate feelings. As we mature, we learn how to express liking, love, respect, empathy, hostility, and pride—a complex set of emotions. The functional competency of expressing **feeling** is primarily relational. We let people know how much we value (or don't value) them by the emotions we express.

We all use language to express our feelings, but being competent at it requires that we do so in an appropriate and effective way. Many people find themselves unable to communicate well when it comes to their own emotions: Elliot might express his frustration with his staff by yelling at them; his staff might respond by mocking Elliot at a local pub after work. Elliot could have said, "I'm feeling *worried* that we're not going to make the deadline on this project"; someone on his staff could have said, "I'm feeling *tense* about making the deadline, too, but I'm *confused* about why you yelled at me." There are also times when we choose to avoid expressing feelings that we judge to be inappropriate or risky in a given situation (Burleson, Holmstrom, & Gilstrap, 2005). For example, when Abby's boyfriend tries to talk about sharing an apartment next semester, Abby might find herself changing the subject to avoid admitting that she doesn't think she's comfortable taking that step.

CONNECT

As indicated, sometimes competent language use means knowing when to withhold information or avoid topics. This is particularly important when developing and maintaining interpersonal relationships (Chapter 7). For example, *strategic topic avoidance* allows you to steer the conversation away from discussing your friend's recent painful breakup until she is ready to discuss it.

CONNECT

Using language to express feelings competently can be a powerful addition to your communication skills in a variety of settings. In a small group (Chapter 9), you need to express your frustration with the fact that you're doing most of the work. In an organization (Chapter 11), you might save your company time and money by effectively sharing your concerns about a project.

Using Language to Express Creativity

What do Edward Cullen, Wolverine, Madea, and Sheldon Cooper have in common? Each is the product of the imagination of a writer or storyteller. And regardless of whether they were conceptualized as part of a novel, comic book, or screenplay, each character and his or her story was primarily expressed through language.

Imagining is probably the most complex functional competency. It is the ability to think, play, and be creative in communication. Children pretend to do something or to be someone (a superhero, a cartoon character, a person from a movie). Adults continue to enjoy this kind of creative communication. The way a song is worded, the way a play is scripted, and the way special effects coordinate with the message delivered in a film—these function to entertain us by stimulating our imaginations. On the job, imagining is the ability to use language to convey a vision for a project to your coworkers (such as an architect using words to explain blueprints and models). In a debate, imagining skills enable you to think ahead of your opponent, to put words to each side of an argument, and to use language in ways that are logical and convincing.

Using Language as Ritual

When little Josie said "thank you" for her cookie, it was a sign that she learned the fifth functional competency: ritualizing. **Ritualizing** involves learning the rules for managing conversations and relationships. We begin learning these rules as children: peekaboo games facilitate learning turn-taking in conversations. Learning to say "hi" or "bye-bye" or "please" means internalizing politeness rituals. Later, teasing, joke telling, and even gossiping may be early lessons in how to manage relationships.

In adulthood, ritualizing effectively means you say and do the "right" thing at weddings, funerals, dinners, athletic events, and other social gatherings. Simple exchanges, like telling a bride and groom "congratulations" or offering condolences to a grieving friend, are some of the ways we ritualize language; but our ritualizing is not always that formal, nor is it limited to big events.

● **THE RAUCOUS COMEDY** *Death at a Funeral* could be a handbook for what *not* to say or do at this ritually somber and respectful ceremony.

Problems with Language

"I think we're still in a muddle with our language, because once you get words and a spoken language it gets harder to communicate" (Ewalt, 2005, para. 1). The famous primatologist Jane Goodall made this point when explaining why chimpanzees get over their disputes much faster than humans. They strike out at each other and then offer each other reassuring pats or embraces, and *voilà,* argument over. Not so with people: words can be really hard to forget.

As you've probably experienced, words can lead to confusion, hurt feelings, misunderstandings, and anger when we blurt things out before considering them (and their effects) carefully (Miller & Roloff, 2007). We sometimes speak too vaguely and fail to consider the timing of our words. We sometimes use labels in ways others don't appreciate, reveal bias through our words, or use offensive, coarse language. And when we put such hastily chosen words in e-mails or post them on Twitter or Facebook, they become "permanent," and we may have great difficulty taking back what we have said (Riordan & Kreuz, 2010).

Abstraction and Meaning

Language operates at many levels of abstraction, meaning that it can range from being very vague to very specific. You might talk in such broad, vague terms that no one knows what you are talking about ("Stuff is cool!"), or you can speak so specifically that people may think you are keeping notes for a court case against them: "I saw you at 10:32 P.M. on Friday, January 29, at the right-hand corner table of Harry's Bar with a six-foot-tall, brown-haired man wearing black jeans, boots, and a powder blue T-shirt."

The famous linguist S. I. Hayakawa (1964) illustrated the specific versus the general levels of abstraction by constructing an **abstraction ladder** (see Figure 4.1). The top rungs of the ladder are high-level abstractions: these are

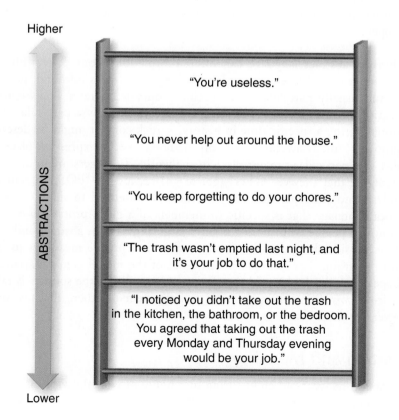

Higher

ABSTRACTIONS

"You're useless."

"You never help out around the house."

"You keep forgetting to do your chores."

"The trash wasn't emptied last night, and it's your job to do that."

"I noticed you didn't take out the trash in the kitchen, the bathroom, or the bedroom. You agreed that taking out the trash every Monday and Thursday evening would be your job."

Lower

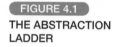

FIGURE 4.1

THE ABSTRACTION LADDER

● **SKATEBOARDERS HAVE** their own jargon for their fancy flips and tricks. If you're not a skateboarder, an "ollie" might seem like a foreign concept.

the most general and vague. Lower-level abstractions are more specific and can help you understand more precisely what people mean. "Request something interesting from Netflix" is a high abstraction that allows a wide range of choices (and the possibility of some really bad movies). Saying "I'd like to watch an action film tonight" (lower abstraction) is more likely to get you something you'll enjoy, while naming the exact movie ("Get *Iron Man 2*") ensures satisfaction.

But even though lower abstractions ensure clarity, high abstractions can accomplish certain communication goals. Here are a few examples:

▶ *Evasion.* We employ highly abstract language as a means of **evasion**, to avoid providing specific details. A teenager might tell her parents that she is "going out with some friends." Her parents might counter by demanding less abstract answers: "Where exactly are you going to be? Which particular friends are you going with?"

▶ *Equivocation.* Another form of high-level abstraction is **equivocation**, using words that have unclear or misleading definitions. Equivocation may be used strategically to get out of an uncomfortable situation, as when a friend asks what you think of her new sweater—which you think is hideous—and you reply, "It's . . . *colorful.*"

▶ *Euphemisms.* Sometimes we employ highly abstract **euphemisms**, inoffensive words or phrases that substitute for terms that might be perceived as upsetting. For example, you might say that your uncle "passed on" rather than "died" or that your mother had a "procedure" rather than an "operation."

Finally, abstract language can offer information about your affiliations and memberships. For example, **slang** is language that is informal, nonstandard, and usually particular to a specific group; it operates as a high-level abstraction because meanings of slang are known only by a particular group of people during a specific time in history. A rock concert might be described as "groovy," "totally awesome," or "off the hook"—each expression places the speaker in a particular time or place in the world. Teenagers might alert each other online that they've "GTG" (got to go) because of "POS" (parent over shoulder), and their parents are none the wiser. Related to slang is **jargon**, technical language that is specific to members of a given profession or interest group or people who share a hobby. Jargon may seem abstract and vague to those outside the group, but conveys clear and precise meanings to those within the group. For example, when a fan of the model game Warhammer 40K speaks of "kit bashing," other fans understand that the speaker is taking parts from two different models and mixing them together. The rest of us, however, would probably just stare blankly.

Situation and Meaning

Imagine a three-year-old child sitting in a house of worship with his parents. He's having a great time banging his stuffed toys around until his mother grabs them away during a silent part of the service. Clearly upset, the child curses at her. Mom's face turns bright red, and she escorts her little one out to the car.

Semantics involves the relationship among symbols, objects, people, and concepts and refers to the *meaning* that words have for people, either because

real communicator

NAME: Snowden Wright
HOMETOWN: Meridian, Michigan
OCCUPATION: Administrative assistant at Columbia University Graduate School of Business
FUN FACT: I own a copy of every Pauly Shore movie made prior to 2002.

The orders came to me in two different ways. First, the waitresses screamed them through the window that connected the dining area with the kitchen. "Cheeseburger, bloody," they said. "Eighty-six the toms." Second, the orders came to me written on little white tickets. "G-C-squared, SP-SW," one read. "Healthy side, x basket." It was my first day working as a short-order cook, and I was already out of my league. The waitresses yelled louder and louder through the window. The little white tickets piled higher and higher. My problem wasn't that I couldn't keep up with the orders; my problem was that I didn't understand what the orders meant.

The Westside Grill, I soon learned, has its own language that relies on a lot of restaurant-specific jargon to convey information between the servers and the cooks. For example, when the waitresses say, "Cheeseburger, bloody, eighty-six the toms," they mean a customer has ordered a cheeseburger, cooked rare, hold the tomatoes. When an order ticket reads, "G-C-squared, SP-SW, healthy side, x basket," it means—through a series of acronyms—that a customer has ordered a grilled chicken wrap, cut in half, on a spinach tortilla, with Swiss cheese, a side order of fruit, and an extra basket.

I knew from my college courses on communication that if I didn't learn this language— quickly— I'd be having a pretty awful time at work. So I set about figuring it all out. On my

first day, I reinforced the spoken information by repeating the orders aloud (hoping to confirm, in front of the waitresses, that I understood what they were saying), but I also withheld the fact that I did not understand them (again, hoping to confirm, in front of the waitresses, that I'm a pretty smart guy). Later that day, when things were slower in the dining area, I questioned the waitresses about what the orders meant, but rather than describing their answers, the waitresses gave me blank, humorless stares. "What?" they said. "You don't speak English?" Great. You can see how thought and language work in this situation. A "healthy side" seems like a pretty vague abstraction to me (aren't cucumbers and carrots healthy sides?), but to the waitresses of the Westside Grill, the words clearly mean "side of fruit." I had to keep this in mind as I set about making my summer job work out.

Through trial and error and sheer persistence, asking questions when necessary and observing my coworkers, I became fluent in the Westside Grill's language. I understood not only the words spoken by the waitresses but also those written on the little white tickets. My language skills grew so developed that I even introduced new vocabulary to the kitchen. "To hockey-puck" a burger, for example, means to cook it well done. Sometimes the waitresses hear the new words and ask me to explain them. "What?" I say. "You don't speak English?"

of their definitions or because of their placement in a sentence's structure (syntax). Our little friend in the example understood the relationship between the word he used and the concept of being unhappy; he was upset about losing his toys, so he uttered the same words he had probably heard a family member use when unhappy with someone or something. He may have also observed strong responses from others to that word, so he thought it would be effective in get-

WIREDFORCOMMUNICATION

Across the Technological Divide

"I need help! My computer just froze. I was working on a document and it just froze."

"Did you try a clean boot? Or a selective startup with extraneous drivers turned off?"

"Huh?"

In a world that's becoming increasingly dependent on technology for even the most common activities, we are likewise becoming increasingly dependent on the people who keep the systems running—the information technology (IT) gurus who staff the help desks at companies and campuses around the world.

When the technologically challenged meet the technologically gifted, there is more than just a knowledge and skills gap between them—there's a language gap. The IT experts often find themselves at the mercy of callers who swamp the help desks with vague and fanciful descriptions of system failures, viruses, crashed hard drives, or indefinable bugs that have rendered them technologically paralyzed. Techies, on the other hand, are often perplexed by clients who can't comprehend the instructions or advice they are being given.

The biggest hurdle to communication between techies and laypeople is jargon. As in most professions, technicians use terms that are clear and precise within the IT world but seem odd or meaningless to those outside the profession. However, jargon plays an important role: it enables professionals to describe complex systems or processes quickly, and helps professionals to identify one another (Perrin, 2007). The phrase "booting up," for example, was coined to describe the process through which a computer starts up, accesses its own memory, and gets ready to work; it was as though the computer was "pulling itself up by its bootstraps." Thirty years ago, this bit of technical jargon was used by a few insiders; today, it's a part of the everyday language, even making its way into other usages (such as taking a personal day or vacation to "reboot" yourself).

Most IT professionals recognize the need to avoid jargon when dealing with less technologically proficient clients and colleagues. "We tend to use our own jargon because it is very specific to our job and serves as a sort of shorthand in relaying information about the problem quickly," admitted one self-proclaimed techie. "But if you ask us what we mean, we will tell you—in nontechnical English, even!" ("Perception of IT professionals," 2003).

THINK ABOUT THIS

❶ Think about the unique language of your job or of the discipline in which you are majoring. Have you picked up any jargon that might seem confusing to someone outside the field?

❷ What kinds of technical words and phrases have become part of your everyday language? Have you ever "Googled" anyone? Would you think it odd if you had to explain the meaning of the verb *Google* to someone in a conversation?

❸ What kinds of jargon have you been exposed to via television, film, and novels? Do you find some medical jargon familiar having watched many seasons of *House* or *Grey's Anatomy*? Do you feel at ease with legalese from time spent watching *Law & Order*?

ting what he wanted. What he had not learned was **pragmatics**, the ability to use the symbol systems of a culture appropriately. He may have gotten a few laughs by cursing in front of his family at home, but he hadn't yet learned that it was inappropriate

what about you?

How Vague Are You?

Circle the response you'd most likely give in each of the following situations:

1. A friend asks what you'd like to do tonight.
   A. "Oh, whatever you want."
   B. "I heard about a party on Garden Street."
   C. "I'd like to rent *Juno* and make Indian food."

2. You have to evaluate an employee who has been late frequently.
   A. "We have guidelines around here, you know."
   B. "I need you to try harder to be on time."
   C. "I want you to be here at 8:55 each morning."

3. A member of a group you belong to suggests that everyone contribute $50 for a wedding present for another member.
   A. "Wow, that's pretty generous!"
   B. "What specifically are we going to buy?"
   C. "I'm willing to contribute $25 for a gift certificate to his favorite restaurant."

4. You're asked to give a speech about your athletic success to a high school sports team.
   A. "I'm no good at that sort of thing."
   B. "What goal do you have in mind?"
   C. "I can't commit to speaking this fall."

5. Your father asks if you'll be coming home for the holidays this year.
   A. "I have a life, you know."
   B. "I'll do the best I can."
   C. "I can visit for three days, December 27 to 29."

If you responded "a" to most items: Vague language (high abstraction) is your specialty. In addition, you put the responsibility on others rather than taking it upon yourself.

If you responded "b" to most items: You avoid being too vague or specific but do wind up using questions to avoid a specific answer.

If you responded "c" to most items: You are good at specific, low-abstraction language, and you take responsibility for your actions in your language.

to use the word outside of the home. When you acquire language, you learn semantics, but when you learn *how* to use the verbal symbols of a culture, you learn pragmatics.

The Limits of Labeling

"Feminist." The literal definition of the term is "a person who advocates equal social, political, and all other rights for women and men." But who are these people who label themselves feminists? In our years of teaching undergraduates, we've heard plenty of students note that feminists are women who hate men and care only about professional success. But as the communication professor Andrea McClanahan (2006) points out, "There is no way to tell what a feminist 'looks' like. Feminists are young, old, women, men, feminine or masculine, and of varying ethnicities" (para. 5).

Feminists also hail from different religious backgrounds, causing some interesting discussions about the labels believers choose regarding their feminist viewpoints. When a group of Spanish Muslims approached city officials in Barcelona, Spain, about sponsoring a conference on Islamic feminism, one official responded with shock, noting that "Islamic feminism" must surely be a contradiction or an oxymoron (Nomani, 2005). Similarly, the evangelical organization Christians for Biblical Equality, which is com-

---

EVALUATINGCOMMUNICATIONETHICS

Résumé Language

You've just graduated with a B.A. in communication and are on the hunt for an entry-level position in marketing. You know that your résumé is strong in terms of your degree, relevant coursework, and good grades, but you're a bit worried that you may not have enough real-world experience. Since you had to work full time to pay college expenses, you couldn't afford to take the kinds of unpaid internships that look so impressive on a résumé; you waited tables all through college instead and graduated in five years instead of four.

You discuss these concerns with a friend who suggests making some changes in the language of your résumé. First, she suggests changing your entry date for college to make it look like you finished the degree in four years. Second, she suggests you cast your restaurant experience as a type of marketing internship in which you developed "people skills" and "sales skills" that helped you "analyze and synthesize" consumers and products. Finally, she tells you to use your cover letter to describe yourself as "a team player" who is "attentive to detail" and has "proven creativity."

You're worried that some aspects of your résumé might not be impressive enough, but you're not entirely sure that padding your résumé with vague language and empty jargon is the way to go. What will you do?

THINK ABOUT THIS

❶ Is it crucial that an employer know how long it took you to earn your B.A.? Is it unethical to simply note the date you finished it?

❷ Will you follow your friend's suggestion to use vague expressions like "team player"? In what ways might you use more precise terms to describe yourself?

❸ Rather than dressing it up as "marketing experience," might there be an honest way to use your restaurant experience to your advantage here?

● **WHAT DOES A FEMINIST** look like? Stereotypes may cause you to believe that the professional woman on the left is a feminist. But the woman on the right, Mukhtar Mai, is a feminist too. A devout Muslim, she also supports and champions Pakistani rape victims.

mitted to the equality of men and women in the home, the workplace, and the church, surveyed members about whether or not they label themselves feminists. Fred Gingrich noted his dilemma: "I consider myself a Christian feminist, though I am cautious about the contexts in which I share that. Not because I am ashamed of the label, but because I don't want it to be a stumbling block to dialogue" (quoted in Greulich, 2005, para. 2). Others have eschewed the feminist label entirely because of its connection to liberal politics. Recently, prominent conservative female politicians have donned the label "mama grizzly" to express the fierceness of pro-life, limited-government women (Torregrosa, 2010).

What these examples reveal is that the labels we choose for our beliefs affect how we communicate them to others (and how others respond). As these examples show, when we place gender, ethnic, class, occupation, and role labels on others, we sometimes ignore individual differences (Sarich & Miele, 2004). So if you think all feminists are liberal, secular, career-oriented women, you may miss out on the opportunity to understand the feminist views of your aunt who is a stay-at-home mom or your male neighbor who is a Conservative Jew, since they may be very comfortable being a mom and a feminist, a man and a feminist, and a religious person and a feminist.

Sometimes our use of labels goes beyond ignoring individual differences and moves into the realm of bias. Derogatory labels, such as racial and ethnic slurs, demean and disenfranchise entire groups of people. To find empowerment, however, members of a particular group or co-culture will sometimes adopt these labels *within* a group. Consider, for example, the evolution of the word *queer*. Its literal definition means "strange, odd, or suspicious," and it has a history of being used as a derogatory term for gay, lesbian, and transgendered people. But in recent years, the word has been "taken back" and found empowerment in queer theory and queer studies, which have helped to legitimize LGBT (lesbian, gay, bisexual, and transgender) studies in academia.

AND YOU?

Has anyone ever labeled you in a way that truly irritated or offended you? What terms did they use? Are you aware of any biased language that frequently seeps into conversations among your friends, family, or coworkers? How might you consider addressing such biases?

The federal government and organizations take derogatory labels that hurt and demean others quite seriously. Professional organizations typically provide employees with information regarding their *harassment* and *sexual harassment* policies, which are intended to protect employees from feeling threatened or attacked because of their race, religion, abilities, or other personal traits. We discuss this important issue in Chapter 11.

The Dangers of Biased Language

Some labels are easily identifiable as derogatory terms. Others, however, are infused with more subtle meanings that influence our perceptions about the subject. This is known as **biased language**. For example, referring to an older person as "sweetie" or "dear" can be belittling (even if kindly intended) (Leland, 2008). In particular, older individuals struggling with dementia are sensitive to language that implies that they are childlike ("Did you eat your dinner like a good girl?" "How are we feeling today?") because they are struggling to maintain their dignity and self-respect (Williams, Herman, Gajewski, & Wilson, 2009).

When language openly excludes certain groups or implies something negative about them, we often attempt to replace the biased language with more neutral terms, employing what is known as **politically correct language**. For example, the terms *firefighter, police officer,* and *chairperson* replaced the sexist terms *fireman, policeman,* and *chairman,* reflecting and perhaps influencing the fact that these once male-dominated positions are now open to women as well. In other cases, politically correct terms evolve around group preferences, with groups redefining the ways in which they want to be described or labeled: terms such as *physically challenged* or *differently abled* have largely replaced the term *handicapped.*

Critics of political correctness, however, argue that attempts at sensitivity and neutrality can undermine communication. They note that political correctness focuses attention on rhetorical arguments rather than real issues underlying language, that it substitutes euphemisms for clarity when dealing with difficult subjects, and that it makes communication more difficult by placing certain words and phrases off limits. But others note that there is value in always trying to be sensitive—and accurate—when we make choices regarding language.

Profanity, Rudeness, and Civility

When CBS picked up the Twitter-based sitcom *$#*! My Dad Says* and adapted it for television, the network faced one crucial challenge: how to express on television the somewhat raunchy language that over a million Twitter fans had embraced and found funny. Recent years have seen an increase in swearing and other rude language in real life as well as in media, and perceptions about what terms are acceptable and appropriate for broadcast are continually changing. For example, media reviewer Edward Wyatt noted that the word *douche,* once considered inappropriate, had been used at least seventy-six times in 2009 on twenty-six prime-time network series like *The Vampire Diaries* and *Grey's Anatomy.* Wyatt claimed that several curse words seldom heard on television just ten years ago had, by 2009, become "passé from overuse" (2009, p. A1). In fact, some critics believe that public outrage over sex, violence, and profanity seems to have waned in recent decades (Steinberg, 2010).

Profanity includes words or expressions considered insulting, rude, vulgar, or disrespectful. The words get their social and emotional impact from the culture's language conventions. For example, swearing can be a powerful expression of emotion, especially anger and frustration, but the perception of swearing as offensive is dependent on the context and the relationship (Jay & Janschewitz, 2008). For instance, Jet Blue flight attendant Steven Slater gained national fame in August 2010 when he responded to a barrage of insults from a passenger with his own colorful language (as he quit his job by jumping down the plane's emergency chute). While we don't advocate responding to profanity with profanity, many people viewed Slater's response as "reasonably hostile." Tracy (2008)

COMMUNICATIONACROSSCULTURES

Teaching Twain

It is considered a classic of American literature, a truly groundbreaking novel that thumbed its nose at convention when it was published in 1885 and continues to challenge ideas about race, relationships, and language more than a century later.

At a time when respectable books were written in upper-middle-class English—and when slavery was still fresh in American memory—Mark Twain's *Adventures of Huckleberry Finn* told the story of the unlikely relationship between a free-spirited white boy and a fugitive slave, Jim, in everyday language. Twain carefully constructed Jim and Huck's conversations with words, inflections, and phonetic spellings that can shock modern readers. Most notably, Twain uses the "N-word" over two hundred times.

The book itself remains controversial as scholars and critics continue to argue about Twain's characters. It is consistently at or near the top of the American Library Association's annual list of books banned or challenged by parents or school boards. John Wallace, a former public school administrator, calls it "racist trash" and says that its use of the N-word is offensive, no matter what the context or how teachers try to explain it (D. L. Howard, 2004). Yet others come to the book's defense, noting that it was written as satire and that Twain's intention was "to subvert, not reinforce, racism" (Kennedy, 2003, p. 108). Temple University professor David Bradley notes that the word must be taken in the context of the times and situation: "What was Twain supposed to do, call them African-Americans?" (Rabinowitz, 1995, para. 16).

Teachers of American literature often find themselves struggling with self-censorship as they grapple with whether or not to speak the word aloud in class, since it may cause students to feel hurt and offended. This was certainly the case for Professor Alan Gribben of Auburn University at Montgomery, who created a revised edition of the work that replaces the N-word with the word *slave*. Professor Gribben explains: "I'm by no means sanitizing Mark Twain. The sharp social critiques are in there. The humor is intact. I just had the idea to get us away from obsessing about this one word, and just let the stories stand alone" (quoted in Bosman, 2011, para. 2). But critics passionately disagree, accusing Professor Gribben's publisher of censorship and sanitizing history. Author Jill Nelson notes that changing Twain's carefully chosen words to suit contemporary mores and eliminate hurt feelings "is an abdication of a teacher's responsibility to illuminate and guide students through an unfamiliar and perhaps difficult text" (Nelson, 2011, para. 3).

THINK ABOUT THIS

❶ What meaning does the N-word carry for you? Does it seem appropriate to use it in a scholarly discussion? How do you feel about its being printed (or not printed) in this textbook?

❷ If an instructor chose to use the word in class, how might he or she do so in a way that would be sensitive to students? Can students investigate the word's meaning and history without using it?

❸ Does avoiding saying (or printing) the word give it more or less power?

❹ What is your opinion on Gribben's new edition? Are his editorial changes sensitive and helpful, or is he sanitizing history?

● The sitcom *$#*! My Dad Says*, though not as brusquely profane as its title might suggest, illustrates the widening repertoire of terms that are considered acceptable and appropriate for media.

argues that language attacking people exhibiting bad behavior in local governance meetings is viewed the same way.

Whether our language is viewed as rude or "reasonably hostile" is also based on the culture and times. What it does have to do is meet some standards of **civility**, the social norm for appropriate behavior. Crude, offensive, vulgar, and profane language can create uncomfortable and unproductive relationships and work environments. Communication business specialists Rod Troester and Cathy Mester (2007) offer five guidelines for the production of more civil language in the workplace—but most of them are applicable outside the business context too:

▶ Use no words rather than offensive ones.

▶ Use words appropriate to your specific listener.

▶ Choose temperate and accurate words over inflammatory ones when commenting on ideas, issues, or persons.

▶ Use objective, respectful, nondiscriminatory language.

▶ Use clean language at all times when at work.

Language in Context

You learned about the importance of context in Chapter 1 as part of our model of communication competence. Context is particularly important to our study of language in three ways: language reflects, builds on, and determines context.

▶ *Language reflects context.* The language we use reflects who we're around, where we are, and what sort of cultural factors are at play—that is, the context we're in. In fact, we each have sets of complex language behaviors or "files" of language possibilities called **speech repertoires**. We call on different speech repertoires to find the most effective and appropriate language to meet the demands of a given relationship, situation, or cultural environment.

▶ *Language builds on context.* At the beginning of this chapter, we wondered about the difference between calling your stepmother "Mom" or "Lisa." It's an example of language building on context. If your stepmother raised you and is your primary maternal figure, you might well want to call her "Mom." But if your relationship is strained, you are close to your own biological or adopted mother, or Lisa entered your life once you were an adult,

AND YOU?
Consider the various situations you find yourself in over the course of a given day—at home, in the classroom, at a student activity, on the job, and so on. Do you have different speech repertoires for each situation? Does your language change further depending on who is present—your mother, your best friend, your professor?

you may well prefer to call her by her name. As you develop relationships, you learn how people prefer to be addressed (and how you are comfortable addressing them) and you adjust your language accordingly.

▶ *Language determines context.* We can also *create* context by the language we use. If your professor says, "Call me Veronica," one context is created (informal, first-name basis, more equal). If she says, "I'm Dr. Esquivel," you will likely have expectations for a more formal context (less personal, less equal). You would choose your speech repertoires accordingly—you're more likely to tell "Veronica" about your weekend plans than "Dr. Esquivel."

With these points in mind, let's consider how language works within our relationships, our situations, our cultures, and in mediated settings.

The Relational Context

Kathryn Stockett's bestseller *The Help* (2009), and the 2011 film adaptation, is a fascinating representation of the relationships between black domestic servants and their white employers in Mississippi in the early 1960s. The dialogues (told in different voices) ring true because they reflect the relationships between and among women of different races, social classes, and experiences. While we don't live in the South in 1960, we nonetheless choose different language to communicate in different relationships: you don't speak to your grandmother the way you speak to your best friend, and we (college professors) don't speak to our students the way we speak to our colleagues. That's because language both reflects and creates the relational context. Let's consider some examples.

Michelle and Chris have been dating for a few weeks. After a movie one night, they run into one of Chris's colleagues. When Chris introduces Michelle using the term *girlfriend,* Michelle is surprised. She hadn't thought of their relationship as being that serious yet. The English language allows us to communicate the status of many of our relationships quite clearly: mother, brother, aunt, grandfather, daughter, and so on. But as with *partners,* discussed at the beginning of the chapter, the language we use when communicating about other types of relationships can be confusing. Chris and Michelle, for example, are in the somewhat undefined state of "dating." When Chris uses the term *girlfriend* as a label for Michelle, this implies a more defined level of intimacy that Michelle isn't yet sure she feels. Chris certainly had other options, but each has its own issues. For example, if Chris had said that Michelle is a *friend,* it might have implied a lack of romantic interest (and might have hurt Michelle's feelings). The fact is, we have very few terms to describe the various levels of intimacy that we have with friends and romantic partners (Bradac, 1983; Stollen & White, 2004).

Labels can also confer status and create understandings between and among individuals. If you say, "I'd like you to meet my boss, Mr. Edward Sanchez," you are describing both Mr. Sanchez's status and the professional relationship that you have with him. The introduction of Mr. Sanchez as your boss notes that he has a degree of power over you, so it tells others what language is appropriate in front of him (for example, tell no stories that would be professionally

CONNECT

The different language we use in different relationships is often affected by unique *communication climates* or atmospheres that encompass relationships. This is certainly true when experiencing interpersonal conflict (Chapter 8). For example, if you and your brother experience a *supportive climate,* your conflicts will likely be characterized by careful, considerate words and an openness to hearing each other's thoughts.

AND YOU?

How do you label your romantic partner? Do you use different terms around different people in different situations? How do the terms you choose for each other affect your understanding of the status of the relationship?

embarrassing). Similarly, you might introduce a coworker by saying "Grace and I work together" to avoid implications of superiority or inferiority. In such a way, you use language—and different levels of abstraction—to create or reflect the context of the relationship in a way that satisfies you and takes into account the needs of others.

The Situational Context

As with the relational context, different situations (being at a job interview, in a court of law, or at your Uncle Fred's sixtieth birthday party) call for different speech repertoires. Your language should always show that you are mindful of your situational context. Sometimes this point actually determines the literal language you speak (English, Spanish, Japanese) as individuals use different languages or dialects to reflect and establish rapport with a particular group in a particular situation. So you might speak English in the classroom or on the job but use another language with your family at home—perhaps that's how you were raised, and your use of this language in the home creates a special bond between family members (Bourhis, 1985; Gudykunst, 2004).

Language can also reflect how comfortable we are in a given situation. For example, we use **high language**—a more formal, polite, or "mainstream" language—in business contexts, in the classroom, and in formal social gatherings (as when trying to impress the parents of your new romantic interest). We use the more informal, easygoing **low language** (often involving slang) when we're in more comfortable environments—watching a football game at a sports bar or enjoying movie night in your basement.

Research also tells us that our sex and gender can interact with our situation to have a powerful effect on our language use. For example, women and men adapt their language use to same-sex versus mixed-sex situations. When women speak with other women, they tend to discuss relationships and use words that are more affection-oriented (concerned with feelings, values, and attitudes). Men chatting with other men use more instrumentally oriented language (concerned with doing things and accomplishing tasks) (Reis, 1998). Research also reveals how socially constructed gender comes into play in workplace situations. Occupations that have been traditionally defined as "masculine" or "feminine" often develop a job culture and language that follow suit. Male nursery school teachers (a traditionally "feminine job") and fathers doing primary child care may employ feminine language at work; female police officers (a traditionally "masculine" job) may adopt more masculine language on patrol (Winter & Pauwels, 2006). But as we've learned, competent communication

● The formal, high language that this young woman employs while at work with her colleagues will differ from the more casual, low language that she probably uses when relaxing at home or socializing with friends.

is about figuring out the most effective and appropriate ways of interacting in a given situation—and that often involves putting aside gendered speech "appropriate" for our sex: a successful male manager should use language that reflects liking and respect when developing relationships in the workplace, and a successful female manager should use direct language to clarify instructions connected to an important task (Bates, 1988).

The Cultural Context

Throughout this book, we remind you about the relationship between culture and communication (particularly in Chapter 3). It may indeed be common sense to assume that communication differences exist between speakers of different languages as we see in stories of "bad translations." For example, when U.S. Secretary of State Hillary Clinton gave her Russian counterpart a lighthearted gift meant to symbolize U.S. hopes to "reset" ties with Moscow, translators labeled the novelty "reset button" with the Russian word *peregruzka*, which means "overloaded" or "overcharged" rather than "reset." Luckily, the Russian minister had a sense of humor about the gift and all was well, but it could have been taken as an insult and thus been problematic for international relations. Translational challenges, however, are merely the tip of the iceberg. Since we can't write an entire textbook on this topic for the purposes of your introductory class, we'll focus on just a few points, including the relationship among culture, words, and thoughts; the relationship between gender and language; how our region—where we grew up or where we live now—affects the words we use; and how we can accommodate others through verbal communication choices.

Culture, Words, and Thought

Early in this chapter, we talked about how our thinking affects our language use. But can our language use affect our thoughts? A study of the Pirahã tribe of Brazil finds it can (Gordon, 2004). The Pirahã language does not have words for numbers above two—anything above two is simply called "many." When researchers laid a random number of familiar objects (like sticks and nuts) in a row, and asked the Pirahã to lay out the same number of objects in their own pile, tribe members were able to match the pile if there were three or fewer objects. But for numbers above three, they would only approximately match the pile, becoming less and less accurate as the number of objects increased. In addition, when researchers asked them to copy taps on the floor, the Pirahã did not copy the behavior beyond three taps. Researchers concluded that the limitation of words for numbers above two prevented the Pirahã from perceiving larger numbers (Biever, 2004).

The results of this study support the **Sapir-Whorf hypothesis**, a claim that the words a culture uses (or doesn't use) influence thinking (Sapir & Whorf, 1956). In other words, if a culture lacks a word for something (as the Pirahã lack words for higher numbers), members of that culture will have few thoughts about that thing or concept. Two ideas, linguistic determinism and linguistic relativity, are related to the Sapir-Whorf hypothesis. **Linguistic determinism** is the idea that language influences how we see the world around us, while **linguistic relativity** holds that speakers of different languages have different views of the world. For example, some languages (like Spanish, French, and German) assign a gender to objects. This is a bit of a foreign concept to many native speakers of English because English is gender-neutral—English speakers simply say *the shoe* whereas a Spanish speaker marks the word as masculine (*el zapato, el* being the masculine article); a French speaker marks the word as feminine (*la chaussure, la* being the feminine article). Some researchers wondered if marking an object as masculine or feminine changes a speaker's mental picture of the object. They asked German and Spanish speakers to describe a key (*key* is a masculine word in German and a feminine word in Spanish) and found that German speakers described the object in traditionally masculine terms (*hard, heavy, jagged, metal, serrated,* and *useful*) while Spanish speakers used traditionally feminine terms (*golden, intricate, little, lovely, shiny,* and *tiny*) (Cook, 2002; Moran, 2003; Wasserman & Weseley, 2009).

Gender and Language

If a man says, "It's a guy thing," one Web site claims, you can translate that as meaning to women, "There is no rational thought pattern connected with it, and you have no chance at all of making it logical" ("Men's secret language," 2010). Do "guys" speak a language unique to themselves? Cultural and situational factors deeply affect our thinking and perception of gender roles, and gender roles, in turn, are often inscribed with "different languages" for the masculine and the feminine (Gudykunst & Ting-Toomey, 1988). The idea that men and women speak entirely different languages is popular fodder for comedy, talk shows, and pop psychologists, so let's identify what actual differences have contributed to that view.

Deborah Tannen's classic 1992 analysis of men and women in conversation outlined the way that women and men enacted gendered identities as they talked about simple tasks or engaged in routine conversations. Tannen found that women primarily saw conversations as negotiations for closeness and connection with others, while men experienced talk more as a struggle for control, independence, and hierarchy.

Consider how social expectations for masculinity and femininity might play out in men's and women's conversation styles, particularly when negotiating power (who has more control in a given relationship). Powerful controlling language may be used to define limits, authority, and relationship. Less controlling language is used to express affection, defining the affiliation level in the relationship. Let's look at a few examples.

▶ *Interruptions.* Male speakers are thought to interrupt others in conversation more than female speakers, but the situation and the status of the speakers are probably better predictors of interruptions than biological sex (Pearson, Turner, & Todd-Mancillas, 1991). For example, female professors can be expected to interrupt male students more often than those male students interrupt the professors, owing to the difference in power and status. When status and situation are neutral, men tend to interrupt

CONNECT

Gendered language often affects mixed-sex small group settings. Women are typically encouraged to build rapport, using affectionate language to keep the peace and share power (Chapters 3 and 9). Men are rewarded for taking charge of a group and using direct, action-oriented language. Competent communicators must be aware of these differences in style and must promote group communication that encourages all members to share and challenge ideas in order to achieve group goals.

women considerably more often than women interrupt men, according to Zimmerman and West (as cited in Ivy & Backlund, 2004).

▶ *Intensifiers.* Women's speech patterns, compared with men's, contain more words that heighten or intensify topics: ("*hot* pink," "*so* excited," "*very* happy") (Yaguchi, Iyeiri, & Baba, 2010). Consider the intensity level of "I'm upset" versus "I'm *really* upset." Attaching *totally* to a number of verbs and adjectives is a popular way to express intensity ("She's *totally* kidding" or "He's *totally* awesome!").

▶ *Qualifiers, hedges, and disclaimers.* Language that sounds hesitant or uncertain is often perceived as being less powerful—and such hesitations are often associated with women's speech. *Qualifiers* include terms like *kind of, sort of, maybe, perhaps, could be,* and *possibly; hedges* involve expressions such as "I think," "I feel," or "I guess" ("Oh, I guess we can go to Disney World instead of Europe for vacation"). *Disclaimers* discount what you are about to say and can head off confrontation or avoid embarrassment: "It's probably nothing, but I think . . ." or "I'm likely imagining things, but I thought I saw . . ." (Palomares, 2009).

▶ *Tag questions.* Another sign of hesitancy or uncertainty associated with feminine speech is the *tag question,* as in "That was a beautiful sunset, wasn't it?" or "That waitress was obnoxious, wasn't she?" Tag questions attempt to get your conversational partner to agree with you, establishing a connection based on similar opinions. Interestingly, some research reveals that tag questions are not always examples of hesitancy or uncertainty. As noted in a study by Spender (as cited in Ivy & Backlund, 2004), sometimes they come across as full-fledged threats—for example, "You're not going to smoke another cigarette, *are you?*"

▶ *Resistance messages.* Differences in the way men and women express resistance can have serious consequences. Specifically, date rape awareness programs advise women to use the word *no* when a male partner or friend makes an unwanted sexual advance. But a woman might instead say, "I don't have protection," choosing vague or evasive language over the direct *no* to avoid a scene or hurt feelings. Men, however, sometimes perceive an indirect denial as a yes. Women's use of clear messages, coupled with men's increased understanding of women's preference for more indirect resistance messages, can lead to more competent communication in this crucial area (Lim & Roloff, 1999; Motley & Reeder, 1995).

In summary, research has corroborated some differences in communication style due to sex (Kiesling, 1998), but many of those differences paled when context, role, and task were considered (Ewald, 2010; Mulac, Wiemann, Widenmann, & Gibson, 1988; Newman, Groom, Handelman, & Pennebaker, 2008). What this means, essentially, is that while an individual's sex may have some influence on his or her communication style, gender—the cultural meaning of sex—has far more of an influence. Furthermore, a number of research studies have found that conversational topic, age, setting/situation, and the sex

AND YOU?

What are your personal thoughts on sex, gender, and language? Do you think men and women speak different languages, or do you feel that we all speak more similarly than differently? How do your thoughts and opinions match up with the research we've cited in this chapter?

composition of groups have just as much influence on language usage as gender (summarized in Palomares, 2008). As Mary Crawford (1995) noted, studying language from a sex-difference approach can be misleading, as it treats women (and men too) as a homogenous "global category," paying little attention to differences in ethnicity, religion, sexuality, and economic status.

In fact, in more recent work, Tannen (2009, 2010) focuses on how we present our "face" in interaction and how language choices are more about negotiating influence (power, hierarchy), solidarity (connection, intimacy), value formation, and identity rather than about sex (Tannen, Kendall, & Gorgon, 2007). Through decades of research, Tannen and others have shown us that we are less bound by our sex than we are by the language choices we make; thus, regardless of whether we are male or female, we can choose to use language that gives us more influence or creates more connection—or both.

Geography and Language

Our editor from New Jersey assures us that even in such a small state, it makes a big difference if you are from North Jersey or South Jersey. (The status of people from the middle part of the state remains unclear, at least to us!) People in North Jersey eat subs (sandwiches that you buy at 7-Eleven or QuickChek) and Italian ice (a frozen dessert); the night before Halloween, when shaving cream and toilet paper abound, is Goosey Night or Cabbage Night; and "the city" is, of course, New York City. People from South Jersey eat hoagies (typically from a convenience store called Wawa) and water ice; the night before Halloween is Mischief Night; and going to "the city" means taking a trip to Philadelphia.

As this example illustrates, even speakers of the same language who grow up a mere fifty miles apart find that the culture of their environment affects their language and their understanding of the world. Now, the world won't end if you walk into 7-Eleven and order a hoagie (though you might confuse the person preparing your sandwich), but other examples are more extreme. A British friend moved Ottawa, Canada, and needed to do some grocery shopping. Disappointed with the cuts of meat on display, she asked the butcher if he could give her a joint. The butcher stared back at her with a shocked look on his face, and she couldn't understand why. She, of course, wanted a large roast; he, however, thought she was asking if he could find her some marijuana. And then there's

● **IS THIS A SUB** or a hoagie? Perhaps a hero or just a plain old sandwich?

our friend Ada, who kindly shared an embarrassing moment with us (and is allowing us to tell you). When she came to the United States from Hong Kong, she knew she had to give up some of her Britishisms in order to communicate more effectively with her American-born classmates at Wesleyan University. This was never more apparent than when she asked a classmate for a rubber (to correct some mistakes in her notebook). She wanted an eraser; he thought she was asking for a condom. Needless to say, she was a bit perplexed by his response: "Maybe after class?"

Accommodation

As discussed in Chapter 3, one tool that can be helpful when we communicate with individuals from different cultures or co-cultures is *accommodation*, changing our communication behavior to adapt to the other person (Giles & Smith, 1979). As both Chapter 3 on culture and communication, and Chapter 5 on nonverbal communication illustrate in more detail, cultures and co-cultures signal their identification with their particular groups by using specialized language, accents, or vocabulary; they maintain or assert their group identity in this way, sometimes even exaggerating behaviors to keep others out or to signal their contempt for people in another group (Hecht, Jackson, & Ribeau, 2003).

Code switching and **style switching** are types of accommodation in which communicators change their regular language and slang, as well as their tonality, pitch, rhythm, and inflection, to fit into a particular group. These language accommodations may be ways to survive, to manage defensiveness, to manage identity, or to signal power or status (Bourhis, 1985). Police officers routinely employ this type of accommodation, adopting the street slang or foreign phrases used by citizens in the neighborhoods they patrol, and using more formal, bureaucratic language when interacting with superiors, filling out reports, or testifying in court.

Mediated Contexts

Have you ever sent an e-mail or a text message that was misunderstood by the recipient? It has happened to all of us—and that's often because our e-mails, text messages, tweets, and wall postings lack the nonverbal cues and hints that we provide in face-to-face conversation. So if you text your spouse to say that you both have to spend Friday night with your slightly quirky Aunt Ethel, and he texts you back "Great," is he really excited? Is he being sarcastic? "Great" could mean either thing, but you can't see his nonverbal reaction to know if he's smiling or grimacing and rolling his eyes. That's why, when communicating in the context of technology, language must be very clear to be most effective (Walther, 2004).

For example, language that is more intense (powerful, committed, strong, not neutral) gets more responses in e-mail surveys, likely because it directs attention to important points (Andersen & Blackburn, 2004). And people in computer-mediated groups who use more powerful language are seen as more credible, attractive, and persuasive than those who use tentative language (hedges, disclaimers, and tag

AND YOU?

Think back to where you grew up—whether in the United States or abroad. Are there any terms that you use that would cause confusion to others who speak your native tongue? Have you ever been in a situation where you've used a regional term that caused an embarrassing miscommunication?

● **USING MEDIA** increases the need for clear language choices.

questions) (Adkins & Brashers, 1995). On the other hand, a recent study of an international adolescent online forum found that it was *not* powerful language that led to students being elected as "leaders" (Cassell, Huffaker, Tversky, & Ferriman, 2006). The students who were elected leaders made references to group goals and synthesized other students' posts. This group-oriented language was seen as more persuasive and effective than language pushing individual or personal goals.

Interestingly, sex and gender can influence the language you use with technology. In computer-mediated games, for example, people who were assigned avatars of their own gender were more likely to use gender-typical language (more emotional expressions, apologies, tentative language if assigned a feminine avatar) than those assigned mismatched avatars (Palomares & Lee, 2010). Another study found that people infer a person's sex from language cues online (amount of self-disclosure, expression of emotion) and conform more to computer-mediated partners when they believe them to be male (Lee, 2007).

But technology affects language use in broader ways as well, including the proliferation of English as the language of the Internet. Individuals in Salt Lake City, São Paulo, and Stockholm can all communicate digitally, often in English. Critics often claim that because English dominates the mass media industries, the values and thinking of English speakers are being imposed on the non-English-speaking world. Nevertheless, many non-Western countries have benefited from this proliferation, with countless jobs being relocated to places like India and Hong Kong (Friedman, 2007). The fact is, every day brings increasing language diversity to the Internet, and Internet-based translators make it much easier to translate material into innumerable languages (Danet & Herring, 2007).

Despite the controversies surrounding English and the Internet and mass media, technology has, in some sense, created a language of its own. The language of text messaging and chat rooms frequently relies on acronyms (IMO for "in my opinion," LOL for "laughing out loud"), which have come to be used and understood in a variety of other contexts. The need for these acronyms is influenced by the fact that this context for communication is meant to be rapid and direct: any system that reduces the number of keystrokes improves the speed and efficiency of the medium. At the same time, however, it's important to keep text language in its appropriate context. If your professor writes you an e-mail regarding your recent absences from class, it's probably not a good idea to respond with "NOYB, IMHO" (none of your business, in my humble opinion). It's inappropriate on several levels—it shows a lack of respect for your instructor (obviously!) but also a lack of understanding regarding context. E-mail etiquette requires more than just a string of acronyms; complete sentences are usually appreciated by the message recipient.

BACK TO ▶ Our Partners

Our discussion of the word *partner* and its various meanings made it clear that the labels we choose are incredibly powerful—and can be fraught with communication complications.

▶ The word *partner* has several denotative meanings, as we discussed earlier. But it can also have powerful connotative meanings. Let's look at romantic couples who choose the term *partner*. When some people hear an individual refer to his or her "partner," they may assume the individual is gay or lesbian—and may have positive, negative, or neutral reactions based on their cultural background. Others may receive the term suspiciously, feeling that the individual is trying to hide his or her marital or legal status. Still others may react favorably, believing that *partner* is a term that marks equality in romantic relationships.

▶ Abstraction plays an important role in the use of the term *partner*. Saying "This is my boyfriend" or "This is my business partner" is a low-level abstraction, offering others a clear definition of your status. But the term *partner* is a high-level abstraction, keeping your status and relationship considerably more vague.

▶ Considering the relational, situational, and cultural context is one way to make the term *partner* less abstract and vague. If you let your chemistry professor know that your "partner" needs some help with an experiment, the instructor understands that you mean your lab partner rather than your romantic partner or the person you play tennis with. Similarly, when introducing the love of your life to your elderly great-aunt, you might want to use a less ambiguous term. Your aunt may be of a generation that did not use the term *partner* to apply to a love interest.

 Activities

1. Take a look at a piece of writing you've produced (an essay, your résumé, or an e-mail to a friend). Do you use high or low levels of abstraction? Is your choice of language appropriate for the communication contexts involved? (For example, is your essay written in a way that is mindful of your relationship with your professor and the academic setting?)

2. Describe the similarities and differences you find in the language you use and the language a close friend or family member of the opposite sex uses over the course of a single conversation. What did you notice? Were there any misunderstandings or power struggles in this conversation? How do your findings match up with what the research we presented tells us?

3. Examine the language you use in computer-mediated-communication. Are there subtle ways in which you and your communication partners negotiate influence and create connectedness? Are any language choices related to sex or gender? What differences do you find in the language you use in mediated contexts from those in face-to-face contexts?

Now that you have finished reading this chapter, you can:

Describe the power of **language**—the system of symbols we use to think about and communicate experiences and feelings:

▶ Words are symbols that have meanings agreed to by speakers of a language (p. 98).

▶ A **denotative meaning** is the accepted definition of a word; its **connotative meaning** is the emotional or attitudinal response to it (p. 99).

▶ **Cognitive language** is what you use to describe people, things, and situations in your mind (p. 100).

▶ Correct **grammar**, the rules of a language, helps ensure clarity (p. 100).

▶ Learning words and how to use them effectively is the process of **communication acquisition** (p. 101).

Identify the ways communication functions for people, the five functional communication competencies:

▶ As an instrument of control (p. 102).

▶ For **informing**, including four aspects: questioning, describing, reinforcing, and withholding (pp. 102–103).

▶ For expressing **feelings**, letting people know how we value them (p. 103).

▶ For **imagining**, communicating a creative idea (p. 104).

▶ For **ritualizing**, managing conversations and relationships (p. 104).

Label communication problems with language and discuss how to address them:

▶ The **abstraction ladder** ranks communication from specific, which ensures clarity, to general and vague (pp. 105–106).

▶ Some communication situations may call for abstractions: **evasion**, avoiding specifics; **equivocation**, using unclear terms; or **euphemisms**, using substitutions for terms that might be upsetting (p. 106).

▶ **Slang** is a group's informal language; **jargon** is a group's technical language (p. 106).

▶ **Semantics** refers to the meaning that words have; **pragmatics** refers to the ability to use them appropriately (pp. 107–110).

▶ We ignore individual differences when we place gender, ethnic, or other role labels on people (p. 111).

▶ **Biased language** has subtle meanings that influence perception; using **politically correct language** is an attempt at neutrality (p. 112).

▶ **Profanity** includes words or expressions that are considered insulting, rude, vulgar, or disrespectful, while **civility** involves language that meets socially appropriate norms (pp. 112–114).

Describe how language reflects, builds on, and determines context:

▶ We use different **speech repertoires** to find the most effective language for a given situation (p. 114).

▶ We use language to create or reflect the context of a relationship (pp. 114–115).

▶ Some situations call for formal language, **high language**, while in more comfortable environments, **low language**, often including slang, is appropriate (p. 116).

▶ The **Sapir-Whorf hypothesis** suggests that our words influence our thinking (p. 117).

▶ **Linguistic determinism** is the idea that language influences how we see the world; **linguistic relativity** holds that speakers of different languages have different views of the world (pp. 117–118).

▶ Assuming gender differences in communication can be misleading, yet some differences in masculine and feminine language exist. The use of interruptions, intensifiers, qualifiers, hedges, disclaimers, and tag questions are linked with feminine versus masculine speech patterns (pp. 118–119).

▶ The culture of the geographical area affects language (pp. 120–121).

▶ **Code switching** and **style switching**, changing language use as well as tone and rhythm, are two types of *accommodation*, changes we make to our language to adapt to another person's communication style (p. 121).

▶ Communication technology has made English the dominant world language and has created a global society. But the Internet also continues to create a language of its own (p. 122).

No dialogue is needed to convey Carl and Ellie's love for each other.

chapter 5

Nonverbal Communication

Can you tell a compelling, believable, and heartwarming love story in just four minutes—without using any words? The Academy Award–nominated *Up* (2009) does just that (Docter & Peterson, 2009). After opening with a simple meet-cute between young, quiet Carl and adventurous, talkative Ellie, the sequence that follows offers a montage of life moments, explained simply and graphically: they express affection by holding hands and devotion by the cross-my-heart gesture of their childhood. Their dreams of children are symbolized in visions of baby-shaped clouds, and as those dreams are crushed, their grief is conveyed by Ellie's silent sobs and Carl's quiet gestures of comfort. As the years go by, their plans to travel are shown with paintings and brochures; the financial struggles that thwart them are explained in tiny vignettes that detail home repairs, car troubles, and medical bills. Relying entirely on nonverbal behaviors—beautifully crafted and rendered by the artists at Pixar Studios—and set to a mesmerizing musical score, the sequence manages to clearly convey the events and emotions that shaped these two characters' decades-long romance, as well as Carl's loneliness and isolation after Ellie's death, without a word of dialogue.

The filmmakers at Pixar were no strangers to near "silent" films—their previous offering, the equally stunning and compelling *WALL-E* (2008), included virtually no dialogue for the first forty minutes, in what the British newspaper *The Independent* called "a masterclass in non-verbal communication" (Quinn, 2008, para. 7). During those scenes, the film not only managed to create compelling characters out of a pair of robots and a lone, unspeaking cockroach, but also to explain a fairly complicated story line of environmental devastation in a simple, accessible way.

After you have finished
reading this chapter,
you will be able to

● Describe the power of
nonverbal communication

● Outline the functions of
nonverbal communication

● Describe the set of
communication symbols
that are nonverbal codes

● Illustrate the influences
culture, technology, and
situation have on our
nonverbal behavior

All filmmakers know that telling a story on screen is more complicated than having characters read from a script because filmmaking encompasses nonverbal performances (be it from actors or from animators). These include the visual choices made by the artists and directors, from colors used in a scene's background to the articles of clothing worn by characters. For animators like the team at Pixar, the challenge is even more daunting, as they are tasked with making inhuman objects—be they computer-generated "people" like Carl and Ellie or robots (or fish, toys, or insects)—into believable, humanlike characters that can effectively communicate complex information and emotions. Likewise, in real life, we communicate with many tools other than language. In this chapter, we examine **nonverbal communication**—the process of intentionally or unintentionally signaling meaning through behavior other than words (Knapp & Hall, 2010). This definition encompasses a variety of actions, such as gestures, tone of voice, and eye behavior, as well as all aspects of physical appearance. We begin studying this powerful topic by examining the nature and functions of nonverbal communication before moving on to the nonverbal codes that convey nonverbal messages.

The Nature of Nonverbal Communication

A deaf woman signs a message to a companion. A colleague writes a note to you on a pad of paper during an excruciatingly boring meeting. A man taps his watch to signal to a friend that it's almost time for lunch. In all three instances, communication is taking place without a word being spoken. But not all of all these examples are actually nonverbal communication. Studying the essential nature of nonverbal communication reveals why.

Nonverbal Behavior Is Communicative

As we have noted, you are communicating nonverbally when you convey a message without using any words. But you also communicate nonverbally when you use nonverbal behaviors *in addition* to words: when you smile, frown, or gesture as you speak or when you speak using a particular tone or volume. For example, as a kid, you probably knew when your parents were angry with you because they called you by your full name while using "that tone."

With this information in mind, consider the examples we just gave. American Sign Language (ASL), a visual language with its own grammatical structure used by hearing-impaired individuals in the United States and English-speaking Canada, is still verbal communication. It may be *nonvocal*, indicating that the voice is not used, but it is still a language with gestures as symbols (rather than spoken words) and with its own strict grammar rules. Likewise, the note that your colleague writes to you uses words, so it too is a form of verbal communication. Only the third example is nonverbal communication—tapping a watch signals meaning without any use of linguistic symbols. Yet the example reminds us that nonverbal behavior and verbal communication are connected. Had the friends not made a verbal agreement to meet for lunch, the act of tapping the watch might be really confusing.

● **GIVING SOMEONE** a big hug is an example of nonverbal communication, but communicating with someone using American Sign Language is not.

Nonverbal Communication Is Often Spontaneous and Unintentional

The best poker players think a great deal about nonverbal communication. They know how to bluff, or convince their opponents that they are holding a better (or worse) hand than is actually the case. While their studies of nonverbal communication may not be scholarly, they are practical. A player who figures out an opponent's "tell"—a nonverbal signal that indicates a good or bad hand—can profit from it if he, quite literally, plays his cards right. Mike Caro, a poker professional and author of *The Body Language of Poker*, for example, warns players not to look at the cards as they are laid out on the table, noting that players who look away from "the flop" have a strong hand, and those who stare at it—or at their cards—have a weak one. He also advises players to memorize their hand so that opponents won't see them looking back at their cards and glean cues from this action (Zimbushka, 2008).

Like these players, we often send nonverbal messages unintentionally—we roll our eyes, laugh, slouch, or blush without meaning to display those behaviors. Often without our knowledge, our nonverbal behaviors send powerful messages. Great poker players know that they can't completely eliminate such behaviors—that's why many of them wear sunglasses while playing: they want to mask their eyes so that their opponents can't pick up such subtle and unintentional cues from their eye movements.

Nonverbal Communication Is Ambiguous

Professional players like Caro might have a system for reading nonverbal behaviors, but even they know that it's more of an art than a science. That's because nonverbal communication is often ambiguous. Blinking, stammering, or hesitations in speech can indicate deception. But they can also indicate anxiety or uncertainty. In many cases, you can pick up clues about the meaning of behavior from the situational context. If your friend is sighing deeply and blinking rapidly

You make sense of your world and decode nonverbal behavior through *schemas*, your accumulated experience of people, roles, and situations (Chapter 2). So if you catch your friend in a lie, you might suspect, on the basis of your relational history, that whenever he avoids eye contact with you, he's lying. But competent communicators must think beyond schemas when determining the meaning of nonverbal communication.

● **DOES THIS CARD PLAYER** have a good or bad hand? Who knows? His poker face reveals nothing.

as she heads off to her biochemistry final exam, you're probably safe guessing that she's feeling anxious. But you can't know for sure. Perhaps her boyfriend broke up with her twenty minutes ago and she just doesn't feel like talking about it. This is why we tell our students to regard nonverbal behavior (and poker "tells") as cues to be checked out rather than as facts.

Nonverbal Communication Is More Believable Than Verbal Communication

Imagine you're grabbing lunch with your brother, talking a mile a minute about all your exciting plans for after graduation, but he's staring off into space. Maybe you're just boring him, right? But when you look closer, you notice that his face is ashen, he isn't making eye contact with you, and he hasn't shaved in a few days. You pause and ask, "Hey, is everything OK with you? You seem . . . not yourself." Your brother looks up somewhat startled, tries to smile, and says, "What? Oh! Yes, everything is great."

What just happened is called **channel discrepancy**, a situation in which one set of behaviors says one thing and another set says something different. In this case, your brother's verbal communication says he is fine, but his nonverbal communication says he is not fine at all. So which message do you believe? In most cases, you'll believe the nonverbal message; like most of us, you assume your brother has less control over his nonverbal behaviors so they are more reliable indicators of truth. Research supports your assumption. Studies show that nonverbal behavior carries more importance than verbal behavior when we

► express spontaneous feelings (such as crying) (Burgoon & Hoobler, 2002)

► assess the motives of others and how they present themselves (as with deception)

► express rapport with others (such as showing liking)

► figure out others' meanings when there are not many other behaviors to observe (Grahe & Bernieri, 1999; Knapp & Hall, 2010)

AND YOU?

Have you ever ignored what someone said because the person's nonverbal behavior seemed to contradict the verbal message? Were you able to determine if the nonverbal communication was accurate?

It is important to bear in mind, however, that just because we tend to place more stock in nonverbal communication doesn't mean that we are always right. Your brother might be fine, just as he says he is. Perhaps he is growing a "playoff beard" along with the rest of his hockey team and is thinking about the next day's game rather than listening to you talk about your plans. In fact, even when we know someone very well, we are sometimes unable to detect deception or to read their nonverbal behaviors accurately (Knapp & Hall, 2010; Manusov & Patterson, 2006).

Functions of Nonverbal Communication

Now that we've established the essential nature of nonverbal communication, we can discuss how it helps us interact effectively in relationships. While it is impossible to discuss every purpose that nonverbal behaviors serve, we highlight here the most important ways that nonverbal behaviors work on their own—and in combination with verbal behaviors—to affect your communication.

Reinforcing Verbal Messages

Nonverbal behavior often serves to clarify meaning by reinforcing verbal messages. It does so in three ways: repeating, complementing, and accenting. **Repeating** mirrors the verbal message, offering a clear nonverbal cue that repeats the verbal message. For example, you hold up three fingers while saying "three" or shake your head at a toddler while saying "no." You can also reinforce verbal messages with **complementing**, nonverbal behavior that matches (without actually mirroring) the verbal message it accompanies. For example, when you pat a friend on the back while saying, "You did a great job," you reinforce the message that your friend has done well.

Nonverbal behaviors are also used for **accenting**, or clarifying and emphasizing specific information in a verbal message. For example, if you want your friend to meet you at a local pub at 6 P.M., you can make eye contact as you talk (indicating that you are monitoring your friend's attention level), touch the friend lightly on the forearm and raise your eyebrows as you mention the pub on State Street ("Do you know the one I mean?"), and give vocal emphasis or added volume as you speak the number 6 ("It's important to me that you be there at 6 P.M.").

● **WHEN A TRAFFIC COP** holds out one hand, you know to stop; she doesn't have to scream "STOP!" to get the intended effect.

Substituting Verbal Messages

Nonverbal cues can also be used for **substituting** or replacing words. For example, a traffic officer's outstretched palm substitutes for the word *stop,* and wagging a finger at a toddler can indicate "no" without your saying anything. Substituting is common in situations where words are unavailable (as when communicating with someone who does not speak the same language as you) or when words are inappropriate (in situations that call for silence) or unintelligible (in noisy situations, as in signaling your partner you're ready to leave a party). Substitution can also signal information that you'd rather not say aloud—for example, raising your eyebrows at a friend seated across the table from you when the other friend you're dining with mentions (for the tenth time) that his current internship is paying him *really* well.

Contradicting Verbal Messages

As we noted earlier, if a person's verbal and nonverbal messages seem at odds, we're more likely to trust the nonverbal cues. That's because nonverbal communication also functions as **contradicting** behavior to convey meaning that is the opposite of

AND YOU?

Have you ever experienced (or been responsible for) a failed attempt at sarcasm or teasing via a text message or social network posting? What, in your opinion, caused this communication breakdown? How might it have been avoided?

● **CHLOE THE LABRA-DOODLE:** a smelly, ugly little monster? Certainly not.

the verbal message. Sometimes this is unintentional, as when you clearly look upset but say that nothing is wrong and don't even realize your nonverbal behavior is giving you away. Other times, though, contradicting behavior is initiated on purpose. This may be true of people looking for sympathy or attention—by sighing deeply and remaining otherwise silent, Carolina might be able to get Andy to ask, "What's wrong?" She can keep the attention coming by refusing to answer or tersely stating, "Nothing," so that he responds, "No, really, I'm worried. Tell me what's up." While such tactics can be quite effective in getting attention, they are also somewhat deceptive, intending to take advantage of a partner's concern for selfish purposes.

Contradicting behavior is also part of what makes joking around, teasing, and the use of sarcasm (cutting remarks) so powerful. When you roll your eyes and say, "Wow, that was a captivating lecture," it lets your classmate know, despite your words, that you found listening to your professor about as interesting as vacuuming. Contradicting behavior can work positively as well, as when your friend calls to your beloved dog, "Come here, you smelly, ugly little monster!" Your friend's smile, high pitch, and open arms reveal instead that your dog is pretty adorable and lovable.

Regulating Interactions

Nonverbal cues are also used in **regulating** or coordinating verbal interaction—they help us navigate the back-and-forth of communication in a constructive, appropriate manner. For example, if you pause after saying "Hello" when answering your phone, you are offering the person on the other end a chance to self-identify and explain the purpose of the call. Face to face, you may hold your hand up while speaking as a sign that you are not finished with a task and do not want to be interrupted; raising your hand in a face-to-face classroom setting lets your professor know that you have a question or information to share with the class. Slouching or sitting back may indicate that you don't want to speak or are waiting for someone else to speak before you get involved.

If conversational regulation doesn't go smoothly, there can be negative consequences. For example, if you successfully interrupt others when they are speaking, you may gain influence but others may like you less. This is particularly true for women who interrupt, as social conventions put pressure on women to be polite and meek in conversation. On the other hand, if you allow interruptions, others may perceive you as less influential (Farley, 2008). Naturally, the situational context plays a role here. It's more serious to interrupt (or be interrupted) at a debate or a business meeting, whereas some interruption is acceptable when having a casual conversation with friends.

Creating Immediacy

Perhaps the most "human" of the nonverbal functions is the creation of **immediacy**, a feeling of closeness, involvement, and warmth between people as communicated by nonverbal behavior (Prager, 2000). A number of nonverbal behaviors together help create immediacy: sitting or standing somewhat close to the other person, turning and leaning toward the person, smiling, making eye contact, and giving an appropriate touch. Even adding "smiley face" icons to your e-mail messages can be helpful—they have been found to increase perceptions of immediacy and liking in an environment that otherwise doesn't give you much opportunity for nonverbal communication (Yoo, 2007).

In addition to the classic immediacy behaviors described above, mimicry is sometimes used to enhance immediacy. **Mimicry** is the synchronized and usually unconscious pattern of imitating or matching gestures, body position, tone, and facial expressions to create social connections between people (Carey, 2008). In other words, if your younger brother is really upset about his grade in algebra and tells you about this fact with downcast eyes, a frown, and a sober tone of voice, you would likely respond with similar nonverbal behavior in order to let him know that you care and support him.

Take a moment to imagine how challenging it must be to create these close connections with others if you lack the ability to reproduce a range of nonverbal behaviors. This is precisely where Kathleen Bogart finds herself, as she suffers from Moebius syndrome, a rare congenital condition that causes facial paralysis. She can recognize others' expressions, but she can't produce them herself (Carey, 2010). As such, she finds it difficult to create immediacy as her facial expressions cannot express joy, sorrow, or frustration—nor can she mimic these important emotions to support her relational partners. Since Kathleen can't smile or laugh or frown, she relies on eye contact, hand gestures, posture, and vocal tone to create the connection and warmth of immediacy.

Immediacy behaviors help you form and manage impressions, particularly if you want to have more social influence. The implications for interpersonal relationships are clear: physical contact, eye contact, smiling, and other gestures tell your romantic partner, your family members, and close friends that you love and care for them and that you want to be near them. A particularly powerful example of nonverbal immediacy in the professional world comes from a study of doctors and patients that found that physicians who engage in immediacy behaviors usually have patients who are less fearful of them and more satisfied with their medical care (Richmond, Smith, Heisel, & McCroskey, 2001).

Deceiving Others

If we're honest, most of us will admit on occasion to engaging in **deception**—the attempt to convince others of something that is false (O'Hair & Cody, 1994). Sometimes we deceive others in order to protect them, as when you tell your friend that no one noticed her torn slacks. Other times, we deceive out of fear, as when victims of abuse blame their injuries on falls or accidents. However, deception can come from malicious and self-serving motives. Our neighbor Barbara received a phone call from a friendly guy who claimed to be "with the government." Saying he wanted to make sure that everything was correct in her "file" so she could receive retirement benefits the next year, he asked for her Social Security number and other personal information. Realizing later that she'd been a victim of identity theft, Barbara confided, "I feel so stupid . . . I can't believe I fell for it. But he sounded so sincere" (Barbara Smith, personal communication, January 8, 2010).

Like many of us, Barbara was drawn in by the sound of a warm, friendly voice. In fact, most of us look for the opposite type of behavior to sniff out a liar (Canary,

AND YOU?

Imagine that you are listening to a friend tell a long story in a face-to-face setting. How might you regulate the interaction to show that you're listening or that you'd like to interject a comment? Would these actions change if the conversation were taking place via instant messaging or in a chat room? How so?

● **THE ULTIMATE DECISION?** Stockbroker and investment advisor Bernie Madoff executed the largest Ponzi scheme in history, defrauding his clients of billions of dollars over a period of more than twenty years.

Cody, & Manusov, 2008). We look for people who appear or sound anxious, who avoid making eye contact, who blink frequently, or who have frequent and awkward body movements (Leal & Vrij, 2008). We also suspect people who have dilated pupils and who raise their vocal pitch, as these nonverbal behaviors are less under conscious control, making them more believable than words or other, more controllable nonverbal behaviors (Burgoon, Buller, & Woodall, 1989; Goss & O'Hair, 1988). Research certainly supports the idea that nonverbal behaviors can help us detect lying and deception, but this is not always the case. As Canary, Cody, and Manusov (2008) note, "A liar may appear anxious only if he or she is concerned about the lie or about getting caught. If the lie is unimportant, a communicator may instead be relaxed and controlled. Further, someone who is accused of lying but is in fact telling the truth may show signs of anxiety" (pp. 82–83).

This doesn't mean that we're destined be tricked by those who want to deceive us. We can still look to the power of verbal messages—Barbara could have realized that someone from "the government" would probably have a more official title and would already know her Social Security number. And we can also look to the relational context and situational context of our interaction. If you suspect that your partner is lying to you and you have caught him or her lying in the past, you might have more reason to be suspicious.

Nonverbal Communication Codes

At this point, you've seen how complex nonverbal behaviors work together to accomplish a number of goals or functions. You also have a good sense of what types of actions constitute nonverbal communication—giving someone a hug, making eye contact, or pausing to let someone else speak. In this section, we examine these **nonverbal codes**, symbols we use to send messages without, or in addition to, words. Although we divide these codes into categories for simplicity and clarity, remember that nonverbal behaviors seldom communicate meaning in isolation. Usually, clusters of nonverbal behaviors convey a message—for example, raising your eyebrows and gasping show surprise or shock, with or without any accompanying words. The specific codes we examine here are gestures and body movements, facial expressions, eye behavior, voice, physical appearance, space and environment, touch, and time.

Gestures and Body Movements

On the television show *Lie to Me*, the character Dr. Cal Lightman claims to be able to "read" nonverbal behaviors to detect when someone is lying; he claims, essentially, that he can read "body language." But the way you move your body is not a language at all—shaking your leg while you're sitting or slouching your

AND YOU?

When you attempt to deceive others (as when telling a friend you like her new boyfriend when you don't), are you aware of your nonverbal messages? Do you tend to alter your tone of voice or change your eye contact? What types of nonverbal indications do you look for in others in order to figure out if they're telling the truth?

shoulders has no specific, consistently understood definition. You are observing body movements called **kinesics**—the aspects of gestures and body movements that send nonverbal messages. When Eva turns her body to include Jane in a conversation, or Rodney walks into an interview with confidence, for example, you are witnessing kinesic behaviors—and research shows that you are fairly good at deciphering the emotions of others from their gestures and movements (Montepare, Koff, Zaitchik, & Alberet, 1999), even though you must be careful not to act as if your interpretations are 100 percent accurate.

There are five main categories of body movements that convey meaning: emblems, illustrators, regulators, adaptors, and affect displays (Ekman & Friesen, 1969).

▶ **Emblems** are movements and gestures that have a direct verbal translation in a particular group or culture. They substitute for verbal messages. During his inauguration parade, Barack Obama greeted the marching band from his old high school with a shaka sign—a pinkie and thumb salute that is a common form of greeting in Hawaii. Though it has no direct translation, the shaka sign is widely regarded as a representation of the Hawaiian "aloha spirit," and, depending on context, can be interpreted as hello, good-bye, praise, or a call to "hang loose." As we'll learn later, emblems don't always translate from one culture to another.

▶ **Illustrators** reinforce verbal messages and help visually explain what is being said. Holding your hands two feet apart while saying, "The fish was *this* big!" is an illustrator. Illustrators can also be used to increase influence in relationships, as when we emphasize our words with pointing or sketching a thought in the air (Dunbar & Burgoon, 2005).

▶ **Regulators** help us manage our interactions. Raising your hand and lifting your head, for example, indicate that you want to speak. Raising your eyebrows usually indicates you want information from others (Flecha-García, 2010).

▶ **Adaptors** satisfy some physical or psychological need, such as rubbing your eyes when you're tired or twisting your hair when you're nervous or bored. Adaptors are not conscious behaviors; they are used to reduce bodily tension, often in response to heightened emotional stimulation. They may be more frequent when someone is stressed, impatient, or bored, and are often interpreted as indicators of negative feelings (Goss & O'Hair, 1988).

▶ **Affect displays** are nonverbal behaviors that convey feelings, moods, and reactions. They are often unintentional, reflecting the sender's emotions: slumping in a chair may indicate fatigue or boredom; a fist thrust high in the air indicates joy when your team scores a touchdown. That's not to say that they're *always* unintentional, though: you may purposely set your jaw and hit your fist on the table to indicate your anger or frustration.

Facial Expressions

Consider the character Spock, the half-vulcan, half-human science officer from *Star Trek* who suppresses his emotions at all costs, in the pursuit of pure logic. Both of the actors who have played Spock (Leonard Nimoy in the original

CONNECT

Kinesics is important when delivering a speech as your body movements should support your words. For example, illustrators help clarify a point for your audience; confident posture reassures your listeners that you're prepared and organized. Certain adaptors (like yawning), however, can leave the audience with the impression that you are bored with your own speech. We discuss these issues in Chapter 14.

● **WITH THOSE** Vulcan eyebrows, Spock portrays little emotion!

television series, and Zachary Quinto in the 2009 film) had their human eyebrows replaced with artificial "Vulcan" ones: because Spock's eyebrows—and eye expressions in general—appear less human, his emotions seem less human too.

In fact, humans are wired to use their faces to indicate emotions. Although the reasons behind our facial expressions might be difficult to ascertain, several specific expressions are actually common to all humans, across all cultures (Ekman & Friesen, 1971). A smile, for example, usually indicates happiness; a frown, sadness; raised eyebrows tend to indicate surprise, and wrinkled eyebrows, concern (see Figure 5.1). Irenaus Eibl-Eibesfeldt (1973) observed that blind children, who cannot learn to mimic facial movements through sight, exhibited sadness, anger, disgust, fear, interest, surprise, and happiness in the same way that sighted people exhibit these feelings. Eibl-Eibesfeldt concluded that these seven primary facial expressions are inborn, while most other expressions are learned from our culture. (See also Gagnon, Gosselin, Hudon-ven der Buhs, Larocque, & Milliard, 2010). There is even some recent evidence that pride may be a universally recognized emotion as well (Tracy & Robins, 2008).

The fact that we're fairly adept at deciphering these common expressions of emotion doesn't mean we're experts at decoding all facial expressions—especially since the human face is capable of producing over a thousand different expressions (and as many as twenty thousand if you take into account all of the combinations of the different facial areas) (Ekman, Friesen, & Ellsworth, 1972; Harrigan & Taing, 1997). This is partly because our emotions can be concealed by facial management techniques, ways of consciously manipulating our faces to give off a particular expression. One common facial management technique is **masking**, replacing an expression that shows true feeling with an expression that shows appropriate feeling for a given interaction. Actors use masking all the time—but you also use masking techniques when you smile at customers at the

FIGURE 5.1

CROSS-CULTURAL PRIMARY FACIAL EXPRESSIONS Research shows that these seven expressions of emotion exist in all cultures and are inborn.

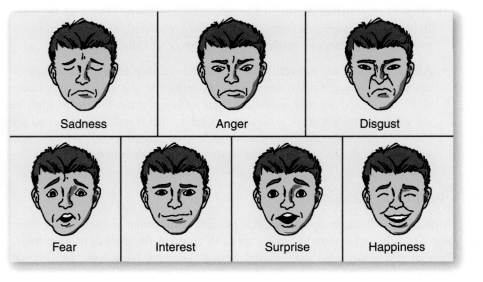

restaurant where you work even though you're really in a horrible mood and just wish they'd leave (Richmond, McCroskey, & Payne, 1991).

Eye Behavior

The film *Harry Potter and the Deathly Hallows*, Part I (2010), finds Harry and his friends Ron and Hermione hidden away from the evil Voldemort as they attempt to complete a particular quest in a time of all-out war. Words are often inadequate and inconvenient for expressing the intense emotions they feel during their plight, yet we never doubt what the characters are feeling. We clearly see the soft eyes of love between Ron and Hermione, and we certainly can't miss Harry's terrified glances as he wonders what has become of his loved ones back at Hogwarts and beyond. **Oculesics** is the study of the use of the eyes to communicate, and it covers the importance of the eyes in communication across the lifespan.

Researchers found that newborn infants (two to five days old) stared significantly longer at faces offering a direct gaze rather than an averted one. The babies also oriented themselves more often toward the face that made eye contact with them. Previous studies also confirmed that babies as young as three months old would smile less when adults averted their gaze, though the smiling would return when adults resumed eye contact (Farroni, Csibra, Simion, & Johnson, 2002).

There are some cultural variations in gaze with children. For example, European American parents gaze more at their children; this is particularly true between mothers and sons. Mexican American parents, on the other hand, spend less time making eye contact with children. In return, children gaze more directly at fathers in European American homes than in Mexican American homes (Schofield, Parke, Castañeda, & Coltrane, 2008). Perhaps children in Mexican American homes gaze less directly at fathers as a sign of respect or because of the cultural hierarchy of the family.

The human gaze remains important beyond childhood. You might make direct eye contact with a hiring manager in a job interview in the United States to make a stronger impression. And you will likely use eye behavior to send messages in more personal relationships. For example, the way you look at a friend is likely not the same way you look at your significant other and certainly not the way you look at someone you dislike immensely. Each glance can send a message of liking, loving, attraction, or contempt (see Table 5.1 on p. 138).

Voice

When Roger Ebert lost the ability to speak due to complications from thyroid cancer, family, friends, and fans of the legendary film critic thought they'd never hear his voice again. He was able to communicate using a computer equipped with text-to-speech technology, but of course it didn't sound like him. A company in Scotland approached him, saying it could create a customized voice for his computer, using the many hours of audio commentary Ebert had recorded over the years. When he unveiled his new "voice" to his wife, she was moved to tears: while the voice still had the stilted speech pattern that typifies computerized speech, it

CONNECT

Despite differing cultural norms regarding direct eye contact, it remains an important part of giving speeches and succeeding in job interviews in the United States. In both situations, eye contact signals respect for your audience and confidence in your abilities and preparedness. You learn more about the challenges of eye contact, and how to move past them, in Chapter 14 and the Interviewing Appendix.

AND YOU?

How do you feel about making eye contact with others (fellow classmates or your professor) when speaking in the classroom? With strangers when you lock eyes in the grocery store or on an elevator? When interacting with people who have higher status (such as a hiring manager or boss)?

TABLE 5.1

THE POWER OF EYE CONTACT

Function of Eye Contact	Example	Image
Influences attitude change	Looking at someone to get the person to trust you or comply with your wishes	
Indicates a degree of arousal	Glancing across a crowded room to signal attraction or interest; looking at a customer attentively in the interest of receiving positive evaluations—and sales (Ford, 1999)	
Expresses emotion	Soft eyes of loving looks; frightened eyes of a startled person; hard eyes of an angry person	
Regulates interaction	Looking more at a conversational partner when listening; regulating eye contact to assume or give up the speaking role (Wiemann & Knapp, 1999)	
Indicates power	Direct, prolonged gaze to convey dominance; avoidance of eye contact to signal submissiveness	
Forms impressions	Making eye contact with an audience to communicate confidence and sincerity	

Source: Leathers (1986). Adapted with permission.

sounded like Ebert, whom she had not heard speak for more than three years (Hare, 2010).

The vocalized sounds that accompany our words are nonverbal behaviors called **paralanguage**. Text-to-speech programs try to mimic human speech, and indeed, the custom program developed for Roger Ebert is able to replicate certain aspects of his paralanguage—specifically, the pitch, tone, and volume of his real voice. **Pitch** in language involves variations in the voice that give prominence to certain words or syllables. Vocal **tone** is a modulation of the voice, usually expressing a particular feeling or mood; you may notice your friend sounds "down" or hear the excitement in your teammate's revelry about your win. Vocal **volume** is how loud or soft the voice is—think of the softness of a whisper or the thunder of an angry shout.

● **ALMOST FOUR YEARS** after losing the ability to speak due to complications from thyroid cancer, Roger Ebert found his voice once again with the aid of a customized text-to-speech computer program.

In addition to pitch, tone, and volume, paralanguage also involves behaviors like pauses, vocal quality, and the rate and rhythm of speech. It exhibits qualities like hoarseness, smoothness, or deepness, and it may sound precise, clipped, slurred, or shrill. We all have preferences about which voices are most attractive—and while individual tastes do vary, research points to some general preferences. For example, we find angry, demanding voices annoying—and whiny voices *really* annoying (Sokol, Webster, Thompson, & Stevens, 2005). Look no further than your favorite radio DJs or newscasters to examine the vocal qualities people enjoy the most. There's a reason why these individuals are able to make a living with their voices: they do not sound shrill or nasal, but tend to have smooth voices and find a middle ground between precise and fluid speech. Pronunciation matters too—and can identify individuals as coming from another country or another section of a country. Thus, people in Texas talk about the city of "*Hew*-ston," while New Yorkers might point to "*How*-ston" Street, even though both locations are spelled "Houston."

The ability of the voice to influence communication also includes our **vocalizations**, paralinguistic cues that give information about our emotional or physical state, such as laughing, crying, sighing, yawning, or moaning. Other vocalizations simply replace words or create nonword fillers in conversations. You might clear your throat to get someone's attention, or use "Shhhh" to quiet a crowd, and most of us tend to insert the sound "umm" into conversation when we're taking a moment to think. Some of these vocalizations help regulate conversations; referred to as **back-channel cues**, the "ah . . . um . . . uh, uh" vocalizations signal when we want to talk versus when we are just encouraging others to continue their talking.

Using vocalizations like "uh-huh" can help others perceive you as an effective listener (Chapter 6). When a loved one discusses a difficult situation, you want to allow the person to speak and not constantly interrupt with your own words. Vocalizations tell your partner that you're listening and that you're actively engaged in the conversation.

Physical Appearance

Reality television's *What Not to Wear* stylists Clinton Kelly and Stacy London are experts at redoing the appearance of real-life people who have been nominated by their friends and family for makeovers. What you wear—or the way you fix your hair or makeup—doesn't really speak to your abilities or define you as a person, but it communicates a message about you nonetheless. In fact, the

● **REALITY SHOW** *What Not to Wear* aims to turn fashion victims into fashion victors—and, in polishing the individual's appearance, also improve his or her self-confidence and how he or she is perceived by others.

Chapter 11 explains that the artifacts you exhibit in a professional setting both reflect and shape the organization's culture—its beliefs, values, and ways of doing things. Competent communicators must be mindful of the messages their artifacts send in light of the larger organizational picture.

initial impression your appearance makes may affect your future interactions with others (Burgoon et al., 1989; DeKay, 2009).

Most people in Western society are well aware of the significance of appearance. Research shows that society affords attractive people certain advantages. For instance, attractive students receive more interaction from their teachers (Richmond et al., 1991); and "good-looking" job candidates have a greater chance of being hired (Molloy, 1983; Shannon & Stark, 2003). Jurors find attractive defendants innocent more often (Efran, 1974), although discussion and deliberation can mitigate this bias (Patry, 2008). Appearance affects not only perceptions of attractiveness but also judgments about a person's background, character, personality, status, and future behavior (Guerrero & Floyd, 2006). In fact, the psychologist Nancy Etcoff (1999) claims that all cultures pursue and value attractiveness as a matter of survival.

Perceptions about appearance and attractiveness are inferred from physical characteristics like body shape and size, facial features, skin color, height, and hair color but also from the clothing you wear, which can reveal quite a bit about your status, economic level, social background, goals, and satisfaction (Crane, 2000; Sybers & Roach, 1962). For example, many uniforms are often associated with lower-status jobs, such as working in a fast-food restaurant, while more formal attire (business suits) and specific uniforms (doctors' coats, judges' robes) are associated with higher-status occupations.

We also infer a great deal of meaning from the things that adorn our body, known as **artifacts**—accessories carried or used on the body for decoration or identification. For example, the expensive Rolex watch that your uncle wears sends a very different message about wealth and status than a ten-dollar watch would. Other artifacts, such as briefcases, tattoos, earrings, nose rings, nail polish, and engagement and wedding rings, also convey messages about your relational status, your gender, and even how willing you are to defy conventions (as in a tongue piercing).

Space and Environment

In addition to the messages your body, its movements, and its adornments convey, you also send nonverbal messages by the spaces that surround you and your communication partners. We examine three such factors here: proxemics, territoriality, and environment.

Proxemics

Ben's first job involved a coworker Lucas, who was a close talker—a person who stands very near when speaking to others. "During shifts when I'd be on with this guy, I'd always have to try to find some excuse to be away from the counter," Ben said. "If we were both behind the counter together, he'd talk so close that I'd end up completely backed into a corner, with the counter digging into my back, just hoping for someone to rob the place so there'd be an excuse to get out of the situation" (Ben Edwards, personal communication, April 2, 2011). Ben's intense discomfort with Lucas was due to **proxemics**, the study of the way we use and communicate with space.

COMMUNICATIONACROSSCULTURES

THINK ABOUT THIS

The Great Uniform Debate

Clothing can communicate social status, group affiliation, gender identity, and socioeconomic status, among other things. During adolescence especially, we use clothing to create messages that express who we are—or who we want to be. Today's adolescents wear everything from miniskirts to full-length jackets to T-shirts with sexual or explicit messages on them and often focus on brands and lines of clothing as defining individual status and identity. Such trends have given rise to some debate about proper attire in public schools in the United States. And while the argument sometimes centers on money and violence, a good portion of the dialogue focuses on what clothing communicates to other students and about the institution. However, in the past decade, this trend has been changing thanks to the adoption of uniforms by some school systems (Cox, 2005).

Proponents suggest that uniforms communicate more than just a preppy look. Uniforms communicate belonging by showing who is supposed to be in the school and who is not, as well as school pride (Wilde, 2008). What is more important is what uniforms do *not* allow to be communicated—gang affiliations and socioeconomic status (Caruso, 1996). A uniform, it is argued, forces students to leave such affiliations at the door of the school. As former President Clinton noted in his 1996 State of the Union address, which focused on stronger families and a safer world for children, "If it means that teenagers will stop killing each other over designer jackets, then our public schools should be able to require their students to wear school uniforms." By reducing negative messages, those in favor of school uniforms hope to encourage learning and allow students to reduce stereotyping.

But opponents suggest that uniforms communicate something negative—conformity and intolerance toward difference (Caruso, 1996). Such was the case in France in 2003 when two sisters were barred from entering a school building because their headscarves did not conform to the school's uniform policy. Their father contended that the dress policy encouraged religious intolerance in an area where about half the students were Muslim (Schofield, 2003). Some youth co-culture theorists, such as Dick Hebdige, even contend that clothing, along with other nonverbal indicators, assist youth in questioning the dominant culture and creating their own identity and self-esteem, a skill that is important to develop during adolescence.

Whatever the outcome of the uniform debate, one thing is clear: clothing in the youth culture communicates volumes about both the individuals and the corresponding institutions (Hebdige, 1999).

❶ What other items, besides clothing, non-verbally communicate information about a high school student?

❷ When you were in high school, what styles did you wear, and what did these clothing items communicate about you? If you now have or have had teen children, what do or did they seem to be communicating about themselves?

❸ Do you believe that uniforms reduce stereotyping by class and status in society? Explain your answer.

❹ Is this more of an issue in high schools and middle schools than in elementary schools? What would you do if your college or university suddenly adopted a uniform policy?

what about you?

You and Your Artifacts

Take a look at the following list of artifacts. Do you make use of or wear any of these items? If so, what does the artifact mean to you, personally, about your identity? What messages might the artifact send to others?

Artifact Type	What Does It Mean to Me?	What Does It Say About Me?
Jewelry (necklaces, rings, watches, cuff links)		
Perfume or cologne		
Body piercings (tongue rings, nose rings, eyebrow piercings)		
Tattoos		
Specific hairstyles (Mohawk, shaved, braided, long, disheveled)		
Clothing labels or logos		
Eyewear (sunglasses, eyeglasses versus contact lenses)		
Other accessories (scarves, belts, high-heeled shoes)		

Professor Edward Hall (1959) identified four specific spatial zones that carry communication messages (see Figure 5.2).

▶ *Intimate* (0 to 18 inches). We often send intimate messages in this zone, which is usually reserved for spouses or romantic partners, very close friends, and close family members.

▶ *Personal* (18 inches to 4 feet). In the personal zone, we communicate with friends, relatives, and occasionally colleagues.

▶ *Social* (4 to 12 feet). The social zone is most comfortable for communicating in professional settings, such as business meetings or teacher-student conferences.

▶ *Public* (12 feet and beyond). The public zone allows for distance between the interactants, such as public speaking events or performances.

Your personal space needs may vary from these space categories (and these vary according to culture too; Hall "normed" these zones for different cultures around the world). How close or distant you want to be from someone depends quite a bit on whom you're dealing with, the situation, and your comfort level. You might well enjoy being physically close to your boyfriend or girlfriend when you are taking a walk together, but you're probably not going to hold hands or embrace during class. Gender also plays a role as research says that groups of men walking together will walk faster and typically leave more space between themselves and others (Costa, 2010). But regardless of your personal preferences, violations of space are almost always uncomfortable and awkward and can cause relational problems.

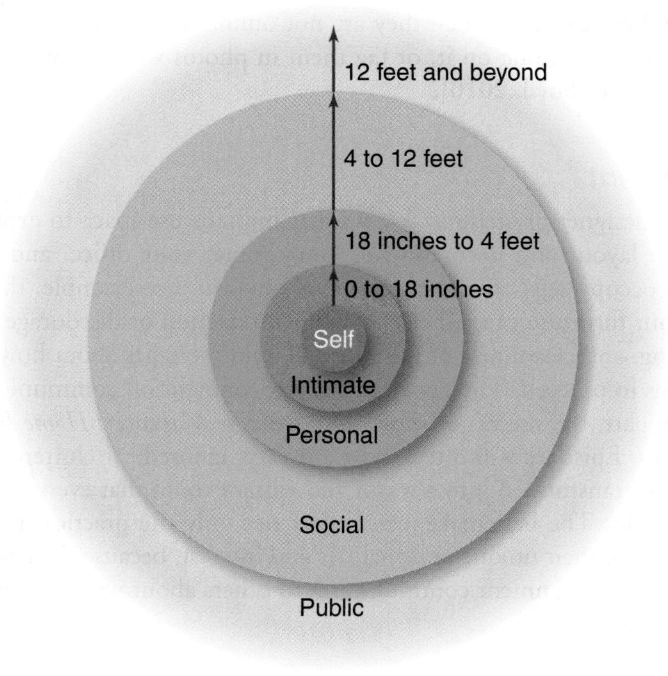

12 feet and beyond

4 to 12 feet

18 inches to 4 feet

0 to 18 inches

Self

Intimate

Personal

Social

Public

FIGURE 5.2

ZONES OF PERSONAL SPACE The four zones of personal space described by Edward Hall indicate ranges that generally apply across cultures.

● **SHELDON COOPER'S** seat on the couch is his kingdom. The *Big Bang Theory* character has established his regular spot as personal—and strictly guarded—territory.

Territoriality can have an impact on group communication, as we generally feel more in control of situations on our own turf (Chapters 9 and 10). Think about this the next time a professor breaks you up into random groups. Do you enjoy moving across the room from your usual seat, or do you prefer your group members to come to you? Chances are good that a new "territory" will affect your communication.

Proxemic messages are not limited to the real world. In the online virtual world *Second Life*, you create your own space, in which you and your avatar move. Research finds that the avatars use proxemic cues to send relational messages and structure interaction, much as people do in real life (Antonijevic, 2008; Gillath, McCall, Shaver, & Blascovich, 2008).

Territoriality

Closely related to proxemics is **territoriality**—the claiming of an area, with or without legal basis, through continuous occupation of that area. Your home, your car, and your office are personal territories. But territories also encompass implied ownership of space, such as a seat in a classroom, a parking space, or a usual table in a restaurant. When territoriality is encroached on, the territory is usually defended by its claimant. If you're a fan of *The Big Bang Theory*, then you know never (ever) to take Sheldon Cooper's seat on the couch as you will be met with a haughty lecture.

Territoriality operates in mediated contexts as well. Just as we do with physical spaces in the real world, we claim our Twitter and Facebook pages by naming them and decorating them with our "stuff," we allow certain people ("friends") access, and we "clean up" our space by deleting or hiding comments. Recent research shows that young people are more adept at managing their space on Facebook than are their parents (Madden & Smith, 2010). Some clean up their wall on a regular basis, deleting status updates and wall posts as often as they make them. Others use what has become known as a "super logoff": they deactivate their accounts when they are not online so that "friends" cannot see their wall, post anything on it, or tag them in photos while they're metaphorically not around (boyd, 2010).

Environment

Any home designer or architect knows that humans use space to express themselves. The layout and decoration of your home, your office, and any other space you occupy tells others something about you. For example, the way you arrange your furniture can either encourage interaction or discourage it; the décor, lighting, and cleanliness of the space all send messages about how you want interactions to proceed. The power of the environment on communication may explain, in part, the success of shows like *Extreme Makeover: Home Edition* and *Clean House*. Episodes will often show a dreary, ignored, or cluttered unlivable space that is transformed into a warm and vibrant room that everyone suddenly wants to be in. The best makeovers reflect not only the practical needs of the family, but also their unique personalities and interest, because the designers understand that environment communicates to others about who we are and what we are about.

Touch

Touch is the first communication experienced in life. A newborn baby is soothed in the arms of her parents; she begins to learn about herself and others as she reaches out to explore her environment. The study of touch is termed **haptics**, and it remains an important form of communicating throughout life. We hug our loved ones in happy and sad times, we reassure others with a pat on the back, and we experience intimacy with the caress of a spouse.

There are as many different types of touches as there are thoughts and reactions to being touched. Scholar Richard Heslin's (1974) intimacy continuum provides insights into how our use of touch reflects our relationship with a communication partner:

▶ *Functional-professional touch* is used to perform a job. How would your dentist perform your root canal or your hairstylist get rid of your split ends if he or she didn't touch you?

▶ *Social-polite touch* is more interpersonal than functional-professional touch. It is often a polite acknowledgment of the other person, such as a handshake.

▶ *Friendship-warmth touch* conveys liking and affection between people who know each other well. Examples might be hugging your friends or offering your brother a pat on the back.

▶ *Love-intimacy touch* is used by romantic partners, parents and children, and even very close friends and family members. Examples include kissing (whether on the mouth or on the cheek), embracing, and caressing. This type of touch communicates deep closeness.

▶ *Sexual-arousal touch* is an intense form of touch that plays an important part in sexual relationships. It often reveals intimacy—as between spouses or romantic partners—but is also used in nonintimate relationships that are sexual in nature.

Another classification system for touch distinguishes among a dozen different kinds of body contact (Morris, 1977). Table 5.2 illustrates these types of contact in connection with Heslin's intimacy continuum.

Clearly, touch has a powerful impact on our relationships. In fact, it is one of the factors related to liking and sustaining liking in healthy marriages (Hinkle, 1999). Our reassuring touch also lets our friends know that we care and serves to regulate social interactions, as when beginning or ending an interaction with a handshake. However, this is not to say that all touch is positive. Bullying behaviors like kicking, punching, hitting, and poking are inappropriate forms of touch, unless inside a boxing ring.

Gauging the appropriate amount of touch for a given situation or relationship is also very important for communication. For example, dating partners usually expect touch, but someone who wants "too much" (such as constant hand-holding) can be perceived as needy or clingy. Withholding touch

AND YOU?

Are you repelled by touches from strangers? What about touches from people who are not your age (children or the elderly)? What about being touched by a colleague or a professor—someone you have a professional relationship with? Does it depend on the situation? Explain your answer.

Type of Contact	Purpose	Intimacy Type
Handshake	Forming relational ties	Social-polite
Body-guide	A substitute for pointing	Social-polite
Pat	A congratulatory gesture but sometimes meant as a condescending or sexual one	Social-polite or sexual-arousal
Arm-link	Used for support or to indicate a close relationship	Friendship-warmth
Shoulder embrace	Signifies friendship; can also signify romantic connectiveness	Friendship-warmth
Full embrace	Shows emotional response or relational closeness	Friendship-warmth
Hand-in-hand	Equality in an adult relationship	Friendship-warmth
Mock attack	An aggressive behavior performed in a nonaggressive manner, such as a pinch meant to convey playfulness	Friendship-warmth
Waist embrace	Indicates intimacy	Love-intimacy
Kiss	Signals a degree of closeness or the desire for closeness	Love-intimacy or sexual-arousal
Caress	Normally used by romantic partners; signals intimacy	Love-intimacy or sexual-arousal
Body support	Touching used as physical support	Love-intimacy

communicates a message of disinterest or even dislike, which has the potential to damage a relationship, whether with a friend, a romantic partner, or a colleague. Obviously, it's important to adjust touch to individual expectations and needs (and culture, as we explain later in the chapter).

Time Orientation

Imagine that you are late for a job interview. If you are the interviewee, you realize that you've probably lost the job before you even have a chance to say a word—your lateness sends a message to the employer that you don't value punctuality and his or her time. If you are the interviewer, however, it's completely acceptable for you to keep the interviewee waiting. In fact, by making the person wait, you are asserting your status by clearly conveying that you have control.

As discussed in Chapter 3, **chronemics** is the study of how people perceive the use of time and how they structure time in their relationships. This is a form of nonverbal communication because your use of time sends a message without a single word. A person's *time orientation*—his or her personal associations with the use of time—determines the importance that person ascribes to conversation content, the length of the interaction, the urgency of the interaction, and punctuality (Burgoon et al., 1989). For example, when you are invited to someone's home for dinner, it is normal to arrive about ten minutes after the time suggested (in the United States, anyway—lateness norms vary considerably across cultures). It shows consideration for your host not to arrive too early or too late (and possibly ruin the dinner!). Similarly, spending time with others communicates concern and interest. For example, good friends will make plans to spend time together even when it's inconvenient. So while it's nice to spend time with your friend Paul when you're working on your group project for your psychology class, it's not the same as spending time with him when you don't *have* to, as you would when you're helping him clean out his garage or watching a soccer match.

Using time to send a message can be confusing, however. How long do you wait to text or call someone you met at a party to see if he or she might want to grab a meal with you? Right after you've left the party may seem too eager, but a week later may suggest you are not really interested. Research shows that we do use people's response rate (how quickly they return e-mails, texts, etc.) as an indication of interest and immediacy, but the situation and context also make a considerable difference (Döring & Pöschl, 2009; Ledbetter, 2008).

AND YOU?
What kind of message does it send if you are habitually late to class? What about showing up late to work? On the other hand, what kind of message is sent by showing up early for a party or to pick up a date?

Influences on Nonverbal Communication

Pick any individual nonverbal code—let's say a kiss. A kiss can mean lots of different things in different places, between different people in different situations. A kiss is a friendly manner of greeting between the sexes and with friends of the same sex throughout much of southern Europe and Latin America. This is not necessarily the case in the United States and Canada, where kissing tends to be reserved for immediate family, romantic partners, or very close friends. You might kiss your romantic partner differently in front of your family members than you would when you're alone. And if you're sending an e-mail to your eight-year-old niece, you might end it with a big wet kiss, signaled by the emoticon :-X. Clearly, nonverbal communication must be considered in context in order to both understand its meaning and to use it appropriately. Here we consider how culture, technology, and situation all serve as powerful influences on our nonverbal behavior.

Culture and Nonverbal Communication

Hold up one hand, with your thumb and two middle fingers folded in, and wave it at a crowd of people. That's what then President George W. Bush and members of his family did before cameras during inaugural festivities. The next day, newspapers in Norway ran photos of a smiling Jenna Bush holding her hand in the "Hook 'em Horns" salute to the University of Texas Longhorns (her alma mater), with a headline reading "Shock Greeting from Bush Daughter" (Douglass, 2005). Why all the fuss over a gesture of support for a college football team? Because in Norway (and

● **JENNA BUSH** thought she was showing her support for the University of Texas Longhorns—not giving a Satanic salute!

indeed, in heavy metal co-cultures around the world), the gesture is commonly understood as a satanic salute.

As this example illustrates, nonverbal communication is highly influenced by culture. What may be an innocent gesture in one group, context, region, or country can convey a different and possibly offensive message elsewhere. But culture's impact on nonverbal communication goes far beyond miscommunication through gestures. It affects everything from eye behavior to touch to facial expressions—and includes time orientation and notions of physical attractiveness, both of which we explained in Chapter 3.

Consider the need to be sensitive to culturally linked nonverbal communication in the academic and professional world. For example, in the United States, we are accustomed to making direct eye contact when speaking to someone, whether a colleague, a supervisor, or a professor. Similarly, in the Middle East, engaging in long and direct eye contact with your speaking partner shows interest and is helpful in determining the sincerity and truth of the other person's words (Samovar, Porter, & Stefani, 1998). However, in Latin America, Japan, and the Caribbean, such eye behavior is a sign of disrespect. You can imagine the misunderstandings and negative perceptions that might take place during an interview between a hiring committee of professors at a university in Guatemala and their potential new colleague from Saudi Arabia.

Similarly, much interesting research has been done on culture's effect on touch. Some cultures are **contact cultures** (for example, Italy) (Williams & Hughes, 2005) and depend on touch as an important form of communication, whereas other cultures are **noncontact cultures** and are touch-sensitive or even tend to avoid touch. Latin American, Mediterranean, and Eastern European cultures, for example, rely on touch much more than Scandinavian cultures do. Public touch, linked to the type of interpersonal relationship that exists and the culture in which it occurs, affects both the amount of touch and the area of the body that is appropriate to touch (Avtgis & Rancer, 2003; McDaniel & Andersen, 1998). Social-polite touch, for example, involves a handshake between American men but a kiss between Arabic men. And some religions prohibit opposite-sex touch between unmarried or unrelated individuals.

Research has also offered some interesting insights into the relationship between sex and gender and nonverbal communication. Women usually pay more attention to both verbal and nonverbal cues when evaluating their partners and deciding how much of themselves they should reveal to those partners, whereas men attend more to the verbal information alone (Gore, 2009). Women engage in more eye contact than men, initiate touch more often, and smile more (Hall, 1998; Stewart, Cooper, & Steward, 2003).

Such differences are not necessarily biologically based. For example, Judith Hall and her colleagues note that learning environments may foster difference, with mothers using more varied facial expressions with their daughters because they believe that women are more expressive (or are supposed to be more expressive) than men. A more emotionally expressive and varied environment in childhood may well lead to more opportunities for nonverbal skill development for women (Hall, Carter, & Hogan, 2000). Adult gender roles may also play a part. Since women are expected to look out for the welfare of others, smiling—as well as other affirming nonverbal behaviors—may help meet situational, gendered expectations (Hall et al., 2000). This very point may also help explain why women exhibit greater sensitivity to nonverbal messages. They tend to exhibit more signs of interest (such as head tilts and paralinguistic encouragers like "uh-huh" and "ah") and also decode others' nonverbal behaviors more accurately, particularly those involving the face (Burgoon & Bacue, 2003).

Mediated Nonverbal Communication

At a conference, a colleague told an interesting story about nonverbal communication and e-mail—a story that you may have experienced from both sides. She asked her students to submit their assignments via e-mail by midnight on the date they were due. At 1:00 A.M., she received a frantic e-mail from one of her students, Aaron, explaining that various laptop malfunctions had prevented him from sending his speech outline until then. As Aaron typically provided quality work and never missed deadlines, our colleague was not concerned and did not intend to penalize him. So she simply wrote back "Got it" to let him know she had received his outline. When she later saw Aaron in class, she was shocked to learn that her e-mail worried him. He took her short response as a sign of annoyance for his lateness; she meant the response as a quick assurance. In the end, Aaron noted, "If you had used a smiley face, I would have known what you meant."

As you've learned throughout this chapter, when you speak with someone face to face, you've got a number of nonverbal codes at your disposal. But not all communication occurs face to face or even on the telephone, where you can use *paralinguistic cues* (vocal tone, rate, pitch, volume, sighs) to offer information even in the absence of visual cues. When you write a letter or send an e-mail, IM, or text message, many of the nonverbal channels you rely on (eye contact, paralanguage, and so on) are unavailable.

However, the lack of nonverbal cues in mediated communication does not mean that users are content to do without. With the rise of electronic written communications, such as text messaging and Internet chat rooms, a whole series of creative substitutions for nonverbal cues can be found: capital letters to indicate shouting or creative use of font sizes, colors, and typefaces to provide emphasis, random punctuation (#@*&!) to substitute for obscenities, and animations, figures, diagrams, and pictures to add visuals to messages. Punctuation (or the lack of it) can help readers "hear" the intonation of what is being said (many people say that they "hear" their friend's e-mails in that friend's "voice"). As Aaron noted in our example, some individuals expect others to use emoticons in mediated texts to help clarify meaning—whether to express emotion or to signal that something we say is a joke. Emoticons can also strengthen the intensity of a message, add ambiguity (was that *really* a joke?), or indicate sarcasm (Derks, Bos, & von Grumbkow, 2008). One study in Japan even found that college students use positive emoticons as a "flame deterrent"—to try to prevent emotional misunderstandings that

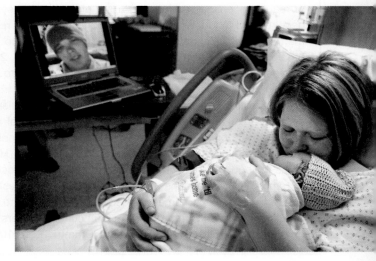

● **TECHNOLOGY HAS BECOME** so advanced that a father stationed in Iraq is now able to witness his child's birth in the United States—via webcam!

AND YOU?

Have you ever taken an online or distance-learning course? Were you happy with the instruction and the amount of interaction? It is challenging to both present and respond nonverbally in courses offered online. What are the most effective ways to do this, based on your experience?

might upset others (Kato, Kato, & Scott, 2009). Since we can't truly hear voice inflection or see facial expressions in many mediated situations, the effective use of the keyboard and computer graphics can nevertheless help to create a sense of nonverbal immediacy (O'Sullivan, Hunt, & Lippert, 2004).

As technology becomes more widely available and affordable, it's likely that our electronic communication will become open to more nonverbal channels: Skype and similar services, for example, allow us to have visual as well as audio and text contact. With refinements, speakers have the potential to be even more persuasive than in face-to-face conversation as they can monitor nonverbal cues electronically. Similarly, group and interpersonal social interactions across distances can be more involved and responsive (Bailenson, Beall, Loomis, Blascovich, & Turk, 2005).

WIREDFORCOMMUNICATION

THINK ABOUT THIS

War Games Without Weapons, Sometimes Without Words

It's probably no surprise that soldiers benefit from virtual reality training offered in computerized war games. But soldiers abroad need to learn to dodge more than bullets: in different cultures, they need to learn to navigate different norms and rules of nonverbal communication.

American soldiers stationed in Iraq, for example, have discovered the hard way that gestures that are innocent in the United States can be quite offensive in Iraqi culture (and vice versa). For example, showing the soles of your feet is considered rude in Iraq; proximity while speaking, head bowing, and handshakes can also lead to misunderstanding. In one instance, an Iraqi man gestured at a female soldier by rubbing his fingers together. He was indicating friendship; she thought he was making a lewd sexual gesture.

This is where Tactical Iraqi, a virtual reality game created for the U.S. military, comes in handy. *Wired* magazine reports that "players navigate a set of real-life scenarios by learning a set of Arabic phrases, culturally relevant gestures and taboos. . . . A speech-recognition system records and evaluates the responses. Accurate responses allow the soldier to build a rapport with other characters and advance to the next level" (Cuda, 2006). The point is to help soldiers understand the Iraqi gestures, as well as to know how Iraqis are likely to perceive gestures that are considered innocent in the United States.

Interestingly, the game, though intended for soldiers, has no weapons or combat of any kind. It focuses instead on mutual understanding, with soldiers attempting to gain the trust of their companions in order to rebuild war-torn communities. The game's technical director, Hannes Vilhjalmsson, notes the power of nonverbal communication in this process: "I got a kick out of removing the weapons and replacing them with gestures" (Cuda, 2006). The success of such games has led the U.S. military to invest even more in simulation games—dubbed "first-person cultural trainers"—that help prepare troops for intercultural communication (Drummond, 2010).

① Do you think soldiers can learn communication skills from a video game? Do you think this method of training would be more or less effective than classroom instruction?

② Why is establishing competent communication so important for soldiers in Iraq? Do you think such training would have been more or less important for soldiers in Europe during World War II?

③ The company that created Tactical Iraqi is considering a civilian version of the game. Would it be useful to engage different cultures in the United States in virtual reality play? How might its technological format affect its usefulness for various co-cultures (age, education, socioeconomic status, and so on)?

The Situational Context

Dancing at a funeral. Raising your Starbucks cup to toast your professor. Making long, steady, somewhat flirtatious eye contact with your doctor. Wearing a business suit to a rock concert. Do these situations sound strange or potentially uncomfortable for everyone around you? The situational context has a powerful impact on nonverbal communication. Recall from our model of competent communication in Chapter 1 that the situational context includes spheres like the place you are in, your comfort level, the event, current events, and the social environment.

Now imagine dancing at a wedding, toasting your friend's accomplishment, flirting with an attractive friend, or wearing a business suit to a job interview. In each instance, the situational context has changed. Situational context determines the rules of behavior and the roles people must play under different conditions. Competent communicators will always consider the appropriateness and effectiveness of nonverbal communication in a given context.

Two of the primary factors involved in situational context are the public-private dimension and the informal-formal dimension. The **public-private**

EVALUATINGCOMMUNICATIONETHICS

Tongue Rings at the Office

You've just graduated from college and have landed an interview for an assistant position at a public policy firm that specializes in childhood education. It's a great position with lots of room for advancement and the ability to be active in an area that really interests you.

The only problem is that it's a fairly conservative office culture, and because the company works closely with lawmakers, lobbyists, educators, and the media, employees are expected to dress in traditional business attire at all times. You worry that you won't fit in: you consider yourself a true bohemian, and the thought of wearing a suit—or losing your beloved tongue piercing—feels somewhat false to you. You know that if you remove the stud from your tongue, the piercing will likely close up, so taking it out for this interview will probably mean taking it out for good.

A friend of yours works for a conservative financial firm; she, too, has a pierced tongue and says that people don't really notice it unless you show it to them. She says that even now, several years into her tenure there, only a few close colleagues know about it; if her boss is aware of it, he's never mentioned it to her.

But you know that the job you want involves interacting with more than just colleagues and clients—there's potential for media contact, and if your piercing is captured on camera, it will send a nonverbal message not only about you but also about the organization. You're certain you could get through the interview without anyone knowing about the piercing, but what if you get the job? What should you do?

THINK ABOUT THIS

❶ Does the piercing even matter? What type of message does the tongue stud send?

❷ Should you just buy the conservative suit for your interview and kiss the tongue ring good-bye? Is it ethical to present an image that works for the job, even if it's incongruous with the way you see yourself?

❸ Would it be more ethical to present yourself as you are and use your verbal communication skills to show the interviewer that you're qualified, competent, and right for this job? Might this render your clothing and artifacts less important?

dimension is the physical space that affects our nonverbal communication. For example, you might touch or caress your partner's hand while chatting over dinner at your kitchen table, but you would be much less likely to do that at your brother's kitchen table or during a meeting at city hall. The

real communicator

NAME: Octavia Spencer
HOMETOWN: Montgomery, Alabama
OCCUPATION: Actress
FUN FACT: I was so excited about a friend's three-year-old's birthday party that I sang karaoke with the children, played in the pirate ship fort, and looted the treasure chest.

I've always wanted to work in the film industry, though I never dreamed it would be in front of the camera. But in 1995, I got a small part opposite Sandra Bullock in the hit film *A Time to Kill*, and I was on my way. Since that time, I've had a number of roles on stage, screen, and television. I'm known for my comedic timing and was named on *Entertainment Weekly's* Web site in their esteemed list, "25 Funniest Actresses in Hollywood," in April 2009.

What I do want everyone reading this interview to realize is that my success is tied to a number of the topics you're studying right now—particularly nonverbal communication. For example, pretty much anyone can read a script out loud, but *how* you read it is what counts in this industry. The tone of voice, the timing, the pause that is just long enough to get people to look up and pay attention—these are the keys to getting (and staying) employed!

Vocal cues alone are incredibly important in acting. When I was the voice of "Minny" on the audio version of the book *The Help* (Kathryn Stockett's *New York Times* bestseller), I had to study the appropriate accents, timing, and inflections to make my performance truly authentic. Later, when I played the same role for the film, I realized just how much more meaning and feeling I was able to communicate when I could

use facial expressions and body movements to express my character.

Most of my roles are comedic and, let me tell you, acting in comedies isn't a barrel of laughs. It's incredibly challenging work. Facial expressions in particular have to be appropriate and come at just the right moment (otherwise, they seem phony or worse—they aren't at all funny). Often there are ten different facial expressions I have to produce in less than one minute to show surprise, hurt, outrage, confusion, acceptance, determination, confidence, liking, disgust, and pleasure. Oh, and it has to appear natural too.

In addition, the way I tilt my head or hold my body changes the information I'm trying to convey. For example, I played Dr. Evilini, a witch with dual personalities, on *Wizards of Waverly Place*. As one personality, my head was bent, and my voice low pitched with a diabolical, screeching laugh. The other personality had a normal voice, and I kept my body erect, though my eyes were always wide with expression. Because the show's target audience was primarily comprised of children, every movement was exaggerated to ensure its comedic value.

At the end of the day, I am truly grateful to be doing something that I absolutely enjoy—and none of it would be possible without a close study of nonverbal communication.

informal-formal dimension is more psychological, dealing with our perceptions of personal versus impersonal situations. The formality of a situation is itself given away by various nonverbal cues, such as the environment (your local pub or a five-star restaurant), the event (a child's first birthday party or a funeral), the level of touch (a business handshake or a warm embrace from your aunt), or even the punctuality expected (a wedding beginning promptly at 2:00 P.M. or a barbecue at your friend Nari's house going from 6:00 P.M. to whenever) (Burgoon & Bacue, 2003). Competently assessing the formality or informality of the situation affects your use of nonverbal communication—you might wear flip-flops and shorts to hang out at Nari's, but you probably wouldn't wear them to a wedding and certainly wouldn't wear them on a job interview.

If your nonverbal communication does not appropriately fit the public-private and formal-informal dimensions, you'll likely be met with some nonverbal indications that you are not being appropriate or effective (tight smiles, restless body movements, gaze aversion, and vocal tension). The situational context matters when you consider your nonverbal behavior.

BACK TO ▶ Pixar Animation Studios

 At the beginning of this chapter, we considered how animators at Pixar use elements of nonverbal communication to tell elaborate stories in films like *Up* and *WALL-E*. Let's reconsider some of the ways nonverbal codes operate in these and other films.

▶ The directors of *Up* used simple visual cues to highlight the characters so their appearance provides insights into their personalities. Carl is very squarish in appearance, so he's perceived as boxed in, in both his house and his life. Eight-year-old Explorer Scout Russell is round and bouncy—like Carl's balloons, reflecting his optimistic, energetic personality. These nonverbal elements carry subtle yet influential messages.

▶ Animators study human kinesics to make decisions about how their animated characters should move. To animate the aged Carl, they studied their own parents and grandparents and watched footage of the Senior Olympics. If Carl moved like eight-year-old Russell, the credibility of the film would be compromised.

▶ It takes talented voice actors to bring a script to life. The veteran actor Ed Asner breathed life into Carl, delivering not only his lines, but also believable vocal cues—grunts, sighs, speaking through clenched teeth—that made those lines more human and real. But for the roles of young Ellie and Russell, the directors chose nonactors who would give genuine, unpolished performances full of childish energy—the goal was for them to sound more like real children than actors reading from a script.

THINGS TO TRY Activities

1. Record a new episode of your favorite scripted television show. Try watching it with the sound turned all the way down (and closed captions turned off). Can you guess what's going on in terms of plot? How about in terms of what the characters are feeling? Now watch it again with the sound on. How accurate were your interpretations of the nonverbal behaviors shown? How successful do you think you would have been if it were an unfamiliar show, one with characters you don't know as well?

2. Shake up your clothing and artifacts today. Wear something completely out of character for you, and consider how people react. If you normally dress very casually, try wearing a suit, or if you're normally quite put together, try going out wearing sweatpants, sneakers, or a T-shirt; if you're normally a clean-shaven man, try growing a beard for a week, or if you're a woman who never wears makeup, try wearing lipstick and eyeliner. Do you get treated differently by friends? How about strangers (such as clerks in stores) or any professionals (such as doctors or mechanics) with whom you interact?

3. Observe the nonverbal behaviors of people leaving or greeting one another at an airport or a train station. Do you think you can tell the relationship they have from their nonverbal behaviors? Describe the variety of behaviors you observe, and categorize them according to the codes and functions detailed in this chapter.

4. Try smiling (genuinely) more than you usually do—and with people you might not usually smile at. See what happens. Do you feel differently about yourself and others? Do others respond with more smiles of their own? (A group of thirty of our students tried this one day and reported back that they thought they had made the whole campus a happier place—though there were a few people they encountered who remained their solemn selves.)

5. Play with text-to-speech features on your computer. Compare the way the machine reads a passage of text to the way you would read it. Do you have a choice of voices to choose from, and is there one you prefer? Would you rather listen to an audiobook performance by a noted actor, or a computer-generated voice reading the same material?

Now that you have finished reading this chapter, you can:

Describe the power of nonverbal communication:

▶ **Nonverbal communication** is the process of signaling meaning through behavior other than words. It is often spontaneous and unintentional, and its meaning may be ambiguous (pp. 128–130).

▶ When **channel discrepancy** occurs, words and actions don't match, and nonverbal behaviors are more likely to be believed than verbal ones (p. 130).

Outline the functions of nonverbal communication:

▶ Nonverbal communication reinforces verbal communication in three ways: **repeating** (mirroring the verbal message), **complementing** (reinforcing the verbal message), and **accenting** (emphasizing a part of the verbal message) (p. 131).

▶ Nonverbal cues can be used for **substituting** or replacing words (p. 131).

▶ Nonverbal communication also functions as **contradicting** behavior, conveying the opposite of your verbal message (p. 131).

▶ Nonverbal cues are used in **regulating** or coordinating verbal interaction (p. 132).

▶ A feeling of closeness, or **immediacy**, can be created with nonverbal behaviors. **Mimicry** can enhance immediacy if perceived as sincere (pp. 132–133).

▶ Individuals with good nonverbal communication skills may practice **deception**, with good or bad intentions (p. 133), when they attempt to use nonverbal behaviors to convince others of something that is false.

Describe the set of communication symbols that are **nonverbal codes**:

▶ **Kinesics**, the way gestures and body movements send various messages, includes **emblems** (movements with direct verbal translations in a specific group or culture), **illustrators** (visually reinforcing behaviors), **regulators** (interaction management cues), **adaptors** (unconscious release of bodily tension), and **affect displays** (indications of emotion) (pp. 134–135).

▶ Seven primary facial expressions are inborn and are recognizable across all cultures: sadness, anger, disgust, fear, interest, surprise, and happiness (p. 136).

▶ **Masking** is a facial management technique whereby we replace an expression of true feeling with one appropriate for a given interaction (p. 136).

▶ **Oculesics** is the study of the use of the eyes in communication settings (p. 137).

▶ How we pause, the speed and volume of our speech, and the inflections we use are vocalized nonverbal messages called **paralanguage** (p. 139), including **pitch** (vocal variation that gives prominence to certain words or syllables), **tone** (vocal modulation that expresses feelings of moods), **volume** (how loud or soft words are spoken), and a variety of other factors.

▶ **Vocalizations** are paralinguistic cues that give information about the speaker's emotional or physical state, such as laughing, crying, or sighing (p. 139).

▶ **Back-channel cues** are vocalizations that signal vocally but nonverbally that you do or don't want to talk (p. 139).

▶ **Artifacts**, accessories used for decoration and identification, offer clues to who we are (pp. 139–140).

▶ **Proxemics**, the study of the way we use and communicate with space, depends on the cultural environment and is defined by four specific spatial zones: intimate, personal, social, and public (pp. 140–144).

▶ **Territoriality** is the claiming of an area, with or without legal basis, by regular occupation of the area (p. 144).

▶ The study of touch as a form of communication, or **haptics**, depends on the relationship with the communication partner (p. 145).

▶ **Chronemics** is the study of how people perceive the use of time (pp. 146–147).

Illustrate the influences culture, technology, and situation have on our nonverbal behavior:

▶ **Contact cultures** are more likely to communicate through touch, whereas **noncontact cultures** may even tend to avoid touch (p. 148).

▶ Gender influences communication, with behaviors traditionally associated with femininity, such as smiling, often perceived as weak (pp. 148–149).

▶ In mediated communication, capitalization, bold-faced terms, and emoticons are used as nonverbal cues (p. 149).

▶ Competent nonverbal communication relates to the situation; the **public-private dimension** is the physical space that affects our nonverbal communication, and the **informal-formal dimension** is more psychological (pp. 151–153).

A doctor's ability to effectively listen to a patient can literally mean the difference between life and death.

chapter 6

Listening

Erno Daniel looks for "stealth germs." As a physician and author of *Stealth Germs in Your Body* (2008), he's on the lookout for conditions caused by bacteria, viruses, and other microbes that can go undiagnosed and untreated until they manifest themselves as something serious later on. While his clinical medical experience helps him to diagnose hidden, chronic, or low-grade infections, he can't run hundreds of tests on every patient. He can, however, listen to them.

Unfortunately, not all physicians listen effectively; in fact, one study found that, on average, doctors interrupt patients only eighteen seconds after they begin to speak (Appleby, 1996); they quickly try to jump to a diagnosis, relying on familiar technical knowledge, and fail to hear the patient's whole story. Financial pressures in the health care industry often limit the amount of time doctors can spend with their patients, and so many can't or don't take the time to listen to the full details of the conditions that afflict patients and may contribute far more to their health situation than the first symptom they disclose.

But Daniel, and other doctors like him, follow the advice of Sir William Osler, who, early in the twentieth century, urged his fellow physicians, "Listen to the patient: He is telling you the diagnosis" (quoted in Appleby, 1996, para. 1). Thus Daniel asks patients to tell him when their symptoms started; he asks them where they've traveled, what they've eaten, when the symptoms became more acute, and what else is going in their lives. Early in his career he used this strategy to discover that an infectious organism in the water of a small community was causing many people to have ulcerlike symptoms; at the time, it was thought that all these symptoms were due to stress, but Daniel's listening skills led him to find the treatable infectious cause. It was only through his "stealth listening" that these stealth germs were discovered.

chapter outcomes

After you have finished reading this chapter, you will be able to

- Outline the listening process and styles of listening
- List the reasons why we listen
- Identify challenges to good listening and their remedies
- Identify attitudinal and ethical factors that inhibit listening
- Describe how contexts affect listening

On our elementary school report cards, we are judged on our ability (or inability) to listen. "Listens well" and "Follows directions" are high praise for young children (Edwards & Edwards, 2009). But somewhere in the years that follow, we stop thinking about listening as a crucial skill. "I listen well" probably isn't a line on your résumé, like being able to speak German or knowing the ins and outs of JavaScript. Yet professors, employers, and (as illustrated above) medical professionals often note that effective listening is a crucial skill. In fact, listening pioneer Ralph Nichols claimed that listening helps us achieve our most basic human need: to understand and be understood (Beall, 2006; Floyd, 2006; Nichols, 2006; Purdy, 2006; Wolvin, 2006). As you saw in our opening vignette, both doctors and patients must listen effectively in order to make accurate diagnoses, make crucial decisions about treatment, and implement effective regimens essential to health.

In this chapter, we examine the very nature of listening—how we hear, process, come to understand, and then respond to the communication of others. We learn why listening is so important and why we so often fail to listen effectively. Throughout, we offer a variety of concrete tools and techniques that can be used every day to make us more effective and more competent listeners.

How We Listen

How many times have you had the radio on, only to realize you weren't listening to it? You know you heard the music, and you may have sung along. But just moments after it ends, you can't recall the name of the song or how the DJ introduced it. You were thinking about something else or simply not paying enough attention to retain what you heard.

Although the two are often confused, hearing and listening are not the same thing. **Hearing** is, essentially, the physiological process of perceiving sound. It's the process through which sound waves are picked up by the ears and transmitted to the brain. Unless there is a physical reason why hearing does not take place, it is an involuntary process—you can't turn it on or off. But you can, to some degree, decide what sounds you're going to notice. This is where listening comes in.

Listening is the process of recognizing, understanding, accurately interpreting, and responding effectively to the messages you hear. It is much more than just hearing words or an ability to recall information (Janusik, 2005; Todd & Levine, 1996). Listening involves *processing* what others say and do, paying attention, and understanding (Thomas & Levine, 1994), as well as *creating* messages that respond to the speaker and are directed toward achieving goals (Janusik, 2005; Wiemann, Takai, Ota, & Wiemann, 1997). In this section, we examine how this crucial process works.

The Listening Process

The listening process occurs so quickly that we may think of it as automatic, but in fact, listening involves a complex web of skills. We can develop and improve

● **THERE'S A BIG** difference between hearing a song on the radio and listening to a friend express concern about a personal issue.

those skills by focusing on the voluntary parts of the process, as detailed in the following sequence of steps:

1. *Selecting.* Since hearing is involuntary, we cannot choose what we hear. When you are faced with competing stimuli—say, the sounds of the television in the next room, the dishwasher running, and your roommate Brett complaining about his economics midterm—you will need to choose one sound over the others. This is a process called **selecting**.

2. *Attending.* Working hand in hand with selecting is **attending**—the additional step of being willing to *focus attention* on both the presence and the communication of someone else. If you select Brett's voice (deciding that it's more interesting than the sound of the running dishwasher); the next step is to attend actively to his words and message. Attending is a particularly important step to be aware of, as it is not always easily achieved. If your other roommate Elton has the TV tuned in to your favorite show, it makes attending to Brett's message much more difficult. One trick that can certainly help in this process is to be silent; research shows that this improves listening effectiveness (Johnson, Pearce, Tuten, & Sinclair, 2003).

3. *Understanding.* While talking about his midterm, Brett mentions the disagreement he had with his professor over the wording of an essay question. He throws around phrases like "aggregate supply" and "reciprocal demand." You've never studied economics, so you barely understand a word he's saying. **Understanding**—interpreting and making sense of messages—is a crucial step in the listening process because it is what enables us to interpret meaning. When you don't understand easily, you need to take a more active role in listening. For example, you might ask Brett questions to learn more about his situation (Husband, 2009).

4. *Remembering.* As a student, you know that it's important to recall information from class during an exam and in real-life situations. **Remembering** or recalling information is a part of the listening process that contributes to perceptions of competence in interaction far beyond the classroom (Muntigl & Choi, 2010). If you don't recall what happened in your conversation with Brett, he might be annoyed later on when he tells you about how his dilemma turned out.

5. *Responding.* Although we tend to think of listening as merely receiving messages, responding to messages is an important part of the process. **Responding** involves generating some kind of feedback or reaction that lets others know that you have received and understood their message. So when Brett wonders if he should talk to his professor and you say, "That sounds like the best course of action given the importance of this exam for your grade," it lets him know that you fully comprehend his concern.

Though the steps in the listening process may seem to happen without much conscious thought, they are the result of a series of quick decisions that we make when communicating with others. **Active listening**, then, involves being an active participant in making choices about selecting, attending, and so on. A failure to make such active choices is called **passive listening**. Passive listeners must frequently have information and instructions repeated to them; they may misinterpret messages or ignore them altogether. Such passive listeners are often seen as less competent by the people around them. After all, you probably wouldn't pour your heart out to someone who rarely chooses to listen to your voice over the sound of the dishwasher or television.

Our goal, then, is **listening fidelity**, the degree to which the thoughts of the listener and the thoughts and intentions of the message producer match following their communication (Fitch-Hauser, Powers, O'Brien, & Hanson, 2007; Mulanax & Powers, 2001). Active listening can play an important role in achieving this goal.

Personal Listening Preferences

If you think about it, the time you spend listening to your professors, other students, family members, and friends consumes a large part of your day—in fact, listening consumes more time than reading or writing (as we illustrate in Figure 6.1). Your use of communication technologies often fuses these categories; for example, reading a post that your friend wrote on your Facebook wall is also "listening" to the message your friend is conveying[1]. Clearly, listening is, and will remain, a vital communication skill no matter how technology continues to evolve (Janusik & Wolvin, 2009).

But how, exactly, are you listening? Four distinct preferences, or styles, emerge when it comes to listening—regardless of whether the communication is face to face or mediated through the use of technology (Barker & Watson, 2000; Watson, Barker, & Weaver, 1995):

▶ **People-oriented listeners** listen with relationships in mind. They tend to be most concerned with other people's feelings, are usually quite good at assessing others' moods, and are able to listen in a nonjudgmental way.

▶ **Action-oriented listeners** are usually focused on tasks; they organize the information they hear into concise and relevant themes. Action-oriented listeners tend to keep the discourse on track and so are often valuable in meetings and as members of teams and organizations.

---

[1]The time you spend communicating on social networking sites and cell phones hasn't yet been worked into listening research at this time.

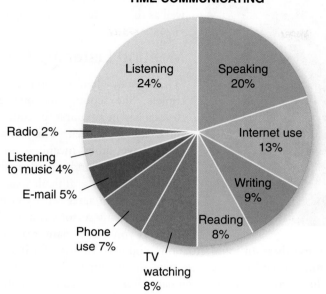

TIME COMMUNICATING

- Listening 24%
- Speaking 20%
- Internet use 13%
- Writing 9%
- Reading 8%
- TV watching 8%
- Phone use 7%
- E-mail 5%
- Listening to music 4%
- Radio 2%

FIGURE 6.1

TIME COMMUNICATING
Time spent by college students in communication activity, including personal computer time, multitasking, weekday and weekend time with work, family, friends, and school. Listening to mediated communication channels comprises the most time.

(*Source*: Janusik & Wolvin, 2009)

▶ **Content-oriented listeners** are critical listeners who carefully evaluate what they hear. They usually prefer to listen to information from sources they feel are credible and critically examine the information they receive from a variety of angles. Content-oriented listeners are usually effective when information is complex, detailed, and challenging.

▶ **Time-oriented listeners** are most concerned with efficiency; they prefer information that is clear and to the point and have little patience for speakers who talk too much or wander off topic. They prefer time limitations on the listening interaction.

While some people show a clear preference for one style over another, about 40 percent of people score high on two or more listening styles, adapting their listening styles to different situations (Barker & Watson, 2000). Thus, you may be more content-oriented when you are listening to a debate and need to analyze the information received in order to make a judgment; you might be more people-oriented when you are consoling a friend because you care about maintaining the relationship; you might favor action-oriented listening at a meeting on a group project, or time-oriented listening when you are working under a tight deadline.

Why We Listen

A court stenographer depends on honed and specialized listening skills to record court proceedings accurately. But is he listening differently than, say, the judge or the jury? Does he listen the same way when he is at the movies, reading Twitter posts, or chatting with friends? Probably not. In this section, we discuss

AND YOU?
Consider the examples of listening styles we've given here. Do you favor a particular listening style? Are you able to adopt different styles in different situations?

● WHEN *MODERN FAMILY*
parents Claire and Phil Dunphy
sit their children down for a
family meeting or lecture,
Haley, Alex, and Luke must
listen more comprehensively
than they would during casual,
everyday interactions with
Mom and Dad.

When listening for
informational purposes,
you may ask *primary* and
secondary questions,
which first seek informa-
tion and then clarify the
speaker's message (see
the Interviewing Appendix).
Secondary questions are
particularly useful in job
interviews because they
show the interviewer that
you are an engaged
listener who desires to
learn more specific
information about the
position and organization.

the different ways in which we listen, as
well as the benefits of listening well.

Meeting Listening Goals

"Please listen." Jenn is a young mother with
triplets. She repeats this phrase a dozen
times a day in a request for control over her
three active children. This simple request
could have other meanings—a desire to
have someone understand where you're
coming from on a difficult issue or a push
for someone to agree with you on a topic.
There are many reasons you want others to
listen to you—and many reasons why you
need to listen to others. In some situations, you need to listen for information; in
others, you must listen for ideas, emotions, or enjoyment. You listen to comprehend, to evaluate, to communicate empathy, and to appreciate (Steil, Barker, &
Watson, 1983). And sometimes you listen in all of these ways at once.

Informational Listening

When you listen to a weather report on the radio, attend a lecture, or hear the
details of your significant other's day at work, your primary goal is to process
and accurately understand what's being said. This process, called **informational
listening** (sometimes referred to as *comprehensive listening*), is used to understand
a message. It is basic to your existence, because you could not accomplish much
if you didn't understand the information, ideas, and opinions communicated by
others. As a student, you spend a good deal of your time engaged in informational listening as you try to understand the concepts and information that your
instructors present to you. Persons giving you directions, providing instructions,
or telling a story all require informational listening from you.

   Questions are important aids to informational listening (and can be used to meet
all types of listening goals). *Questioning techniques* are inquiries that a listener can
make to coordinate what the speaker is saying with what the listener is hearing. Asking such questions signals that listening *is* occurring; it also indicates to the speaker
that you are tuned in and interested. Questions can also help the speaker become
more effective by getting to the points that will do the listener the most good.

Critical Listening

While most of our listening is informational at its most basic level, we sometimes
need to go a step further, to making a judgment about the nature of a message.
When you evaluate or analyze information, evidence, ideas, or opinions, you are
engaged in **critical listening** (sometimes called *evaluative listening*). This type of
listening is very valuable when you cannot take a message at face value. Most of
us probably need to employ this type of listening when we are considering a big
financial purchase like a car. Don bought his last car from a friend of a friend,
and failed to ask enough questions. If he'd listened more critically, he would
have found out the car had been in two accidents.

It's probably obvious that *critical thinking* is a necessary component of critical listening. When you think critically, you assess the speaker's motivation, credibility and accuracy (Has she presented all the facts? Is the research current?), and ethics (What does she stand to gain from this?).

If you'd like to improve your critical listening, there are four points to keep in mind:

► *Determine the thesis or main point of the speaker's message.* This isn't always an easy task, particularly if you are stuck listening to a speaker who rambles on and on without ever seeming to make a point. But you can watch for key words and phrases like "What I'm trying to say . . ." or "The issue is . . ." or "Okay, here's the deal . . ."

► *Focus your efforts.* The truth is that listening is sometimes hard work. You might need to store up energy (for example, not head into your three-hour large group lecture after working out or frantically finishing a paper), concentrate, and avoid distractions (a topic we will discuss shortly).

► *Decode nonverbal cues.* As you learned in Chapter 5, your communication partner tells you quite a bit through nonverbal behavior. Your friend might reveal sadness or anger in ways that don't come across in his verbal message; your professor might hint at some information that will be on a test by sharing it slowly and loudly or even repeating it.

► *Use your memory.* Clearly, it helps to actually remember what a speaker tells you. If you're in a classroom situation or on a job interview, note-taking can help jog your memory. If you're listening to a classmate share concerns about a group project (a situation where note-taking might be awkward), try to make mental associations with her words. For example, if she is concerned that Benjamin in your group is being far too controlling, you might think "bossy Benjamin" to remember her complaint.

Empathic Listening

Think of someone whom you would describe as a "good listener." Chances are, you've thought of someone who allows you to communicate your feelings and is a sensitive, caring, and open receiver of your messages. When we engage in **empathic listening**, we are attempting to know how another person feels; it involves listening to people with openness, sensitivity, and caring. Empathic listening can provide emotional support for someone in need or comfort someone when tragedy or disappointment has struck and is particularly important in medical situations. Doctors, nurses, and other health care providers must listen compassionately to the seriously ill. They need to determine the mental and emotional state of the patients and their families to decide how much information should be disclosed to them at a particular point in time. Empathic listening helps manage the emotions of people confronting adverse events, and can help uncover erroneous assumptions that may be contributing to their anxieties (Iedema, Jorm, Wakefield, Ryan, & Sorensen, 2009; Rehling, 2008).

When you are listening empathically, it's often helpful to **paraphrase** the thoughts and feelings being expressed. This involves *guessing* at feelings

CONNECT

Empathic listening relies on appropriate nonverbal communication (Chapter 5). In addition to paraphrasing messages, you let your partner know you're listening by leaning in, nodding, and making eye contact. Your tone of voice and your vocalizations—like the supporting "mmm-hmm"—also show empathy. The combined effect of your verbal and nonverbal messages tells your partner that you care.

AND YOU?

Whom do you call when you have exciting news or when you're feeling down? What makes this person a good listener? Are you a good listener in return when this person calls you?

and rephrasing what you think the speaker has said. That's because empathic listening is person-centered (Burleson, 1994). It recognizes and elaborates on others' feelings, giving them some degree of legitimacy. The empathic listener reflects the feelings and thoughts of the speaker without suggesting an answer or solution (Fent & MacGeorge, 2006; Shotter, 2009). Just remember not to overdo paraphrasing, as this makes for a pretty awkward conversation and your partner may feel ridiculed (Weger, Castle, & Emmett, 2010).

real communicator

NAME: Dan Long
HOMETOWN: San Jose, California
OCCUPATION: Software support technician
FUN FACT: I have run several marathons.

I've got a tech job. I provide software support for an Internet service provider that allows doctors and patients to communicate in a safe and secure environment. (For instance, doctors can prescribe medication via the service provider.) The most time-consuming part of my job is talking to clients—doctors, medical educators, and patients—to help them troubleshoot problems. There are certain barriers to competent communication in these interactions: (1) I talk almost exclusively to strangers, people with whom I have no previous relationship; (2) I communicate with clients almost exclusively over the phone, missing out on nonverbal cues; and (3) I speak tech-heavy "computerese," and they often do not. Because of these barriers, it's especially important that I be an active listener.

Recently, a prestigious doctor called me. He was unable to use our software as designed. In the hopes of gauging his mood, I paid particular attention to the tone of his voice. Was it calm, tired, frustrated, confused, inquisitive, or bitter? He was frustrated, and so I responded in such a way as to let him know that his message had not only been received but empathetically understood. I said something like, "Ah, yes, new software can be really frustrating. I totally understand."

Once a relationship (however small) has been established, I must become an action-oriented listener. We had a task to accomplish—figuring out why the doctor couldn't access the software—and we needed to do so in a time-efficient manner. He's got to go save lives and stuff.

Instead of being a passive listener, I adopted a questioning technique. I asked probing questions like, "Are you using a PC or a Mac? What Internet browser are you using? Do you know how to clear cookies out? No? OK, what happens when you click on X? Do you see an error message? In the address bar, can you read me the number at the end of the URL?" Probing questions got the doctor to focus on the things that would do me, as the troubleshooter, the most good.

When we still hadn't solved the problem, I paraphrased what he'd told me. I said: "OK, you're on a PC and you're using the latest version of Internet Explorer. When you—"

"Well," he broke in, "I don't know if I'm using the *latest* version of Internet Explorer."

Aha! I helped him update the browser, he was able to access the software, and we hung up the phone. Everyone was happy. As he reached for his stethoscope, I answered the next call.

Appreciative Listening

The fourth goal of listening is enjoyment. **Appreciative listening** is used when your goal is simply to take pleasure in the sounds that you receive. Listening to music, poetry, narrations, comedy routines, plays, movies, and television shows all qualify as appreciative listening situations (Christenson, 1994). Some people find this type of listening so important that they schedule time to do it—that's why we buy tickets to concerts and other performances or tell our family members to not bother us when *America's Got Talent* is on. Appreciative listening can also help relieve stress, unclutter the mind, and refresh the senses. We can't help but wonder if this is why credit card and health insurance companies play classical music while they keep callers on hold for twenty minutes—not that it keeps most of us from being irritated. Table 6.1 illustrates ways in which you can accomplish each of the four listening goals we have discussed in this section.

● **SOMETIMES** we listen for the pure enjoyment of the sound of a jazz artist, a string quartet, or a rock band.

The Value of Listening Well

So now you know how we listen and what types of listening we do, but let's face it, we're all busy. Listening is probably a skill we can sometimes do without or short-change, right? Hardly. Listening is crucial to winning at Trivial Pursuit and running for class president, from knowing how to change a tire to knowing how to argue for a better grade or a pay raise. Put simply, listening affects more than your ability to communicate: it enables you to live a productive, satisfying, and healthy life.

Type	Description	Strategies
Informational	Listening to understand, learn, realize, or recognize	Listen for main ideas or details; take speaker's perspective; use memory effectively
Critical	Listening to judge, analyze, or evaluate	Determine speaker's goal; evaluate source of message; question logic, reasoning, and evidence of message
Empathic	Listening to provide therapy, comfort, and sympathy	Focus on speaker's perspective; give supportive feedback; show caring; demonstrate patience; avoid judgment; focus on speaker's goal
Appreciative	Listening for enjoyment of what is being presented	Remove physical and time distractions; know more about originator (author, artist, composer); explore new appreciative listening opportunities

TABLE 6.1

LISTENING GOALS

● **DAVE RIFE,** owner of fast-food franchise White Castle, poses as a new hire in his own company, listens carefully, and takes directions from a veteran employee.

Effective Listening Helps Your Career

Effective listening is greatly valued and rewarded professionally. Employers report that effective listening is related to job satisfaction, performance, and the achievement of the organization's goals (Cooper, 1997; Gray, 2010). In fact, surveys of *Fortune* 500 company personnel reveal that listening is one of the most important skills that a college graduate can possess (Wolvin & Coakley, 1991). In the professional world, employees who are good listeners are seen as alert, confident, mature, and judicious—qualities that result in professional rewards. It's important to note that employers also value employees who can listen effectively in a variety of contexts. For example, a manager might expect her assistant to listen carefully to directions on a project, but also listen for tone or points of confusion in an e-mail from a customer. Similarly, employees must listen carefully to others during teleconferences and WebEx meetings, despite potential distractions like background noise or malfunctioning equipment (Bentley, 2000).

New employees aren't the only people who need to listen well in professional situations. In order to be strong leaders, established professionals need to listen to others, make them feel heard, and respond effectively to them (Stillion Southard & Wolvin, 2009). The CBS reality series *Undercover Boss* features CEOs who go "undercover" in their companies. Unrecognized by employees, they listen more than anything—by asking questions, hearing about the reality of work life for people at all levels of the organization, and probing for insights into what works and doesn't. In most instances, the CEO returns to make positive changes in the company's operations—and improve the communication with employees as well.

Effective Listening Saves Time and Money

One of the reasons that professionals value listening skills so much is simply because good listeners save time by acting quickly and accurately on information presented to them. You comprehend more when you listen well (Rubin, Hafer, & Arata, 2000), so if you actively listen to your instructor's remarks about an upcoming exam, you can save time by studying more effectively. If you listen carefully when someone is giving you driving instructions to get from point A to point B, you'll be more relaxed and more likely to show up on time.

Good listeners can avoid costly errors: businesses lose millions of dollars each year because of listening mistakes alone (Rappaport, 2010; Steil, Summerfield, & de Mare, 1983). Repeated or duplicated tasks, missed opportunities, lost clients, botched orders, misunderstood instructions, and forgotten appointments can cost companies money—as can failing to listen to customers on an organizational level. In 2009, the makers of Tropicana orange juice changed the packaging of its products with little fanfare, causing loyal customers to deluge the company with letters and e-mails of complaint. Company officials quickly responded and reverted to the recognizable label (an orange with a straw protruding from it), but they could have avoided the costly fiasco

AND YOU?

Can you think of a time when poor listening cost you something? Have you ever missed test instructions? Missed meeting a friend or a team practice? Do you think these lapses reflect the value (or lack of value) you placed on these events?

if they had listened to their customers in the first place (Wiesenfeld, Bush, & Sikdar, 2010).

Effective Listening Creates Opportunities

Good listeners don't just avoid mistakes; they find opportunities that others might miss. A real estate agent who truly listens to what a young couple is looking for in their first home and comprehends their financial constraints is more likely to find the clients a home that truly works for them; an entrepreneur who listens to fellow diners at a popular restaurant complain that no place in town serves vegetarian fare might find an opportunity for a new business. Even writing a textbook like the one you are reading involves listening. As authors, we must listen to our peers, who help us decide what topics and scholarship to include. We must listen to the students who have reviewed our manuscript to find out what kinds of examples and issues will make communication scholarship most relevant to them. And we must listen to our editors, who help us make the material more clear and engaging.

● **HOW WILL** your real estate agent help you find your dream home if he doesn't listen to and comprehend your desire for high ceilings and hardwood floors?

Effective Listening Strengthens Relationships

Throughout this book, we note that relationships depend on good communication in order to thrive. That means that we need to be aware of our perceptions and our verbal and nonverbal messages, but it also means that we need to understand the role that listening plays in our relationships. Have you ever had a friend who just talked about himself or herself without ever allowing you to share your own thoughts or concerns? Does your roommate or a colleague send text messages or update Facebook while saying, "I'm listening"? Perhaps they're hearing, but listening seems unlikely.

In new relationships, competent listening is required for partners to learn more about each other; a failure to do this usually results in less attraction and more negative emotions (Knobloch & Solomon, 2002). As your relationships progress, listening remains a top priority. For example, you won't be inclined to continue making self-disclosures to a friend who isn't showing you involved listening behaviors. Similarly, you can significantly reduce your partner's stress in a challenging situation by letting him or her talk through difficult events while you listen actively (Lewis & Manusov, 2009).

Listening Challenges

Despite the tremendous benefits of listening well, we all fail to listen effectively at times. We may find ourselves unable to listen to material (or a speaker) that we find boring; we may have trouble focusing when we have a lot on our mind, are in a rush, or are coming down with a cold. In this section, we discuss **listening barriers**, factors that interfere with our ability to comprehend

As relationships develop (Chapter 7), communication content changes, as do listening behaviors and goals. When you were in the *initiating* and *exploratory stages* of your friendship with Michelle, you likely used informational listening to discover her hobbies. But during the *intensification stage*, critical and empathic listening likely became more important as you sought to analyze, understand, and connect on a deeper level.

information and respond appropriately. But don't despair! Listening can be improved by training, so in each section, we offer advice to overcome these barriers to become more competent listeners (Nichols, Brown, & Keller, 2006).

Environmental Factors

When the New Orleans Saints won the Superbowl in January 2010, Saints quarterback Drew Brees invited his one-year-old son down to the field to join the celebration. The stadium was noisy enough to warrant a pair of protective earmuffs to shield the toddler's ears from the cumulative and irreversible hearing loss that comes from constant exposure to loud noises (Cohen, 2010). In another stadium later that year, thousands of loud trumpets called vuvuzelas drew criticism from broadcasters, players, and fans during the 2010 World Cup in Johannesburg, South Africa (Longman, 2010).

Loud noise, such as the noise we experience at sporting events and rock concerts or when working around heavy equipment, is only one of the environmental factors that impair our ability to listen (and sometimes even hear). For example, it's usually easier to listen in one-on-one situations because groups involve more people competing for your listening ear and attention (Beatty & Payne, 1984). It can also be difficult to listen when there are distractions in your environment: the TV is on, you've got a view of the beach out of your window on a sunny day, your baby is crying, your allergies are driving you crazy, or the acoustics of a room cause the speaker's voice to echo. Similarly, some local transit systems can be as loud as a rock concert (around 120 decibels), so you may not want to listen to your mom describe her difficult work situation while sitting on the Washington, D.C., Metro (Childs, 2009). Even the temperature or air quality in a room can make it difficult to listen effectively.

If you know that environmental factors will distract you from a listening situation ahead of time, there are several things you can do to improve your attention. For example, there's a classroom on one of our campuses that is always cold, even if it's 90 degrees outside. So we warn our students to dress appropriately—freezing in a tank top is not an excuse for not listening and taking notes during a lecture! You may need to take similar steps to deal with environmental factors that would otherwise negatively impact your listening. You can choose the best time and place for a discussion, avoiding, for example, busy public places when planning for an intimate conversation or a study group discussion. And if you must attend a lecture with a lot of rowdy individuals who make it difficult to listen, try to get to the meeting early to pick a seat closer to the speaker, which will make it easier to hear and to limit the amount of competing visual stimuli. Seemingly small steps like this can boost your listening success quite a bit.

Hearing and Processing Challenges

Environmental factors can explain many situations where it is difficult to hear and therefore listen. But sometimes the difficulty lies not in the situation, but in a physical or medical issue. For example, the ability to hear does decline with age, and this hearing loss affects not only the ability to hear words but also the nonverbal aspects of speech (tone, pitch, range, and so on) (Bellis & Wilber, 2001; Villaume & Brown, 1999). Stereotypes of older adults portray them as unable to engage in normal conversation because of cognitive decline when the reality is often that they have to work harder to separate the sounds they hear (Murphy, Daneman, & Schneider, 2006). And hearing challenges are not an issue faced solely by older people; accidents, diseases, stress and anxiety, or physical differences can also cause varying degrees of hearing impairment (Roup & Chiasson, 2010).

It's important to note, however, that hearing loss (even total hearing loss) does not mean that an individual is unable to listen competently. For example, deaf individuals often speak of "listening with their eyes," and research notes that those who cannot hear physically are quite competent at decoding nonverbal behaviors such as gestures, facial expressions, and eye behaviors that can reveal a speaker's emotions (Grossman & Kegl, 2007). In addition, individuals who use American Sign Language as a primary language also listen to each other and encode and decode messages in much the same way as two friends speaking Japanese, English, French, or any other vocal language.

● **LISTENING** is not reserved for those with the ability to hear. These two friends are sharing ideas through sign language.

Many individuals who have perfect hearing also face listening challenges. *Attention deficit disorder* (ADD) can impair one's ability to focus on information and tasks, and can make listening particularly difficult. Another processing challenge is *auditory processing disorder*, a learning disability that makes it difficult for individuals to process information they hear. Individuals who have these disorders learn to employ specific strategies in order to focus on and understand spoken information: they might adjust their environment, for example, by always sitting in the front of the classroom or always studying in the quietest section of the library. They might rely more heavily on written or visual cues when trying to learn new information or make use of paraphrasing to confirm that they've received and processed messages correctly. They take great pains to focus on only one listening task at a time, because, as we'll learn in the next section, multitasking can be a formidable listening challenge even for those who don't suffer from these disorders.

Multitasking

If listening well amid environmental distractions is difficult, it can be nearly impossible when your attention is divided among many important tasks. **Multitasking**—attending to several things at once—is often considered an unavoidable part of modern life. We routinely drive, walk, cook, or tidy up while listening to music, talking on the phone, communicating on social networking sites, or watching television.

We may truly believe that we're giving fair attention to each task, but research shows that our ability to attend to more complicated chores—driving, listening to a lecture, cooking a new recipe—suffers when we multitask. That's because our ability to focus is limited—we wind up toggling our attention between various tasks, alternating from one to another, and our efficiency and accuracy decrease substantially (Wallis, 2006). And while it's true that to some degree individuals who grew up in the electronic age surrounded by television, PlayStations, and iPods can multitask better than those who grew up without such distractions, it's still largely a myth that multitasking can be done well: regardless of age or experience, the brain is limited in its ability to process information during multitasking (Wallis, 2006).

So what are realistic remedies for this listening barrier? One remedy is discipline: vow to silence your cell phone, log out of Facebook, and refrain from

COMMUNICATIONACROSSCULTURES

Listening with Your Eyes

In the city of Rochester, New York, people listen differently. Movies are shown with captions of dialogue. Telephones flash rather than just ring. That's because the city hosts the nation's largest population of deaf and hearing-impaired residents and is home to the National Technical Institute for the Deaf, part of the Rochester Institute of Technology (RIT) (York, 2006). On campus and in the surrounding city, Deaf culture mingles with the larger culture of the hearing, and listening takes on a new dimension.

Deaf culture defines itself not by hearing ability (or lack of it) but through the shared code of language. American Sign Language (ASL) is the most common signed language in North America, and it is quite distinct from spoken language. For example, ASL is not a code of nonverbal gestures that translate word for word into spoken English but rather a completely different language, rich with unique meanings and nuances (Hott & Garey, 2007; Siple, 2003).

Among the deaf, eye contact, appearance, time, and touch play key roles in understanding others. When communicating, deaf people rely more heavily on nonverbal cues than most hearing people do. This can cause confusion. Most hearing people, for example, are uncomfortable maintaining eye contact for prolonged periods of time; but for a deaf person, breaking eye contact—or failing to make it in the first place—is a sign of indifference or disinterest. Deaf people use touch to greet one another and facial expressions, body movement, and gestures to convey meaning; from their perspective, the verbal communication of the hearing can seem lifeless and dull (Siple, 2003).

In fact, the visual nature of sign language has given rise to a unique form of poetry that must be performed rather than read. And just as written poetry makes use of devices like rhyming, line division, and alliteration, signed poetry takes advantage of the visual nature of sign—for example, repeating similar hand movements and orientations to make visual "rhymes" and incorporating facial expressions and other nonverbal cues.

Source: Dirksen Bauman (2003).

THINK ABOUT THIS

❶ How can hearing people become better listeners when they communicate with deaf people? How can deaf people improve their listening skills in the hearing world?

❷ If you are able to hear, does it strike you as surprising that in Deaf culture, you might be labeled as deficient in the realm of nonverbal communication? How might this influence how you view your own communication skills?

❸ What kinds of mediated communication do both hearing and deaf people share? Can individuals use them to overcome communication barriers between hearing and deaf people?

❹ What kind of meaning might be lost if a poem born in ASL were to be translated into written form? Can a nonsigner truly appreciate the performance of a signed poem?

texting for a specified period. Another remedy is to be mindful and considerate of others. You may think it's not a big deal to send text messages during a classmate's presentation in your human communication course, but if the roles were reversed, you might worry your speech was boring or that your skills as a speaker were truly lacking (Mello, 2009; Stephens & Davis, 2009). This point goes for interpersonal interactions as well—if you're texting Rodney or playing Words with Friends with Denise while you're engaged in a face-to-face conversation with Alex, you might be sending Alex an unintended message about how much (or how little) you value his company.

Boredom and Overexcitement

Sometimes it's just hard to listen to a speaker whose voice lulls you off to sleep or whose presentation is lifeless; it can be equally hard to listen to a perfectly competent speaker who is giving a presentation on a boring topic. The truth is, when something (or someone) seems overwhelmingly dull, we can wind up daydreaming. There are so many more interesting things to think about: weekend plans, that interesting person you met at a party on Friday night, what you want to do after graduation. Even creating a mental grocery shopping list might seem more interesting than listening to a particular speaker. Nonetheless, boring information may still be important information that is worth your attention.

● **YOUR ABILITY** to accomplish tasks would undoubtedly be stretched too thin if you attempted to write a paper, browse Web sites, and carry on a phone conversation simultaneously.

On the flip side, overexcitement may also distract us from listening effectively, even if the speaker is saying something that you might normally find really engaging. If you're consumed by plans for an upcoming vacation or you're wondering how you're going to study for two midterms while writing a twenty-page paper and putting together a lab report, it can be difficult to listen to competing messages.

There are ways to improve your listening skills in situations where you are prone to boredom or overexcitement. You can be a better listener by becoming more conscious about the situation. Think about how *you* would deliver the information being discussed and how you would restructure it or give examples; in the process, you may find yourself listening more attentively and avoiding boredom. Avoid daydreaming by taking notes and relating the information to your own life examples. If you're in an interpersonal situation—and you're sick of listening to your friend Carla complain for the hundredth time about her problems with Professor Jones—you might discuss your concerns with her or try to put yourself in her shoes.

Attitudes About Listening

You probably haven't spent much time analyzing your attitudes and feelings about the act of listening (who has?). Yet sometimes our attitude is the very thing that causes us to struggle when communicating with others. Let's examine three examples here.

Talking Seems More Powerful Than Listening

In many Western societies, people tend to think that talking is powerful, so *not* talking must be less than powerful. Because we fail to value the power of listening, we tend to neglect it. Michael listens only to plan what he's going to say

WIREDFORCOMMUNICATION

THINK ABOUT THIS

Multitasking: An Attention Deficit Epidemic

Alicia is sitting in a history lecture hall, typing notes as her instructor runs through a PowerPoint presentation detailing Santa Anna's siege on the Alamo. As her IM window pops up, she takes a moment to read a note from a classmate who missed yesterday's lecture and was hoping to borrow her notes; they exchange messages before she toggles back to her notes and tunes back in to the lecture. Alicia doesn't realize it, but in the time it took her to attend to that message, she missed five minutes of the fifty-minute lecture.

For many people, modern life means spending the bulk of one's time plugged in to any number of electronic devices, from iPads to cell phones to laptops. Many people like to brag about their ability to multitask, and with the right technology, we can do six things at once. But should we?

Some experts think not. According to cognitive researchers, the human brain doesn't really multitask, it just divides its attention. That means we're never really paying attention to more than one thing at a time; we're just constantly moving between tasks. And the more tasks, the more likely we are to make mistakes (Wallis, 2006).

Recent evidence suggests that multitasking doesn't just affect our ability to focus at a specific time—it actually has lasting effects on the way we think and react even when we're determined to focus on just one thing. "The technology is rewiring our brains," notes Nora Volkow, one of the world's leading brain scientists (qtd. in Richtel, 2010, para.13). And while there is some evidence of benefits to multitasking, on the whole, those identified as multitaskers are far less adept at filtering out extraneous information in order to focus on what is important (Richtel, 2010). This important part of the listening process—selecting—suffers when we try to attend to several things at once.

Psychiatrist Edward Hallowell notes that multitasking can lead to attention deficit trait (ADT), a condition with symptoms similar to those of attention deficit disorder (ADD), including distractibility, restlessness, impulsiveness, and irritability. However, he notes that it is caused by environmental factors: a person with ADD always has symptoms, but a person with ADT is able to relax when he or she is in the setting that induces the symptoms (Steptoe, 2006). Hallowell points to those who spend the bulk of their time responding to e-mails and voice mail and being interrupted by phone calls and IMs. Technology invades their lives and leaves them little time to process their thoughts. "What your brain is best equipped to do is to think, to analyze, to dissect and create," Hallowell notes. "And if you're simply responding to bits of stimulation, you won't ever go deep" (as cited in Gilbert, 2005). So for those of us who divide our attention among various beeps, buzzes, and other inputs, it might be worth taking some time to unplug and reboot.

① What kinds of activities do you know distract you and affect your ability to listen? Are there any tasks that you feel you can do without affecting your listening?

② Do you ever listen to music while you study? How carefully are you really listening to it? Is it just background noise that you actually tune out?

③ Does it bother you when people attend to other things—checking e-mail, Web surfing, and such—when you are speaking to them?

next; he's not interested in what his wife has to say, only in making *her* listen to *him*. Katrina thinks she already knows what others will say; when her sister is speaking to her, she nods quickly and says, "Yeah, yeah, I know." Both Michael and Katrina would likely be better communicators and experience healthier relationships if they remembered that listening empowers.

A frequently recommended suggestion for listening well is simply to stop talking. Sounds simple, right? It's easier said than done; you have to adjust to a new speaking-to-listening ratio. That means you talk less and listen more, being sure to raise your awareness of your listening time. If a desire to dominate the conversation creeps up on you, just remind yourself that through the act of listening you are empowering communication partners to reveal their thoughts, insights, fears, values, and beliefs (Fletcher, 1999); you are also freeing yourself to connect, enlarge, and comprehend multiple concepts and connections (Dipper, Black, & Bryan, 2005). In the long run, you may even get more influence in relationships as people come to think you understand them, relate to them, and confirm them. As they feel more confident about your caring for them, they give *you* more influence.

Overconfidence and Laziness

Randall walked into a status meeting certain that he knew everything that was going to be said. As he confidently sat through the meeting only half listening to his colleagues tossing ideas around, his boss began asking him questions that he was unprepared to answer. The root of Randall's problem lies in overconfidence—he assumed that he didn't need to pay attention because he already knew everything. Overconfidence frequently leads to laziness—we use our high expectations of ourselves as an excuse not to prepare or plan in advance or pay attention during the communication transaction.

Listening Apprehension

You may be aware that many people suffer from public speaking anxiety. But did you know that many people also struggle with concerns about listening? **Listening apprehension** (also called *receiver apprehension*) is a state of uneasiness, anxiety, fear, or dread associated with a listening opportunity. Listening to your boss give you a reprimand about your performance, listening to someone else's personal problems, or listening to highly detailed or statistical information can trigger listening apprehension, which compromises your ability to concentrate on or remember what is said (Ayres, Wilcox, & Ayers, 1995).

Students with high listening anxiety have lower motivation to process information in the classroom, which can affect overall academic performance (Schrodt, Wheeless, & Ptacek, 2000); confident individuals usually understand information better than their less confident peers (Clark, 1989). So it is important to assess your ability to listen effectively and to spend time developing your listening confidence. What do you think about your own listening apprehension? You may have a better idea after you complete the self-assessment on page 174.

Unethical Listening Behaviors

In addition to environmental factors, hearing challenges, multitasking, boredom, overexcitement, and attitudinal factors, our own selfishness and defensiveness can come into play in a major way when listening. We may all be guilty of such

CONNECT

Believe it or not, public speakers must listen to the audience to help the audience listen to the speech. Chapter 14 describes the importance of interacting *with* the audience rather than speaking *at* your listeners: Are they yawning, looking confused, laughing, or nodding in agreement? By watching for such verbal and nonverbal cues, competent speakers adjust elements of their speaking (rate, pitch, volume, and so on) to meet the audience's needs.

behavior from time to time (Beard, 2009; Lipari, 2009). The behaviors that we discuss in this section—defensive listening, selective listening, selfish listening, hurtful listening, and psuedolistening—are all aspects of incompetent communication. They will not benefit you in any way personally or professionally. But with careful attention and the development of positive listening behaviors, they can be overcome (Gehrke, 2009).

Defensive Listening

If you've ever read the *Harry Potter* series of books or seen the movies, you know that Harry Potter can't stand Professor Snape, and Professor Snape despises Harry Potter. To some extent, the mutual dislike is earned: Snape often singles Harry out for punishment, and Harry frequently disrespects Snape. Throughout the series,

what about you?

Your Listening Apprehension

Lawrence Wheeless has developed a test that identifies listening areas that can cause apprehension. Some of these areas are listed below. Answer the following questions to get an idea of your listening apprehension level.

Score your answers to the following questions according to whether you strongly agree (1), agree (2), are undecided (3), disagree (4), or strongly disagree (5).

_____ 1. I am not afraid to listen as a member of an audience.

_____ 2. I feel relaxed when I am listening to new ideas.

_____ 3. I generally feel rattled when others are speaking to me.

_____ 4. I often feel uncomfortable when I am listening to others.

_____ 5. I often have difficulty concentrating on what is being said.

_____ 6. I look for opportunities to listen to new ideas.

_____ 7. Receiving new information makes me nervous.

_____ 8. I have no difficulty concentrating on instructions given to me.

_____ 9. People who try to change my mind make me anxious.

_____ 10. I always feel relaxed when listening to others.

Scoring: Add up your scores for items 1, 2, 6, 8, and 10. Now add up your scores for items 3, 4, 5, 7, and 9. Subtract the total of the second set of answers from the first total to get a composite score. If your final score is positive, you have a tendency toward listener apprehension; the higher the score, the more apprehension you report. If your final score is negative, you have little or no apprehension.

Source: Wheeless (1975). Adapted with permission.

their preconceived notions of one another hamper their communication. When Snape tries to teach Harry a crucial skill, Harry refuses to listen to his valuable advice and corrections. In Harry's eyes, Snape is picking on him yet again, trying to make him feel like a failure, so he simply shuts down and responds with anger. Snape, on the other hand, refuses to acknowledge any talent or hard work on Harry's part. Both characters, because of their mutual dislike and distrust, are guilty of **defensive listening**, responding with aggression and arguing with the speaker without fully listening to the message.

We've all been in a situation where a speaker or communication partner seems to be confronting us about an unpleasant topic. But defensive listeners who respond with aggressiveness and who argue before completely listening to the speaker experience more anxiety, probably because they anticipate not being effective in the listening encounter (Schrodt & Wheeless, 2001). If you find yourself listening defensively, we offer some tips to help you in Table 6.2.

● **HARRY POTTER** and Professor Snape may have their issues, but Harry's defensive listening isn't going to help him learn Occlumency.

Selective Listening

When you zero in only on bits of information that interest you, disregarding other messages or parts of messages, you are engaging in **selective listening**. Selective listening is common in situations when you are feeling defensive or insecure. For example, if you really hate working on a group project with your classmate Lara, you may only pay attention to the disagreeable or negative things that she says. If she says, "I can't make it to the meeting on Thursday at eight," you shut off, placing

TABLE 6.2

STEPS TO AVOID DEFENSIVE LISTENING

Tip	Example
Hear the speaker out	Don't rush into an argument without knowing the other person's position. Wait for the speaker to finish before constructing your own arguments.
Consider the speaker's motivations	Think of the speaker's reasons for saying what is being said. The person may be tired, ill, or frustrated. Don't take it personally.
Use nonverbal communication	Take a deep breath and smile slightly (but sincerely) at the speaker. Your disarming behavior may be enough to force the speaker to speak more reasonably.
Provide calm feedback	After the speaker finishes, repeat what you think was said and ask if you understood the message correctly. Often a speaker on the offensive will back away from an aggressive stance when confronted with an attempt at understanding.

Selective listening can also be influenced by our attributions—personal characteristics we use to explain other people's behavior. If you believe that your classmate Lara is lazy, you may listen only to messages that support your attribution. Competent communicators avoid selective listening by verifying their perceptions, seeking thoughtful explanations, and moving past first impressions in order to understand communication partners (Chapter 2).

another check in the "Lara is lazy and awful to work with" column of proof. However, you might miss the rest of Lara's message—perhaps she has a very good reason for missing the meeting, or perhaps she's suggesting that you reschedule.

Selective listening can work with positive messages and impressions as well, although it is equally unethical in such situations. Imagine that you're a manager at a small company. Four of your five employees were in place when you took your job, but you were the one who hired Micah. Since hiring well makes you look good as a manager, you might tend to focus and brag to your boss about Micah's accomplishments and the feedback from others in the organization on Micah's performance. He may well be a great employee, but it's important to listen to compliments about other employees as well, particularly when it comes time to consider promotions.

To improve our communication, particularly when we're feeling apprehensive or defensive, we must face communication messages honestly—that is, we must not avoid particular messages or close our ears to communication that's uncomfortable. Being mindful of our tendency to behave in this manner is the first step in addressing this common communication pitfall.

Selfish Listening

Selfish listeners listen for only their own needs—or even for their own unethical purposes. Essentially, a selfish listener only hears the information that he or she finds useful in achieving specific goals. For example, your colleague Lucia may seem really engaged in your discussion about some of the recent negative interactions you've had with Ryan, your significant other. However, it's possible that she's only listening to get a sense of the weaknesses in your relationship because she has a romantic interest in Ryan and wouldn't be disappointed to see the two of you end your relationship.

But selfish listening can also be **monopolistic listening**, or listening in order to control the communication interaction. We're all guilty of this to some degree—particularly when we're engaged in conflict situations. You may hear your father voicing his concerns about financially supporting you this semester (after some lackluster grades), but you may not be deeply considering his points if you're using his words to plot your own response in order to get your own way.

Hurtful Listening

Hurtful listening also focuses on the self, but it's a bit more direct—and perhaps even more unethical—than selfish listening. *Attacking* is a response to someone else's message with negative evaluations ("Well, Leon, that was a pretty stupid thing to say!"); *ambushing* is more strategic. By carefully listening, the ambusher finds weaknesses in others—things they're sensitive about—and pulls them out at strategic or embarrassing times. So if Mai cried to Scott about the fact that she failed her calculus final and Scott is later looking for a way to discredit Mai, he might say something to the effect of "I'm not sure that Mai is the right person to help us draw up a budget. Math isn't exactly her strong suit, is it, Mai?"

At other times, our listening isn't meant to be intentionally hurtful, but we can still end up offending others or being inconsiderate of their feelings. **Insensitive listening** occurs when we fail to pay attention to the emotional content of someone's message, instead taking it at face value. Your friend Adam calls to tell you that he got rejected from Duke Law School. Adam had mentioned to you that his LSAT scores made Duke a long shot, so you accept his message for what it appears to be: a factual statement about a situation. But you fail to hear the disappointment in his voice—whether or not Duke was a long shot, it was his top choice as well as a chance to be geographically closer to his partner, who lives in North Carolina. Had you paid attention to Adam's nonverbal cues, you might have known that he needed some comforting words.

Pseudolistening

When you become impatient or bored with someone's communication messages, you may find yourself engaging in **pseudolistening**—pretending to listen by nodding or saying "uh-huh" when you're really not paying attention at all. One of the many downsides of pseudolistening is that you can actually miss important information or risk offending your communication partner and damaging the relationship. Pseudolistening is a common trope in television sitcoms—when Homer Simpson nods absently (daydreaming, in fact, about food or some other inappropriate topic) even though he hasn't listened to a word his boss has said, we find it funny and perhaps a little familiar. But in real life, implying that we have listened

AND YOU?

Do you know any people who engage in the unethical behaviors described? Is it frequent behavior or a rare slip? How do these tendencies affect your interactions with those people? Do you ever find yourself engaging in such behaviors?

EVALUATINGCOMMUNICATIONETHICS

THINK ABOUT THIS

Listening When You're Sick of Hearing

You were happy to lend your friend Jamie a sympathetic ear as Jamie worked through a difficult divorce earlier this year. You were by Jamie's side when the divorce papers were filed; you went to the bank to help open up a bank account and hunted for a new apartment together. And of course, as a single person yourself, you were there to empathize as Jamie faced the prospect of heading back into the dating world. You agreed to be each other's date when attending parties with all of your coupled-up friends and made plans to check out a speed-dating party together as sort of a gag.

But now, only eight months after the divorce, Jamie is in the throes of a new romance with an attractive new coworker. You can't help but feel a bit jealous—you've been single for more than three years; it doesn't seem fair that Jamie should find love so quickly. What's worse is that Jamie insists on spending as much time as possible with this new love—often at the expense of time with you. You want to support and be happy for your friend, but you're finding it very difficult to listen to discussions about day hikes and movie nights and sports outings. You find yourself continually avoiding the subject of dating, and as a result, you notice that Jamie seems less interested in talking to you. Somewhat relieved, you start to avoid talking to Jamie at all. You're not all that surprised when Jamie suddenly asks you why you're mad. But you don't really know what to say. You know why you're avoiding your friend, but you're sort of embarrassed about your reasons. What should you say?

❶ Should you tell Jamie the truth? Is it ethical to hide your true feelings from a friend? What might happen if you just say, "I'm embarrassed to say that I'm feeling a bit jealous. I'm feeling bummed about my own love life, and I miss having you as my similarly single friend"?

❷ What are Jamie's ethical responsibilities here? Has your friend been listening to you? Should Jamie have been able to sense your sensitivity about the situation from the way you've responded?

❸ What kinds of unethical listening behaviors might be at work here? Are you avoiding? Is Jamie ambushing?

when we have not can have disastrous consequences: we miss instructions, neglect tasks that we have implied we would complete, and fail to meet the needs of others.

Listening in Context

Chances are, you've recognized bits of yourself or your friends scattered throughout this chapter. We have all, at one time or another, felt defensive, nervous, bored, or lazy and found that we were less effective listeners because of it. But you probably don't feel that way all the time. You might find yourself to be a great listener in certain situations and weak in others. That's because, like every other part of communication, our listening skills and abilities are affected by context (Bommelje, Houston, & Smither, 2003). In this section, we examine the ways in which the context of communication influences listening.

The Relational and Situational Listening Contexts

Imagine this scenario. You're a shy, introverted person, standing in a crowd of people at a party or a conference. You positively hate events like this, vastly preferring interpersonal or very small group activities. Your friend Yvonne asked you to come here, but, as usual, she is late. You've given up on going to the movies with Yvonne since it's pointless to pay $12 for a ticket when you'll miss the first half hour of the film anyway. Suddenly, Yvonne calls you on your cell phone and begins a hasty explanation: "I'm sorry I'm late but . . ." You may well hear Yvonne's excuse, but are you listening?

The situation we're in and the relationship we have with other communicators at any given time have a profound effect on our communication (as you've likely discovered in earlier chapters). When you're in a place you're unfamiliar with or when you're feeling uncomfortable with your surroundings or the formality of an event (such as a funeral, a wedding, or a professional conference), you may experience the sort of listening apprehension that we discussed earlier. And in some situations, such as a party, environmental noise can contribute to listening problems. We've all been in a situation where there are so many people talking or loud music playing that you literally have to scream to be heard, and it feels like it takes all of your energy and concentration just to make out a conversational partner's words. Clearly, such situations make communication more challenging.

The relational context is also at play in this scenario. As great a friend as Yvonne is, you perceive her chronic lateness as a sign that she doesn't value your time or friendship. So when Yvonne attempts to explain why she is late on this occasion, you hardly pay attention, offering no empathy and not thinking deeply about the message. Perhaps it's another excuse about car trouble or running into an old friend on her way to meet you, but perhaps it isn't. The only way that you'll find out is to listen actively.

The Cultural Listening Context

In various parts of the United States and abroad, you will encounter listening behaviors different from your own. As you travel or do business across the country or the world, you'll likely find it necessary to understand and adapt to listening differences.

MATT GROENING

● **WHAT MIGHT** Mr. Burns be saying here? Homer Simpson doesn't know because he's pseudolistening.

CONNECT

As you learned in Chapter 3, cultures vary in their comfort with emotional expression. Some cultures have a tendency toward *understatement* (downplaying emotion) while others favor *hyperbole* (exaggerating emotion). As a competent communicator, you must listen carefully to assess your partner's emotional state and needs based on this important cultural variation.

When you think about traits and habits that make someone a "good" listener or a "bad" listener, you're often thinking about how your culture judges listening ability. For example, indirect styles of communication, common in Eastern cultures like China and Japan, require listener-responsible communication that saves face for the speaker. So a listener would be expected not to question the speaker directly, to construct meaning and understanding from the context of the situation, and to accommodate the speaker's needs more than the listener's (Lustig & Koester, 2006). Speaker-responsible listening, common in Western cultures like the United States and Canada, is more direct; the speaker usually tells the listener what he or she wants the listener to know. The listener can ask direct questions without offending the speaker, and both speaker and listener may be assertive without threatening the relationship or making the situation uncomfortable.

● **WHEN TWO PEOPLE** from different backgrounds address each other, they must be mindful of the culturally influenced behaviors and expectations that are at play.

In addition to the actual listening behaviors themselves, *perceptions* of appropriate listening vary among cultural groups. One study of competence and listening found that U.S. Caucasians are perceived as expressive listeners who exhibit nonverbal facilitators (like nodding, saying "mmm-hmmm," and the like). Caucasians also use more questioning techniques to clarify and comprehend the speaker's message. Latinos and Asian Americans are perceived as somewhat less expressive than whites, and African Americans are perceived as the least expressive listeners among these groups (Dillon & McKenzie, 1998). If you are comfortable or aware of only the preferred listening style of your own culture, miscommunication can occur. So Jennifer, a Colombian American, speaking with Jonathan, an African American colleague, might judge Jonathan as an ineffective listener if he is less expressive than she would hope as she complains about their mutual boss. She needs to remember that culture—including gender—is at play in this situation. In traveling around the globe, you will also find that expressiveness is viewed very differently in different cultures. Whereas many Westerners consider deep feelings private (or to be shared only with intimate relational partners), other cultures, including Hindus in Fiji and the Ommura in New Guinea, do not regard private feelings as sacrosanct; they communicate a variety of emotions to others in order to build shared experiences and expressions (Brenneis, 1990). Some suggestions that can help you communicate with people of different cultures are offered in Table 6.3.

A discussion of culture would not be complete without thinking about how your concepts of masculinity and femininity affect your perceptions of listening competence. For example, men in the United States are usually discouraged from expressing intense emotions in public (Brody, 2000). This reluctance to react emotionally to information may give the appearance that men are not listening. Expectations about appropriate feminine behavior encourage women to exhibit *more* verbal and nonverbal feedback when listening, such as nodding and smiling more, and using more encouraging filler words ("Really?" "Oh, wow," "Right"). Most research indicates that an individual's role (being a parent, for example) accounts for more listening differences than the sex of the listener does (Duncan &

TABLE 6.3

TIPS FOR COMMUNICATING ACROSS CULTURES

Tactic	Explanation	Example
Recognize cultural differences	When communicating with someone from a different culture, keep in mind that factors such as country of origin, religion, gender, educational level, and socioeconomic status all play into our values and beliefs about communication. If you can, learn about the person's background, and ask questions.	If your future mother-in-law is a devout Catholic from France and you are a nonreligious person from St. Louis, you might want to learn more about French culture and Catholicism; you might ask your fiancée questions about how to get to know Mom.
Clarify behaviors as appropriate	Pay attention to the cultural needs of the listener. If you find that cultural differences are preventing good communication, tell the speaker or be silent to observe context and nonverbal behaviors.	"I don't think I'm understanding you correctly. Can you say that in another way for me, please?"
Adjust to differences	Ask more questions if necessary; ask the speaker to work with you to bridge the gap between cultural differences.	"I'm sure I'm not getting the complete picture. Can you give me an example of the problem to help me understand it better?"

Fiske, 1977; Johnston, Weaver, Watson, & Barker, 2000). Nonetheless, listening stereotypes are still powerful and make their way into entertainment and advertising at every level. In the episode "I Am Peter, Hear Me Roar," *Family Guy*'s Peter decides to get in touch with his feminine side and calls his buddy Quagmire "just to talk"—he wants to listen to what's going on with his friend and have his friend listen to him in turn. Quagmire is so uncomfortable with this situation that he slams down the phone!

Such differences are not necessarily biologically based, however. Listener behavior is not consistent in all situations. For example, in brief debates, South African men engaged in more of these supportive verbal and nonverbal cues when they addressed female audiences, indicating that situational and relational context may be more powerful than gendered expectations (Dixon & Foster, 1998).

● **THE GANG** from *Family Guy* believes that listening—and the verbal and nonverbal expressions that accompany it—is for women only!

The Technology Listening Context

Anish Patel could have walked across campus to attend his microeconomics course in person. But why bother, when the lecture is streaming live over the campus network? Instead of listening with his classmates in a crowded lecture hall, he watches on his laptop in the comfort of his own apartment (Gabriel, 2010).

Russell Hampton is both a father and the president of a book and magazine publishing unit of Walt Disney Company. When he was driving his daughter and her teenage friends to a play, he listened to their conversation about an actor in a Disney movie and tried to join in the conversation. Suddenly, the girls became very quiet. Russell could see his daughter texting in the rearview mirror and chided her for being rude and ignoring her friends. He later discovered that all three teens were texting each other—so that they could listen to one another without Russell listening to them (Holson, 2008).

As these two examples illustrate, technology can be both helpful and hurtful to the listening process. Anish Patel might listen more effectively in a classroom with the energy of live interaction where questions can be asked and notes compared, but Anish might also be able to process the lecture more effectively by rewinding and listening again to sections of the lecture without distraction. Russell Hampton might be hurt that his daughter and her friends shut him out of their conversation, but their texts give them a powerful way of listening to one another.

Listening to messages in various technological contexts requires a lot more effort than other forms of communication. For example, when you talk on the phone, you rely on verbal messages as well as vocal nonverbal messages (tone of voice, speaking rate, silences, and so on) because you lack other nonverbal cues such as body movement and eye behavior. But when you read your mom's e-mail or you text your significant other, you often lack both components.

For this reason, you must be sure to listen actively to the cues you do have at your disposal. When your friend Sheila capitalizes a word in an e-mail, she's giving emphasis to a particular point; you can show her that you've listened by making sure to address that particular point. In general, you show your communication partners that you've listened to their e-mails when you respond to all of the questions or concerns that they raised. You're not listening competently if you respond to your father's questions about when you're coming home next with an e-mail that details what you had for lunch. Similarly, you listen well when you enter a chat room and read the sequence of comments before responding (rather than blurting out a response to the first post you see).

And of course, using technology competently also involves consideration of the receiver of your message. Consider how your friend Eddie in Milwaukee would want to hear the news that you've broken up with his cousin whom you've been dating for two years: through a text message? On Twitter? Over the phone? You'll want to choose the channel that is the most effective and appropriate for the occasion.

BACK TO Stealth Listening

We started this chapter with a discussion of the role of listening in doctors' diagnoses of illness and disease. Let's consider the ways that listening skills and barriers affect the doctor-patient interaction and health care in general.

▶ Effective listening involves thoughtful and intelligent *active* interactions with patients, not just a smiling bedside manner. For doctors like Erno Daniel, active listening means engaging patients and carefully assessing what they say, and inviting them to say more, a form of informational listening. On another level, Daniel's diagnoses involve critical listening—a constant mental process of testing and refining alternate hypotheses that might explain the symptoms and findings at hand (Lawson & Daniel, 2010).

▶ It's not just the doctor who has listening responsibilities. Daniel (2008) provides worksheets to help patients inform their doctors about their symptoms and their lives (p. 273). Patients should also come prepared to ask questions—What causes are possible? What tests could give clues? What multiple processes or conditions might be at work in my case?—and carefully listen to the responses (p. 274).

▶ Listening apprehension is a huge listening barrier for many patients. Patients may be concerned or preoccupied with anxiety about their own health, fears that their concerns will sound foolish, or feelings of embarrassment or modesty during a medical exam. Such situational and environmental concerns often serve to increase listening apprehension.

THINGS TO TRY ▶ Activities

1. Describe a time when you listened well. How do you know you listened well? Where were you? Who were you with? What were your goals? Did you adapt your listening to the situational, cultural, or relational context? What can you learn from this successful listening experience to guide you in future listening challenges?

2. Practice listening with your eyes as discussed in this chapter. When you go to your next class, observe your instructor or whoever is speaking. Form an overall impression of the speaker from nonverbal cues such as body movements, eye behavior, and tone of voice. What emotions do they suggest? Do they match the verbal message being conveyed?

3. As you become a more critical listener, inquire about inconsistencies when you observe them in conversation. For example, if your friend offers you verbal and nonverbal messages that contradict each other, let him or her know. Be careful to avoid being defensive here. Instead of saying, "You're sending me mixed messages," say, "I'm confused about what you mean. You said you were happy with the decision, but you frowned and sighed at the same time."

4. Practice listening styles that are less familiar to you. Some people don't paraphrase well; others are uncomfortable being person-centered. The best way to try this out is to look back at the chapter and think about the discussions that made you feel uncomfortable ("I could never do that"). Then give it a try in a context that might benefit you. For example, if you tend to be an empathic, person-centered listener in group meetings and your meetings always run late because of it, try being a more time-centered or action-centered listener.

5. Keep a log of how you "listen" with technology. Is it easier—or more difficult—for you to select, attend, remember, understand, and respond? Compare your experiences with friends. Do some of your friends or family prefer the technology or do they value face-to-face listening more?

Now that you have finished reading this chapter, you can:

Outline the listening process and styles of listening:

➤ **Hearing** is the physiological process of perceiving sound; **listening** is the process of recognizing, understanding, and interpreting the message (p. 158).

➤ We improve listening skills by focusing on the voluntary parts of the process: **selecting**, choosing one sound over others; **attending**, focusing on the message or sound; **understanding**, making sense of the message; **remembering**, recalling information; and **responding**, giving feedback (pp. 159–160).

➤ **Active listening** involves making choices about selecting, attending, and so on, and is more competent than **passive listening** (p. 160). **Listening fidelity** is the degree to which the thoughts of the listener agree with the intentions of the source of the message following their communication (p. 160).

➤ **People-oriented listeners** listen with relationships in mind (p. 160).

➤ **Action-oriented listeners** focus on tasks (p. 160).

➤ **Content-oriented listeners** carefully evaluate what they hear (p. 161).

➤ **Time-oriented listeners** prefer information that is clear and to the point (p. 161).

➤ Most people develop multiple listening preferences (p. 161).

List the reasons why we listen:

➤ **Informational listening** is used to understand a message (p. 162).

➤ In **critical listening**, you evaluate or analyze information, evidence, ideas, or opinions, and use critical thinking (pp. 162–163).

➤ **Empathic listening** is an attempt to know how another person feels, often using **paraphrasing** to recognize and elaborate on the other's feelings (pp. 163–164).

➤ **Appreciative listening** is used when the goal is simply to appreciate the sounds, such as music (p. 165).

Identify challenges to good listening:

➤ **Listening barriers** are factors that interfere with our ability to comprehend information and respond appropriately (pp. 167–168).

➤ Allergies and crying babies are examples of environmental factors that impair our ability to listen (p. 168).

➤ Hearing loss challenges can be overcome with understanding of nonverbal behaviors (pp. 168–169). Processing challenges (for example, ADD) are faced by many who have normal hearing.

➤ **Multitasking**, attending to several things at once, limits focus on any one task (pp. 169–170).

➤ A boring speaker or topic can be hard to follow, and on the flip side, overexcitement can be distracting (p. 171).

➤ Talking may be regarded as more powerful than listening (pp. 172–173).

➤ Overconfidence may cause us not to pay careful attention during communication (p. 173).

➤ **Listening apprehension**, anxiety or dread associated with listening, may hinder concentration (p. 173).

Identify attitudinal and ethical factors that inhibit listening:

➤ **Defensive listening** is responding with aggression and arguing with the speaker, without fully listening to the message (pp. 174–175).

➤ **Selective listening** is zeroing in on bits of information that interest you, disregarding other messages or parts of messages (pp. 175–176).

➤ Selfish listeners listen for their own needs and may practice **monopolistic listening**, or listening in order to control the communication interaction (p. 176).

➤ **Insensitive listening** occurs when we fail to pay attention to the emotional content of someone's message and just take it at face value (p. 176).

➤ **Pseudolistening** is pretending to listen while not really paying attention (p. 177).

Describe how various contexts affect listening:

➤ Different situations (a crowded party, a professional conference) create different challenges (p. 178).

➤ The dynamics of the relationship between communicators can also change how you listen (p. 178).

➤ As in all aspects of communication, the cultural context affects listening behavior (pp. 178–180).

➤ It may seem that we don't listen when we communicate electronically, but technology is an important context for listening (pp. 180–181).

PART TWO

Interpersonal Communication

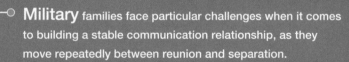
Military families face particular challenges when it comes to building a stable communication relationship, as they move repeatedly between reunion and separation.

7

Developing and Maintaining Relationships

Mary Marquez is a U.S. Army wife. She's strong; she has to be. For a good part of the year, she manages her job, two teenage sons, the house and its bills and maintenance, and her relationships, all while missing—and worrying about—her husband, Justin. When Justin is home, Mary obviously wants to spend time with him. But as soon as she's feeling comfortable and connected, he's sent off to some other part of the world and she's on her own again.

Mary and Justin are like many other families whose military-related separations put a strain on their communication and relationships. Justin and Mary often don't know when and where Justin will deploy; even when the deployment has been scheduled, dates often fluctuate. This uncertainty puts a strain on every member of the family as they struggle between the independence they must have during the deployment and the connectedness they desire when they are all together (Merolla, 2010b). Some military spouses deal with it by not dealing with it at all—that is, by engaging in arguments about other matters or by shutting down communication completely. But Mary and Justin work on their communication. They hide notes for one another around the house while he is home. When he is away, they plan times when they can connect online, and during those conversations they try to focus on "normal," routine things like talking about their days or discussing a book they are both reading. Mary said these behaviors "made it feel more routine and made it feel like he wasn't so far away" (Sahlstein, Maguire, & Timmerman, 2009, p. 431).

The distance and time zone differences can make connecting in real time difficult, though; when family members miss a connection, it can lead to hard feelings and misunderstandings. For example, one of Mary's friends described how disgruntled her husband became when she and the kids weren't at home waiting for his call.

chapter
outcomes

After you have finished reading this chapter, you will be able to

- Explain key aspects of interpersonal relationships
- Describe how and why we form relationships
- List the advantages and disadvantages of relationships
- Describe the factors that influence self-disclosure
- Outline the predictable stages of most relationships

As you learned in Chapter 1, people need to be in relationships with other people, plain and simple. After all, relationships help us meet our needs for companionship and intellectual stimulation and also help us meet our physical needs. Could Frodo of *The Lord of the Rings* have survived without the help of his friend Samwise Gamgee, who provided him with the protection and the love necessary to stave off the evil effects of the ring? Of course not! And the military families we described here are no different. They need one another; their relationships are important to their survival too.

In this chapter, we focus on **interpersonal relationships**, the interconnections and interdependence between two individuals. To understand these relationships, we need to be aware of the role communication plays in them. **Interpersonal communication** is the exchange of verbal and nonverbal messages between two people who have a relationship and are influenced by the partner's messages. You engage in interpersonal communication in your most intimate relationships—when you sit down to a heartfelt conversation with your significant other or when you catch up with your childhood best friend. But you also engage in interpersonal communication when you talk with your professor about your midterm grade and when you chat with your waiter at Chili's. Even though your relationship with your mom is probably more important to you than your relationship with a barista at Starbucks, competent communication in both relationships allows you to meet personal needs and achieve goals, whether it's support after a hard day's work or getting the right cup of coffee.

So let's take a closer look at interpersonal relationships and the communication that takes place in them by examining the types of relationships we form, why and how we do so, and what happens once we're in them.

Types of Interpersonal Relationships

Martin asks Pete, "Do you know my friend Jake?" Pete responds, "I've met him once or twice. He seems OK." In two short sentences, we gain information about relationships at play among these three men: to Martin, Jake is a friend; to Pete, he's just an acquaintance. Each of us is involved in multiple relationships, and we distinguish between them in countless ways. We have acquaintances, colleagues, friends, close friends, family members, romantic partners, virtual strangers we see all the time (like the Starbucks barista), and so on. In fact, every person has a complex **relational network** or web of relationships that connect individuals to one another. In this section, we focus on family relationships, friendships, and romantic partnerships, as well as online relationships.

Family

Who's your family? For some people, the term *family* refers to immediate relatives who live in the same household. For others, it means a more extended family that includes grandparents, aunts, uncles, and cousins. Still others use the term to describe groups of people with whom they are intimately connected and committed, even without blood or civil ties. Participants in Alcoholics Anonymous, fraternal organizations, and religious communities often consider one another to be family.

But for our purposes, a **family** is a small social group bound by ties of blood, civil contract (such as marriage, civil union, or adoption), and a commitment to care for and be responsible for one another, usually in a shared household.

Family relationships constitute the first and most basic relationships in our lives. From them, we learn communication skills and develop characteristics that affect how we interact with other people throughout our lives. TLC's reality series *Little People, Big World* revolves around the daily family life of the Roloffs, led by parents Matt and Amy, who are both dwarfs (little people) and their four children. It is moving to learn about the struggles that Matt, Amy, and their son Zach (who is also little) face living in a world where everything is built for people over four feet tall, but what's truly endearing about the show are the relationships and communication between the family members. How does Zach relate to his average-height twin, who is nearly two feet taller than he is? How do idealistic dreamer Matt and logical planner Amy communicate about important family decisions? Through all of the mishaps around their Oregon farm, the Roloffs deal with one another with openness, affection, discipline, humor, and sarcasm—qualities that reveal strong family communication (see Table 7.1 on p. 190). Moreover, Matt and Amy impart to their children the beliefs, values, and communication skills they need to face life's challenges, to feel loved and secure, and to achieve success both professionally and personally (Ducharme, Doyle, & Markiewicz, 2002). The communication of such beliefs and values is essential for enriching family life and positively developing younger family members (Canary & Dainton, 2003; Guerrero, Andersen, & Afifi, 2007; Mansson, Myers, & Turner, 2010).

Friendship

As individuals grow and interact with people outside their families, they establish new, nonfamily relationships. **Friendship** is a close and caring relationship between two people that is perceived as mutually satisfying and beneficial. Friendship benefits include emotional support, companionship, and coping with major life stressors (Rawlins, 1992, 2008). Children who form successful friendships with

As you learn about interpersonal relationships, remember the competent communication model from Chapter 1. There is no right way to communicate with friends, family, or romantic partners because competent communication considers relational, situational, and cultural contexts. You may feel comfortable sharing personal information with your father; your friend Julie may not. You and your significant other may develop a communication style that simply wouldn't work for your brother and his girlfriend.

● *LITTLE PEOPLE, BIG WORLD* depicts struggles and triumphs that any family can relate to while also representing dwarfism in mainstream media.

TABLE 7.1

FAMILY COMMUNICATION QUALITIES

Communication Standard	Examples
Openness	• Being able to talk when something is wrong • Talking about sensitive issues like sex or drugs • Sharing feelings
Structural stability	• Having at least one person in the family whom everyone listens to and obeys • Dealing with emotional issues only when everyone can handle them
Affection	• Being loving and affectionate with one another • Saying affectionate things like "I love you"
Emotional and instrumental support	• Helping each other • Being able to count on each other • Knowing support will be there
Mind reading	• Knowing what's going on with each other without asking • Understanding how the other feels without discussing it
Politeness	• Never being rude or inconsiderate • Not talking back
Discipline	• Having clear rules for family members • Knowing that there are consequences for breaking family rules
Humor or sarcasm	• Being able to tease other family members • Poking fun at each other
Regular routine interaction	• Meeting regularly to discuss things • Setting aside time to communicate
Avoidance	• Avoiding topics that are too personal • Agreeing to skirt issues that are painful

Dr. John Caughlin at the University of Illinois conducted three studies of 1,023 undergraduate students and found that people generally agree that these ten qualities constitute "excellent family communication" (2003).

others perform better academically and demonstrate fewer aggressive tendencies than those who do not (Doll, 1996; Hartup & Stevens, 1997; Newcomb & Bagwell, 1995; Rawlins, 1994; Weisz & Wood, 2005). And secure, stable friendships and family relationships serve to enhance children's ability to process communication behaviors (Dwyer et al., 2010).

Although everyone has a personal opinion as to what qualities a friend should possess, research finds agreement on six important characteristics of friendship (Pearson & Spitzberg, 1990):

▶ *Availability*—making time for one another

▶ *Caring*—feelings of concern for the happiness and well-being of each other

▶ *Honesty*—being open and truthful with each other, even if that means saying things that are hard to hear (Shuangyue & Merolla, 2006)

AND YOU?

What characteristics do you consider most important in your friendships? How do they compare to the characteristics mentioned in the research? Do your friends meet your expectations? As a friend, do you exhibit the characteristics you listed as most important?

▶ *Trust*—being honest and maintaining confidentiality

▶ *Loyalty*—maintaining relationships despite disagreements and framing differences as positive (Baxter, Foley, & Thatcher, 2008)

▶ *Empathy*—communicating the ability to feel what each other is feeling and experiencing

The extent to which you and your friend share these characteristics helps build the relational context of your relationship, as you learned in Chapter 1. The amount of trust, loyalty, honesty, and other characteristics that you experience together affects you as you construct and decode messages.

Romantic Relationships

What ideas, thoughts, and feelings come to mind when you think about romantic relationships? Do you think of romantic dinners, jealousy, butterflies in your stomach? Perhaps you think about sex or about commitment and love (Tierney, 2007).

Most people associate love with romantic relationships. But *love* can be used to describe feelings other than romantic ones, including our feelings for our families, friends, pets, or anything that evokes strong feelings of like or appreciation (as in "I love the Philadelphia Eagles" or "I love the seven-layer burrito at Taco Bell"). But we typically define **love** within the context of relationships, as a deep affection for and attachment to another person involving emotional ties, with varying degrees of passion, commitment, and **intimacy**, or closeness and understanding of a relational partner (Sternberg, 1988). And there are many types of love that can characterize different relationships—or even the same relationship at different times. For example, the love between Anna and Mario, married for fifty-seven years, is probably not exactly the same as it was when they were first married. Studies involving hundreds of people revealed six categories of love: *eros* (erotic, sexual love), *ludus* (playful, casual love), *storge* (love that lacks passion), *pragma* (committed, practical love), *mania* (intense, romantic love), and *agape* (selfless, romantic love) (Hendrick & Hendrick, 1992; Lee, 1973). These types of love are explained in detail in Table 7.2. Some relationships may be characterized by only one of these types of love, while others may move through two or more types of love over the course of time.

The complexities of romantic love can be astounding, but one thing is clear: the desire to attain it is as universal as it is timeless. In fact, the value of relationships and the characteristics that comprise love and commitment between two people are fairly consistent regardless of culture, though in countries where marriage is voluntary and divorce is accessible, there are more positive associations with marriage than in countries where less freedom exists (Fowers, Fışıloğlu, & Procacci, 2008). Studies also show that relational harmony has both physical and psychological benefits, as you can see in Figure 7.1 (Parker-Pope, 2010a). Same-sex couples in long-term,

● **OPRAH WINFREY AND GALE KING'S** decades-long friendship illustrates the benefits and joys that can result from a close, caring relationship.

One of the best ways to react with empathy is through *empathic listening* (Chapter 6). By paraphrasing your friend's words and using caring facial expressions and body movements (Chapter 5), you encourage your friend to share what's on his mind—even if you have never had the experience that he's describing.

TYPES OF LOVE

Type	Description	Explanation
Eros	Beauty and sexuality	Sex is the most important aspect of erotic love. This type of relationship is quite intense, both emotionally and physically. The focus is on beauty and attractiveness.
Ludus	Entertainment and excitement	*Ludus* means "play" in Latin, and the ludic lover views love as a game. Ludic love does not require great commitment.
Storge	Peacefulness and slowness	*Storge* is a type of love that lacks passion and excitement. Storgic lovers often share common interests and activities but rarely disclose any feelings about their relationship.
Pragma	Deed, task, work	In Greek, *pragma* means "life work." Pragmatic lovers are extremely logical and practical. They want a long-term relationship with an individual who shares their goals in life.
Mania	Elation and depression	This is the love that is often referred to as "romantic love." It exhibits extreme feelings and is full of excitement and intensity, but it reaches a peak and then quickly fades away.
Agape	Compassion and selflessness	In this type of love, the individual gives willingly and expects nothing in return. This type of lover can care for others without close ties; a deep relationship is not necessary for agapic love to develop.

FIGURE 7.1

EFFECTS OF RELATIONAL HARMONY Drawing on research from Parker-Pope (2010a) on marital discord, this figure represents some of the benefits that happy relationships might expect.

(*Source*: Parker-Pope, 2010a.)

Psychological Health
Fewer mood swings
Less risk of depression
Lowered levels of stress
  hormones

Physical Health
Lowered risk of diseases
  like diabetes and heart
  disease

Healing
Stronger immune system
  and quicker healing

● **ROMANTIC COUPLES,** regardless of sexual orientation, age, race, or ethnicity, all enjoy similar benefits of being in a relationship: intimacy and commitment.

committed relationships share the same benefits of meaningful commitment (such as life satisfaction and general well-being) as other romantic couples (Kurdek, 1989; Lipman, 1986), and cohabiting unmarried couples enjoy greater well-being than single people (though not as much as married couples) (Brown, 2000; Horwitz & White, 1998).

Perceptions of love and romance are also somewhat consistent across cultures: one study found that among Americans, Chinese, Japanese, and Koreans, differences in notions of love were not pronounced, and respondents from all four countries reported that happiness and warmth were associated with love (Kline, Horton, & Zhang, 2005).

Online Relationships

Holly and Delia's friendship began long before they met face to face. As regular readers of a social commentary journal, the two women began posting in the journal's chat room. Over time, they developed a friendly conversation that led to direct texting correspondence. When Holly found herself traveling on business to Delia's hometown of Phoenix, the two finally met.

For years, online relationships were thought to be rather impersonal, lacking the richness of nonverbal cues found in face-to-face relationships (Tidwell & Walther, 2002). But Joe Walther (1996) found that mediated communicators often took advantage of the lack of some nonverbal cues to gain greater control over both their messages and their presentation of self. His **social information processing theory** (SIP) (1996; Walther & Parks, 2002) argues that communicators use unique language and stylistic cues in their online messages to develop relationships that are just as close as those that grow from face-to-face content—but using text takes time, so it takes longer to become intimate. Online communicators often even develop what Walther (1996) calls **hyperpersonal communication**, communication that is even *more* personal and intimate than face-to-face interaction. Freed from the less-controllable nonverbal cues (such as personal appearance or nervous fidgeting), online communicators can carefully craft their messages and cultivate idealized perceptions of each other (see Walther & Ramirez, 2009). Indeed, relational partners often feel less constrained in the online environment (Caplan, 2001). As we saw with Holly and Delia above, they can develop rich and meaningful relationships both

WIREDFORCOMMUNICATION

Electronic Romance: Still Romantic?

Ashton Kutcher likes to flirt with his wife, Demi Moore, electronically. He texts her at parties. He posts about her on Facebook. He is a prolific Twitterer, frequently professing his love for her in 140 characters or less for his more than six million followers. "There's something fun about sharing secrets with your date while in the company of others," Kutcher says, noting that he thinks of texting as the modern-day equivalent of whispering in a loved one's ear. And he likens posts on Facebook and Twitter to public proclamations of love, like sending flowers to the office. "You are declaring your love for everyone to see. Who doesn't like to be publicly adored?" (Kutcher, 2010, para. 5–6).

There's no denying that electronic communication is an essential part of modern romance. Many couples first meet online, through chat rooms or dating sites, and their initial explorations of the relationship often occur through written words, electronically transmitted. Some people worry that in the process, couples are neglecting romance or that they are presenting filtered versions of themselves, developing different—if not necessarily false—personas through carefully crafted and thoroughly edited witticisms sent via electronic means.

Self-disclosure and uncertainty reduction are crucial to the formation of romantic relationships, and clearly the degree to which we engage in these practices is affected by whether we communicate face to face or through mediated channels. We are generally suspicious of information posted on dating sites, but once we are in relationships our mediated communication tends to be more intimate and direct than our nonmediated communication (Tidwell & Walther, 2002). Studies have shown that commitment and involvement tend to be higher in "real space" relationships than in relationships that exist entirely in cyberspace (Cornwell & Lundgren, 2001).

So, while it's possible to begin and explore new relationships through mediated channels, and mediated communication can play a role in maintaining relationships once they are established, it's clear that meaningful relationships require some real-world contact. Even Kutcher (2010) notes that no amount of electronic communication can replace face-to-face interaction: "The reality is that we communicate with every part of our being and there are times when we must use it all" (para. 7).

THINK ABOUT THIS

❶ How are romantic texts, e-mails, and posts different from the celebrated love letters of the Victorian era? How are they the same? Do they shape romantic relationships in different ways?

❷ What are the risks and rewards of self-disclosing through mediated communication versus face to face? Do the risks and rewards change as the relationship develops?

❸ If you were to create a profile for yourself on a dating site, how carefully would you construct it? If you were reading another person's profile as a prospective partner, how carefully would you critique it?

online and off (Anderson & Emmers-Sommer, 2006; Antheunis, Valkenburg, & Peter, 2010; Parks & Roberts, 1998; Pauley & Emmers-Sommer, 2007).

In a similar manner, romances can also bud and be maintained through the use of electronic media. Many couples today first "meet" online through a dating site like Match.com or eHarmony, and their initial interactions are entirely electronic; only after communicating via site interfaces, e-mail, and perhaps phone calls and texts do they eventually meet face to face. Established couples maintain long-distance relationships by using e-mail, video chat, texts, Facebook, and phone calls to communicate feelings. As with friend relationships, such couples tend to communicate greater intimacy than geographically close partners; they are more likely to avoid conflict and problematic topics when using these media (Stafford, 2010). On the other hand, their online communication may avoid the very communication behaviors that are necessary to manage the future of the relationship face to face.

In all types of relationships, online communication enables us to maintain intimacy with others over great distances. Sharing photos, videos, and stories on Facebook, Twitter, or personal blogs allows us to share our lives with family and friends in other states and countries. And regular texting, video chats, phone calls, and e-mail messages keep partners close and aware of each other's lives (Bergen, 2010; Maguire, 2007; Maguire & Kinney, 2010; Mansson, Myers, & Turner, 2010; Merolla, 2010a; Stafford, 2005). So where once a group graduating from college or leaving the military would scatter around the country or region and gradually lose touch, today these individuals can much more easily remain parts of one another's daily lives if they choose to make use of all or some of the available media.

Other online relationships include online communication that is merely part of the larger relationship. For example, work colleagues frequently e-mail each other or video chat throughout the day. However, they still see each other in the hallways, in the cafeteria, or even at regional meetings where they communicate face to face. In fact, some married and cohabiting couples report that they will use computer-mediated communication to discuss their conflicts, even though they could handle it face to face, because it helps them remain less emotionally involved and defensive (Quenqua, 2010). Perhaps this is because e-mail or Facebook messages do not require immediate responses, allowing the communication partners time to formulate appropriate and thoughtful messages.

Why We Form Relationships

We've already established that romantic relationships are a timeless and universal desire. But what about other types of relationships like those you have with friends, colleagues, or family members? You might expect that collectivist cultures (like Japanese culture) would place more importance on relationships than fiercely individualistic cultures like we find in the United States. But research fails to demonstrate large differences between these culture types, revealing instead that individuals in all cultures value their relationships (Diener & Diener, 1995; Endo, Heine, & Lehman, 2000; Landsford, Antonucci, Akiyama, & Takahashi, 2005). In this section, we examine why everyone forms relationships and which factors influence the formation of particular relationships.

AND YOU?

Do you have any relationships that exist strictly online? Do you consider these relationships different from other ones in your life? Are they more intimate or less?

Functions of Relationships

In U.S. prisons today, more than twenty-five thousand inmates are serving their time in solitary confinement—removed from the general prison population, isolated in small cells with little human contact (Sullivan, 2006). It's a measure that prison officials feel is necessary to maintain order, but some activists worry about the harshness of this form of punishment. They hold that, since human beings form and maintain relationships in order to satisfy basic human needs—to provide companionship, to provide stimulation, and to meet goals—it is cruel to deny those basic needs (Ramirez, Sunnafrank, & Goei, 2010).

Companionship

Humans feel a natural need for companionship, and we all long for **inclusion**—to involve others in our lives and to be involved in the lives of others. Thus loneliness can be a real motivation—in some cases, the primary motivation—behind some people's desire for a relationship. In fact, psychological problems such as anxiety, stress, depression, alcoholism, drug abuse, and poor health have all been tied to loneliness (Canary & Spitzberg, 1993; Segrin & Passalacqua, 2010). Depriving prisoners of companionship may be an effective form of punishment, but it may also be damaging to them on a psychological level, dashing any hopes for eventual rehabilitation.

Stimulation

People have a need for intellectual, emotional, and physical stimulation (Krcmar & Greene, 1999; Rubin, Perse, & Powell, 1985). Nobody enjoys being bored! So we seek out diversions: watching TV or listening to music. But interaction with another person provides a unique kind of stimulation because it occurs on a personal level and frequently provides multiple types of stimulation at once. In fact, the emotional communication we receive when our partners are involved with us contributes to our relational satisfaction (Guerrero, Farinelli, & McEwan, 2009).

Consider some of the communication relationships you have with various people over the course of a day. You might chat with your roommates or your family in the morning about the fact that you're nervous about an upcoming exam. You see your professor at office hours to share an interesting story that you think relates to the class. You check up on your old high school buddies on Facebook to see who complains the most about the workload at their universities. And then you meet up with your significant other, who greets you with a warm hug after a long day. It's also possible, of course, for you to find multiple forms of stimulation in one person.

These innate needs for stimulation are what cause many people to feel that solitary confinement is unethical and immoral. Senator John McCain (2008), recalling the more than five years he spent as a prisoner of war in Vietnam, noted: "As far as this business of solitary confinement goes—the most important thing for survival is communication with someone, even if it's only a wave or a wink, a tap on the wall, or to have a guy put his thumb up. It makes all the difference" (para. 1).

Achieving Goals

Some people enter into relationships to achieve particular goals. Sometimes the goal is simply satisfying the needs we have discussed earlier: to alleviate loneli-

● **SENATOR JOHN MCCAIN** cites communication with fellow prisoners of war, even if fleeting, as one of the factors that helped him survive solitary confinement in Vietnam.

ness, for example, or to provide stimulation. Other goals are more practical: if you have dreamed all your life about working in finance, you might seek relationships with influential people in that field through networking via your college alumni group or through an internship.

Often your initial motivation for developing a relationship with a particular individual is to see what that person can do for you or how he or she can help you. This is the argument that is put forward by those who feel that solitary confinement is justified. When particularly dangerous prisoners are kept in isolation, they are unable to form relationships that might help them to accomplish dangerous goals (such as gang memberships or terrorist networking) (Sullivan, 2006).

Interpersonal Attraction

Hollywood movies often deal with troubled relationships and deceiving relationships, but the movie *Julie and Julia* is different. While the movie revolves around a young blogger attempting to find purpose in her life by cooking her way through Julia Child's famous cookbook, it plays against the reality of Child's life: her love of cooking and her marriage to Paul Child is the refreshing background against which everything else happens (Parker-Pope, 2010b). The film depicts not only the exciting beginning of relationships, but also the possibility of happy, easy, fun, interesting relationships in which people can remain attracted to one another for a lifetime.

As discussed previously, we seek relationships to meet basic needs for companionship, stimulation, and goal achievement. But our reasons for forming specific relationships are as individual and complex as we are and are rooted in our unique needs and motivations, which develop and change over the course of our lives (Westmyer, DiCioccio, & Rubin, 1998). Let's turn to the proximity, physical attraction, and similarity influences on our likelihood of establishing particular relationships.

Proximity

As practical and unromantic as it sounds, one of the first criteria of relationship formation is simple **proximity**, or nearness. Think about how many of your friends you got to know because they sat next to you in elementary school, competed with you on the swim team, lived on the same dorm floor, or worked with you at Starbucks. Proximity is not just something we need in order to meet other people—it's what enables us to interact in ways that form and develop relationships.

Physical proximity was once the most important factor in determining and maintaining relationships. You were unlikely to ever meet someone who did not live nearby; and if you were to move away from a neighborhood, switch schools, or change jobs, you would likely lose touch with old friends and eventually make new friends in your new surroundings. But as noted earlier, modern technology allows us to redefine proximity: we have physical proximity with those whom are physically near to us, but we have virtual proximity with those whom we are able to interact regularly through mediated channels, even if they are physically quite far away. Nonetheless, if persons are not in physical

AND YOU?

Do you rely on different relational partners for companionship, stimulation, or goal achievement? Do you have some relationships that provide all three functions?

● *JULIE AND JULIA'S* depiction of Julia Child's supportive and stimulating marriage to husband Paul is a look at the best of what interpersonal attraction can become: deep, lifelong companionship.

proximity and fail to establish and maintain virtual proximity—for example, if they avoid social networking or don't have access to a computer—the chances of forming or maintaining long-distance relationships dwindle.

Physical Attraction

While culture plays a powerful role in our ideas about physical attraction (Chapter 3), it's important to remember that we all have schemas about attractiveness (Chapter 2). So while you might find Jordan very attractive, your friend Cameron might not because Jordan reminds her of a previous awful romantic partner or because Jordan is the spitting image of Cameron's brother.

If you've ever watched a makeover show like *What Not to Wear* or *The Biggest Loser*, you've no doubt seen at least one client or contestant who expressed a belief that an improved physical appearance would enhance his or her prospects for love and career success. And as you've learned in earlier chapters, your physical appearance does indeed play an important role in attracting others, especially in the very early stages of a relationship, when first impressions are formed. People who are considered beautiful or attractive are often perceived as kinder, warmer, more intelligent, and more honest than unattractive people, and they have earlier opportunities for dating and marriage (Canary, Cody, & Manusov, 2008).

But before you wonder if your social worth is based solely on your physical attractiveness, remember two things. First, beauty is largely in the eye of the beholder, and individual tastes vary due to a multitude of factors too numerous to discuss in this chapter. Beauty is also a concept that changes frequently based on cultural standards. For example, among the Padaung tribe of Southeast Asia, women wrap rings around their necks to push down their collarbones and upper ribs, giving the illusion of extremely long necks. The Padaung consider a long neck a sign of beauty and wealth; Western standards of beauty are not the same. In addition, our communication has a large impact on perceptions of beauty. For example, Levinger (as cited in Canary, Cody, & Manusov, 2008) notes that "initial impressions of a beautiful person are outweighed by subsequent interaction" with the person and that "an ugly person may gradually or suddenly become attractive for reasons other than a change in physical appearance" (p. 250). So your ability to use verbal and nonverbal messages appropriately and effectively probably has a lot more to do with your attractiveness than the perfection of your smile or the size of your jeans.

Similarity

The notion that "opposites attract" is so common in popular culture that many people take it as a simple, undeniable truth. But despite the popularity of the concept (and not to offend any of you romantics out there), research shows that our attraction to others is often based on the degree of *similarity* we have with another person, whether through shared hobbies, personality traits, backgrounds, appearance, attitudes, or values (Gonzaga, Campos, & Bradbury, 2007). In short, people look for (and tend to be happiest with) others who are, in one way or another, like themselves. For example, consider close friends Liza and Cheryl. Liza is an African American student from Denver, a literature major, and a tomboy who lives and dies with the Broncos. Cheryl is a white student from Boston, majoring in engineering; she hates sports but follows fashion and rarely steps out of her dorm room without her hair and makeup done. To an outsider, they seem like a mismatched pair. But ask either of them what they have in common, and they'll roll off a list of similarities: both grew up in urban neighborhoods, attended all-girl Catholic high schools, love indie rock, and take great pride in being able to quote J. R. R. Tolkien on cue. So long as the relational partners feel that they have much in common, as Liza and Cheryl do, they feel similar and attracted to one another.

Communication researchers have several ideas to explain how the degree of similarity works in relationships: attraction-similarity, matching, and genetic similarity (Amodio & Showers, 2005; Berscheid, 1985; Byrne, 1971; Fehr, 2001; Morry, 2005; Rushton, 1990). The **attraction-similarity hypothesis** suggests that the extent to which we project ourselves onto another person is the direct result of the attraction we feel for that person. Greater attraction to an individual leads to perceptions of greater similarity. The **matching hypothesis** also deals with attraction, positing that we seek relationships with others who have comparable levels of attractiveness. Finally, the **genetic-similarity hypothesis** argues that two individuals who hail from the same ethnic group are more genetically similar than two individuals from different ethnic groups. The impact of the hypothesis is that we tend to help, favor, and form relationships with people from our own ethnic groups (Rushton, 1980). Nonetheless, physical and social attraction coupled with more societal acceptance is contributing to more pervasive intercultural relationships (Balaji & Worawongs, 2010; McClintock, 2010). And as people from various cultures interact more and more, they have opportunities to practice relational skills (like self-disclosure and empathic listening) and see similarities in each other (Jin & Oh, 2010).

Managing Relationship Dynamics

When it comes to relationship advice, you don't need to look far for what seems like "expertise." The self-help aisles at every bookstore (and the headlines on many magazines) are brimming with advice on managing and maintaining healthy relationships. While Dr. Phil proffers advice to his television audiences and Candace Bushnell (the real-life counterpart of *Sex and the City*'s Carrie Bradshaw) offers some interesting insights and advice, communication scholars explore the way we manage relationships in a far more scientific way. In this section, we explore the dynamics of relationships on the assumption that our connections to others are constantly changing, growing, and evolving throughout our lives (Conville, 1991; John-Steiner, 1997; Knapp & Vangelisti, 2008).

Costs and Rewards

Every relationship has advantages and disadvantages for the parties involved. A close friendship may offer companionship and intimacy, but you will also need to accept your friend's negative personality characteristics and invest time in working through difficult situations together. **Social exchange theory** explains this process of balancing the advantages and disadvantages of a relationship (Cook, 1987). Relationships begin, grow, and deteriorate based on an exchange of rewards and costs.

Rewards are the elements of a relationship that you feel good about—things about the person or your relationship that benefit you in some way. There are *extrinsic rewards*, which are those external advantages you gain from association with another person (such as social status or professional connections); *instrumental rewards*, which are the resources and favors that partners give to one another (for example, living together to save on rent and utilities); and *intrinsic*

what about you?

Determining Your Own Costs and Rewards

Consider the following list of traits and behaviors, and decide which you consider rewards and which you consider costs in a romantic relationship. Write R1 next to rewards that you feel you must have from your partner and R2 next to those you see as less important. Write C1 next to costs that you simply couldn't tolerate from your partner and C2 next to costs that you could live with.

_____ Laughs at my jokes

_____ Is affectionate

_____ Is physically attractive

_____ Fits in with my friends

_____ Fits in with my family

_____ Makes inappropriate jokes or comments

_____ Dislikes sharing emotions

_____ Ignores my feelings

_____ Is career-oriented

_____ Wears clothes I dislike

_____ Has views about religion different from mine

_____ Has views about children similar to mine

_____ Has an exciting personality

_____ Overlooks my shortcomings

_____ Has annoying friends

_____ Shares similar dreams for the future

_____ Is likely to be financially successful

_____ Enjoys very different hobbies and activities

_____ Comes from a close-knit family

_____ Is of a different race or from a different culture

There is no official scale to help you grade this self-assessment; its purpose is to help you clarify your goals and desires for a relationship. Now think of a romantic relationship that you have been in or are currently in. How well does your partner meet your expectations regarding costs and rewards? Just for fun, retake the quiz with friendship rather than romance in mind, and see whether or not your evaluation of rewards and costs changes.

rewards, which are the personally satisfying rewards that result from an exchange of intimacy (for instance, intellectual stimulation or feelings of safety) (Rempel, Holmes, & Zanna, 1985). **Costs**, by contrast, are the things that upset or annoy you, cause you stress, or damage your own self-image or lifestyle. If you find your relationship too costly (for example, there is a lot of conflict, jealousy, or infidelity), you may decide to engage in negative behaviors or end the relationship (Dainton & Gross, 2008; Guerrero, La Valley, & Farinelli, 2008).

The social exchange of costs and benefits is inherently complicated. You might wonder, for example, why *The Good Wife*'s Alicia Florrick (or any of the real-world political wives who inspired the character) would stand by her husband after he humiliated her with an affair that became public. But the benefits of her marriage (including the love and the history she shares with her husband and the stability the marriage provides for her children) might outweigh the costs (such as her personal humiliation or her subsequent distrust of her husband).

Reducing Uncertainty

We begin to weigh the costs and rewards involved in a relationship at its beginning stages. Early in a relationship, uncertainty creates excitement at the prospect of a new friendship to enjoy or romance to explore. But uncertainty is uncomfortable. That's why we need to use a variety of techniques to get to know one another.

According to **uncertainty reduction theory**, when two people meet, their main focus is on decreasing the uncertainty about each other (Berger & Calabrese, 1975). The less sure you are of the person's qualities, the way the person will behave, or what will happen, the higher the degree of uncertainty. Thus, reducing uncertainty increases your ability to predict that person's behavior. As two people—college roommates, coworkers, romantic partners—reduce uncertainty between them, they uncover similarities, become better at predicting what the other will do or say, and thus develop more comfort with continuing the relationship.

In order to reduce uncertainty and increase the likelihood of a closer relationship, you must obtain information about your new relational partner. If you're a fan of the *Twilight* series, you know that upon first noticing each other at school, Edward and Bella each used several strategies to find out more information about the other. Bella asked her classmates about Edward; she watched how he behaved in the halls and made observations about how he presented himself. Eventually, she questioned him directly. Edward, finding his ability to read minds useless on Bella, was forced to employ similar strategies. And, unless you too can read minds, you've likely employed those same strategies yourself. Depending on the situation, three types of strategies may work well: passive strategies, active strategies, and interactive strategies.

Passive Strategies

Most college students who live on campus are faced with the somewhat awkward prospect of sharing a small space with a complete stranger. The first thing Shawna did when she received word about her new roommate, Ramona, was

● *THE GOOD WIFE*'S **ALICIA FLORRICK** must carefully weigh the costs and benefits of remaining with her husband after discovering his affair and enduring a public scandal.

It's important to reduce uncertainty in all communication contexts. For example, in Chapter 12 we discuss audience analysis, which allows you to learn about the people who will listen to your speech. By understanding your audience's expectations, learning about their opinions of your topic, and carefully considering their demographics, you can reduce uncertainty and determine the most effective way to reach them.

to enter her name and hometown into Google. She quickly found Ramona's public profile on Facebook and learned that she is a concert pianist and an avid knitter who sometimes sells her creations through Etsy.com (see Antheunis, Valkenburg, & Peter, 2010).

Shawna engaged in a passive uncertainty reduction strategy. **Passive strategies** involve observing others in communication situations without actually interacting with them. Often, you may also analyze their reactions to others familiar to you when you believe they are not under a lot of pressure to conform to social roles (when you think you get an "honest read" of them). Without Ramona knowing it, Shawna had already found out quite a bit about her. Social networking allows us to monitor others with relative ease, but we use passive strategies in other, unmediated ways as well whenever we observe others going about their day-to-day business as we try to get a sense of what they are like.

Active Strategies

Active strategies let you obtain information about a person more directly, by seeking information from a third party. For example, Shawna may discover (via Facebook) that she and Ramona have one friend in common. In that case, Shawna might contact this individual to see how much she knows about Ramona. Does she party a lot? Does she like to keep the room fairly neat? Does she snore?

Active strategies can be particularly useful when the information you are seeking could be potentially awkward for a new relationship. For example, Shawna might wonder if Ramona will be tolerant of the fact that she would be uncomfortable having significant others spend the night in their dorm room. Thus, she might chat with the mutual friend to get a sense of how open Ramona might be to this arrangement in order to be prepared to discuss it with Ramona when they arrive on campus.

Interactive Strategies

Sometimes you will need to find out important information about a relational partner via **interactive strategies**, or speaking directly with them rather than observing them passively or asking others for information. When they "meet" for the first time (be it on Facebook, in person, or via phone or e-mail), Shawna might ask Ramona what kind of music she likes, what major she is pursuing, and why she chose this particular school. Although direct questioning is helpful in reducing uncertainty, it also entails risks. If you ask questions that are perceived as too forward or inappropriate (for example, "What are your religious beliefs?"), you might do more harm than good.

Dialectical Tensions

Weighing costs against benefits and reducing uncertainty are not the only challenges we face in developing relationships. In any relationship, it is common to experience contradictions or opposing feelings about your relational partner and about the relationship itself (Baxter & Erbert, 1999; Pawlowski, 1998). When a love relationship becomes serious, for example, one or both partners might find themselves mourning their old, single lifestyle, despite the benefits of commitment.

Relational dialectics theory holds that **dialectical tensions** are contradictory feelings that tug at us in every relationship. These tensions can be external (between the partners and the people they interact with) or internal (within their relationship). Many types of dialectical tensions are possible, but we focus on three internal tensions that dominate research: *autonomy* versus *connection, openness* versus *closedness,* and *predictability* versus *novelty* (Baxter & Simon, 1993). Note that dialectics exist along a continuum; they are not all-or-nothing trade-offs or alternatives but rather ranges of options that need to be continually negotiated and adjusted (Baxter, Braithwaite, Bryant, & Wagner, 2004). Also, these tensions are natural and normal—experiencing them does not indicate that your relationship is falling apart!

Autonomy Versus Connection

Teresa and Marie are as close as sisters can be. Identical twins, they have always done everything together—from their first breaths of air right on through their college educations. As they grew older, loosening these bonds was a real struggle. Marie remembers bursting into tears at her bridal shower and explaining, "It's just that I've never had a party all to myself before." (See Hazel, Wongprasert, & Ayres, 2006.)

In all close personal relationships—family connections, romantic relationships, and friendships—there is a tension between independence (autonomy) and dependence (connection). In other words, we struggle because we want to be our own person while also being a part of something else: a couple, a family, or a group. It's a tension that can result in hurt feelings. Attempts to express autonomy can be easily misunderstood—children's attempts to express their own identities are often seen as acts of rebellion or defiance, while romantic partners risk alienating their loved ones when they pursue certain interests or activities alone. On the other hand, we can be seen as nagging when we try to force connectedness on our relational partner: if we drag our partners off to yoga class against their wills or to a sporting event in which they have no interest, we're more likely to alienate them than to bring them closer.

Openness Versus Closedness

Every superhero from Batman to Superman knows about this tension. To become close, individuals must share information with their relational partners. However, by disclosing information, they reveal a part of their private selves that then becomes vulnerable. The tension comes as partners strive to find a balance between sharing information (openness) and a desire to keep some things private (closedness). Chuck Bartowski, on the spy comedy *Chuck,* wants to maintain a close relationship with his sister, Ellie, but he can't tell her about his secret life. While Chuck is out saving the world, Ellie worries that he's not living up to his potential, that he's unhappy and unfulfilled, wasting his technical skills and intellect working at a local electronics chain store. The tension between Chuck's duty to his country and duty to his family take a toll on his relationship with Ellie.

Without the excuses of double lives and national security, most people need to disclose some private information to those with whom they have relationships in order to facilitate a perception of involvement and deep understanding. Even when we take into account cultural differences (see Chapter 3), relational intimacy is consistently advanced by self-disclosure (as we develop more fully below) (Chen & Nakazawa, 2009). But it is not always a good idea to reveal to your partner every thought that comes to your mind. Contrary to the notion that there should be "no secrets between us," relational dialectics researchers argue that much information

● **THREE'S A CROWD** (sometimes). Perhaps no familial relationship plays out the delicate balance between autonomy and connection as clearly as that of multiple-birth siblings.

AND YOU?
Consider your relationship with your oldest friend or with a close family member. Evaluate the ways in which dialectical tensions have manifested themselves in that relationship over the years. Have these tensions shifted over time? Is there one particular tension that continues to crop up?

● **CLAIRE AND PHIL FOSTER** love each other, but they're a little bored with their regular routine, which leads them to shake things up—with hilarious consequences—in *Date Night*.

might be better left unsaid. The comparison you make in your mind between your current romantic partner and an attractive celebrity is a good example.

Predictability Versus Novelty

Which is more important to you, safety and security or excitement and novelty? This third dialectical tension assumes that most people have a simultaneous need for stability through predictable relational interaction as well as a need for new and exciting experiences in personal relationships. On the one hand, partners seek daily routines and stable patterns of interaction: Colin and Casey, for example, enjoy the comfort of their evening routine of dinner and television, as well as their usual Friday night at their favorite diner. At the same time, every relationship needs some degree of spontaneity and novelty. This is why Colin and Casey have made plans to travel to Japan next summer and why they find enjoyment in working together on odd projects—such as building their own computer or learning to cook Thai food—that shake up their routine.

Self-Disclosure and Interpersonal Relationships

Do you remember Angelica from Chapter 2 (p. 56)? In case you've forgotten her, she's in debt over her head because of the lifestyle she leads (expensive vacations, a new car, a nice apartment, and so on). When she divulges her personal financial mishaps to a friend, she is self-disclosing, revealing very personal information. As you've likely experienced in your own life, self-disclosure has a powerful impact on the development of interpersonal relationships (Samter, 2003). The process of choosing what information to disclose to others and when has long fascinated communication researchers and scholars. In the sections that follow, we look at the ways in which we choose to divulge or withhold personal information and how those decisions affect relationships.

Social Penetration Theory

In many relationships, a primary goal is to increase intimacy, or relational closeness. **Social penetration theory** (SPT) explains how partners move from superficial levels to greater intimacy (Altman & Taylor, 1973). SPT uses an onion as a metaphor to describe how relationships move through various stages: just as you might peel off layer after layer of an onion in an attempt to reach the core or center, a relational partner attempts to reach the most intimate thoughts and feelings at the other partner's "core" (see Figure 7.2).

According to SPT, each layer contains information that is increasingly more private and therefore more risky to divulge to someone else. The outer layer represents aspects of the self that are obvious and observable, such as appearance and nonverbal behavior. Successive layers become more private and less obvious to

FIGURE 7.2

SOCIAL PENETRATION THEORY (SPT) MODEL According to the SPT model, relational partners peel away layers of intimacy to reach each other's cores.

COMMUNICATIONACROSSCULTURES

Socializing Around the World over Drinks

Alcohol has long been used to grease the wheels of interpersonal communication. Greeks cut loose with shots of ouzo, Czechs argue about football in beer halls, Japanese businessmen close deals over cups of sake, and urban American women trade stories while sipping cosmopolitans. Alcohol is used to forge and strengthen social bonds all over the world. And according to Tom Standage's book *A History of the World in Six Glasses,* this isn't a recent phenomenon: in one form or another, alcohol has been a social lubricant for roughly twelve thousand years.

Between 10,000 and 4000 B.C.E., inhabitants of the Fertile Crescent discovered that grain could be fermented into beer, an alcoholic beverage that was far safer to drink than the potentially disease-ridden water of Mesopotamia. The rise of beer occurred at a pivotal time when humans were switching from a nomadic, hunting and gathering lifestyle to a more settled farming existence. As people settled down, cities formed, and neighbors became permanent, beer took on significant importance as a social drink. Sumerian pictograms from 3000 B.C.E. show two people drinking beer through straws from the same vessel.

Standage (2005) observes:

> The most likely explanation . . . is that, unlike food, beverages can be shared. When several people drink beer from the same vessel, they are all consuming the same liquid; when cutting up a piece of meat, in contrast, some parts are usually deemed to be more desirable than others. As a result, sharing a drink with someone is a universal symbol of hospitality and friendship. It signals that the person offering the drink can be trusted, by demonstrating that it is not poisoned or otherwise unsuitable for consumption. (p. 18)

Our tradition of clinking glasses can be traced back to this ancient Middle Eastern practice; imbibers are symbolically reuniting their glasses into a single vessel of shared liquid.

The use of alcohol as a centerpiece for interpersonal interaction dates back a long way—ancient Egyptians would greet each other with the phrase "Beer and bread," which meant "Have a good day." But despite this common original starting point, modern rituals and practices vary widely from one culture to the next. In Spain, home entertaining isn't very common, so friends and neighbors get together at local bars. In the nineteenth century, Andalusian bartenders began putting slices of sausage or ham on top of their customers' wineglasses to keep insects out. And suddenly Spain had *tapas* (the verb *tapar* means "to cover"). Korean rituals emphasize the social aspect of drinking—you fill your companion's glass, not your own—and encourage the "keep 'em coming" philosophy— it's considered disrespectful to allow your drinking companion's glass to get empty.

THINK ABOUT THIS

❶ The Qur'an forbids the consumption of alcohol. Does the absence affect communication between non-Muslim drinkers and Muslim nondrinkers?

❷ Drinking on the job is frowned on in corporate America. But at work-related lunches and dinners, businesspeople often run up considerable bar tabs. Why might alcohol be encouraged in one setting but discouraged in the other?

❸ Do you think there are topics that people feel more comfortable talking about when sharing a glass of wine with a family member or meeting a friend at a pub? How might your answers be influenced by the culture you come from?

others: at each layer, partners assess the costs and benefits of the relationship and of disclosing information to each other. If costs exceed rewards, it is unlikely that the partners will move inward toward the more deeply concealed layers. So upon getting to know Jorge, for example, you might find that despite his boisterous, funny exterior, he sometimes suffers from some fairly serious bouts of depression, which he manages with medication. But Jorge must choose to reveal this information: it is a part of him that only his closest, most trusted friends know, and it's something that he's likely to reveal only as a relationship becomes closer and more intimate.

Communication Privacy Management

Communication privacy management (CPM) **theory** helps explain how people perceive the information they hold about themselves and whether they will disclose or protect it (Petronio, 2000, 2002). CPM explains why Celeste, for example, will boldly share her religious beliefs, whereas Eddie will keep his faith intensely private. CPM theory presumes that people believe they own their private information and need to set up boundaries to control the potential risk that may make them vulnerable (Petronio, 2004).

Central to the notion of privacy management are two key features of relationships. First, privacy management can be affected by dialectical tensions such as openness versus closedness, discussed earlier in the chapter. You want to share information in order to increase intimacy with your partner, but it may be risky to do so, and maintaining private information is a worthy goal in its own right. Second, privacy management requires cultural, situational, and relational rules or expectations by which people must be willing to abide. For example, it would likely be considered impolite for you to ask your boss about his medical condition because that topic is far too private for a work context in many cultures, and you are unlikely to have that level of personal intimacy with your manager. Yet that type of disclosure is expected in close relationships (Derlega, Winstead, Mathews, & Braitman, 2008).

If there is a threat to your privacy boundaries (for example, your trusted friend told your secret to someone else), you experience **boundary turbulence** and must readjust your need for privacy against your need for self-disclosure and connection (Guerrero, Andersen, & Afifi, 2007; Theiss, Knobloch, Checton, & Magsamen-Conrad, 2009). Boundary turbulence occurs in mediated situations too. If you have personal information about someone else, do you have the right to post it on Facebook? What about inside jokes or pictures taken at a party—do you have the right to share them with others? Judgments are made about you based on the appearance and behavior of your "friends" on Facebook, so you can see how complex privacy management becomes in mediated situations (Walther, Van Der Heide, Kim, Westerman, & Tong, 2008).

Strategic Topic Avoidance

Certain topics are simply too sensitive for some people to confront openly. **Strategic topic avoidance** is used by one or both relational partners to maneuver the conversation away from undesirable topics because of the potential for embarrassment, vulnerability, or relational decline (Dailey & Palomares, 2004). As

AND YOU?

Do you post any personal information on social networking sites? What kind of information are you willing to reveal? What kind of information do you consider too private to share in mediated contexts?

we touched on in our discussion of communication privacy management, there are also topics we avoid because we are culturally trained to do so. For example, prior relationships, negative information, dating experiences, money issues, and sexual experiences are largely considered inappropriate for public communication (Baxter & Wilmot, 1985; Dailey & Palomares, 2004; Guerrero & Afifi, 1995). So if you're hanging out in the office lunchroom and your colleague asks you how big your bonus was this year, you could proclaim that it's none of his business, but research shows that you'd be better off to use a less direct avoidance tactic, such as keeping silent, deflecting, giving an unrelated response, lying, or simply ending the conversation (Dailey & Palomares, 2004).

Like other issues related to self-disclosure, there are some ethical considerations regarding pursuing and avoiding topics. Is it appropriate for parents to disclose the private details involved in their impending divorce to their children? They may mean well (for example, they may want to reduce uncertainty for their children), but they may use such strategies unethically (such as if each parent offers his or her own side of the story in order to be viewed in a better light than the other parent). In addition, adolescent children may suffer emotionally and view the disclosures as inappropriate (Afifi, McManus, Hutchinson, & Baker, 2007). Every relationship is unique, and as we have discussed, relational partners may experience different degrees of comfort with self-disclosure at various points.

Research into strategic topic avoidance illustrates both benefits and detriments. Most people in healthy relationships, for example, report that topic avoidance seems to work best when partners are sensitive to each other's concerns and when polite and accommodating strategies are used (Dailey & Palomares, 2004). In other words, the divorcing parents' relationships with their children might remain positive if they allow the kids to bring up the divorce in their own time. You may find that some of your relational partners are more comfortable disclosing personal history at a slow rate, especially about sensitive issues such as childhood abuse, financial problems, medical diagnoses, substance abuse, or complications experienced in prior relationships.

AND YOU?
What topics do you consider strictly off-limits? Are there some topics you are willing to discuss with some people but not with others? How do you inform others of your unwillingness to discuss these topics?

● **FANS OF** *The Office* have watched Jim and Pam's romance mature through several relationship stages over the years.

Stages of a Relationship

Although every relationship is unique, several scholars argue that relationships go through somewhat predictable stages (Knapp & Vangelisti, 2000). Communication differs during each stage as relational partners select messages that are individualized for the stage they perceive themselves to be in (Avtgis, West, & Anderson, 1998). Not every relationship will experience every stage—our assessments of costs and rewards will determine how the relationship will change. So if you feel like you're not getting something out of your relationship with a new friend early on, you're probably going to move to end the relationship rather than take it deeper. A number of interpersonal researchers have outlined relational stages—some in more detail than others—and they all have in common the stages we develop in the following sections (see Figure 7.3).

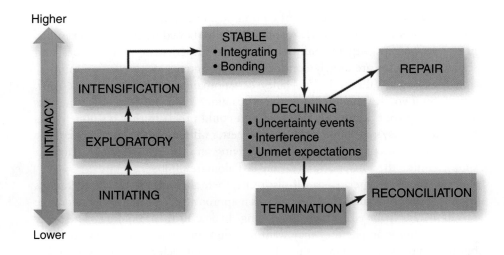

Higher

INTIMACY

Lower

FIGURE 7.3

TYPICAL STAGES OF A RELATIONSHIP Most of us will move between these eight stages over time in our interpersonal relationships.

It can be awkward to verbally indicate that you want a relationship to end or to move beyond the initiating stage. You wouldn't tell a new classmate, "I don't like you. Stop talking to me." Luckily, nonverbal communication helps you address this issue. You can indicate like or dislike with facial expressions, posture, use of space, or touch, as we discuss in Chapter 5. Then you must hope this individual properly decodes your message! (See Chapter 1.)

Initiating Stage

The **initiating stage** of a relationship is one in which you make contact with another person. You might say hello to the person sitting next to you in class and ask his or her name. If you think about the number of new people you initiate with on a given day, you won't be surprised to learn that most relationships don't move beyond this stage. Just because you say "Good morning" to the woman who sold you a bagel doesn't mean the two of you will be chatting on the phone later today. But you will likely use your first impression of a person to gauge whether or not you're interested in moving forward with the relationship (Canary, Cody, & Manusov, 2008).

Exploratory Stage

In the **exploratory stage**, you are seeking relatively superficial information from your partner. You make small talk, asking things like "Do you watch *Mad Men*?" or "How many brothers and sisters do you have?" In this stage, you're not likely to reveal anything too deep or personal; you're still testing the waters, so to speak. You might e-mail the person a link to a funny YouTube video. This stage is also where a number of monitoring strategies are at work to reduce uncertainty. In addition to the small-talk questioning we mentioned, you're likely to observe your partner closely in order to learn more about his or her attitudes and behaviors. As in the initiating stage, you'll want to invest further in the relationship if the rewards seem high.

Intensification Stage

The **intensification stage** occurs when relational partners become increasingly intimate and move their communication toward more personal self-disclosures. This stage includes the use of informal address or pet names ("honey," "darling") as well as "we" talk ("We're going to the concert on Friday night, right?" "Where are we going for your birthday next week?"). Relational partners in this stage also understand each other's nonverbal communication to a greater degree and often share their affection with one another ("What would I do without you!") (Knapp & Vangelisti, 2000).

Stable Stage

By the time partners reach the **stable stage**, their relationship is no longer volatile or temporary. They now have a great deal of knowledge about one another, their expectations are accurate and realistic, and they feel comfortable with their motives for being in the relationship. According to Goss and O'Hair (1988), relationships reach the stable stage when uncertainty about each other (and the relationship) reduces to the point where partners feel comfortable understanding their preferences and goals for each other. That doesn't mean, however, that stable relationships are set in stone, as the partners and their goals can still change.

Knapp and Vangelisti (2000) note two substages that occur during the stable stage. First, we see relational partners **integrating** or "becoming one." You and your roommate Dana now cultivate common friends, develop joint opinions ("We loved that movie!"), and share property ("Where did you put our new toaster?"). People also treat you as a pair—one of you would never be invited to a party without also inviting the other one. If the relationship progresses beyond integrating, **bonding** takes place when two partners share formal symbolic messages with the world that their relationship is important and cherished. Before concerns about HIV, children and teens used to become "blood brothers" or "blood sisters" to show their attachment to one another. Engagements, weddings, civil unions, and entering into legal contracts (such as buying a house together) are common ways to reveal a bonded romantic couple.

Life's challenges inevitably arise for partners in a stable relationship, so each individual will need to determine if the benefits of the relationship (such as intimacy or companionship) outweigh the costs that these challenges represent. The relationship can evolve to meet those challenges and remain stable. This is why Marge puts up with Homer's antics on *The Simpsons*. However, if one or both partners feel that the costs outweigh the benefits, the relationship may go into decline. For a few tips on developing and maintaining stable relationships, see Table 7.3 on page 210.

● **SUPERSTARS** Jay-Z and Beyoncé Knowles epitomize the stable stage of a relationship: love, familiarity, comfort—and they prove that it's possible to reach this stage even as a Hollywood couple!

Declining Stage

Have you noticed your partner criticizing you more often, refusing to talk about issues important to you, getting defensive, or speaking with contempt? If these behaviors are occurring more often than positive behaviors in your relationship, it is probably in decline (Gottman & Silver, 1999). Three factors typically lead to the **declining stage**, when the relationship begins to come apart. These are uncertainty events, interference (concerning family, work, timing, money, or the like), and unmet expectations.

STRATEGIES FOR
MANAGING STABLE
RELATIONSHIPS

Strategy	Examples
Remember what made you interested in the relationship in the first place.	• Sharing inside jokes • Visiting favorite places (for instance, a coffee-house where you used to meet)
Spend quality time together.	• Sharing your day-to-day activities • Exploring new hobbies and interests • Taking part in activities like going to the movies or sporting events
Be understanding.	• Empathizing with your partner's concerns, dreams, fears, and so on • Avoiding unnecessary judgments • Trying to see conflict-causing situations from your partner's point of view
Express affection.	• Proclaiming how important your partner is ("You're a great friend" or "I love you") • Doing something nice or unexpected for your partner without being asked
Have realistic expectations.	• Not comparing your relationships to others • Accepting your partner's strengths *and* weaknesses
Work on intimacy.	• Maintaining a trusting, open environment where self-disclosure is possible • Offering supportive, positive messages, particularly during stressful times • Revealing your commitment by showing and sharing that you are invested in the relationship

Sources: Dindi & Timmerman (2003); Gilbertson, Dindi, & Allen (1998); Goffman (1971); Harvey, Weber, & Orbuch (1990); Stafford (2003); Vangelisti & Banski (1993).

Uncertainty Events

Events or behavioral patterns that cause uncertainty in a relationship are called **uncertainty events**. Uncertainty events in a relationship may be caused by competing relationships (romantic or platonic), deception or betrayal of confidence, and sudden or unexplained changes in sexual behavior, personality or values, or the degree of closeness between partners (Planalp & Honeycutt, 1985). One or both partners are left wondering about the cause of the events and their significance for the relationship. Imagine how you would feel if your romantic partner suddenly started withholding information from you or if a close friend began engaging in activities that you found offensive. Uncertainty events may be sudden and very noticeable (betrayal of confidence, for example), or they may be subtle and escape immediate attention (your sister stops returning your phone calls).

Interference

When Patrick becomes involved in a serious romantic relationship, his best friend and roommate, Dennis, feels abandoned. Jason wants to get married, but Norah is not ready. Emma and Leigh are finding that financial troubles are putting a strain on their relationship.

These are just some of the many obstacles that may pop up in a relationship and interfere with its growth. Timing, the family or friends of one or both partners, and problems with work or money can all contribute to the decline of a relationship. For example, a *Money* magazine study of one thousand spouses found that 84 percent of married couples reported money as a culprit in marital distress and that money beats sex and in-laws as a source of arguments in the marriage ("Money," 2006). Partners often view money differently because of upbringing, spending habits, and gender (Blumstein & Schwartz, 1983). And money isn't solely an issue for committed couples; it can also cause strain in friendships. Consider the friction that occurs when executive A.J. pressures his best friend, schoolteacher Danny, to join him at pricey restaurants, on ski trips, and at sporting events that Danny can't afford.

Unmet Expectations

Whenever people enter into a relationship, they form ideas as to what they think will or should happen; these expectations influence how we send messages to and receive them from our partners. Unrealistic expectations can create problems in

EVALUATINGCOMMUNICATIONETHICS

THINK ABOUT THIS

Money and Relationship Strife

You have a pretty good relationship with your parents, but money has also been a source of conflict with them. You're the first in your family to attend college, and you're working thirty hours a week to contribute toward your living expenses and tuition. You've taken out a hefty amount of money in student loans as well. You know that money is tight for your parents, and you are grateful for the help that they can provide. Your mother, for example, sends generous packages of food, and your father and stepmother pay for your car insurance. But still, money is a constant concern for you.

Recently, you discovered that you could qualify for a particular scholarship and a grant—money for college that does not need to be repaid—if you can prove that your income falls into a certain bracket. The only way to make that happen is to declare yourself independent from your parents' care. But that would have some negative financial consequences for them, as they would no longer be able to claim you as a deduction on their tax return. You decide to discuss the issue with your father, hoping that he will see the situation from your point of view, but he does not. In fact, he becomes so angry that he threatens to cut you off altogether—no more car insurance money and no place to live during the summer internship you've arranged near your father's town. He tells you that if you want to be independent, you should be completely independent.

Either way you look at it, your relationship with your father has been affected. If you do declare yourself independent, you will lose his assistance and gain his wrath. If you don't, you will resent him deeply for causing you additional financial stress. You want to repair your relationship with him . . . but how?

❶ Can you put yourself in your father's position and empathize with him? What are your responsibilities here as an ethical listener?

❷ In light of the information you have gleaned from this chapter, how would you prepare to have a conversation about repairing the relationship no matter which decision you make? What repair tactics could you consider using?

❸ Construct a conversation that allows for relationship repair (based on the decision that you make regarding your independence). What might that conversation be like? What communication skills could you use? How will you ensure that the conversation is ethical?

a relationship: if Hannah believes that true love means never arguing, she might well interpret her boyfriend Liam's criticism of her messy apartment as a sign that they're simply not meant to be together. Realistic expectations, by contrast, can increase relational satisfaction and improve interpersonal communication (Alexander, 2008). Luisa, for example, has learned that her friend Emily is simply never going to remember her birthday. It's not a sign that Emily doesn't care; it's just that Emily isn't good with dates and times. Instead, Luisa focuses on all of the kind things that Emily does for her, like sending her funny postcards from her business travel or offering to watch the dogs when Luisa had to fly to Las Vegas for a funeral.

Relationship Repair

A relationship in decline is not necessarily doomed to failure: partners may attempt to save or repair their relationship by changing their behavior, interactions, or expectations. If you have a strong commitment to someone else, particularly in a romantic relationship, you often perceive problems as less severe, so you are more likely to reduce conflict and increase the likelihood of repairing the relationship (Miczo, 2008). **Repair tactics** should include improving communication, focusing on the positive aspects of each partner and of the relationship itself, reinterpreting behaviors with a more balanced view, reevaluating the alternatives to the relationship, and enlisting the support of others to hold the relationship together (Brandau-Brown & Ragsdale, 2008; Duck, 1984).

As these tactics suggest, partners hoping to repair a relationship must focus on the benefits of their relationship rather than the source of a particular argument (see Table 7.3 on p. 210; many of the tactics noted for managing stable relationships are also useful for repairing them). Listening to each other and trying to take each other's perspective is usually key here. Relational partners should also remind themselves about the attractive qualities that sparked the relationship in the first place (for example, how Talia can make Greg laugh and how Greg can make Talia feel at ease with her emotions). Partners may also try to increase their intimacy by offering more self-disclosures and spending quality time together (Blumstein & Schwartz, 1983). If a relationship is in serious decline, however, and seems beyond repair, the partners may need to seek professional help or outside support.

Termination Stage

Try as they might, not all relational partners stay together. (If they did, we wouldn't be subject to countless sad songs, bad poems, and heart-wrenching screenplays!) The **termination stage**, or end of a relationship, usually comes about in one of two ways (Davis, 1973). The first is *passing away,* which is characterized by the gradual fading of a relationship; it loses its vitality, perhaps because of outside interference or simply because partners don't make the effort to maintain an intimate relationship. Also, if partners spend less time together as a couple, communication and intimacy may decline, leading to dissatisfaction and a perception of different attitudes. This is why romances and friendships sometimes deteriorate when one partner moves away or why marriages and outside friendships change when kids come into the picture. The second way

TABLE 7.4

TERMINATION STRATEGIES FOR ROMANTIC RELATIONSHIPS

Strategy	Tactics	Examples
Positive-tone messages	Fairness	"It wouldn't be right to go on pretending I'm in love with you when I know I'm not!"
	Compromise	"I still care about you. We can still see each other occasionally."
	Fatalism	"We both know this relationship is doomed."
Deescalation	Promise of friendship	"We can still be friends."
	Implied possible reconciliation	"We need time apart; maybe that will rekindle our feelings for each other."
	Blaming the relationship	"It's not your fault, but this relationship is bogging us down."
	Appeal to independence	"We don't need to be tied down right now."
Withdrawal or avoidance	Avoid contact with the person as much as possible	"I don't think I'll be able to see you this weekend."
Justification	Emphasize positive consequences of disengaging	"It's better for you and me to see other people since we've changed so much."
	Emphasize negative consequences of not disengaging	"We will miss too many opportunities if we don't see other people."
Negative identity management	Emphasize enjoyment of life	"Life is too short to spend with just one person right now."
	Nonnegotiation	"I need to see other people—period!"

Source: Canary, Cody, & Manusov (2008), pp. 278–286. Adapted with permission.

relationships often end is in *sudden death*—the abrupt, and for at least one partner, unexpected termination of a relationship. This might happen if your spouse or romantic partner has an affair, or if you decide that you can no longer tolerate a friend's emotionally manipulative behavior. Communicating your desire to end a relationship can be difficult, particularly in romantic relationships; some messages useful for terminating romantic relationships are listed in Table 7.4.

Reconciliation

Is there any hope for a terminated relationship? Soap operas and sitcoms certainly say so—but it's true in real life as well. **Reconciliation** is a repair strategy for rekindling an extinguished relationship. Attempting reconciliation entails a lot of risk—one partner might find that the other partner is not interested, or both partners might find that the problems that tore them apart the first time remain or have even intensified. But research reveals that there are a few tactics that can help the partners mend the relationship (O'Hair & Krayer, 1987; Patterson & O'Hair, 1992):

▶ *Spontaneous development:* The partners wind up spending more time together. Perhaps a divorced couple is involved in their son's school or two ex-friends find themselves helping out a mutual friend.

▶ *Third-party mediation:* The partners have a friend or family member mediate the reconciliation.

▶ *High affect:* The partners resolve to be nice and polite to one another and possibly remind each other of what they found attractive about the other in the first place.

▶ *Tacit persistence:* One or both partners refuse to give up on the relationship.

real communicator

NAME: Chad Ludwig
HOMETOWN: Shreveport, Louisiana
OCCUPATION: Director, Video Entertainment, Disney Online
FUN FACT: I won an Elvis impersonator contest.

My wife and I met in college when we were both eighteen and had only our personal needs to worry about. Our communication was fairly straightforward—we would talk face to face about our feelings, and we grew accustomed to each other's nonverbal cues. When we graduated and lived far apart for two years, however, it was much harder to maintain our relationship. Luckily, we were able to adapt. We doubled our efforts to actively listen to each other (even without many of the nonverbal behaviors we had previously relied on) and, through trial and error, we learned what topics were best to discuss over the phone versus over e-mail. We also set specific times to call each other so we'd always be able to look forward to the next conversation. And we were among the first people we knew to invest in webcams (I know, I'm old . . .) so that we could actually *see* each other every once in a while . . . even though the connection was painfully slow by today's standards. Still, seeing the smiling face I loved from across the ocean made all the difference in the world.

We also realized the importance of some regular face-to-face time and did everything we could to see each other in person (thank you, credit cards and frequent flyer miles!). When we were in the same room, we found that we could clarify where we stood on our relational issues and address any misunderstandings.

Married with a child now, we have to adapt our relationship even more as we address increasingly complex topics—for example, child-rearing decisions, financial expenditures, and extended family obligations. Like many couples, we have to address these potentially inflammatory topics while we both hold down extremely demanding full-time jobs. When my wife is traveling for work and stressed because her flight has been canceled, I have to think carefully about how best to tell her that our son hit his head on the coffee table during a "special trick" he was performing. In other words, we still have many (many!) opportunities to practice all the skills we've honed over the years. Thank goodness for the advanced technology that constantly helps us stay in touch throughout the day or when we travel—we frequently e-mail about our family calendar, text to say "I'll be home in ten minutes to walk the dog," use meeting invitations to recall who's bringing our son to preschool on any given day, and say good night via cell phone when we're away from home.

The communication patterns we've established over the past decade help us tremendously. I think I know when my wife is frustrated and tired without her telling me, and she understands that I'm not angry with her when I appear stressed after a long day at work. Nonetheless, all relationships take work—"maintenance behaviors," I think my college communication professor called it.

▶ *Mutual interaction:* The partners begin talking more often following the dissolution, perhaps vowing to remain friends after their breakup.

▶ *Avoidance:* The partners avoid spending time together and begin to miss each other.

If you think about couples in popular culture who have broken up and gotten back together—Ross and Rachel on *Friends*, for instance—you can clearly see some of these strategies at work.

AND YOU?

Have you ever been able to restore a relationship that you thought was irreparably damaged? Have you ever ended a relationship but secretly believed that you would repair it at some point in the future?

BACK TO Mary and Justin

At the beginning of this chapter, we met Mary and Justin, a couple struggling to maintain a close and functional family life during Justin's regular military deployment. Let's consider how they deal with the strains of time, distance, and uncertainty in light of what we've learned in this chapter.

▶ Military spouses often take on the role of single parents, making new rules and routines for interaction with the children when their partners are gone. When the soldier returns, these communication behaviors are not familiar to him or her, so communication may become strained. When Justin is home, he and Mary talk a lot about how they should guide and discipline their sons, so that the boys feel consistency whether Justin is home or not— and so that they manage the dialectical tension of autonomy-connection.

▶ Technology can help some military families keep abreast of one another's lives. Depending on what technologies are available (and when), families can talk every day or schedule a time to video chat. They can also engage in activities together, even though they are far apart. Mary and Justin like to choose a book that they can both read independently and then discuss when they have time together. They also pray together at an agreed-upon time, even though they are not connected physically or electronically. These simple but meaningful activities help them to feel a sense of closeness despite the distance between them.

▶ Sharing family news—whether big ("Doug made the basketball team") or small ("Daniel was home from school today with a bit of a cold")—helps to keep Justin involved in the family's day-to-day activities. Mary and Justin's discussions of the routine details of their daily lives help them to increase feelings of intimacy.

▶ Sahlstein, Maguire, and Timmerman (2009) urge military couples to develop better communication skills to handle separation and reunion times. For example, Justin worries that if he self-discloses his emotions (particularly negative ones) about his experiences that he may be seen as weak, but he also knows that talking about them with Mary (who shows support without judgment) helps him deal with his experiences (another example of the openness-closedness dialectic).

THINGS TO TRY ▶ Activities

1. List one family relationship, one friendship, and one romantic relationship in which you are or have been involved. For each of these relationships, list at least five self-disclosures you made to those individuals, and describe how each revelation advanced relational intimacy. Now list at least five self-disclosures you wish you had *not* made to each of these individuals. Did these inappropriate self-disclosures increase or decrease your intimacy? Reflect on these lists as you self-disclose in future relationships.

2. Consider a romantic relationship that has ended. Using the stages outlined in this chapter, create a time line of the relationship. Include significant communication episodes that encouraged the relationship to move into another stage as well as any stages that may have been skipped. Reflect on your level of satisfaction at each stage, and note any changes you would have made at that point. If any stages were omitted from the time line, reflect on why. Based on your experiences in this relationship, did you or will you communicate differently with later romantic partners?

3. As a new romantic relationship begins, keep a journal of the communication events that occur. In this journal, indicate the stage you perceive the relationship to be in (based on the stages in this chapter). List key communication events that increase or decrease attachment in the relationship. Reflect on and include in your journal your level of satisfaction with the relationship and if and how you would like the relationship to proceed.

4. In small groups in your class, discuss how popular culture and films portray interpersonal relationships, considering specifically relationship stages. Discuss communication techniques that the characters might have used to produce different relationship outcomes. Analyze how accurately the communication behaviors of the characters themselves and those they use in their relationships reflect real-life communication episodes.

Now that you have finished reading this chapter, you can:

Explain key aspects of interpersonal relationships:

▶ **Interpersonal relationships**, the interconnections between two individuals, are influenced by **interpersonal communication**, the exchange of verbal and nonverbal messages between two people who are influenced by their partner's messages (p. 188).

▶ We all have a complex **relational network** or web of relationships. We have **family** relationships, **friendships**, and romantic partners, in addition to acquaintances, colleagues, and others (p. 188).

▶ **Love** is a deep affection for another person with varying degrees of passion, commitment, and **intimacy**, or closeness and understanding (p. 191)—and is important to romantic relationships.

▶ **Social information processing theory** explains that virtual relationships develop much like those that grow from face-to-face contact but that the process often takes longer to become more intimate. Online relationships have the potential to develop even more personal and intimate relationships than face-to-face ones, a phenomenon known as **hyperpersonal communication** (pp. 193–194).

Describe how and why we form relationships:

▶ Humans have a natural need for companionship and **inclusion**—a need to share our lives with others (p. 196).

▶ Relationship formation involves a number of types of attraction. For attraction to occur, a relationship requires **proximity**, or nearness (p. 197).

▶ Research shows that similarity influences attraction; supporting evidence includes the **attraction-similarity hypothesis**, the **matching hypothesis**, and the **genetic-similarity hypothesis** (p. 199).

List the advantages and disadvantages of relationships:

▶ **Social exchange theory** (p. 199) explains how we balance the advantages and disadvantages in our relationships.

▶ **Rewards** are what make you feel good about the relationship and may be extrinsic, instrumental, or intrinsic. **Costs** are aspects of the relationship that upset you (pp. 199–201).

▶ According to **uncertainty reduction theory**, a relationship priority is to decrease the uncertainty between partners through the use of **passive**

strategies (which involve observing others without actually interacting—pp. 201–202), **active strategies** (which involve seeking information from a third party—p. 202), and **interactive strategies** (which involve communicating directly with the person—p. 202).

▶ **Relational dialectics theory** holds that **dialectical tensions** arise when opposing or conflicting goals exist in a relationship (p. 202).

▶ Individuals may struggle to find a balance between independence (autonomy) and dependence (connection), openness and closedness, and predictability and novelty (pp. 202–204).

Describe the factors that influence self-disclosure:

▶ **Social penetration theory** explains how relational partners move toward intimacy, the primary goal of many relationships (p. 204).

▶ **Communication privacy management theory** helps explain how people perceive the information they hold about themselves and how they disclose it (p. 206). **Boundary turbulence** arises when violations occur in a relationship that make it necessary to readjust the disclosure versus privacy.

▶ **Strategic topic avoidance** is used to maneuver the conversation away from topics that make people feel vulnerable (p. 206).

Outline the predictable stages of most relationships:

▶ The **initiating stage** is the first contact (p. 208).

▶ In the **exploratory stage**, there is superficial communication (p. 208).

▶ More self-disclosure occurs in the **intensification stage** (p. 208).

▶ In the **stable stage**, expectations are accurate and realistic. We see partners **integrating**, or becoming one, and **bonding**, sharing messages about their relationship with the world (p. 209).

▶ In the **declining stage**, **uncertainty events**, interference from outside the relationship, and unmet expectations take a toll, though **repair tactics** may reverse the decline (pp. 209–212).

▶ In the **termination stage**, the relationship fades away (passing away) or is unexpectedly terminated by one partner (sudden death) (pp. 212–213).

▶ **Reconciliation** is a repair strategy for rekindling an extinguished relationship (p. 213).

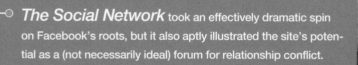

The Social Network took an effectively dramatic spin
on Facebook's roots, but it also aptly illustrated the site's potential as a (not necessarily ideal) forum for relationship conflict.

chapter

8

Managing Conflict in Relationships

If you believe the story detailed in the film *The Social Network*—and most evidence suggests that you shouldn't—Mark Zuckerberg invented Facebook as revenge against his ex-girlfriend (O'Brian, 2010). Feeling angry after she dumped him, Zuckerberg begins posting nasty things about his ex on his personal blog and then goes on to develop the site that will eventually become the most ubiquitous (and profitable) social networking site on the Internet.

Zuckerberg's intentions for Facebook were undeniably exaggerated for dramatic effect in the film, but the fact remains that his invention can be a blunt weapon for individuals seeking to air grievances. Facebook, like MySpace and Twitter, provides a fairly open forum for communication as well as for users to voice opinions and complaints to everyone they know—and plenty of people they don't—with ease. Slamming on celebrities, talking smack about sports teams, deriding political parties and government policies, and maligning social groups and co-cultures are common practices on Facebook. Confrontational posts are often met with confrontational comments, and online bullying is not unusual. Chances are you've witnessed or even become embroiled in a Facebook conflict yourself.

What starts out as a complaint or an observation can quickly develop into a nasty conflict or even an investigation. Just ask Joe Lipari, who in 2010 posted what he thought was a sarcastic but benign comment about his experience at his local Apple Store. A Facebook "friend"—probably more of an acquaintance who was unfamiliar with Lipari's sarcastic sense of humor—misread his post (a paraphrased line from the film *Fight Club*) as a threat against the store and alerted authorities. A few hours after posting what he thought was a funny, if perhaps mean-spirited, complaint on Facebook, police were knocking on Lipari's door, searching his apartment, and questioning him as a suspected terrorist (Calhoun, 2010).

219

After you have finished reading this chapter, you will be able to

- Describe the factors that lead to productive conflict
- Identify conflict triggers in yourself and others
- Explain the forces that influence how people handle conflict
- Evaluate and employ strategies for managing conflict in different situations
- Compare levels of resolution in conflict outcomes

Dealing with conflict—be it with a romantic partner, a family member, a colleague, a classmate, or a business or institution—can be hard. Some people avoid it altogether, while others lash out aggressively. Some vent their anger on Facebook, where they can be more confrontational than they might be willing to be in a face-to-face encounter. But, of course, there is also a fair amount of middle ground that falls between covering our ears and posting aggressive comments in a public forum. There are also lots of ways in which we can not only manage conflict, but also grow and learn from it. In this chapter, we'll take a look at some of the root causes of conflict and examine the ways in which we engage in conflict with others. We'll then consider productive ways in which to manage conflict in our relationships as well as conflict outcomes.

Understanding Conflict

You've undoubtedly had countless conflicts in your life, from arguments with siblings over who would wash the dishes to the painful task of ending romantic relationships. But just what is conflict, anyway? **Conflict** is not simply an argument or a struggle: it's a negative interaction between two or more interdependent people, rooted in some actual or perceived disagreement.

Scholars like to distinguish between conflict—which is inevitable and sometimes cannot be resolved—and **conflict management**, which refers to the way that we engage in conflict and address disagreements with our relational partners. For example, consider Lisa and Steven Bradley, a couple who seemed to have it all: a beautiful home, four expensive cars, designer clothes, dinner out (or ordered in) every night. But they had a secret: Lisa spent lavishly without consulting Steven, and Steven stewed about it without ever confronting Lisa. Like countless Americans today, even the relatively well-off Bradleys were spending more than they earned, essentially living on credit. Though they rarely fought about it, Lisa and Steven were struggling to keep up with their bills and were on the brink of divorce (Greenhouse, 2006; Oprah.com, 2008).

For Lisa and Steven, the conflict was rooted in differing ideas about money, credit, and financial priorities. And they chose to manage their conflict by avoiding discussion and confrontation, which in this case wasn't particularly helpful. As the Bradleys eventually discovered—and as you'll see throughout this chapter—conflict can be managed productively or unproductively. Let's examine these two approaches to conflict and consider the costs and benefits of each one.

Unproductive Conflict

If you haven't already guessed, Lisa and Steven's approach to managing their conflict over money was an unproductive one. **Unproductive conflict** is conflict that is managed poorly and has a negative impact on the individuals and relationships involved. For Lisa and Steven, the costs involved in unproductive conflict, both in dollars and in terms of its impact on their relationship, were clear.

In many respects, our relationships—including those with families, friends, colleagues, and romantic partners—are defined by the way we manage conflict. But a damaged relationship isn't the only negative outcome that can stem from unproductive conflict. Researchers have discovered that when conflict is handled poorly, those involved can experience medical problems, including emotional distress (Davies, Sturge-Apple, Cicchetti, & Cummings, 2008), mood disorders (Segrin, Hanzal, & Domschke, 2009), heart disease, and immune deficiency (Canary, 2003). In one study, ill-handled father-daughter conflicts led to an increase in eating disorders in the young women, while productively managed conflict seemed to reduce eating disorder behaviors (Botta & Dumlao, 2002). Finally, studies on couples have demonstrated that unproductive conflict leads to aggression in relationships (Olsen & Golish, 2002) and can result in violence, particularly by men against their female partners (Feldman & Ridley, 2000).

● **EVEN WITH MATTERS** as simple as making plans for a Friday night, we may be uncompromising and create unproductive conflict or discuss the options, reach an agreement, and act on it.

Productive Conflict

Not all conflict is negative, though. In fact, conflict can be as valuable as it is inevitable! Conflict that is managed effectively is called **productive conflict**. We often do not even notice the conflicts that we handle productively, as when two people quickly reach a compromise over some issue on which they disagree (like whether to eat at the Olive Garden or Pizza Hut), without argument or confrontation. But productive conflict can also follow unproductive conflict, as when Lisa and Steven, fed up with the debt and realizing that their marriage was in jeopardy, began to confront and work on their financial and relationship problems. On the advice of a financial planner, they took on additional work to increase their income, and they made some deep cuts in their monthly budget. By addressing the problem collaboratively—facing the reality of their debt, agreeing on their financial priorities, setting a budget, and making decisions about money together—the couple began both resolving their financial problems and healing their relationship.

It is important to note that productive conflict does not necessarily mean a successful resolution of conflict. Results of a recent study on dating couples revealed that most conflicts do not result in resolution, and that a couples' satisfaction is determined more by the strategies used to manage conflict than the outcome of the argument (McGinn, McFarland, & Christensen, 2009). That's because such productive management strategies can actually benefit the parties involved, whether they're couples, friends, families, or even communities. Let's look at a few examples.

Productive Conflict Fosters Healthy Debate

To believe that conflict can be productive rather than destructive, you have to actively engage in it. There is no greater intellectual exercise than exploring and testing ideas with another person. And like a sport, it can get competitive, as evidenced by the popularity of debate teams in high schools and colleges and the media fanfare surrounding political debates during major elections. In fact, active and lively debate allows us to exchange ideas, evaluate the merits of one another's claims, and continually refine and clarify each other's thinking about

Few people enjoy conflict, but avoiding it can have negative consequences. In Chapter 9, we discuss *groupthink*—when groups focus on unity and conflict avoidance rather than openly discussing alternative solutions to problems. If your student organization president makes an irresponsible suggestion on how to spend funds and you and the others keep silent, conflict may be avoided—but at a cost.

the issue under discussion. A respectful debate between two candidates can help voters make decisions about whom they wish to support in an upcoming election; similar debates on the floors of Congress allow representatives to go on record with their opinions on bills being considered and to try to persuade their colleagues to consider their positions. When government leaders fail to engage in such debates—when they evade questions or block a bill from going to debate on the floor of the legislature—they are formally engaging in the same kind of unproductive conflict avoidance that individuals use when they refuse to discuss sensitive or difficult subjects.

Conflict and healthy debate can also be a useful part of everyday life. Let's say that you want to buy a new hybrid car. Your spouse, however, isn't as keen on the idea. You argue that your current car is costing more and more money to maintain, and the savings in gas that a hybrid car allows will make up for the initial investment. Your spouse points out that you have only a limited amount of money in your joint savings account, which the required down payment would significantly diminish. Not only that, but the monthly payments on this new car would have a significant impact on your budget. By engaging in a healthy debate, you and your spouse are better able to evaluate the pros and cons of buying this new car.

Productive Conflict Leads to Better Decision Making

Healthy debate serves a real purpose in that it helps individuals and groups make smarter decisions. By skillfully working through conflicting ideas about how to solve a problem or reach a goal, we identify the best courses of action. That's because a productive conflict provides an arena in which we can test the soundness of proposed ideas. Suggested solutions that are logical and feasible will stand up to scrutiny during the decision-making process, while weaker solutions are likely to be exposed as flawed. So by engaging in productive discussion about your conflict, the real costs and impact of a new car are revealed, and you and your spouse are able to come up with a workable solution: you will continue driving the old car while sacrificing this year's vacation and dinners out to put an additional $350 every month into a special savings account toward the purchase of a secondhand hybrid car in one year.

● IN *GOING THE DISTANCE*, Erin and Garrett work at overcoming the hurdles of a new long-distance relationship by communicating regularly.

Productive Conflict Spurs Relationship Growth

Differences of opinion and clashing goals are inevitable in any relationship. And that can be part of what keeps our relationships fun and interesting! But it's how the partners *handle* the disagreements that arise that determines whether their bond will grow stronger. As two individuals—be they romantic partners, friends, roommates, or colleagues—work through their disagreements productively, they build on the relationship (Dainton & Gross, 2008). For example, in the film *Going the Distance*, a budding romance between Erin and Garret is put to the test when Erin must return to graduate school on the opposite coast just six weeks after they meet. The trials of negotiating a long-distance romance almost kill the relationship. But once they are able to clear a few logistical hurdles—each seeking new jobs in closer proximity, in an extremely difficult job market—they are able to be together again. Undoubtedly, the very difficult struggle to maintain a relationship over three thousand miles helped to solidify their commitment. To paraphrase the German philosopher Friedrich Nietzsche, that which does not kill a relationship can indeed make it stronger.

AND YOU?

Have you ever let a small conflict grow into a bigger one simply because you avoided engaging in conflict management? On the other hand, are there times when avoiding conflict is more productive than trying to address it?

Conflict Triggers

▶ "He was drinking from the milk carton again. I caught him. It's so disgusting—I have to use that milk too, you know!"

▶ "Is there any point to making lunch plans with Abby? She's always breaking them."

▶ "My boss is at it again. I swear, she would throw me underneath a truck if it would make her look good."

Do any of these scenarios seem familiar? Everyone has one—a "hot button," something that drives you absolutely mad when it happens. It could be your sister leaving her dirty exercise clothes on the bathroom floor or your mother asking about your grades every single day. But you know it when it happens—and conflict often ensues.

The fact is, conflicts arise for a number of reasons. People often have conflicting goals, beliefs, or ideas; we face competition for scarce resources, such as money or time. We experience misunderstandings, and unfortunately, we lose our tempers. And sometimes we encounter people who are deceitful or uncooperative or who intentionally undermine our efforts to achieve our goals. In the following sections, we'll examine a few common conflict triggers (Sanford, 2010).

The best way to account for unusual behavior may be to ask if your perceptions are accurate. In Chapter 7, we discuss *interactive strategies* that help you to reduce uncertainty and get information directly from a person. You might tell a friend, "I sense that you're angry with me because you haven't talked to me today. Am I right?" Such questions allow your friend to clarify perceptions and may eliminate unnecessary conflict.

Inaccurate Perceptions

Misunderstandings are a common—and regrettable—cause of conflict. For example, in the movie *The Break Up*, partners Brooke and Gary fight over the giving and taking in their relationship. Brooke is frustrated that she frequently accompanies Gary to baseball games (which she does not particularly enjoy), but Gary never takes her to the ballet, despite her desire to see a performance. While it may seem that Gary is selfish and uninterested in Brooke's desires, Brooke does have a role in this conflict. Gary points out that Brooke never told him she dislikes baseball—he thought they were mutually enjoying the games. Also, Brooke never shared her desire to attend the ballet—so how would Gary know to surprise her with tickets? Had they communicated openly, they could have avoided these perceptual errors altogether and potentially saved their relationship.

● *GREY'S ANATOMY'S*
Callie and Arizona find their relationship put to a critical test when they reveal their opposing views on having children.

Incompatible Goals

Since much communication is goal-driven, conflicts are bound to arise when goals are perceived as incompatible (Canary, 2003). On *Grey's Anatomy*, for example, the happy and committed relationship between Callie and Arizona is shattered by their different ideas about children: Callie realizes that she wants to settle down and start a family, but Arizona is certain that she never wants to have children. When couples differ on such serious life decisions, it can be extremely difficult to resolve conflict to both partners' satisfaction. But even among relational partners who are in agreement on big life decisions, other goals are likely to come into conflict. For example, couples that are committed to having a family have conflicts about the timing, number, and rearing of children.

Unbalanced Costs and Rewards

Your roommate is annoyed that you keep eating her food; you are annoyed that she doesn't clean the bathroom—ever. Evie is feeling overlooked and underpaid at work. Tom and Angela are angry that they seem to be the only ones willing to initiate activities and programs for the PTA at their daughter's school. As you learned in Chapter 7, conflict often arises when we are struggling to get a share of some limited resource, such as money, time, or attention. According to some researchers, we treat our interpersonal relationships almost like financial exchanges; we tally up our *rewards* (what we're getting from a relationship) and compare these to our *costs* (what we're putting into the relationship). If we think our costs are outweighing the rewards, then conflict may likely be triggered.

Provocation

Of course, not every conflict arises out of natural differences between individuals' goals or perceptions. The hard truth is that people can be uncaring or even aggressive at times. While conflict is indeed a natural part of every relationship, a great many conflicts arise through **provocation**—the intentional instigation of conflict. Research by Dan Canary (2003) reveals a wide range of events that can spark intense negative emotions in a relationship:

▶ *Aggression.* Aggressive behaviors are an obvious form of provocation. Such behaviors range from verbal intimidation to physical threats. Fear and defensiveness (along with even more aggression) are common responses to such behavior.

▶ *Identity management.* When someone insults you, it can threaten your identity. Threats to identity management range from mild insults ("Man, you have a messy car") to condescending remarks ("I'll go slowly so you can keep up") to attacks on one's values or religion and racial or ethnic slurs. The reverse is also true, as evidenced by a study revealing that those who feel entitled to admiration from others engage in high amounts of identity management. As such, their self-image goals cause conflict and hostility in their relationships (Moeller, Crocker, & Bushman, 2009).

▶ *Lack of fairness.* When someone uses more than a fair share of resources, it commonly leads to conflict. So when one sibling dominates the computer or the space in a shared bedroom, conflicts are bound to erupt.

▶ *Incompetence.* When someone you work with or depend on performs poorly, the person is in a sense provoking conflict. Feelings of anger and resentment occur when a lab partner fails to bring needed supplies or write her share of the lab report.

▶ *Relationship threats.* When a relationship comes under threat, conflict is likely to arise. If your romantic partner reveals things that suggest he or she has other interests ("I saw my ex yesterday"), you feel jealousy, anger, or insecurity. But not all threats to relationships are so cut and dried: a young child can see a new baby as a threat to his relationship with his parents; you might see a new, talented coworker as a threat to your career.

You may have noticed that most provocations are closely related to strong, unpleasant emotions: conflict often springs out of fear, anger, frustration, sadness, or insecurity. But as you will see, the factors that influence all communication—situation, culture, gender, personality, and so on—also influence the way that we handle conflict. We'll consider these and other factors in the next section.

● **JOHN MAYER** may be an award-winning musician, but his growing reputation for making incendiary comments about race, celebrities, and himself has earned him nothing but a poor public image.

AND YOU?

What kinds of behaviors provoke you the most? Are there times when you provoke conflict with others, perhaps even on purpose?

Factors Affecting Conflict

We've just looked at triggers that can cause a conflict to crop up between people. But once a conflict arises, several specific forces can influence how the people involved handle the conflict. We examine these forces next.

CONNECT

Cultural context has a strong impact on power dynamics. In Chapter 3, we discuss *high- and low-power-distance cultures*, which differ in their expectations and acceptance of the division of power among individuals and groups. In intercultural group settings—where members and leaders may have different attitudes about power dynamics—it's a good idea to discuss the dynamics openly to make conflict more productive and enhance group communication (Chapter 10).

Power Dynamics

When one person has power over another, that dynamic can cause one or both of the people to handle conflict unproductively. Power dynamics are often at play in the workplace, where your boss determines the nature of your work and can fire, promote, or transfer you. If you and your boss disagree about some issue at work, your boss may pull rank, saying something like "I'm in charge here." But power dynamics also come into play in more intimate relationships. For example, if you are dependent on your parents for tuition, shelter, food, or anything else, they may use that power to control your behavior, perhaps pressuring you to choose a specific school or major or making bold declarations about how you should spend your time.

Dan Canary and his colleagues have studied the effects of power on romantic relationships. They note, for example, that unhealthy relationships are often characterized by too much dependence of one partner on the other, control of one partner, and an inability to communicate boundaries, among other things (Canary, Cody, & Manusov, 2003). You can imagine what happens when conflict enters such an unbalanced relationship. In some cases, the partner with more power may engage in activities that make the other partner fearful and compliant, such as making threats, bullying, or intimidating. Let's say that Chris and Amy are considering purchasing their first home together and that Amy is just starting up her own freelance writing gig. Amy now relies on Chris's full-time job for health insurance and a stable income. In a relationship where power is balanced and healthy, Chris would be supportive of Amy's new venture and would want to come to a mutual decision about the type of home that they purchase, understanding that Amy will be spending most of her time in the house, working out of a home office. But if the balance of power is skewed in Chris's favor—either because he is domineering or because Amy refuses to voice her opinions—Chris may engage in some of the tactics we mentioned. You could imagine him saying, "Well, I am the one *paying* for the house," or, "Fine, I guess we'll just keep throwing away money on rent," if Amy suggests that perhaps Chris's top-choice house isn't what's best for them.

It's important to bear in mind that differences in power aren't limited to material resources. In any relationship, one person has power over another if he or she controls something that the other person values. For example, when you are angry with your best friend, you may ignore her, depriving her of the benefit of spending time with you. You might also withhold affection from your romantic partner or your children if they bring about any type of conflict that upsets you. In fact, some people—even entire cultures—will shun individuals whose behavior they disapprove of. For example, old-order Amish communities in the United States and Canada may shun members who are baptized in the faith and transgress the moral order of the church (for example, purchasing a car or marrying someone outside the community). Shunning may prevent community members from eating with the shunned individual or conducting business with him or her (Kraybill, 2007). Although this may seem a bizarre practice to outsiders, it is actually a reflection of the fact that the Amish actively seek a difference in power, valuing the governing of the church and the needs of the community over the power of individuals.

Attitudes Toward Conflict

If you watch the show *30 Rock*, you know that Jack Donaghy (Alec Baldwin) loves to engage in conflict. He relishes the opportunity to renegotiate an actor's contract or fight with his ex-wife, and he is highly critical of his colleague, Liz Lemon (Tina Fey), who spends much of her time avoiding conflict and defusing conflicts among her staff. These different attitudes toward conflict influence how willing Jack and Liz are to discuss disagreements and how productively they handle conflict. Certain attitudes about conflict in general (for instance, "Conflict is always bad") or about specific disagreements can cause people to avoid dealing with it. For example, you might steer clear of conflict for any of the following reasons:

▶ You don't consider the particular disagreement important enough to merit discussion.

▶ You dislike arguing or debating issues.

▶ You fear that openly acknowledging and talking about a disagreement will destroy the relationship.

▶ You don't believe that the current time or place is appropriate for talking about a particular disagreement.

● **ON** *30 ROCK,* Jack relishes interpersonal conflict, while Liz will do anything to avoid it. Ironically, the two friends manage conflict between themselves very productively.

AND YOU?

Think of an attitude you have about conflict that is making it difficult for you to talk productively about dis-agreements with someone in your life. For example, do you believe that discussing conflict will destroy your relationship? What steps might you take to begin let-ting go of this unproductive attitude?

Another reason that some people avoid dealing with conflict is that they're reluctant to discuss certain topics with particular people, a behavior known as **communication boundary management** (Petronio, 2000). For instance, you might be unwilling to discuss your spouse's annoying habits with your brother, who is feeling anxious and upset about the fact that he hasn't been able to find a relationship since his divorce. Why? Because you not only want to be considerate of your brother, but also want to prevent him from becoming more distant from you if he perceives you as insensitive or petty. Similarly, stepchildren may avoid discussing certain topics with their stepparents because they worry that doing so might create conflict in their relationship (Golish & Caughlin, 2002).

COMMUNICATIONACROSSCULTURES

Culture of Nonviolence

On April 16, 2007, a gunman brutally shot and killed thirty-two individuals in one of the deadliest mass-shooting rampages in United States history (Hauser & O'Connor, 2007). The murders at Virginia Tech seemed to stem from the gunman's anger at wealthy students (CNN.com, 2007). After the shootings, many people were understandably angry themselves—at the gunman, at the school, and at the system for failing to prevent this tragedy (Johnson, Williams, Jansing, & Stewart, 2007). According to attribution theory (also termed the self-serving bias), blaming others, whether in one-on-one conflicts or large groups, is a natural reaction (Landau, 2003).

Consider, then, another shooting that occurred at an American school less than a year before the massacre at Virginia Tech. On October 2, 2006, an armed gunman entered a small one-room schoolhouse in the Amish community of Nickel Mines, Pennsylvania. The gunman, who was not Amish, took hostages and eventually lined up all the girls and began firing. Seven children were shot—five of them fatally—before the gunman, knowing that state troopers were closing in, turned his weapons on himself and committed suicide (Dewan, 2006).

Like the shootings at Virginia Tech—and those that have occurred at various schools around the United States in recent years—the murders at Nickel Mines shook the nation. But while members of the mainstream American culture reacted with anger, shock, and a need to assess blame, the pacifist Amish were fervent in their desire to forgive and actually embraced the gunman's family in the aftermath of the tragedy (Goodstein, 2006). When asked how the Amish community was dealing with the loss of these young girls, one grandfather told the press, "We must not think evil of this man" (CNN.com, 2006). Another member of the community noted, "He had a mother and a wife and a soul and now he's standing before a just God."

THINK ABOUT THIS

1 Is forgiving those who do harm an acceptable outcome for a conflict of this magnitude? Did the reaction of the Amish to their children's killer and to his family effectively resolve the conflict, or was it rather a way of managing it?

2 How do the reactions of these Amish survivors differ from those expressed by Americans after the Virginia Tech shootings? What about after 9/11?

3 The Amish forgive those involved in conflict with them because of their deeply held religious beliefs. Are there other reasons for forgiveness that can be useful in a conflict?

4 What is your reaction to the information on Amish forgiveness in light of what we learned about Amish shunning earlier in the chapter?

Communication Climate

Conflicts can stem from certain atmospheres, or feelings, surrounding different relationships. This is known as a **communication climate**. According to Folger, Poole, and Stutman (1997), climates represent the dominant temper, attitudes, and outlook of a group and provide continuity and coherence in mutual activities.

How might you determine what type of climate you may face when engaging in conflict with others? We suggest three likely possibilities: uncertain, defensive, and supportive (Gibb, 1961). The AMC television series *The Walking Dead* illustrates the ways different climates affect conflict management.

▶ **Uncertain climates** are those in which at least one of the people involved is unclear, vague, tentative, and awkward about the goals, expectations, and potential outcomes of the conflict situation. Many conditions can create uncertain climates, including unfamiliarity with the people, the surroundings, or the topic at hand. In uncertain climates, communicators are hesitant to take action, and conflict management can bog down. On *The Walking Dead*, a small group of individuals who escape a zombie epidemic outside of Atlanta manage to band together in order to survive. Clearly there are innumerable uncertainties in this postapocalyptic world: What if the zombies find their camp? How will they obtain necessary supplies? What if one of the group members is attacked? But this confusion is compounded by the overwhelming fear and hesitancy of many of the individual characters, who can't seem to decide on plans or a clear course of action to ensure their continued safety.

▶ **Defensive climates** are those in which the people involved feel threatened. It is an atmosphere of mistrust, suspicion, and apprehension. On *The Walking Dead*, protagonist Rick Grimes is attacked and captured by a father, Morgan Jones, and his son who have survived the epidemic. When Grimes awakens, he finds himself tied up and bound to a bed, face to face with the

● **AS THE FEW** escapees of a zombie epidemic band together in the post-apocalyptic *Walking Dead* series, they find themselves in a variety of communication climates: from initial defensive mistrust of one another to supportiveness and cosurvival.

understandably agitated, suspicious, and fearful father. Jones proceeds to interrogate Grimes harshly in order to ascertain if he has been exposed to the zombie virus—and he doesn't hesitate to let Grimes know that the wrong answer or move will lead to his demise.

▶ **Supportive climates** are ideal because they offer communicators a chance to honestly and considerately explore the issues involved in the conflict situation. Communicators are open to one another's ideas and feelings and together construct a reality that induces productive resolution of the problems that instigated the conflict in the first place. On *The Walking Dead*, supportive climates are hard to find. But individuals—friends, spouses, siblings, and even strangers—do work to manage problems among themselves by exploring issues and being sensitive to one another's feelings. For example, friends Dale and Andrea manage to share their sentiments about Andrea's decision to remain behind at the doomed Center for Disease Control facility and resolve their conflict with mutually beneficial results.

How do you move from a defensive or uncertain climate to a supportive one? Your first task is to make sure you know which climate you are experiencing. Your gut instincts are helpful with this task; how you feel is a credible guide. Beyond feelings, however, you can make some formal assessment of the climate situation. What are your past experiences with this topic, this person or group, these conditions? How do you feel things turned out? Once you know the climate you are in, you can take steps to move toward a supportive climate. Figure 8.1 offers several communication steps to help you find your way to supportive conflict climates.

Culture and Conflict

Culture and conflict are clearly linked. If we consider how important culture is to our identities and how pervasive conflict is in our lives, we can begin to understand how culture influences and guides our conflict experiences. Differences

FIGURE 8.1

STEPS TO REACHING A SUPPORTIVE CLIMATE

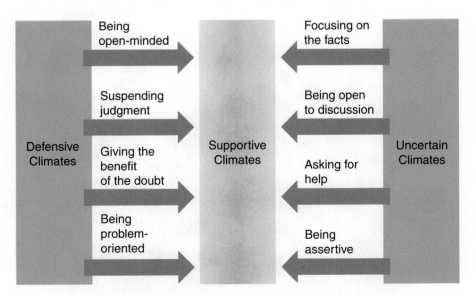

in cultural values, beliefs, and attitudes can lead to conflict directly, and they can also affect how individuals perceive conflict, what their goals are for conflict, and how conflict is handled. Let's examine two of the innumerable cultural influences on conflict: individualist versus collectivist cultures and sex and gender.

Individualist Versus Collectivist Cultures

Research in the area of race, ethnicity, and conflict often examines differences between individualist, low-context cultures and collectivist, high-context cultures. As you learned in Chapter 3, *individualist cultures* emphasize personal needs, rights, and identity over those of the collective or group, while *collectivist cultures* emphasize group identity and needs. In addition, you'll recall that people rely more on social norms and nonverbal communication than on what is actually said in *high-context cultures*. In *low-context cultures*, people are expected to say what they mean.

According to Ting-Toomey and her colleagues (2000), European Americans are individualist and low-context, while Latinos and Asians are collectivist and high-context. Thus, European Americans tend to view conflict as a necessary way to work out problems and feel that specific conflict issues should be worked out separately from relational issues. For Latinos and Asians, on the other hand, conflict is perceived as having a negative effect on relational harmony, and conflict issues cannot be divorced from relationships. Because conflict is viewed as damaging to relationships, Asians tend to avoid conflict and often use less direct communication than their more individualist American counterparts (Merkin, 2009; Trubisky, Ting-Toomey, & Lin, 1991).

When it comes to power in relationships, individualist, low-context cultures rely on and compete for tangible power resources. For example, people with power can reward and punish others; power is often asserted through threats and direct requests. In collectivist, high-context cultures, however, power is about gains or losses in reputation and is displayed subtly through indirect requests. Communication during conflict in individualist, low-context cultures is expected to be clear and direct, whereas in collectivist, high-context cultures, people are supposed to pick up on subtle cues and vague verbal messages. So whereas a Canadian parent might assert, "I'm angry with you because you used my car without asking," a Vietnamese parent may stare at his son or daughter, wait for an acknowledgment of wrongdoing, and then ask, "Why did you take the car without asking?" Understanding these very influential differences between cultures can help us understand how confusion, frustration, and miscommunication can happen when communicating across cultures.

Sex and Gender

In the 2010 film *The Kids Are All Right*, mothers Jules and Nic are worried about their teenaged son, Laser, who appears withdrawn. They ask him, over and over, if there's anything he wants to talk about. They complain that his friend Clay is a bad influence. They ask him for reasons why he sought out his biological father without telling them. But Laser simply does not want to talk. While such nagging female/noncommunicative male stereotypes are standard in fiction and film, there is some evidence to suggest that, in fact,

● IN *THE KIDS ARE ALL RIGHT*, mothers Jules and Nic and adolescent son Laser play out the typical imbalance of communicativeness between females and males.

women are more inclined to voice criticisms and complaints, and men tend to avoid engaging in such discussions.

Researcher John Gottman (1994) has studied marital conflict and the differences in conflict behaviors between men and women. He believes that four destructive behaviors are predictors of relationship dissolution: criticism and complaints, contempt, defensiveness, and stonewalling. He calls these behaviors the "four horsemen of the apocalypse." Criticism is attacking your partner's character, especially when the criticism is weaved into the complaint; contempt is attacking your partner's sense of self-worth; defensiveness is making yourself the victim; stonewalling is refusing to engage in conflict and withdrawing from the interaction. Gottman (1994) found that women tend to criticize more than men and that men tend to stonewall more than women. Recent research also suggests that sex and gender influence satisfaction level with regard to certain conflict management strategies. Afifi, McManus, Steuber, and Coho (2009) found that when women perceived that their dating partner was engaging in conflict avoidance, their satisfaction level decreased, but avoidance did not cause the same dissatisfaction in men.

The outcome of such behavioral patterns does not mean inevitable doom for relationships. According to Gottman's Web site, gottman.com, one way of improving conflict is to focus on the bright side of the relationship and give five positive statements for every one negative. In other words, Veronica may well have reason to be upset that Brent continually stonewalls her when she attempts to bring up the topic of marriage. But while she seeks productive ways to address this area of conflict, she might do well to remember the reasons she's interested in marrying him in the first place. Similarly, Brent might try to focus on Veronica's traits that bring joy to his life—her sense of humor, her ambition, and her adventurous nature—rather than constantly viewing her attempts to discuss "settling down" as a nagging criticism.

AND YOU?

Do you see yourself as more of a feminine or masculine individual? In what ways have gender differences influenced the conflicts you've experienced with people whose gender is different from yours?

When we think of these aspects of conflict and culture, it is important to remember that cultural values are not either/or. Assuming that cultures are at one extreme or the other is dangerous because it can lead people to believe that differences in culture mean irreconcilable differences in conflict. It may be difficult to understand others' cultural values, and we may feel compelled to persuade others to see things the way we do, but competent communication in conflict means understanding and respecting differences while working to "expand the pie" for both parties. Even in the most uncomfortable and frustrating conflict situations, we can learn a great deal about others and ourselves through culture.

● **THE COFOUNDER** of Wikipedia, Jim Wales, allegedly broke up with his girlfriend on his Wikipedia page. Perhaps this wasn't the best choice!

Communication Channel

In many communication situations, we don't think much about which available channel to choose in order to deliver a message. Not so when it comes to conflict. If you've ever sent flowers as a way of apologizing, left a voice mail on a weekend to let an instructor or colleague know you've missed a deadline, or delivered bad news via text message, chances are you chose that channel as a way of avoiding engaging in conflict face to face. But conflict and communication channels are often intertwined: conflict can arise from poor channel choices, as we perceive things differently depending on the channel used (see Chapter 2). But even more interesting is the powerful way that channel choice influences conflict management.

Of course, some practical considerations can influence which channel we select to communicate with someone else about a disagreement. For example, if you live far away from your sister, and you and she need to address an issue that has come up between you, you may decide to talk about it by phone rather than make the long journey to have a face-to-face conversation. However, our reasons for choosing one channel over another are often rooted in emotions. If you're intimidated by someone you're in a conflict with, you may feel safer communicating with them by e-mail than over the phone or face to face. But beware: managing conflict with close friends or romantic partners through electronic channels can come across as insensitive and even cowardly. Just ask anyone who found out that a relationship was over via a changed "relationship status" on his or her significant other's Facebook page!

Online Anonymity and Conflict

On a related front, the relative anonymity of electronic communication has emerged as a new factor that influences conflict, particularly in the generation of heated and unproductive electronic exchanges in Internet forums, in e-mails, and through social networking sites (Shachaf & Hara, 2010). Of course, people have long been able to provoke conflict anonymously—for example, prank phone calls were common in the days before caller ID. But the Internet has

A lack of nonverbal communication can pose problems when handling conflict via mediated channels (Chapter 5). If you text an apology to your friend, he can't see your facial expressions to appreciate how sorry you are. Emoticons do help display feelings (☺!), but competent communicators must consider if nonverbal communication is needed for a particular message. When dealing with conflict, it might be better to speak face to face or over the phone so that nonverbal behaviors such as tone of voice can be decoded.

provided a vast arena for **flaming**—the posting of online messages that are deliberately hostile or insulting toward a particular individual. Such messages are usually intended only to provoke anger and can ignite flame wars between individuals when friendly, productive discussions give way to insults and aggression. In many cases, the root cause of these conflicts is not even a disagreement but one person's misinterpretation of another's message (as with Joe Lipari's pseudo-threat on the Apple Store detailed in the chapter opener).

Flaming should be distinguished from **trolling** which is the posting of provocative or offensive messages to whole forums or discussion boards in order to elicit some type of general reaction (Morzy, 2009). Trolls often use their online anonymity to intentionally stir up conflict and create damage in an online community; research reveals that they are often motivated by boredom, attention seeking, and revenge (Shachaf & Hara, 2010).

Technological channels are also an arena for even more aggressive conflict behaviors, such as **cyberbullying**—multiple abusive attacks on individual

---

AND YOU?

Consider a recent conflict. What channel did you select to communicate with the other person? How did the communication channel affect the quality of the exchange? Did the channel you chose lead to a productive conflict or an unproductive one? Why?

WIREDFORCOMMUNICATION

Virtual Conflict: Flaming, Trolls, and Mods

Internet forums are, in a sense, a grand experiment in free speech. A trip to an open forum on just about any topic—from *American Idol* to the war in Afghanistan—is likely to yield astute critiques and interesting perspectives—as well as lots of irrelevant, incoherent, offensive, and inflammatory banter. That's because for the most part, Internet forums are both interactive and uncensored: users are able to post whatever they want. It's up to the network of users to self-police the interaction, keep it on topic, and eliminate any rude or irrelevant chat. For example, experienced forum users often warn, "Do not feed the trolls," in an attempt to prevent other users from taking the bait and responding to obnoxious messages designed to provoke (Cambria, Chandra, Sharma, & Hussain, 2010). And while some studies do reveal that forum members understand the value of ignoring the messages (Sobkowicz & Sobkowicz, 2010), others find it too hard—or too immoral—to walk away from hateful, vitriolic posts online (Hardaker, 2010).

Moderated forums, by contrast, trade complete openness for order. Forum moderators—commonly known as mods—set strict rules for posts, often review all posts before making them public, and have the power to censor or ban specific posts. At the fiercely moderated television commentary site *Television Without Pity*, for example, moderators set clear and strict rules and regularly review discussion threads to eliminate posts that fall off topic or are repetitive. While some critics claim that the moderators do so to rid the site of bad language or positions at odds with the moderators', most critics see a clear advantage to the site's authoritarian moderation of its boards: the discourse is civil and literate, and conflicts between posters are respectful and productive (Stevens, 2007).

THINK ABOUT THIS

❶ Do you participate in Internet forums? Do you prefer moderated or open forums? What makes you prefer one over the other?

❷ Which is more important, a free-speech open forum or a managed, productive conflict? Do you think it's necessary to trade off one for the other?

❸ Does self-policing work on the Internet? What circumstances might inhibit a group's ability to self-police?

targets conducted through electronic channels (Erdur-Baker, 2010). Social networking sites like MySpace and Facebook offer an open forum for bullies, who demean or threaten individuals. Sociologists and educators point out that traditional bullying, while highly unpleasant, is also extremely intimate; cyberbullying, by contrast, makes use of e-mails, instant messages, and text messages to deliver cruelty to its victims, often anonymously (Maag, 2007b). Among teens and preteens, the problem has serious consequences, as evidenced by the suicide of a thirteen-year-old Missouri girl, Megan Meier. Moments after receiving a message that "the world would be a better place without you" from a boy she'd connected with through MySpace, Megan ran to her closet and hanged herself with a belt. Megan had been corresponding and flirting with this boy, Josh Evans, for months before he viciously turned on her. He told her that he had heard she was terrible to her friends and that he was no longer interested in being friends with her. A few other teens who were linked to Josh's profile also joined in on the attack, sending her hate-filled messages. In the aftermath of her suicide, it was revealed that the boy didn't really exist and was in fact a creation of the mother of a former friend of Megan's (Maag, 2007a).

In some cases, cyberbullies—so empowered by their anonymity—entirely disregard expectations surrounding particular situational contexts. After seventeen-year-old Alexis Pilkington took her own life, her friends and family set up a Facebook memorial page to remember Alexis and to share their mutual grief. Sadly, alongside messages honoring this young woman's life were lewd, hateful, and inappropriate messages indicating that Alexis "got what she deserved." A family friend summarized the bullies' attempt to create controversy and conflict in such an inappropriate time and space: "Children want to mourn their friend, and there are posts of photos with nooses around her neck. It's disgusting and heartless" (Martinez, 2010, para. 6).

● **SOMETIMES THE** competition for a lone piece of pie can mask larger emotional issues.

Strategies for Managing Conflict

A number of strategies might be employed to manage any conflict. To get an initial sense of these strategies, let's consider a common, very simplistic scenario: Leslie is sitting with her twin sister, Kathy, at the dinner table after a family meal. There's one last piece of key lime pie (or whatever kind of pie you like best), and both sisters want it.

In certain conflict situations, such as a competition for a piece of pie, the people involved can resolve the conflict—that is, bring it to an end—in just seconds. But when the conflict is more complex or when a seemingly simple disagreement is a symptom of a larger problem between people, resolving the situation will require more time and thought. If Leslie is growing resentful of always having to share everything with Kathy—her room, her friends, her laptop, her iPod, her clothes—their conflict is bigger than a piece of pie. Resolving it may require a more involved approach, such as honest, lengthy dialogue about Leslie's resentments and possible ways for her to have

CONFLICT STRATEGIES: THE KEY LIME PIE INCIDENT

Type	Description	Examples
Escapist	Conflict is avoided or prevented; goals may not be important; conflict is not seen as a viable alternative	• Relinquish the pie ("You can have the pie")
Challenging	Individual goals are pursued; relationship is threatened	• Take the pie ("That's my piece of pie") • Fight for the pie ("Oh, no, it's not")
Cooperative	Pursuit of mutual interests; problem-solving approach emphasized; relationship is preserved	• Share the pie • Flip a coin for the pie • Broker a deal for the pie ("I'll do the dishes if you let me have the pie")

more things she can call her own. Nonetheless, the strategies we use for managing conflict, be they simple or complicated, generally fall into one of three basic categories: escapist, challenging, or cooperative (see Table 8.1).

Escapist Strategies

One way for Leslie to manage the conflict is to make a decision to avoid it, and let Kathy have the pie, even though she really wants it for herself. Through such **escapist strategies**, people try to prevent or avoid direct conflict. Perhaps they want to steer clear of a confrontation because they're afraid a direct conflict would hurt the other person or the relationship. Or maybe they wish to postpone dealing with the conflict until a more convenient time, when they can talk at length about it with the other person. Another reason for selecting this type of strategy might be to force the other person to raise the issue instead of having to do so themselves.

In certain situations, escapist strategies can be harmless and practical, offering a quick resolution to issues that are relatively unimportant (like pie), and can help maintain relationships that might be damaged if conflict erupted over every little thing. Stafford (2010) found that couples in long-distance relationships engage in greater conflict avoidance than couples in geographically close relationships, but notes that this strategy is effective for long-distance partners' relational maintenance because it minimizes differences and maximizes positive affect. But such strategies may be unproductive if they continually prevent people from dealing with issues that need addressing: if Leslie always defers to Kathy, for example, resentment is likely to brew between the sisters. The pie could become a tipping point for a larger issue, prompting Leslie to take a different approach. In fact, recent research has found that continual avoidance of conflict in families negatively impacts family strength and satisfaction (Schrodt, 2009).

Challenging Strategies

If Leslie decides that she wants the pie more than she wants to avoid fighting with Kathy, she might demand the entire piece for herself, at her sister's expense. Such **challenging strategies** promote the objectives of the individual who uses them, rather than the desires of the other person or the relationship. Challenging strategies are often referred to as assertiveness. Assertive people are generally effective at handling conflicts because they don't let negative emotions like anxiety, guilt, or embarrassment get in the way and they stand up for what they believe is right.

Challenging strategies may or may not strengthen the relationship of the people involved, depending on the situational context and how the strategy is employed. For example, if Leslie becomes aggressive with Kathy and rudely demands the last slice of pie, she's probably not doing much to be considerate of her sister or to strengthen their bond. However, research does reveal that there are times when challenging others has positive benefits. For example, Canary, Cunningham, and Cody (1988) found that people tend to employ challenging strategies when they feel the need to defend themselves from a perceived threat. So, you would rightly be assertive when the friend you came to a party with attempts to get behind the wheel of a vehicle after consuming alcohol. Drunk driving is a threat to your, your friend's, and the public's well-being. In fact, your friend may later mention that he is grateful to you for thwarting his attempts to engage in such a risky activity, thus strengthening your friendship.

In some relationships, challenging strategies are accepted as part of a relational context that is generally open and forgiving. To illustrate, perhaps Leslie and Kathy are so close and feel so confident of their love for one another that Leslie knows a moment of selfish behavior on her part will be overlooked or forgiven by Kathy (and vice versa). Conversely, if the relationship is not really valued, challenging strategies can enable individuals to get what they want without any consequential losses, since maintaining the relationship is not a priority. For example, Leslie might adopt a challenging strategy if she were in competition with a stranger for the last piece of pie while on the lunch line at school.

Cooperative Strategies

Of course, the most practical and fairest way for Leslie to manage this conflict is to propose a compromise, offering to split the last piece of pie with Kathy. If Leslie decides to share the pie, she is attempting to arrive at the best outcome for both partners in this relationship. Strategies that benefit the relationship, serve mutual rather than individual goals, and strive to produce solutions that benefit both parties are called **cooperative strategies** (Zacchilli, Hendrick, & Henrick, 2009).

AND YOU?

Are there certain people with whom you engage in more challenging strategies than others? Do you engage in conflict with strangers more or less than you do with people who are important to you?

● **WHILE KIERAN** might be sure he wants to join the Army, negotiating alternatives with his mother might allow him to explore his choices and uncover other options.

Whether the issue is pie or child custody decisions, several tactics are useful in cooperative conflict management. For example, let's consider a larger issue that is causing conflict within a family: twenty-year-old Kieran wants to drop out of college to join the Army. His mother is very upset and wants him to continue his education. A number of strategies can help them manage the conflict cooperatively.

real communicator

NAME: Anonymous
HOMETOWN: Chicago, Illinois
OCCUPATION: Police officer
FUN FACT: Due to security reasons, officer must remain anonymous

I'm a police officer in Chicago. Cops on TV are always running around with their guns drawn or tossing bad guys against brick walls, and while I do some of that, of course, I'd say that over 90 percent of my job is spent communicating with people. And most of that time is about managing conflict.

In my first few years out of the academy, I responded to a lot of domestic disputes. Neighbors call in about other neighbors making too much noise; spouses and parents call in about fighting in the home. These are unproductive conflicts: screaming, destruction of property, and all too often violence. And few things have the potential to escalate unproductive conflict like uniformed men and women coming into your home with guns, right?

The first thing I do is use my eyes to see if physical injuries are apparent or if a crime has been committed. If so, it's a domestic violence situation, and I arrest the perpetrator, taking him or her to jail. The conflict is temporarily resolved. Most of the time, however, these calls are incidents of domestic *disputes*. A crime hasn't been committed. I can't make an arrest. And my job becomes much more difficult. Now I have to manage conflict—through mediation.

First off, I don't use any challenging strategies as I might with a drug dealer on the street.

I stay nonaggressive (I am, after all, in someone else's home). I try not to lean forward, I stay out of people's faces, and I speak in a monotone. I try to exude calmness, because everyone else in the place is freaking out.

One time, I had a man who simply wouldn't stop screaming at and about his wife: *I hate her! I hate her guts!* As calmly as possible, I asked, "You hate who?" He said, *I hate my wife!* I looked shocked and said, "Sir, you hate your *wife*?" I kept the questions coming. In the academy they call this verbal judo, the sword of insertion. In communication classes, it's called probing. I asked the man simple questions, getting him down to facts, getting him to think about things reasonably, as opposed to thinking about them emotionally.

Sometimes, I'll turn to one party and say, as respectfully as possible, "Listen, I know I don't have a right to ask you to leave your own house, but maybe there's a cousin's place you can go crash at for the night, or maybe you can go take a long walk and cool down." It's not a win-win or lose-lose resolution; it's a separation, a temporary one. It's an escapist strategy, a prevention of further unproductive conflict, a rain check on the situation until a better time, when heads are cooler. Often that's the best I can do. I've got other homes to go to, other conflicts to manage.

Focus on Issues

With any issue, it's very important that the discussion remain centered on the matter at hand and steer clear of any personal attacks. If Kieran's mother boldly declares, "You are irrational and thoughtless. Who drops out of college with only one year left?" she's making the argument personal and isn't considering the fact that Kieran may well have thought through the ramifications of his decision. Such **verbal aggressiveness**—attacks on individuals rather than issues—are

what about you?

Hitting Above and Below the Belt

The concepts of argumentativeness and verbal aggressiveness are important to the study of conflict management because the first is more likely to produce positive outcomes than the second. Examine the items below, and mark each one according to how you feel about most conflicts (1 = true, 2 = undecided, 3 = false).

——— 1. Arguing over controversial issues improves my intelligence.

——— 2. I really come down hard on people if they don't see things my way.

——— 3. I am good about not losing my temper during conflict situations.

——— 4. Some people need to be insulted if they are to see reason.

——— 5. I prefer being with people who disagree with me.

——— 6. It is exhilarating to get into a good conflict.

——— 7. I have the ability to do well in conflict situations.

——— 8. It is not hard for me to go for the throat if a person really deserves it.

——— 9. I know how to construct effective arguments that can change people's minds.

——— 10. I avoid getting into conflicts with people who know how to argue well.

——— 11. I know how to find other people's personal weaknesses.

Scoring: Add your scores for items 1, 3, 5, 6, 7, and 9. Reverse your scores for items 2, 4, 8, 10, and 11 (1 = 3, 3 = 1); after converting the numbers, add all of these scores to your previous total. If you scored between 11 and 18, you are prone to argumentativeness. If you scored between 26 and 33, you are likely to be verbally aggressive when you are in conflict situations. If you scored between 19 and 25, you are probably neither very argumentative nor very aggressive.

Source: From Infante, D. A. (1988). Adapted with permission of the publisher.

common, especially in the media (witness the personal assaults that characterize political campaigns and celebrity gossip), but they are also unproductive. Research by Roberto, Carlyle, Goodall, and Castle (2009) suggests that parents' verbal aggression toward their children can negatively impact relationship satisfaction and is associated with nonsecure attachment styles among young adult children. Further, when verbal aggression is used by supervisors toward their subordinates in the workplace, it can negatively affect employee job satisfaction and commitment (Madlock & Kennedy-Lightsey, 2010).

Such personal attacks do little to foster cooperation and usually succeed only in putting the other person on the defensive and making the interaction more heated. So, Kieran's mother would do better to keep the focus on Kieran's decision ("I really don't like the idea of your dropping out of school when you're halfway finished with your degree") than to focus her criticisms on Kieran himself.

Debate and Argue

CONNECT

In Chapter 7, we discuss the relational repair tactics that help partners shift the focus from the problems to the benefits of their relationship. By separating the issues from the person, partners can remember why they value each other in the first place. Instead of telling your roommate that she is inconsiderate and messy, remember that she makes you laugh and prepares your meals when you're sick. *Then* approach her to work out your issues.

As noted earlier in this chapter, when we engage in conflict by debating the issue at hand, we exchange more ideas, reach better decisions, and foster stronger, healthier relationships. Healthy debate is therefore a cornerstone of cooperative conflict management. A number of tactics can help foster debate.

One is **probing**—asking questions that encourage specific and precise answers. If Kieran's mother asks probing questions ("Why do you want to join the Army now when you're so close to graduating?"), she'll get a better understanding of why and how he's come to this decision. Likewise, Kieran will get a better sense of his mother's feelings if he asks similar questions of her ("Why is it so important to you that I finish my degree now?").

Probing can help parties explore the pros and cons of an issue, encouraging either side to consider both the positive and the negative aspects of it. This allows one individual to clarify his or her argument to the other and the other to critique it. Kieran, for example, might note that the job market for college graduates in his major is completely flat, and so he sees the Army as a solid employment opportunity. His mother might point out that he'll still have to pay back all his college loans, with or without his degree, and that all that expenditure will have amounted to little if he doesn't finish. Kieran's mother might also play the role of **devil's advocate**—pointing out the worst-case scenarios ("There's a war going on. What if you get hurt or killed?")—to make sure her son has considered all the possible outcomes of his decision (and revealing her own fears in the process).

Consider Options and Alternatives

Offering—and potentially negotiating—alternatives is a useful tactic for cooperative conflict management. Kieran's mother might suggest, for example, that he join the Army Reserve instead, which would allow him to finish school while also serving his country and ensuring a career if he wants to go on active duty after graduation.

Consider the Importance of the Outcome

Obviously, a disagreement over a serious issue like quitting school to join the Army clearly warrants serious debate. But many of the conflicts in which we find ourselves embroiled (like disputes over pie) don't seem all that important. Nevertheless, it's important to clarify that the issue will have consequences. For example, Kieran's mother might emphasize that the Army is not a job he can simply quit if he doesn't like it.

Reassure Your Partner

To resolve a conflict cooperatively, a straightforward explanation of your good intentions might be in order. When Kieran's mother tells him, "Please, I just want to talk about this to make sure I understand your reasons before you make a rash decision," she's stating her desire to resolve the disagreement, showing him that she respects his feelings and intelligence, and reassuring him that she wants to engage in a discussion with him, not simply tell him what to do.

> **AND YOU?**
> Think of a person with whom you have recently had a disagreement who isn't willing to discuss the situation with you. What might be causing this reluctance? And which technique might best help you draw the person into discussion about your conflict?

Conflict Outcomes

As we noted earlier, conflict cannot always be resolved. But every conflict does, eventually, have some outcome. Regardless of how they engage in it, the conflict between twins Leslie and Kathy will produce some outcome: one or the other sister may get the pie, the two might share the pie, or neither might get any pie at all.[1] Conflict outcomes fall into several categories (see Table 8.2 on p. 243).

Compromise

You may buy into the idea that compromising is always the easiest and best way to resolve a conflict. Sometimes that may be true, as when a compromise involves sharing a piece of pie; other times, however, it may prove more challenging, as when you must set up a schedule for using a jointly owned computer or split the cost of some shared item with a roommate or neighbor. With most **compromises**, both sides give up a little to gain a little.

Compromises can be arrived at through **trading**, whereby one partner offers something of equal value in return for something he or she wants. Separated parents who must navigate joint custody arrangements might strike compromises regarding time spent with their children: Maggie offers Sean extra weekends with their boys in the spring if he'll let her have them for Christmas for the second year in a row. On the other hand, a committed

---

[1]Research on conflict types has been conducted in the communication field for many years, and many terms are given for the types you will read about in this section. An excellent source that describes these conflict types (using many different terms) is a comprehensive review by Oetzel and Ting-Toomey (2006).

couple with young children might bargain for time spent away from the family: Dan stays home on Friday while Ann goes to the movies with her sister; Ann stays home on Sunday while Dan plays golf with a friend.

Other options might include **random selection** (for example, Maggie and Sean could flip a coin to decide who gets the kids for Christmas) or, when appropriate and practical, taking a vote (having the kids weigh in on where they want to go and when).

The advantage of compromise is that it lets you and the other person quickly resolve or avert a conflict by agreeing on a decision-making method. However, important relationships can suffer if the people involved are *always* making compromises. That's because compromising means giving up *some* of what you want, even though you're getting a little of something else in return. After a while, that can get tiresome. With romantic partners, close friends, and family members,

EVALUATINGCOMMUNICATIONETHICS

THINK ABOUT THIS

The Accidental Relationship Counselor

You and your sister Ellen are close in age—she's only a year younger than you—and are very close friends. And while it was weird when Ellen began dating your best friend, Steve, during your junior year of high school, over the past few years you've gotten used to them being together. They've been dating for three years now, and you still hang out with them all the time, both individually and as a couple.

But lately you've been noticing that their relationship isn't as close as it used to be. Even though you all commute to the same community college, you've noticed that Ellen and Steve aren't always together the way they used to be. While you and Steve navigated the campus together as freshmen last year, Ellen is tackling her first year at school in a more independent manner. She is making lots of new friends, joining campus clubs, and spending a lot of time away from Steve (and you). While you're happy to see your little sister spreading her wings, you worry about her future with Steve.

Making things worse, Steve is confiding his doubts about the relationship in you—he tells you that he thinks Ellen might be interested in other guys and asks you if she has mentioned anyone in particular. He then mentions that there is girl in one of his classes who he thinks might like him. Meanwhile, Ellen mentions that she's disappointed in the way Steve is handling college. When the three of you had lunch recently, Ellen publicly vented her frustration at Steve: "You still act like you're in high school. You have all the same friends, all the same interests. Don't you want to experience something new?" As awkward as that encounter was, you feel even worse when Ellen later confides to you privately: "I feel like maybe it's time we broke up. What do you think?"

You always knew that the day might come when Steve and Ellen split up, but you never imagined you'd feel so caught in the middle. You know that Steve loves her and wants to stay together, but at the same time you know that Ellen isn't entirely happy in the relationship. What will you do?

❶ You know that both Ellen and Steve rely on you as a friend (and in Ellen's case, as family). How can you maintain your relationships with both of them even as their relationship with each other is falling apart? Is it fair of them to involve you at all?

❷ What outcomes are possible here? Can you provide advice to help them stay together? Should you?

❸ What do you think of Steve mentioning another girl? Would it affect you differently if Ellen were just a friend, and not your sister?

Incident	Dispute	Outcome
The Great Compromise, 1767	In forging the U.S. Constitution, disagreement emerges between small states that want equal representation in the legislature and large states that want representation to be apportioned according to population.	Win-Win (via Win-Lose): The framers created a bicameral Congress, consisting of the Senate, which offers equal representation (small states win, large stages lose), and the House of Representatives, which gives larger states a bigger voice (large states win, small states lose). In the long run, the bicameral Congress serves the interests of both large and small states (win-win).
Montgomery Bus Boycott, 1955–1956	Following the lead of Rosa Parks, African Americans in Montgomery, Alabama, begin walking to work and school rather than riding on segregated buses.	Win-Lose: African Americans in Montgomery rely heavily on public transportation, so the decision to boycott the buses presents some serious hardships for them. But since they constitute three-fourths of the ridership on city buses, their actions translate into a major loss of revenue. Their hardships pay off: in June 1956, a federal court rules that Alabama's law requiring segregated buses is unconstitutional.
Don't Ask, Don't Tell, 1993–2010	President Bill Clinton tries to eliminate restrictions on homosexuals' serving in the military; he is met with opposition from conservatives and some members of the armed forces. In 1993, a compromise is struck that prohibits the military from investigating individuals' sexuality but still allows dismissal of military personnel if their homosexuality becomes known.	Lose-Lose turned Win-Lose: Neither side is satisfied with the compromise. Congress repealed the rule in 2010, allowing gays and lesbians to serve openly.
Apple Corp. v. Apple Computer, 1978–2010	A lawsuit from the Beatles-founded music company challenges the American computer maker's use of the Apple name and logo. An initial compromise that limited each company's use of the logo, specifically in relation to selling music, was challenged when music became a digital commodity in the 1990s.	Win-Win: After nearly three decades of litigation, the matter was finally settled in 2007. Both companies were satisfied with the agreement, in which Apple Computer purchased full rights to the name and logo but licensed it back to Apple records for use on CDs and music sales. The Beatles catalog was finally made available on iTunes in November 2010.

TABLE 8.2

CONFLICT OUTCOMES: THE GOOD, THE BAD, AND THE UGLY

● **MANY PEOPLE STAY** in jobs they hate because they fear the unknown. But this way, nobody wins: you're unhappy and you do your job poorly, which affects those who depend on you.

it often feels better to come up with more creative, thoughtful approaches to ongoing conflicts that lead to "win-win" resolutions.

Win-Win

When both participants in a conflict discuss the situation and arrive at a solution that fully satisfies each of them, the conflict has been resolved in a win-win manner. Thinking back to the key lime pie incident, if sisters Leslie and Kathy use that conflict to work through their issue of having to share everything, they may be able to arrive at a variety of solutions to the problem and strengthen their relationship in the process. They might agree to pool their money for a second computer or come up with a system for sharing certain items of clothing while placing others off limits. Through such "win-win" solutions, both parties can meet their own goals (unlimited computer access, a bigger wardrobe), help the other with her goals, and improve their relationship.

Lose-Lose

Of course, there are times when a conflict is resolved without either side getting what it wants. If Leslie decides that if she can't have the pie, nobody can and tosses it in the trash, she's resolved the conflict at hand, even though she didn't get what she wanted. While such outcomes seem childish, they are in fact relatively common. Individuals often stay in jobs that they hate and do them poorly because they don't see the possibility for other outcomes; in such cases, both the individual and the employer lose, along with any customers or clients who depend on them.

Separation

By contrast, individuals who quit jobs opt for a different outcome: **separation**. Removing oneself from a situation or relationship is a clear way to end a conflict without necessarily creating clear wins or losses for either party. For example, suppose you're renting an apartment from a friend who, as the landlord, never repairs burst pipes or fixes the fridge when it breaks, even though you pay your rent on time every month. You've tried to reason with him; you've even tried to guilt him into reimbursing you for the money you've spent on repairs he should have paid for. But nothing has worked. In this case, the best resolution to this conflict may be to simply pack up your things and move.

Allocation of Power

Yet another way to resolve conflict is to decide, with the other person, which of you will have the power to make certain decisions in the relationship. For example, in a couple, one individual may be dominant on one issue (such as

AND YOU?

Have you ever opted for separation as a way to end a conflict—with a friend, a romantic partner, or a roommate? Was it difficult for you to separate? Are there some relationships for which separation would never be an option?

finances) while the other makes the decisions on others (such as child rearing); in a work environment, several employees may split the responsibilities of a given project, with one member making financial decisions, another in charge of creative ones, and a third in charge of communicating all those decisions to others outside the group.

BACK TO The Social Network

At the beginning of this chapter, we talked about the film *The Social Network* and how in real life people often use Facebook status updates as a means of airing grievances and dealing with conflict. Let's consider how the concepts we've learned about in this chapter play into social networking conflicts.

▶ When you're dealing with conflict, it's important to consider the forum, especially in mediated communication. Although Mark Zuckerberg's personal blog reveals that he did indeed insult a woman on the night he began working on SmashFace (the precursor to Facebook), there is no evidence that he created the site as a means of revenge. The idea of letting off steam by complaining about others online, however, is not terribly original. Facebook, Twitter, and personal blogs turn something that, in a face-to-face setting, would be a simple letting off of steam among a few friends into something public and permanent, which can never be taken back.

▶ While some of the conflicts dramatized in the film *The Social Network* are fictional, others, including disputes over who actually conceptualized and owned Facebook, are matters of public record. Zuckerberg was initially hired by twins Cameron and Tyler Winklevoss and Divya Narendra to write code for a social network they were developing. He instead launched his own site, which they claim he stole from them. Though they tried to settle the matter in Harvard's Honor Court, they wound up suing Zuckerberg for a share in the company. In this type of dispute, avoiding conflict might have cost them millions—if not billions—of dollars.

▶ When using Facebook to vent about a conflict, it's important to be aware of your goals. Announcing one's divorce or changed relationship status on Facebook can be helpful if your goal is to inform your friends of what you're going through without having to detail or live through painful events all over again as you tell person after person what is going on. But using it as a forum to insult or complain about your ex is a less productive means of conflict management.

▶ It's also important to consider relational context when posting on Facebook. Will everyone in your friend list understand your references, your sense of humor, and your intentions? Joe Lipari's close friends probably got the joke when he paraphrased a violent threat from *Fight Club* in his status update, but someone from the region surrounding his hometown (where the police complaint originated) took it seriously enough to alert authorities.

THINGS TO TRY ▶ Activities

1. The engagement in and resolution of interpersonal conflict are often key factors in romantic comedies (like *Life As We Know It* and *When Harry Met Sally*), as well as in buddy-driven action films (such as *Shanghai Noon* and *The Other Guys*). Try watching such a film, and pay attention to the way in which the principal characters engage in conflict with one another. How does their conflict management lead to relationship growth?

2. For an interesting look at conflict and debate, you need not search further than the U.S. Congress. Debates on the floor of the Senate and House of Representatives are broadcast on C-SPAN and provide an interesting glimpse into the way that conflict and argument shape new laws and policy. In addition to observing how this process works, pay attention to the way that strict rules regarding time and etiquette keep the debate relatively diplomatic. For a comparison of rules in the House and Senate, go to http://www.senate.gov/reference/resources/pdf/RL30945.pdf.

3. Read the advice column in your daily paper or an online magazine. Bearing in mind what you've read in this chapter, consider the nature of the interpersonal conflicts discussed. What are the precursors to the conflicts? What kinds of tactics does the columnist suggest using to manage and resolve the disagreements?

4. This week, if you have a disagreement with a friend, roommate, romantic partner, family member, or boss, identify *one* change you could make to manage and resolve the conflict more productively. For example, could you suggest a compromise? Look for a broader range of promising solutions to your disagreement?

Now that you have finished reading this chapter, you can:

Describe the factors that lead to productive conflict:

▶ **Conflict** is a negative interaction between interdependent people, rooted in disagreement (p. 220).
▶ **Conflict management** refers to how relational partners address disagreements (p. 220).
▶ **Unproductive conflict** is conflict that is managed poorly and that has a negative impact (p. 220).
▶ **Productive conflict** is healthy and managed effectively. It fosters healthy debate, leads to better decision making, and spurs relationship growth (p. 221).

Identify conflict triggers in yourself and others:

▶ Many conflicts are rooted in errors of perception (p. 223).
▶ Incompatible goals can spark conflict (p. 224).
▶ Conflicts arise when the costs of an interpersonal relationship outweigh the rewards (p. 224).
▶ **Provocation**, the intentional instigation of conflict, arises when one party demonstrates aggression, a person's identity feels threatened, fairness is lacking, someone you depend on is incompetent, or an important relationship is threatened (pp. 224–225).

Explain the forces that influence how people handle conflict:

▶ Power dynamics affect relationships in which there is an imbalance of power (pp. 226–227).
▶ Attitudes about conflict in general or about specific disagreements can cause people to avoid dealing with it (p. 227).
▶ People may be reluctant to discuss certain topics with particular people, behavior known as **communication boundary management** (p. 228).
▶ **Communication climate** varies, and may be **uncertain**, **defensive**, or **supportive** (pp. 229–230).
▶ Cultural issues, such as gender expectations, religious beliefs, and being from an *individualist culture* versus a *collectivist culture,* have a strong influence on conflict (pp. 230–231).

▶ Our reasons for choosing certain channels may be rooted in emotions or practical considerations (p. 233).
▶ The Internet provides an arena for **flaming**, posting hostile online messages to an individual; **trolling**, posting hostile online messages to a more general group; and **cyberbullying**, abusive attacks through electronic channels (pp. 233–235).

Evaluate and employ strategies for managing conflict in different situations:

▶ **Escapist strategies** avoid direct conflict and are good for quick resolutions but may leave issues unresolved (p. 236).
▶ **Challenging strategies** promote the interests of individuals who use assertiveness to get their way (p. 237).
▶ **Cooperative strategies** benefit both parties (p. 237).
▶ A focus on the issues avoids **verbal aggressiveness**, attacks on individuals (pp. 239–240).
▶ **Probing**, asking questions that encourage precise answers, and playing **devil's advocate**, pointing out worst-case scenarios, are two techniques for healthy debate (p. 240).
▶ Other useful tactics include negotiating alternatives, clarifying the importance of the outcome, and reassuring your partner of your good intentions (pp. 240–241).

Compare levels of resolution in conflict outcomes:

▶ With **compromise**, which may involve **trading** or **random selection**, both parties give up something to gain something (pp. 241–242).
▶ A solution that satisfies all parties is win-win; a lose-lose solution has no winner (p. 244).
▶ **Separation**, removing oneself from the situation, is a form of resolution, as is making a decision to allocate power for certain decisions (p. 244).

Group and Organizational Communication

PARTICIPANTS in the Susan G. Komen 3-Day for the Cure rely on one another more than anything else to walk a full sixty miles and stand up against breast cancer.

Curtis walks for his wife. Danielle walks for her mother. Lynette walks for herself. And Cindy walks for her young granddaughter in the hope that she'll never hear the four terrifying words that changed Cindy's life forever: "You have breast cancer."

Every year, the organization Susan G. Komen for the Cure plans "3-Day," sixty-mile walks to raise funds for breast cancer all over the United States—from Philadelphia to Dallas to San Francisco. Individuals are required to raise a minimum of $2,300 to participate, and they must devote a significant amount of time to training (mentally and physically) for the challenge of the walk.

Sounds overwhelming, doesn't it? And yet thousands of men and women (over 220,000 since 2003) gladly devote their time and effort to participate ("Susan G. Komen," 2011a). They host bake sales and car washes and join with others to plan larger events—like fashion shows and golf tournaments—to raise money. They find support from virtual personal trainers and volunteer training walks as they prepare their bodies for the challenge. And let's not forget the power of the Internet! Susan G. Komen for the Cure hosts online forums so that participants have a virtual space to encourage and support one another, before and after the walk.

By the time the 3-Day for the Cure weekends arrive, participants know that they are enveloped in a group more powerful than any individual. They are members of a community that shares goals, drive, and, quite often, the experience of being touched by breast cancer, either personally or through the struggle of a loved one. As one participant noted, "The reason we get together might be sad, but when we're together [it's about] sisterhood, and family, and teamwork that I really haven't experienced anywhere else" ("Susan G. Komen," 2011b). And that teamwork certainly comes in handy when rain pours down, calves get sore, blisters form, and ice packs just aren't enough. Anywhere a participant looks is a fellow teammate ready to point out their shared commitment: "Sixty miles. I can do that."

After you have finished reading this chapter, you will be able to

- List the characteristics and types of groups and explain how groups develop

- Describe ways in which group size affects communication

- Identify the influence of networks in groups

- Define the roles individuals play in a group

- Identify key issues affecting group communication and effectiveness

As you will recall from earlier chapters, communication between two individuals (a dyad) is far more complicated than many of us assume. In a dyad, both participants simultaneously deliver, receive, and interpret messages presented through verbal and nonverbal means—and these messages can be misunderstood in light of perceptual differences or faulty listening. So consider how much more complex things can get when you add more people to the communication scenario! When three or more people come together, their interactions and relationships—and their communication—take on new characteristics, as you can see in our discussion of the 3-Day for the Cure walks. In this chapter, we'll learn more about group communication, how groups operate, and the factors that influence their communication.

Understanding Groups

Your family sitting down to dinner. Ten adults on a bus to Cleveland, Ohio. Your fraternity or sorority at an event. A group of coworkers sitting down for a drink at the end of a shift. Six exasperated parents sitting in a doctor's office with sick kids. Each of these examples involves multiple people (sometimes crowds of people) engaged in some activity—and most of us would probably say that these are examples of "groups of people." But are they really groups? We'll explore what it actually means to be in a group, in addition to understanding what types of groups exist and how those groups develop in the first place.

Characteristics of Groups

For our purposes, a **group** is a collection of more than two people who share some kind of relationship, communicate in an interdependent fashion, and collaborate toward some shared purpose. When we break that definition down, we can identify three key characteristics that make a group something other than just a collection of individuals:

▶ *A shared identity.* Members of a group perceive themselves as a group. That is, they share a sense of identity with other members of the group: they recognize other members of the group, have specific feelings toward those individuals, and experience a sense of belonging in the group. Thus, a variety of people who identify themselves as part of a group (political parties, for example, or fan organizations) are as much a group as a baseball team or a string quartet.

▶ *Common goals.* Members of a group usually identify with one another because they have one or more goals in common. Goals may be very specific—coming up with an ad campaign for a new project or organizing a mission trip for a congregation—or they might be quite general, such as socializing or discussing books or films. In either case, a shared sense of purpose helps define a group, even when there is some disagreement about specific goals or ways of achieving them.

▶ *Interdependent relationships.* Members of a group are connected to one another and communicate in an interdependent way. Simply put, the behavior of each member affects the behavior of every other member. This interdependence is fostered by the way that group members adopt specific roles and collaborate to accomplish goals. These goals might be very specific (completing a specific task) or very general (socializing).

Looking back at the examples that we opened this section with, you can probably guess that your family, your sorority or fraternity, and your pals at work constitute a group. You share an identity with the other members and have feelings about them (for better or worse); you likely have common goals, and you are interdependent—that is, you rely on them, and they on you, for love, friendship, or professional growth. This is not the case with the strangers on a bus to Cleveland. They might share a goal (getting to their destination), but they are not interdependent, and they do not share an identity. The same point can be made for the parents waiting in the office of the pediatrician.

Size and proximity were once major factors in group creation, but the ease with which modern technology allows individuals to communicate with others means that these factors are no longer as relevant to group formation as they once were. Four friends chatting over coffee at your local Starbucks constitute a group; so do twenty individual photographers who've never met but who contribute to a group photo pool on Flickr. In both cases, the individuals are joined by shared goals, shared identity, and interdependence; these three key factors—not size or proximity—determine group status. Of course, not all groups are alike. Let's take a look at different types of groups.

● **BANDMATES** such as the members of TV on the Radio must share a sense of identity, communicate interdependently, and collaborate to achieve their shared goal of creating music.

Group Types

Groups can take many forms. The most common among them are called **primary groups**—long-lasting groups that form around the relationships that mean the most to their members. Your family constitutes one primary group to which you belong; your friends are another.

In addition to primary groups, there are groups defined by their specific functions (for instance, support groups, study groups, and social groups). However, any one of these groups can perform multiple functions. Alcoholics Anonymous (AA), for example, is primarily a **support group**—a set of individuals who come together to address personal problems while benefiting from the support of others with similar issues. But AA is also a **social group**, as membership in the group offers opportunities to form relationships with others. And finally, as a group with a specific mission—to help members manage their struggles with alcohol and addiction—AA is also a **problem-solving group**.

While all groups are to some degree social, some groups are more task-oriented than others. **Study groups**, for example, are formed for the specific purpose of helping students prepare for exams. A **focus group** is a set of individuals asked by a researcher to come together to give their opinions on a specific issue (Frantz, 2007; Sinickas, 2000). For example, when a new TV pilot is getting ready to air, a network will assemble a focus group to gauge how the public might respond to the pilot.

Perhaps the most task-oriented and goal-driven type of group is the **team**—a group that works together to carry out a project or a specific endeavor or to compete against other teams. Sports teams are an obvious example, but teams are also common in large organizations or as subsets of other groups: an Army unit

---

WIREDFORCOMMUNICATION

From Group to Smart Mob

In 2011, demonstrations rocked Cairo, Egypt, as young people organized protests to demand political change. In 2010, a seemingly random crowd of shoppers in Bristol, in the United Kingdom, suddenly erupted into an epic lightsaber battle that lasted for two and a half minutes, then ended just as quickly.

What do these two stories have in common? They're both examples of smart mobs or large groups of individuals who act in concert, even though they don't know each other, and who connect and cooperate with one another, at least initially, via electronically mediated means (Rheingold, 2002). Smart mobs were first identified in 2001, when calls for protest in the Philippines spread via text message, gathering more than a million people to a nonviolent demonstration in Manila within four days. Largely hailed as the world's first "e-revolution," the Manila protests quickly and peacefully brought about the resignation of President Joseph Estrada. While the revolution itself was, of course, grounded in frustrations that had been building for many years, social media provided a key tool in organizing these protests and fueling their momentum. In the years since, as electronic devices have become even cheaper and more available, smart mobs have emerged as a fairly common form of group behavior.

Like all electronic social networks, smart mobs are grounded in a shared desire for communication and rely on affordable devices that offer instantaneous communication. But smart mobs have two important additional characteristics that a generic social network lacks: a shared goal and a finite time frame (Harmon & Metaxas, 2010). Simply communicating is not enough to make a smart mob—there must be a tangible goal (be it a flash mob dance-off at a shopping mall or a carefully orchestrated political protest on the steps of a national capitol) that is organized via mediated communication and achieved quickly and effectively.

Traditional groups and organizations recognize the efficiency and immediacy of smart mobs, and make use of social networks to encourage smart mob behaviors in order to meet specific goals. For example, in 2010, the humanitarian group Oxfam used its existing social network to encourage members and nonmembers alike to donate to money for immediate relief. By mobilizing donors in this manner, the group was able to meet its fundraising goal of $100 million in immediate aid to earthquake-stricken Haiti in just five weeks.

THINK ABOUT THIS

❶ Many social movements benefit from social networks, but is it fair to credit electronic communication with bringing about social change? How did groups like the American civil rights movement organize demonstrations, and how did their demonstrations differ from modern smart mobs?

❷ In an effort to quell the uprisings in Egypt in 2011, the Egyptian government blocked citizens' access to the Internet, yet protests continued. What does this say about the pervasive nature of electronic communication? What does it say about the role of electronic communication in causing and fueling action?

❸ Have you ever witnessed the beginning tremors of a smart mob in any of the social networks of which you are a part? What kinds of goals might motivate you to join a smart mob?

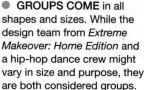

● **GROUPS COME** in all shapes and sizes. While the design team from *Extreme Makeover: Home Edition* and a hip-hop dance crew might vary in size and purpose, they are both considered groups.

might select a few members to form a reconnaissance team; a community group might nominate a team of individuals to take charge of its annual fundraiser.

One of the more noteworthy types of groups in today's organizations is the **self-directed work team**, a group of skilled workers who take responsibility for producing high-quality finished work (Douglas, 2002). In self-directed work teams, members bring complementary skills and experiences that enable the team to accomplish more than any individual member could achieve independently (Katzenbach & Smith, 1993). Self-directed work teams have proliferated in the last few decades in a variety of organizations and industries (Beyerlein, 2001; Yandrick, 2001).

In self-directed work teams, many typical management functions are completely controlled by the team members. For example, members arrange their own schedules, buy their own equipment, and set their own standards for productivity, quality, and costs. They conduct their own peer evaluations, bring in new members, and coordinate future plans with management. The theory is that when people have more control over their work, they have a more positive attitude and are more committed to the group.

Perhaps the most dramatic impact of self-directed teams is the improved performance and behavior of employees throughout the organization. In enterprises characterized by self-directed teams, the environment is marked by cooperation rather than competition. (See Table 9.1 on p. 256 for tips on working in a self-directed work team.)

Of course, the lessons of self-directed work teams extend far beyond work situations. Collaborative software programs (most commonly known as opensource pages or wikis) allow many individuals to collaborate on a written project, creating, editing, and linking content and reviewing the work of others.

AND YOU?

In your first job out of college, do you think you would prefer to work as part of a self-directed work team or in a more traditionally arranged team where a manager takes control? What would be the advantages of each?

TABLE 9.1

SELF-DIRECTED WORK TEAMS: TIPS FOR WORKING COLLABORATIVELY

Action	Considerations
Define a clear purpose for the team	What are the team's goals—short term *and* long term?
Foster team spirit	Build a sense of energy, excitement, and commitment in your team by engaging in team-building activities and events, rewarding members who demonstrate commitment, and identifying new challenges for the team to take on.
Train	Working on a self-directed team may be a new experience for some members. See if your organization can provide training to help members understand and implement the defining practices of self-directed teams.
Clarify expectations	Make sure all members of the team understand what's expected of them in terms of their roles and performance. For example, what functions will each member serve? How, specifically, will the team define "success"?
Set boundaries	Articulate where the team's responsibilities begin and end. If necessary, remind members that they are working in the service of the organization and that they need to stay focused on their specific purpose.

Sources: Capozzoli (2002); Nelson (2002); Rosenthal (2001).

Group Development

If you've ever become wrapped up in a reality TV show such as *Survivor, The Biggest Loser*, or *Top Chef*, you know how fascinating and dramatic group interactions can be. In each of these shows, a season typically opens with the forming of a group: cast members always start off as strangers but are quickly thrust into a group situation—sharing a living space and working together to accomplish certain tasks. As the season progresses, the group members bond, conflicts erupt, and alliances are forged and reforged. In fact, much of the drama in reality television stems from the tensions that arise between cast members as they struggle to work with—or against—one another. Contestants on *Survivor*, for example, must team up to work on certain challenges, such acquiring food, building shelter, completing an obstacle course, or solving a puzzle. Of course, these "reality" shows are often manipulated—contestants are selected at least in part for their TV "presence," and scenes are edited to heighten the drama. But the shows do reflect some basic truths about how groups develop (Wheelan, 1994). Research shows that as a group progresses, it goes through five specific stages, memorably called forming, storming, norming, performing, and adjourning (Tuckman, 1965). Using *Survivor* as an extended example, let's take a look at each stage.

Forming

When a group first comes together, its members are unsure how to act around one another, are nervous about how others perceive them, and aren't clear on what roles they'll be playing within the group. In this **forming** stage, group members try to negotiate who will be in charge and what the group's goals will be. The primary purpose of this stage is for group members to make friends,

Beginning a relationship with a group isn't so different from starting a new interpersonal relationship. In both contexts, we reduce uncertainty about our relational partners so that we feel secure and confident about roles, interactions, and so on. So whether you're beginning a new romance or forging a new student organization, try the passive, active, and interactive strategies that we discuss in Chapter 7 (see pp. 201–202).

come to a point where they feel that they "fit in," and learn more about one another and the group's objectives. Once individuals feel accepted, they can begin to identify with the group (Moreland & Levine, 1994). On *Survivor*, contestants are initially divided into two groups or "tribes." Contestants don't usually have much say regarding which tribe they'll become a part of: they might be randomly selected or assigned to a tribe based on factors like gender (seasons 6 and 9), age (season 21), or even race (season 13). Almost immediately, tribe members begin sizing up their competition—making judgments about one another's strengths, weaknesses, trustworthiness, and likeability.

● ON *SURVIVOR: NICARAGUA*, Shannon quickly decides that teammate Jud is a "dumb blond" and dubs him "Fabio." The nickname sticks, but not the impression: "Fabio" is the last survivor standing and wins the million-dollar prize.

Storming

After forming, group members move into the **storming** stage, in which they inevitably begin experiencing conflicts over issues such as who will lead the group and what roles members will play. On *Survivor*, a tribe member who shows prowess in gathering food or making fire, for example, will become valued, while members who seem weak are not. This process is shown in harsh relief as tribe members continually assess each of their fellow contestants during periodic "tribal councils." Group members who are a detriment to the groups' goals—or who pose a threat to individual goals—are voted off.

Norming

During the **norming** stage, norms emerge among members that govern expected behavior. **Norms** are recurring patterns of behavior or thinking that come to be accepted in a group as the "usual" way of doing things (Scheerhorn & Geist, 1997). During this stage, group roles also solidify, and a leader emerges. On *Survivor*, some tribe members take on leadership roles or present themselves as likeable heroes (like Rupert Boneham, season 7) or ambitious villains (like Richard Hatch, season 1); other contestants draw on specific strengths (such as physical prowess or fishing expertise) to make themselves invaluable to their fellow tribe members. In addition, group identity grows stronger as members begin to realize the importance of their roles within the group and the need to cooperate to accomplish goals.

Performing

Once the group has established norms, the action shifts to accomplishing tasks. During the **performing** stage, members combine their skills and knowledge to work toward the group's goals and overcome hurdles. On *Survivor*, tribemates work together on group challenges, such as building a shelter for the tribe. They might also endeavor to work together on physical challenges to earn rewards for the tribe.

Adjourning

Many groups—though clearly not all—eventually disband. For groups whose project or task has come to an end, there is an **adjourning** stage. The group members reflect on their accomplishments and failures as well as determine whether the group will disassemble or take on another project. To mark this stage, some groups hold a celebratory dinner or simply say thank you and good-bye. Alternatively, some groups may decide to continue to work together on new tasks. Members may also opt to maintain friendships even if they will no longer be working together. On reality shows like *Survivor*, some or all of

real communicator

NAME: Stephanie Lam
HOMETOWN: Hong Kong, China
OCCUPATION: Youth trainer
FUN FACT: My dream is to watch my favorite soccer team, Chelsea, play at their headquarters in Stamford Bridge, England.

I work at the Hong Kong Federation of Youth Groups (HKFYG), an organization dedicated to developing a pool of young leadership talent for the future of Hong Kong. Specifically, I am a professional trainer in youth team building. We use experiential learning at the HKFYG. I don't teach students in a traditional, lecture-style delivery. Instead, the students gain experience on their own, in groups. We are trained to help these groups teach themselves, to develop their own perceptions about a concept. For example, a couple of years ago, we sent twenty kids to South Africa for the Cathay Pacific International Wilderness Experience. The overriding aim was to have students learn about the environment, which is important for them as future decision makers.

My first job was to get these twenty students to think of themselves as more than just a collection of individuals. They needed to think of themselves as a team, a group that must work together to solve problems and accomplish goals. To do that, I concentrated a lot of my energy on the formation stage of group development. Building initial rapport and fostering team spirit are vital to a group's future success. In South Africa, the kids were encouraged to have a giant mud fight with one another (not that they needed much encouragement!). It brought them closer to nature and to one another. It got the students enthusiastic, and an enthusiastic group

is a more cohesive group. And a cohesive group is better at achieving goals.

Next, I helped the group build self-confidence, giving the students incrementally more difficult tasks to accomplish. First, they went snorkeling in the Indian Ocean, with the aim of exploring a reef ecosystem and learning the importance of its conservation. Then they participated in a sociocultural exchange: as a group, they had to learn how to fish and prepare food in the traditional way of the local Tsonga culture.

Next—and here's where it got tough—they had to build a Tsonga boat and race it down the river, competing against other teams. It was important that I phrase the goal as a problem to be solved: build a boat. I established clear standards for success: floating. And with the help of the Tsonga people, I identified the resources the group would need to accomplish that goal: the tools and materials necessary to build a boat.

With a clearly defined common goal, the students were forced to communicate more effectively. Members of the group started to feel—if they hadn't already—that they were connected; their communication became interdependent.

When it was all over, students discussed and debated environmental problems and opportunities. I think that because they became better at group communication, they became better individual communicators as well.

the contestants typically return for a reunion episode of the season, where they discuss the game. Some contestants' friendships endure long past the end of the show; others profess their dislike or use the reunion as an opportunity to make amends with tribemates with whom they have conflict.

Group Size and Communication

AND YOU?

Think about your experience as part of a group to which you no longer belong—an old job, your high school class, or a club that you're not a part of anymore. Did the group go through all five phases described here?

When you chat with an instructor in her office, you probably speak freely and informally. The two of you may exchange questions and comments rapidly, interrupt one another, and prompt each other for more information. But when you sit in a classroom with that same professor and a roomful of other students, the nature of your communication changes—you would be out of line if you interrupted when she was speaking; you might be expected to raise your hand, defer to other students who are already speaking, or not ask questions at all.

What has changed? Why is the nature of your communication so different in the classroom from the way you converse in her office? When a situation changes from a dyad to a group, communication becomes more complex. In this section, we'll take a look at how group communication grows more complex as the number of individuals increases.

Size and Complexity

The basic logistics of communication—the need to take turns speaking and listening, for example—grow more complex the larger a group gets. You might find it fairly easy to keep up an instant message chat with one friend online, but when a third person joins the conversation, the communication becomes muddied and complicated. This complexity creates the need for increasingly structured exchanges among members. Specifically, the bigger the group, the more its communication takes on the following characteristics:

● **WHEN YOU'RE** chatting with a professor during office hours, you are the focus of your professor's attention. However, in the classroom, you have to respect that other students want to speak as well!

▶ *Interaction is more formal.* Group communication simply cannot work in the same kind of informal way that dyadic communication occurs, due to the need to include more communicators in the discourse. Individuals

participating in a group may feel the need to obtain permission to speak, and they may also be reluctant to interrupt a speaker.

▶ *Each member has limited opportunities to contribute.* Participants may want or be required by a leader to share "floor time" with other group members. Such time constraints can inhibit the quality and quantity of their contributions. Even without a formal leader, in larger groups a few members tend to dominate much of the talk, while the less assertive members tend to remain quiet.

▶ *The communication becomes less intimate.* The greater the number of participants, the less comfortable participants feel self-disclosing or voicing controversial opinions.

▶ *The interaction consumes more time.* As more participants are invited to contribute or debate, the interaction takes longer to complete.

▶ *Relationships become more complex.* As more participants are added, the relationships become more complex. In the dyad, of course, there is only one relationship—that between person 1 and person 2.

As indicated by Figure 9.1, adding just one person to a dyad means that each of the three members of the new group must now deal with four potential relationships—one between persons 1 and 2; another between persons 1 and 3; a third between persons 2 and 3; and finally, the group relationship among all three participants. The number of relationships at play multiplies with each additional participant that joins a group: in a group of four, there are 11 potential relationships; in a group of five, there are 90; a six-member group involves 301 relationships; and so on.

FIGURE 9.1

COMPLEXITY OF GROUP RELATIONSHIPS Each time a person is added to a group, the number of potential relationships increases substantially.

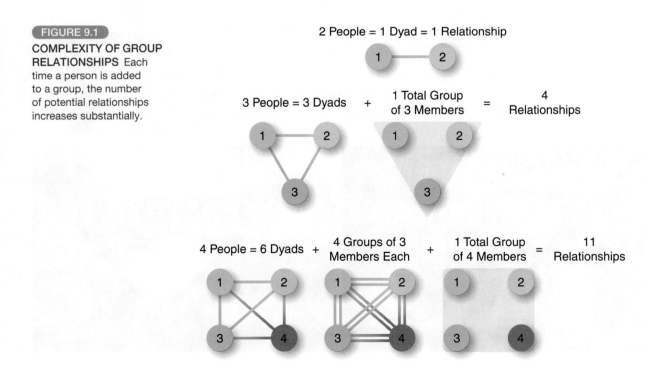

Size and the Formation of Cliques

In the comedy series *The Big Bang Theory*, geniuses Leonard and Sheldon are roommates and close friends. Sheldon, the quirky theoretical physicist, is extremely socially awkward and rarely takes kindly to new people or situations. Inevitably, when Leonard starts dating their neighbor, Penny, Sheldon has a difficult time adapting to his friend's new time commitments. In fact, he even winds up trying to trail along on Leonard and Penny's dates and frequently interrupts them when they wish to enjoy time alone. Even if you've never behaved quite like Sheldon, perhaps you've felt like he does—you love hanging out with your best friend, but whenever her boyfriend is around, you feel like you might as well be invisible. That's because your presence has changed the nature of the communication from dyadic to group communication, but the other two people haven't adjusted their communication behavior. They've remained a dyad, forming a subgroup that leaves you the lone outsider.

As a group's size increases, similar problems arise. **Cliques** (or coalitions) emerge—small subgroups of individuals who have bonded together within a group (Wilmot, 1987). Cliques are a common part of group life—they're a fixture in middle and high schools. You have your marching band kids, your football players, the "in" crowd, the art students, and so on. Many people think that they will escape cliques once high school ends, but this is usually not the case. In college, you might be tempted to form cliques with others in your major, your dorm, or a particular organization. In office settings, members of cliques or coalitions typically sit next to each other in meetings, eat lunch together, share the same opinions about what's going on in their organization, and support one another's positions.

When cliques take shape in a group, communication becomes more challenging because members are no longer dealing only with other individual members. Rather, they must navigate relationships and figure out how to communicate with entire subgroups. In addition, **countercoalitions**, in which one subgroup positions itself against another on an issue, can leave anyone who isn't affiliated with a subgroup in a very awkward position.

CONNECT

As you learn in Chapter 3, we define ourselves by our group memberships, with a tendency toward favoring our *ingroup* members and comparing ourselves to (and sometimes excluding) *outgroup* members. While it may be a natural tendency to form cliques with those who share our affiliations, competent communicators must remember to be inclusive of various groups and co-cultures—particularly in team and organizational settings.

● **LEONARD AND PENNY'S** budding relationship turns *The Big Bang Theory* into a big awkward-fest because best friend Sheldon fails to pick up on social cues and give the couple privacy.

Group Size and Social Loafing

On many education and learning blogs, you can find students and instructors complaining about one of the most dreaded assignments of all time: the grueling group project. Consider the following post from an angry group member: "In the 21 courses that composed my MBA program, I had to do a total of seven group projects. I won't bore you with all the gory details, but there were people who didn't do their work, control freaks who wouldn't allow anyone else's input, you name it. Group projects should be abolished." At first glance, doesn't it seem that group projects should be easier than working solo? There are more minds to share in the work and more people to try out ideas with. But what we all dread is having group members who don't pull their own weight. The fact is, the larger a group, the more prone members may become to **social loafing**—failing to invest the same level of effort in the group that they'd put in if they were working alone or with one other person. Social loafing affects all kinds of group activities, from sports competitions to professional work assignments. Even on cut-throat competitions like *Survivor*, there are always a few contestants who manage to make it through to the final simply by keeping their heads low and letting their teammates do most of the work.

Clearly, social loafing affects both participation and communication in groups (Comer, 1998; Shultz, 1999). When a person fails to speak up because he or she feels shy around a lot of people, the person is engaging in social loafing. Social loafing also results from the feelings of anonymity that occur in large groups. The larger the group, the more difficult it is for an individual member's contributions to the group's efforts to be evaluated and measured. Thus a member may put in less effort, believing that nobody will notice that he or she is slacking off or, conversely, that he or she is working hard. Social loafing even occurs in large electronic networks: some members of an online discussion group, for example, may actively engage in the discourse by posting regular messages, while others—known as lurkers—may just read others' posts and

---

EVALUATINGCOMMUNICATIONETHICS

THINK ABOUT THIS

Sketchy Behavior

You have recently formed a comedy troupe with four other friends: Calvin, Eddie, Meredith, and Sylvia. Your first live show with the group is in just a few weeks, and your group has written and rehearsed five sketches. But you and Calvin have had doubts about one sketch, written by Eddie and Sylvia, since day one. Rather than voice your concerns, you and Calvin have been trying to come up with an alternative sketch. During a late-night session, the two of you come up with an idea for a sketch that in your opinion outclasses the one you've been having problems with.

It is now a few days before the show, and the two of you have decided, independent of the other members, that the weaker sketch needs to be changed in favor of the one you've written. You are concerned about how this will look and have a nagging feeling the other members are going to perceive your writing of this sketch as a selfish way to push your work over that of your teammates, but you feel strongly that the new sketch will make the show a greater success. Calvin suggests that you present your sketch to Meredith, since she was not involved in writing either sketch. "If we convince Meredith that our sketch is the stronger one," Calvin reasons, "we'll be able to point to her opinion as a truly objective opinion—she's got no agenda."

You're pretty certain that Meredith will prefer your sketch, not only because you feel it is better but also because it features a role that Meredith would love to play. And you know that if you talk to Meredith beforehand, you'll have a clear majority in favor of your sketch should the decision be put to a vote. But is this ethical?

❶ What role did group communication play in this scenario? Might cliques have been involved? What were other communication options?

❷ Is it unethical to attempt to gain Meredith's vote even if you honestly believe that it's in the best interest of the group?

❸ What ethical implications arise from approaching Meredith with the new sketch? Should the sketch be presented to the entire team at the same time? Is it fair to tempt Meredith with a juicy role in exchange for her vote?

contribute very little. According to Nagel, Blignaut, and Cronje (2009) these "read-only participants" can distract from the formation of a virtual community and undermine others' perceptions of the credibility and influence of the messages people post (Rains, 2007).

Group Networks

Just as a group's size strongly influences communication within the group, so do networks. **Networks** are patterns of interaction governing who speaks with whom in a group and about what. To understand the nature of networks, you must first consider two main positions within them. The first is *centrality*, or the degree to which an individual sends and receives messages from others in the group. The most central person in the group receives and sends the highest number of messages in a given time period. At the other end of the spectrum is *isolation*—a position from which a group member sends and receives fewer messages than other members.

A team leader or manager typically has the highest level of centrality in a formal group, but centrality is not necessarily related to status or power. The CEO of a company, for example, may be the end recipient of all information generated by teams below her, but in fact only a limited number of individuals within the organization are able to communicate directly with her. Her assistant, in fact, may have a higher degree of centrality in the network. As you might imagine, networks play a powerful role in any group's communication, whether the group is a family, a sports team, a civic organization, or a large corporation.

In some groups, all members speak with all others regularly about a wide range of topics. In others, perhaps only a few members are "allowed" to speak directly with the group's leader or longest-standing member about serious issues. In still other groups, some members may work alongside one another without communicating at all. There are several types of networks, including chain networks, all-channel networks, and wheel networks (see Figure 9.2) (Bavelous, 1950).

Chain Networks

In a **chain network**, information is passed from one member to the next rather than shared among members. Such networks can be practical for sharing written information: an e-mail, forwarded from person to person along a chain, for example, allows each person to read the original information from other prior

AND YOU?

What group are you spending most of your time in these days? What type of communication network exists in the group? Is that network helping the group achieve its goals? If not, what changes might the group make to operate more effectively?

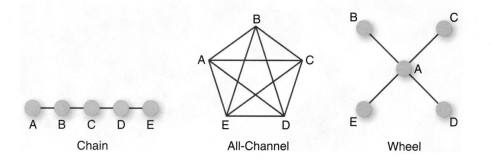

FIGURE 9.2

GROUP COMMUNICATION NETWORKS

Source: Scott (1981), p. 8. Adapted with permission.

Chain   All-Channel   Wheel

recipients. But this form of group communication can lead to frustration and miscommunication when information is conveyed through other codes, such as spoken words. It can be like a game of telephone, where the message gets distorted as it progresses down the chain. Person A tells person B that their boss, Luis, had a fender bender on the way to work and will miss the 10:00 A.M. meeting. Person B tells person C that Luis was in an accident and will not be in the office today. Person C tells person D that Luis was injured in an accident; no one knows when he'll be in. You can imagine that Luis will be in a full-body cast by the time the message reaches person G!

All-Channel Networks

In an **all-channel network**, all members are an equal distance from one another, and all members interact with each other. When people talk about roundtable discussions, they're talking about all-channel groups: there is no leader, and all members operate at equal levels of centrality. Such networks can be useful for collaborative projects and for brainstorming ideas, but the lack of order can make it difficult for such groups to complete tasks. Imagine, for example, that you're trying to arrange a meetup with a group of friends. You send out a mass e-mail to all of them, to determine days that will work, and you ask for suggestions about where to meet. Each recipient can simply hit "reply all" and share their response with the group. By using an all-channel network, the entire group learns that Friday is not good for anyone, but Saturday is; and while a few people have suggested favorite spots, there's no consensus on where to go. That's where wheel networks come in.

Wheel Networks

Wheel networks are a sensible alternative for situations in which individual members' activities and contributions must be culled and tracked in order to avoid duplicating efforts and to ensure that all tasks are being completed. In

● **THE COPYEDITING TEAM** in a newsroom works as a wheel network. All of the copyeditors report to one copy chief, who regulates the copyediting style.

a **wheel network**, one individual acts as a touchstone for all the others in the group; all group members share their information with that one individual, who then shares the information with the rest of the group. Consider the example above: as the sender of the initial e-mail, you might take on a leadership role and ask everyone just to reply to you. Then you could follow up with a decision about time and place to meet and send that out to everyone else. Wheel networks are common in sororities and fraternities, with the chapter president at the center. All other officers must report to the president, and the president must report back to the officers on the status of the others. Such groups have the lowest shared centrality but are very efficient (Leavitt, 1951).

Understanding Group Roles

If you've watched the cast of *House* over the past few seasons, you know that the diagnostic physicians at Princeton-Plainsboro Teaching Hospital tend to take on certain roles on their team. Dr. Eric Foreman is relatively reserved; he listens carefully but also tends to ask blunt questions to gather important information on patients. Medical student Martha Masters typically encouraged group harmony and ethical communication with patients. And then there's Dr. Gregory House, the team leader, who is well known for pushing his own agenda and openly mocking his underlings. The fact is that we all tend to fall into particular roles in the various groups we belong to, and these roles influence group communication. There are three types of roles—task, social, and antigroup. Let's look at each of them in turn.

Task Roles

In some cases, a role is defined by a task that needs doing, and a person is asked or appointed to fill it (or he or she volunteers). Such **task roles** are concerned with the accomplishment of the group's goals—specifically, the activities that need to be carried out for the group to achieve its objectives. For example, your role on a committee charged with organizing a sorority rush party might be to post advertisements for the event in key locations around campus and in the campus newspaper.

Task roles can also be specifically related to the group's communication; for instance:

▶ An *information giver* offers facts, beliefs, personal experience, or other input during group discussions ("When the sisters of Chi Omega posted their ad in the student lounge, they had good attendance at their rush party").

▶ An *information seeker* asks for additional input or clarification of ideas or opinions that members have presented ("Jane, are you saying you're not comfortable with the party theme we're proposing?").

▶ An *elaborator* provides further clarification of points, often adding to what others have said ("I agree with Ellie about selecting Currier & Chives as our caterer; my friend works there, and she's a great cook").

● **ALTHOUGH MIKE** "The Situation" Sorrentino has been known to anger his *Jersey Shore* housemates with clueless disrespect, he also fancies himself the "house parent" and makes an effort to extinguish disputes among the friends.

▶ An *initiator* helps the group move toward its objective by proposing solutions, presenting new ideas, or suggesting new ways of looking at an issue the group is discussing ("How essential is it that we schedule the rush party for the last Friday of the month? If we moved it a week later, we'd have more time to find the right band").

▶ An *administrator* keeps the conversation on track ("OK, let's get back to the subject of when to schedule the party") and ensures that meetings begin and end on time ("We've got five minutes left; should we wind up?").

▶ In an online forum, the person who coordinates and sometimes screens the members' comments is called the *moderator* or *master*. An *elder* is the name given to an online group member who has participated a long time and whose authority is respected by the less experienced *newbies*.

Social Roles

Some group roles evolve to reflect individual members' personality traits and interests; such roles are called **social roles**. For example, a nurturing housemate might unofficially fill the role of "house parent"—baking cookies for everyone, listening compassionately to people's problems, and making everyone feel taken care of. Consider these additional examples of social roles (Anderson, Riddle, & Martin, 1999; Benne & Sheats, 1948; Salazar, 1996):

▶ A *harmonizer* seeks to smooth over tension in the group by settling differences among members ("OK, you both want the party to succeed; you just have different ideas about how to get there").

▶ A *gatekeeper* works to ensure that each member of the group contributes to discussions ("Tonya, we haven't heard from you yet on this question of when to schedule the party. What are your thoughts?").

▶ A *sensor* expresses group feelings, moods, or relationships in an effort to recognize the climate and capitalize on it or modify it for the better ("I'm registering a lot of frustration in the committee right now. Let's take a break and reconnect in half an hour").

Each member in a group can play task and social roles. For example, though Evelyn was appointed chairperson of the rush party committee, she also serves as the group's unofficial harmonizer because she has a knack for mitigating tensions between people. Members can also adopt a personal or task role if they believe the role is needed but no one else seems to be willing to fill it. To illustrate, by the end of the rush party committee's first meeting, Candace noticed an air of excitement infusing the gathering as ideas for the party theme began flying back and forth. Wanting to build on that excitement and channel it into commitment to the group's cause, she took on the role of sensor. As the meeting came to a close, each member took a moment to explain what tasks she would be responsible for that week. When Candace's turn came, she told the other members, "I'm really excited about all the progress we made today. I think that with this kind of enthusiasm, we're going to throw the best rush party in our history!" The meeting ended on a high note, and members adjourned eager to dig into their tasks.

Antigroup Roles

Unlike task and social roles, **antigroup roles** create problems because they serve individual members' priorities at the expense of group needs. You've probably seen evidence of these antigroup roles in the groups you belong to:

▶ A *blocker* indulges in destructive communication, including opposing all ideas and stubbornly reintroducing an idea after the group has already rejected or bypassed it ("None of the dates any of you proposed will work for the party. It really needs to be five weeks from today, as I said earlier").

▶ An *avoider* refuses to engage in the group's proceedings by expressing cynicism or nonchalance toward ideas presented or by joking or changing the subject ("Well, whatever, I'm guessing it's not a big deal if this party doesn't even happen, right?").

▶ A *recognition seeker* calls attention to himself or herself by boasting or by going on and on about his or her qualifications or personal achievements ("I planned a gathering for a women's studies group last year, and it went really well. People still talk about it! So trust me on this one").

▶ A *distractor* goes off on tangents or tells irrelevant stories ("Does anyone know what happened on *Grey's Anatomy* last night? I missed it").

Competent leadership can address problematic antigroup roles. As you learn in Chapter 10, a *directive leader* might lay out tasks to thwart a distracter; a *supportive leader* might thank each member for his or her contributions, preventing a recognition seeker from claiming the glory. Leaders have the power to affect norms and roles, encouraging group members to make productive contributions.

> ▶ A *troll* is someone in an online group who intentionally inserts irrelevant and inflammatory comments into the discussion in order to stir up controversy.

To mitigate the impact of these antigroup roles, members can revisit the norms the group has established and make the changes needed to improve group communication (for example, "All ideas get a fair hearing"). People fulfilling certain task or social roles can also help. For instance, if you're a gatekeeper, you can prompt an avoider to contribute her opinion on a proposal that the group has been considering. Research also indicates that positive and proactive responses to avoiders and blockers can help establish individuals as leaders in their organizations (Garner & Poole, 2009). For example, in online groups, masters frequently encourage group members to not "feed the troll"—do not respond or take the bait of abusive comments.

Role Conflict

Imagine that you work at a local retail store and you've been promoted to store manager. As part of your new role, you will have to manage staff members who are working as individual contributors at the store. Several of them are also your close friends, and you all used to be at the same level in the store.

Role conflict arises in a group whenever expectations for a member's behavior are incompatible. The roles of manager and friend are inherently in conflict. After all, as a manager, you'll have to evaluate staff members' performance. And how can you give a good friend a poor performance review and still remain friends?

As you might imagine, role conflict can make group communication profoundly challenging, and there are no easy answers to this kind of dilemma. In the case of the retail store, you might decide not to give your friend a negative review in the interest of saving the friendship. Or perhaps you'll decide to give candid constructive feedback to your friend on his performance. But you'll try to constrain the damage to your friendship by saying something like "I hope you know I'm offering this feedback as a way to help you improve. As your friend and manager, I want to see you do well here."

Additional Factors Affecting Group Communication

In addition to size and networks, numerous other factors affect communication within groups—most notably cohesion, groupthink, norms, clarity of goals, and individual differences. In the sections that follow, we explore each of these additional factors in more detail.

Cohesion

Cohesion is the degree to which group members have bonded, like each other, and consider themselves to be one entity. A cohesive group identifies itself as a single unit rather than a collection of individuals, which helps hold the group

AND YOU?

Have you ever been in a leadership role among a group of friends? Have you ever been subordinate to a friend in a group situation? Did any conflict arise, and if so, how did you resolve it?

together in the face of adversity. In fact, cohesion is an important factor in generating a positive group temperament, or *climate*, in which members take pride in the group, treat each other with respect, feel confident about their abilities, and achieve higher success in accomplishing goals. Such positive climates can also foster optimism and confidence in the face of obstacles. A self-confident, cohesive group tends to minimize problems, eliminate barriers, and cope well with crises (Folger, Poole, & Stutman, 2001).

Much research has focused on how cohesion affects a group's effectiveness and communication. In general, cohesive groups perform better than noncohesive groups on decision-making tasks (for example, selecting a course of action more quickly and making more informed choices) (Carless & DePaola, 2000). Nonverbal communication is also influenced by group cohesion. Yasui (2009) found that cohesive group members often repeat and build on one another's gestures. This collaborative process indicates a shared imagination and agreement about the ideas they are proposing.

● **A DISRESPECTFUL** or unreasonable boss risks weakening the cohesion of his or her team of employees, fostering a negative group climate, and ultimately reducing the team's effectiveness.

You can determine group cohesion in two ways. First, take a look at how the participants feel about their own membership in the group. Members of a cohesive group are enthusiastic, identify with the purposes of the group, and tell outsiders about its activities. Even positive, constructive argumentation (as opposed to verbal aggressiveness) can be a sign of group cohesiveness (Anderson & Martin, 1999). Second, consider how well the group retains members. A cohesive group will retain more members than a noncohesive group. That's why employers are often concerned with employee turnover—the number of people leaving and joining the staff. Not only do the arrival and departure of staff cost time and money for retraining and such, but they also affect—and reflect—group cohesion. The more that members receive satisfaction and fulfill their needs through their group participation, the more cohesive the group.

Gouran (2003) offers several practical suggestions for increasing cohesion and fostering a more positive group experience:

▶ Avoid dominating other group members.

▶ Stay focused on the tasks the group must accomplish.

▶ Be friendly.

▶ Show sensitivity to and respect for other members.

▶ Demonstrate that you value others' opinions.

▶ Cooperate with other members rather than compete with them.

Clearly, cohesive groups offer tremendous benefits, but too much cohesion can actually cause the group to be unproductive. For example, if you and the other members of your study group enjoy each other's company to the point

In Chapter 4, we discuss *jargon*, vocabulary unique to a specific hobby or profession. Jargon helps build group cohesiveness because it connects members to one another. A group of police officers might speak about perps (perpetrators), vics (victims), collars (arrests), and brass (supervisors)—terms that their mechanic or physician friends would not use. This use of language helps officers bond as a group.

COMMUNICATIONACROSSCULTURES

THINK ABOUT THIS

The International, American Pastime

The typical major league baseball team has a full roster of players and a substantial staff of coaches who work with players on specific skills. There's the general manager, a bullpen coach, a batting coach, a bench coach, and strength and conditioning coaches. There's a bevy of trainers and coordinators. And sometimes, there's a language coach.

America's pastime is, like America itself, a melting pot of diversity. Homegrown players work alongside newly arrived teammates from as nearby as the Dominican Republic and as far away as Japan. Many of these players arrive with much fanfare but with few or no English skills. In order to succeed as part of a team, however, it's crucial that they be able to communicate with their teammates and coaches, both on and off the field. And while the finite rules of baseball (along with the formal nonverbal signals teams develop to communicate on the field) help to create a clear code of communication that all the players share, language barriers can still hamper communication among group members.

Spanish-speaking players may find that they have a slightly easier transition than others because they are likely to find at least a few players or staff members who speak their native tongue. Yet having players split off into Spanish- versus English-speaking subgroups can be a true challenge to team cohesion. As such, the San Diego Padres, like many other major league teams, offer English language classes to help players who are not fluent in English. But the team also takes the opposite approach: they teach basic Spanish to their staff. "It's something I thought was important to make us efficient when dealing with players when we're going to the Dominican [Republic] or with our players who are just coming here and don't have command of the English language yet," said Padres Director of Player Development Randy Smith (Brock, 2010). In a sport that is increasingly recruiting from Spanish-speaking countries, teams are growing bilingual, so Smith's idea is a logical step.

While creating a bilingual organization makes sense, there are some non-native players who speak neither English nor Spanish. In some cases, the best solution is to hire a translator. For example, Japanese star Hideki Matsui is rarely seen unaccompanied by his translator, Roger Kahlon. Translators must suit up to accompany players on the field during practices; they have their own lockers in the team clubhouse (Geffner, 2005). When Matsui led the Yankees to the 2009 championship, Kahlon accompanied him on a float down New York's Canyon of Heroes and was even awarded a key to the city along with the rest of the team (Nelson, 2009). For the Yankees, the language barrier could have been a hindrance to group cohesion. But having a translator on hand made communication easier, making Kahlon a welcome part of the group.

① How important is it to have all the players on a team speak the same language? Would having a single language policy increase group cohesion? What might the downsides of such a policy be?

② Who is responsible for developing a shared code when coaches and players speak different languages? How might the rules of communication be worked out between individuals who speak different languages?

③ What other cultural differences might inhibit communication on a professional sports team? How does multiculturalism and globalization affect other sports?

that you never get your work done, then you'll be unlikely to achieve your goal: doing well on an exam! In addition, excessive cohesion can lead to groupthink, an important group factor that we discuss next.

Groupthink

As you learned in Chapter 8, engaging in productive conflict fosters healthy debate and leads to better decision making. Unity and cohesion are important for groups to operate effectively, but if these qualities are taken to an extreme—that is, if they become more powerful than members' desire to evaluate alternative courses of action—the group can't generate enough diverse ideas to make smart decisions (Miller & Morrison, 2009; Park, 2000).

Consider the tragic explosion of the U.S. space shuttle *Challenger* in 1986. Prior to launch, there had been some concern among many engineers that certain fittings (called O-rings) might fail, but the shuttle launched in spite of these concerns. Eventually, those fittings were indeed found to be related to the explosion, but a large part of the blame for the disaster was laid on communication failures within NASA. Engineers later testified that the climate at NASA made them reluctant to voice their concerns if they couldn't back them up with a full set of data (McConnell, 1987). Indeed, the Rogers Commission (1986), which investigated the disaster, noted that had safety concerns been more clearly articulated—and had NASA management been more receptive to concerns raised by engineers from various departments—it is unlikely that *Challenger* would have launched that day.

The *Challenger* explosion is often pointed to as a classic example of **groupthink**—a situation in which group members strive to maintain cohesiveness and minimize conflict by refusing to critically examine ideas, analyze proposals, or test solutions (Janis, 1982). In a more receptive group climate, a productive

● **SOMETIMES VOICING** dissent is more important than group unity. If the engineers at NASA had shared their concerns, the *Challenger* disaster might not have happened.

conflict over the O-rings might have revealed the problems that the engineers sensed but couldn't quite put their fingers on. The following are some symptoms of groupthink that you should be aware of in all of your group memberships:

▶ Participants reach outward consensus and avoid expressing disagreement so as not to hurt each other's feelings or appear disloyal.

▶ Members who do express disagreement with the majority are pressured to conform to the majority view.

▶ Tough questions are ignored or discouraged.

▶ Members spend more effort justifying their decisions than testing them.

One important way to prevent groupthink is to encourage dissent among members and manage it productively (Klocke, 2007). In fact, some of the same practices for handling interpersonal conflict discussed in Chapter 8 can help you deal constructively with disagreements in a group. For example, frame conflicts as disagreements over issues or ideas, not as evidence of a weak character or some other personal shortcoming in particular members. To illustrate, when someone in the group expresses a dissenting viewpoint, don't say, "It's clear that you aren't as dedicated to our cause as I had hoped." Instead, say something like "It looks like we have some different ideas circulating about how to handle this new problem. Let's list these ideas and talk about the possible benefits and risks of each of them." A recent study by Aakhus and Rumsey (2010) supports this point by noting that productive conflict can generate *more* supportive communication for members of an online cancer support community than simply expecting members to keep dissenting opinions private.

Norms

As you saw earlier in the chapter, over time a group will develop norms. Norms are determined by the group itself and are imposed by members on themselves and each other; they direct the behavior of the group as a whole and affect the conduct of individual members. In a business environment, norms might dictate the kinds of topics that can be expressed in a meeting (Should non-task-related conversation be interjected? Are jokes appropriate?). In an online group, norms might evolve to govern the use of foul language, negative comments, or criticism. For example, a recent study showed that established members of an online anorexia support group allow new members to share pro-anorexic statements in order to establish that they are ill. In time, however, these members are initiated into the group norm that prohibits such unhealthy and negative statements (Stommel & Koole, 2010).

Some norms have a negative impact on communication. For example, suppose a group permits one member to dominate the conversation or allows members to dismiss an idea before discussing its pros and cons. A group with these norms will have difficulty generating enough diverse ideas to make informed decisions. If you find yourself in a group with unproductive norms like these, consider modifying them—this is possible if you approach the task diplomatically (Brilhart & Galanes, 1992). The following three-step process can help:

1. *Express your loyalty and dedication to the group, to show that you have the group's best interests at heart.* For instance, "I've been a member of this school committee for two years now and have hung in there during the tough times as well as the good times. I want to see us be the best we can be."

2. *Cite specific examples of the behavior you find harmful to the group's effectiveness.* To illustrate, "When we didn't take time to explore the pros and cons of the special-ed funding strategy that came up last month, we ended up making a decision that we regretted later."

3. *Ask other members for their opinions about the problem norm you've identified.* If others feel that the norm is still warranted, they may advocate keeping it ("Well, there are some situations where we don't have as much time as we'd like to consider the merits of an idea. During those moments, we need to be able to move ahead with a decision quickly").

With respectful, productive discussion, the group may decide to maintain the norm, change it under specific conditions ("We'll have someone play devil's advocate when time allows"), or abandon it entirely.

Clarity of Goals

Think of the worst group meeting you've ever attended. How would you describe that meeting? Was the conversation disorganized? Unproductive? Confusing? Did all the talking seem like just a lot of hot air and a huge waste of time? Did you leave the meeting with a bad feeling about working with the group again in the future? When people have these kinds of reactions to a group's communication, the culprit is very likely the lack of a clear goal. To communicate productively in any group, members need goal clarity: that is, they must understand what the group's purpose is, what goals will help the group achieve its purpose, how close the group is to achieving its goals, and whether the activities members are engaging in are helping the group move toward its goals.

Goals vary considerably from one group to another. For example, a team in one of your classes may have the simple goal of completing a fifteen-minute in-class exercise and reporting the results to the rest of the class. An urban beautification fundraising committee may have the goal of collecting $4,000 for new landscaping at a neighborhood park.

How can you make sure your group has clear goals? You might suggest the goals yourself. However, you'll get even better results by encouraging the rest of the members to define the group's goals. When members take part in establishing goals, they feel more committed to and excited about achieving those objectives. Research shows that a group is more likely to reach its goals when those goals are communicated in terms that are specific ("Raise $4,000 by the end of March"), inspiring ("Imagine our neighborhood becoming a community of choice for young families"), and prioritized ("We'll need to focus on this goal first and then this other one next") (O'Hair, Friedrich, & Dixon, 2002).

As you learn in Chapter 1, *goal achievement* is an important function of communication in all contexts. Just remember that while it's important for a group to keep the end goal in sight, competent communicators are flexible—they try to maintain interdependence while being open to various ideas on achieving goals. They also recognize that the goal itself may change as group members share ideas and present solutions to problems.

Groups are also more likely to reach their goals if members have some autonomy in deciding how to achieve them. For example, everyone on the urban beautification committee has agreed that the group wants to raise $4,000 by the end of March. But the committee chair decides not to dictate how the group should approach this task. Instead, he invites members to brainstorm ideas for reaching the goal. By encouraging people to come up with ways to achieve the goal, a group leader ensures that members produce a wide range of ideas. And the more ideas the group explores, the more likely its members will ultimately make an informed choice about how to move forward.

Here are some additional communication strategies for setting group goals effectively (O'Hair, Friedrich, & Dixon, 2002):

▶ *Define goals in terms of problems to be solved* (for example, "Our goal is to raise $4,000 to beautify Dixon Park"), not values to be embodied ("Our goal is to be good citizens of this community"). Value-based goals are vague, so it's difficult to know if and when you've achieved them. (What does "being a good citizen" mean in practice, anyway?)

▶ *Establish clear performance standards.* How will your group know when it has succeeded in reaching its goal? For example, "We will have $4,000 in our checking account by the last day of March."

▶ *Identify the resources your group will need to accomplish its goals.* Include such things as members' time, office space, funds, and equipment. By anticipating resources, you avoid getting into a situation where your worthy goal shrivels and dies because it never received sufficient funding or attention.

▶ *Recognize contingencies that may arise.* For instance, "Our goal is to have $4,000 in our account by the end of March, on the assumption that we have good weather for the fundraising campaign we're planning to hold on the town common."

▶ *Determine how you will monitor and report progress toward your group's goals.* Will the group hold a weekly status meeting? Will members circulate daily e-mails to update one another?

Once your group begins working toward its goals, encourage yourself and your fellow members to talk regularly about the decisions you're making and the actions you're taking to ensure that these all support progress toward the goals.

Individual Differences

Members of a particular group may share goals and an identity, but they each bring personal differences to the group as well. And these differences can strongly affect communication. Let's examine how cultural factors and communication apprehension—which vary by individual—affect our ability to communicate in groups.

Cultural Factors

As you've learned throughout this book, culture has a big impact on how we communicate. When a group has culturally diverse members, that diversity can have benefits (such as enabling the group to produce a wide array of viewpoints) as well as challenges (including misunderstandings between members).

As we noted earlier, cultures in nations such as the United States, Great Britain, and Canada are largely individualist. Their members value personal accomplishment and competition and strive to differentiate themselves from one another. In an individualist culture, people place a high value on getting their own opinions heard and appreciated, and so they may strive to have their ideas "win" within the group. In a collectivist culture, people value cooperation and group harmony. They allow group norms (rather than their own personal goals) to have the largest influence on their behaviors and thoughts (Triandis, Brislin, & Hul, 1988). Not surprisingly, this difference can present a challenge when members of these cultures are working together in groups. People from individualist cultures will likely more openly vocalize their disagreement with the others and try to persuade each other, while the collectivists may feel "bulldozed" as they stifle their own objections in order to help the others save face.

Gender and sex differences can also affect group communication largely due to the social expectations of masculine and feminine individuals. For example, research shows that women are socially encouraged to focus on establishing relationships within a group, while men—who are socialized to focus on autonomy and success—tend to pay more attention to completing the task at hand (Baird, 1986). Moreover, masculine individuals seek to display signs of their power while communicating in groups (for example, pointing out their credentials or their achievements), whereas those with a more feminine style are likely to show signs of affection toward each other (Helgesen, 1990). These differences were cleverly mocked on *The Simpsons*, when Springfield elementary is suddenly divided into two separate schools. Lisa enjoys the camaraderie at her new, all girls' school, but is disappointed to find her math class focused not on arithmetic or geometry, but on self-esteem, group sing-alongs, and "feeling math." She winds up dressing up as a boy in order to attend the all boys' school, where she can learn without anyone worrying about hurting people's feelings. Lisa rejected her gender socialization in order to find a more appropriate group setting in which to further her study of her favorite subject (Brooks & Groening, 2006).

Communication Apprehension

The next time you're sitting in your communication classroom or logging on to a discussion forum in your online course, take a peek around. Is there someone who never speaks up or raises a hand? Is there someone who rarely posts thoughts on a discussion board? Perhaps you're assuming that this person has nothing to say or that he or she is a social loafer. Maybe you're right. But it's also possible that this individual feels uncomfortable participating in group conversation even when his or her contribution would clearly help the

AND YOU?
Have you ever misunderstood another member of a group you were involved in because of cultural differences? If so, how did you and the other person deal with the misunderstanding?

● **POOR LISA.** She enjoys the camaraderie of other girls at school, but she wants to learn how to *do* math, not feel it!

MATT GROENING

If you suffer from communication apprehension in groups, you're probably aware of the negative effects it can have on your social and professional life. Luckily, there are many practical strategies for dealing with apprehension, as we discuss in Chapter 14. Check out our tips on desensitizing yourself, visualizing your success, and taking care of yourself in anxiety-producing situations.

group. What explains this communication apprehension? Scholars have identified several causes (Schullery & Gibson, 2001):

▶ *Lack of self-esteem.* When an individual doubts the worth of his contributions, he may decline to speak up in a group. Fear of being wrong, of being mocked, or of creating a bad impression can further lead to communication apprehension.

▶ *Status differences.* Group members who hold a relatively low position in the group's social or political hierarchy may avoid disagreeing with their superiors in the group because they fear retribution from the more powerful persons.

▶ *Unbalanced participation.* When a group member—or a small number of group members—dominates the conversation in a group, the less aggressive members may retreat from communicating. This strongly influences how

what about you?

How Well Do You Interact in a Group Setting?

To test how apprehensive you might be in a group setting, complete the following six items, which are based on the Personal Report of Communication Apprehension (PRCA-24). Use the following scale: 1 = strongly agree; 2 = agree; 3 = undecided; 4 = disagree; and 5 = strongly disagree.

_____ 1. I do not like to participate in group discussions.

_____ 2. Generally, I feel comfortable participating in group discussions.

_____ 3. I am tense and nervous while participating in group discussions.

_____ 4. I like to get involved in group discussions.

_____ 5. I get tense and nervous when I engage in a group discussion with new people.

_____ 6. I am calm and relaxed while participating in group discussions.

Scoring: Use the following formula, in which the numbers in parentheses represent your answers to the six items. (For example, if you answered "4" for item 1, then replace the "1" in the formula with a 4.)

$$18 - (1) + (2) - (3) + (4) - (5) + (6)$$

A score of 24 or above indicates a high level of communication apprehension for participation in group discussions; a score of 12 or below indicates a low level of communication apprehension for this situation.

Source: McCroskey (1982). Adapted with permission.

decisions get made in the group. One classic study found that groups tend to adopt ideas that receive the largest number of favorable comments (Hoffman & Maier, 1964). If most of those comments come from a single member and that person has inaccurate or incomplete information to back up his or her argument, the group risks making a faulty decision.

Some simple techniques can help a group address communication apprehension among members. For example, to ease self-esteem problems, consider starting a group meeting by having each member tell the member to their left what he or she appreciates about that person. To neutralize status differences, have members sit in a circle and invite lower-status members to speak before higher-status ones. To rebalance participation, suggest a norm that calls for everyone to weigh in on ideas presented in the group. Or look for members who are holding back and invite them specifically to contribute their views.

● **AS THE EQUITABLE** group leader of Andy's toys in the *Toy Story* films, Woody takes particular care to hear the input of quieter and more apprehensive members of the group, such as Rex and Slinky Dog.

BACK TO ▶ The "3-Day" Walks

At the beginning of this chapter, we talked about the annual Susan G. Komen for the Cure's 3-Day, sixty-mile walks to raise funds for breast cancer—and the initiation of individual participants into a community that shares their goals, drive, and (quite often) life experiences. Consider the nature of the 3-Day walks in light of what you've learned in this chapter.

▶ It may seem unbelievable that thousands of men and women—most of whom will not speak to each other in the process of the walk—could be considered a group. And yet they develop a shared identity (fighters, survivors, supporters), share common goals (to raise money in an effort to rid the world of the scourge of breast cancer), and develop interdependent relationships (supporting each other's fundraising and training efforts).

▶ Participants in the 3-Day walks fall into several group types. They are certainly examples of a support group: participants share and work through similar struggles and life experiences. In addition, 3-Day walk groups can also be considered problem-solving groups (because they attempt to raise money for a cure) and even primary groups (many walkers go on to develop committed friendships with each other).

▶ As noted, Susan G. Komen for the Cure requires that each participant raise at least $2,300 and commit to training for the walk. While there are opportunities for group training and fundraising, each individual member of the group is still held personally accountable for his or her efforts. This makes social loafing—common in large groups—much more difficult.

THINGS TO TRY Activities

1. Consider a group to which you belong—your communication class, your family, your religious community, etc. Draw a chart that depicts members of the group and the patterns of communication among them. What kind of network does the group most closely resemble?

2. Read up on the history of some influential but now defunct music group (such as the Beatles, Nirvana, or Public Enemy). Did the group go through all the stages of group development outlined in this chapter? How did the group determine roles and establish norms? How did members deal with conflict? How did the eventual disbanding of the group play out?

3. Consider the adjourning phase of group development for a group you were part of that disbanded—Scouts, a sports team, the school newspaper staff—and think about what aspects of the group made for the hardest good-bye from the group. Are high-performing groups hardest to leave? Groups with the clearest established norms? What sorts of closing rituals have you experienced?

4. The telephone game, passing a message from person to person, is fun simply because of the inevitable message distortion that gets revealed at the end. Can you think of a time when a message was passed to you from an indirect source that you discovered to be blatantly wrong? Maybe it was bungled homework instructions or a wrong meeting time or place. Given these sorts of problems, what type of workplace might function best with a chain network?

5. Analyze the group dynamics from five of your favorite television shows. See if you can identify the various social and antigroup role types in each of the groups.

6. The *Challenger* disaster is a classic example of groupthink. Run an Internet search on *groupthink*, and find other historical examples. Have any of these occurred in your lifetime? How are they similar to or different from the *Challenger* incident?

Now that you have finished reading this chapter, you can:

List the characteristics and types of groups and explain how groups develop:

▶ A **group** is a collection of more than two people who have a shared identity, have common goals, and are interdependent (p. 252).

▶ **Primary groups** are long-standing and meaningful groups, such as family groups (p. 253).

▶ Specific function groups include **support groups**, **social groups**, **problem-solving groups**, **study groups**, and **focus groups** (p. 253).

▶ A **team** is a task-oriented group, and a **self-directed work team** is a group with responsibility for producing high-quality finished work (pp. 254–255).

▶ Groups develop through five specific stages: **forming**, **storming**, **norming** (**norms** are recurring patterns of thought or behavior), **performing**, and **adjourning** (pp. 256–257).

Describe ways in which group size affects communication:

▶ The bigger the group, the more interaction becomes formal, less intimate, more time-consuming, and complex, and the less opportunity members have to contribute (pp. 259–260).

▶ The bigger the group, the more likely **cliques** (coalitions)—small subgroups—will emerge, making communication more challenging (p. 261).

▶ A **countercoalition**—a subgroup positioned against another subgroup—may leave unaffiliated members in an awkward position (p. 261).

▶ The larger the group, the more members are prone to **social loafing**, giving less effort (pp. 261–262).

Identify the influence of networks in groups:

▶ **Networks** are patterns of interaction governing who speaks with whom in a group (p. 263).

▶ The member who sends and receives the most messages has the highest degree of centrality; the other end of the spectrum is isolation (p. 263).

▶ In a **chain network**, information is passed from one member to the next rather than shared among members (p. 263).

▶ In an **all-channel network**, all members are equidistant and all interact with each other (p. 264).

▶ In a **wheel network**, one individual is the touchstone for the others (pp. 264–265).

Define the roles individuals play in a group:

▶ **Task roles** involve accomplishment of goals and include information giver, information seeker, elaborator, initiator, administrator, moderator, and elder (pp. 265–266).

▶ **Social roles** evolve based on personality traits and members' interests and include harmonizer, gatekeeper, and sensor (pp. 266–267).

▶ **Antigroup roles** put individual needs above group needs and include blocker, avoider, recognition seeker, distractor, and troll (pp. 267–268).

▶ **Role conflict** arises when expectations for behavior are incompatible (p. 268).

Identify key issues affecting group communication and effectiveness:

▶ **Cohesion**, how tightly group members have bonded, helps hold the group together in the face of adversity and helps to create a positive climate (p. 268).

▶ **Groupthink** occurs when members minimize conflict by refusing to critically examine ideas and test solutions (p. 271).

▶ Norms direct the behavior of the group, sometimes negatively, requiring modification (p. 272).

▶ Goals should be specific, arrived at by group decision, clearly defined, supported with the necessary resources, and able to be monitored (pp. 273–274).

▶ Individual differences—including cultural factors and varying levels of communication apprehension—can create communication challenges in groups (pp. 274–277).

In the face of unenthusiastic colleagues, an unsupportive public, and minimal funding, the ever optimistic and vigilant Leslie Knope prevails as an effective director of the Department of Parks and Recreation.

Leadership and Decision Making in Groups

Parks and Recreation's Leslie Knope loves her job. As deputy director of the Department of Parks and Recreation in the small town of Pawnee, Indiana, she is a committed public servant who is quite simply thrilled to be a part of local government. And while she may seem naive or even delusional (she describes the citizens who scream at her during town meetings as "people caring loudly at [her]"), she is, in fact, an effective and essential leader.

The people she works with are decidedly less enthused. Her boss, Ron, believes that the government, and he himself, should "do as little as possible," and his assistant, April, is an expert in thwarting any work that comes his way. (Want a meeting with Ron? April will happily pencil you in for Marchtember Oneteenth.) Colleague Tom seems preoccupied with his side project as a club promoter. And while state auditor Chris may be the only person on earth more optimistic than Leslie, his optimism is usually thwarted by his pragmatic colleague, Ben, who is charged with making the difficult cuts needed to balance the budget.

But Leslie is always focused on her goals, whether it's building a park where there once was a pit or reviving the town's long forgotten Harvest Festival, even as the local economy collapses. She works doggedly; even when crippled by flu, she makes it to a meeting and manages to get a majority of the town's businesses to participate in the Harvest Festival. She also has a well-earned reputation for being kind, honest, and ethical, which proves to be an asset: when Leslie asks the Pawnee police department to provide security at the festival on a volunteer basis, the chief agrees, no questions asked. "Leslie Knope gets as many favors as she needs," he says, "because she's the kind of person who uses favors to help other people."

What makes a leader? Skills? Character? Power? An ability to make decisions? And is it possible for groups to exist, if not thrive, without someone like Leslie Knope taking on an effective and inspiring leadership role? In this chapter, we continue our discussion of group communication by examining two additional processes that often emerge in groups: leadership and decision making. These two processes are tightly interrelated: a group's leader affects how the group makes decisions, and the decisions a group makes affect how the leader operates. When leadership and decision making work together in a constructive way, a group stands the best possible chance of achieving its goals. To understand how these processes influence a group's effectiveness, let's begin by taking a closer look at group leadership.

Understanding Group Leadership

It's a word that's constantly tossed about in political campaigns, highlighted on résumés, and used in book titles and biographies. But just what is *leadership*? Scholars have grappled with the task of defining leadership for many years. Consider these classic definitions:

- ▶ "The behavior of an individual when he [or she] is directing the activities of a group toward a shared goal" (Hemphill & Coons, 1957, p. 7)

- ▶ "Interpersonal influence, exercised in a situation, and directed, through the communication process, toward the attainment of a specified goal or goals" (Tannenbaum, Weschler, & Massarik, 1961, p. 24)

- ▶ "An interaction between persons in which one presents information of a sort and in such a manner that the other becomes convinced that his [or her] outcomes . . . will be improved if he [or she] behaves in the manner suggested or desired" (Jacobs, 1970, p. 232)

Notice that two key terms—*direction* and *influence*—show up or are hinted at in these definitions. That's because in its most essential form, **leadership** is the ability to direct or influence others' behaviors and thoughts toward a productive end (Nierenberg, 2009). This capacity for influence may stem from a person's power or simply from group members' admiration or respect for the individual. Because influence involves power over others, let's take a look at power—what it is and where it comes from.

Five Sources of Power

If you've ever seen the classic Steven Spielberg film *Jaws,* you know that it is, on the surface, the tale of a small coastal town being terrorized by a nasty, man-eating shark. But at the heart of the tale is the interaction among a group of men, each of whom bears or takes some responsibility for ridding the waters of the treacherous animal. First, there's the town's mayor, whose main priority is protecting the local economy. Second, there's the town's new chief of police, who's thrust into the story when the first body washes ashore not long after his arrival.

● **QUINT, CHIEF BRODY,** and Matt Hooper each bring something different to the shark-hunting mission, and derive their power from different sources.

Also playing a role are Matt Hooper, a young marine biologist who studies sharks, and the local shark hunter, a war-scarred fisherman who goes only by the name of Quint. Over the course of the film, each man demonstrates leadership that is firmly rooted in the nature of the power he possesses.

Researchers have identified five types of power—legitimate, coercive, reward, expert, and referent (French & Raven, 1959).

▶ **Legitimate power** comes from an individual's role or title. The president, your supervisor at work, and the coach of a team all possess legitimate power as elected or appointed leaders. In *Jaws,* the elected mayor of Amity Island, Larry Vaughn, has some degree of legitimate power, as does Martin Brody, the chief of police, though his power is subordinate to the mayor's.

▶ **Coercive power** stems from a person's ability to threaten or harm others. A harsh dictator who keeps his people under threat of violence or economic hardship holds such power, but so does a boss who threatens to dock or demote employees if they step out of line. In *Jaws,* the mayor—whose primary concern is protecting the town's economy, which is dependent on the summer tourist season—uses this kind of power to influence or override decisions made by the police chief. He hired Chief Brody, and he can fire him.

▶ **Reward power** derives from an individual's capacity to provide rewards. For example, your boss might offer all the people in your department a paid day off if they work late three nights in a row on an important project. In the film, the mayor relies on reward power: hundreds of local fishermen set out to catch the shark in hopes of winning a monetary reward.

▶ **Expert power** comes from the information or knowledge that a leader possesses. Expert power is divided in *Jaws.* Faced with any other kind of homicide, Brody's credentials as a former New York City police officer might have given him a fair amount of expert power. But as a newcomer, he gets little respect from the islanders, especially the fishermen, who think of him as a city slicker without sea legs. The scientist, Matt Hooper, who studies sharks, fares a little bit better. But Quint, who has decades of shark-hunting experience, quickly emerges as the true expert, garnering the respect of his crewmates.

▶ **Referent power** stems from the admiration, respect, or affection that followers have for a leader. The popular kids in your high school may have had

COMMUNICATIONACROSSCULTURES

Trying to Change a Culture of Violence

Is violence a virus? Can it be contained and controlled—like the spread of HIV or tuberculosis? Gary Slutkin thinks it can. He's the founder of CeaseFire, a Chicago-based group that focuses on stopping gang-related violence in the city's most troubled neighborhoods. The group, featured in the 2011 independent documentary *The Interrupters*, works by identifying violent situations that have the potential to snowball into more violence. By keeping an ear to the street (and the local emergency rooms), group members are able to intercede with gang members, for example, who would normally seek retribution.

Crucial to CeaseFire's operations is its credibility. Most of the men and women employed by the group to intercede are former felons—and often former gang members—who have strong ties to the community and the gang culture. Many of them were identified and recruited while serving time in jail and were hired upon their release from prison to serve as CeaseFire's "conflict interrupters." And that is their role: when a situation arises that the group feels is likely to erupt into violence (a shooting, a turf war, even an insult hurled), conflict interrupters seek out the individuals involved and try to pressure them not to seek revenge, to keep their guns at home, and to let the matter go. After one gang-related shooting in Chicago in 2010, for example, conflict interrupters who had histories with the two gangs were able to negotiate a treaty before any retaliations took place (Slutkin, 2011).

The reasoning behind the group's practices links with Slutkin's background as an epidemiologist, someone who studies factors affecting health and illness in a population. Years earlier, while trying to contain an outbreak of cholera in a Somalian refugee camp, he learned that the best way to change the behavior of a group was to have members of the group take the lead. In that instance, he found that training Somali birth attendants to identify, treat, and prevent the disease was the most effective way of stopping it from spreading, because members of the group were more likely to take the advice of someone from within their own culture. "Copying and modeling the social expectations of your peers is what drives your behavior," Slutkin noted (qtd. in Kotlowitz, 2008, para. 20). The idea for using former felons and gang members as leaders to prevent violent escalations in inner cities is based on the same principle (Kotlowitz, 2008).

THINK ABOUT THIS

❶ Why is it important that CeaseFire's violence interrupters come from the gang culture? Does their history as felons who've served time truly empower them?

❷ What practical and logistical benefits does hiring members of the community offer CeaseFire? Would Slutkin himself be able to identify and track down individuals who might seek retribution?

❸ What kinds of leadership skills are needed to change the culture of violence in these communities? Should the conflict interrupters employ the same kinds of leadership skills in dealing with the community that the project's founder might use in managing them?

the power to influence other students' style of dress or way of behaving simply because others admired them. In *Jaws,* Quint demonstrates this kind of power: when he relays his story as a survivor of the USS *Indianapolis* during World War II, Brody and Hooper gain a new sense of understanding of, and admiration for, his obsession with killing sharks.

It's important to note that these types of power are not exclusive of one another; indeed, most leaders wield several, if not all, of these types of power. Quint, for example, demonstrates legitimate power as captain of his own vessel as well as expert and referent power. Note also that individuals gain power only if others grant it to them. That's true to some degree even of coercive power: for example, Brody could have chosen to quit his job early on rather than to acquiesce to the mayor. Thus group members often decide to allow a particular individual to lead them.

Shared Leadership

With so many sources of power, it's not surprising that in some groups, several individuals take on leadership roles, each drawing from different sources of power. Thus leadership is shared by a few members of the group who divvy up the power and take control of specific tasks. For example, imagine that your sorority is planning a trip to Jazz Fest in New Orleans. As chair of the social committee, you take care of organizing the group for the event—publicizing the trip and recording the names of individuals who are interested in going. Another sorority sister, Eva, takes care of booking a block of hotel rooms in the French Quarter and negotiating a group rate. Lily, the chapter president, gets in touch with the sister chapter at Louisiana State University to arrange a meetup. Meanwhile, Keisha, your chapter's community outreach chair, organizes a fundraiser on campus in the hope of raising money for Habitat for Humanity in New Orleans so that your sorority may present the organization with a generous check during your visit.

When the talents and powers of each group member are leveraged through shared leadership, members feel more satisfied with the group process and more motivated to perform (Foels, Driskell, Mullen, & Salas, 2000; Kanter, 2009). As a result, the group is more likely to achieve its goals. Probably for these reasons, many businesses and professional organizations in the United States are moving toward a shared-leadership model, whereby they give people at lower levels of the organization decision-making and leadership responsibilities (Krayer, 2010).

Leadership Styles

What is the best way to lead a group? Should you accept input from the members or rule with an iron fist? Do you focus mainly on the task at hand or help resolve relationship problems? It turns out that there is no one "best" style of leadership. Rather, scholars argue that effective group leaders, whether they're leading alone or sharing power with someone else in the group, adapt their leadership styles to the needs of the group or the situation at hand. Four possible styles are discussed here—directive, participative, supportive, and achievement-oriented—each of which works best under different conditions (Gouran, 2003; Pavitt, 1999).

AND YOU?

Consider three groups to which you belong. Is there a clearly established leader for each group? If so, what type of power does this leader have? Do you find certain types of power more ethical or appropriate than others? Explain your answer.

Shared leadership is at the heart of the *self-directed work team* we describe in Chapter 9, where sharing leadership goes beyond improving group member motivation to allow members to set standards for the group, conduct peer evaluations, bring in new members, and coordinate plans with management. The end result is often goal achievement and a sense of cooperation rather than divisive competition among members.

● *LAW AND ORDER'S*
Lieutenant Van Buren never leaves her detectives hanging; she gives them specific and thorough directions for every step of a case.

Directive

A **directive leader** controls the group's communication by conveying specific instructions to members. This style works best when members are unsure of what's expected of them or how to carry out the group's tasks. Directive leaders can move their group in the right direction by charting next steps in the group's tasks and clarifying the group's goals, plans, and desired outcomes. For example, an instructor must tell students how to complete an assignment or guide them through an in-class exercise. Similarly, Lieutenant Anita Van Buren on NBC's *Law and Order* takes a directive approach in guiding how her detectives handle specific cases: she offers guidance in determining which leads to follow, whom to bring in for questioning, and what information to follow up on. She also has the final say on when to approach the district attorney for warrants, oversees the questioning of witnesses and suspects, and disciplines her detectives when they overstep their bounds.

Participative

A **participative leader** views group members as equals, welcomes their opinions, summarizes points that have been raised, and identifies problems that need discussion rather than dictating solutions. This style works best when group members are competent and motivated to take on the task at hand. Such leaders typically guide and facilitate rather than giving instructions to group members. Many online topic forums and blogs are moderated by participative leaders—they allow discussion among members of the group to take off in many directions, and they contribute right along with everyone else. But they also step in when needed to remind inappropriately contributing members of the purpose of the discussion.

Supportive

A **supportive leader** attends to group members' emotional needs. This style is especially helpful when members feel frustrated with a task or with each other. Supportive leaders can best apply this style by stressing the importance of positive relationships in the group, reminding members of the group's importance, and expressing appreciation for members' talents and work ethic. Consider Tim Gunn of *Project Runway*. He acts as a leader and mentor figure to the aspiring designers, helping them visualize their designs and talk through their frustrations and encouraging team members to communicate with each other, listen to each other, and "make it work." He is always profuse in his praise, and even when a particular design doesn't impress him, he is encouraging and positive in his criticism.

Achievement-Oriented

An **achievement-oriented leader** sets challenging goals and communicates high expectations and standards to members. This style works best when group members see themselves as competent and are motivated to excel at their tasks.

What Type of Leader Are You?

Choose the answer that best describes what you might do in each situation.

1. Your chemistry professor assigned a full-semester group project and has asked you to take the lead in your group because chemistry is your best subject. When it comes down to assigning your tasks to the other group members and getting the project done, what do you do?

   A. Ask a lot of questions. Who knows, someone else may know just as much as you, but is too shy to act on it.

   B. Get down to business! You know the facts, so you immediately delegate work to each member of the group.

   C. Assume you're working with very smart people and allow everyone a chance to say what direction the group should take.

   D. Don't want to hurt anyone's feelings, so you ask for input and watch everyone's emotional reactions to ensure that everyone is happy.

2. You organized a study group to prepare for your history final exam and invited a handful of other hardworking students from class. Another classmate, Scott, shows up. Scott is rarely prepared for class and isn't contributing to the group. What do you do?

   A. Start asking Scott questions in areas you think he might be knowledgeable. You hope that by inviting him to participate, he will begin contributing to the group.

   B. Don't really notice if Scott is contributing or not because you're too busy organizing the group's class notes.

   C. Try to get Scott to participate but don't go out of your way too much. If he is to be an equal member of the group, he has to reach out too.

   D. Become concerned with Scott's feelings. You move your chair next to his and ask how he's doing. This may slow the group's progress, but at least it includes Scott.

3. Managing a local, casual restaurant has its ups and downs, and today is one of the downs. Customers have been complaining that the waiters and waitresses have not been friendly, so you've decided to call a "worker meeting" to address the problem. What do you do at the meeting?

   A. Tell the workers what the customers said and then sit back and listen to everyone's responses.

   B. Explain the problem and offer possible solutions while delegating particular tasks (such as checking in on customers) to specific individuals.

   C. Tell your workers about the complaints and explain that you're shocked—you could never have imagined that this scenario would happen.

   D. Open the group meeting by having each member state what's been on his or her mind lately; you figure personal problems may affect the working environment.

If your answers are mostly A's: You are a participative leader.
If your answers are mostly B's: You are a directive leader.
If your answers are mostly C's: You are an achievement-oriented leader.
If your answers are mostly D's: You are a supportive leader.
(A mix of answers indicates a diverse leadership style.)

● WITH MR. SCHUESTER'S achievement-oriented leadership, the New Directions choir gleefully sees one of its goals met: winning Regionals.

In addition to setting lofty goals, such leaders encourage outside-the-box thinking, compare the group with other high-performing groups, and keep members focused on tangible outcomes. Will Schuester, the leader of the New Directions show choir on *Glee*, has an achievement-oriented leadership style. He sets a clear goal for the club—to qualify for and compete at a national competition—and in preparation, he has members check out competitors and create their own new and unique singing routines.

Competence and Ethics

An ability to mix and match leadership styles to suit your group's needs is an essential skill for a leader. But to be a truly competent leader requires other skills as well. The most effective leaders remain focused on their group's goals, and they hold both themselves *and* the group accountable for achieving those results. They treat all group members in an ethical manner. They also have credibility with their group. That is, members see them as knowledgeable, experienced, believable, and respectable—even if they don't like their leader personally. Finally, competent leaders use skilled communication techniques, such as describing a compelling vision of success and acknowledging the group's valuable talents, to inspire members to contribute their best.

But not all leaders demonstrate these qualities. Some use unethical tactics to try to acquire and keep control over an entire group or individual members within a group. These tactics can include **bullying** or behaviors such as harsh criticism, name-calling, gossip, slander, personal attacks, or threats to safety or job security (Smith, 2005). It can also include offensive gestures, ignoring, withering looks, or a sarcastic tone of voice. Bullies may

In many organizational contexts, bullying behaviors can escalate to illegal *harassment*, communication that hurts and offends, creating a hostile environment. Victims of bullying may find our tips in Chapter 11 (p. 333) helpful for dealing with such unethical behavior in a group, in an organization, or even in an interpersonal relationship.

try to manipulate group members by withholding needed information, excluding them from meetings, or insisting on unrealistic deadlines or expectations. Unfortunately, such unethical tactics can prove successful for some leaders to some degree. Take chef Gordon Ramsay on the reality TV series *Hell's Kitchen*. Aspiring chefs are split into two teams that are pitted against each other in challenges while also preparing and serving dinner to a roomful of diners. Ramsay is very particular about how he wants the food to taste and look. If something is not up to par, he often screams profanities at the contestant responsible for the mistake, even tossing the offending dishes on the floor. Ramsay has no qualms about insulting any of the contestants or getting personal; in a fit of anger, he will hurl insults about contestants' appearance, ethnicity, or professional background. While his anger and derogatory statements are usually met by a grim "Yes, chef," and while he may gain the respect of some of the contestants, some do tire of being abused on a regular basis and break down or walk out.

● **GORDON RAMSEY'S** constant belittlement of *Hell's Kitchen* contestants creates a very hostile work environment. Only the brave and thick-skinned need apply!

EVALUATING COMMUNICATION ETHICS

Leading the Interns

You are currently working as an assistant to an editor at a reputable music magazine, and among your responsibilities is leading a group of young, aspiring summer interns. You find this task especially rewarding because as a college student, you suffered through a number of magazine internships in order to get your foot in the door, so you hope that you can make this internship rewarding for the students in your department.

Back when you were an intern, you worked with an assistant named Bradley, who was in a position similar to the one you're in now. Bradley always seemed to pass off his boring, menial tasks—such as filing, answering his boss's e-mail, and setting up appointments—to the interns so that he could sit and listen to new records in an attempt to further his career in rock criticism. You and the other interns were willing to take on just about any task in order to get a good recommendation, but you always slightly resented Bradley, feeling that he had used you and others in your group.

Since you started working long hours at your assistant job, however, you've wondered if Bradley actually had the right idea. Like Bradley, you aspire to be a music critic, and the mundane tasks of your job are beginning to frustrate you. Such tasks are, however, part of your job description—they are what every assistant does.

You want to have time to talk to writers, to write or edit copy, and to be able to sit in on pitch meetings. Bradley kept you from such experiences as an intern because you were too busy fetching lattes for his boss. The problem is, now you need to get lattes for your own boss, and this is keeping you from gussying up your own portfolio. Yet here are new, young interns willing and eager to do anything to get ahead, perhaps even taking over those menial tasks. What should you do?

THINK ABOUT THIS

❶ Was Bradley wrong, or was he just doing what any aspiring journalist would do to free up his time? Do you have a greater understanding for his struggle in light of your own position?

❷ Is it OK to pawn your work off on unpaid college students, even if they're willing to do it?

❸ As the group's leader, do you have a responsibility to these interns to ensure that they get the most from their internship experience?

Culture and Group Leadership

As you'll recall from Chapter 3, culture can strongly shape the way people approach leading a group and the ways in which members respond to a leader. Let's look at three particular factors—gender, high versus low context, and power distance—that prove to be particularly powerful when leading a group.

Gender and Leadership

Would you vote for a female presidential candidate? A 2007 Gallup poll found that 88 percent of Americans said they would vote for a well-qualified female president to lead the nation (Kohut, 2007). You may well recall the passion and drive behind many of Hillary Rodham Clinton's supporters when she made her historic bid for the presidency in 2008. But why the concern over a leader's biological sex? Is there really a difference between men and women as leaders?

With a few key exceptions, research has provided little support for the popular notion that men and women inherently lead differently, though scholars Eisenberg, Goodall, and Trethewey (2010) note that the popular idea of men and women communicating and leading differently has persisted. In essence, we may assume that men have a masculine style of leadership, emphasizing command and control, while women have a feminine style of leadership, emphasizing more nurturing communication environments. For example, some research has suggested that feminine leaders think of organizations as webs of relationships, with leaders at the center of the web, in contrast to the more traditionally masculine view of organizations as pyramids with a leader at the top. Feminine leaders may also view the boundaries between work and personal life as fluid and may communicate their understanding of employees' need to balance professional and personal obligations (Helgesen, 1990; Mumby, 2000; Rosener, 1990).

Interestingly, a study by Sarah Rutherford (2001) notes that men and women's leadership styles are often dictated by factors other than sex and gender, such as the general communication style of the group or organization. In the marketing department of an organization Rutherford studied, for example, 47 percent of the managers were women, yet the department had a decidedly masculine style, perhaps due to the competitive and confrontational nature of a business that favored a less nurturing response. You might contrast this with the leadership style of Sun-Joo Kim, the chairman and chief executive of luxury-goods company MCM Worldwide, who leans on motherhood as a model of leadership and seeks to run her business with her heart (Covel, 2008). Such a style might well work in an organization that values and promotes nurturing, sharing, and other traditionally feminine values.

However, regardless of the leadership style encouraged by a division or organization, 84 percent of female respondents in Rutherford's (2001) study believed that women manage differently from men, while 55 percent of men believe the same—supporting Eisenberg, Goodall, and Trethewey's (2010) point that the idea of sex differences can be hard to shake. That said, we encourage you to remember the concept of *behavioral flexibility* discussed in Chapter 2. Leadership is a complicated and messy topic, and it seems clear that men and women—when leading a business or even a student organization—must look for opportunities to use the best skills from both traditional styles of leadership at the right time for ethical purposes, regardless of their biological sex.

Context and Power Distance

Two additional factors at play in this discussion are context and power distance, terms we introduced in Chapter 3 that are worth reconsidering within a larger discussion of leadership. For example, you may recall that people from high-context cultures (such as Japan) tend to communicate in indirect ways, while those from low-context cultures (like the United States) communicate more directly (Hall, 1976). Imagine, for example, a manager tasked with keeping a team on target to meet a very tight deadline. A leader from a high-context culture might simply present a calendar noting due dates and filled with tasks and competing projects; she would rely on her team to get the point that the deadline is in trouble and expect team members to offer solutions. A leader from a low-context culture, on the other hand, would be more likely to clarify the situation directly: "I'm moving the deadline earlier by two weeks; that means you'll need to accelerate your work accordingly." The ways in which group members respond will also be influenced by culture: group members from a high-context culture might communicate in a similarly indirect way with their leader ("We have some concerns about the new deadline"), while those from a low-context culture would be more direct ("Sorry, we can't make the new deadline").

In addition to high- and low-context cultures, power distance is a cultural difference that affects how groups communicate. As we learned in Chapter 3, *power distance* is the extent to which less powerful members of a group, be it a business organization or a family, accept that power is distributed unequally. This means that a person who is leading a group in a high power distance culture and wants all members to offer their ideas in a meeting might need to make a special effort to encourage everyone to participate in the discussion, whereas in a group with low power distance, members are likely to offer their opinions without much prodding. For example, a manager in a software development company in Hong Kong (a region with high power distance) may need to reassure her employees that she does want to hear what they think and does want them to take the initiative in developing new ideas and products.

● **IN A LOW POWER DISTANCE** culture, meetings might feel like roundtable discussions, where everyone gets a chance to speak. In a high power distance culture, meetings are usually more hierarchical.

Decision Making in Groups

As you learned in Chapter 9, the communication between group leaders and members strongly influences how a group makes decisions. And because of the large numbers of exchanges and people involved, decision making in a group differs markedly from decision making by one individual or between just two people. For one thing, in a group, a complex set of forces influences decision making. These forces also influence how a group progresses through the decision-making process. In the following sections, we examine each of these topics in detail.

Forces That Shape a Group's Decisions

Experts have identified three forces—cognitive, psychological, and social—that strongly affect how groups and their leaders discuss and arrive at decisions (Hirokawa, Gouran, & Martz, 1988). Going back to the devastating *Challenger* example from Chapter 9, let's take a deeper look at these forces.

Cognitive Forces

Cognitive forces consist of group members' thoughts and beliefs. These affect how everyone in a particular group perceives, interprets, evaluates, stores, and retrieves information, which in turn influences the group's decisions.

Cognitive forces influenced the NASA officials who made the fateful decision to launch the *Challenger* shuttle, a subject you read about in Chapter 9. The officials discounted the credibility of key information available to them at the time, and they drew incorrect conclusions from the data. They also wrongly believed that the shuttle system was sound, which made them overly confident in their ability to have a successful launch.

Psychological Forces

Psychological forces refer to group members' personal motives, emotions, attitudes, and values. In the *Challenger* disaster, lower-level NASA decision makers had initially recommended postponing the launch until the day warmed up. But when higher-ups pressured them to reverse their recommendation, they caved in—perhaps because they were worried about losing their jobs if they didn't go along.

The decision makers also changed their attitudes about which criteria to use for postponing a shuttle launch. Previously, NASA rules dictated that a launch wouldn't take place if anyone doubted its safety. But with the *Challenger*, the rule had changed: the launch would proceed unless someone presented conclusive evidence that it was unsafe. Engineers' qualms about the launch didn't constitute conclusive evidence, so they hesitated to express their concerns. And the launch proceeded.

Social Forces

Social forces are group standards for behavior that influence decision making. In the *Challenger* disaster, engineers were unable to persuade their own managers and higher NASA officials to postpone the launch. They tried to prove that it was *unsafe* to launch rather than take the opposite (and possibly more effective) tactic: showing that no data existed to prove that the launch was *safe*.

The Problem-Solving Process

To make decisions, groups and their leaders often go through a six-step process (Dewey, 1933). To illustrate these steps, consider EcoCrew, a group of sixteen environmentally active students at a West Coast community college who wish to resolve environmental problems in their community.

Identifying the Problem

The EcoCrew group has scheduled its first meeting in the student union lounge. Susan, who initially had the idea of forming EcoCrew, is the group's designated leader. Deciding to adopt a participative leadership style, Susan invites each person to give his or her perception of the problem the group will set out to address. "No debate or questions until we have all voiced our perceptions," Susan says. Members pipe up with a number of issues and activities they'd like the group to address. "The campus bookshops and food courts need to eliminate plastic bags," says one; "the beaches are covered with litter during the winter months," says another.

By inviting members to voice their concerns one at a time, Susan is providing an opportunity for the group to identify and define several problems. Once all the members have presented their views, Susan encourages the group to discuss the various proposed definitions of the problem and agree on one that EcoCrew can productively address. The group decides that litter, both on campus and on the nearby beach, is the most immediately troubling environmental issue.

Having defined the problem it wants to address, EcoCrew has gotten off to an effective start. According to researchers, many groups don't spend enough time identifying the problem they want to tackle (Gouran, 2003). Without a clear, agreed-on problem, a group can't work through the rest of the decision-making process in a focused way.

Analyzing the Problem

Having decided to tackle litter cleanup as its primary mission, EcoCrew begins to analyze the problem. Susan suggests that each member carry a diary for one week as they travel around campus and the surrounding area and note where the litter is most concentrated and how much litter they see. When the group meets again the following week, all members agree that the two biggest litter problems in the area are on the beaches and in the wooded areas surrounding the campus parking lots. Several members note that the trash cans on the beaches are not being emptied often enough by city sanitation workers; they appeared to be overflowing with trash, which was being blown out of the cans by the gusting ocean wind.

Generating Solutions

Once the EcoCrew team has identified and analyzed the problem, the next step is to come up with a solution. Susan starts asking for ideas from the group and

AND YOU?
How do cognitive, psychological, and social forces affect decision making in groups you're currently involved in? Have these forces ever caused your group to make a poor decision? If so, how?

Brainstorming and *clustering* can help you in both public speaking and small group settings. When choosing a topic, both strategies allow you to generate ideas based on our interests, your audience's interests, and your time constraints (Chapter 12). In a group, brainstorming and clustering allow you to identify and discuss solutions from a variety of perspectives to ensure that the solution meets the needs of the group.

● **WRITING DOWN** any ideas that your team has on a whiteboard can be a great way to get the creative juices flowing.

writes them down on a whiteboard. "Just give me any ideas you've got," Susan says. "We'll evaluate them later."

This technique, called *brainstorming*, encourages members of a group to come up with as many ideas as possible without judging the merits of those ideas yet. The intent is to prompt fresh thinking and to generate a larger number of potential solutions than a group might arrive at if members evaluated each idea as it came up. As the EcoCrew members throw out idea after idea, the whiteboard grows dense and colorful with possibilities (see Figure 10.1).

Once the members have run out of new ideas, they'll need to narrow down the list. To help them focus on the one or two strongest ideas, Susan invites them to define the criteria that eventual solutions will have to meet. First, Susan reminds them that the primary goal would be to reduce litter on the beach. Another member, Wade, then points out that at this point, the group has no budget, so it needs to limit its initial efforts to tasks that have little or no cost. Another member, Larissa, notes that because the group has a relatively small membership, it should focus on things either that the group can manage on its own or in which the group could encourage nonmembers to participate. The group concludes that an acceptable solution must meet these key criteria.

FIGURE 10.1

SUSAN'S WHITEBOARD

- More trash cans!
  - Can we provide these?
  - Get the city to provide?
- Covered trash cans that keep litter in—wind-resistant?
- Increase city sanitation pickups!
  - Letter writing/e-mail campaign?
  - Contact the mayor?
- Beach cleanup?
  - Massive volunteer beach cleanup event
  - Monthly volunteer beach cleanup?
- Antilitter advertising? "Don't pollute!"
  - Flyers/posters would create more litter.
  - Permanent signs/billboards? $$$$

Evaluating and Choosing Solutions

Once EcoCrew has generated its list of possible solutions, group members have to evaluate the pros and cons of each idea to consider how well it meets the criteria the members have defined. For example, one member, Kathryn, points out that the lack of funding makes replacing the garbage cans out of the question and would make an antilitter advertising campaign difficult, if not impossible. Wade notes that organizing a beach cleanup would cost next to nothing: they could all volunteer to get together to pick up garbage and clean up the beach. Larissa adds that if they get the word out, they'd also be able to attract additional volunteers—and potential new members—from outside the group to participate. Thus the group decides to launch a monthly beach cleanup; this would be a regular social event that could raise awareness of the group, encourage nonmembers to participate and new members to join, and involve little to nothing in terms of cost.

Implementing the Solution

Implementing a solution means putting into action the decision that the group has made. For EcoCrew, this means making plans for the regular beach cleanup. The group focuses first on logistics—setting dates and times. One member, Allison, volunteers to act as a liaison with the county sanitation department to see if it can provide trash bags and picks for the volunteers and to arrange for the sanitation trucks to pick up the trash once it's been bagged.

Larissa adds that with a bit of legwork, the group could turn the cleanup into a large community event; she volunteers to arrange for an end-of-day gathering and to see if she can get her mother's sandwich shop to donate food. Wade notes that he can probably get his roommate's band to entertain free of charge as well.

Assessing the Results

Once a group has implemented a solution it has decided on, members should evaluate the results. Evaluation can shed light on how effective the solution was and whether the group needs to make further decisions about the problem at hand. For EcoCrew, it will be helpful to assess the first event in terms of how well it met the three key criteria:

● **AFTER THEIR BEACH** cleanup, the EcoCrew team needs to assess the results. The first question should be: "Was the beach cleaner after our event?"

▶ Was the beach cleaner at the end of the day as a result of the group's efforts? Before-and-after photos of the beach reveal a very successful cleanup.

▶ Did the event wind up costing the members any money? Thanks to the donations of local restaurants and supplies provided by the county sanitation department, the event cost the group absolutely nothing.

▶ Did the event attract volunteers from outside the group? Fifteen nonmembers participated in the cleanup, among them several schoolchildren who attended with their parents.

AND YOU?

Consider the six steps to problem solving we've just discussed. If Susan, the leader of EcoCrew, had chosen a different leadership style, would this have affected how the problem-solving steps were carried out? If so, how? What has your experience been in solving problems in groups with different types of leaders?

By revisiting these criteria, the group is able to tweak its plan for the following month's cleanup event. Larissa suggests that the members pitch in a few dollars to place an ad in the local paper thanking the volunteers and donors and announcing the date of the next cleanup. Wade follows up by suggesting that the group make a pitch at the local elementary school to get more kids and their families involved. Kathryn volunteers to submit a brief story about the cleanup, along with photos of the event and the results, to the campus newspaper. And Susan suggests holding a raffle at the next event, with half the proceeds paid out in prizes and half retained by the group, to get a small budget started to cover future ads and expenses.

Leadership in Meetings

EcoCrew was able to identify a problem, create a solution, and implement it very successfully. Much of the planning and implementation took place in meetings. Group leader Susan was able to direct the discussion and manage the deliberations in ways that kept the group focused and invited input from all participants. Indeed, meetings—be they face to face, over the phone, online, or through a combination of media—are an integral part of many group activities. But they are not always successful, and the failure of a meeting often rests on the shoulders of the group leader.

Consider Julia, a freelance Web designer who works from a home office. On Friday, Julia received an e-mail from her biggest client, Jacob, asking her to phone in to a meeting with the sales team to discuss marketing materials related to the launch of the new Web site she's designing for his skateboard manufacturing company. Struggling with several competing deadlines, Julia dreaded spending an hour or two listening to a group of people she'd never met discuss parts of the project with which she had little to do. But she reluctantly confirmed that she could take part in the meeting the following Monday.

After spending the better part of Monday morning reviewing her design for the project and outlining a few ideas for ways it could be teased into the marketing campaign, Julia dutifully dialed in to the conference room at the designated time, only to find herself placed on hold—complete with irritating piped-in music—for twenty minutes before the team picked up. The meeting that followed was equally frustrating: Jacob spent the better part of an hour describing the content of the site, how it would work, and the potential for revenues it would generate for the team of salespeople, who were entirely unfamiliar with the project. Julia—who was responsible only for creating the look and functionality of the Web site and had nothing to do with content or sales—sat miserably watching the clock, grateful that at least the team couldn't see her as she scribbled angry doodles and notes to herself.

Meetings can be integral to group decision making, but they can often be unproductive and frustrating. Ineffective meetings are one of the top time wasters cited by workers: one survey of more than thirty-eight thousand workers worldwide found that people spend more than five working hours per week in meetings, and about 70 percent of the respondents felt that most meetings weren't productive (Microsoft, 2005). In this section, we'll analyze meetings

Planning a meeting can be similar to planning a speech, particularly regarding audience analysis (Chapter 12). In both contexts, you must be aware of the expectations and goals of others involved (your audience or attendees): Why are they present? Why should they listen to you? How is the meeting or speech relevant to them? In addition, you need to consider the situational context for the event (location, room setup, and so on) in both contexts to ensure that it won't inhibit communication.

from a communication perspective and consider how they can be best used to arrive at better decisions and solutions. We'll discuss how technology has changed meetings—and how it hasn't. Most important, we'll show that effective leadership is crucial to conducting effective and productive meetings.

Planning Meetings Effectively

Let's consider all the reasons why Julia found the meeting we've just described so frustrating. First, it was a bad time: she was struggling to meet deadlines and really didn't want to stop working to sit in on a meeting. What's worse, she probably didn't really have to be there either—the client was using the meeting to inform the sales team about the site as a whole, not to discuss anything that dealt with Julia's design. Further complicating the issue were the facts that the meeting didn't start on time, Julia had not met anyone on the sales force before, and the medium used—speakerphone—limited Julia's communication with the team in concrete ways. Put simply, the meeting was poorly planned.

Proper planning is crucial for successful meetings. Making a few decisions beforehand and taking steps to clarify goals and logistics for the team can lead to more effective decision making during the meeting itself. Yet research has shown that as many as 30 percent of groups do not plan meetings effectively (or at all), even though planning can improve decision-making quality by as much as 35 percent (Gouran, 2003). There are several steps that group leaders can take to plan meetings more effectively.

Justify the Meeting

Before calling a meeting, a group leader should consider what he or she wants to accomplish and assess whether a meeting is even necessary to meet that goal. If there are no clear goals for a meeting, it's impossible for any goals to be met as a result of it. What's more, the leader needs to ensure that only those whose presence is necessary in order to meet the goals or who would truly benefit from attending are included. While not a typical meeting, a good example of this is when Harry Potter first begins to assemble Dumbledore's Army in *Harry Potter and the Order of the Phoenix*. He determines the goals of the meetings (to teach other students how to defend themselves in the face of Voldemort's return to power) and invites only students that he knows will use the training and won't derail the meeting.

In many cases, meetings can be avoided altogether or made smaller and more efficient by asking team members to contribute information ahead of time or simply picking up the phone to ask someone a question when one arises (Conlin, 2006).

● **EVERYONE PRESENT** at the Dumbledore's Army gatherings is well aware of the goal of these meetings: to learn how to fight and defend themselves against the evil Voldemort.

Clarify the Purpose and the Participants

If a meeting is necessary, it is the responsibility of the leader to clearly articulate the goals of the meeting and the roles of everyone who is to attend. Think back to Julia's situation. Her client, Jacob, wants to get his sales force interested and excited about the launch of the Web site. Getting the sales force together to view the beta version and get feedback on it might seem like a good way to brainstorm ideas for marketing. But Jacob failed to clarify what he wanted to accomplish at the meeting and what Julia's role would be. Jacob might have made a more efficient use of Julia's time if he'd simply discussed elements of the design with her prior to the meeting or asked her to outline a few key features for him and then used her information in his meeting with the sales force without any need for Julia to attend.

Set an Agenda

President Dwight D. Eisenhower noted, "I have often found that plans are useless, but planning is indispensable." Creating a plan is a valuable phase in decision making, even if the plan itself isn't followed to the letter in the end. Setting an agenda is crucial.

An **agenda** for a meeting should detail the subject and goal of the meeting and logistics like time, place, or log-in or conference call information. It should set a schedule for the meeting as well so that participants will know how much time to block out for the meeting and so that the group leader can manage time effectively during the meeting itself. It should list or include any materials that participants would need to have read or reviewed in advance of the meeting so that everyone arrives with the appropriate background on the issue. Think of your agenda as a checklist—an essential component of meeting success (Gawande, 2009). A sample agenda for Jacob's meeting is provided in Figure 10.2.

Managing Meetings Effectively

So you now see that meetings can go well—or they can go horribly off track. During a meeting, it is the responsibility of the leader to manage the discussion in ways that help the group communicate while remaining focused on the meeting's goal. The following steps can help.

Arrive Prepared

In a 2005 interview, veteran businessman and writer Simon Ramo estimated that he's attended forty thousand meetings during his career, so he has a strong sense of what works and what doesn't. When running a meeting, the most important thing for a leader to do, Ramo advised, is to be prepared. If you've planned properly, you are fully aware of your goals for the meeting and familiar with all the background information you'll need.

Keep the Group Focused

It's also important to know who the participants are. You should have a sense beforehand of which participants are likely to be the biggest contributors, as well as who will likely need to be kept on track or prevented from going off on tangents.

Meeting with sales team to discuss marketing strategies for new SlickBoards Web site.

Date: March 24, 2012
Time: 10:00 A.M.–12:00 P.M. (EST)
Location: Conference Room 2. Call-in number 555-555-0823.

AGENDA

I.   Welcome
     A. Quick introduction of core team working on Web site
     B. Introduce purpose of meeting—to discuss the marketing
        strategies for the new SlickBoards Web site
II. Why do we need a new SlickBoards Web site?
     A. Overview of our current Web site and its deficiencies
     B. Present the concept of the new Web site, why we needed a
        revamp, and how it improves on the old site
III. What will be on the new SlickBoards Web site?
     A. Outline all the new information about the products that
        will be on the Web site and how it will increase sales
     B. Explain how clients will be able to customize their SlickBoard
        directly on the new Web site
IV. How should we market this new Web site?
     A. Discuss the focus of the marketing campaign: What's the
        message?
     B. Brainstorm how to get the message out
     C. Distill list of ideas; assign roles
V.   Conclusion and follow-up
     A. Take any questions or concerns
     B. Establish next meeting time and what should be accomplished
        by then

FIGURE 10.2

JACOB'S AGENDA Although Jacob's meeting agenda is very well organized, there is no indication that Julia needs to be present for it, or that she plays a role in this meeting.

One member might bring up a topic that's not on the agenda, and others might be unnecessarily long-winded. When these things occur, Ramo advised, "As tactfully as possible, interrupt to move the discussion along" ("Why Most Meetings Stink," 2005). This might be as simple as saying, "We're getting off the subject here," and bringing the group back to the main topic of the meeting.

Of course, as the meeting progresses, it is likely that the goal may be redefined or new goals may emerge. "Keep the objective of the meeting constantly in your mind so you'll keep moving toward the goal," Ramo advised. "But if the goal changes during or because of the meeting, be prepared to invent Plan B."

Summarize Periodically

As a group explores and settles on decisions, it's important that someone (a leader or any member) regularly summarize what has happened. Summaries provide members with opportunities to confirm, correct, or clarify what has occurred so far during the conversation. Summaries thus help ensure that everyone in the group is in agreement about what the group has decided, what steps it will be taking next, and how members are to carry out their designated tasks.

CONNECT

To keep a group focused and productive, you must employ effective listening skills (Chapter 6). You might think that leaders should talk more than listen, but without *informational, critical,* and *empathic listening* skills, they miss opportunities to learn new information from others or to analyze ideas that might help the group achieve goals.

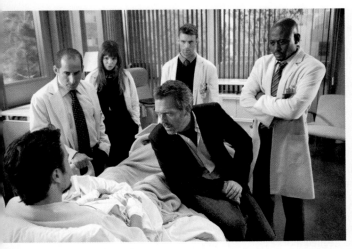

● **ALTHOUGH THE DIFFICULT** Dr. House would sooner create conflict than manage it, his team of doctors does succeed in working together through disputes to diagnose difficult medical cases.

Keep an Eye on the Time

Nobody likes to waste time, and nobody likes sitting through a long meeting when a short one would do. Group leaders need to be aware of time constraints to keep their meetings running efficiently and to respect the time pressures on the other members. When large groups are involved or when the agenda includes many topics or issues, it can be helpful to impose *time limits* on certain components of the discussion. When a decision must be made, taking an informal vote on a decision—a tactic called a **nonbinding straw poll**— can help you move the group forward.

Manage Conflict

As you saw in Chapter 8, the best decisions are usually those that have come from productive conflict (Kuhn & Poole, 2000; Nicotera, 1997). When group members deal with conflict productively, they ask clarifying questions, challenge one another's ideas (in a respectful way), consider worst-case scenarios, and revise proposals as needed to reflect new information and insights. This process leads to sound decisions because it enables group members to generate the widest possible range of ideas as well as test each idea's pros and cons. Any idea that survives this rigorous process has a fighting chance of delivering the hoped for results when it's put into action. The diagnostic team on *House* provides an interesting take on this process: doctors bounce ideas for treatments off of one another and point out possible outcomes and side effects of each one.

The other advantage of productive conflict is that the group members who engage in it feel a sense of ownership of the group's final decision. That's because they've had a hand in exploring and arriving at the decision. And when people share ownership of a decision, they're more likely to feel committed to carrying it out. Thus, decisions made through productive conflict have a greater chance of being implemented. That's a good thing, since even the most brilliant decision is useless unless a group puts it into action.

For this reason, making decisions by consensus is often a better approach than making decisions by majority vote. According to the consensus approach, everyone must agree on the final decision before it can be implemented. Consensus enhances members' feeling of ownership and commitment to carrying out the decision. But as you might imagine, it takes more time than deciding by majority vote. Still, because of its power to enhance commitment from group members, consensus should be used whenever time allows.

Follow Up

After the meeting has concluded, group members should implement their decisions and take stock of the results as well as the experience of working together. A simple follow-up e-mail that details the decisions reached at the meeting can ensure that everyone came away with the same perceptions and is aware of what each person must do to keep the group moving toward its goal.

AND YOU?

Do you have experience with group conflict, as either a group member or leader? If so, how was this conflict handled? Did conflict strengthen or weaken the communication between group members?

real communicator

NAME: Jim Simons
HOMETOWN: Marietta, GA
OCCUPATION: Project manager at an architecture firm
FUN FACT: I've worked on projects all over the world, from Thailand to the United Arab Emirates.

I'm a project manager at an architecture firm. Clients come to us and say, "We own this building site, and we want to use it productively, but we don't exactly know what form that should take." Maybe they know they want an office building with retail at the street level and parking underground, and they want us to get the maximum square footage for the property—or maybe they know much less. Once the client's request gets to me, I can put together a team.

For this task, it's important for a team to consist of varied professionals: me (the project manager), senior architects, creative designers, junior architects, and consultants (structural engineers, for example). We will need to work together to produce the product that the client has asked for.

I go into the first team meeting highly prepared and I try to keep the atmosphere loose and informal. I dress professionally, but not in a manner that may intimidate others. I provide food to give even the most disinterested team member a reason to become interested. Once the bagels have been passed around, I go to work outlining the goals of the meeting. I identify the problem and I make explicit what the group must accomplish. I tell the team *everything* I know about the client's request—the problem at hand needs to become everyone's problem. Open and honest communication is vital at this stage.

In a diverse group, people hear things differently. One way to clarify the message is to invite questions—misunderstandings will become exposed and can be cleared up. At this point, the meeting becomes a dialogue among equals with me serving more as a moderator. I keep an eye on the clock, but I'm careful not to cut people off too early. Architects are creative, and creative people need the opportunity to express their ideas. It's all about respecting and getting to know the individuals on your team and learning their strengths and weaknesses.

Once our task has been explicitly identified, I adopt an achievement-oriented leadership style. I delegate responsibilities. I give everyone on the team ownership over some component of the project, so that each individual can be his or her own supervisor on that particular component—whether it's the building's core, the exterior enclosure, the form, the numbers, or the mechanical system. Thus clear goals are established for each participant and interaction between team members will begin.

That's the first meeting. In the next meeting, each team member makes a brief presentation. This meeting is about reconciling solutions. My job here is twofold: (1) to bring group members' creative ideas back to the original task, the client's request, and (2) to summarize, summarize, summarize. Through explicit summaries, I hope to facilitate dialogue and cooperation and create order and cohesion out of a number of different ideas. I need to walk out of this meeting with a particular solution, a story to sell. Next, I will make an informational and persuasive presentation to the client. But that's a different story. I've got to wear a suit and tie in *that* meeting.

WIREDFORCOMMUNICATION

Bridging Space and Time

Outsourcing, combined with time zone differences between members of a virtual team, means that groups can literally work around the clock (Kuo & Yu, 2009). Sharyn, an account manager in Seattle, can spend all day on her accounts and send them to Indira in Bangalore at day's end, to be processed overnight and returned to Sharyn before her day begins the next morning.

Indeed, having workers in another time zone work while folks at the home office sleep can save an entire business day, which can be very beneficial when working on time-sensitive projects. Even as technology makes building virtual teams easier and more common, in far-flung, virtual environments, seemingly mundane tasks (such as scheduling or conducting a meeting) can become logistically difficult and personally taxing (Lira, Ripoll, Peiró, & Orengo, 2008). Frustrating delays can arise when one member of the team has a question for another team member who is on a different continent. Research demonstrates that as computer-based team meeting time increases, lower levels of positive affects and good feelings toward the group diminish (Johnson, Bettenhausen, & Gibbons, 2009). If Sharyn neglects to include some vital piece of information in the files she forwards to Indira, the project can be delayed for an entire day because of something that Sharyn could have provided in a matter of minutes if she were working at the same time as Indira.

Leaders of virtual teams must also grapple with unique challenges when trying to build team cohesion and trust among coworkers who will most likely never meet face to face (Montoya, Massey, Hung, & Crisp, 2009). Sharyn and Indira, for example, never talk but are in constant contact via e-mail. If either one of them has a question or complaint about the other's work, it's unlikely that they'll ever be able to resolve the conflict productively by talking to each other. It's up to their supervisor or group leader to handle the problem between them.

Managing meetings between virtual groups—even groups in the same time zone—can also be a challenge. Telephone conference calls, for example, typically involve members of one group on a speakerphone with other team members, either individuals or other groups, connected at the other end. In such situations, the larger group tends to dominate the discussion, and smaller groups or individuals find themselves left out. It is up to the group leader to manage such situations. One easy way to do it, noted one expert, is to "send people to their rooms"—that is, to have each team member sit at his or her own desk (rather than in groups) and dial in to the same conference call (Snyder, 2003). This way, the team consists of a group of individuals rather than a collection of small, competing groups.

THINK ABOUT THIS

❶ What can a group leader do to foster communication among team members in different locations and time zones?

❷ Should team members be expected to make themselves available via e-mail, text message, or telephone during nonworking hours to attend to questions or problems that might arise? What problems might this kind of communication cause?

❸ Can virtual teams ever build group relationships if they can never communicate in real time?

Using Technology in Meetings

Technology has changed the nature of meetings in both positive and negative ways. Obviously, the ability to set up virtual meetings through teleconferencing and videoconferencing (such as voice over Internet Protocol services like Skype and iChat) makes it possible for groups to collaborate over long distances. That's how Julia, the freelance designer, is able to "attend" a meeting with her client and his sales staff without actually having to leave home. Such virtual links can be beneficial for a team that needs to actively communicate about some issue or problem. But it also can be ineffective; the fact that everyone

● **RESEARCH INDICATES** that group members work better face to face initially, but that individuals who are familiar with each other and established as a team also work productively with video-conferencing technology.

can be included doesn't necessarily mean that everyone *must* be included. Julia, for example, did not need to sit in on the meeting with the sales team; she had little to add and gained nothing by being there. Further, the ability to share information with team members quickly and efficiently via e-mail and file sharing has enabled teams to avoid some meetings altogether (Conlin, 2006). Julia and Jacob, for example, might have done well to e-mail a link to the beta version of the site to the entire sales team rather than having a meeting to discuss it in the abstract.

But is there a difference between face-to-face meetings and virtual meetings? Research indicates that face-to-face teams perform better initially but that once the group is established, virtual teams actually do better at brainstorming, while face-to-face teams perform better on tasks that require negotiation or compromise (Alge, Wiethoff, & Klein, 2003; Salkever, 2003). Savvy team leaders, then, will bring their teams together for face time early in the process, if possible, so that team members can get to know one another and get a sense of the others' styles and personalities. But as the teams develop, electronically mediated communication—especially e-mail—can often take the place of face-to-face group meetings.

Group Decision Support Systems (GDSS) are computer programs specifically designed to help groups (whether face to face or long distance) collaborate and make more effective decisions (DeSanctis, Poole, et al., 2008). They provide tools to facilitate and evaluate meeting management, problem identification, idea generation, discussion, and organization (Lewis, 2010). Research has found that although GDSS use is not always effective, groups can benefit from GDSS if they have complex tasks and a good facilitator to help them with the technology (DeSanctis, Poole, et al., 2008). These systems are also effective when the group already has solid relationships and open communication among its members.

Evaluating Group Performance

Groups that intend to work together and meet on a regular basis should evaluate their decision-making performance periodically. By assessing how well the group makes decisions, achieves its goals, and solves problems, a group can identify and address areas needing improvement. Think of your group as an automobile: to make sure your car keeps running smoothly, you have to take stock of how it's operating and adjust a few things as needed (such as giving it a tune-up or replacing the tires). When evaluating your group's performance, it's helpful to assess the group's overall effectiveness as well as the performance of individual members and leaders.

Albert Kowitz and Thomas Knutson (1980) have done extensive research evaluating groups as a whole. They recommend assessing three aspects of a group's performance: the informational, the procedural, and the interpersonal.

Informational Considerations

Ask yourself whether your group is working on a task that requires everyone's expertise and insights. If not, the group doesn't actually need to be a group! In this case, it should select a different task or assign just one or two members to deal with the current task.

If the task does require contributions from all members, how well is the group doing on this front? For example, are members conducting needed research and inviting one another to share information during group gatherings? Does the group know when it needs to get more data before making a decision? Does the group analyze problems well? Come up with creative solutions? Offer opinions respectfully? Elaborate on problems, concerns, and solutions?

● **THINK ABOUT** whether each group member's expertise is necessary to achieve a goal. If not, they don't need to be present.

By regularly assessing these aspects of information management in your group, you can identify where the group is falling short and address the problem promptly. For instance, if you notice that the group rushes to make decisions without getting all the facts first, you could say something like "I think we need to find out more about the problem before we take action."

Procedural Effectiveness

How well does your group coordinate its activities and communication? Key things to evaluate on this front are how the group elicits contributions, delegates and directs action, summarizes decisions, handles conflict, and manages processes.

For example, do some members talk too much while others give too little input? If so, the group needs someone to improve the balance of contributions. Simply saying something like "Allie, I think we should hear from some other people on this subject" can be very effective.

Or does your group tend to revisit issues it has already decided on? If so, you can expect many members to express frustration with this time-wasting habit. A leader or another member can steer the group back toward its current task by saying something like "OK, what we've been talking about is . . ." or "I'm not sure revisiting this previous decision is helping us deal with our current problem."

Finally, what does your group do when things become tense during a meeting? Another sign of procedural effectiveness is a group's ability to release tension. For example, someone cracks a joke or tells a funny story. Or a member says, "Well, the temperature in this room just dropped a few degrees!"—prompting everyone to acknowledge the tension and then resume the discussion.

Interpersonal Performance

How would you describe the relationships among the members of your group while everyone is working together to accomplish a task? If these relationships are strained, awkward, or prickly, the group probably won't function effectively. Observe how group members behave on the following four fronts:

▶ Do they provide *positive reinforcement* for one another—for instance, by showing appreciation for each other's contributions and hard work?

▶ Do members seem to feel a sense of *solidarity* with one another—for example, by sharing responsibility for both successes and failures?

▶ Do members *cooperate freely* with one another, fulfilling the responsibilities they've agreed to shoulder and pitching in when needed?

▶ Do members demonstrate *respect* for one another—for example, by keeping disagreements focused on the issues or positions at hand rather than on personal character?

If you can answer yes to these four questions, your group scores high on interpersonal performance.

As you evaluate interpersonal performance, you are essentially determining what type of *climate* your group has developed. As we discuss in Chapter 8, *supportive climates*—in which individuals are open to and supportive of one another's ideas—often have an advantage in being effective and achieving goals.

BACK TO ▶ Parks and Recreation

 At the beginning of this chapter, we talked about Leslie Knope, a midlevel government bureaucrat in the fictional town of Pawnee, Indiana. Let's take a look at Leslie's leadership and decision-making skills in light of what we've learned in this chapter.

▶ At Pawnee Town Hall, there is a clear hierarchy of legitimate power. As deputy director, Leslie's power is subordinate to Ron's, but in many ways, their relationship is an example of shared leadership: Ron's commitment to "doing as little as possible," as well as his genuine affection for Leslie and his respect for her work ethic, means that he leaves her in charge of pretty much everything. But while Leslie takes responsibility for the day-to-day running of the department, decision-making power still lies largely with Ron.

▶ Leslie has an achievement-oriented style of leadership. She identifies a goal and then does everything in her power to make that goal happen. Her commitment, enthusiasm, and optimism are infectious, motivating everyone around her—from her apathetic coworkers to local businesses and other departments—to help pitch in to make it happen.

▶ In addition to her legitimate power, Leslie has a substantial amount of referent power—she is as committed to behaving ethically as she is to providing services to the people of Pawnee. Her ethics and character inspire the police to work for free during the Harvest Festival. And when auditors suggest laying Leslie off as a way of balancing the department budget, Ron steps up and offers to take the layoff himself, noting, "If you fire Leslie, you might as well get rid of the entire department."

THINGS TO TRY ▶ Activities

1. Arrange an interview with the chair, president, or director of an organization to determine how the various groups within the organization operate. How closely do these groups conform to the decision-making process discussed in this chapter? Report what you have learned to the class.

2. Create a chart that lists the four leadership styles described in this chapter (directive, participative, supportive, and achievement-oriented). Evaluate the leaders of each of the different groups in which you participate—your boss at work, your professors, the resident assistant of your dorm—in terms of their leadership style. Where do they fall on your chart? Do some fit more than one category? Do some fit none?

3. Select a city, state, or campus problem that is relevant to the members of your class. Form a group to solve the problem using the six-step decision-making process described in this chapter.

REAL REFERENCE ▶ A Study Tool

Now that you have finished reading this chapter, you can:

Describe the types of power that effective leaders employ:

▶ **Leadership** is the ability to influences others' behaviors and thoughts toward a productive end (p. 282).

▶ **Legitimate power** comes from an individual's role or title (p. 283).

▶ **Coercive power** stems from the ability to threaten or harm others (p. 283).

▶ **Reward power** is derived from the ability to bestow rewards (p. 283).

▶ **Expert power** comes from the information or knowledge an individual possesses (p. 283).

▶ **Referent power** stems from the respect and affection that followers have for a leader (p. 284).

▶ Most leaders will use more than one type of power, and often leadership is shared by more than one individual (p. 285).

Describe how leadership styles should be adapted to the situation:

▶ The best leaders adapt their leadership styles to the situation (p. 285).

▶ A **directive leader** gives specific instructions; this is a good choice when members are unsure of expectations (p. 286).

▶ A **participative leader** views members as equals, inviting collaboration; this is effective when members are competent and motivated (p. 286).

▶ A **supportive leader** attends to members' emotional needs; this is helpful when members are frustrated or discouraged (p. 286).

▶ An **achievement-oriented leader** sets challenging goals and has high expectations; this is useful when members are motivated to excel (pp. 286–288).

▶ The best leaders behave ethically and avoid **bullying** (p. 288).

Identify how culture affects appropriate leadership behavior:

▶ Masculine leadership—valuing hierarchy and control—and feminine leadership—valuing nurturance and caring—may stem more from organizational situations and constraints than from deeply entrenched sex differences (p. 290).

▶ Leaders from high-context cultures tend to make suggestions rather than dictating orders or imposing solutions (p. 291).

▶ Group members in a high power distance culture typically defer to those with higher status (p. 291).

List the forces that shape a group's decisions:

▶ **Cognitive forces** are members' thoughts, beliefs, and emotions (p. 292).

▶ **Psychological forces** refer to members' personal motives, goals, attitudes, and values (p. 292).

▶ **Social forces** are group standards for behavior that influence decision making (p. 292).

Explain the six-step group decision process:

▶ Identify and define the problem (p. 293).

▶ Analyze the problem (p. 293).

▶ Generate solutions, identifying the criteria that eventual solutions will have to meet (pp. 293–294).

▶ Evaluate and choose a solution (p. 295).

▶ Implement the solution (p. 295).

▶ Assess the results (p. 295).

List behaviors to improve effective leadership in meetings:

▶ To ensure a well-planned meeting, assess whether the meeting is necessary, ensure that those present are necessary, ask for information in advance, articulate goals, and set an **agenda** (pp. 297–298).

▶ To manage the meeting, you should arrive prepared; keep the group focused; summarize periodically; keep an eye on the time, perhaps using a **nonbinding straw poll** to help move things along; manage conflict; foster productive conflict; and follow up after the meeting (pp. 298–301).

▶ Use technology effectively, arranging a face-to-face meeting for the start-up, but as the team develops, allowing mediated communication. **Group Decision Support Systems** (GDSS) are computer programs specifically designed to help groups collaborate and make more effective decisions (p. 303).

Demonstrate three aspects of assessing group performance:

▶ Informational considerations: Does the group require all its members? Does it need more data? Does it come up with creative solutions? (p. 304)

▶ Procedural effectiveness: Does the group coordinate activities and communication? Manage problems? (p. 305)

▶ Interpersonal performance: Do the group members reinforce one another? Feel a sense of solidarity? Cooperate freely? Respect one another? (p. 305)

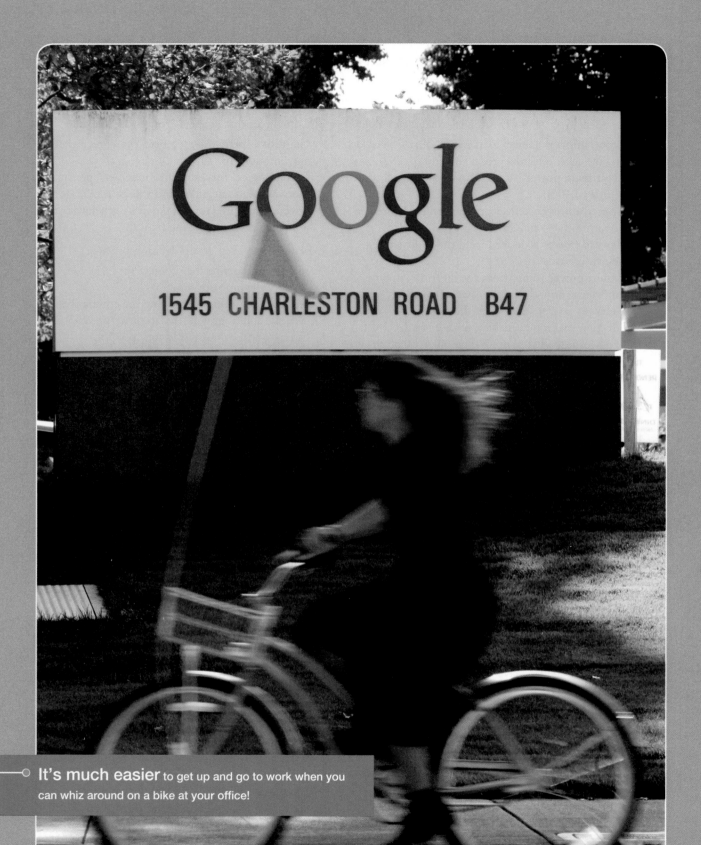

It's much easier to get up and go to work when you can whiz around on a bike at your office!

chapter 11

Communicating in Organizations

Would you work harder or more efficiently if your employer provided you with free gourmet meals whenever you were hungry? Would a midday massage increase your creativity? Wouldn't life be easier if you could just get your laundry done while you're at work?

Folks at Google, one of the fastest-growing companies in the world, think it might. With a belief that happy employees are productive and creative employees, they built their sprawling campus in Mountain View, California, with a focus on fun. "Our atmosphere may be casual," the company notes, "but as new ideas emerge in a café line, at a team meeting or at the gym, they are traded, tested and put into practice with dizzying speed—and they may be the launch pad for a new project destined for worldwide use" (Google, 2009). Workers literally scoot—or bike—from office to office. Walls are covered with whiteboards where workers scrawl graffiti and cartoons that turn random thoughts into innovative ideas (Google, 2011a).

But is a fun place to work enough to fuel the kind of innovation that makes companies like Google work? Probably not. That's why the company does more than just let its people play: it gives them room—and time—to think. Google's policy requiring engineers to spend 20 percent of their time on personal pet projects has yielded a few major innovations, including Google Suggest, AdSense for Content, and Orkut (Google, 2011c). The creative culture also leads to a few failures, such as Google Wave, a real-time collaboration app that never really caught on. When the company pulled the plug on it in August 2010, then-CEO Eric Schmidt offered no apologies: "Remember, we celebrate our failures. This is a company where it's absolutely okay to try something that's very hard, have it not be successful, and take the learning from that" (Siegler, 2010). This commitment to keeping employees happy and encouraging creativity has paid off. Just ask the people at *Fortune* magazine, who have ranked Google among the top five best companies to work for four years in a row ("100 Best," 2011).

The management at Google takes a particular interest in communication. The company cares about how employees communicate with one another, how management communicates with employees, and even what the office setting communicates about the company. And while not every workplace lets its employees take afternoon naps, these larger points about Google's communication hold for most **organizations**, groups with a formal governance and structure. You see this in action every day: your college or university, student groups, fraternity, religious community, volunteer organizations, and state and local governments are all actively involved in the process of communicating messages about themselves and their members. This is why we stress that **organizational communication**, the interaction necessary to direct an organization toward multiple sets of goals, is about more than meeting agendas and skills or getting along with moody bosses. It is at work in your life *right now* (Eisenberg, Goodall, & Trethewey, 2010). So it's important that we understand these organizations and how we communicate in them. In this chapter, we'll look at several approaches to managing organizations, issues related to organizational culture, important contexts for communicating in organizations, and common issues facing organizations today.

Approaches to Managing Organizations

For as long as humans have been working together toward shared common goals, we've been trying to figure out how to organize ourselves to achieve success. Whether we're talking about effective ways to build a castle, establish a town in the wilderness, or run a factory, preschool, or student government, it's useful to learn the various approaches to managing organizations. Over the centuries, these approaches have changed quite dramatically, and the changes have had important implications for how people in organizations work together and communicate. In the following sections, we'll take a quick trip through time to see how this evolution has played out, beginning with the classical management approach and moving on to the human relations, human resources, and systems approaches.

Classical Management Approach

In classic children's novel *Charlie and the Chocolate Factory,* Charlie, an impoverished youngster, wins a tour through the most magnificent chocolate factory in the world, run by the highly unusual candymaker Willy Wonka (portrayed in the 2005 film version by Johnny Depp). As Charlie tours the factory with a small group of other children, he sees an army of small men called Oompa Loompas. Each Oompa Looma is charged with performing a specific task: some do nothing but pour mysterious ingredients into giant, clanking candymaking machines; others focus on guiding the tour boats that ferry the children along rivers of sweet liquid. Still others work only on packing finished candies into boxes as the candies come off the assembly lines. You could almost compare the chocolate factory to a car and each worker to a specific part with a specific job— seat belt, brakes, steering wheel, and so on.

To Charlie, the factory might be a novelty or a curiosity, but to organizational communication scholars, it's a pretty clear example of the **classical**

● **WHETHER YOU'RE** part of a fraternity trying to rush new members or part of Greenpeace's efforts to save the oceans, your organization communicates its beliefs and goals to the outside world.

management approach—an approach that likens organizations to machines, with a focus on maximizing efficiency. Not surprisingly, classical management reached its peak during the Industrial Revolution in the nineteenth century—a time when factories and machinery were proliferating rapidly in various parts of the world, particularly Europe, North America, and Japan.

Classical management depends on two central ideas, both of which have strong implications for communication. The first is a **division of labor**, or the assumption that each part of an organization (and each person involved) must carry out a specialized task in order for the organization to run smoothly. This is exactly what you see in *Charlie and the Chocolate Factory:* each worker has a very specific job, and there is little reason for individual workers—or groups of workers on different tasks—to communicate with one another. Classical management approaches also favor **hierarchy**, which refers to the layers of power and authority in an organization. To illustrate, in Willy Wonka's chocolate factory, Willy has the most power to control the working conditions, rewards, and other aspects of life for all the creatures who work in the factory. His team of lower-level "managers" (such as the head of the Oompa Loompas) have somewhat less power. And the assembly-line workers themselves have almost no power at all. As illustrated, communication in such situations usually flows from the top (management) down to the bottom (the lowest-level workers). It's unlikely that a worker pouring chocolate would contact Willie Wonka to make suggestions for improving the factory.

Human Relations Approach

If reading about the classical management approach makes you want to protest that you're a person, not a machine, you're not alone. Critics of such organizational practices became more vocal during the Great Depression and World

AND YOU?

Are you involved with or familiar with any organizations that favor hierarchy and a division of labor? What are the pros and cons for communication in such organizations?

● **THESE OOMPA LOOMPAS** from *Charlie and the Chocolate Factory* are responsible for rowing a boat down this chocolate-filled river and not much else!

War II, times characterized by massive social and economic changes in the United States. For example, scholars Eric Eisenberg, Bud Goodall, and Angela Trethewey (2010) discuss the work of Mary Parker Follett (1868–1933), a Boston social worker who developed new and seemingly radical ideas about leadership, community, and communication. She believed that "only cooperation among people working together in groups under a visionary leadership produced excellence in the workplace, the neighborhood and the community" (p. 72). That's a far cry from the classical management approach. Follett and others set the stage for the **human relations approach** to management, which considers the human needs of organizational members (enjoying interpersonal relationships, sharing ideas with others, feeling like a member of a group, and so on).

The benefits of this approach came into sharper focus in the 1930s when Harvard professors Elton Mayo and F. J. Roethlisberger conducted an experiment at Western Electric's Hawthorne plant in Cicero, Illinois, in order to discover why employees were dissatisfied and unproductive. The researchers separated workers into two different rooms. In one room, the researchers slowly increased the amount of light; in the other, the amount of light was held constant. Much to the researchers' surprise, both groups of workers showed an increase in productivity, regardless of the amount of light they were exposed to. Why? It turns out that the employees were motivated by the increased attention they were receiving from management rather than the increased amount of light (Eisenberg, Goodall, & Trethewey, 2010).

In organizations managed with the human relations approach, communication takes on a different flavor than in companies managed through the classical approach. Managers express more interest in employees (for example, encouraging them to give their best on the job), and they emphasize the notion that "we're all in this together," so employees have a greater sense of belonging to a larger cause or purpose. Similarly, organizational members are encouraged to interact on a more personal level, allowing for satisfying exchanges of thoughts and ideas.

Human Resources Approach

The human relations approach was an improvement over the classical one in terms of bettering workforce productivity. But it didn't take into account employees' own goals and motivations for success. While incorporating the basics of human relations, the **human resources approach** takes things one step further by considering organizational productivity from the workers' perspectives and considers them assets who can contribute their useful ideas to improve the organization (Miller, 2009).

In Chapter 16, we will introduce you to Abraham Maslow and his hierarchy of needs, which asserts that people must fulfill basic needs (such as obtaining food and shelter) before they can achieve higher needs (such as finding friendship, love, and enjoyable work). As you will discover, Maslow's work is particularly useful when discussing persuasive speaking, but it has also had a powerful impact on communication in organizations. For example, in consideration of Maslow's work, managers learned that their workers would be more productive if management tended to their higher-level needs (such as self-fulfillment) in addition to their lower-level needs (such as worker safety). Boston Consulting Group encourages employees to pursue social causes that are important to them; in 2009, for example, the company pulled employees off of projects and sent them to Haiti to provide help after the earthquake ("100 Best," 2011).

Maslow's ideas also play out in other organizational situations. Imagine that you're a new member of a synagogue and you're not quite sure how to get involved. Your rabbi might find that you have a knack for working with kids; he or she might motivate you to become a more productive member of the community by telling you that you have a gift for teaching and encouraging you to fulfill your potential by volunteering with the Hebrew school class each week. Similarly, your manager at the tutoring center where you work ten hours a week might take the time to find out what you really value about your job. If you particularly enjoy tutoring Spanish, he or she might be interested in setting you up with students struggling in this subject: you'll be more engaged with your job, and the students will receive high-quality help, which can lead to improved grades and increased interest in tutoring services. Everyone wins.

● **THE HUMAN RESOURCES** approach takes into consideration your needs and interests.

The Systems Approach

You can see that human relations and human resources had a huge impact on the plight of organizational members. No longer is an employee a "cog in the machine" of the classical approach; an employee is now a person with feelings and ambitions who is a valuable, contributing member of an organization. But note that neither approach considers the importance of *both* the individual *and* the organization as a whole. This realization led to the **systems approach**, which views an organization as a unique whole made up of important members who have interdependent relationships in their particular environment (Monge, 1977). This means that no individual can work in isolation; no company, group, or team can insulate itself from the interactions of its members; and outside forces can change the communication processes of organizations.

Figure 11.1 on page 315 shows how a college or university works as a system. Its members include faculty, students, office staff, financial aid staff, and the bursar, all of whom have relationships with one another. The college exists within an environment, which includes other systems that directly affect it. These other systems might be the city and state where the college is located, the legislature that sets tuition, local employers who offer students full-time or part-time jobs, the families that the students come from or live with, and the high schools that supply many of the students.

Two of the most important components of organizations as systems are openness and adaptability. **Openness** in a system refers to an organization's awareness of its own imbalances and problems. For example, in our university example, let's say that our college begins receiving messages from local elementary schools that the university's student teachers seem ill prepared for the classroom. The university has two choices: it can ignore this feedback about the health of its program, or it

real communicator

NAME: Pat Driscoll
HOMETOWN: Belle Harbor, NY
OCCUPATION: Online producer
FUN FACT: While working as an NBC page, I was "fired" live on the *Today* show by Donald Trump.

When I was in college, majoring in communication, I remember hoping that I'd one day work for a company that takes a human resources approach to organizational communication. I didn't want to end up like the Charlie Chaplin character in *Modern Times*, the guy who works on an assembly line and then gets sucked into the machine, his body pulverized by giant wheels, cogs, and levers.

Today I work as a writer-producer for black20.com, a comedy network on the Internet. Thankfully, black20—like all organizations with an HR approach—stresses interpersonal relationships and the sharing of ideas. It's how we make comedy.

Black20 was founded by three friends who worked together at a major television network, and many people who have joined the company have a personal relationship with one of the original three. In other words, we're all friends—which makes for a unique organizational culture. There are supervisors, but we share responsibilities. Producers work with writers who work with the on-air talent who are themselves writers and producers. We get to work at 10:00 A.M., and everyone stays until that day's work is done.

Because of the human relations approach, quirky ideas can quickly snowball into a polished comic video. For instance, a black20 employee was—for no discernible reason—singing the Feist song "1-2-3-4" in a vampire accent. Because every office door in the company is always open, I overheard him. I came into his office and said,

"What if Dracula loved pop hits?" From there we started singing different songs in Dracula's accent. We figured he'd probably be a fan of Puff Daddy's "Bad Boys for Life" and Kid Rock's "Bawitdaba." A video was taking shape.

I went to one of my bosses—he's more like a mentor, actually—and he laughed. With most jobs that's probably a bad sign, but not here. We held a meeting, which is an informational presentation in which the audience is made up of heckling class clowns. Everyone's ideas were mapped out on a whiteboard. Instead of one music video, we decided it would be funnier to do a fake commercial selling a CD called (in a takeoff of those *NOW! That's What I Call Music* compilations) *NOW! That's What Dracula Calls Music*. We spent hours debating how the video should be approached, how particular lines should be spoken, whether to film Dracula at a cemetery or popping out of a coffin (we went with both). We took all ideas, and—as always—majority ruled.

Since we're all friends, I have the utmost trust in the people I work with. No one is trying to outdo the other. And because we're young comedians working at a start-up Web site, each of us realizes that our career is riding on the person next to us. There's a sense of common goals and interdependence. I just happen to work at a place in which the common goal is pretending to sell a CD that doesn't exist sung by a fictional neck-biting vampire. That's my job. Somebody's got to do it.

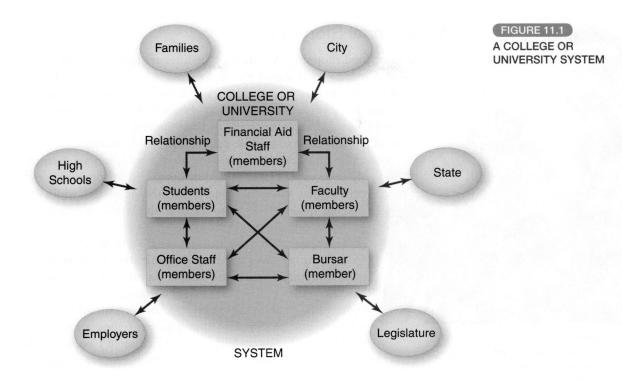

FIGURE 11.1

A COLLEGE OR
UNIVERSITY SYSTEM

can look to correct the problem, perhaps restructuring its elementary education program with feedback from local educators, professors, students, and government and policy representatives. The latter choice clearly helps the organization move forward by allowing for change and growth in light of changing times and circumstances. This ability to adjust is known as **adaptability**. And at the heart of it all is communication. If everyone involved in the system, from students to professors to principals, keeps to themselves and never voices concerns or ideas, the system can become closed and collapse under the weight of its own problems.

Communicating Organizational Culture

The management approaches you learned about in the preceding section can cause one organization to feel quite different from another. If you were working in a nineteenth-century factory that valued classical management, you probably wouldn't have team birthday parties or picnics the way you might under the management of the human resources approach, which values individuals. Yet understanding how different organizations come to give off different vibes is more complex than simply understanding their management styles. We must come to understand **organizational culture**, an organization's unique set of beliefs, values, norms, and ways of doing things (Harris, 2002). What's particularly fascinating to scholars in our discipline is the pivotal role that *communication* has in both the shaping and the expression of organizational culture. We'll elaborate on this topic in the sections that follow, looking at the popular Trader Joe's grocery store chain.

AND YOU?

Think of a situation when an organization you belonged to was faced with criticism. Was the organization open to suggestions for change, or was it closed off from such discussions? What was the end result?

Organizational Storytelling

Do you enjoy food shopping? We don't. The lines are long, the store light-ing is never flattering, and there's always someone who leaves a cart in the middle of the aisle so that you can't pass. But if you're lucky enough to live near a Trader Joe's, you might have a very different experience when pur-chasing groceries: employees smile and recommend their favorite salsa, food prices remain reasonable despite nationwide increases, and the colorful South Seas décor gives the place a bold, fun appearance. This is because Trader Joe's has developed an organizational culture that values a friendly, neighborhood feel while of-fering quality food from all over the world at seemingly reasonable prices.

One of the ways that Trader Joe's forms and ensures its cultural values is through **organizational storytelling**, the communication of the company's values through stories and accounts, both externally (to an outside audience) and internally (within the company). An organization telling a story isn't so different from a parent telling a story to a young child. Just as fairy tales and children's books teach kids important lessons, like the dangers of talking to strangers, organizational stories help would-be customers and potential members answer the question "What is this company all about?" or "Why should I support or join this organiza-tion?" They also help employees and current members of an organization under-stand why they work for a company or support a particular organization (Aust, 2004; Boje, 1991). James and Minnis (2004) also note that when the organization is a for-profit business, "Good communicators use storytelling to sell products, generate buy-in and develop and cultivate corporate culture" (p. 26).

What Trader Joe's stories communicate and shape their organizational culture? We'll look at several examples. First, consider the stories that the store itself tells us. As we noted earlier, it looks different from other grocery stores. Employees wear sneakers and Hawaiian shirts, hand-lettered signs tout low prices, and someone with really nice penmanship takes the time to write puns on a giant chalkboard ("Leaf it to us to give you your favorite bagged salads"). The message is clear: we're fun, we've got cool stuff, and we're cheap. Trader Joe's Web site and newsletter (*Trader Joe's Fearless Flyer*) also present fun drawings, facts about the company, and cleverly written highlights of featured products (anyone up for some Spanish gazpacho soup or Lemon Raspberry Zinger bundt cake?).

In addition, like many successful organizations, Trader Joe's makes use of metaphors in its storytelling. A *metaphor,* you may recall, is a figure of speech that likens one thing to something else in a literal way, although there is no literal connection between the two (Jacobs & Heracleous, 2006). You probably use metaphors often: "This classroom is a freezer" or "This assignment is a night-mare." Trader Joe's metaphor is, essentially, "We are a ship." Ships are associated with travel, perhaps even vacation, which highlights the company's commitment to provide quality products from all over the world. The employees at Trader Joe's are all crew members, including the captain (store manager) and the first mate (assistant store manager) (Lewis, 2005). Each member is essential to keep-

● **AT TRADER JOE'S,** employees always have bright smiles—and plenty of tasty food recommendations!

ing the ship running; no one is expendable. These titles communicate Trader Joe's commitment to being employee-friendly, which in turn leads to friendly employees and happy customers.

Trader Joe's also makes use of stories about **organizational heroes**, individuals who have achieved great things for the organization through persistence and commitment, often in the face of great risk (James & Minnis, 2004; Schulman, 1996). Trader Joe's employees and would-be customers alike all learn about "Trader Joe" himself, a Stanford University M.B.A. graduate named Joe Coulombe who opened a chain of Pronto Market convenience stores in the Los Angeles area during the 1950s. In the 1960s, 7-Eleven stores invaded southern California, threatening to crush Joe's business. Rather than admit defeat, Coulombe changed his tactics: trusting that the burgeoning airline industry would entice more Americans to travel—and that those Americans would want to find the foods they enjoyed abroad once they were back home—Coulombe began stocking imported foods other convenience stores didn't carry. Thus began the first Trader Joe's in 1967 (Hoover, 2006).

Learning About Organizational Culture

Could someone who dislikes people, Hawaiian shirts, and exotic foods find a successful career at Trader Joe's? According to Cohen and Avanzino (2010), **organizational assimilation** is the process by which newcomers learn the nuances of the organization and determine if they fit in. Studies suggest that successful assimilation is often based on a newcomer's ability to figure out and make use of behaviors that will be appropriate and effective in a given organization (Mignerey, Rubin, & Gorden, 1995). Typically, new organizational members are quite motivated to get these behaviors figured out because the uncertainty of not knowing what to do or say can be challenging (Cohen & Avanzino, 2010). Organizations understand this as well and generally seek to help. That's why religious organizations often have new-member meetings or classes and employers often have an orientation program to acquaint newcomers with the organization.

At Trader Joe's, for example, new employees are subject to the group "huddle," when all staff members at the store come together in a circle to share information and introduce themselves, perhaps noting where they're from or how long they've been with Trader Joe's. The idea is to make each new employee feel like part of the team (or in this case, crew) and to get to know everyone. You can imagine a new employee walking away from the huddle thinking, "OK, these people value friendliness and team building," which in turn reflects what Trader Joe's values and communicates to customers. A new employee at a different organization who eats lunch alone in a corner would likely experience a very different set of values.

Similarly, an additional perk of working for Trader Joe's is the free samples. Employees are always encouraged to try new products and even make up recipes for everyone to try (Lewis, 2005). The benefit of this is that employees become actively engaged with the products: they feel personally connected to the products and can make heartfelt recommendations to customers, thereby furthering Trader Joe's value of a friendly, interactive shopping experience.

Organizational storytelling can also help new individuals assimilate. For example, stories illustrate praiseworthy and unacceptable behaviors, reflecting the values of an organization (Meyer, 1995). Imagine you're new at a part-time job at your local library. The environment seems really laid back and casual, but not about everything. The children's librarian, Faith, approaches you and says, "Did you hear that the boss screamed at Shira this morning for being five minutes late? Her car wouldn't start, but he didn't care. She's in the bathroom crying right now." Your boss could tell you two hundred times that being on time matters in this organization; he could leave countless memos in your mailbox stating the same thing. But neither is as effective or as powerful as the message that your colleague is weeping in a bathroom stall after getting yelled at for violating the boss's rules.

Relational Contexts in Organizations

In the fictionalized version of NBC/Universal depicted on *30 Rock*, Jack Donaghy was in his element. The network, owned by General Electric (a subsidiary of the Sheinhardt Wig Company) embraced a classical approach: writers and actors on the show report to Liz Lemon, who in turn reports to Jack. But when the network is sold to Kabletown, Jack is challenged by the new organizational culture: the CEO insists on hugs instead of handshakes and invites low-level employees to eat in the executive dining room. Jack worries about these changes, from the open office hours to the memos containing emoticons: "If this is how Kabletown does business, I don't know if I have a future here!" (Fey, Hubbard, & Riggi, 2011). We laugh as Jack learns to navigate the new organizational culture at NBC and the way it affects his communication with his managers, peers, and employees. Let's consider each of these relationships in turn.

Supervisor-Supervisee Relationships

Few relationships are parodied as often as the relationship between supervisors and the people they manage. Think of Homer Simpson reporting to Mr. Burns, or the gang on *The Office* dealing with former manager Michael Scott. We often enjoy portrayals of the "bad" boss or the "crazy" boss who causes employees to sit around the lunch table complaining, even though in real life, most bosses are fairly reasonable people. Perhaps we find pleasure in these portrayals because supervisors, inherently, have power over us. Bosses negotiate our salaries and approve our vacation time; they might determine our hours or whether or not we get promoted. There are supervisory roles in nonworkplace situations as well. Your priest may require you to attend premarital counseling sessions before he will agree to marry you and your fiancé; you have to get your student government president to approve your idea for this year's budget before you can actually plan to do anything with that money. And

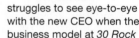

● **JACK DONAGHY** struggles to see eye-to-eye with the new CEO when the business model at *30 Rock* transitions from a classical management approach to a more human relations–centered approach.

to achieve anything worthwhile with your supervisor, the two of you must be communicating regularly.

If you're involved in a professional, community, or student organization where people are reporting to you, don't be a Mr. Burns! You should know how to get the most out of your conversations with the people you supervise. Often you can improve communication by following just a few simple steps:

▶ Schedule adequate time for important conversations. For example, if you are the president of a student organization and you need to speak to the treasurer about his messy bookkeeping, don't do it in the ten minutes you have between classes. Set up an appointment, and allow adequate time to discuss the problem and generate solutions.

▶ Minimize distractions or interruptions in order to give your full attention to your supervisee or employee.

▶ Ask supervisees for suggestions and ideas. For example, if you're working as a manager in a bank, you might ask the tellers for suggestions to make the work schedule more equitable.

▶ Demonstrate that you're listening when a supervisee is speaking to you, giving appropriate verbal and nonverbal responses, such as paraphrasing what you're hearing and nodding.

Even if you manage several people, you almost certainly report to a supervisor yourself—and it's important that you be able to communicate competently in this context as well. You can certainly follow the guidelines regarding listening and avoiding distractions that we mentioned earlier, but there are a few additional points to consider when you're the person with less power:

▶ Spend some time thinking about what you'd like to say to your boss. What are the main points you want to make? What do you hope to achieve through this discussion? It's embarrassing to start talking with a supervisor only to realize that you forgot what you wanted to say.

▶ Then spend some time *rehearsing* what you want to say to your manager. You might even ask a friend or family member to rehearse the conversation with you so that you can hear yourself speak.

▶ When you speak with your manager, try to avoid being emotional or hurling accusations such as "You always . . ." or "You never. . . ." It's typically more productive to be specific and logical and to ask for clarification: "When you removed me from the Edwards project, I took that to mean that you didn't think I was capable of handling it. Am I misunderstanding something?"

▶ Remember to be open-minded in discussions (whether with your boss or with other members of your organization). In the example above, for instance, your boss may have taken away a particular project because he or she has something else in store for you. Be an active listener.

▶ Keep the lines of communication open. Misunderstandings or unfocused goals are often the result of a lack of clear communication.

CONNECT

In addition to the tips we list here, competent communication with your boss will also include competent use of nonverbal communication (Chapter 5). Be sure to make appropriate eye contact, avoid fidgeting, and use an appropriate tone of voice. Shifty eyes, rapid movements, or a sarcastic tone can make you come across as guilty, hostile, or anxious—not desirable when discussing a difficult situation with your manager.

For competent communication in the evolving relationship between mentor and protégé, you need to understand key aspects of the relational context—history, goals, and expectations—discussed in Chapter 1. As a protégé, you might be uncomfortable if your company mentor asked you for professional advice; it might be equally awkward to ask your mentor for advice on searching for a new job when you first meet. Such communication defies expectations.

Mentor-Protégé Relationships

Somewhat related to the supervisor-supervisee relationship is the mentor-protégé relationship. A **mentor** is a seasoned, respected member of an organization who serves as a role model for a less experienced individual, his or her **protégé** (Russell & Adams, 1997).

If a new employee or member of an organization has a supervisor or access to some other person in a position of authority, does he or she really need a mentor? Doesn't that just muddy the waters and create confusion for the newcomer? Research shows that mentoring actually provides a number of key benefits for everyone involved (Jablin, 2001). For one thing, it accelerates the protégé's assimilation into the organization and its culture, which helps the newcomer become productive faster and thus helps the organization meet its goals (particularly in reducing the number of members leaving an organization) (Madlock & Kennedy-Lightsey, 2010). Protégés win too: in one study, protégés reported that mentors helped make their careers more successful by providing coaching, sponsorship, protection, counseling, and ensuring they were given challenging work and received adequate exposure and visibility (Dunleavy & Millette, 2007). Protégés experience greater job satisfaction, and the mentors benefit by receiving recognition as their protégés begin to achieve in the organization (Kalbfleisch, 2002; Madlock & Kennedy-Lightsey, 2010).

Many colleges and universities set up mentorships for incoming students in order to help them adjust to life at the college or perhaps even life away from home. In many cases, second-, third-, or fourth-year students agree to be "big brothers" or "big sisters" to help the newcomers figure out campus parking, where to get a decent sandwich between classes, or which professors to take or avoid. First-year students may then become mentors themselves in future years. As you can imagine, the communication between mentor and protégé changes over time in this example. At first, the protégé may rely quite heavily on the mentor, since everything in the college environment is new and perhaps somewhat frightening. However, as the first-year student adjusts and begins to feel comfortable and self-assured, he or she will rely less and less on the mentor. By the next fall, the protégé may well be on an equal par with the mentor, and the relationship may have turned into a friendship or may have dissolved entirely. Understanding that mentor-protégé relationships go through four distinct stages— initiation, cultivation, separation, and redefinition—can help both parties adjust to these natural changes. See Table 11.1 for more on these stages and the communication that takes place during each.

If you are new to an organization—be it a community college, a house of worship, or a job—and a mentorship interests you, you can see if the organization has a formal program. If such a program does not exist, you can still find a mentor, albeit in a more informal way. Consider the following tips (Kram, 1983):

● **WITH COLLEGE MENTORING** programs, older students help new arrivals to acclimate, from navigating an unfamiliar campus to completing those first daunting class assignments.

TABLE 11.1

STAGES IN MENTOR-PROTÉGÉ RELATIONSHIPS

Stage	Communication Goal	Mentor Responsibilities	Protégé Responsibilities
Initiation	Get to know one another	• Show support through counseling and coaching • Help protégé set goals	• Demonstrate openness to suggestions and loyalty to the mentor
Cultivation	Form a mutually beneficial bond	• Promote the protégé throughout the organization (for example, by introducing him or her to influential people) • Communicate knowledge about how to work best with key people and what the organization's culture is	• Put new learning to use (for example, by forging relationships with influential people) • Share personal perspective and insights with mentor
Separation	Drift apart as protégé gains skill	• Spend less time with protégé	• Take more initiative in the organization • Strive for development or promotion
Redefinition	Become peers	• Occasionally provide advice or support as needed	• Stay in touch with mentor at times if additional advice is required

▶ Ask your peers (colleagues, members of a congregation, and so on) to recommend individuals who might be interested in serving as a mentor.

▶ Identify people who have progressed in the organization in ways that interest you, and determine whether one of them would make a good mentor.

▶ Build rapport with someone you think would be an effective mentor. Ask if he or she would like to sponsor you in a mentor-protégé relationship. Explain why you think he or she would be a good mentor, and describe your qualifications as a protégé—such as your ability to learn or to cultivate networks quickly.

Peer Relationships

One of the most fun aspects of watching the television show *Grey's Anatomy* is keeping track of the web of relationships among the staff at Seattle Grace Mercy West Hospital. Workplace friendships, secret crushes, full-fledged romances, and bitter resentments could definitely keep your night interesting! Yet these interactions also interest us as scholars because such **peer relationships** reveal the importance of **peer communication**, communication between individuals at the same level of authority in an organization. Researchers, management coaches, and popular magazines warn that Americans are spending more and more time in the workplace, leaving less time for outside personal relationships. Yet we all need

● **THE *GREY'S ANATOMY*** surgeons spend so much time at Seattle Grace Mercy West Hospital that their work life *is* their social life—and what results is a complex web of peer relationships.

When communicating with peers in organizations, remember *communication privacy management* (Chapter 7), which helps you understand how people perceive and manage personal information. You may decide that certain topics, such as your romantic life, are off-limits at work. You must determine for yourself what is private in different relationships—and it's also wise to consider the cultural expectations of your organization before sharing.

friends and confidants. So where do we find them? You guessed it—in the organizations we devote time to, particularly the organizations we work for. Research, however, seems to say some contradictory things about whether or not this phenomenon is healthy.

In a survey of more than five million workers over 35 years, 29 percent of employees say that they have a "best friend" at work (Jones, 2004). This statistic matters: Out of the approximately three in ten people who state that they have a best friend at work, 56 percent are engaged with, or enjoy, their work, while 33 percent are not engaged. Only 11 percent are actively disengaged and negative about their work experience. On the other hand, of the seven in ten workers who do not have a best friend at work, only 8 percent are engaged, whereas 63 percent are not. The remaining third of employees without a workplace best friend are actively disengaged from their work (Gallup, cited in Jones, 2004). These findings have powerful implications for employers: having a workplace best friend makes workers seven times more likely to enjoy their work and consequently be more productive. Perhaps this is the thinking behind organizational initiatives to help employees get to know one another— office picnics, hospital softball teams, and school Frisbee and golf tournaments.

But there's also a potential downside to these workplace intimacies. One is that the relationships may not actually be so intimate after all. *Management Today* warns that professional friendships are often based on what is done together in the workplace. While that may be beneficial for finding personal support on work-related issues, the friendship can easily wither and die when the mutual experience of work is taken away ("Office Friends," 2005). Privacy and power also come into play, since sharing personal details about your life can influence how others see you in a professional setting. For example, Pamela, an insurance broker from Chicago, did not want her colleagues or boss to know that she was heading into the hospital to have a double mastectomy in order to avoid breast cancer. But she did tell her close friend and colleague, Lisa. When Pamela returned to the office, there was a "get well soon" bouquet of flowers from her boss waiting on her desk. Lisa had blabbed; Pamela felt betrayed and had the additional burden of her colleagues' knowing this private, intimate detail about her life (Rosen, 2004). It's also important to remember that friendships in the workplace—and all organizations—are going to face trials when loyalty and professional obligations are at odds.

Please don't take this to be a warning against making friends in the organizations you belong to. Relationships with colleagues and other members of organizations can be both career-enhancing and personally satisfying; many workplace friendships last long after one or both friends leave a job. But it's important to be mindful as you cultivate such relationships. The following tips can help (Rosen, 2004):

► *Take it slow.* When you meet someone new in your organization (be it your job or your residence hall association), don't blurt out all of your personal details right away. Take time to get to know this potential friend.

▶ *Know your territory.* Organizations have different cultures, as you've learned. Keep that in mind before you post pictures of your romantic partner all over your gym locker for the rest of the soccer team to see.

▶ *Learn to handle conflict.* If your friend Alisha from a particular student organization wants to run for president despite the fact that you plan to run as well, talk it out. Manage the conflict or awkwardness before it becomes problematic.

▶ *Don't limit yourself.* It's OK to take the time to make friends outside of your fraternity or sorority or outside of your job!

▶ *Accept an expiration date.* Sometimes friendships simply don't last outside of the context they grew in. You may have found that you lost some of your high school friends when you started college; this point is also particularly true for friendships on the job. Accept that life sometimes works out like this and that no one is to blame.

AND YOU?

Who are your three closest friends? Are they members of any organizations that you belong to? If so, has your joint membership affected the friendship in any particularly positive or negative ways? Explain your answer.

EVALUATINGCOMMUNICATIONETHICS

More Than Friends at Work

You've begun to notice that two colleagues at work, Cheryl and Michael, are spending an inordinate amount of time together, and you suspect that they may be romantically involved—or at least engaged in a very strong flirtation. They work together on several projects, so it's natural that they spend a lot of time together, but you—along with a few of your colleagues— are beginning to be annoyed by the amount of time the two spend in one or the other's office, chatting about personal and other nonwork issues and generally goofing off during working hours. Both of them are beginning to fall behind on their work, and their slacking off is affecting the performance of your entire department. You've approached Michael about it, noting that "people are beginning to notice" how much time he spends with Cheryl. They cooled it for a few days after that, but gradually, they returned to their old behavior.

Personally, you don't have a problem with the two of them having a relationship outside the office. Although the company has a policy requiring employees to disclose any romantic relationships between coworkers, you think the policy is an invasion of privacy and you don't agree with it at all. But the constant chatter and goofing off that they do at the office is beginning to affect your own work, not to mention feeding the gossip mill around the water cooler, thus distracting other members of your team from getting their work done.

You've considered speaking to your boss, who works on a different floor and isn't aware of Cheryl and Michael's day-to-day behavior, or even talking to human resources about it. But you're reluctant to "rat them out," especially because you're not even sure that the two are actually romantically involved. What should you do?

THINK ABOUT THIS

❶ What's the real issue here, Cheryl and Michael's relationship or their behavior? If they acted more professionally at work, would the status of their romantic relationship matter?

❷ How does your opinion of the company policy on dating at work factor into your decision? Does the impact of your coworkers' flirtation change your opinion of the policy?

❸ What other approaches could you take to get Cheryl and Michael to change their behavior? Is going over their heads your only option?

Challenges Facing Today's Organizations

Diversity is a word you likely hear a lot nowadays. We use it throughout this book to highlight the importance of understanding and respecting people from various co-cultures with experiences different from our own. But you also hear about companies needing to "diversify" and the importance of tailoring messages to a "diverse" audience. What does it all mean? It means that today's organizations need to branch out and be open to new ideas and experiences. They must make use of new communication technology and address colleagues and other organizations worldwide. Organizational members must find ways to balance the multitude of pressures for their time and must learn to be tolerant of each other's differences and behave competently and respectfully at all times. We examine these important issues in the sections that follow.

Communication Technology

Advances in communication technology—including instant messaging, professional and social networking sites, and videoconferencing—enable members of organizations to communicate more easily, particularly with clients and colleagues who work offsite or in home offices. But they've also introduced new challenges for organizations.

First, there's the question of figuring out which channel is most appropriate for a particular message in an organizational setting. We discussed this point in earlier chapters—you might, for example, text a friend an apology if you're too embarrassed to call her. But there are additional ethical and legal considerations when choosing channels in organizations. If you're a manager, you simply cannot fire someone in an e-mail with the entire department copied. Rather, you would need to have a private face-to-face meeting—or perhaps a phone call if the employee works elsewhere in the country or the world. This is an illustration of **media richness**, the degree to which a particular channel is communicative (Daft & Lengel, 1984, 1986). Media richness theory suggests that people must consider the number of contact points a particular channel offers for a message (Montoya, Massey, Hung, & Crisp, 2009). Face-to-face communication is the richest because it allows for verbal and nonverbal contact. Speaking on the phone is slightly less rich because it allows for verbal contact and some limited nonverbal contact (tone of voice, rate of speaking, and so on) but removes the opportunity to communicate with body movements. Text messages are even less rich because they lack most nonverbal cues and need not be responded to immediately. The level of richness people expect in their communication vehicles depends on their goals. So if you need to tell the treasurer of your student organization that your meeting has been moved to a different room, you can just text her. However, if you needed to discuss the fact that you noticed a $250 discrepancy on the books, you'd have better luck with a face-to-face conversation.

Research shows that most people do make conscious decisions about which communication vehicle to use based on the situational and relational context. Table 11.2 offers a look at various organizational goals and people's perceptions about the most competent channel for achieving those goals.

● **IF YOU HAVE** something sensitive to discuss with a colleague, it's better to do so in a face-to-face situation rather than with a text message.

With such a variety of communication technologies available to organizational members to keep in close contact with one another, it should come as no surprise that people wind up using technology to achieve personal goals as well. Twenty years ago, employees might get in trouble if they spent too much time making personal phone calls on the job. So consider how much more distracting it can be to have the ability to bank online, text your romantic partner, and read your brother's blog during the day. Sixty-nine percent of workers admit that they access the Internet at work for nonwork-related purposes, and many of them are quite busy on social networking sites like Facebook (Schweitzer, 2007). Richard Cullen of the Internet filtering company SurfControl, for example, states that Facebook alone may be costing Australian businesses $5 billion a year due to decreased worker productivity (West, 2007).

What's more is that organizations aren't just concerned about *when* you're updating your status, but also about *what* you're posting—particularly whether or not you're posting comments about the organization or individuals associated with it. Consider, for example, the 2011 case of Natalie Munroe, a high school English teacher who was suspended and faced termination over unflattering comments she made about her students on her personal blog. The blog

Task	By E-Mail	By Phone	In Person
Edit or review documents	67%	4%	26%
Arrange meetings or appointments	63%	23%	12%
Ask questions about work issues	36%	17%	44%
Bring up a problem with one's supervisor	6%	6%	85%
Deal with sensitive issues	4%	9%	85%

TABLE 11.2

EMPLOYEE SURVEY OF APPROPRIATE COMMUNICATION CHANNELS FOR ORGANIZATIONAL TASKS

Source: Pew Internet & American Life Project Email at Work Survey, April–May 2002; *N* = 1003; margin of error = ± 3%.

was relatively anonymous—Munroe never used her full name or identified individual students—and was only followed by nine friends and family members. In addition, the vast majority of posts had nothing to do with the school, the students, or the teaching profession (Werner, 2011). But as with many other high-profile social networking suspensions and terminations, organizations have a keen interest in the way employees represent them in the virtual world.

Concerns over employee Internet use have led many organizations to an increase in workplace **surveillance** or monitoring of employees to see how

WIREDFORCOMMUNICATION

Back to the Future

Back in the 1980s, when the Internet emerged and the prices of personal computers began to fall, there were countless predictions regarding the effects of an Internet-connected populace on communities, cities, and workplaces. In 1984, *Time* magazine estimated that by 1999, as many as ten million corporate employees would be working from home, electronically connected to coworkers and supervisors via the World Wide Web, fax, and phone. The prevailing wisdom was that as telecommuting became cheaper and easier, the importance of the office as a work environment would lessen: fewer people would commute to work, traffic jams would become a thing of the past, and cities would become obsolete (Grieves, 1984).

In the years since these predictions took hold, the Web has indeed become pervasive. It is estimated that today, some thirteen million corporate employees are working from home more than eight hours each week. Online learning programs allow students to enroll in colleges and universities hundreds or even thousands of miles away and take classes from home. Telecommuting is indeed becoming a part of the nature of work, education, and play in the twenty-first century. Logic would suggest that such ease of communication would make distance a nonissue in the postindustrial world, and employers would be happy to do away with expensive corporate offices in pricey cities in favor of cost-saving electronic offices for their employees. Yet despite 1980s notions about the future of the workplace, telecommuting hasn't replaced corporate offices or university centers or even lessened their importance. Consider, for example, that in recent years, Hewlett-Packard—once a trailblazer in telecommuting—has focused on bringing more workers back into the office to facilitate brainstorming and teamwork (Holland, 2006). Why do location and distance still matter?

It turns out that although the Internet is great for sharing and exchanging information, it is less useful when it comes to completing other functions of communication, such as expressing affiliation and influencing others. That's why electronic communication simply cannot replace the value of "face time," especially between employers and employees: we rely heavily on face-to-face communication in order to build trust (Harford, 2007). It turns out that even telecommuters need to have some face time with their bosses and colleagues in order to communicate well.

THINK ABOUT THIS

❶ Do you think that organizations benefit more from having employees work face to face or from having employees work from home? Does it have to be one way or the other?

❷ What communication benefits does telecommuting offer employees? What does it offer the organization?

❸ How can organizations ensure that telecommuting staffers are able to develop strong working relationships? How can they build "face time" into a virtual team?

they're using technology (Ball, 2010; Williams, 1993). On some levels, monitoring seems to make sense, particularly when employees are spending time on questionable nonwork-related activities. Yet it still raises several important ethical questions: Does monitoring constitute an invasion of employees' privacy? Should workers accept monitoring as a fact of organizational life? These questions are stimulating important research and lively debates in legal circles, but no one seems to have a clear answer. One thing seems obvious, however: in any organization, you'll be much more productive if you limit the amount of time you spend using communication technologies for personal matters.

Globalization

Daily direct flights to locations around the world, instant messaging and video-conferencing, international wire transfers—we're living in an age where the other side of the world is an instant message away. Globalization is the buzzword in today's society—you hear it on the evening news, read about it in magazines and newspapers, and see the evidence of it in your everyday life. If you've bought something with a "Made in China" sticker or if you've recently seen a foreign film at your local theater, you've experienced the effects of globalization. **Globalization** is the growing interdependence and connectivity of societies and economies around the world.

Globalization is especially evident in the business world. Increases in communication technology and the convenience of travel have allowed companies to expand their labor force beyond geographical boundaries. More often than not, when you call customer service for help on the DVD player you bought in the United States, the person who picks up the phone is in India. More and more services are being outsourced to developing countries, where wages and operating costs are lower. Take Kenneth Tham, a high school sophomore in California. Most afternoons, he signs on to an online tutoring service, TutorVista. His tutor is Ramya Tadikonda, a twenty-six-year-old mother in Chennai (formerly Madras), India. TutorVista's president, John J. Stuppy, thinks that in this day and age, global tutoring makes the most sense because it makes "high-quality, one-on-one tutoring affordable and accessible to the masses" (Lohr, 2007). This example highlights a few of the benefits of globalization. U.S. companies benefit from the lower costs of operating in developing countries, and people in those countries benefit from better-paying jobs and a higher quality of life.

While globalization has torn down some of the barriers to legitimate commerce between countries, it has also made unethical labor practices easier. **Human trafficking**, the recruitment of people for exploitative purposes, is an example of the darker side of globalization. As wages rise in countries that have grown past the early stages of development, there is a need for even cheaper labor to be shipped in from even poorer countries, such as Cambodia and Bangladesh. Workers are lured in by shady labor brokers with false promises of high wages. The workers pay their brokers huge sums of money for this opportunity, only to work for paltry sums of

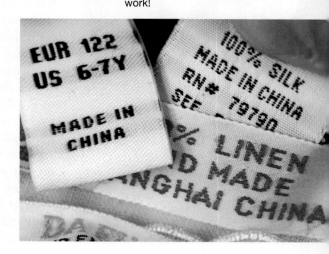

● **HAVE YOU EVER** bought something in the United States with a "Made in China" label? That's globalization at work!

money and often in unsavory working conditions. The story at Local Technic, a Malaysian company that makes cast aluminum bodies for hard disk drives, is a typical example of the forced labor that has increased with globalization. An unnamed executive at Local Technic admits that most of the company's guest workers have been duped into working there. He insists it's not the company's fault: sleazy brokers promise more than the company can afford. However, once the workers arrive and find out they've been taken for a ride, they can't quit, because under Malaysian law, they have had to sign multiyear contracts and surrender their passports to their employer. The parts made at Local Technic are used in virtually every name-brand machine on the market, thus implicating companies like Western Digital that have used components made by Local Technic. Although Western Digital is a member of the Electronics Industry Citizenship Coalition (EICC), which aims to improve industry working conditions, its relationship with Local Technic sends a conflicting message (Wherfritz, Kinetz, & Kent, 2008).

Globalization is a powerful force, and its impact on organizations is undeniable. However, without clear global labor laws, unethical practices such as human trafficking are difficult to control and police.

● **BURNOUT IS THE HARMFUL** result of prolonged labor and stress, as well as a reminder of how vital it is to strike a manageable balance between work and life.

Work-Life Balance

Diane is a single mom with a seven-year-old son. She works forty hours a week as a receptionist in a medical office and is currently completing class work to become a dental hygienist. She is also the "room parent" for her son's second-grade class and is frequently called on to help bake for classroom celebrations and to chaperone class trips. Luis is a nineteen-year-old sophomore at a state university. He is working two part-time jobs to help meet the cost of tuition and is taking six classes with the hopes of graduating one semester early. He dreams of studying in France next year and would love to live in foreign-language housing in order to improve his French, but he's not sure how he could add the mandatory conversation hours to his already overbooked schedule.

These two individuals have different lives, different goals, and different constraints. Yet they have one thing in common: they are sinking under intense pressures from the organizations in their lives. We've already indicated that Americans are spending more and more time on the job, making it increasingly difficult to enjoy outside relationships. But other types of organizations make huge demands on our time as well. If you are a parent, you may, like Diane, find that your child's school or the PTA simply expects you to be available for events. As a college student, you may discover that taking on too many classes and academic responsibilities prevents you from enjoying other aspects of the college experience, such as joining a particular club, volunteering, or just hanging out with friends. In any of these examples, the end result is often **burnout**—a sense of apathy or exhaustion that results from long-term stress or frustration. Burnout hurts its victims as well as the organizations and communities they belong to. Many researchers maintain that burnout leads to negative self-evaluations and emotional exhaustion

(Hallsten, Voss, Stark, & Josephson, 2011; Maslach, 1982). And no wonder: television shows and movies celebrate glamorous people who manage to work hard, play hard, meet the partner of their dreams, raise adorable kids, and look great doing it all. So we ask, "Why can't I do it all too?" Yet the more we try, the more we burn out.

Many workplaces are aware of the dangers of burnout and implement programs to assist employees with **work-life balance**, which involves achieving success in one's personal and professional life. Such programs include flexible work arrangements, paid vacation, and onsite child care. In addition, more and more companies are recognizing that they must top their competitors in offering new and creative work-life options in order to recruit the best job candidates. According to a survey by the Association of Executive Search Consultants, 85 percent of recruiters have seen outstanding candidates reject

COMMUNICATIONACROSSCULTURES

Work-Life Balance: Around the Globe and Around the Block

If you're like most Americans, chances are that when you consider a job or career, you think not only about salary but also about benefits. As we learned in this chapter, some of the most appealing companies to work for offer enticements like flexible work hours, in-house dining, child care, and even laundry services. These kinds of perks are relatively new, still largely unexpected, and rare enough that the companies offering them are able to fill their staff rosters with the best talent. But what about the most basic benefit of any job—time away from the job?

Two weeks of vacation time is standard in most American companies—but it's not guaranteed. There are no laws in the United States requiring employers to give their employees any paid vacation time or paid holidays. According to recent studies, the average private sector worker in the United States receives only about nine paid vacation days per year and six paid holidays. Almost one in four American workers has no paid vacation or holidays at all. Of course, most successful American companies do offer vacation time to employees, even if they are not required by law to do so. But lower-wage workers typically receive fewer paid days off (seven on average) than higher-wage workers (an average of thirteen) (Ray & Schmitt, 2007).

In other rich nations, things are quite different. Australia, New Zealand, and European Union countries are required to give each employee a minimum of twenty paid vacation days per year; in some European countries the number is as high as twenty-five or thirty. At least ten vacation days are guaranteed in Canada and Japan. In some of these nations, laws are designed to ensure that employees actually take the time off: in Portugal, Spain, and Switzerland, for example, employers are prohibited from offering incentives like additional pay to get employees to give up their vacation time (Ray & Schmitt, 2007).

THINK ABOUT THIS

❶ Does it surprise you that vacation time is not mandated in the United States but is mandated in most other wealthy nations? Do you think that Americans would be more or less productive if they had more vacation time?

❷ Consider the cultural variations discussed in this chapter and in Chapter 3. How is the largely masculine, individualist culture of the United State reflected in American policies on and attitudes toward vacation time?

❸ What are your expectations for paid time off from work? Do you expect to be paid for holidays like Independence Day and Thanksgiving? Are your feelings about religious holidays different from your expectations for national holidays?

a job offer because the position didn't provide enough work-life balance (Ridge, 2007).

Yet even in seemingly supportive work environments, many employees are still unable to balance their work and their personal life. For some, this is a choice: "I never go on vacation," says New York City real estate agent Ellen Kapit. "And when I do, I have my computer, my Palm, my e-mail, and my phone with me at all times" (Rosenbloom, 2006). For employees like Kapit, choosing the organization over other areas of life may be a sign of ambition, pride, guilt, a sense of overimportance, or simply a love of work, according to Ellen Galinsky, president of the Families and Work Institute (as cited in Rosenbloom, 2006). Yet it can also be a sign of fear. CBS News (2010) reports on a recent survey by the Conference Board Research Group noting that only 43 percent of today's workers feel secure in their jobs (down from 47 percent in 2008 and 59 percent in 1987). The sad truth remains that in far too many workplaces, there is an unspoken rule that if you take a vacation, put your family first, or have outside interests that take up a lot of time, you are not committed to the organization.

So if you're feeling burned out or on the verge of collapsing from organizational pressure, what should you do? This question is at the forefront of a great deal of research in sociology, psychology, business, and communication. Here are a few tips that various scholars, medical doctors, and other professionals find helpful (Mayo Clinic, 2006):

> ▶ *Keep a log.* Track everything you do for one week, including school- and work-related activities. Note which activities are nonnegotiable (such as taking a mandatory math class), and decide which other commitments matter the most to you. Consider cutting commitments that are not fulfilling or necessary.

> ▶ *Manage your time.* Organizing your life can help you feel more in control of your circumstances. Set up specific times to study, work, and have fun—and try your hardest to stick to your schedule.

> ▶ *Communicate clearly.* Limit time-consuming misunderstandings by communicating clearly and listening carefully to the important people in your life.

> ▶ *Nurture yourself.* Set aside time each day for an activity that you enjoy, such as watching a particular TV show, working out, or listening to music.

> ▶ *Get enough sleep.* Enough said!

Sexual Harassment

There are days when none of us like being at work or at school, particularly when the weather is nice or there's some other fun activity to take part in. Imagine, however, if your main reason for not wanting to head to class or to your job is fear. For many women and men around the world, a fear of being bullied or harassed in the workplace, on campus, or in other settings is far too common. **Harassment** is any communication that hurts, offends, or embarrasses another person, creating a hostile environment. It can take many forms, such as antagonizing people about their sex, race, religion, national origin, sexual orientation, age, or abilities (Federal Communications Commission, 2008).

One particularly offensive type of harassment is **sexual harassment**, which the U.S. Equal Employment Opportunity Commission (EEOC) (2011) defines as follows: "Unwelcome sexual advances, requests for sexual favors, and other

what about you?

Are You Off Balance?

1. Which statement best describes you after you leave work for the day?
   A. I don't think about work again until I arrive the next morning.
   B. I usually check my work e-mail before bed.
   C. I check my work e-mail or make calls three or four times during the evening.

2. A big project requires you to stay late to meet a deadline. You think to yourself:
   A. "This is happening way too much. I'll have to talk to my supervisor about it."
   B. "Oh, well, I'll take off a little early next week to make up for it."
   C. "I wonder if Bud, the night watchman, will bring me a sandwich like he always does."

3. Which statement best describes what you usually do on vacation?
   A. I kick back, relax, and savor the time off.
   B. I check in with my organization at least once so that people know I'm available.
   C. I continue to check my e-mail because you never know when an emergency might arise.

4. It's Tuesday, and you arrive home at 5:30 P.M. How do your housemates or family react?
   A. They say hello and discuss dinner plans.
   B. They act surprised—they never know if you'll be on time or not.
   C. They wonder if you've been fired because you're home so very early.

5. What are you most likely to do to manage your time at home?
   A. Organize chores and write to-do lists
   B. Try to run errands on days off from work or school
   C. Tackle chores and errands one at a time as needed

If your answers are mostly A's: You're leading a fairly well-balanced life—congratulations! You may, however, need to give your organization more priority now and then, particularly during time-sensitive projects.

If your answers are mostly B's: You're striking a great balance! Keep up the good work.

If your answers are mostly C's: You're likely headed toward burnout. Consider some of the strategies we discuss to find more balance.

Source: CNN.com/living (2008). www.cnn.com/2007/LIVING/personal/07/30/wlb.quiz.balance/index.html. Adapted with permission.

Cultural differences, like those discussed in Chapters 3, 4, and 5, can lead to perceptions of harassment when communicators fail to remember the cultural context. Gestures that are entirely appropriate in one culture might be considered offensive elsewhere. The same can be said for verbal messages such as commenting on an individual's appearance. Companies and communicators should take time to clarify perceptions and adapt messages in order to avoid miscommunication.

verbal or physical harassment of a sexual nature . . . when it is so frequent or severe that it creates a hostile or offensive work environment or when it results in an adverse employment decision (such as the victim being fired or demoted)." Specific conduct that can create such an environment may include sexist remarks, embarrassing jokes, taunting, displays of pornographic photographs, and unwanted physical contact such as touching, kissing, or grabbing.

How big a problem is sexual harassment? Well, over 90 percent of *Fortune* 500 companies have reported cases of sexual harassment (Keyton, Ferguson, & Rhodes, 2001), and in fiscal year 2010, the EEOC (2011) received 11,717 complaints of sexual harassment. In addition, the American Association of University Women Educational Foundation notes that nearly two-thirds (62 percent) of two thousand college students surveyed in 2005 said that they had been subject to sexual harassment in college (National Organization for Women [NOW], 2006). Women are most commonly the victims of sexual harassment, but men can also experience its negative effects. In fact, 16.4 percent of the charges filed with the EEOC in 2010 were complaints from men (2011). In addition, three-quarters of lesbian, gay, bisexual, and transgendered (LGBT) students report that they have experienced incidents of sexual harassment on campus (NOW, 2006). These statistics are clearly problematic, but what is even more challenging is that victims often feel shame and embarrassment, preventing many of them from filing official complaints. For example, only seven percent of students say that they reported sexual harassment to a member of their college or university; LGBT students in particular report that they are extremely angry and embarrassed by their experience (NOW, 2006). Still other victims fear that they will lose their jobs if they speak out—particularly if they are harassed by a boss or other individual with power (Vijayasiri, 2008; Witteman, 1993).

Sexual harassment costs organizations millions of dollars every year and robs individuals of opportunities, dignity, and sense of self-worth. For this reason, organizations have instituted official codes of conduct and clear definitions and penalties for sexual harassment. Many even offer training to educate organizational members. For example, some programs discuss gendered communication, noting that women socialized in feminine nurturing are more likely than men to disclose personal information in the workplace. Men, who tend to be more private about personal information at work, may interpret that behavior as flirting and may respond with a sexual advance. Similarly, men may use smiling, extensive eye contact, and touch as signals that they are sexually attracted to someone, while many women use these same nonverbal behaviors to demonstrate their interest in a conversation topic and their support of the person who is speaking (Berryman-Fink, 1993). By understanding and being aware of such communication differences, incidents can be prevented before they happen. Nonetheless, when incidents do occur, victims should recognize that the law is on their side; they should feel empowered to take action against an illegal act. If you are a victim of sexual harassment—or even if you think you might be—consider the following communication strategies:

▶ Clearly and firmly tell the harasser that his or her advances are not welcome.

▶ Immediately report the incident to someone who can assist you: a trusted professor, a counselor, or your boss. If the harasser is your boss, you can contact a representative in your organization's human resources department.

▶ Document each incident in writing. Include a description of the incident, the date, the person or persons involved, and any action you took.

▶ If anyone else in the organization witnessed the harassing behavior, have each witness verify the details of the incident and add that information to your documentation.

Likewise, be careful not to inadvertently behave in a harassing manner yourself. For example, if a friend e-mails a dirty joke or pornographic photo to you at work, *don't forward it to anyone else in the organization.* It's not appropriate under any circumstances. And if your organization is like many, it may well fire you on the spot.

BACK TO Google

At the beginning of the chapter, we explored life at Google's Mountain View, California, headquarters. Life there seems like a techie paradise, a place where the best and the brightest minds in computer engineering work and play around the clock. Let's revisit the Googleplex and consider how and why the people at Google structured their organization—and organized their offices—in this particular way.

▶ The organizational structure at Google shows little in the way of corporate hierarchy. There is, however, a strong emphasis on creating networks of individuals who share ideas and work together, and the company's interest in keeping employees challenged and happy (reflected most clearly in the policy of allowing engineers time to pursue nonwork-related projects) shows the influence of the human resources approach.

▶ Google takes pride in its story as a company focused on the goals of building the perfect search engine and of creating fast, easy, and practical tools for accessing the ever-growing amount of information on the Web. The company's founders often say that Google "is not serious about anything but search" (Google, 2011b). They take pride in the company's reputation as one where work represents a challenge rather than a chore.

▶ Google is in many respects the face of technology and innovation today. It is interesting to note, however, that the company also sees the value in old-fashioned, face-to-face communication. The cafés, gyms, sofas, and layout of offices encourage employees to meet and mingle, bounce ideas off one another, and work out problems together. Decidedly low-tech whiteboards abound to capture ideas and inspiration as they occur.

 Activities

1. Compare two organizations that you belong to or have regular contact with (such as a social organization, a volunteer organization, or a company). What type of management approach does each of these two organizations have? Also think about how the two organizations differ in their organizational culture. Be specific about how their values, artifacts, slogans, or assimilation practices vary.

2. Workplace comedies and dramas typically play off situations that really arise in organizational settings. Watch a few episodes of such workplace sitcoms as *The Office*, *30 Rock*, and *Parks and Recreation* or workplace dramas like *Grey's Anatomy* and *House*, and reflect on the different organizational contexts shown. What are the supervisor-supervisee relationships like? Are there any mentor-protégé relationships? What about peer relationships? How do these various relationships affect the way their organization functions?

3. In this chapter, we talked about some of the challenges that today's organizations face, including work-life balance, sexual harassment, and communication technology. Does your organization—be it a college or university, a club or campus organization, or a business—also tussle with some of these challenges? What challenges are specific to your organization? How might your organization minimize or adapt to some of these challenges?

ration, the focus of this chapter. The next step focuses on organization, which we'll talk about in Chapter 13. Then in Chapter 14, we will discuss the causes of speech anxiety and offer techniques that you can use to manage any concerns you may have. For now, know that being concerned with giving a speech is natural, but preparation and solid effort can make you a successful speaker, for this sort of skill building will enable you to conquer your nervousness (Bodie, 2010; Schroeder, 2002).

Clarifying the General Purpose of Your Speech

In the real world, choosing a topic and purpose for a speech is seldom a difficult task. You speak because you volunteered—or were forced—to speak on a topic for which your expertise is relevant to the situation. For example, you are a public health nurse giving a community presentation on the importance of early

AND YOU?

Have you ever experienced the power of a speech? Think about a specific presentation that you've seen—be it a watershed national event or a more personal experience such as a eulogy at a loved one's funeral. What about the speech stirred your emotions?

COMMUNICATIONACROSSCULTURES

THINK ABOUT THIS

Private Pain and Public Speaking

There are people who will do just about anything to avoid public speaking. In the minds of many people, the fear of public speaking is worse than the fear of death, disease, or serious illness (Wallace, Wallace, & Wallechinsky, 2004). And then there are those who cannot *not* speak out—people whose lives have been forever altered by events, illness, crime, and even death. For many victims, patients, and survivors, speaking publicly about their ordeals has proved to be a valuable tool for personal healing and public change.

Consider Carolyn McCarthy, a New York nurse, wife, and mother whose life was anything but public until her husband was murdered and her son injured in a gun massacre on the Long Island Rail Road in 1993. McCarthy suddenly emerged as a public figure, a spokeswoman for the victims and families of victims injured and killed by assault weapons. Unhappy with her congressional representative's record on gun control laws, she ran for Congress in 1996—and won. "All [I] wanted to do was make something come out of a horrible situation," said the freshman congresswoman in 1996 (as cited in Barry, 1996, para. 27).

Others find that adversity simply takes their public life in a different direction. The actor Michael J. Fox had been a household name since he was a teenager, appearing first in the television series *Family Ties* and later as the star of such feature films as *Back to the Future* and *Teen Wolf*. Diagnosed with Parkinson's disease in 1991, he semi-retired from acting in 2000, in the midst of an Emmy-winning run on the sitcom *Spin City*, and founded the Michael J. Fox Foundation, an organization devoted to funding research in hopes of a cure for the disease. Despite the debilitating physical effects of the disease, which include shaking and involuntary movement of the body, as well as difficulty speaking, Fox chose to remain a public figure, speaking at congressional hearings on stem cell research and becoming, in effect, the public face of the disease. "The time for quietly soldiering on is through," Fox told senators. "The war against Parkinson's is a winnable war, and I have resolved to play a role in that victory" (Fox, 2002, para. 147).

❶ In what ways were the public lives of McCarthy and Fox similar? How were they different?

❷ How does adversity inspire public speaking and, indeed, public life? In American culture, what defines a public figure?

❸ How does celebrity culture relate to public speaking? Is a movie star more capable of drawing support for a cause than an ordinary citizen?

❹ Is a shooting victim or the family of that victim more credible on the issue of gun control than someone whose life has not been touched by gun violence?

screening for breast or prostrate cancer; your candidate for student government president wants you, as campaign manager, to make the nominating speech; or you are presenting a group gift at a farewell party for a colleague who is off to join the Peace Corps. Often the parameters for a speech are quite general: a high school valedictorian or keynote speaker, for example, has to write a speech that both honors and inspires a large group. The possibilities for such speeches are endless. This communication class may provide a similar challenge—finding a speech topic and purpose that fit within your instructor's guidelines, which may range from very specific ("give a five-minute speech defending the constitutional right to free speech") to quite vague ("give a persuasive speech").

Speaking assignments usually fit within one of three general purposes: informative, persuasive, and special-occasion.

● **PRESIDENT FRANKLIN D. ROOSEVELT** was able to inform a wide audience about events around the country through his radio broadcasts.

Informative Speeches

In our information society, managing and communicating information are keys to success (Berrisford, 2006). *Informative speeches* aim to increase your audience's understanding or knowledge by presenting new, relevant, and useful information. Such speeches can take a variety of forms. They might explain a process or plan, describe particular objects or places, or characterize a particular state of affairs. You can expect to give informative speeches in a variety of professional situations, such as presenting reports to supervisors or stakeholders, running training sessions for a company (for example, new employee orientation), and formal education speaking (for example, K–12 teaching or teaching a community nutrition class).

Consider the storied Fireside Chats that President Franklin D. Roosevelt delivered during the 1930s and 1940s. Through the then-emerging medium of radio, Roosevelt was able to reach, inform, and reassure a vast number of Americans suffering through the Great Depression and, later, the Second World War. A brief excerpt from his first such address, delivered shortly after he took office and in the immediate aftermath of widespread bank failures, is offered as Sample Speech 12.1. Note how Roosevelt describes what happened with the banks in clear and simple language.

SAMPLE SPEECH 12.1 ────────────────────

Fireside Chat on the Bank Crisis

FRANKLIN D. ROOSEVELT

● Roosevelt clearly states his purpose at the beginning of his speech.

● I want to talk for a few minutes with the people of the United States about banking—with the comparatively few who understand the mechanics of banking but more particularly with the overwhelming majority who use banks for the making of deposits and the drawing of checks. I want to tell you what has been done in the last few days, why it was done, and what the next steps are going to be. I recognize that the many proclamations from State Capitols and from Washington, the legislation, the Treasury regulations, etc., couched for the most part in banking and legal terms, should be explained for the benefit of the average citizen. . . .

First of all let me state the simple fact that when you deposit money in a bank the bank does not put the money into a safe deposit vault. It invests your money in many different forms of credit-bonds, commercial paper, mortgages and many other kinds of loans. . . . In other words the total amount of all the currency in the country is only a small fraction of the total deposits in all of the banks. •

What, then, happened during the last few days of February and the first few days of March? Because of undermined confidence on the part of the public, there was a general rush by a large portion of our population to turn bank deposits into currency or gold—a rush so great that the soundest banks could not get enough currency to meet the demand. The reason for this was that on the spur of the moment it was, of course, impossible to sell perfectly sound assets of a bank and convert them into cash except at panic prices far below their real value.

By the afternoon of March 3 scarcely a bank in the country was open to do business. Proclamations temporarily closing them in whole or in part had been issued by the Governors in almost all the states.

It was then that I issued the proclamation providing for the nation-wide bank holiday, and this was the first step in the Government's reconstruction of our financial and economic fabric. . . . •

Source: From "On the Bank Crisis," radio address by Franklin Delano Roosevelt delivered March 12, 1933. Retrieved from "Fireside Chats by Franklin D. Roosevelt" at the Franklin D. Roosevelt Presidential Library and Museum, http://www.fdrlibrary.marist.edu/031233.html

• Note how Roosevelt explains how banking works in very simple terms for those listeners who might not be familiar with the process.

• Here Roosevelt begins to lay out and explain his plan for addressing the crisis so that listeners feel more comfortable about what's going on.

Persuasive Speeches

Persuasive speeches are very common in daily life and are a major focus of public speaking classes (R. Smith, 2004). You may think that persuasion is a dishonest tactic used to coerce someone into doing or believing something, but that is not necessarily the case. Rather, *persuasive speeches* are intended to influence the attitudes, beliefs, and behaviors of your audience. Although they often ask for a *change* from your audience, persuasive speeches can also reaffirm existing attitudes, beliefs, and behaviors: a politician speaking at a rally of core constituents probably doesn't need to change their minds about anything, but she uses persuasive speaking nonetheless to get them excited about her platform or energized for her reelection campaign. In other cases, persuasive speech is a more straightforward call to action. In Sample Speech 12.2, for example, the entertainer and human rights activist Ricky Martin urges members of the international community to step up efforts to put an end to human trafficking. A United Nations goodwill ambassador, Martin offers both facts and statistics related to this global crime, outlines efforts to combat it, and calls for support.

SAMPLE SPEECH 12.2

Speech at the Vienna Forum

RICKY MARTIN

As a musician, activist, and universal citizen, I thank the United Nations Global Initiative to Fight Human Trafficking for allowing the Ricky Martin Foundation to share our commitment to end this horrible crime. Since this modern day form of slavery has no geographical boundaries, the truly international reach of this unprecedented forum is an essential platform to combat this global nightmare.

My commitment toward this cause was born from a humbling experience. In my 2002 trip to India I witnessed the horrors of human trafficking as we rescued three trembling girls [who were] living on the streets in plastic bags. Saving these girls from falling prey to exploitation was a personal awakening. •

I immediately knew the Foundation had to fiercely battle this scourge.

That was six years ago. . . . Since then the Foundation expanded and launched People for Children, an international initiative that condemns child exploitation. The project's goal is to provide awareness, education, and support for worldwide efforts seeking the elimination of human trafficking—with special emphasis on children.

This unscrupulous market generates anywhere from $12 to $32 billion dollars annually, an amount only surpassed by the trafficking of arms and drugs. . . . My hope is to secure every child the right to be a child through a not-for-profit organization conceived as a vehicle to enforce their basic human rights in partnership with other organizations, social responsible corporations, and individuals. . . . •

I am certain that our voices, together with the power of other organizations that work against this horrible crime, will continue to galvanize efforts to prevent, suppress, and punish human trafficking.

Changing attitudes and human behavior is difficult, but never forget that multiple small triumphs over a long period of time are tantamount to social change.

As a foundation that supports the objectives of this historic forum which aims to put this crime on the global agenda, be certain that:

We will continue to tell the world that human trafficking exists; we will keep educating the masses; and we will keep working on prevention, protection and prosecution measures in our campaigns to alleviate the factors that make children, women and men vulnerable to the most vicious violation of human rights.

Human trafficking has no place in our world today. I urge you to join our fight. React. It's time. •

Source: From "Speech at the Vienna Forum" by Ricky Martin, United Nations Global Initiative to Fight Human Trafficking, February 13, 2008. Retrieved from www.ungift .org/ungift/en/vf/speeches/martin.html

• Note how Martin effectively uses a real-life, personal experience to awaken his audience to the horror of the situation.

• Here Martin lays out facts about this international crime and clearly describes his persuasive goal for his speech.

• Note Martin's call to action. He hopes to persuade his audience members to get involved in the fight and not sit passively while this international crime continues to rob victims of their very personhood.

Special-Occasion Speeches

Special-occasion speeches use the principles of both informative and persuasive speaking for special occasions, such as introducing a speaker, accepting an honor or award, presenting a memorial, or celebrating an achievement. Almost certainly at some point in your life you will be called on to deliver a speech at a wedding, a toast at a retirement party, or a eulogy at a funeral. Special-occasion speeches are frequently delivered on the world stage as well. In 2005, for example, Bruce Springsteen inducted fellow rockers U2 into the Rock and Roll Hall of Fame. An excerpt of his speech is presented in Sample Speech 12.3. As you'll see, the speech is intended to bring everyone listening to the same conclusion: that this band is a true icon of rock and roll that changed the sound and scope of popular music.

SAMPLE SPEECH 12.3

U2 Rock and Roll Hall of Fame Induction

BRUCE SPRINGSTEEN

Uno, dos, tres, catorce. That translates as *one, two, three, fourteen.* That is the correct math for a rock and roll band. For in art and love and rock and roll, the whole had better equal much more than the sum of its parts, or else you're just rubbing two sticks together searching for fire. A great rock band searches for the same kind of combustible force that fueled the expansion of the universe after the big bang. . . .

It's embarrassing to want so much, and to expect so much from music, except sometimes it happens—the Sun Sessions, Highway 61, Sgt. Pepper, the Band, Robert Johnson, *Exile on Main Street, Born to Run*—whoops, I meant to leave that one out (laughter)—the Sex Pistols, Aretha Franklin, the Clash, James Brown . . . the proud and public enemies it takes a nation of millions to hold back. This is music meant to take on not only the powers that be, but on a good day, the universe and God himself—if he was listening. It's man's accountability, and U2 belongs on this list. . . . •

They are both a step forward and direct descendants of the great bands who believed rock music could shake things up in the world, who dared to have faith in their audience, who believed if they played their best it would bring out the best in you. They believed in pop stardom and the big time. Now this requires foolishness and a calculating mind. It also requires a deeply held faith in the work you're doing and in its powers to transform. U2 hungered for it all, and built a sound, and they wrote the songs that demanded it. . . .

Now the band's beautiful songwriting—"Pride (In the Name of Love)," "Sunday Bloody Sunday," "I Still Haven't Found What I'm Looking For," "One," "Where the Streets Have No Name," "Beautiful

● **JENNIFER HUDSON** might have imagined giving a toast at a friend's wedding, but until her Oscar nomination, she probably hadn't considered preparing for such a public and important acceptance speech.

● Springsteen compares U2 to other accomplished, well-known artists in order to show the level of their success.

Day"—reminds us of the stakes that the band always plays for. It's an incredible songbook. In their music you hear the spirituality as home and as quest. How do you find God unless he's in your heart? In your desire? In your feet? I believe this is a big part of what's kept their band together all of these years. . . .•

This band . . . has carried their faith in the great inspirational and resurrective power of rock and roll. It never faltered, only a little bit. They believed in themselves, but more importantly, they believed in "you, too." Thank you Bono, the Edge, Adam, and Larry. Please welcome U2 into the Rock and Roll Hall of Fame.

Source: From "Bruce Springsteen Inducts U2 into the Rock and Roll Hall of Fame, March 17, 2005." Retrieved from http://www.u2station.com/news/archives/2005/03/transcript_bruc.php. Used with permission of Bruce Springsteen.

• Here Springsteen lists U2's impressive accomplishments.

AND YOU?

Have you ever attended a speaking event where the speaker did not behave appropriately for the occasion? How did it make you feel as a listener?

Analyzing Your Audience

As you will quickly discover, **audience analysis**—a highly systematic process of getting to know your listeners relative to the topic and the speech occasion—is a critical step in the speech preparation process (O'Hair, Stewart, & Rubenstein, 2010; Yook, 2004). Because you are asking the audience members to accept your message—to learn new information; to change their attitudes, beliefs, or behaviors; or to recommit themselves to a cause or organization—it is important for you to know where they are starting from. You must consider not only their expectations, but also the unique situational factors affecting them, as well as their demographic backgrounds, while anticipating their reaction to your speech. Gaining this understanding will be crucial to choosing a topic that will resonate with them.

Considering Audience Expectations and Situational Factors

People naturally bring different sets of expectations and emotions to a speech event (O'Hair, Stewart, & Rubenstein, 2010). And as with other forms of communication discussed in this book, competent public speaking involves understanding and acknowledging the expectations of your communication partners—in this case, your audience.

Audiences are likely to have expectations about your speech based on the speaking situation, the information their culture provides about public speaking, and even their knowledge about you as an individual or as a speaker. For example, think about the types of expectations you bring to a wedding toast or a valedictorian's speech. Would you expect a best man to use his microphone time to talk about the fact that the bride is untrustworthy because she cheated on her taxes last year? This would clearly defy tradition and cultural expectations. Similarly, as we learned from some Russian colleagues, an American businessperson giving a speech in Moscow might defy audience expectations by coming right to the point when informing them about a particular technology. In Russia, audiences expect speeches to favor storytelling rather than direct fact sharing.

CONNECT

Analyzing expectations in a speaking situation may seem difficult, but you frequently do this work in other communication contexts. As we learn in Chapter 7, relational partners must address each other's expectations in order for the relationship to grow. Similarly, the speaker must remember the audience's expectations for the speaking occasion (level of formality or appropriate language, for example) in order to be competent and successful.

Audiences can also be influenced by a variety of situational factors that you cannot always plan for. Be aware of issues such as the time of day of your speech, events happening in the outside world, or the comfort and attractiveness of the room—because these issues do matter. Our publishing colleagues at Bedford/St. Martin's will be presenting our book to the company's sales representatives at a sales convention. They always pray, "Please, anything but the 3:00 P.M. Friday speech slot"—the last time slot of the meeting. They know that they'll have to be even more enthusiastic and on top of their speech when they're giving it to an audience exhausted after days of meetings and eager to return home to friends and family.

● **THE BANE** of a school presenter's existence? Fidgety kids who would much rather poke their neighbors than pay attention.

Considering Audience Demographics

Although understanding audience expectations and situational factors is an important component of audience analysis, it is only one of the important steps. You should also examine your audience's demographics. **Demographics** is the systematic study of the quantifiable characteristics of a large group. An audience analysis might focus on co-cultural statistics such as gender, socioeconomic status (including income, occupation, and education), religious and political affiliation, family status (married, single, divorced, partnered, with children, without children), age, and ethnic background. Other statistics that might be relevant include student enrollment status (full time or part time), student residential status (living on campus or off campus), major area of study, or the geographical regions your fellow students hail from.

Understanding such statistics can lead speakers to topics that will be of interest and will carry meaning for specific audiences. For example, one of the most easily quantifiable and useful demographic statistics to consider is the age range of your audience. If you have a good sense of how old most of your audience members are, you'll be able to choose a topic that is relevant to concerns of their generation and ensure that the examples and anecdotes you use in your speech will resonate with the age groups you are addressing.

As we learned in Chapter 3, some audience characteristics will be more *salient*—or significant—in some speaking situations than in others. For example, if your audience members are mostly Latina women in their fifties who have survived breast cancer, their status as survivors is not likely to be salient if you are informing them about the importance of maximizing their annual contributions to their 401(k) plans before retiring in the next ten years. But if you are persuading a group to contribute money to the American Cancer Society in order to support new research campaigns, their experience fighting cancer should be firmly in your mind as you develop and deliver your speech.

Now, you're probably thinking, "How can I possibly know all of the demographics of my audience members?" You're right, of course. You can't necessarily know that the guy who sits three rows back on the left side of the classroom

AND YOU?

Have you ever found yourself feeling disconnected from a speaker, be it a course instructor or a politician, because he or she failed to consider your age, gender, sexual orientation, or ethnic background? Conversely, have you ever found a speaker very effective because he or she did consider such factors?

is a heterosexual Libertarian genetics major from a working-class family and a Christian who works part time at the deli around the corner from his off-campus apartment. But you can look for some general traits and trends. For example,

real communicator

NAME: Amy Talluto
HOMETOWN: New Orleans, Louisiana
OCCUPATION: Freelance Web designer and fine artist
FUN FACT: I like to gobble at flocks of wild turkeys to see if I can get a gobble back. So far I enjoy about a 90 percent return.

I'm a visual artist. I do some photography, some ink and pencil drawings, but mostly I paint landscapes. Thickets, cascading rivers, Silver Pond in Montana. Not too long ago, I was asked to go out to Eastern Illinois University and speak to about fifty graduate students getting their master's in the visual arts. I was asked to talk about my work.

My work? What do you want me to say?

So first things first. This was an informational presentation on my work. But what specifically did I want my audience to learn? What, as my undergraduate public speaking professor might ask, was my purpose?

I didn't know exactly. So I started thinking about who would be in my audience and what they might want to hear about. Well, they're artists—photographers, painters, sculptors, graphic designers. They think visually, and they probably learn visually too. Also, and just as important, they're students, many of them young, many of them putting together a body of work for the first time.

So I knew my presentation would have to be visual (pretty obvious, since I was asked to speak about my visual work). And I decided, based on this understanding of my audience, to focus my presentation on the creative process: how a finished landscape painting gets finished. Traditionally, visiting artist lectures are done using a projector and slides and consist of a straightforward march of single images projected on a large screen. Click. Click. Click. Dust coming off the top of the carousel. I wanted to do something different. I wanted to juxtapose (and enhance) the images of my finished landscapes with the source photos I used as references, in-progress painting sequences, and images of New York and the Chelsea gallery district. I wanted to visually show my creative process. To do that, I went to PowerPoint.

Uploading my digital photos onto Power-Point, I was able to zoom in and out, show exactly what I wanted to show. And knowing my audience, I kept text to an absolute minimum. I avoided those long bulleted lists. (With one exception: I had noticed, while attending traditional slide-based artist lectures, that the audience often repeatedly asked about basic details of the works—like the size, year completed, or medium—disrupting the flow of the discussion. So I used PowerPoint to add that brief information next to each image during my slide show.)

I didn't just let the images speak for themselves, however. I had to present them. I elaborated on each image verbally, and I didn't work off the cuff. Before the presentation, I used the "Notes" feature in PowerPoint to type my own text references for the verbal discussion. These notes were for my eyes only and would not appear onscreen. I was able to save my slide show to Microsoft Word, which automatically arranged all of my hidden text notes and paired them with thumbnails of my art images, creating the perfect reference document as I went through my presentation. The audience was then free to visually enjoy the large images while listening to me speak.

visit your college or university Web site to get a sense of the demographic breakdown of your school. Most schools make data available on factors like age, race, gender, and religion and often provide information on the percentage of students receiving financial aid, the number of students living on campus versus those who commute, full-time versus part-time students, and so on.

There are some limitations of demographic information that deserve mention here. Sometimes speakers—including politicians and advertisers—mistakenly apply stereotypes to demographic groups or overgeneralize about common views of group members. And, in some cases, the results of demographic data collection can be flawed or even downright wrong (Sprauge, Stuart, & Bodary, 2010). Because of this, it's important to be mindful in the way you use demographic information. For example, your class may be 75 percent Catholic, but

---

WIREDFORCOMMUNICATION

THINK ABOUT THIS

In a Click, Lectures Become Interactive

One of the challenges of public speaking has always been that the communication is, for the most part, one-way. And while some audiences might provide lots of feedback (in the form of applause, boos, silence, hysteria, and so on), others might not even want to pay attention. When dealing with a passive audience, speakers generally have little chance for real dialogue and interaction. But teachers are finding new technology that allows their once passive student audience to actively engage in their lectures.

Through the use of remote controls commonly referred to as "clickers," lecturers at hundreds of colleges and universities (and even some elementary and secondary schools) are able to pose questions to large groups of students and, within a minute or two, tally up all the answers and display the results (Steinberg, 2010a). The technology is changing the nature of lectures. "It's not like an hour-long lecture where the professor is droning on and everybody goes to sleep because they don't know what's important," explained one physics professor. "It lets the lecture turn into a two-way conversation" ("Classroom Clickers," 2005).

The clickers supply both lecturers and audiences with instant feedback. "I've found that in [the lecture] setting, you find yourself thinking, 'Well, what are they thinking?'" noted one instructor. "I use it to take their pulse" ("No Wrong Answer," 2005). Students answering questions get instant feedback as well. "You don't have to wait for someone to sit back and grade them by hand," one student said of classroom assignments. "Right away you're able to get your answers back" ("Classroom Clickers," 2005).

Students have responded positively, as the anonymity of the device allows them to share their opinions with their instructors without revealing them to their peers. And the simplicity with which the clickers make the lecture interactive helps them to stay engaged. "I actually kind of like it," noted one student. "It does make you read. It makes you pay attention. It reinforces what you're supposed to be doing as a student" (Steinberg, 2010b).

❶ What other advantages does the clicker give the speaker? What kinds of new challenges might it pose?

❷ How does the clicker change the nature of the lecture? Does it change the relationship between speaker and audience? Or does it simply change the interaction between them?

❸ If you were giving a speech to an audience armed with clickers, what kinds of questions would you ask? How might the audience's responses change the nature or style of your speech? Could you make those changes on the fly?

● **ANGELINA JOLIE** often dons stylish all-black outfits in her role as an activist, but she alters her image based on the audience and context: formal wear for a press conference, casual clothes for field work.

that doesn't *automatically* mean that they'll be interested in a speech related to the church. That's why it's important to anticipate how your audience members might respond to your speech—even before you officially choose your topic and conduct your research.

Anticipating Your Audience's Response

As speech instructors, we openly confess that we get tired of hearing speeches on gun control, abortion, and euthanasia. It's not that these topics aren't worthy of thoughtful public discourse. Rather, we've just heard the same arguments over and over, and we're interested in learning about new topics, such as the process involved in preparing homemade barbecue sauce or easy steps to cut personal spending in order to save for retirement. All audience members feel this way from time to time. You may be required to attend meetings at work that have nothing to do with your projects or your job; you may sit through a sermon at your house of worship that feels unrelated to your life experiences. When you are the speaker, it's always useful to remember these experiences and to do your best to ensure that you don't cause your audience to react the same way! Considering a few practical points, and adapting your speech accordingly, can certainly help:

▶ *Consider audience motivation.* Is your audience choosing to listen to your speech or are they required to attend? Voluntary audiences tend to be motivated to listen because they have *chosen* to hear what you say. The audience members in your class, however, are usually required to listen—and some of them may be entirely unmotivated to do so. Therefore, you must work to choose a relevant, engaging topic that they will care about and to engage them with your delivery skills (a topic we'll address in Chapter 14).

▶ *Seek common ground.* Do you and your audience members share certain opinions or experiences with one another? If so, you can capitalize on this **homogeny**—or sameness—by delivering a message that will keep their attention. For example, when his university changed their taxation policies for graduate students receiving stipends, Eduardo delivered a speech informing his fellow students of the steps they would need to take to ensure proper tax withholding. It didn't matter that the students hailed from assorted fields and departments because they were all stuck dealing with the same confusing tax questions.

▶ *Determine prior exposure.* Audience members' interest in your speech may differ greatly depending on whether or not they have previously been exposed to your ideas and your arguments. Having a general sense of what they know about the topic—and how they have reacted to it in the past—will help you prepare. For example, if your informative speech on vegetarian cooking seemed to go over really well with your classmates, then it's reasonable to think that they might be interested in hearing a persuasive speech on the health and financial benefits of a diet with more produce and less meat.

▶ *Consider disposition.* Your audience's preexisting attitudes toward a particular message—or even toward you as a speaker—can have an impact on how they receive your speech. If you are a company executive informing employees that they will not be receiving an annual pay raise, you can assume your audience will be angry with the message (and may well dislike you as a speaker). You would be well advised to focus on areas of agreement, seek common ground, and attempt mutual understanding rather than sweeping changes in attitudes. (We will address how to adjust your speech to receptive, hostile, and neutral audiences in Chapter 16).

As was the case on gathering demographic information on your audience members, you may wonder exactly *how* you go about finding information to anticipate your audience's reaction to your speech. Luckily, there are a few steps you can take that may yield incredibly helpful information.

▶ *Observe people.* People-watching is a hobby for some, but a must for speakers! You can learn a lot by casually observing those around you. How do they react to topics discussed in class—particularly if the topics are controversial? What types of speakers do they seem to respond to? (Consider, for example, how they react to your instructor or other student speakers in the classroom.)

▶ *Get to know people.* This may seem like common sense, but you'd be surprised how often students complete a course without making personal connections. Talk to a few people who sit next to you in class or engage in online chatting with those in your virtual course. Ask questions. Learn more about your classmates' hobbies, life situations, and other factors that might help you develop an effective speech.

▶ *Survey and interview your audience.* You might also want to assess your audience on a more formal level. After receiving approval from your instructor, you might develop and distribute a short questionnaire to determine your classmates' opinions on a topic you're considering for your speech. Or you might talk with several members of a student organization to get feedback on your topic before you deliver your speech at the next group meeting.

CONNECT

When surveying and interviewing your audience to help anticipate their response to your speech, it's important to develop the most useful questions possible. For example, you'll want to consider whether to ask *open, closed,* or *bipolar questions* to get the information you need. And you'll want to avoid unethical directed, leading, and loaded questions. See the Interviewing Appendix for more information.

▶ *Use the Web.* Do a Web search for opinion polls on your topic, especially polls that gauge the views of college students or other key demographic groups in your audience. Examine the kind of attention the issue has been getting on campus or in the local media (such as the school's newspaper or Web site).

All of the information you gain about your audience members—from their expectations and situational constraints to their demographics and possible reactions—sets the stage for you to move forward in developing an effective and appropriate speech. The next step is officially choosing your topic.

Choosing Your Topic

Choosing a topic can seem like a daunting task, but it doesn't have to be. As noted, you'll want to consider the audience's expectations for the speech and topics that will interest them, taking their demographics into account. In this course, you may have some guidance, in that your instructor—arguably your most important audience member—will likely have given you a specific assignment. Be certain of your instructor's expectations for your speech, asking questions if necessary, to ensure that your topic and speech are appropriate. Then, it's time to start thinking about your topic. In searching for a good topic, you might try two proven strategies for generating ideas: considering personal interests and brainstorming or clustering.

Finding a Topic That Intrigues You

It's hard to give a persuasive speech about something you don't find particularly inspiring or an informative speech on a topic you know nothing about. Finding a speech topic that is truly interesting to you will serve you well as you prepare your speech, making you more motivated to research and refine the topic and generating an enthusiasm in you as a speaker that will impress your audience.

But when you have a variety of interests, it can be hard to pinpoint one to speak about. One way to get started is to write up a list of topics that interest you. For example, take a look at the variety of interests listed in Table 12.1. Creating a thorough and detailed list of topics that interest you—or even looking at topics that interest other people—can be a great tool for stimulating ideas for your speech.

Brainstorming and Clustering

Once you've determined a very general topic—by focusing either on an area of interest to you or on a general topic assigned by your instructor—you'll need to start amassing information, thinking creatively, and considering problems and solutions related to your topic. This is a process known as **brainstorming**. You might begin by considering what you already know

● **CHOOSING** a topic from among numberless ideas and interests will call for some thinking and writing. Get creative!

TABLE 12.1

PERSONAL INTEREST TOPICS

Personal Experiences	Controversial Issues	Current Events	Hobbies	Beliefs and Values
• Camping trips • Life-threatening event • Education • Organizations • Accomplishments • Military service • Volunteer work	• Smoking bans • Driving age • Drinking age • Same-sex marriage • Immigration • Prayer in public schools	• Global warming • Budget deficits • Space flights • Sporting events • Musical performances • National health care • Revolutions in the Middle East	• Skiing • Cooking • Camping • Automobile restoration • Gardening • Shopping • Online gaming • Social networking	• Spirituality • Social justice • Environmentalism • Humanitarianism • Political beliefs • Mysticism • Supernatural events • Retribution • Gun control

Source: O'Hair, Stewart, & Rubenstein (2007), tab. 7.4, p. 98. Adapted with permission.

about your subject. For example, if you are giving a two-minute speech describing a place, you might consider a very specific place (the corner table by the window at your favorite coffeehouse) to a very general place (the Midwest).

You might also consider using a technique called clustering (R. E. Smith, 1993). **Clustering** is technique for identifying potential speech topics. It begins with a core idea from which the writer branches out into a web of related thoughts and ideas. It's similar to brainstorming, but rather than generating a list of ideas, clustering "spills" its ideas onto paper. To begin, simply write a main word or phrase in a circle; then create a web or collection of ideas inspired by the nucleus word or phrase. See Figure 12.1 for a sample of clustering for the nucleus phrase *country music*. As the process continues, you'll be struck by

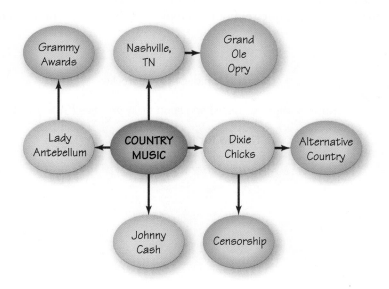

FIGURE 12.1

EXAMPLE OF A WEB OF ASSOCIATIONS PRODUCED BY CLUSTERING Thinking about "country music" can lead to numerous possible speech topics.

some concepts that might be suitable topics for your speech. In a sense, it's like Googling your own brain, starting out with a word or concept and branching to form a web of links to related thoughts.

Narrowing Your Topic

Now that you have searched for potential topics, it's time to make a choice. Your goal is to select the topic that best meets the following three criteria:

1. Is it a topic you are interested in and know something about?
2. Does the topic meet the criteria specified in the assignment?
3. Is it a topic that your audience will find worthwhile?

Once you are satisfied that your topic meets these criteria, you can begin to consider how to break down your topic further so that it is more specific and manageable. This will aid you a great deal in your research (a topic we will discuss later in this chapter) since it is considerably easier to find information on a specific topic (traditional Jewish foods served for Passover) than an extremely general one (the Jewish faith). One way to narrow down your topic is to break it up into categories. Write your general topic at the top of a list, with each succeeding word a more specific or concrete topic. As illustrated in Figure 12.2, you might begin with the very general topic of cars and trucks and then narrow the topic down a step at a time until you focus on one particular model (the Chevy Tahoe hybrid) and decide to persuade your listeners about the advantages of owning a hybrid vehicle with all of the SUV amenities.

Determining the Specific Purpose of Your Speech

Once you've narrowed your topic, you'll need to zero in on a specific purpose for your speech. You might begin by asking yourself, "Precisely what is it about my topic that I want my audience to learn, do, consider, or agree with?" A **specific purpose statement** expresses both the topic and the general speech purpose in

FIGURE 12.2

NARROWING YOUR TOPIC
Start with a general idea and become increasingly specific until you have a manageable topic for your speech.

General topic: Cars and trucks

Narrow slightly: Trucks and sport utility vehicles (SUVs)

Narrow further: SUVs only

Narrow further: Hybrid SUVs

Narrow further:
Chevy
Tahoe
Hybrid

action form and in terms of the specific objectives you hope to achieve with your presentation.

Let's consider an example. Imagine you are giving a persuasive speech on volunteerism, a topic you feel very strongly about. Your general purpose and specific purpose might look like this:

Topic: Volunteer reading programs

General purpose: To persuade

Specific purpose: To have audience members realize the importance of reading with local elementary school children so that they sign up for a volunteer reading program such as Everybody Wins

There is an additional level of specificity to consider when preparing your speech. It is called the *thesis statement*—you're probably familiar with this term from high school or your college composition course. We help you understand and develop your own thesis in the next section.

Developing a Thesis Statement

Once you have homed in on your topic, general purpose, and specific speech purpose, you can start to encapsulate your speech in the form of a **thesis statement**, a statement that conveys the central idea or core assumption about your topic. The thesis statement must clearly summarize what you want the audience to get out of your speech, but is not the same thing as your specific purpose statement; as noted, it is more specific. Revisiting the example about volunteer reading programs, note how your thesis statement works with your general purpose and specific speech purpose and how it expresses the core idea that you want your listeners to walk away with:

Thesis statement: Volunteers who read with local elementary school children through programs such as Everybody Wins improve young lives by enhancing children's self-esteem and expanding their possibilities for academic success.

Can you see how the thesis statement works? Offering a solid thesis statement your audience will remember long after your visual aids have faded from their minds will help you achieve your general purpose and your specific purpose: to persuade your listeners to get out there and read with local kids. For additional examples of thesis statements, see Table 12.2.

Researching the Topic

Anyone can make a speech—to stand on a stump or at a podium and speak on one matter or another is a birthright in the United States, regardless of whether or not what you are saying is useful, interesting, or even truthful. But a good speech should offer listeners something new, some information, insight, perspec-

CONNECT

Your thesis statement helps you stay focused on your goals for communicating with others in a public speaking situation. But staying focused on goals also matters in communication contexts such as running a meeting. As we discussed in Chapter 10, clearly stating the purpose of your meeting and organizing your agenda around it helps everyone stay focused and makes you more likely to achieve your goals.

TABLE 12.2

GENERATING A THESIS STATEMENT

Topic	General Purpose	Specific Purpose	Thesis Statement
Low-carbohydrate diets	To inform	To inform listeners about low-carbohydrate diets so that they can make good decisions about their own eating habits	Before choosing to start a low-carbohydrate diet, it is important to have a thorough understanding of how carbohydrates affect your body and what the possible benefits and risks of the diet are so that you can make an informed decision about your health.
Study-abroad programs	To persuade	To have listeners realize that studying abroad is an exciting opportunity and encourage them to consider spending a semester taking classes in another country	Studying abroad is an amazing opportunity to learn about another culture, to enhance your educational experience, and to make yourself more appealing to prospective graduate schools and employers.
My grandparents	To honor an amazing couple on their fiftieth wedding anniversary (special occasion)	To celebrate with my family and my grandparents' friends in light of this happy milestone in their lives	In big and small ways, my grandparents have shared their fifty years of love and commitment with their family, their congregation, and their students, having been dedicated teachers for three decades.

tive, or idea that they didn't have before. Such original thoughts are usually the product of both deep reflection and careful research.

In a speech, research is information that helps support the points that you make, strengthening your message and credibility. For many students, the prospect of researching for a speech or presentation might seem boring, overwhelming, or both—and it can be. But if you are working with a topic that intrigues you and you approach your research in a practical way, the research process can be better than you think.

Types of Information to Consider

A wealth of material is available to enliven your speech and make it more effective. Listeners respond best to a range of information, so try to include a variety of types of support materials in your speech, including testimony, scholarship and statistics, anecdotes, quotations, and comparisons and contrasts.

Testimony

When you need to prove a point about which you are not an authority, incorporating the voice of an expert into your speech can lend it some validity. **Expert testimony** is the opinion or judgment of an expert, a professional in his or her field. Opinions from doctors, coaches, engineers, and other qualified, licensed professionals serve as expert testimony. In a speech about knee surgery, for example, you might cite an orthopedic surgeon when explaining the difference between arthroscopy and knee replacement surgery. **Lay testimony** is the

The type of information you choose for your speech should be influenced by its general purpose. If you are persuading your audience (Chapter 16) or giving a speech for a special occasion, try using personal anecdotes to touch your audience emotionally. When informing your audience (Chapter 15), make sure that your use of anecdotes illuminates your topic and doesn't persuade the audience to think a certain way about it.

opinion of a nonexpert who has personal experience or witnessed an event related to your topic. In a speech on weather disasters, you could provide the testimony from a witness who survived a tornado.

Scholarship and Statistics

If you can bolster testimonies with hard numbers and facts, you'll be more effective as a speaker. **Scientific research findings** carry a lot of weight with audiences, particularly if your topic is related to medicine, health, media, or the environment. For example, in a speech about educational television programs, a speaker might point out that studies have found that children who watched *Sesame Street* as preschoolers were more likely to enjoy elementary school and to achieve higher grades even in high school (Huston & Wright, 1998).

Numbers can impress an audience more than mere words. **Statistics**—information provided in numerical form—can provide powerful support for a speech. Statistics reveal trends, explain the size of something, or illustrate relationships. They can be made more meaningful when paired with or made part of *factual statements*—truthful, realistic accounts based on actual people, places, events, or dates. For example, when speaking about domestic violence, you might use a combination of statistics and factual statements to back your statement that a person is more likely to be killed by a family member or close acquaintance than a stranger:

> Out of 13,636 murders studied in the United States, 30.2% of the victims were murdered by persons known to them (4,119 victims), 13.6% were murdered by family members (1,855 victims), 12.3% were murdered by strangers (1,676 victims), and 43.9% of the relationships were unknown (investigators were not able to establish any relationship). (U.S. Department of Justice, 2010)

Anecdotes

While facts and statistics are useful for gaining credibility, they can also be boring and easily forgotten. An effective way to breathe life into them—and into your speech in general—is to flesh it out with personal details that give faces to statistics and facts and make them part of a memorable and cohesive story. **Anecdotes** are brief, personal stories that have a point or punch line. The statistics on murder presented above would be greatly enhanced if they were paired with one or two personal stories that bring them down to a more intimate and relatable level. Anecdotes can be pointed or emotionally moving; they can also be humorous or inspiring. When used well, they add a personal and memorable element to your speech.

Quotations

You can also call on the words of others to lend your speech a sense of history, perspective, and timeless eloquence. *Quotations,* repeating the exact words of another person, are usually most effective when they are brief, to the point, and clearly related to your topic. You might quote a historical figure, a celebrity, a poet, or a playwright. For example, in a speech about motivation, you could quote Michelangelo: "The greatest danger for most of us is not that our aim is too high

AND YOU?

What type of supporting information do you find most compelling in speeches? Expert testimony? Statistics? Anecdotes? Why? Do you find that your preference depends on the topic of the speech? Why or why not?

and we miss it but that it is too low and we reach it." Your sources do not need to be famous—you may be motivated to quote a friend or family member: "My grandfather always told me, 'An education is never a burden.'" Be sure to point out the source of your quote and, if necessary, explain who the person is or was.

Comparisons and Contrasts

Comparisons and Contrasts have the potential to liven up your speech and make it more memorable for your audience. You might also consider playing these tools off of each other to make an even bigger impression. *Comparisons* measure the similarity of two things. In a comparison, the likeness or resemblance of two ideas or concepts are pointed out. *Contrasts* show dissimilarities among two or more things. By illustrating differences, speakers can make distinctions among ideas they are discussing. A speech on school funding, for example, might call attention to disparities between schools by providing contrasting descriptions of the equipment in their science labs or gyms. You could follow that up by contrasting statistics on their students' average test scores or graduation rates.

Researching Supporting Material

Of course, the facts, statistics, anecdotes, and other supporting material that you want for your speech won't come out of thin air. Now that you've got your list of ingredients for your speech, you'll need to do some shopping—that is, you'll need to go out and find the material. Here's how.

Talk to People

● **SURVEYING LOCAL FARMERS** about the effects of factory farming and mass-produced food on their livelihood will likely give you some interesting insights and quotations to use in your speech.

If you're looking for testimony, narratives, real-world examples, and anecdotes, you'll need to start talking to people. You may be looking for experts in a particular field or people who have had firsthand experience with an event or occurrence, which can be a challenge. You can start by *networking*—making connections with people you don't know through people you do know. Searching through literature and Internet resources is another way to track down people who may be able to provide support for your speech.

Another useful reason to talk to people is to conduct a survey. **Surveys** involve soliciting answers to a question or series of questions related to your topic from a broad range of individuals. Conducting a survey can give you a sense of how a group of people view a particular event, idea, or phenomena. For example, if you are giving an informative speech on fear of terrorism in the United States, you might randomly select students on campus and ask them how safe they feel from terrorist attacks. Results from surveys can be discussed to back up your points ("Of the forty students with whom I spoke, only twelve felt that a terrorist attack is likely in this region of the United States").

Search the Literature

Published literature lets you reach beyond your own knowledge and experience and can be a valuable resource for supporting material for your speech. If you're giving a speech on hip-hop music, for example, you're likely to find some great material in the pages of magazines like *Vibe* and *Rolling Stone*. If you're looking for studies on mental health issues affecting rescue workers after Hurricane Katrina, you might search through newspaper archives or scholarly journals such as the *New England Journal of Medicine*.

Most current publications are available in searchable databases in libraries; some can even be accessed via the Internet (though you may have to pay a fee to download complete articles). Such databases give you access to a wealth of stored information. The Internet Movie Database (www.imdb.com), for example, is a great example of a commonly used database. A source of information on film, television, and even video games, it is accessible online for free and is growing daily.

Another type of secondary resource is a **directory**. Directories are created and maintained by people rather than automatically by computers. Because human editors compile them, directories often return fewer links but higher-quality results. Directories guide you to the main page of a Web site organized within a wider subject category. You can also access useful literature through **library gateways**—collections of databases and information sites arranged by subject, generally reviewed and recommended by experts (usually librarians). These gateway collections assist in your research and reference needs because they identify suitable academic pages on the Web. In addition to scholastic resources, many library gateways include links to specialty search engines for biographies, quotations, atlases, maps, encyclopedias, and trivia. There are also a number of "virtual libraries" that exist only on the Internet. Some well-known library gateways and directories are identified in Table 12.3.

Make the Internet Work for You

Twenty years ago, the first stop on any research mission would have been the library. Today, the Internet puts a multitude of information at your fingertips, accessible at any hour. Navigating the vast sea of information—not to mention misinformation—available on the Internet can be daunting, and if you don't search wisely, it can be a waste of time. A solid knowledge of search tools can therefore make your searches more fruitful and efficient.

TABLE 12.3

USEFUL INTERNET SEARCH SITES

Library gateways	Digital Librarian *www.digital~librarian.com*
	Internet Public Library *www.ipl.org*
	Living Web Library *www.livingweb.com/library/search.htm*
	New Canaan Library *www.newcanaanlibrary.org*
Directories	Academic Info *www.academicinfo.net*
	LookSmart *www.looksmart.com*
	Open Directory Project or DMOZ *www.dmoz.org*

● **WE RELY HEAVILY** on the internet for our research needs. In fact, *google* has become a legitimate verb in our everyday language!

An Internet **search engine** is a program that indexes Web content. Search engines such as Google, Yahoo!, Metacrawler, and Bing search all over the Web for documents containing specific keywords that you've chosen. Search engines have some key advantages—they offer access to a huge portion of publicly available Web pages and give you the ability to search through large databases. But they frequently return irrelevant links, and they don't index the "invisible Web"—databases maintained by universities, businesses, the government, or libraries that cannot always be accessed by standard search engines. If a search engine fails to produce useful results, try a **metasearch engine**—a search engine that scans multiple search engines simultaneously. Metasearch technology delivers more relevant and comprehensive results than a search engine.

Evaluating Supporting Material

Once you've gathered a variety of sources, you must critically evaluate the material and determine which sources you should use. After all, your credibility as a speaker depends largely on the accuracy and credibility of the sources that you cite in your speech as well as the appropriateness of the sources for your topic and your audience.

Credible Sources

In today's media, anyone can put up a blog or a Web page, edit a wiki, or post a video to YouTube. What's more, a large and growing number of opinion-based publications, broadcasting networks, and Web sites provide an outlet for research that is heavily biased. Consequently, it is always worth spending a little time evaluating **credibility**—the quality, authority, and reliability—of each source you use. One simple way to approach this is to look at the author of the material and evaluate his or her credentials. This means that you should note if the author is a medical doctor, Ph.D., attorney, CPA, or other licensed professional and whether he or she is affiliated with a reputable organization or institution. For example, if you are seeking statistics on the health effects of cigarette smoke, an article written by an M.D. affiliated with the American Lung Association would be more credible than an editorial written by your classmate.

Up-to-Date Sources

In most cases, you'll want to use the most recent information available to keep your speech timely and relevant. Isaiah, for example, is speaking to a group of potential clients about his company's graphic design services. If, during his speech, he makes reference to testimonials from satisfied clients in 2008 and earlier, the audience may wonder if the company has gone downhill since then. For this reason, always determine when your source was written or last updated; sources without dates may indicate that the information is not as timely or relevant as it could be.

Accurate Sources

When compiling support for your speech, it is important to find accurate sources—sources that are true, correct, and exact. A speaker who presents inaccurate information may very well lose the respect and attention of the audience. There are several ways to help ensure that you are studying accurate sources. Considering the credibility of the source and whether it is up-to-date, as just mentioned, is a start. In addition, accurate sources are "exact" sources, meaning that they offer detailed and precise information. A source that notes that more than 33,000 people died as a result of automobile accidents in the United States last year is less accurate than a source that notes that 33,808 people died in such accidents. The more precise your sources, the more credibility you will gain with your audience.

Relevant Sources

Audiences are impressed with speakers who support their speeches with information that is relevant to the topic. If you are speaking to persuade an audience to donate time and money to the American Cancer Society, you might cite statistics, testimonials from doctors, or personal anecdotes from cancer survivors—but you probably would not need to talk about the biological process of cancer growth in the human body. Although such information may be accurate and interesting, it is not necessarily relevant to your topic or the purpose of your speech.

One way of demonstrating the relevance of your supporting material is through its *timeliness,* its connection to its time and the subject under discussion. Timely information is not the same as new or up-to-date information: in fact, examples, research, and studies that are quite old can be timely if recent events have rendered them relevant. For example, if Lea decides to inform her audience about high gas prices in 2011, she might use examples and statistics from the oil crisis of 1973 in her speech because the 2011 situation makes discussions of historical oil shortages and price hikes relevant. Such a discussion, however, would have been less interesting and relevant to audiences in 2000, when gas prices were relatively low.

Compelling Sources

Support material that is strong, influential, interesting, and believable is considered to be *compelling* information. Information that is convincing and persuasive helps your audience understand, process, and retain your message. A speaker might note that 65 percent of adults were sending and receiving texts in September 2009 and that 72 percent were texting in May 2010. However, adults do not send nearly the same number of texts per day as teenagers (twelve- to seventeen-year-olds), who send and receive, on average, five times more texts per day than adults (Lenhart, 2010). Now those are some compelling statistics!

To be compelling, your supporting material should also be *vivid.* Vivid material is clear and vibrant, never vague. For example, in a speech about the 2004 cicada invasion of the Washington, D.C., area, Ana might reference a source describing these bugs as large insects, about one and a half inches long, with red eyes, black bodies, and fragile wings; she might also use a direct

The sources you cite in your speech are part of your *self-presentation* to your audience (Chapter 2). If your sources are outdated or from your cousin's blog, you will present a self that says, "I am unprepared and I didn't research my topic thoroughly." Conversely, if you offer statistics, facts, and stories from a variety of current, reliable, and compelling sources, you present yourself as trustworthy, prepared, and competent—and your audience is more likely to consider what you're saying.

quotation from a D.C. resident who notes that "there were so many cicadas that the ground, trees, and streets looked like they were covered by an oil slick." Such vivid (and gross) descriptions of information interest listeners. Look for clear, concrete supporting details that encourage the audience to form visual representations of the object or event you are describing.

Reliable Sources

A reliable source will show a trail of research by supplying details about where the information came from. A reputable publication will supply a thorough list of references, either as endnotes or footnotes. Examining this list—and perhaps even investigating a few of the sources—will help you determine the validity of the material. Similarly, in news writing, source information is integrated into the text. A newspaper or magazine article, for example, will credit information to named sources ("Baseball Commissioner Bud Selig said . . .") or credentialed but unnamed sources ("One high-ranking State Department official said, on condition of anonymity . . .").

The Internet poses special problems when it comes to reliability due to the ease with which material can be posted online. Check for balanced, impartial information that is not biased, and note the background or credentials of the authors. If references are listed, verify them to confirm their authenticity. Web sites can be quickly assessed for reliability by looking at the domain, or the suffix of the Web site address. Credible Web sites often end with *.edu* (educational

what about you?

Assessing Your Sources

After you have gathered a variety of sources, critically evaluate the material and determine which sources you should use in your final speech. Here is a checklist of questions to ask yourself regarding your supporting material:

_____ 1. Are my sources credible?

_____ 2. Are my sources up to date?

_____ 3. Are my sources accurate?

_____ 4. Are my sources relevant?

_____ 5. Are my sources compelling?

_____ 6. Are my sources reliable?

As noted throughout the chapter, if you cannot answer "yes" to these questions, then you will likely benefit from additional research time. The more credible, up to date, accurate, relevant, compelling, and reliable your sources, the more credible and trustworthy you will be as a speaker—and the better you will be able to inform or persuade your audience.

institution), *.mil* (military site), or *.gov* (government). Most people are familiar with *.com* (commercial business). Be aware of addresses that contain a tilde (~) because this usually indicates a personal Web page that may not necessarily contain dependable information.

Ethical Speaking: Taking Responsibility for Your Speech

As a responsible public speaker, you must let ethics guide every phase of planning and researching your speech. But what does it mean to be an ethical speaker? The short answer is that it means being responsible: responsible for ensuring that proper credit is given to other people's ideas, data, and research that you have incorporated into your presentation, as well as being responsible for what you say (and how you say it) to your audience. Let's review, starting with what happens when you fail to cite your sources properly: plagiarism.

Recognizing Plagiarism

Plagiarism is the crime of presenting someone else's words, ideas, or intellectual property as your own, intentionally or unintentionally. It is a growing problem and is not limited to the written word—or to students (Park, 2003). In March 2011, German Defense Minster Karl-Theodor zu Guttenberg resigned after it was revealed that he had plagiarized large portions of his doctoral thesis (McGroarty, 2011). Most universities and colleges have clear definitions of plagiarism and enforce strict penalties regarding the issue. In fact, we wouldn't be surprised if your professor included information about your school's plagiarism policy in your syllabus. If so, *read this document carefully*. The syllabus is like your contract with your professor; by enrolling in the course, you have agreed to follow it.

Despite the problems associated with plagiarism, many students, writers, and speakers remain unsure of how, when, or why they must credit their sources. In fact, many people are shocked to find that they can be guilty of plagiarism with a seemingly unimportant error, like simply failing to include quotation marks or mistakenly deleting one little footnote when completing a paper or speech. To avoid making the same mistake, keep careful track of where all your material comes from and document it properly. In Chapter 13, we will explain how to document your sources in your speech; for now, we will focus on the important role of taking accurate and thorough notes during the research phase.

Taking Accurate Notes

The noted historian Doris Kearns Goodwin was accused of using passages from three other books in her own work without proper attribution. After settling with the wronged authors and making corrections to her book, Kearns explained that the misrepresentation had been the result of a crucial error she had made during the note-taking phase. "Though my footnotes repeatedly cited [another author's] work, I failed to provide quotation marks for phrases that I had taken verbatim, having assumed that these phrases, drawn from my notes, were my words, not hers" (Goodwin, 2002, para. 3).

> **AND YOU?**
>
> How do you feel about the fact that even unintentionally using someone else's words, ideas, or intellectual property is still plagiarism? Does it seem unfair that you might suffer severe consequences (such as being expelled) even if you do something without intent? Why or why not?

As this example shows, keeping track of all your outside material and its sources can be one of the most challenging aspects of conducting research. That's why taking accurate notes is so critical. To keep yourself organized, consider using note cards to keep track of references separately. Or place all of your references into an electronic document, such as a word processing file or a note-taking application on your smart phone or computer. Regardless of the format you choose, each card or entry should contain the quote or material you want to use, along with pertinent information, such as author name, publication information (title, volume, publisher, location, date), and relevant page numbers from the source. In addition, each card or entry should note whether the material is copied *verbatim* (word for word) or *paraphrased* (put into your own words). When your research is complete (or nearly complete), you'll be able to shuffle these individual cards or entries around as you develop your speech without losing track of their sources. Two sample note cards are shown in Figure 12.3.

FIGURE 12.3

SAMPLE NOTE CARDS

INTELLECTUAL THEFT/Internet Piracy

SOURCE: Scott Turow, Paul Aiken, and James Shapiro: "Would the Bard Have Survived the Web?" Op-Ed, in *The New York Times*, February 15, 2011, p. A29. Verbatim:

"The rise of the Internet has led to a view among many users and Web companies that copyright is a relic, suited only to the needs of out-of-step corporate behemoths. Just consider the dedicated 'file-sharers'—actually, traffickers in stolen music, movies, and, increasingly, books—who transmit and receive copyrighted material without the slightest guilt." (p. A29)

INTELLECTUAL THEFT/Internet Piracy

SOURCE: John P. Mello, Jr., "Avatar Tops Most Pirated List for 2010." *PCWorld*, December 22, 2010, retrieved from http:// www.pcworld.com/ article/214676/avatar_tops_most_pirated_list_for_2010.html. Paraphrased:

Avatar is the most pirated movie of the year, with more than 16.5 million illegal downloads through BitTorrent alone. Runners-up were *Kick Ass* with 11.4 million illegal downloads and *Inception* with 9.7 million.

You'll also need to keep a **running bibliography**—a list of resources you've consulted. There are various styles of organizing these resources (including styles dictated by the Modern Language Association, American Psychological Association, and so on), so make sure to ask your instructor what his or her preference is if you're required to hand this document in. Regardless, all styles generally require you to list the following information:

▶ The complete name of each author, or origin of the source if no author is named ("National Science Foundation Web site," or "*New York Times* editorial")

▶ The title and subtitle of the source (article, book chapter, Web page) and of the larger work in which it appears (magazine, newspaper, journal, book, Web site)

▶ The publication date of the source; for Web sources, date of publication and date of access; for journals, volume and issue numbers

▶ For books, publisher and city of publication; for Web resources, the complete URL

▶ Page numbers for the material used and for the entire work being cited

We present an example of a running bibliography in APA style in Figure 12.4.

References

Boutin, P. (2010, December). The age of music piracy is officially over. *Wired.* Retrieved from http://www.wired.com/magazine/2010/11/st_essay_nofreebird/

Johns, A. (2010). *Piracy: The intellectual property wars from Gutenberg to Gates.* Chicago: University of Chicago Press.

Mellow, J. P., Jr. (2010, December 22). *Avatar* tops most pirated list for 2010. *PCWorld.* Retrieved from http://www.pcworld.com/article/214676/avatar_tops_most_pirated_list_for_2010.html

Turow, S., Aiken, P., & Shapiro, J. (2011, February 15). Would the Bard have survived the Web? [Op-ed]. *The New York Times.* Retrieved from http://www.nytimes.com/2011/02/15/opinion/15turow.html

U.S. Department of Justice, Federal Bureau of Investigation. (n.d.). Risks of peer-to-peer systems. Retrieved from http://www.fbi.gov/scams-safety/peertopeer

FIGURE 12.4

SAMPLE RUNNING BIBLIOGRAPHY IN APA STYLE

EVALUATINGCOMMUNICATIONETHICS

Plagiarism: Intentional or Unintentional?

You and Tivya are good friends, and you have been studying together for your speech communication course. You are both working on informative speeches about popular culture during specific periods in history. You've been doing quite a bit of research on popular sitcoms from the 1970s, while Tivya has been researching children's programming from the 1990s. Tivya typically struggles with introductions and conclusions when preparing speeches, but she tells you that she's pretty sure she has a perfect opener for this one.

When Tivya gives her speech, the class enjoys it because your friend has engaged their interest by asking them to remember watching certain cartoons or playing with certain toys that were popular in the 1990s. She even brings in a few toys from her own childhood as props! But you notice that the opener—indeed, several areas of the speech—seems just a little too similar to an e-mail that had gone around earlier that year titled "Remember the 90s." You're a bit startled. Is it possible that Tivya has intentionally copied the e-mail and presented it as her own original work? Or might she have read the e-mail long ago and internalized it to the point that she thinks it's her own material?

In some respects, all work is derivative: it carries the influence of all the things we've read, seen, and heard throughout our lives. But even though it's a given that any piece of writing will have been influenced by the work of others, it is the writer's responsibility to ensure that the work one produces is truly one's own. Borrowing words from another source, even unintentionally, is plagiarism. In 2006, a young novelist was accused of doing just that. Kaavya Viswanathan, a sophomore at Harvard University, had just published her first book, *How Opal Mehta Got Kissed, Got Wild, and Got a Life,* when reporters from the *Harvard Crimson* accused her of having taken numerous passages from another writer's work. Viswanathan's novel was pulled from bookstores and revised for a second printing. The author issued an apology, claiming that as a high school student, she had read both *Sloppy Firsts* and *Second Helpings,* the two Meghan McCafferty novels from which she was accused of stealing. "While the central stories of my book and hers are completely different, I wasn't aware of how much I may have internalized Ms. McCafferty's words," Viswanathan said in a statement. "I am a huge fan of her work and can honestly say that any phrasing similarities between her work and mine were completely unintentional and unconscious" (Memmot, 2006).

Intentional or not, plagiarism is extremely problematic. It's a common enough mistake among writers and speakers, but what of your friend Tivya? Intentionally or unintentionally, she had plagiarized that e-mail quite extensively. Her grade, her status in school, and her reputation are at stake. What should you do?

THINK ABOUT THIS

1 How is Tivya's mistake plagiarism? How about Kaavya Viswanathan's? How are these cases similar, and how are they different? In either case, does it matter if the plagiarism is intentional or unintentional?

2 Was Viswanathan's apology statement appropriate? What kinds of steps could Tivya take to address her mistake? Should she tell her instructor? Should you?

3 Imagine that as the instructor or publisher, it is your responsibility to respond to an instance of plagiarism. How would you handle the situation?

Speaking Ethically and Responsibly

Your responsibility as a speaker goes beyond simply giving credit to others' work; you need to take responsibility for what *you* say.[1] If you use inflammatory, hurtful, or hateful language—even if it is language that is quoted from another source—it is you who will bear the brunt of the audience's reactions. Providing a footnote or endnote can reinforce your points, but it cannot excuse you from taking responsibility for them.

The First Amendment to the U.S. Constitution guarantees every citizen the right to free speech, but not all speech is ethical. As a public speaker, you are responsible for providing your audience members with all of the necessary information for them to make accurate, appropriate decisions about you and your message. The speeches by Chinese leader Deng Xiaoping, who tried to intimidate Chinese citizens into revealing the whereabouts of leaders of the unsuccessful 1989 student uprising in Tiananmen Square in Beijing, were unethical and coercive. In addition, it's important to recognize that the right to free speech in this country is not without limits. As Supreme Justice Oliver Wendell Holmes wrote in 1919, the Constitution "would not protect a man falsely shouting fire in a theater and causing a panic" (*Schenck v. United States,* 1919). Speech that endangers people—for example, speech that incites riots, advocates the unlawful overthrowing of the government, or causes unnecessary panic—would not only be ethically questionable but might be illegal as well (*Gitlow v. New York,* 1925; *Schenck v. United States,* 1919).

Although everyone has different standards for ethical communication, the qualities of dignity and integrity are universally seen as core to the idea of ethics. *Dignity* is feeling worthy, honored, or respected as a person; *integrity* is incorruptibility—the ability to avoid compromise for the sake of personal gain (Gudykunst, Ting-Toomey, Sudweeks, & Stewart, 1995). Basic rules for ethical speaking require that we adhere to four principles: we should strive to be trustworthy, respectful, responsible, and fair in our speeches (Day, 1997).

▶ *Trustworthiness* refers to being honest with your audience about the goal of your message and providing accurate information.

▶ By treating people right, you are showing *respect.* In public speaking, respect is shown by focusing on issues rather than on personalities, allowing the audience the power of choice and avoiding excluding the audience in discussions.

▶ As a *responsible* public speaker, it is your job to consider the topic and purpose of the speech, evidence and reasoning of the arguments, accuracy of your message, and honest use of emotional appeals.

▶ Ethical public speakers must be *fair* by presenting alternative and opposing views to the audience. A fair speaker will not deny the audience the right to make informed decisions.

[1]Much of this discussion was inspired by the work of Michael Josephson, founder and president of the Joseph and Edna Josephson Institute of Ethics in Marina del Rey, California.

AND YOU? Consider your own personal opinions about ethical speaking. Would you add anything to the four principles noted here? If so, what characteristics would you cite?

● **WHILE THE** First Amendment allows anyone to step up on a soapbox and say whatever he or she wants to say, it's still important to refrain from unethical or derogatory speech.

BACK TO Steve Jobs

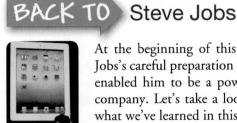

At the beginning of this chapter, we talked about how Steve Jobs's careful preparation and intimate knowledge of his projects enabled him to be a powerful public speaker on behalf of his company. Let's take a look at his presentation skills in light of what we've learned in this chapter.

▶ Clearly, Steve Jobs enjoyed technology. But he also knew the importance of preparation and practice. If he relied entirely on presentation aids, he would have fallen flat during inevitable technical glitches. While technology played a role in his presentations, it was his research and preparation that truly shined.

▶ Jobs also knew his audience. Apple fans are a unique and loyal breed of consumer—when he took the stage, he was essentially preaching to the choir. The audience was always eager to hear what he had to say and see what he had to show. He didn't bother talking about competing products, because he knew the crowd was more interested in hearing about Apple products.

▶ Prior exposure played a role in the way Jobs presented his products. The original iPod, launched in 2001 along with the iTunes Store, was a revolutionary device, and Jobs's presentation was full of surprises for his audience. When introducing later iterations and new generations of the device, Jobs focused only on new features and options.

▶ The company also limits prior exposure by maintaining a high level of secrecy about products in development. When Jobs introduced a *new* product, there was little chance that the crowd had already heard anything more than rumors about it beforehand, which affected how Jobs presented information to the audience.

THINGS TO TRY Activities

1. Think back to a memorable speech you've witnessed, either in person or through the media. What kind of speech was it? Was the speaker trying to inform, persuade, or celebrate? Was he or she successful in that endeavor? Did the speech change the way you felt?

2. Tune in to a few news pundits—for example, Bill O'Reilly, Rachel Maddow, Randi Rhodes, or Rush Limbaugh—on the radio or on television. Listen carefully to what they say, and consider how they back up their statements. Do they provide source material as they speak? Can you link to their sources from their online blogs? How does the way they back up their points or fail to back them up influence your perceptions of what they say?

3. Take a look at your school's policy on plagiarism. Does your school clearly define what acts constitute plagiarism? How harsh are the punishments? Who is responsible for reporting plagiarism? How is the policy enforced?

4. The next time you read something—a magazine article, a political blog, a work of nonfiction, a chapter in a textbook—take time to think about the research presented in it. What kinds of research did the authors do? How do they back up their statements? What kinds of research materials do they include?

Now that you have finished reading this chapter, you can

Describe the power of **public speaking** and how preparation eases natural nervousness. Identify the purpose of your speech:

▸ *Informative speeches* aim to increase the audience's understanding and knowledge of a topic (p. 342).

▸ *Persuasive speeches* are intended to influence the beliefs, attitudes, and behaviors of your audience (p. 343).

▸ *Special-occasion speeches* are given at common events (like weddings and funerals), and many of us will deliver them at some point in time (p. 345).

Conduct **audience analysis**—the process of getting to know your audience:

▸ It is important to understand and appreciate your audience's expectations for the speech as well as key situational factors (pp. 346–347).

▸ Knowing **demographics**, the quantifiable characteristics of your audience, will help you identify topics that the audience would be interested in learning about (p. 347).

▸ You will want to anticipate your audience's response by considering their motivation, seeking common ground (**homogeny**), determining prior exposure, and considering disposition (pp. 350–351).

▸ You can learn about your audience by observing people, getting to know people, conducting interviews and using surveys, and using the Web (pp. 351–352).

Choose an appropriate topic and develop it:

▸ Speak about something that inspires you (p. 352).

▸ Use **brainstorming** to amass information, think creatively, and consider problems and solutions related to your topic (p. 352).

▸ Hone your topic by **clustering**, creating a web of thoughts and ideas about your topic on paper (p. 353).

▸ A **specific purpose statement** expresses the topic and the general speech purpose in action form and in terms of the specific objectives you hope to achieve with your presentation (pp. 354–355).

▸ Narrow your topic and write a **thesis statement**, a summary of your central idea (p. 355).

Support and enliven your speech with effective research:

▸ Include **expert testimony**, the opinion of an authority, or **lay testimony**, opinion based on personal experience (pp. 356–357).

▸ **Scientific research findings** carry weight in topics on medicine, health, media, and the environment; **statistics**, information in numerical form, can clarify your presentation (p. 357).

▸ **Anecdotes**, relevant personal stories, bring the human experience to the speech (p. 357).

▸ **Surveys** will add the point of view of a larger range of people (p. 358).

▸ Use databases to find material, such as **directories**, **library gateways**, **search engines**, and **metasearch engines** (pp. 359–360).

Cull from among your sources the material that will be most convincing:

▸ Take time to evaluate the **credibility**—the quality, authority, and reliability—of each source you use (p. 360).

▸ Up-to-date information convinces the audience of its timeliness (pp. 360–361).

▸ Citing accurate and exact sources gains audience respect (p. 361).

▸ Relevant information supports the core topic (p. 361).

▸ Compelling information is influential and interesting (p. 361).

▸ Reliable sources provide reputable information (pp. 362–363).

Give proper credit to sources and take responsibility for your speech:

▸ Avoid **plagiarism**, presenting someone else's intellectual property as your own (p. 363).

▸ Keep accurate track of all your references to avoid unintentional errors (p. 363).

▸ Keeping a **running bibliography**, the list of resources you've consulted, will free you from having to write the same information over and over (p. 365).

▸ Honor the basic rules for ethical speaking (p. 367).

Although the President of the United States is the sole figure to deliver the State of the Union address, he works with a whole team of writers and advisors behind the scenes to put the final speech together.

Organizing, Writing, and Outlining Presentations

The Constitution of the United States of America makes a simple demand of the president. "He shall from time to time give to the Congress Information of the State of the Union, and recommend to their Consideration such Measures as he shall judge necessary and expedient" (art. 2, sec. 3).

For much of our nation's history, the State of the Union address was a lengthy letter to Congress read to members of the Senate and House by a congressional clerk. But over time it has evolved into an elaborate and highly politicized annual affair that allows the president to present major ideas and issues directly to the public: the Monroe Doctrine (James Monroe, 1823), the Four Freedoms (Franklin D. Roosevelt, 1941), and the War on Terror (George W. Bush, 2002) were all detailed for the American people during State of the Union addresses (Longley, 2007).

And so each January, White House speechwriters face the daunting task of addressing both Congress and the nation with a speech that outlines what is going on in foreign and domestic policy in a way that flatters the president and garners support for his agenda for the following year. As if that weren't a sufficiently difficult task, speechwriters must also navigate a deluge of requests from lobbyists, political consultants, and everyday citizens eager to get their pet project, policy, or idea into the president's speech. "Everybody wants [a] piece of the action," lamented former White House speechwriter Chriss Winston in 2002. "The speechwriter's job is to keep [the speech] on broad themes so it doesn't sink of its own weight." Matthew Scully (2005), one of President George W. Bush's speechwriters, concurred: "The entire thing can easily turn into a tedious grab bag of policy proposals."

chapter
outcomes

After you have finished
reading this chapter,
you will be able to

- Organize and support
  your main points

- Choose an appropriate
  organizational pattern for
  your speech

- Move smoothly from
  point to point

- Choose appropriate and
  powerful language

- Develop a strong
  introduction, a crucial
  part of all speeches

- Conclude with the
  same strength as
  in the introduction

- Prepare an effective
  outline

Imagine that you are building a bridge, a skyscraper, or even a humble little house. You might start with a picture of it in your head, but before you can build it, you need to form a solid foundation and develop a framework that is structurally sound. Any architect will tell you that even the most exciting and lofty designs are useless without these two crucial components. Skimp on either one, and your structure will crack, shift, or collapse.

Building a speech follows a similar process. Whether you are writing a national address for the president of the United States or a three-minute presentation for a communication class, you will be unable to make your point if your speech is not structurally sound. As we discussed in Chapter 12, you begin with your idea and then build your foundation with research and a clear thesis statement. The next step is to develop your framework—the overall structure of your presentation. In this chapter, we'll focus on organizing all of your ideas and information into a clear and practical framework and integrating them into a well-written speech. Let's begin by considering the main points of your speech.

Organizing Your Speech Points

You've got your purpose, your research, and your thesis. But before you jump into the deep end of the pool and begin writing, it's best to organize your ideas—to set out the points you want to make, examples you plan to use to support them, and the basic order in which you want to present them. And you will want to do all of this *before* you write your introduction or conclusion. In this section, we'll focus on identifying your main points and developing your supporting points, in addition to considering useful ways to arrange those points and connect them in your speech.

Identifying Your Main Points

First and foremost, you must determine the **main points** of your speech, which are the central claims that support your specific speech purpose and your thesis statement (which you learned about in Chapter 12). That is, you need to identify and organize key ideas that will lead the audience members to accept or consider what you are asking them to do, believe, or consider.

Before you begin developing your main points, you may be wondering how many you will need in your speech. Unfortunately, there is no hard-and-fast answer because each speech is unique (for example, you'll probably have more main points in a forty-five-minute speech addressing the shareholders of a company than you will in a seven-minute persuasive speech for your speech class or a three-minute toast at a wedding). However, the general rule is that audiences have trouble remembering more than three or four main points. This will generally serve you well for the purposes of your human communication course, but always check with your instructor if you have questions.

With this in mind, let's consider how main points work in action. Let's say you're giving a persuasive speech advocating for listeners to vote in favor of removing unhealthy candy and soda vending machines from your local high school in order to combat obesity. What key points do you think will influence your listeners to vote this way? Perhaps they would be motivated to do so if they knew the scope of the problem:

Main Point 1: Obesity in children and adolescents is a growing, national health problem in the United States.

You'd likely further your argument by connecting the types of food and beverages in vending machines to the obesity problem:

Main Point 2: Vending machines typically offer food choices and beverages with low nutritional value in addition to excess fats and refined sugars.

Finally, they might want to hear about some success stories to motivate them to take action:

Main Point 3: Several major school districts successfully removed soda pop machines from their schools with positive benefits.

Note that each main point includes only one major idea. This prevents you from overwhelming your audience with too much information and makes it a whole lot easier for you to supply the examples, testimonies, statistics, and facts to back up each point. When in doubt about developing your main points, ask yourself "Does this point prove my thesis? Does it help me achieve my specific purpose?" If you can confidently answer yes, then you're on the right track.

Supporting Your Main Points

Each main point—as well as your speech as a whole—is fully fleshed out with the use of **subpoints** that provide support for the main points. Subpoints utilize your research to back up your main points in the same way that your main points back up your thesis statement and specific purpose; you can use a similar test to check their usefulness, asking yourself, "Does this bit of information back up my main point?" For example, two subpoints under our main point about obesity as a growing national health threat might be:

▶ The Centers for Disease Control and Prevention notes that 19.6 percent of children and 18.1 percent of adolescents in the United States are obese (Centers for Disease Control, 2010).

▶ According to the Office of the Surgeon General, Type 2 diabetes—which is linked with obesity—has increased dramatically in children and adolescents (U.S. Department of Health & Human Services, 2007).

Like main points, subpoints may—and often should—be backed up with more information, referred to as *sub-subpoints*.

CONNECT

When deciding which types of material to use to support your speech points, keep the cultural context in mind (Chapters 1 and 3). Cultural variables affect the type of research audience members respond to. For example, if your audience consists of concerned parents of teenagers, they will likely be responsive to statistics and facts about the long-term health effects of vending machine food.

● **THINK OF YOUR MAIN POINTS** and subpoints as Russian *matryoshka* dolls— each sub-subpoint should nest inside a subpoint, which should nest inside your main point.

FIGURE 13.1

HIERARCHY OF POINTS
Note how many sub-subpoints support a smaller number of subpoints. Each subpoint supports the main point. And the main point supports your thesis.

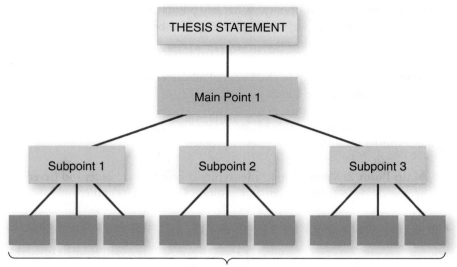

Well-chosen supporting points will naturally fall under your main point in a clear hierarchy of ideas that will form the basic outline of your speech. Each main point should be supported by a number of coordinating subpoints, each carrying equal weight, as well as sub-subpoints that carry less weight. The resulting structure reflects a pyramidlike hierarchy of ideas: a foundation of many sub-subpoints supports a structure of fewer but larger subpoints, which in turn support a few main points, which together support the thesis statement and ultimately your specific purpose. This structural hierarchy of points, depicted in Figure 13.1, ensures that you've presented a coherent and sturdy argument in support of your thesis and specific purpose. Later in the chapter, we'll show you how to use an outline to detail this hierarchy of points in a text format, but next we'll consider helpful ways to arrange your points.

Arranging Your Points

Think for a moment of a family photo album. If you were to put one together that covered your entire life, how would you arrange it? You could work chronologically, simply placing the photos in the order in which they were taken. You might expand on that chronological approach by trying to arrange the photos in a way that tells the story of your family, with photos of your parents before you were born and of family milestones like weddings and new babies. Alternatively, you might arrange it by topic, with separate sections for family events and school events; you might even have a separate section for each family member with sections or pages dedicated to each person's sporting events, birthday parties, proms, and graduations.

You have similar options when preparing a speech. During the process of sorting out your main points and subpoints, you may have taken the initial step of arranging your ideas in some sequence. Here are some common arrangements, or patterns, to consider.

AND YOU?
Organizing your main points and subpoints for a speech may seem overwhelming, but you've likely done this type of work before. Good, clear writing—whether an academic paper or an important letter—requires similar organization. Think of a particular piece of writing you were nervous about—a term paper or a private message to a potential romantic partner. What was the purpose of your writing? How did you go about organizing your main points?

Chronological Pattern

Often it makes sense to organize your points according to time: what happened first, second, and so on. A **chronological pattern** presents the main points of a message forward (or backward) in a systematic, time-related fashion. For example, you might use a chronological presentation when speaking about the development of Picasso's style over the course of his life or in describing the events leading up to the Cuban Missile Crisis. A chronological organization can be especially useful when analyzing a step-by-step process, such as a presentation on how to use a new computer program.

Topical Pattern

Also known as a *categorical pattern,* the **topical pattern** is based on organization into categories, such as persons, places, things, or processes. Thus you might use it to describe the various departments in an organization, the characteristics of a successful employment interview, or the reasons for giving a charitable contribution to a specific organization.

One key concern when selecting this approach is the sequencing of topics—which topic to offer first, second, and so on. Depending on the circumstances, the best approach is often ascending or descending order—that is, according to the relative importance, familiarity, or complexity of the topics. The **primacy-recency effect** can also offer some guidance in that it notes that audiences are most likely to remember points you raise at the very beginning, or at the very end, of a message. In other words, you might consider placing your strongest (or what you believe to be your most exciting, compelling, or interesting) point first or last so that your audience members keep it in mind long after you end your presentation.

● **DECIDING HOW** to organize your speech, like deciding how to arrange family photos, can be tricky because you have many options to consider: you can do it chronologically, topically, or even spatially.

Spatial Pattern

The geographical or **spatial pattern** arranges main points in terms of their physical proximity to or position in relation to each other (north to south, east to west, bottom to top, left to right, outside to inside, and so on). As an organizational pattern, it is most useful when describing objects, places, or scenes in terms of their component parts. Thus you might describe the physical layout of a media-enhanced classroom or the Mall in Washington, D.C., using a spatial pattern of organization.

Problem-Solution Pattern

If you're trying to call an audience to action to address a particular problem, the **problem-solution pattern** of organization can be especially effective. This pattern involves dramatizing an obstacle and then narrowing alternative remedies down to the one that you recommend. The message is organized to focus on three key points:

1. There is a problem that requires a change in attitude, belief, or behavior.

2. A number of possible solutions might solve this problem.

3. Your solution is the one that will provide the most effective and efficient remedy.

Topics that lend themselves to this pattern include business, social, economic, and political problems for which you can propose a workable solution. For example, you might use it when proposing a new course evaluation system for your college or suggesting a plan for reducing college loan debt.

Cause-Effect Pattern

With the **cause-effect pattern**, you attempt to organize the message around cause-to-effect or effect-to-cause relationships. That is, you might move from a discussion of the origins or causes of a phenomenon (for example, rising fuel costs) to the eventual results or effects (increases in the cost of airplane tickets). You can also work in reverse, starting with a description of present conditions and then examining apparent or possible causes. The choice of strategy is often

EVALUATINGCOMMUNICATIONETHICS

THINK ABOUT THIS

The Ethics of Using Research

Your condo association has asked you to give an informative presentation about the dangers of certain breeds of dogs as pets at the next association meeting. The board intends to use your speech as a springboard for passing a resolution to ban these animals from the community. Several residents have raised particular concerns about your elderly neighbor's large dog, a chow–German shepherd mix.

You research the issue carefully and find conflicting information. You find powerful examples in some widely publicized mauling cases, including the death of a San Francisco woman who was attacked by her neighbors' Presa Canarios outside of her apartment in January 2001 and the June 2005 case of a twelve-year-old boy killed by his family's own pet pit bulls. You have also read that some homeowners' insurance companies deny coverage to individuals who own certain dog breeds, such as Rottweilers, Dobermans, pit bulls, Presa Canarios, chows, and wolf hybrids because of risks associated with these breeds (Treaster, 2002). At the same time, however, a veterinarian friend reminds you that any individual dog, regardless of breed, is unlikely to pose a threat to the community. Indeed, some veterinarians warn that small, seemingly docile dog breeds can pose more of a threat to safety than large dogs (Treaster, 2002).

On a personal level, you would love to see these "dangerous" dog breeds banned from the complex—you were bitten by a Doberman when you were a child and have been terrified of most dogs ever since. But you also empathize with your neighbor who lives alone and got his dog after his home was burglarized. And you know that while his dog is very protective of the home, barking loudly whenever someone comes near the property, he's well trained and has never shown signs of being vicious.

You know that your job is to inform your listeners, not to persuade them toward one side or the other. But as you prepare to use your supporting material for your presentation, you wonder what sort of ethical obligations you face as you inform the condo association members.

❶ Consider what you've learned from your research. Is it more important to be honest and truthful with your audience, to honor the wishes of the condo association board who asked you to speak, or to prevent your neighbor from possibly losing his pet?

❷ Think about some of the potential ethical dangers of crossing the line between an informative and a persuasive speech in this case. Where might you be tempted to persuade your audience? How can you keep your speech strictly informative?

❸ Might there be some middle ground? Could you adjust the topic to focus on verifiable facts? For example, you could investigate whether banning dogs would lower the insurance premiums paid by the association as well as premiums on individual homeowners' insurance policies. Would this be ethical?

based on which element—cause or effect—is more familiar to the intended audience: if you're talking about fuel prices, for example, it might be best to start with the cost of gasoline—a very familiar expense—and work backward from there. The cause-effect pattern of organization is especially useful when your purpose is to get your audience to agree with or understand your point, rather than to call people to action.

Narrative Pattern

Speakers often tie their points together in a way that presents a vivid story, complete with characters, settings, plot, and imagery. This is called a **narrative pattern**. However, most speeches built largely on a story (or a series of stories) are likely to incorporate elements of other organizational arrangements. For example, you might present a story in a cause-effect design, in which you first reveal why something happened (such as a small aircraft crash) and then describe the events that led up to the accident (the causes).

Motivated Sequence Pattern

The **motivated sequence pattern**, created more than seventy years ago by the noted public speaking scholar Alan Monroe, is a five-step plan for organizing a speech that can be useful in a variety of contexts. Based on the psychological elements of advertising, the motivated sequence pattern includes five phases, which may be modified to suit the desired outcome of your speech:

1. *Attention:* the speaker gains the interest of the audience.
2. *Need:* the speaker addresses an unmet need apparent to the audience.
3. *Satisfaction:* the speaker proposes a solution that satisfies the need.
4. *Visualization:* the speaker illustrates how the solution meets the need.
5. *Action:* the speaker demonstrates how the solution may be implemented.

Monroe argued that when constructed effectively, speeches incorporating the five-step plan motivate listeners. Presentations that lend themselves to the motivated sequence include persuasive presentations, inspirational speeches, graduation addresses, and motivational talks. For a more detailed discussion and examples of Monroe's Motivated Sequence, please see pp. 492–493 in Chapter 16.

Connecting Your Points

When you're pulling together, supporting, and arranging your points, you may find yourself falling into what we like to call the "grocery list trap." Essentially, this is where your speech begins to seem like a very thorough list of good, but seemingly unrelated, ideas. You may recall from the chapter-opening vignette that White House speechwriters struggle with this very issue each year when preparing

● **WHEN ORGANIZING** your speech in a narrative pattern, put your feet in a storyboard artist's shoes. Visualize your outline as a storyboard, and think of your speech points as scenes.

the president's State of the Union Address. So, how do you move smoothly from one point to another? The key lies in your use of transitions, signposts, and internal previews and summaries.

Transitions

Transitions are sentences that connect different points, thoughts, and details in a way that allows them to flow naturally from one to the next. Clear transitions cue the audience in on where you're headed with the speech and how your ideas and supporting material are connected. They also alert your audience that you will be making a point. Consider the following examples of transitions:

COMMUNICATIONACROSSCULTURES

Evidence, Popular Culture, and the "*CSI* Effect"

"We've got a match." If you watch *CSI* or any of its several spin-offs, you know that those words are usually the clincher in a comparison of evidence from the murder scene to something belonging to a suspect—be it DNA, carpet fibers, or bullets. The popular procedural drama is based on the premise that stalwart and brilliant teams of forensic scientists can and will work tirelessly to find and present evidence that indisputably solves crimes.

In fact, most of the evidence presented by the show's crime scene investigators is far from indisputable, and the show's portrayal of forensic science is sometimes closer to science fiction than science fact. Fiber evidence, for example, can be examined for possible connections, but no scientist would be able to testify under oath that a specific fiber came from a specific vehicle. As Lisa Faber, supervisor of New York City's police crime lab, notes, "The terminology is very important. On TV, they always like to say words like 'match,' but we say 'similar,' or 'could have come from' or 'is associated with'" (quoted in Toobin, 2007, para. 5). Only DNA evidence really comes close to what most scientists would consider mathematical certainty (Toobin, 2007). The show misleads juries about the technology available to prosecutors—much of the tech shown is beyond the reach of most departments or simply does not exist—as well as the time frame for obtaining results and the human resources that are devoted to crime scene investigation (Toobin, 2007).

Some legal scholars worry that the popularity of shows like *CSI* may bias juries in several ways. There is a possibility that jurors who follow the shows believe they have developed some level of expertise about forensic evidence, or at the very least some expectation that the kinds of evidence presented on *CSI* will be available for every case, a theory that has become known as the "*CSI* effect." While there is no evidence that watching such programs has any impact on trial outcomes, there are some indications that watching the show may influence the way jurors perceive the quality of police work in investigations as well as their behavior during deliberations (Thomas, 2006).

THINK ABOUT THIS

1 Do you watch shows like *CSI*, *Bones*, and *Cold Case*? How realistic do you think they are? Does popular culture have an impact on how individuals perceive evidence? Would it affect you if you were on a jury?

2 If you were on a jury in a criminal trial, what would your expectations for evidence be? Would you be willing to convict someone based on a fiber sample, even if the expert witness described it as "similar" rather than "a match"?

3 Do you think that shows like *CSI* have an ethical responsibility to depict forensic science more realistically? Or is it the audience's responsibility to separate entertainment from reality?

▶ "I've just described some of the amazing activities you can enjoy in our National Parks, so let me tell you about two parks that you can visit within a three-hour drive of our university."

▶ "In addition to the environmental benefits of reducing your energy consumption, there are some fantastic financial benefits that you can enjoy."

Notice how the transitions in both examples also serve to alert your audience that you will be making a point that you want them to remember. Transitions are, therefore, essential to making your points clear and easy to follow.

Signposts

Effective speakers make regular use of **signposts**, key words or phrases within sentences that signify transitions between points. Think of signposts as links or pivot points at which you either connect one point to another ("similarly," "next," "once again,") or move from one point to a related but perhaps opposing or alternative point ("however," "on the other hand"). Consider the following examples:

▶ "*Another way* you can help to fight puppy mills is to boycott pet stores that sell animals from disreputable sources."

▶ "*The third problem* with our current emergency room system is not surprising: there simply isn't enough money to fund our ERs."

Table 13.1 on page 380 details various examples of signposts and considers how they function effectively to achieve a specific purpose.

Internal Previews and Internal Summaries

Like a good map that shows travelers points along the way to their destination, **internal previews** prime the audience for the content immediately ahead. They often work best in conjunction with **internal summaries**, which allow the speaker to crystallize the points made in one section of a speech before moving to the next section. For example:

▶ "So far, I have presented two reasons why you should enroll your puppy in obedience school. First, it benefits your dog. Second, it benefits your family. Now I will address my third point: that taking your dog to obedience school benefits your neighborhood."

▶ "Now that I have explained what asthma is and the two main types of asthma, allergic and nonallergic, I will discuss what you can do to avoid an asthma attack."

By first summarizing and then previewing, the speaker has created a useful transition that gracefully moves the speech forward while offering audiences an opportunity to synthesize the information already received.

● **DIRECT THE AUDIENCE** from one point in your speech to the next with signpost words or phrases, such as "similarly" or "on the other hand. . . ."

TABLE 13.1
USEFUL SIGNPOSTS

Function	Example
To show comparison	Similarly In the same way In comparison
To contrast ideas, facts, or data	On the other hand Alternatively In spite of
To illustrate cause and effect	It follows, then, that Consequently Therefore Thus
To indicate explanation	For example In other words To clarify
To introduce additional examples	Another way in which Just as Likewise In a similar fashion
To emphasize significance	It's important to remember that Above all Bear in mind
To indicate sequence of time or events	First, Second, Third Finally First and foremost Once Now, Then Until now Before, After Earlier, Later Primarily
To summarize	As we've seen Altogether Finally In conclusion

Source: O'Hair, Stewart, & Rubenstein (2007), p. 181. Adapted with permission.

Using Language That Works

Now you know quite a bit about the main points of your speech—you know how to identify them and support them, you have ideas on arranging them, and you know how to move between them. But how will you describe and explain the points themselves? That's the focus of this section: making competent language choices that bring your ideas to life right before your audience's eyes. The words that you choose for your speech are clearly powerful, so it's important to think about them *now,* while you're preparing and writing your speech, so that you can eventually incorporate them into your actual presentation.

Respect Your Audience

As noted earlier, communication involves not only what we say but also how others perceive what we say. Most audiences are composed of both men and women from many different cultures, races, religious backgrounds, lifestyles, and educational levels. Therefore, it is important to use unbiased and appropriate language that makes the entire audience feel included and respected.

Keep It Simple

Albert Einstein once advised, "Make everything as simple as possible, but no simpler." The physicist's wisdom applies to language as well. Speakers and writers who use unfamiliar or inappropriate language are not as effective as those who speak directly and in terms that their audience can readily understand and interpret. This is not to say that you should "dumb down" your points, only that you need to make your points in a language that is clear, simple, and unambiguous so that your audience can follow what you are saying. In addition, there is no speaker quite as dreaded as the long-winded speaker. (Admit it—you've been to a wedding or sports award banquet where the best man or honoree droned on seemingly forever. We've all been there!) A speaker who repeats the same points or uses six examples when one would suffice will quickly lose audience interest. If you keep your speech short and to the point, you'll have a better chance of reaching your audience with your intended message.

Use Vivid Language

Language paints a picture for an audience. The more vivid your terms, the more the audience members can use their imaginations and their senses. For example, if you say you have a car, your listeners get a vague impression of a forgettable fact. If you tell them that your father drove a faded orange 1972 Volkswagen Beetle with a dent in the left fender and a broken taillight, you'll give them a very clear and memorable picture of this vehicle. Over our years of teaching human communication, we've had many students become frustrated with us about our insistence on "painting a picture with words"; too many times we've heard, "But I have these great eye-catching slides and props!" We'll elaborate more on the use of presentation aids in the next chapter, but for now, remember that your words count—often even more than your PowerPoint slides.

Incorporate Repetition, Allusion, and Comparisons

In 1851, American abolitionist and women's rights activist Sojourner Truth delivered an effective and memorable speech at the Women's Convention in Akron, Ohio. The speech, now known as "Ain't I a Woman?" is effective not only because of its powerful message about the evils of slavery and the mistreatment of women, but also because Truth's passionate use of language helped make a lasting impression on her listeners. Consider, for example, her use of repetition, allusion, and comparisons. (See Sample Speech 13.1.)

CONNECT

Part of using language your audience understands involves a careful consideration of *jargon*—technical language specific to a particular industry, organization, or group (see Chapter 4). Jargon might be useful among a very homogenous group, but it can alienate audience members in other settings. A doctor might use medical jargon when addressing colleagues but needs to use everyday terms when addressing other groups.

● **AUDIENCE MEMBERS** wouldn't conjure this clear and memorable picture in their minds unless it was painted with vivid language by the speaker.

● **SOJOURNER TRUTH'S** "Aint I a Woman?" speech uses vivid and effective language to presuade.

I Sell the Shadow to Support the Substance.
SOJOURNER TRUTH.

● Notice how Truth encourages the audience to extend this existing belief about women to her as she too is a woman.

● Truth invokes religious stories that are familiar to the audience members in her effort to persuade them.

SAMPLE SPEECH 13.1

Ain't I a Woman?

SOJOURNER TRUTH

Well, children, where there is so much racket there must be something out of kilter. I think that 'twixt the negroes of the South and the women at the North, all talking about rights, the white men will be in a fix pretty soon. But what's all this here talking about?

That man over there says the women need to be helped into carriages, and lifted over ditches, and to have the best place everywhere. Nobody ever helps me into carriages, or over mud-puddles, or gives me any best place! And ain't I a woman? Look at me! Look at my arm! I have ploughed and planted, and gathered into barns, and no man could head me! And ain't I a woman? I could work as much and eat as much as a man—when I could get it—and bear the lash as well! And ain't I a woman? I have borne thirteen children, and seen most all sold off to slavery, and when I cried out with my mother's grief, none but Jesus heard me! And ain't I a woman? ●

Then they talk about this thing in the head; what's this they call it? [member of the audience whispers "intellect"] That's it, honey. What's that got to do with women's rights or negroes' rights? If my cup won't hold but a pint, and yours holds a quart, wouldn't you be mean not to let me have my little half measure full?

Then that little man in black there, he says women can't have as much rights as men, 'cause Christ wasn't a woman! Where did your Christ come from? Where did your Christ come from? From God and a woman! Man had nothing to do with Him.

If the first woman God ever made was strong enough to turn the world upside down all alone, these women together ought to be able to turn it back, and get it right side up again. And now they is asking to do it, the men better let them. ●

Obliged to you for hearing me, and now old Sojourner ain't got nothing more to say.

Source: From Sojourner Truth, "Ain't I a Woman?" speech delivered at the Women's Convention in Akron, Ohio, May 1851. Retrieved from http://www.feminist.com/resources/artspeech/genwom/sojour.htm

Repetition

Repetition—saying certain terms, phrases, or even entire sentences more than once—can help increase the likelihood that the audience will remember what matters most in your speech. In Truth's speech, she repeats "Ain't I a woman?" several times. This repetition highlights each of the injustices she feels and influences audience members to consider Truth deserving of the rights and privileges withheld from her.

Allusion

An *allusion* is making vague or indirect reference to people, historical events, or concepts to give deeper meaning to the message. Allusions can be useful in evoking emotions or responses without making direct statements. They can also ground your speech, providing context that goes beyond what you are saying. In Truth's "Ain't I a Woman" speech, for example, she uses allusion with the words "If the first woman God ever made was strong enough to turn the world upside down all alone, these women together ought to be able to turn it back, and get it right side up again." She is alluding to the biblical figure Eve, who ate the forbidden fruit from the tree of the knowledge of good and evil, and consequently upset the harmonious balance between God and humankind. Yet Truth does not take time to explain this story. She knows that her audience will be familiar with her reference, so she uses allusion to add power and emotion to her message.

Comparisons: Similes and Metaphors

One of the most common and useful tools in public speaking is the figure of speech known as the *simile*. A simile uses *like* or *as* to compare two things. Truth uses a simile to conjure up the images of her strength and fortitude when she states "I could work as much and eat as much as a man—when I could get it—and bear the lash as well!" In your speech, you might employ a simile, such as "Fog enveloped the city like a heavy blanket."

Like similes, *metaphors* liken one thing to another in a literal way, even though there may be no literal connection between the two. A metaphor presents a comparison as a statement of fact—it does not contain the word *like* or *as*—but it is not expected to be taken as a fact. You might use a metaphor, such as "The fog was a heavy blanket over the city," to add imagery to your speech.

Writing a Strong Introduction

Any journalist knows that the single most important part of a news story is the lead: without an effective lead paragraph, nobody will proceed to paragraph two. Like a lead paragraph, the introduction to your speech must accomplish three crucial tasks: it must grab your audience's attention, it must offer a preview of your main points, and it must give your listeners a sense of who you are and why they should want to hear what you have to say. Recall that *primacy effect* discussed earlier in this chapter. Your introduction is the first thing your audience will hear; it therefore sets the tone and the stage for the rest of your speech.

Capture Your Audience's Attention

Finding a creative, attention-grabbing opening can be a struggle, but in the end it will be well worth the effort, for your first words can and do make a big impression on your audience (Hockenbury & Hockenbury, 2002). If you open with something as boring as "Hi, my name is . . ." or "Today I'm going to talk

CONNECT

In Chapters 5 and 14, you learn about nonverbal aspects of speech such as rate, pauses, tone, volume, and pitch. In many cases, these factors can help you use repetition effectively. For example, if you repeat a phrase with an upward inflection of voice followed by a pause, you will help the audience anticipate the next line and enhance their retention of your main points.

CONNECT

Your speech introduction is the first impression you give your audience. But introductions are important in other contexts as well. The Interviewing Appendix shows how your résumé and cover letter give a potential employer an introduction to you and your abilities. If your résumé has typos or other errors, your first impression will be less than stellar—just as a disorganized or inappropriate speech introduction leaves a negative impression with your audience.

AND YOU?

Take a look at your research. Of all the evidence you have gathered for your speech, what jumps out at you? Did you come across any statistics that shocked you? Did you encounter any individuals whose stories touched you—with humor, sadness, or surprise? Think about how any of the statistics, facts, anecdotes, and quotes you've gathered might be worked into an effective introduction.

about . . ." your audience may conclude that there's nothing more interesting to follow. In many cases, you'll write—or at least finalize—your introduction after the bulk of your speech is complete. This is an advantage because you will approach your introduction armed with your main points and your supporting material—and probably a few ideas on how to make it lively! Consider the following suggestions.

Use Surprise

It is likely that during research on your topic, you came across a fact, statistic, quote, or story that truly surprised you. Chances are that such information will likewise come as a surprise to your audience. A startling statement uses unusual or unexpected information to get an audience's attention. For example, in a speech on sleep deprivation, you might begin your speech as follows:

> Did you know that every semester, university students are legally drunk for one week straight? Yet despite feeling drunk, they never drink a drop of alcohol. During finals week, students at the University of Oklahoma sleep an average of five hours per night. Sleep deprivation—characterized by getting five hours or less of sleep per night—can affect reaction time and mental sharpness. After being awake for seventeen hours straight, a sleep-deprived person has the reaction time and mental sharpness of someone with a blood alcohol concentration of 0.05, which is considered legally drunk throughout most of Europe.

Tell a Story

As discussed in Chapter 12, anecdotes can be useful illustrations for your speech. Real-world stories can be particularly effective when worked into your opening, where they can make audiences feel invested in a person before they even know what your thesis is. For example, Miriam is pretty sure that her audience will roll their eyes or begin fiddling with their iPhones if she simply informs her audience that she's going to discuss the secret costs of credit cards. But what if she opens with a story? For example:

> A few months ago, my friend Monica—not her real name—decided that she positively *needed* to own a pair of Jimmy Choo boots. Now, I'll admit, these were some amazing boots: black leather, calf-high, four-inch heels. But they cost—are you sitting down?—$895.00. Like most of us, she didn't have that kind of cash lying around, so she bought the boots on credit and figured that she would pay them off month by month. Despite the fact that she diligently puts $50 toward her payment each and every month, it's going to take Monica 102 months—more than eight years—to pay for those boots. In addition, she'll pay over $750 in interest, which is almost as much as the boots cost in the first place!

By telling a story, Miriam puts a familiar face on her subject; she's also caught the attention of anyone who's ever had the experience of really wanting something they couldn't afford—which is pretty much anyone!

Start with a Quote

Leading with a quotation is a convenient and interesting speech opening. Quotes can connect you as a speaker to real people and real situations. For example, Kenneth is preparing an informative speech on Alzheimer's disease. In his opening, he uses a quote from former president Ronald Reagan, who passed away in 2004 after a ten-year struggle with the disease:

> "I now begin the journey that will lead me to the sunset of my life." That's how Ronald Reagan, upon learning he would be afflicted with Alzheimer's disease, described the illness that would eventually rob him of the eloquence, wit, and intelligence that had defined him as an actor, politician, and president. I'm here today to talk about the tragedy of Alzheimer's disease.

Quotations can come from familiar sources, like Reagan, or from everyday people (Kenneth might quote his mother, who described the time she cared for her Alzheimer's-afflicted father as "the greatest challenge I've ever taken on, and also the greatest honor.") Table 13.2 offers tips for using quotes wisely.

Ask a Question

Posing a question is a great way to get the audience's attention and to make people think. Rather than simply presenting some bit of information, posing a question invites listeners to react, in effect making them participants in the speech.[1] For example, "Would you leave your child in a room full of anonymous strangers? No? Then why would you allow your child to participate in online chats?" Here again, saying something startling can add to the effect: not only have you

TABLE 13.2

USING QUOTES WISELY

Use quotes worth using.	Don't quote something that you could say or explain more effectively in your own words; paraphrase instead, with an attribution to the original source.
Use relevant quotes.	Even the prettiest bit of prose is useless if it doesn't support your points.
Include a clear attribution.	Whether you're quoting Shakespeare or your six-year-old nephew, it's important that audiences know who said what.
Is the quote from a notable source?	Cite not only the author in your speech but also the date and the work in which the quote appeared, if relevant.
Double-check for accuracy.	You do not want to misquote anyone in your speech, so it's important that you proofread your copy against the original. If you've used an online quote source, it is wise to double-check the quote against additional sources known to be reliable because many online quotes fail to provide accurate source information.

---

[1] Asking questions is an effective way of gaining participation in many communication contexts; see O'Hair, O'Rourke, and O'Hair (2000).

● **YOU DON'T HAVE TO TURN YOUR SPEECH** into a stand-up comic performance, but a good opening joke will pique the audience's interest.

gotten your listeners' attention by saying something provocative, but you've also asked them to internalize what you've said and to react to it. As a result, they're likely to be more interested in and open to what you're about to say.

Make Them Laugh

Humor is another effective way to begin your speech. Usually, humor that is brief, relevant to your topic, and makes a point is most effective. For example, consider this opening, which makes the audience laugh but is clearly tied to the main topic of the speech on the effects of multitasking: "I find that the key to multitasking is to lower your expectations. Sure, I can do two things at once—if I do them poorly! Today, I want to talk about the hazards of multitasking."

Introduce Your Purpose and Topic

As you were capturing your audience's attention with stories, questions, quotations, and so on, it's likely that you gave them a fairly overt introduction to your topic. It is *essential* that your introduction clearly establishes what your speech is about and what you hope to achieve by speaking (by incorporating your thesis statement). Imagine that you just caught your audience's attention with the description of a fun-filled and active day: kayaking on a pristine lake, hiking in a rain forest, rock climbing on a craggy coastline, and so on. You would then introduce your thesis: "All of these activities—and many more—are available to you in one of our nation's most diverse protected spaces: Olympic National Park. I hope to persuade you to visit and to take advantage of all this park has to offer."

Preview Your Main Points

Another key goal for your introduction is to provide a preview of the main points that will be covered in the body of the speech. Tell the audience the points that you will discuss in the order that you will talk about them. For example, if you are giving a speech about why students should enroll in an art course, you might say: "There are two reasons why every college student should enroll in an art course. First, it provides students with a creative outlet, and second it teaches students useful and creative ways of thinking about their own subjects of study." Audiences prefer to listen to speakers who are prepared and have a plan the audience can follow; by previewing, you offer a mental outline that your listeners can follow as they attend to your speech.

Connect with Your Audience

Another goal for your introduction is to establish a relationship with your listeners, providing them with a sense of who you are and why they should listen to what you have to say. Like participants in an interview, the members of your audience will come to your speech with three points in mind. They will be curious about the nature of your speech: will it be boring, interesting, or inspiring? They'll also be wondering what they will get from it: will the speech be worth their time and attention? Finally, they will be curious about you as a speaker: will they like you? Should they trust you? Your introduction should provide enough information to allow the audience to make accurate assumptions about your speech and about you.

One way that a speaker can establish a relationship with the audience is to demonstrate why listeners should care about the topic. First, make sure that you verbally link the topic to the audience's interests. One way to do this is to show the topic's relevance. As discussed in Chapter 12, consider timeliness to show how your topic is related to current events or local interests. You should also try to appeal to your listeners' personal needs—let them know what's in it for them. For example, a college recruiter speaking at a high school might talk about what his school offers prospective students. He might also touch on recent local or national events to show the relevance of the school's curriculum: "I've been told that many students in this room participated in the Mock United Nations program last summer. If that experience has piqued your interest in international diplomacy, you might want to consider Sterling College. Our outstanding international relations program offers internships with the United Nations in New York and the State Department in Washington, D.C."

Writing a Strong Conclusion

There's a reason why courtroom dramas like TV's *Law and Order* almost always include footage of the hero lawyer's closing statements. When a wealth of evidence, testimony, and facts have been presented, it's easy for juries (and television audiences) to get bogged down in the details and lose track of the bigger, more dramatic picture. For any speaker—be it a college sophomore in front of a communication class or a fictional lawyer in front of a mock courtroom—it is important to end a presentation with a compelling and pointed conclusion. Once again, the *recency effect* reminds us that the conclusion is the *last* thing the audience will hear in your speech, and it is likely what they will remember most. As such, a speech conclusion must address a number of functions.

● **ONE OF THE MOST CRUCIAL** moments in a trial is the closing statement. It's the lawyer's last chance to make his or her case to the jury.

Signal the End

Your conclusion should alert the audience that the speech is coming to a close. You might do that by using a transitional phrase, such as "In conclusion," "Finally," or "Let me close by saying. . . ." Such phrases serve as signposts, telling audiences that you're about to conclude and asking for their full attention one last time. Remember to keep it brief. Audiences do not like to be overwhelmed with a lot of new information at the end.

real communicator

NAME: Jon Clarke
HOMETOWN: Rockaway Beach, New York
OCCUPATION: Stand-up comic and freelance writer
FUN FACT: My first screenplay, *Idiots in the Atlantic,* was featured at the New York Film and Video Festival.

I wasn't a huge fan of my mandatory college public speaking course. But as much as I hate to admit it, it has helped me out quite a bit in my profession as a comedian. For example, in order to make connections with the people in my audience, I have to pick up on physical cues—are they bored, are they entertained, should I keep going with this bit? I have to make equal amounts of eye contact—particularly hard when the lights on stage are so bright that you physically can't see anyone (in those cases, I just fake it and act as if I can see them). But probably the most helpful thing I learned was how to outline a presentation, or in my case, a routine.

You hear this all the time: start with a joke. But in stand-up comedy, everything's got to be a joke. The first joke has to be a particular kind—it has to be my "persona setter." It has to indicate the type of person I am, what ideas I'm concerned with. Lately I've been starting out with "I'm nerdy but not a *complete* nerd. I used to hang out with the cool kids in school, but I was always waiting for them to beat me up." Now everything I say after that first joke gets filtered through that persona: nerdy but not too nerdy.

After that first joke, I go into my bits. Comedy routines are made up of bits. Bits are about a minute long apiece, and they've got four or five jokes in them. But which bits should go next to one another? This is a big challenge for me when I'm putting together a routine. I do this one about *Sesame Street* on how Cookie Monster can't eat cookies. After that, I can either go into more pop culture stuff (I've got a bit on Spike TV), or go into family stuff (my mother always told me never to talk to strangers; that first day of school was tough). It all depends on the audience that night. Is it college kids who might appreciate Spike TV references? If not, I've got to drop that particular bit.

Even after I know which bit goes where, it's very difficult to actually get there. I used to spend about twenty seconds making the transition from *Sesame Street* to Spike TV, saying things like "Well, I watched a lot of TV as a kid, and I still do. I love TV. The other day, I was sitting on my couch, flipping channels, and I see this Spike TV. . . ." But in comedy, those kinds of segues might as well just be dead air. I want to do them because I have this writerly impulse to flesh things out and have people know me, but the audience is only there for the jokes, and details that don't contribute to the jokes have got to go. Instead of wasting time trying to labor a transition from one bit to the other, I allow my audiences to make thematic connections. I'm talking about *Sesame Street,* and now I'm talking about Spike TV. They can put it together in their heads.

When there's a minute left to go, a light will go on at the back of the club. That's how I know that it's time for me to go into wrap-up mode. I try to end with fast jokes. And as soon as I get a big laugh, I'm out of there. I thank the audience, reintroduce the emcee, and get off the stage before the audience's energy can flag.

A routine usually takes six to eight minutes. The better it is organized—if the persona-setting opening joke is nice and quick and the subsequent material fits that persona well; if bits follow one another logically, allowing transitions to be implicit rather than laboriously explicit—the better the routine goes. Sometimes it feels like it's over in a flash, like a dream, and I'm feeling great all week. Sometimes those six to eight minutes take an eternity. But it's always exciting.

Reinforce Your Topic, Purpose, and Main Points

The conclusion of your speech is the last opportunity you'll have to reinforce the topic and purpose of your speech as well as to remind your audience about the key points you want to live on in their memories. In other words, competent speakers should reiterate this essential information so that listeners are able to mentally check off what they have heard and what they should remember. For example, "Today, I discussed the benefits of seeing your physician for an annual physical, even when you're feeling perfectly fine. Not only can this simple visit offer peace of mind right now and help to prevent costly medical conditions in the future, but it may also save your life if you have an underlying medical problem that requires early diagnosis and treatment."

Make an Impact

Your conclusion should be memorable and interesting for your audience members. All your efforts developing your points and sharing your research will have been in vain if your audience doesn't care to keep anything you've said in mind! Several techniques discussed in the section on introductions can be useful for memorable conclusions as well.

Quotations

To wrap up a speech, speakers often use quotes from historical figures, writers, philosophers, or celebrities. Take care in choosing a quote so that you leave the audience with something to think about. For example, if you are concluding a speech that illustrates the importance of friendships, you might quote the writer Edna Buchanan: "Friends are the family you choose for yourself" (www.ednabuchanan .com). A strong quotation helps make an unforgettable impression.

Statements and Questions

In some types of speeches, it can be especially effective to end with a statement or question that drives home your main point. This rhetorical device is important for conclusions because you want to emphasize the points you made during your speech and have the audience feel connected to your ideas. For example, you might end a speech explaining how to change the oil in your car with a simple statement that sums up your thesis: "Remember, the best way to protect your car is to change the oil every three thousand miles— and it's something you can do yourself." Alternatively, you might make the same point in question form: "Why pay someone else to change the oil in your car, when you can do it yourself in about fifteen minutes, for about a quarter of the price?"

A Final Story

Stories are also as effective for conclusions as they are for introductions. Stories should always tie in to your speech topic, be relatively short, and make a related point. For example, if you are advocating a college-level foreign-language requirement for your university, you might tell this well-known tale: "Mother

Mouse was crossing the street with her three children. She got about halfway across when she saw a cat, crouched and ready to pounce upon them. The cat and Mother Mouse eyeballed each other for two to three minutes. Finally, Mother Mouse let out an enormous 'WOOF!' The cat ran away. Mother Mouse turned to her children and said, 'NOW do you see the advantage of a second language?'"

Challenge the Audience to Respond

The point of a speech (whether informative or persuasive) is to learn something new, right? As the speaker, you must also consider what you want your audience to do with the information you are providing. According to O'Hair, Stewart, and Rubenstein (2010), in an informative speech, you should challenge your audience members to make use of the information. If you've taught them the steps of making homemade hummus, maybe they will buy some pita bread and try it themselves! Or you may extend an invitation to your listeners: "Please join me on Wednesday evening for a town hall meeting on this subject. Our local congressperson will be there to listen to our concerns. I will have the sign-up sheet in the back of the room for you at the end of my presentation."

In most persuasive speeches, the challenge will come through a **call to action** that challenges listeners to act in response to the speech, see the problem in a new way, or change their beliefs, actions, and behavior (O'Hair, Stewart, & Rubenstein, 2010). For example, "Sign this petition. In doing so, you will make a difference in someone's life and make our voices heard" or "Don't forget to vote next Tuesday!"

AND YOU?

What kind of impression would you want to leave your audience with? What is the one thing you'd like people to remember about you and your speech?

Outlining Your Speech

At this point, you have all of the building blocks for a successful speech. Now you're ready to pull all of your hard work together in the form of an **outline**—a structured form of your speech content (Fraleigh & Tuman, 2011). This will be incredibly helpful to you as a speaker because an effective outline helps you confirm that your points are arranged clearly and properly, ensures that you've cited your all-important research, and assists you in your speech delivery. (In fact, many instructors require students to turn in an outline before the presentation. Be sure to check on your instructor's preferences.)

You may already be familiar with the basics of outlining from your high school courses or from your college composition class. Nonetheless, a refresher is always useful, which is why we'll begin with a discussion of the essentials of outlining before we move to types of outlines and the heart of this section: the preparation and speaking outlines.

Essentials of Outlining

In every phase of outlining, basic guidelines will help you structure and prepare your speech. A solid outline will clearly reveal the structure of your arguments and the hierarchy of your points.

► *Use standard symbols.* What an outline does, essentially, is put the hierarchy of points visualized in Figure 13.1 into a text format. To do this, outlines generally use roman numerals, letters, and standard numbers to indicate different levels of importance in the hierarchy.

I. Main Point

   A. Subpoint

   B. Subpoint

      1. Sub-subpoint

      2. Sub-subpoint

If you need to break down the sub-subpoints even further, you may use lowercase letters (a, b, etc.) to create sub-sub-subpoints.

WIREDFORCOMMUNICATION

Bullets to the Brain

There is something sinister in the world of technology. You've undoubtedly been exposed to it, at work or at school. It's probably in your home computer. But it's not a virus. You probably paid to have it there. And according to one of the nation's leading experts, it's making all of us stupid.

Edward Tufte is a professor of political science, computer science and statistics, and graphic design at Yale University and has been academia's most influential voice on the subject of the visual display of information for over two decades. He is an expert on the use of graphs and visual aids to explain any number of types of information, from train schedules to empirical data. He uses computers all the time to crunch numbers and present quantitative information. But Tufte is no fan of slideware. And slideware—specifically, Microsoft's PowerPoint—is everywhere.

The problem, Tufte (2003) explains, is that programs like PowerPoint force presentations into an outline format, with little development beyond a series of bulleted lists. Because a typical slide contains a mere forty words—about eight seconds of reading—presentations become a succession of short, boring lists of facts, presented out of context and with little room for evaluation. In schools, where PowerPoint has become a common teaching tool, Tufte finds the problem even more alarming. By forcing information into short, bulleted lists and colorful graphics, such tools teach students to create infomercials rather than reports and to write ad copy rather than sentences.

Visual aids can indeed be a valuable asset for a presentation, and Microsoft's program is, Tufte concedes, a useful tool for managing and presenting slides. But often presenters rely on the program to design the content of their speeches rather than to enhance it, and Tufte finds that a program's format "routinely disrupts, dominates, and trivializes content." The best remedy? Focus on content. "If your numbers are boring, then you've got the wrong numbers," Tufte writes. "If your words or images are not on point, making them dance in color won't make them relevant."

THINK ABOUT THIS

❶ The use of bulleted lists predates Microsoft PowerPoint—instructors and presenters have made use of overhead projectors and slide shows for decades. Why is Tufte being so hard on Microsoft?

❷ We've spent much of this chapter talking about the importance of outlining and of communicating your final outline clearly to your audience. How is that different from presenting your outline in slide form?

❸ Are there some subjects or types of speeches that lend themselves to PowerPoint presentations? Are there others that don't?

▶ *Use subdivisions properly.* It is basic logic that a whole of anything—a sandwich, a doughnut, or an outline heading—can never be split into fewer than two pieces. Therefore, as you divide your ideas from main points to subpoints, remember that each numbered or lettered entry must come in a series of at least two points: if you have a I, you must have a II; if you have an A, you must have a B; and so on.

▶ *Separate the parts of your speech.* It is typically helpful to label your introduction, conclusion, and even your transitions to distinguish them from the body of your speech (your main points and supporting subpoints).

▶ *Call out your specific purpose and thesis.* Many instructors want students to include this pertinent information at the top of the outline, so check with your instructor to determine his or her preference. You may feel that you already know this information by heart, but it can be truly helpful to see it at the top of your outline page in order to ensure that all of your main points support the purpose and thesis. Also, you may wind up tweaking them a bit as you work your way through the outlining process.

▶ *Cite your sources.* As discussed in Chapter 12, it is extremely important to give proper credit to sources that you cite in your speech. As you work on the outline, you should always mark where a specific point requires credit. Directly after the point, either insert a footnote or a reference in parentheses; once you complete the outline, arrange the references in order on a separate sheet headed "Works Cited," "Notes," or "References." Citations can be presented in a variety of formats, including styles dictated by such organizations as the Modern Language Association (MLA) and the American Psychological Association (APA). See Figure 13.2 on page 400 for a sample of how you might handle references in APA format. Your instructor may have his or her own preferences about how to handle citations, so when in doubt, ask.

▶ *Give your speech a title.* Once all of your ideas and points are organized on paper, you can give your speech a catchy title that captures its essence. You might also consider using a provocative question as the title or part of a memorable quotation that you will use in the body of the speech.

At every phase of development, you should review your outline to ensure that your organization is sound. When you review your outline, you should see a clear hierarchy of points reflected in each tier of your structure. A weak link in the outline—an unsupported argument, an unrelated point—reveals an overall weakness in the way you've presented and defended your thesis. A solid outline shows not only how well you've organized your material but also how each point is supported by two or more subpoints, making a stronger case for your thesis statement. It also shows the scope and validity of your research by detailing your evidence with complete citations.

Styles of Outlines

There are three basic approaches you can take to outlining your speech, which vary according to the level of detail. All three formats—sentence

● **ALTHOUGH HOMER SIMPSON** typically eats a whole doughnut in one big bite, he does, on occasion, split it up. Even he knows you can't split it into less than two bites!

outlines, phrase outlines, and key-word outlines—can be valuable tools in developing and eventually delivering your speech. In most cases, you'll move from one format to another as you progress from preparing your speech to actually delivering it.

Sentence Outline

The first type of outline is the **sentence outline**, which offers the full text of your speech, often the exact words that you want to say to your audience. Sentence outlines are generally used as you develop and prepare early drafts of your speech because they help you become more comfortable with all aspects of your speech; they are typically not ideal for your actual presentation because many speakers wind up reading directly from the outline, missing out on valuable eye contact with the audience. Consider the following example from Sample Speech Outline 13.1 (see p. 397) regarding sleep deprivation:

II. There are many causes of sleep deprivation, according to the Centers for Disease Control and Prevention.

    A. Busy work and family schedules contribute to sleep deprivation.

        1. As college students, many of us are trying to handle full-time course work and full- or part-time jobs to help pay for tuition, in addition to maintaining relationships with loved ones.

        2. New parents are often incredibly sleep deprived as they attempt to adjust to life with an infant as well as those infamous nighttime feedings.

        3. Shift workers (including police officers, nurses, pilots, and so on) often having trouble establishing good sleep habits since their schedules change frequently and they are sometimes required to work the night shift.

    B. Late-night television and Internet use can also interfere with the ability to fall asleep or can prevent individuals from adhering to a bedtime.

    C. The use of caffeine and alcohol can also make it difficult to fall asleep and stay asleep.

    D. Some medical conditions—including insomnia and obstructive sleep apnea—also make sleeping incredibly difficult.

Phrase Outline

A **phrase outline** takes parts of sentences and uses those phrases as instant reminders of what the point or subpoint means. Consider the following example:

II. Many causes of sleep deprivation (CDC)

    A. Busy work and personal lives

        1. Students struggling with school and work

        2. New parents adjusting to baby schedule

        3. Shift work disrupts sleep

B. Using TV or computer late at night

C. Use of caffeine and alcohol

D. Medical conditions—insomnia and sleep apnea

The phrase outline is often the preferred format because it offers speakers a clear road map of their presentation, with reminders of key points and phrases. Yet it also keeps speakers on their toes, allowing them to deliver a speech rather than simply read it.

Key-Word Outline

A **key-word outline** is the briefest possible outline, consisting of specific "key words" from the sentence outline to jog the speaker's memory. This type of outline allows the speaker to maintain maximum eye contact with the audience, though the speaker must be *extremely* familiar with the content of the speech to be comfortable using this type of outline. An example of a key-word outline is as follows:

II. SD causes (CDC)

    A. Family and work

        1. College students

        2. New parents

        3. Shift workers

    B. Television and Internet

    C. Caffeine and alcohol

    D. Medical conditions—insomnia, apnea

● **AS YOU DEVELOP YOUR SPEECH**, you'll transition from a more detailed preparation outline to a speaking outline that will equip you for the actual presentation.

From Preparation Outline to Speaking Outline

In most public speaking situations, you will use the basics you've learned to create two outlines. The first is a **preparation outline** (sometimes called a *working outline*), a draft that you will use, and probably revisit and revise continually, throughout the preparation for your speech. The function of a preparation outline is to firm up your thesis statement, establish and organize your main points, and develop your supporting points. From the preparation outline, you will eventually develop a **speaking outline**, or *delivery outline,* which is your final speech plan, complete with details, delivery tips, and important notes about presentational aids (which we will discuss in Chapter 14).

In most cases, it will be entirely acceptable for you to use a sentence outline when working on your preparation outline (though, as always, check with your instructor if you will be submitting a formal version of your outline before presenting your speech). As you move toward a final speaking outline, it's best to switch from a sentence format to a phrase or key-word approach (or a combination of the two). To do this, look at your full sentences, and pull out key words or phrases that will jog your memory as you speak; boil down longer passages into quick headers that will serve as guideposts for your more extemporaneous delivery. Sample Speech Outline 13.1 shows the full progression from preparation outline to speaking outline.

Your speaking outline should also include **delivery cues**, brief reminders about important information related to the delivery of your speech that are for your eyes alone. We'll talk in greater depth about your delivery in Chapter 14, but for now, be aware that you'll likely want to remind yourself to show a presentation aid or speak slowly at the beginning of the speech, when you are the most nervous. These points should be noted in your outline. Table 13.3 offers additional delivery cues that may be helpful to you.

Another important aspect of your speaking outline is that it should contain notes for your **oral citations**, the references to source materials that you mention in the narrative of your speech. After a sentence or phrase in your outline,

TABLE 13.3

USEFUL DELIVERY CUES

Delivery Cue	Purpose	Example as It Might Appear in Your Outline
Transition	A segue from one topic or idea to another; might be a simple reminder that you're changing tone here or a specific example or story that takes the speech from one topic to another	• [TRANSITION] • [TRANSITION: Use dog story!]
Timing and speaking rate	A reminder to use a specific speaking rate, either for emphasis or to quell anxiety	• [Slow down here] • [Speed up here] • [Repeat for emphasis]
Volume and nonverbal behavior	A reminder to raise or lower your voice at particular points in your speech or to use particular gestures or body movements for emphasis	• [Louder] • [Softly] • [Thump on podium] • [Count out on fingers]
Sources	Sources for cited material	• [Dowd, M. (2007, May 23). Pass the clam dip. *The New York Times.*]
Statistics	Statistics for reference, with source	• [U.S. Census Bureau: 64% of voting-age citizens voted in 2004, 60% in 2000]
Quotations	Exact wording of a quotation you plan to use	• [Dwight D. Eisenhower: "I've always found that plans are useless, but planning is indispensable."]
Pronunciations	Phonetic reminders for difficult-to-pronounce names or words	• [Hermione (her-MY-uh-nee)] • [Kiribati (kee-ree-BAHSS)]
Visual aids	Reminder for when to incorporate particular visual aids	• [Census chart] • [Show model]

Source: O'Hair, Stewart, & Rubenstein (2007), tab. 13.2, p. 201. Adapted with permission.

AND YOU?

How do you outline? Do you think of an outline as a hard-and-fast map, written before you begin writing and strictly adhered to throughout the process? Or do you start with a rough outline, revising and refining the organization as you move through the writing process?

you might simply place the source in parentheses so that you remember to give credit. For example, the key words "SD-financial costs (Skerritt, HBR)" should prompt you to say: "Sleep deprivation costs businesses more than $3,000 per employee, annually, in terms of lowered productivity, according to a recent report by Patrick Skerritt in *The Harvard Business Review*." For material quoted word for word from the source, the oral citation must clarify that the material is in fact quoted rather than your own expression ("As Skerritt notes, 'This doesn't include the cost of absenteeism—those with insomnia missed an extra five days a year compared to good sleepers'"). In such instances, you will likely want to use full sentences in your outline, rather than key words or phrases, to ensure that you do not misquote or misrepresent your source.

Finally, you should choose a comfortable format for using your speaking outline in front of your audience. You may transfer the outline to note cards, which will enable you to flip through notes quickly; alternatively, you might create virtual note cards on your smart phone or tablet. And, of course, some speakers prefer to use a standard-size sheet of paper. In many classroom situations, your instructor will indicate the preferred format.

what about you?

Assessing Your Outline

To ensure that your speech is well organized and that your thesis is soundly supported, use the following checklist as you are preparing your outline.

- ▶ Is there a clear hierarchy of points in my outline?
- ▶ Are my points each supported by at least two subpoints?
- ▶ Do I call out the parts of my speech, including the introduction, transitions, and conclusion?
- ▶ Have I incorporated my research into my outline effectively?
- ▶ Have I worked oral citations into my outline to avoid unintentional plagiarism?
- ▶ Does my outline offer a complete list of references for all of the research I cite in my speech?
- ▶ Does my speaking outline provide important delivery cues that will help me when I present?
- ▶ Have I verified the style of my outline with my instructor (for example, a sentence outline for a preparation outline, or a phrase outline for a speaking outline)?

If you cannot answer "yes" to each of these questions, then you will likely benefit from additional work on your outline. Remember, the more effort you put into addressing these details, the better prepared and the more confident you will be when it is time to deliver your speech.

SAMPLE SPEECH OUTLINE 13.1

From Preparation Outline to Speaking Outline

Title: Sleep It Off: Understanding the Dangers of Sleep Deprivation
General Purpose: To inform
Specific Speech Purpose: To inform my audience about the dangers of sleep deprivation so that they may take appropriate steps to avoid this troubling medical issue.
Thesis Statement: You must understand the causes and effects of sleep deprivation—as well as simple steps you can take to avoid it—in order to improve your life now and avoid costly personal and social ramifications.

Sample Preparation Outline •

Introduction

  I. Do you ever feel like you're struggling to juggle relationships, work, and classes? Many of us do, and often enough, the first thing we cut out of our busy daily routine is sleep. •
 II. For better or worse, the human body needs an adequate amount of sleep to function properly, and my research indicates that we simply aren't getting enough of it.
III. You must understand the causes and effects of sleep deprivation, as well as simple steps to take to avoid it, to improve your life now and avoid costly personal and social ramifications. •
 IV. Today I will speak about sleep deprivation. I will begin by explaining what it is, before moving on to its causes and effects, and examining simple solutions to the problem. •

Transition: So what exactly is sleep deprivation?

Body

  I. In a personal communication with Dr. Arkeenah Jones, a family physician, on March 15, 2011, she noted that sleep deprivation is a condition in which a person does not get enough sleep, which can lead to chronic exhaustion. •

  A. The National Sleep Foundation's 2009 survey notes that 70 percent of adults sleep less than eight hours per night, and 40 percent sleep less than the minimum recommended seven hours per night.

  B. The results of the survey I passed out last week reveal that 30 percent of people in this very classroom get less than six hours of sleep on weeknights.

Transition: By a show of hands, how many people in this room *like* to sleep? • I thought so. So, if we enjoy sleeping so much, why are we not getting enough of it?

• Note that the speaker uses a sentence outline style throughout the preparation outline.

• The speaker opens with an attention-getting question and offers a response that the audience will likely relate to.

• Thesis statement

• Preview of main points

• Main point 1

• The speaker keeps her audience involved in the speech by asking questions.

II. There are many causes of sleep deprivation, according to the Centers for Disease Control and Prevention. •

A. Busy work and family schedules contribute to sleep deprivation.

1. As college students, many of us are trying to handle full-time course work and full- or part-time jobs to help pay for tuition, in addition to maintaining relationships with loved ones. •

2. New parents are often incredibly sleep deprived as they attempt to adjust to life with an infant as well as those infamous nighttime feedings.

3. Shift workers (including police officers, nurses, pilots, and so on) often having trouble establishing good sleep habits because their schedules change frequently and they are sometimes required to work the night shift.

B. Late-night television and Internet use can interfere with the ability to fall asleep or can prevent individuals from adhering to a bedtime schedule.

C. The use of caffeine and alcohol can also make it difficult to fall asleep and stay asleep.

D. Some medical conditions—including insomnia and obstructive sleep apnea—also make sleeping incredibly difficult.

Transition: As we've seen, busy schedules, overuse of media, the intake of alcohol and caffeine, and medical conditions can all cause sleep deprivation, • but why does sleep deprivation truly matter so much?

III. Sleep deprivation can have negative effects on the health and safety of individuals and the community at large. •

A. According to Dr. Michael J. Breus, a clinical psychologist and writer for WebMD, sleep deprivation decreases performance and alertness.

1. Sleep deprivation decreases workplace productivity, at a cost of more than $3,000 per employee annually, as noted by Patrick Skerritt in the *Harvard Business Review.*

2. Sleep deprivation is a leading cause of automobile accidents, especially among adolescent motorists, according to a February 15, 2010, report by the American Academy of Sleep Medicine. •

B. Dr. Michael J. Breus also notes that sleep deprivation causes relational stress.

1. In my own life, I certainly find that I argue more with friends and family when I'm exhausted than I do when I'm well rested. •

2. The results of the survey I conducted indicate that 55 percent of the members of this class find that "arguing with a loved one" is a problematic outcome of not getting enough sleep.

C. Dr. Arkeenah Jones notes that sleep deprivation affects memory and cognitive ability.

1. In fact, a Centers for Disease Control and Prevention study noted that 23.2 percent of sleep-deprived individuals report difficulties with concentration. Similarly, 18.2 percent report difficulty remembering information.
2. Dr. Pamela Thatcher, a psychology professor at St. Lawrence University, conducted a study in which she discovered that students who pull all-night study sessions typically have lower GPAs than those who do not.

D. Sleep deprivation can contribute to chronic health conditions, including depression, obesity, and diabetes, according to the Centers for Disease Control and Prevention.

Transition: So far, we've discussed the common causes of sleep deprivation as well as its negative—and potentially tragic—effects. At this point you may be wondering how to avoid sleep deprivation altogether. I will discuss several suggestions now. •

• The speaker transitions to her final main point with an internal summary and an internal preview.

IV. You can avoid sleep deprivation with a few simple changes to your daily routine.

A. Make sleeping a priority in your life, along with your other commitments.
B. Have consistent sleep and wake-up times, even on weekends.
C. Don't watch television, play on your laptop, or even study in bed. Try to reserve your bed for sleeping.
D. Don't drink alcohol or consume caffeine too close to bedtime.
E. Dr. Arkeenah Jones recommends contacting your primary care physician or a nurse practitioner in the Student Health Center in order to address underlying medical problems that might affect your sleep.

Transition: Regulating your schedule and developing good habits are essential for preventing sleep deprivation.

Conclusion

I. Sadly, a realization about the dangers of sleep deprivation came too late for Zlatko Glusica, a fatigued pilot whose slow reaction time caused a fatal error in landing an Air India Express flight in 2010. According to a report by Alan Levin in *USA Today*, 158 people—including Mr. Glusica—died. •

• The speaker signals the end of her speech with a tragic story that drives home her main points.

II. As you've seen today, sleep deprivation is a concerning problem for individuals and communities.

    A. It has many causes ranging from busy schedules and media use to caffeine and alcohol consumption and medical problems.

    B. Its effects can be devastating, as I've detailed in this speech.

    C. Luckily, many of us can prevent sleep deprivation by making simple changes to our daily routines. •

III. Now go get some rest . . . after the remainder of today's speeches are over, that is! •

• The speaker reiterates her main points.

• The speaker uses a memorable statement and humor to end her speech.

FIGURE 13.2
REFERENCES (in APA style)

References

American Academy of Sleep Medicine. (2010, February 15). Sleep problems and sleepiness increase the risk of motor vehicle accidents in adolescents. *Science Daily*. Retrieved from http://www.sciencedaily.com/releases/2010/02/100215081728.htm

Breus, M. J. (2004). Sleep habits: More important than you think. In *WebMD: Sleep disorders guide*. Retrieved from http://www.webmd.com/sleep-disorders/guide/important-sleep-habits

Centers for Disease Control and Prevention. (2008, February 28). CDC study reveals adults may not get enough rest or sleep. Retrieved from http://www.cdc.gov/media/pressrel/2008/r080228.htm

Centers for Disease Control and Prevention. (2011). Insufficient sleep is a public health epidemic. Retrieved from http://www.cdc.gov/Features/dsSleep/

Levin, A. (2010, November 18). Air India pilot's "sleep inertia" caused crash. *USA Today*. Retrieved from http://www.usatoday.com/news/world/2010-11-18-airindia18_ST_N.htm

National Sleep Foundation. (2009). Sleep in America poll: Summary of findings. Retrieved from http://www.sleepfoundation.org/article/sleep-america-polls/2009-health-and-safety

St. Lawrence University. (2007, December 1). All-nighters equal lower grades. *Science Daily*. Retrieved from www.sciencedaily.com/releases/2007/11/071130162518.htm

Skerritt, P. D. (2011, January 12). Your health at work: Sleep deprivation's true workplace costs. *Harvard Business Review*. Retrieved from http://blogs.hbr.org/your-health-at-work/2011/01/sleep-deprivations-true-workpl.htm

Sample Speaking Outline

Introduction [Speak slowly! Look at audience!]

I.   Juggling commitments? Many give up sleeping.

II. We need sleep; research = we don't get enough.

III. Be informed about sleep deprivation (SD) to improve life and prevent negative consequences. •

IV. I will discuss SD: what, causes, effects, prevention. •

Transition: What is SD?

Body

I.   SD = not enough sleep; can lead to chronic exhaustion. (Dr. Arkeenah Jones, personal communication, March 15, 2011) •

    A.   70% of adults sleep <8 hours per night, and 40% sleep <7 hours per night. (National Sleep Foundation's 2009 survey) •

    B.   30% of people in class sleep <6 hours on weeknights. (my survey)

Transition: *Like* to sleep? Then why not sleeping? **[Smile, encourage audience response]**

II. SD causes (CDC) •

    A.   Family and work

        1.   College students—course work, jobs, relationship
        2.   New parents—crying, hungry babies
        3.   Shift workers—trouble with consistent schedules

    B.   Television and Internet

    C.   Caffeine and alcohol

    D.   Medical conditions—insomnia and obstructive sleep apnea

Transition: Causes: schedules, media, alcohol/caffeine/medical conditions. Who cares?

III. SD has negative effects for individuals and community. •

    A.   Decreases performance and alertness (Dr. Michael J. Breus, clinical psychologist & writer for WebMD)

        1.   Decreases workplace productivity; costs >$3,000 per employee annually (Patrick D. Skerritt, *Harvard Business Review*)
        2.   Causes auto accidents, especially teens (American Academy of Sleep Medicine, February 15, 2010) •

    B.   Causes relational stress (Dr. Breus)

        1.   True for me!
        2.   55% of class fights with loved ones from SD. (my survey)

    C.   Affects memory and cognitive ability (Dr. Jones)

Side annotations:

• Thesis statement. The speaker is so familiar with her speech purpose and thesis that she only needs a brief reminder.

• Key-word preview of main points.

• Main point 1

• The speaker retains a bit more detail in this subpoint in order to keep her statistics straight.

• Main point 2

• Main point 3

• The speaker makes sure that her oral citations are clear throughout the speaking outline.

1. 23.2% report difficulties with concentration; 18.2% report difficulty remembering info. (CDC)
2. All-nighters lead to lower GPA. (Dr. Pamela Thatcher, psychology professor at St. Lawrence University)

   D. Chronic health conditions—depression, obesity, diabetes (CDC)

Transition: Discussed causes and effects. How to prevent SD?

• In an earlier practice, the speaker noted her tendency to read directly from notes, preventing useful interaction with the audience.

IV. Daily routine changes [**Don't read as list. Look up!**] •

   A. Prioritize sleeping
   B. Consistent sleep and wake-up times
   C. No TV/Internet in bed; just sleep
   D. No alcohol/caffeine close to bedtime
   E. Talk to MD or NP at health center about medical concerns. (Dr. Jones)

Transition: Changes in routine and good habits prevent SD.

Conclusion

• The speaker uses effective delivery cues throughout the speech. Here she reminds herself of a difficult pronunciation.

I. Zlatko Glusica [***Zlat*go Glue*sick*uh***], • fatigued pilot, India Air Express, killed 158 people landing plane. (Alan Levin, *USA Today*, 2010) [**Show image of crash**]

II. SD is concerning problem for individuals and communities.

   A. Causes: busy schedules, media use, alcohol/caffeine/medical problems
   B. Devastating effects
   C. Mostly preventable with simple changes

III. Get some rest!

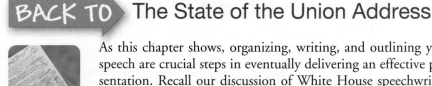

BACK TO ▶ The State of the Union Address

As this chapter shows, organizing, writing, and outlining your speech are crucial steps in eventually delivering an effective presentation. Recall our discussion of White House speechwriters preparing the State of the Union address from the beginning of the chapter. What considerations and challenges will affect their organization and outlines? How will their organization influence their audiences' perceptions of the speech?

▶ Ideas will come in from every direction, so planning and organization are key. David Frum, a former White House speechwriter, observed that "the planning for the next State of the Union really begins the day after the last State of the Union" (as cited in Jackson, 2006).

▶ Speechwriters need to bear in mind that they are writing for two different—albeit not mutually exclusive—audiences. Chriss Winston (2002) points out that members of Congress and Washington insiders judge the speech primarily on its policy content, while everyday Americans tend to look for leadership qualities in the president as well as evidence that he shares their values. The challenge lies in choosing content and language that speak to both groups.

▶ The key to avoiding what Matthew Scully (2005) refers to as a "tedious grab bag of policy proposals" lies in the skillful and artful use of transitions. Instead of jumping from point to point, speechwriters need to find and build unifying themes among the many policies under discussion. Thus George W. Bush's speechwriters were able to draw connections between such issues as cloning and war by focusing on the overall theme of human dignity and human rights. These connections allowed for natural transitions from one issue to the next (Scully, 2005).

▶ Creating unified themes is also crucial to keeping the content (and length) of the speech from spiraling out of control. President Bill Clinton was known for long State of the Union speeches that detailed many policy proposals. President George W. Bush preferred to stick to big ideas. "He's not going to talk about everything under the sun," said one deputy director in advance of Bush's 2006 address; "he's going to be talking about a handful of very big themes" (as cited in Jackson, 2006).

THINGS TO TRY ▷ Activities

1. Take a look at the outline of this chapter in the Contents (pp. xxx–xxxi). Do you see a clear hierarchy of points and subpoints? Within the chapter, how are transitions used to move from point to point? How might the techniques used in this chapter work in your speech?

2. Read a famous or familiar speech (such as Martin Luther King's "I Have a Dream" speech), and create an outline for it. Can you follow a clear sequence of points? Do the subpoints support the speaker's main points?

3. When creating the outline for your speech, write each main point on a separate index card. Spread the cards out on a table, and then pick them up in the most logical order. Does this order match the order of your outline? How did you choose to arrange the topics—spatially, chronologically, or topically?

4. Establishing a relationship with the audience is important when giving a speech. Make a list of all of the possible members of your audience. How do you plan to connect with all members of the audience? Pretend you are giving a speech at your old high school. Will your introduction affect the seniors the same way it affects the principal?

5. Pick a general topic, and try to come up with several different attention getters for that topic. Here's an example for the topic "dogs":

▶ Tell a funny story about your dog.

▶ "Did you know that the human mouth contains more germs than a dog's mouth?"

▶ "In my hometown, there is a dog that walks upright like a human because he does not have any front legs."

▶ "Did you know that approximately 10 million unwanted dogs are euthanized annually in the United States?"

Try this with a topic such as your favorite food, favorite vacation spot, or some other appealing topic.

REAL REFERENCE ▶ A Study Tool

Now that you have finished reading this chapter, you can

Organize and support your main points

▶ Identify your **main points**, the central claims that support your specific speech purpose and your thesis statement (p. 372).

▶ **Subpoints** support your main points using all of the statistics, stories, and other forms of research you discovered on your topic (p. 373).

Choose an appropriate organizational pattern for your speech:

▶ A **chronological pattern** presents main points in a systematic, time-related fashion (p. 375).

▶ A **topical pattern** is based on categories, such as person, place, thing, or process (p. 375). The **primacy-recency effect** argues that audiences are most likely to remember what comes at the beginning and end of messages (p. 375).

▶ A **spatial pattern** arranges points according to physical proximity or direction from one to the next (p. 375).

▶ The **problem-solution pattern** presents an obstacle and then suggestions for overcoming it (p. 375).

▶ The **cause-effect pattern** moves from the cause of a phenomenon to the results or vice versa (p. 376).

▶ The **narrative pattern** uses a story line to tie points together (p. 377).

▶ The **motivated sequence pattern** uses a five-step plan to motivate listeners: attention, need, satisfaction, visualization, and action (p. 377).

Move smoothly from point to point:

▶ Build strong **transitions**, sentences that connect the points so that topics flow naturally (p. 378).

▶ Use **signposts**, key words or phrases that signify transitions (p. 379).

▶ **Internal previews** prime the audience for the content immediately ahead (p. 379).

▶ **Internal summaries** crystallize points in one section before moving on (p. 379).

Choose appropriate and powerful language:

▶ Consider your audience when you choose your words (p. 381).

▶ Use simple, unambiguous words (p. 381).

▶ Be concise (p. 381).

▶ Use vivid language (p. 381).

▶ Use repetition, allusion, similes, and metaphors to make a lasting impression (pp. 381–383).

Develop a strong introduction, a crucial part of all speeches:

▶ Grab listeners' attention with surprise, a good story, a quote, a question, or humor (pp. 383–386).

▶ Introduce your purpose and topic (p. 386).

▶ Preview your main points to provide a mental outline for your audience (p. 386).

▶ Establish a relationship with the audience (pp. 386–387).

Conclude with the same strength as in the introduction:

▶ Signal the end to ask for listeners' full attention, and wrap up quickly (p. 387).

▶ Reiterate your topic, purpose, and main points (p. 389).

▶ Make a final impact with a memorable closing quote, statement, question, or story (p. 389).

▶ Challenge the audience to respond with a **call to action**—what you hope they will do in response to the speech (p. 390).

Prepare an effective outline:

▶ The **outline** puts the hierarchy of points into a text format (p. 390).

▶ The hierarchy of points for a strong outline will show each point supported by two or more subpoints (p. 392).

▶ There are three essential styles of outlines (from most detailed to sparest): **sentence outline**, **phrase outline**, and **key-word outline** (pp. 392–394).

▶ Write a **preparation outline** (or working outline) to organize and develop your speech (p. 394).

▶ The **speaking outline** (or delivery outline) is your final speech plan (p. 394).

▶ Add **delivery cues**, brief reminders about important information, to your speaking outline (p. 395).

▶ **Oral citations**, references to source materials to be included in your narrative, should also be in your speaking outline (p. 395).

Many people feel anxious about delivering speeches—and some even manage to get through life without having to speak publicly. But consider the nervousness and challenges that King George and David Seidler managed to overcome in the process of finding their voices. Both men, in different ways, moved audiences, and in Albert's case, affected an entire nation. As their stories illustrate, with the right tools and plenty of practice, even the most nervous or challenged individuals can become accomplished and engaging speakers. In this chapter, you'll learn the basics of effective speech delivery that will help you connect with your audience and deliver an effective presentation. We begin by acknowledging the nervousness you may naturally experience before moving on to key methods of delivery, guidelines for effective delivery and presentation aids, and tips for practicing your speech.

Understanding and Addressing Anxiety

Jerry Seinfeld once joked, "According to most studies, people's number one fear is public speaking. Number two is death. . . . This means to the average person, if you go to a funeral, you're better off in the casket than doing the eulogy" (as cited in Peck, 2007). Whether Seinfeld's statistics are accurate or not, it's true that speechmaking can cause some level of **public speaking anxiety** (PSA), the nervousness we experience when we know we have to communicate publicly to an audience (Behnke & Sawyer, 1999; Bippus & Daly, 1999). While we might think of PSA as an emotional challenge, it often manifests itself with real physical symptoms, including a rapid heart beat, erratic breathing, increased sweating, and a general feeling of uneasiness. (To determine your own level of PSA, visit James McCroskey's online quiz at www.jamescmccroskey.com/measures/prpsa.htm.)

For some individuals, however, this nervousness goes far beyond giving a speech and extends to such essential speaking tasks as answering a question in class, meeting new people, or voicing an opinion. Noted communication scholar James McCroskey (1977) calls this **communication apprehension** (CA) because it is a more general "fear or anxiety associated with either real or anticipated communication with another person or persons" (p. 78). Clearly, speaking up or speaking out can enhance personal opportunities and career prospects: "Being a poor speaker is the principal reason people don't make it into the executive ranks," noted one professional career adviser (Ligos, 2001).

But don't despair! Whether you suffer from PSA or even the more general CA, you can learn to control your nervousness. In more severe cases, you might consider meeting with a trained professional at your campus counseling center. For less disruptive symptoms, you might simply find comfort in the fact that nervousness is a natural part of life—and that it can actually spur you on to do your best (in the case of a speech, this may mean preparing more thoroughly and practicing more diligently). You may also benefit from the advice we offer here on identifying your anxiety triggers and building your confidence.

Identifying Anxiety Triggers

Before you can conquer your nervousness, you need to identify it. Just what has you so frightened? Research, as well as our personal experiences, points to several key factors, including upsetting experiences, fear of evaluation, and distaste for attention (Ayres, 2005; Bodie, 2010).

Upsetting Experiences

Anna forgot her line in the second grade school play, and the audience laughed. They thought it was adorable, but to Anna, the experience was devastating. It's fairly common for a negative experience in our past to shape our expectations for the future, but it's important to remember that it's never too late to learn or improve on personal skills. Anna needs to think about other skills that she has mastered, despite her initial nervousness: she was anxious the first time she drove a car, for example, and the first time she tried downhill skiing. With practice, she was able to master both—even though she failed her first road test and came home bruised after her first challenging ski run. She needs to approach public speaking with the same kind of "try, try again" attitude.

Fear of Evaluation

Anna's anxiety about public speaking may not be about speaking but about being evaluated on her speaking abilities. In her communication class, she knows that her instructor will grade her speech; in other speaking situations, she worries that her audience will laugh at her words or message. We all feel this way from time to time, but Anna must remember that her instructor will consider other aspects of her speech preparation, including her organization and research. In addition, she should recall that she's not under the intense scrutiny that she imagines: in most public speaking situations—be it a communication class, a wedding toast, or a eulogy—the audience wants the speaker to succeed. In fact, research shows that audiences are usually far less aware of a speaker's nervousness than the speaker is (Sawyer & Behnke, 1990, 1996, 2002). And in any case, Anna should always remember that, as with her road test and her first ski run, she can always just try again if she falls short of her expectations. Keeping the presentation in this perspective will help her to feel less anxiety.

Distaste for Attention

Alonzo loves to sing in the car, in the shower, at concerts, and as part of his church worship team. But he refuses to sing a solo because being the center of attention makes him feel incredibly uncomfortable. While he may be able to avoid singing a solo, he will likely have to speak publicly at some point (whether for a college class, at a church event, or at a wedding or funeral). He can minimize his discomfort with being the center of attention by thinking of his speech as an opportunity to communicate with a group rather than to perform. In other words, if he were to give the best-man speech at his brother's wedding, he'd be communicating with a group of family members and close friends (people who share his love for his brother) rather than putting on a performance. Similarly, when giving a speech for his human communication course, he's still part of the same group as his classmates. His fellow students are in the same position (as nervous speakers) and have similar goals of succeeding at the task at hand.

CONNECT

Since many people are apprehensive about speaking publicly, we might assume that communication apprehension (CA) is limited to this context. However, throughout this book you learn that anxiety can occur in many contexts. Some people experience high levels of CA in interpersonal relationships (Chapter 7) while others get anxious working in groups (Chapter 9). And still others find that interviews (Interviewing Appendix) trigger CA. The techniques in this chapter are useful in all situations where CA occurs.

● **PUBLIC SPEAKING** anxiety manifests itself both psychologically and physically, but it can be overcome by identifying the triggers of anxiety and building confidence.

● **MEDITATING OR PRACTICING** yoga can help you learn to relax your muscles and focus your attention.

Building Your Confidence

Most people can cope effectively with periodic bouts of public speaking anxiety by applying the following advice, which can also be employed for more general cases of communication apprehension.

▶ *Prepare for the unexpected.* Anxiety has positive effects as well, such as driving you to be more prepared. You might, for instance, worry that you will forget all your main points while giving your speech, something that is unlikely to happen if you are prepped with solid notes. By thinking about what might go wrong, you can come up with simple solutions for just about any scenario.

▶ *Desensitize yourself.* Sometimes the best way to get over something is to "just do it." You address your fear of public speaking by making attempts to get up in front of a crowd in less threatening situations (like asking a question in class or at a community meeting). You might even try singing karaoke with friends—nobody expects you to be any good at it, anyway, and it might be fun!

▶ *Visualize your success.* Research shows that people with high speech anxiety tend to concentrate on negative thoughts before giving their speeches (Ayres & Hopf, 1993). In order to reduce those thoughts (and their accompanying anxiety), it's important to spend time imagining positive scenarios and personal success, a technique known as **performance visualization** (Ayres, 2005; Ayres & Hopf, 1992). Imagine yourself standing before your audience with confidence and grace—and it just may happen.

▶ *Take care of yourself.* In order to be productive, remember to take care of yourself in the days leading up to your speech. Be sure to get enough rest. Budget your time effectively by getting your other work out of the way to make room for your speech practice sessions. Try to eat a light meal before the presentation (this is particularly important if you're worried about your stomach growling), and give relaxation techniques (such as deep breathing, yoga, a calming walk, and laughing with friends) a try. After you successfully give your speech, be sure to treat yourself to something nice—it's time to celebrate!

▶ *Practice, practice, practice.* As we've mentioned—and as we'll discuss throughout this chapter—adequately preparing for your speech will increase the likelihood of success and lessen your apprehension or anxiety (Smith & Frymier, 2006). Research demonstrates that confidence does come through preparation and skill building, which means that conducting thorough research, organizing your points, and preparing a useful outline will help you achieve a positive outcome (Schroeder, 2002).

With a more realistic understanding of the role of anxiety—and with these tips for controlling it in mind—let's move on to the various methods of delivery that you may confront over the course of your life as a student, professional, and citizen.

Methods of Delivery

When you think of a great speaker, you might envision someone who speaks eloquently yet sounds as though he or she is speaking without having prepared a written speech. Although that's possible in certain situations, most speakers spend time preparing in the ways we've already discussed in Chapters 12 and 13—they might write out a full speech and then prepare a speaking outline as a phrase or key-word outline. Deciding just how to prepare for your speech affects, and is affected by, your choice of delivery style. We'll examine four specific delivery options and the potential benefits and pitfalls of each.

Speaking from Manuscript

If you've watched the president of the United States deliver the annual State of the Union address, you may have noticed that he alternates between two tele-prompter screens as he reads his speech. That's because he's delivering a speech from manuscript. When you speak from manuscript, you write your entire speech out and then read it word for word from the written text because your allegiance is to the words that you have prepared. Speaking from manuscript is

---

WIREDFORCOMMUNICATION

Facing Your Public Speaking Fears in Virtual Reality

Picture yourself at a podium in front of a huge audience. The people in the audience look bored, even sleepy. As you stand before them, every yawn, cough, and shuffle of their feet echoes in the vast auditorium. You struggle to make eye contact with one person or another, but their responses seem far off, their expressions disconnected from everything you are doing and saying.

This may sound like a very real situation—or a very realistic nightmare. In fact, it's a virtual reality simulation designed to help individuals suffering from public speaking anxiety overcome their fear. Companies specializing in virtual reality therapy (VRT) use 3-D imaging software, video footage, and sometimes mechanized props that simulate movement to create artificial representations of stress-inducing environments. Clients wear helmets, and motion sensors allow them to interact with the virtual reality environment. "It's a therapist's dream," notes one psychologist who has used the simulations to treat certain social anxieties. "To help people deal with their problems, you must get them exposed to what they fear most" (Lubell, 2004).

The effectiveness of VRT on public speaking anxiety is unclear. The technology is not yet widely used. And although some individual therapists using the technology claim success rates as high as 90 percent, there have been no large-scale, scientific studies of the programs (Lubell, 2004). Nonetheless, it does offer individuals a chance to test their skills in front of an audience in a very private and constructive way.

THINK ABOUT THIS

❶ Do you think virtual reality simulations would be helpful aids in preparing for public speaking? Whom might they help more, individuals with moderate speech anxiety or severe speech anxiety?

❷ What are the benefits of practicing in front of a virtual audience? How would it compare to a real one?

❸ What aspects of the public speaking situation do you think a VRT simulation could effectively simulate? What aspects would it be impossible to capture?

common for presidential speeches. That's because they are by nature quite long and will likely be quoted and interpreted throughout the world. A mistake in the delivery of such a speech might not merely embarrass the president but affect world events. Manuscript delivery is useful in any situation where accuracy, time constraints, or worries about misinterpretation outweigh the need for a casual and natural delivery style.

However, manuscript delivery also has a number of downsides. First, it's time-consuming, involving countless rewrites to get the written message exactly right. That's one reason why, although it works for the president (who has a team of speechwriters at his disposal), this is not a form of delivery that students typically use in class. Second, the static nature of reading from a written speech—be it from manuscript in your hand or a teleprompter in front of you—limits your ability to communicate nonverbally. Chained to the written word, you are less able to move around the stage, use facial expressions or hand gestures, or make eye contact with members of your audience. As you'll learn later in this chapter, planning and rehearsal are crucial for overcoming these tendencies when delivering a speech from manuscript.

Speaking from Memory

Speaking from memory is an ancient public speaking tradition referred to as **oratory**. In this style of speaking, you prepare the speech in the manuscript form as just described but then commit the words to memory.

Oratory delivery is fairly uncommon today as a form of public speaking, as it is both time-consuming and risky. A speaker who forgets a word or phrase can easily lose his or her place in the speech, panic, and never recover. But even if every line is delivered perfectly, the very nature of memorization can create a barrier between speaker and audience. Having memorized the speech and rehearsed without an audience, the speaker tends to deliver it as if the audience wasn't there. Such a speech can therefore end up feeling more like a performance, a one-man or one-woman show, rather than a communication situation in which the speaker is engaging with the audience.

Speaking Spontaneously

Impromptu speaking refers to situations where you speak to an audience without any warning or preparation. (Talk about public speaking fears!) When you are unexpectedly called on to speak in class or suddenly motivated to give a toast at a party, you must speak impromptu. The secret to excelling at impromptu speaking is understanding that it's never entirely spontaneous; if you are always prepared to give a speech unexpectedly, no speech is entirely unexpected. The following steps can help you be prepared.

Think on Your Feet

When called on to speak unexpectedly, begin by first acknowledging the person who introduced or called on you, and then repeat or rephrase the question or issue. This will give you a moment to focus on the topic and quickly construct a game plan. Usually you'll want to choose a simple format for responding, such as noting advantages and disadvantages, cause and effect, issues or problems, or

● **SPEAKING FROM** manuscript is a fitting method of delivery for TV newscasters such as Brian Williams, for whom accuracy and time constraints are critical.

In an impromptu speaking situation you should be aware of the relational, situational, and cultural context in which you are communicating (Chapter 1). This knowledge will help you tailor your speech to be appropriate and effective, whether you're giving a toast at a friend's wedding surrounded by her religious family members, or at an international meeting of a professional association surrounded by colleagues.

● **NO PUBLIC SPEAKERS** think on their feet as much as debaters. These political candidates must not only present and defend their sides of key issues but must also anticipate and address what their opponents might say.

agreement or disagreement, and then apply it to the topic. For example, let's say you're a high school teacher attending a board of education meeting. Your principal is speaking on how to maximize the funds allocated toward art and music at your school when he suddenly turns to you and asks you to respond to the proposal. After initially wanting to crawl under a table, you'd likely want to restate your principal's points about the importance of art and music in the lives of many teens and then discuss what you agree with regarding the proposal and what you think could be changed. Or you might talk about the advantages of the proposal, following up with a few disadvantages.

Listen to Others

One of the best ways that you can prepare to speak when you are unprepared to do so is by reflecting on the event you are attending to see if there is something that has been emotionally moving to you. Determine if you have some personal application of a point or an example that a speaker has made that either substantiates or refutes another speaker. Most audiences enjoy hearing speakers tell a brief story that illustrates a point that another speaker made or a theme that an event uses. At a "roast" for a retired quarterback, for example, various teammates shared stories of old times with the audience. When the emcee asked for others to contribute on an informal basis, one participant reflected on an occurrence that a previous speaker had described and added several humorous insights of his own.

Speaking Extemporaneously

Have you witnessed those calm, cool, collected speakers who seem to be making it up as they go along in a surprisingly organized manner? This is called **extemporaneous speaking**.

When you speak extemporaneously, you plan the content, organization, and delivery well in advance, but instead of writing the entire speech out word for word, you speak from an outline of key words and phrases or speaking aids such as slideware programs (for example, PowerPoint). Extemporaneous speaking involves delivering your speech in an impromptu style, even though the speech is neither spontaneous nor unrehearsed. Most speakers favor extemporaneous delivery because they can fully prepare and rehearse their presentations while economizing on time because they need not determine in advance the exact words that they want to use.

One downside to extemporaneous speaking is that it's difficult to have exact or precise timing or wording given the spontaneous nature of the speech. In other words, speakers can easily get off track or become wordy and repetitive. This pitfall may cause speakers with imposed time limits (such as those your instructor sets for you and your classmates) to go over their allotted time.

So what's the secret to succeeding at extemporaneous speaking? You can achieve success and confidence through practice and preparation. Consider the following points:

▶ *Prepare well in advance.* You can begin preparing for an extemporaneous speech as soon as you decide on a topic. Think about some possible points you want to make and how you might support them.

▶ *Don't forget the outline!* You studied outlining in Chapter 13, so we won't repeat that information here except to remind you that your key-word or phrase outline keeps you focused but gives you lots of flexibility with your word choice.

● **WILL FERRELL** and his costars ad-libbed much of *Anchorman*, not unlike what you will do when speaking extemporaneously.

▶ *Practice truly makes perfect.* Do actors or jazz musicians give the exact same performance every single time they perform? Certainly not! But they do practice a lot. When you get really familiar with a script or a musical composition (or a speech), you may indeed memorize parts of it, but a little bit of it will change each and every time, allowing for a more natural delivery.

Guidelines for Effective Delivery

Everything that you have done up to this point, from selecting a topic and researching information to outlining your presentation, is a prerequisite to the big moment: actually delivering your speech. In this section, we'll take a fresh look at a point that we've emphasized throughout this book: how you say something is as important as what you say. That is, audiences receive information not only from the actual words that you speak but also through two channels of nonverbal communication: the vocal and the visual. Let's see how these nonverbal channels play out in your speech.

● **EFFECTIVE SPEAKING** is a crucial skill. Whether you're a sports star giving a press conference or a climbing instructor giving a safety demonstration, you need to know how to deliver your words in an articulate and expressive manner.

Effective Vocal Delivery

Actor Seth Rogen is the rare comedian who uses a monotone voice to great comic effect—his delivery of zinging punch lines in a flat, unchanging tone adds an extra layer of irony to films like *Paul* (2011), *Pineapple Express* (2008), and *Knocked Up* (2007). But listening to him deliver a long speech in the same style would likely lull you to sleep (or perhaps cause you to fantasize about throwing things at the podium).

Obviously, your voice and the language you choose are extremely important components of your speech. But your voice is also a powerful nonverbal factor that affects delivery. By using varying aspects of your voice, you can engage your audience as well as convey confidence and trustworthiness. Through practice, you can learn to control the elements of vocal delivery, which include pitch, volume, rate, pauses, pronunciation, and articulation.

Varying Your Pitch

To be an effective public speaker, you must make use of the range of vocal sounds that the human voice is capable of producing. These variations of sound range from high to low—like musical notes—and are known as *pitch*. You speak in a **monotone** (like Seth Rogen) when you do not vary your pitch at all. And as we indicated, it can be painful to listen to a monotonous speaker. So how do you ensure that you are using your pitch effectively? One way to practice is to record yourself speaking ahead of time to determine if there are places where you need to use more energy and extend your pitch levels.

AND YOU?

Many of us feel awkward when we hear our voices on a recording, but rather than feel uncomfortable, you should learn to embrace your speaking voice. What aspects of your vocal delivery are unique to you? How might you, like Seth Rogen, utilize these features to create a confident speaking style all your own?

Adjusting Your Speaking Rate and Volume

Speakers can use vocal cues to signal to the audience what is important to pay attention to. Just as we use boldface and italic type in the pages of this book to emphasize certain words and phrases, as a speaker you can use audible cues to emphasize certain points.

How fast or slow you speak is known as your **speaking rate**, and it can also be a key factor in effective speaking. You want to speak slowly enough that your audience is able to hear and absorb what you say but quickly enough to capture the urgency and importance of what you are saying. Typically, if you speak faster, compared with surrounding material, you signal your enthusiasm for the content, and the audience's interest will follow. When you slow down, your rate signals a degree of seriousness and concern. You would deliver a persuasive call-to-action speech at a faster pace in order to show and elicit enthusiasm. You would deliver a tribute or dedication, such as a eulogy, at a slower pace to demonstrate sincerity and seriousness.

Changes in *volume*—how loudly or quietly you speak—can also be used to emphasize certain points. What do you want to stand out from your speech for the audience to remember? Is it a statistic, a name, or a product? Think about giving one word or phrase in every few sentences some "punch." This differentiates the word or phrase from its context.

Using Pauses for Effect

A well-placed pause is one of the most powerful tools available to speakers. Because many speakers believe that their entire goal is to talk, they pause too infrequently. But taking a moment between statements, words, or phrases and not saying anything at all can add drama to your speech by offering the audience a moment to reflect on what you have said and building anticipation for what will follow. For example, in Martin Luther King Jr.'s famous "I Have a Dream" speech, King's use of pauses, combined with rhetorical tools like repetition, helped to build drama and anticipation as he delivered his speech.

Speaking Clearly and Precisely

One of the quickest ways to lose credibility with your audience is to mispronounce a word—especially a word that is specifically related to the subject of your presentation. **Pronunciation** is the correct formation of word sounds. Many words in the English language are frequently mispronounced, to the point that individuals are not even aware that they are saying these words incorrectly.

Throughout his presidency, George W. Bush was the butt of countless jokes—often self-deprecating ones—for his frequent errors in pronunciation. But even though Bush sometimes made mistakes in pronunciation, he articulated well. **Articulation** is the clarity and forcefulness with which the sounds are

● AS *SUPERNANNY* JO FROST demonstrates with her proper British accent, certain patterns of pronunciation can make a person sound more intelligent or authoritative.

made, regardless of whether they are pronounced correctly. To speak clearly, even if incorrectly, is to be articulate. All speakers strive to be articulate, but there are several ways in which we routinely sabotage our efforts (O'Hair, Stewart, & Rubenstein, 2007).

When a speaker omits certain sounds in a word, runs words together, and speaks so softly that a listener can hardly hear, the speaker is guilty of **mumbling**. Most people mumble either because they are in a hurry, because they suffer from communication apprehension, or because they are not prepared to speak clearly. And like mispronunciation, mumbling can also be simply a matter of habit.

Audience perceptions about a speaker's skills can be affected by **accents**— patterns of pronunciation that are specific to a certain upbringing, geographical region, or culture. Speakers who hail from different countries, or even different regions or cultures within a country, typically speak with distinctive accents. While the word choices that they make may differ from time to time, the greatest difference that you hear is in their emphasis on syllables and cadence or rhythm while speaking. British speakers tend to emphasize syllables differently

AND YOU?
How do you react when you hear speakers with an accent that is different from yours? Do you find them difficult to understand, or do you make assumptions about them based on the way they speak? How might your own accent be an advantage or disadvantage in your next speaking situation?

COMMUNICATIONACROSSCULTURES

You Sound Like You're From . . .

In a country as large as the United States, diversity means more than a mere ethnic, religious, or racial mosaic. Regional dialects—local speech patterns, including unique pronunciations and vocabulary—create a special challenge for competent communication. English may be a common language, but each of us actually speaks it somewhat differently. And, for better or worse, our regional dialects carry with them certain baggage. For example, Americans tend to perceive midwestern accents as the most "correct," while strong southern and New York City accents are perceived as signs of lower intelligence (Preston, 1998).

That's why many people whose jobs require public speaking go to great pains to shed their regional accents. Many of them head to speech coaches like the late Sam Chwat, the "speech coach to the stars" whose clients included the actors Robert DeNiro and Julia Roberts, as well as a host of corporate executives and public figures who need to unlearn their hometown accent—or learn a new one (Woo, 2011). Chwat, a speech pathologist who had shed his own thick New York accent in order to avoid confusing his clients, told *The New York Times* in 2010, "I have seen a notable rise in the number of self-referred corporate execs who are trying to retain their competitive edge within their corporations, be clearly understood by customers or clients who typecast or stigmatize them by their speech patterns" (as cited in Roberts, 2010). While he made his living recognizing, learning, and teaching the varied nuances of different accents, Chwat didn't feel that having an accent, any accent, was a bad thing. "There is no direct instruction for public speaking and standard articulation," he noted, "and there is no penalty for speaking with an accent" (as cited in Roberts, 2010).

THINK ABOUT THIS

❶ What type of accent do you have? How do you feel it is perceived by others from different regions in the United States or even abroad?

❷ Why do most newscasters tend to speak with a midwestern accent? Why might that accent be considered the most neutral?

❸ If a speaker has a strong regional accent, should he or she try to lessen it when speaking publicly? Are there any public speaking situations where a strong regional accent might be beneficial?

than Americans and speak with different cadences as well. Southern speakers tend to drawl (use a slower pace) and elongate vowel sounds. Speakers from the Northeast tend to omit sounds from the middle of words such as *park* and *word*. Midwestern speakers tend to insert an "r" sound into words such as *wash*.

Effective Visual Delivery

In the same way that a monotone can lull an audience to sleep, so can a stale, dull physical presence. This doesn't mean that you need to be doing cartwheels throughout your speech, but it does mean that you should avoid keeping your hands glued to the podium and that you should look up from your note cards once in a while. Otherwise, you'll be little more than a talking head, and your audience will quickly lose interest. What's more, effective visual cues can enhance a presentation, helping you clarify and emphasize your points in an interesting and compelling way.

Dressing for the Occasion

Recall from Chapter 5 that *artifacts*—accessories carried on the body for decoration or identification—send powerful messages about you. If you're not sure whether or not to cover up your tattoos or keep your tongue ring in, consider your topic, the occasion, your own comfort level, and what you can glean as the comfort level of the audience. And don't forget that your instructor can offer valuable advice and guidance as well.

If you're like most people, you probably hop out of bed in the morning, open your closet, and hope that you have something decent to wear to work or class since you haven't exactly had time for the laundry. However, on the day of your speech—just like the day of a job interview or an important date—you don't want to leave your appearance to chance.

Today you are a speaker, and even though you may be presenting to a group of friends or classmates you see every week, it is imperative that you look the part of someone capable of informing or persuading the audience. Research, for example, indicates that attractive people are more persuasive (Chaiken, 1979). And while you certainly don't need to have a Hollywood-perfect body, an expensive wardrobe, or a killer hairstyle to inform or persuade anyone, you should attempt to look and feel your personal best. You can signal authority and enhance your credibility by dressing professionally in neat, ironed clothing—like a pair of black pants or a skirt, with a button-down shirt or simple sweater (Cialdini, 2008; Pratkanis & Aronson, 2001). You should certainly avoid looking overly casual (by wearing shorts, cut-off jeans, or sneakers), which can signal that you don't take the audience, your speech topic, or even yourself as a speaker seriously.

There may, however, be occasions in which nonformal dress or a surprising aspect of appearance deeply enhances a presentation. For example, a former student of ours always wore her red hair in a long braid. It was part of her personal "uniform" (in addition to jeans and flip-flops). On the day of her presentation, she ditched the flip-flops, but also her hair. You see, our student was giving an informative presentation on alopecia, a condition that causes hair loss. She developed the condition as a young child and felt comfortable and confident that speaking without her trademark red wig would increase her credibility on her chosen topic (see Cialdini, 2008).

Using Effective Eye Behavior

As we noted in Chapter 5, eye behavior is a crucial aspect of nonverbal communication that can be both effective and appropriate when you consider the cultural context in which you are communicating. In Vietnamese culture, for example, it is considered inappropriate and rude to make prolonged, direct eye contact with someone, particularly if that person is of a higher rank or social status. In the many Western cultures, conversely, a lack of eye contact can make a speaker seem suspicious or untrustworthy; in the United States in particular, direct eye contact is one of the most important nonverbal actions in public speaking, essential to signaling respect and interest to the audience (Axtell, 1991). But how can a speaker make and maintain eye contact with a large group of individuals?

One way is to move your eyes from one person to another (in a small group) or one section of people to another (in a large group), a technique called scanning. **Scanning** allows you to make brief eye contact with almost everyone in an audience, no matter how large. To use it, picture yourself standing in front of the audience, and then divide the room into four imaginary sections. As you move from idea to idea in your speech, move your eye contact into a new section. Select a friendly-looking person in the quadrant, and focus your eye contact directly on that person while completing the idea (just make sure you don't pick a friend who will try to make you laugh!). Then change quadrants, and select a person from the new group. Tips for using the scanning technique are offered in Table 14.1.

Incorporating Facial Expressions and Gestures

Have you ever seen an anime cartoon in which a character's face contorts, the jaw dropping unnaturally (sometimes to the floor) and the eyes becoming small white dots? The animator certainly gets the point across—this character is either entirely surprised or seriously confused. Your facial expressions, while not as exaggerated as those of an anime character, serve a similar purpose: they let your audience know when your words arouse fear, anger, happiness, joy, frustration, or other emotions. The critical factor is that your expressions must match the verbal message that you are sending in your speech. As a competent communicator, you

Work in sections	Do not scan from left to right or right to left. Always work in sections and move randomly from one section to another.
Avoid the "lighthouse" effect	You'll look like a human lighthouse (or a lawn sprinkler) if you simply rotate your upper torso from left to right while you talk, looking at no one person in particular.
Look people in the eye	Avoid looking at people's foreheads or over their heads; look them in the eye, even if they are not looking back at you.
Focus for a moment	Remember to pause long enough on an individual so that the person can recognize that you are looking directly at him or her.
Don't jump away	If someone is not looking at you, stay with the person anyway until you've finished your thought. Then move on to another.
Divide large groups	If the audience is too large for you to get to everyone, look at small groups of two or three people sitting together.

TABLE 14.1

TIPS FOR SCANNING YOUR AUDIENCE

are unlikely to smile when delivering a eulogy—unless you are recounting a particularly funny or endearing memory about the deceased.

Like facial expressions, gestures amplify the meaning of your speech. Clenching your fist, counting with your fingers, and spreading your hands far apart to indicate distance or size all reinforce or clarify your message. What is most important about using gestures is that they should be appropriate and natural. So if you want to indicate your deeply held emotional sentiments when persuading your audience about the benefits of becoming a foster parent, but you feel awkward putting your hand over your heart, don't do it. Your audience will be able to tell that you feel uncomfortable and unnatural. Focus instead on what you do feel comfortable with. You might indicate the giant bear hug your foster child greets you with every morning if that feels like a better fit for your personality (Buckley, 1999, p. 209).

EVALUATINGCOMMUNICATIONETHICS

Judging Speeches

Later in this chapter, you will read about Anna Capps (our Real Communicator), and we've talked about the struggles that people with physical challenges (such as King George VI) face when delivering speeches. But how do culture and ethics collide when it comes time actually to judge or assign a grade to a presentation?

Imagine that your speech class is engaging in peer evaluation. In groups of six, you practice delivering your speech before the final presentation to the entire class. You will evaluate your group members' speeches twice—and a portion of your grades will be determined by the improvement they make between the first two practice speeches and then between the final rehearsal and the delivery before the entire class.

One woman in your group, Evelyn, has cerebral palsy, a neurological disorder that permanently affects body movements and muscle coordination. It can have a diverse number of symptoms, but Evelyn struggles most with slurred speech, balance, and exaggerated reflexes. Evelyn is quite comfortable talking about her disability and appears to be a confident speaker. Yet as she talks, you find it somewhat difficult to understand her speech. Because many of her words are slurred, you feel like you're missing a few main points. And as much as you try not to, you find the fact that she sways when she speaks and that she must grip the back of her chair for balance somewhat distracting.

You feel bad making these comments to Evelyn on her first evaluation, and so you focus your remarks on improvements she can make on the outline. But you're worried about how the rest of the class will react to Evelyn and even what sort of grade she might get from your professor (who has a reputation for being a difficult speech grader). You're now facing your second round of evaluations for Evelyn.

THINK ABOUT THIS

❶ Is it ethical to share your concerns with Evelyn? Or is it more appropriate to keep quiet in this situation?

❷ You may have been reading this scenario under the assumption that you do not have any physical challenges. Now imagine that you have speech challenges or that you suffer from a chronic illness. Does this influence your critique of Evelyn's speech? Does it make you more or less comfortable addressing her?

❸ Imagine instead that Evelyn is not a native speaker of English, or that is from a different region of the United States and you find her accent difficult to understand. Is it ethical to address these concerns when judging her speech?

Controlling Body Movements

As you can see, audience members are listening not only to the words of your speech, but also to the way you deliver those words. In addition to eye behavior, facial expressions, and gestures, your audience can't help but notice your body. In most speaking situations you encounter, the best way to highlight your speech content is to restrict your body movements so that the audience can focus on your words. Consider, for example, your **posture**, or the position of your arms and legs and how you carry your body. Generally, when a speaker slumps forward or leans on a podium, rocks back and forth, sways left and right, paces forward and backward, or appears to dance behind a lectern, the audience perceives the speaker as unpolished and listeners' attention shifts from the message to the speaker's body movements.

How do you prevent such movements from happening, particularly if you're someone who fidgets when nervous? One useful technique is called **planting**. Stand with your legs apart at a distance that is equal to your shoulders. Bend your knees slightly so that they do not lock. From this position, you are able to gesture freely, and when you are ready to move, you can take a few steps, replant, and continue speaking. The key is always to plant following every movement that you make.

Connecting with Your Audience

It is through vocal and visual delivery that speakers are able to interact with their audiences—that's what makes public speaking different from just writing a good presentation. When you compose an essay, you write it and it goes off to the reader; it's a linear model of communication (as discussed in Chapter 1). But speaking before an audience is more than just providing information through words; it's an interaction between speaker and audience.

The most talented public speakers are always keenly aware of this. Gifted speakers like Ronald Reagan and Bill Clinton were known for their ability to connect with members of any audience on a very personal level and for their knack for delivering even the most formal speeches in a style that felt conversational, personal, and familiar. That's because both were able to use their words, voices, and gestures to convey the way they felt about a subject. They also spoke directly to their audiences in a way that felt unrehearsed and sincere. Let's now take a look at the way our words converge with our vocal and visual delivery to establish such a connection with the audience. We'll also consider the ways we can adapt our delivery to suit the audience's needs and expectations.

● **PRESIDENT RONALD REAGAN** earned his reputation as a gifted public speaker by recognizing the interaction between speaker and audience and presenting himself as approachable and self-assured.

Expressing Emotion

If you do not feel passion for what you are talking about, you can be sure that your audience will not feel it either. One of your responsibilities is to ensure that throughout your speech, the audience feels the same emotions that you

real communicator

NAME: Anna Capps
HOMETOWN: Cleveland, Georgia
OCCUPATION: Student at Gainesville State College
FUN FACT: I have a cocker spaniel named Lady who always lets me know when someone's at the door.

At Gainesville State College, I took a course called Introduction to Human Communication. On the first day of class, I saw on the syllabus that I would have to deliver two speeches: one informative, one persuasive. You know Jerry Seinfeld's comment about Americans preferring to be in the casket rather than delivering the eulogy? That's me. I had never given a speech in my life. And to make things harder, I'm deaf. Oral communication does not come as easy to me as it does to people who've grown up learning language by hearing language. But I wasn't going to let that stop me. I was going to ace that first speech.

I didn't ace that first speech. It was an informational presentation on gemstones, and I was *so* nervous. I held the lectern in a death grasp. According to my professor, I talked way too fast and didn't establish direct eye contact with my audience. What's worse is that as I was speaking, I could tell things were not going well. My particular disability leaves me visually hyperaware, so I saw confused, puzzled, what-is-she-talking-about looks on my listeners' faces. The hardest part was that it seemed as if the other students were becoming increasingly embarrassed for me. They were not used to hearing my voice and couldn't understand what I was saying. I started to get really frustrated, and that only made me more nervous. I finished my speech (forgetting about half of it) and sat back down in my chair, my face burning.

I learn well from my mistakes, however. For my second presentation, I didn't need to consider a hypothetical worst-case scenario in order to manage my communication apprehension; I'd already lived it! I evaluated what went wrong. One of the problems in my first speech was that my audience didn't understand me. I wasn't speaking clearly. I decided that in the second speech, I'd have to maximize my strengths and play down my weaknesses. I went to disability services and got a sign language interpreter. I also wrote a speech I was more interested in: addressing the smog problem for allergy sufferers. And I practiced and practiced. Was I still nervous when it came time to deliver the speech? Of course. But now I had an attack plan. I would concentrate on my visual delivery, particularly eye contact, as I had to make sure to look at my audience and not at the interpreter. I scanned the room, looking people in the eye—and not only did direct eye contact establish credibility for me as a speaker, but looking at all those people responding positively also made me more confident in myself. Then too—and here is where my hearing disability helped—I have very animated facial expressions. I was able to communicate through gestures, and the audience members who are visually oriented responded to that. By the end of the speech, feeling more assured, I was smiling and standing up straight.

I know that I will have to deliver speeches and face other challenging communication situations in the future (as we all will!). But this experience has given me a huge boost of confidence in many areas of my life, so I know that I can face what's ahead. And the next time I speak in front of a group, I know that I will do a good job. I've already done it once. Who's going to tell me I can't do it again?

do for your subject matter. Many Americans, for example, felt an intimate connection to New York Mayor Rudy Giuliani when he addressed the media in the immediate aftermath of the terrorist attacks on the city on September 11, 2001. Although he remained authoritative and in control, he was also able to express his grief in a way that rang true to everyone watching or listening. When an audience feels that a speaker is simply acting, they may question the sincerity of the message.

Adapting to Your Audience

One common mistake speakers make is to speak to—or even at—the audience. Competent public speakers always think of their presentations as speaking *with* the audience. As discussed earlier, in Western cultures, this generally means making and maintaining eye contact. But it also means listening to audience reactions, paying attention to listeners' body movements, and continually gauging their responses to what you say and do so that you can make adjustments to your speech as you go along. For example, if you observe audience members frowning or squinting, it may be a sign of misunderstanding. You can take this as a cue to slow down or emphasize key points more explicitly. Alternatively, if you notice your audience members responding with smiles, focused eye contact, or even laughter, you probably want to maintain the style of speaking that produced such a positive reaction.

Creating Immediacy with Your Audience

As you learned in Chapter 5, immediacy is a feeling of closeness, involvement, and warmth between people as communicated by nonverbal behavior (Mehrabian, 1971; Prager, 2000). We often think of immediacy as being an important facet of close interpersonal relationships. This is certainly true—but it is also an important component of building trust in the relationship between the speaker and the audience.

Speakers enhance their immediacy with their audience by following many of the guidelines we have already set forward in this chapter: establishing and maintaining eye contact with audience members, smiling, moving toward the audience, using inclusive gestures and posture, speaking in a relaxed or conversational tone or style, and using humor. Research clearly shows that audiences respond favorably to speaker immediacy in a variety of settings (Christophel, 1990; Frymier, 1994; Teven, 2007a, 2007b, 2010; Teven & Hanson, 2004). However, as is the case with interpersonal relationships, immediacy is a two-way street. Audiences help to foster this feeling of closeness and trust by being competent listeners. That is to say, they should be listening actively, responding with eye contact, nodding, and offering nonverbal indications of agreement, surprise, confusion, and so on.

Effective Presentation Aids

Bill Gates is a technology buff, to be sure. He is the man behind Microsoft, the company that invented the ubiquitous presentation software, PowerPoint. So when he gives speeches on behalf of the Bill and Melinda Gates Foundation, it's not surprising that he uses PowerPoint slides to graphically display information on changing death rates from malaria in poor countries and the impact of simple tools like mosquito netting as well as vaccines and other preventatives. But Gates

also thinks outside the technological box when it comes to presentation aids: "Malaria is, of course, spread by mosquitoes," he tells the crowd. "I've brought some here," he adds, as he opens a jar to let a small fleet of (uninfected) insects fly around the auditorium. "There's no reason only poor people should have the experience" (Gates, 2009). This simple presentation aid got the audience's attention and made the fight against malaria familiar to anyone who has ever swatted a mosquito off their arm on a summer evening.

Like Gates, today's speakers have many tools to create dramatic visual presentations that enhance their words and deepen the audience's understanding of the topic. We'll explore how presentation aids work in the sections that follow.

● **BILL GATES** was certainly thinking outside of the box—or the jar!—when he released mosquitoes into the auditorium to aid a presentation on malaria.

The Function of Presentation Aids

You already know that presentation aids can be a valuable asset to a speech, heightening an audience's interest and helping you convey technical information. But remember that a presentation aid should *supplement* your speech, not substitute for the speech. Sure, you may have a moving video or shocking image to share with the audience. But if you haven't researched your topic thoroughly, assembled a useful speaking outline, or even looked up from the podium while speaking, who will care? To be truly useful, presentation aids must enhance your speech, accomplishing three goals:

▶ *Help listeners process and retain information.* Effective presentation aids help the audience see relationships among concepts, variables, or items. Always make a point, refer to the presentation aid, direct the listeners' attention to where you want them to focus, and then restate, reiterate, or rephrase what you have said.

▶ *Promote interest and motivation.* If you show terms, photographs, statistics, tables, and other items that truly reinforce your spoken message, the audience will be more likely to go along with you.

▶ *Convey information clearly and concisely.* There is no comparison between the amount of time it would take you to read a series of figures versus showing them on a table, graph, or chart. A good visual can present a lot of information in a clear, concise, and simple matter, saving the speaker's time for interpretation and elaboration.

Types of Presentation Aids

Students often ask, "What type of visual aid should I use for my speech?" The answer to that question is never entirely straightforward because it depends on your topic, the needs of your individual speech, the time constraints, the constraints of the speaking location, and a myriad of additional factors. What we can share, however, is a look at the dominant types of presentation aids and their general purposes for speakers. We begin by considering props and models before moving on to media clips and images, graphs and charts, posters and transparencies, flip charts and marker boards, and presentation software.

Props and Models

Some things, people, places, or processes are difficult to describe with only words and gestures, making visual aids both effective and appropriate. An object, or **prop**, removes the burden from the audience of having to imagine what something looks like as you speak. For instance, if you are giving an informative speech on the way to tune a guitar, you might find it difficult to explain the process with only words and gestures. Demonstrating the process on an actual guitar would be an effective visual (and audio) aid. You can also be your very own prop! For example, if you're teaching your audience particular moves in Irish dancing, you might do well to display your moves for everyone to see.

● **AN INTERESTING PROP** can be a helpful visual aid. This speaker might have trouble illustrating certain muscles and nerves in the human body without his model.

If a prop is too large to bring into the classroom or too small to be easily viewed by your audience members, consider using a **model**, an appropriately scaled object. One of our past students brought in a small-scale model of the Soviet nuclear submarine the *Kursk* to demonstrate how the vessel tragically encountered problems, exploded, and sank.

Be mindful and considerate when selecting the objects and models you bring to your presentation. You may be surprised to learn how many speakers have brought their pets in for a demonstration—despite the fact that other students in the classroom may have severe allergies. Along the same lines, avoid objects that may be dangerous or even illegal, such as firearms, knives, chemicals, and so on. Think safety first!

Media Clips and Images

Film, television, and Internet video clips can add another dimension to your speech by providing vivid illustrations of topics that are difficult to capture with words alone. For example, if you wanted to persuade your audience to protest the unethical treatment of animals by the food industry, you might show a brief clip from *Food, Inc.*, revealing how thousands of chickens are caged without room to move and without access to natural light.

Similarly, images—pictures, illustrations, or photographs—can enhance your speech by clarifying your words and points. A speaker informing an audience about reconstructive surgery for cleft palate, for example, might show a photograph of a child born with the condition as well as postsurgical photos, rather than trying to describe the condition and outcome only in words. When choosing media clips and images, keep a few points in mind:

▶ Make sure that your classroom is equipped with the equipment you will need to make your selection viewable to your audience.

▶ Keep your video clips short (say, one to two minutes maximum, depending on the length of the speech).

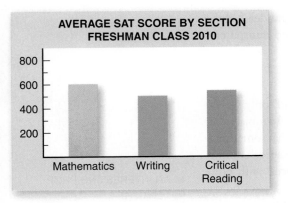

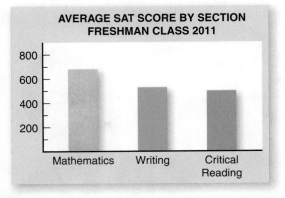

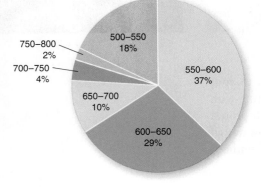

FIGURE 14.1

SAMPLES OF EFFECTIVE GRAPHS Bar graphs use bars of varying lengths to make comparisons. Pie charts depict the division of a whole.

▶ Don't overwhelm your audience with ten illustrations or photographs when two or three would suffice.

▶ Remember that your visual aids should not be the center of your speech; one hundred beautiful pictures will not make up for a lack of research or a poor delivery.

Graphs and Charts

When you're delivering a speech rich in statistics, data, and facts, visual aids can be indispensable presentation tools (see Figure 14.1). You can actually cut your presentation time drastically and increase your listeners' interest by pointing to some figures on a graph rather than reading them aloud, number by number. Graphs take several different forms. **Bar graphs** show the relationship of two or more sets of figures. A figure comparing a freshman class's average SAT scores by section, for example, is well illustrated with a bar graph. **Pie charts** show percentages of a circle divided proportionately; for example, a university admissions office uses a pie chart to reveal the percentage of freshman students scoring in a particular range on an SAT exam. A pie chart should ideally have from two to five segments; under no circumstances should it have more than eight since it will become difficult for the audience to read: if you have too many categories, you can add the smallest ones up and present them in a single segment.

Posters and Transparencies

You may find it helpful to have key words or ideas written out or visually displayed for your audience members to see. In such cases, it may make sense to use posters and transparencies. For example, if you're informing your audience about the Kübler-Ross model of the grieving process, you may wish to have the five stages (denial, anger, bargaining, depression, and acceptance) written down on a poster so that you can point to each stage as you begin to discuss it. Similarly, when persuading your audience about the effectiveness of graphic antidrug campaigns on television, you might want to place a poster of such an ad in clear view for everyone to see.

As with posters, transparencies can greatly enhance your ability to present complex information in your speech. They have an additional advantage in that they can often be rendered ahead of time to look more professional through the use of particular fonts and graphics. Simply purchase low-cost transparency sheets at an office supply store and use a photocopier to duplicate color and black-and-white pages. However, before you even get this far, verify that your classroom is equipped with a transparency projector. If you don't see one, let your instructor know of your plans to use transparencies and he or she will likely be able to request one for the day of your presentation.

When designing posters and transparencies, it's often helpful to keep a few key points in mind:

► Write large and legibly so that your audience members don't strain to understand your visual aid. For transparencies, this usually means choosing at least a twenty-point font.

► Use vivid colors to make your posters and transparencies more appealing.

► Avoid cramming more than one main idea or main point into a poster or transparency sheet unless it has a very specific purpose to enhance your meaning (for example, a collage of photos of missing and exploited children in your area).

► Put the transparency sheets and poster pages in order of use, and number them in case they get shuffled.

► If possible, use a pointer and stand near the poster to limit excessive movement.

► When using transparencies, try to stand near the screen instead of standing at the projector with your back to the audience.

Flip Charts and Marker Boards

Flip charts and marker boards (or chalkboards), which are very common in professional settings, have a distinct advantage for displaying words and ideas over posters and transparencies: they can invite and organize audience participation. For example, when presenting a new health insurance plan to a group of managers, a human resources representative might open the speech by asking the managers, "What aspects of health insurance matter most to your employees?" The audience members may respond with comments like "flexibility" or "low copays," which the speaker can jot down on the flip chart or board. He can then refer to each priority as he addresses them in his speech.

Boards and flip charts are also valuable when you wish to "unfold" an idea, step by step, before an audience, such as a coach using a board to break down a certain defense or offense. Just remember that your use of flip charts and boards should never be distracting. In other words, your audience may become irritated if you're constantly flipping back and forth between pages or running around to point to multiple different diagrams on the board.

Presentation Software

Sitting through hours of slides from your Aunt Sonja's trip to Phoenix is boring enough (with all due respect to our Arizona readers). Sitting through a slide show that essentially repeats your speech outline can be positively unbearable. Presentation software (such as Microsoft PowerPoint, Apple Keynote, and Google Docs), when used appropriately, allows you to have a one-stop home for lots of different visual aids without having to awkwardly move back and forth between different media.

However, presentation software is frequently misused by speakers who plug meaningless text or pointless visuals into slides without considering how to keep the audience's attention. You may, in fact, be familiar with the phrase "death by PowerPoint" (DuFrene & Lehman, 2004). Too often speakers allow their slides to dominate their presentations, attempting to wow the audience with their technical proficiency rather than focusing on interesting points or well-researched evidence. We often warn our students that the fancier and more detailed the digital presentation, the more suspicious we are of the information being presented.

AND YOU?

Think back on a variety of different public presentations you've witnessed—speeches by fellow students, presentations by instructors, political debates, and so on. What is the most effective use of a visual aid that you have encountered? What is the least effective? Why?

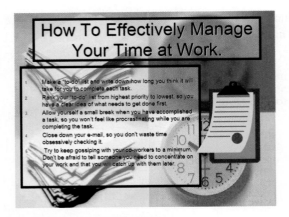

● **BEWARE THE TERRIBLE**
PowerPoint slide! A long
bulleted list of all of your speaking points on a distracting
background is a surefire way
to detract from your speech
and lose your audience's
attention.

If you decide to use presentation software in your speech, here are some tips for developing effective slides:

▶ Become familiar with all of the features and options of your specific software before you begin to plug in your presentation information.

▶ Use as few slides as possible. Remember, more is not always better!

▶ Use a minimal amount of text. Research indicates that restrained and very direct use of bullet points can positively affect audience recall of information (Vogel, Dickson, & Lehman, 1986).

▶ Make sure the font is large enough for easy viewing (we suggest forty-point type for titles and twenty-point type and above for all other text).

▶ Use only design elements that truly enhance meaning.

▶ Be prepared to give the same speech without slides in case of a technology glitch. In other words, make sure your presentation is effective even without your slides.

▶ Prepare and practice in advance! As we will discuss in the next section, you will need to give yourself enough time to organize, reorganize, edit, and feel comfortable moving between slides.

Practicing Your Speech

If there's one key to developing skill as a public speaker, it's practice. Practice transforms nervous public speakers into confident ones and good public speakers into great ones, particularly when speakers pay attention to four important points: remembering the speaking outline, practicing with presentation aids, simulating the speaking situation, and practicing the actual delivery.

Remember Your Speaking Outline

You've heard quite a bit from us about writing your outline and using it for speaking, and you know the benefits of creating a speaking outline consisting of key words and phrases. Now it's time to practice from it. Review your speaking outline to make sure that all of your key words and phrases work as prompts—if you can't remember that the letters "SD" stand for "sleep deprivation," for example, you might need to write that term out.

Practice Using Presentation Aids

Recall our discussion of Steve Jobs's annual keynote presentations in Chapter 12. Clearly, Jobs rehearses his presentations, including his use of presentation software and other technological aids—in fact, he knows it all well enough to work

The words in your speaking outline must prompt you to remember your ideas. During your rehearsal, you'll discover whether you've chosen key words that are at an appropriate level of *abstraction*, or vagueness vs. concreteness (Chapter 4). If the word is too vague, it may not jog your memory under pressure. But if it's too concrete, you may be tempted to read directly from your notes. You will need to practice under realistic conditions to discover the right level of abstraction.

around it when the inevitable technological glitches arise. When practicing with your presentation aids, consider the following tips:

▶ *Eliminate surprises.* If you're using any kind of technology, practice with it long before you deliver your speech. Show up with a DVD that skips or an MP3 clip that didn't download properly, and you may find your presentation stalled.

▶ *Test the facilities in advance.* Be proactive. Will the classroom PC be able to read files created on your Mac? It should, but you'll rest easier if you test it

what about you?

Assessing Your Practice Session

After you have practiced your speech aloud (either alone or in front of a mock audience), critically assess your performance and answer the following questions. *Note:* If you will be practicing in front of a group, you might consider offering your audience members a copy of this quiz so that they can answer questions as they listen to you.

_____ 1. Does your voice project confidence? Authority?

_____ 2. Are you varying your pitch (to avoid being monotonous)?

_____ 3. Are you varying your speaking rate and volume?

_____ 4. Are you articulating well? Are you mumbling? Can other people understand your words?

_____ 5. Does your speech contain words that might pose pronunciation problems for you?

_____ 6. Are you effectively scanning as you rehearse? (If you have others present, are you making eye contact? If not, are you looking at different quadrants of the room you are rehearsing in?)

_____ 7. Do you use occasional gestures to emphasize a point you're making in your speech? Do they feel natural?

_____ 8. Do you animate your facial expressions as you deliver your speech?

_____ 9. Are you able to integrate your presentation aids into your presentation effectively?

_____ 10. Is your speech within the required time limits for the assignment?

_____ 11. Are your speaking notes helpful and effective?

As noted throughout the chapter, if you cannot answer "yes" to these questions, then you will likely benefit from additional rehearsal time. Remember, the more you employ effective visual and vocal delivery—and the better prepared you are with effective and helpful notes—the more competent and confident you will be when you attempt to speak before your real audience.

out beforehand. Likewise, you should do sound checks for video and audio clips to make sure that the entire audience can see and/or hear them.

▶ *Write notes to yourself.* In your outline, make sure that you provide delivery cues to let yourself know when to move to the next item or slide or when to show an image or play a clip. This will help you avoid rushing ahead to get to a particular aid, as well as ensure that you don't forget any.

▶ *Rehearse your demonstrations with a partner.* When your presentation aid is actually a live prop (for example, a student in your own class), you'll need to practice with this person in advance of the presentation.

▶ *Have a backup plan.* What will you do if something malfunctions during your speech? If a video clip won't play, can you tell it as a story? You might have a handout prepared for your audience members, just in case your software doesn't work (or in case someone likes it so much they want to read through it again).

Simulate the Situation

You already know that few people can simply walk up to a podium for the first time and deliver a perfect speech. Seasoned public speakers often look and sound great in large part because they've done it before and done it often. Exposing yourself to some of the more unnerving aspects of public speaking—for example, an audience—can help you become more comfortable. You can do this by simulating some aspects of your speech delivery during your rehearsals. For example:

▶ *Create similar conditions.* Think about the room you'll deliver your speech in: what is its size, space, layout? Keep these things in mind as you rehearse—or even better, arrange to rehearse in the room where you will be speaking. Awareness of these conditions will help you practice eye contact, movement, gestures, and your use of notes.

▶ *Practice in front of someone.* Try practicing in front of someone or, preferably, a few people. One method for getting over anxiety about speaking in front of an audience is to "practice upward": practice first in front of one friend, then two, then three, and so on, until you are comfortable speaking before a fairly large group.

▶ *Keep an eye on your time.* Use a stopwatch or a kitchen timer to stay on target with your allotted speech time. You might even keep track of how much time you spend on each point, particularly if you have a tendency to go into a lot of detail early on or to rush at the end.

Practice Your Delivery

In any speech, your objective should be to communicate a message to an audience. If your message is clear, the audience will connect with it; if it's buried in a sea of mumbling or if it's forced to compete with distracting body language, the audience will miss your point. As you practice, you can improve the aspects of delivery you studied in this chapter and concentrate on your message.

▶ *Focus on your message.* Concentrate on the way that you express an argument, paraphrase a quotation, or explain a statistic. If you focus on your message, the right delivery will usually follow naturally.

▶ *Use mirrors cautiously.* Conventional wisdom has advocated rehearsing in front of a mirror in order to practice eye contact, maximize facial expressions, and assess gestures and movement. But we have mixed thoughts on this because there won't be any mirrors when you deliver the speech; they can also make you feel self-conscious about your appearance, distracting you from the message you want to communicate.

▶ *Record a practice session.* Before you gasp in horror and skip to the next bullet point, please trust us: this really does help. Many teachers and professors even record themselves to get a sense of their presence in the classroom ("Do I favor one side of the room?" "Do I tend to interact with only the front row?"). Recording your performance will allow you to get a sense of how well you project your voice, articulate your points, and use body movements, facial expressions, and gestures.

▶ *Ask for feedback.* See if you can find a person or two to listen to your speech who will give you an honest and constructive critique of your performance. Ask what they remember most about your presentation. Did they focus mostly on your content, or were they distracted by your postures, gestures, or stammering? Were your presentation aids helpful, or were they distracting or confusing?

AND YOU?

After you have practiced in front of one or more friends, family members, or classmates, consider their feedback. Was anything about the feedback surprising? Did they note the strengths and weaknesses that you expected them to pick up on, based on your own self-assessment? If not, how might you incorporate their feedback into your next practice session?

BACK TO ▶ *The King's Speech*

At the beginning of the chapter, we talked about Britain's King George VI, or Albert, who was thrust into a position that demanded public speaking skills even though he struggled with a challenging stammer. Let's think about Albert's journey, as well as that of David Seidler, who was inspired by Albert's story and eventually brought it to the screen with *The King's Speech*, in light of what we've learned in this chapter.

▶ Given his royal position, Albert knew that public speaking would be a part of his life. As such, part of his preparation was to build confidence and overcome anxiety by addressing his stammer through prolonged, and somewhat experimental, speech therapy. Had he not been a prince (and, later, king), he might never have addressed his fear.

▶ As a king in the early twentieth century, Albert had to contend with emerging media—particularly radio—when giving speeches. While he still had to contend with the transactional nature of public speeches (in which he must interact with and adjust to the audience), radio gave him the opportunity to gain confidence and practice: the audience's feedback is limited in radio's linear model of communication.

▶ The audience plays a role in the success of any speech, and it is likely that every British citizen, facing the horror and uncertainty of world war for the second time in a generation, *wanted* the king to succeed. As actor Colin Firth noted, "People knew this man was facing his demons just by speaking to them. I think there was a sense that it cost him something. They found it valiant" (CBS News, 2011b).

THINGS TO TRY ▷ Activities

1. *The King's Speech* centers on Albert's address to the British people on September 3, 1939, at the outbreak of World War II, audio recordings of which are available online. Listen to them, and consider how you would have received the king's message if you were a British citizen at that time. What do you think of his delivery? Do you think your knowledge of his struggles with stammering affect the way you rate his delivery?

2. While in class, select a partner and give a one- to two-minute impromptu speech on a topic of your choice. Your partner will write down both negative and positive feedback to share with you, and you will do the same in return. Then team up with another pair of partners. You and your original partner will take turns giving the same speeches again, incorporating improvements suggested by your partner the first time around. The new partners in your group will likely give both negative and positive feedback. Listen carefully, and apply their advice. Now add another pair of partners to your group, for a total of six people, and give your speech one last time. Think of the feedback from all three sessions. If you received the same negative feedback more than once, you know where further improvement is needed. Did you feel more confident giving your speech the third time than you did the first time?

3. Pay attention to how you meet people and the general first impression you receive from them. Ask yourself what makes you feel the way you do about the person. Does the person make you feel comfortable by smiling at you, looking you in the eye, or coming across as sincere? If you can pinpoint the reasons for your own first impressions, you can better understand what an audience expects from a speaker (and adjust your own behaviors in order to make a good impression).

4. When practicing a speech, pay attention to your gestures and body movements. Practice once using movements that you feel are appropriate and comfortable; then practice in front of a friend, and ask how appropriate your movements actually look. Are you using too many gestures? Two few?

5. Search YouTube for a segment with a speaker giving a speech (the topic does not matter). Turn off the volume so you can only see (not hear) the speech. Analyze the physical speech delivery of the speaker. Make lists of the problems with his or her speech delivery and of things the speaker does well (for example, maintains eye contact). Then watch the speech again, this time with the volume on. Listen carefully to the vocal delivery (such as pitch, rate, and volume) of the speaker. What do you notice about his or her voice? Compare your lists, and note all of your observations as you prepare for your own speech.

Now that you have finished reading this chapter, you can

Identify and control your anxieties:

▶ **Public speaking anxiety** (PSA) is the nervousness we experience when we know we have to communicate publicly to an audience (p. 408).

▶ **Communication apprehension** (CA), fear or anxiety associated with communication, is a common barrier to effective delivery (p. 408).

▶ Common anxiety triggers include upsetting past experiences, fear of evaluation, and distaste for attention (pp. 408–409).

▶ Confidence comes from being prepared, desensitizing yourself, visualizing success (particularly through **performance visualization**), taking care of yourself, and lots of practice (p. 410).

Choose a delivery style that is best suited to you and your speaking situation:

▶ Speaking from manuscript is helpful when you need to get the details 100 percent right but can be static and dull (pp. 411–412).

▶ Speaking from memory, referred to as **oratory**, doesn't invite rapport with the audience and is rare today (p. 412).

▶ Speaking spontaneously—when you're asked to speak with no warning beforehand—is known as **impromptu speaking** (p. 412).

▶ **Extemporaneous speaking** makes the speech look easy and spontaneous, but it's actually based on an outline of key points and practice, practice, practice (pp. 413–415).

Employ effective vocal cues:

▶ Use *pitch* to vary your sound range and avoid a **monotone** (p. 415).

▶ Cue the audience as to what's important by adjusting your **speaking rate** and *volume* (p. 416).

▶ Add drama to the speech by pausing for effect (p. 416).

▶ Speak clearly and precisely: use proper **pronunciation**, practice careful **articulation**, and avoid **mumbling** (pp. 416–417).

▶ If you have an **accent**, be aware of how it might influence your audience (pp. 417–418).

Employ effective visual cues:

▶ Dress appropriately for the speaking occasion (p. 418).

▶ Make brief eye contact with almost everyone, using the technique known as **scanning** (p. 419).

▶ Facial expressions and gestures must match the verbal message of your speech (p. 419).

▶ Maintain a steady, confident **posture** by positioning your legs at a distance equal to your shoulders, with slightly bent knees, in the stance known as **planting** (p. 421).

Connect with your audience:

▶ Share your passion for the topic with your audience through effective use of emotion (pp. 421–423).

▶ Gauge the audience response and adapt to it (p. 423).

▶ Generate *immediacy* with your audience (p. 423).

Enhance your words with effective presentation aids:

▶ Effective presentation aids help listeners process and retain information, promote interest and motivation, and convey information clearly and concisely (p. 424).

▶ Based on the needs of your presentation, you can choose among helpful presentation aid types, including **props** and **models**, media clips and images, graphs and charts (including **bar graphs** and **pie charts**), posters and transparencies; flip charts and market boards, and presentation software (pp. 425–428).

Make efficient use of your practice time:

▶ Make sure the key words in your speaking outline are meaningful prompts (p. 428).

▶ Do a run-through with your presentation aids (particularly the electronic ones), and try to simulate the actual speaking conditions (pp. 428–430).

▶ Focus on the message (p. 430).

Dr. Neil deGrasse Tyson shoulders a hefty load: educating the public about astrophysics. His flair for informative speaking has earned him widespread praise.

Informative Speaking

As a noted astrophysicist and the director of the Hayden Planetarium at the American Museum of Natural History, it's not surprising that people enjoy asking Dr. Neil deGrasse Tyson questions: What happens if you get sucked into a black hole? Why was Pluto demoted to "dwarf planet" status? What is surprising, however, is that people recognize Tyson at all. After all, scientists—even noted scientists—are not often celebrities, and unless you're a fan of the television show *The Big Bang Theory*, astrophysics is a field that seems far removed from everyday life. Yet Tyson has, in many ways, become the face of science today, having written several bestselling books and given lectures around the country. He also hosts the PBS series *NOVA science-NOW* and has made appearances on *The Daily Show*, *The Colbert Report*, and *Jeopardy!*. In 2007, he was voted one of *Time* magazine's one hundred most influential people in the world, and *People* crowned him the "sexiest astrophysicist alive" in 2000 (Lemonick, 2007). He has more than 36,000 Facebook fans and over 124,000 followers on Twitter.

Tyson's popularity is rooted in both his cosmic expertise and his communication skills, which have been recognized by NASA, the Rotary International, and the science advocacy group EarthSky. He has a particular knack for presenting the vast mysteries of the universe in ways that laypeople can understand. During a presentation at the University of Texas, for example, Tyson noted, "We have no evidence to show whether the universe is infinite or finite," before explaining that astrophysicists can only go so far as to calculate a horizon—similar to the horizon line viewed from a ship at sea. He then continued that comparison: "Yet a ship is pretty sure that the ocean goes beyond the horizon of the ship, just as we are pretty sure the universe extends beyond our particular horizon. We just don't know how far" (Tyson, 2009).

Tyson recognizes the challenge of informing the general public about complex scientific and cosmic issues that researchers devote decades to understanding: "It was not a priority of mine to communicate science to the public," Tyson says. "What I found was that enough members of the public wanted to know what was going on in the universe that I decided . . . to get a little better at it so I could satisfy this cosmic curiosity" (cited in Byrd, 2010).

After you have finished
reading this chapter,
you will be able to

○ Describe the goals of
informative speaking

○ List and describe each
of the eight categories of
informative speeches

○ Outline the four
major approaches to
informative speeches

○ Employ strategies to
make your audience
hungry for information

○ Structure your speech to
make it easy to listen to

Like Neil deGrasse Tyson, the best informative speakers share information, teach us something new, or help us understand an idea—whether it relates to cooking, auto mechanics, or astrophysics. Clearly Tyson has a talent for informative presentations. He knows how to analyze his audience members and tailor his presentations to engage them quickly. He organizes his information clearly and efficiently so that listeners can learn it with ease. And he presents information in an honest and ethical manner—he offers facts and data, rather than opinions. In this chapter, we'll take a look at how you can use these same techniques to deliver competent informative speeches in any situation.

The Goals of Informative Speaking

As you'll recall from Chapter 12, the purpose of **informative speaking** is to increase the audience's understanding or knowledge; put more simply, the objective is for your audience to learn something. But to be a truly effective informative speaker, your presentation must not only fill your listeners' informational needs but also do so with respect for their opinions, backgrounds, and experiences. In addition, you want to be an objective speaker, focusing on informing (not persuading) your audience, and you want to be an ethical speaker. In this section, we examine these goals and investigate ways that you can ensure that your speech remains true to them at every phase of development and delivery.

Meeting the Audience's Informational Needs

Effective speakers engage their listeners because they have made the effort to understand the needs of their audience members. This is especially important in informative speaking. You want to avoid delivering a long list of facts that are already common knowledge because the object is for your audience to learn something new. But understanding your listeners' needs goes beyond knowing what they know. It also involves choosing an appropriate topic and making that topic relevant to your listeners. Let's take a look at these points using DNA evidence as an example.

▶ *Gauge what the audience already knows.* Estimating the knowledge level of the audience helps determine where to begin, how much information to share, and at what level of difficulty the audience can understand and still maintain interest. If your goal is to inform an audience of fellow students about DNA evidence, for instance, you should assume that they are not experts on your topic. After all, they aren't scientists or law enforcement agents—and only a few students may be majoring in fields that would provide them with a detailed background about your topic. Your tasks involve describing the procedures related to the collection of DNA evidence (such as saliva and skin cells) and explaining why the criminal justice system uses forensic DNA testing. You might even want to ask your listeners if they feel they are familiar with DNA evidence from watching shows like *CSI* or *Bones*.

▶ *Decide on an appropriate approach to the topic.* Involving your listeners through the appropriate use of language and presentation aids gives them

the impression that you have fine-tuned the speech for a particular group of people. You might present the story of a defendant who was convicted based on DNA evidence or of a convict who was later exonerated by it. Be sure to consider the different types of sources at your disposal: visual images, models, artifacts, fingerprints or footprints, and expert testimony. These sorts of things will captivate your audience and help them remember the new information you are teaching them.

▶ *Make the topic relevant to each member of the audience.* Always specifically connect the subject to the audience by pointing out how it is pertinent and useful to your listeners' lives. For example, you might appeal to your audience members' personal senses of right and wrong when you share stories of felons who "got away with it" being brought to justice in light of DNA evidence. Similarly, you can draw your audience members in by noting the way that such evidence can come to their aid should they ever be the victims of crime themselves.

Informing, Not Persuading

As you learned in Chapter 12, informative speaking serves as the base for persuasive speaking: in many cases, speakers inform audiences in hopes of persuading them to behave in a certain way. In a similar vein, persuasive speakers must first inform their audiences about certain facts and information before they can attempt to influence them. But while these two types of speaking are naturally related, it's important to recognize that informative and persuasive speeches differ in one very important way: an informative speech is intended to be **objective**—it presents facts and information in a straightforward and evenhanded way, free of influence from the speaker's personal thoughts or opinions. A persuasive speech, by contrast, is expected to be **subjective**—it presents facts and information from a particular point of view.

This means, essentially, that when delivering an informative speech, you must always remain objective; if you find yourself expressing an opinion or choosing only facts, information, or other material that supports your personal view, you are in fact delivering a persuasive speech. So when delivering an informative speech, it's important to examine your process at every step in the development of the speech to ensure that you are being truly objective. Some of the issues you'll need to evaluate are examined in Table 15.1 (see p. 438).

Speaking Appropriately and Ethically

Objectivity is not the only ethical consideration you must bear in mind when delivering an informative speech. Because communication is a powerful instrument for influencing people's attitudes,

CONNECT

Meeting your audience's informational needs is important in various contexts. When you're running a group meeting (Chapter 10), gauge what your audience already knows and make the content of the meeting relevant. No one wants to sit through a two-hour meeting on details of a situation that the group members already understand. And don't make your topic—the reason you've gathered—seem confusing or irrelevant.

● **WHEN YOU'RE** speaking to an audience that is knowledgeable about your topic, you don't want to bore them with a long list of facts they already know. Tell them something new!

INFORMATIVE VERSUS PERSUASIVE SPEAKING

	Informative Speeches	Persuasive Speeches
Approach	From a perspective of inquiry or discovery; the speaker researches a topic to find out what information exists and shares that information with an audience.	From a perspective of advocating a position or desired outcome; the speaker researches a topic to find information that supports a particular point of view and then tries to convince an audience to change an attitude or take some action based on that point of view.
Objectivity	The speaker reports information objectively, in the role of a messenger.	The speaker argues a case subjectively and speaks from a particular point of view.
Use of facts and information	The speaker sets out the current facts or state of affairs concerning the topic.	The speaker builds a case that he or she is passionate about and includes information that supports his or her favored position.
Expression of opinions	The speaker may provide others' opinions but refrains from giving his or her own.	The speaker provides others' opinions that support his or her own position or viewpoint; the speaker may mention differing opinions only to rebut or discredit them.

beliefs, and behaviors, we must consider the implications of our actions (Sides, 2000). As we've discussed throughout this book, an ethical speaker has a responsibility to an audience to provide information that is relevant and reliable in a way that is respectful of both the audience and the subject. The types of supporting material you offer (or do not offer) and your motives for speaking on a particular subject reveal quite a bit about you as an ethical speaker. Remember, an ethical speaker provides information in an honest and truthful way and chooses appropriate topics for discussion. A fellow communication professor, who provided helpful feedback on this book, told us that one of her students gave an informative presentation on how to grow marijuana. No matter what your opinion is on the legalization of marijuana, its use is still illegal in the United States, so informing your audience about how to grow it is simply unethical.

Ethical speakers also always remember to avoid plagiarism by orally citing sources and providing a complete list of references at the end of a speech outline. If your speech misinforms your audience in any way, you are not offering an appropriate or ethical informative speech.

AND YOU?

Have you ever had a sense that a speaker was intentionally leaving some information out or that the information was somehow unreliable? How did it make you feel about the speaker? Did it change the way you thought about the information he or she provided?

Topics for Informative Presentations

When it comes to choosing a topic for an informative speech, there are countless options. You can speak, for example, about something very concrete, such as a person, place, thing, process, or event. In many cases, your topic will fit into more than one category: for example, a speech on hip-hop music might include descriptions of the genre (thing) as well as of particular bands (people) and performances (events). You might also talk about the way the music developed over time (process). We'll take a look at eight categories for informative speech topics identified by the communication researchers Ron Allen and Ray McKerrow (1985) in the sections that follow.

People

If there's one subject that fascinates most people, it's other people. That's why shows like A&E television's *Biography* and E! Entertainment Television's *E! True Hollywood Story* enjoy such success; it's why we might sneak a peek at *In Touch Weekly* or the *National Enquirer* when we're stuck in line at the grocery store (even though we're not that interested in the state of Tom Cruise and Katie Holmes's marriage). And it's why you don't hang up the phone when your mother or father says, "Did you hear what happened to your cousin Leah?" The life of another person certainly makes for an interesting informative speech topic. You might lean toward giving a speech about someone who is famous (or infamous)—indeed, audiences are usually receptive to learning about someone who is famous simply because they revere or worship celebrity (Atkinson & Dougherty, 2006). Yet an obscure but interesting person can often be a great topic for a speech as well.

Your audience is an important variable to consider as you choose your topic. Your goal in an informative presentation is to meet the audience's information needs, so you must understand their knowledge and interests. Before you decide to inform your audience about backyard gardening, solicit information about your listeners using the strategies in Chapter 12 (pp. 346–352). If you learn that most of your audience members live in apartments, they probably won't care about gardening in a backyard they don't have.

● **FROM LEGENDARY** movie stars to historic natural disasters, you can develop a compelling informative speech on virtually anything (or anyone!).

The key to giving a successful speech about another person is to focus on the person's human qualities as well as his or her achievements. Bear in mind also that you need not limit your speech to one person. For example, if you are talking about Mother Teresa, who devoted her entire life to helping India's poor, you might draw parallels between her life's work and that of 1999 Nobel Peace Prize nominee Dr. Catherine Hamlin. Known as the "Angel of Ethiopia," Hamlin has provided free medical care to young women suffering from the devastating effects of difficult childbirths. You might go on to talk about similar efforts by other women who have worked on humanitarian efforts in Third World countries, including some who are quite well known (Angelina Jolie) and others who are completely unknown (your aunt Eloise, who joined the Peace Corps at age sixty). In any case, the key is to show not merely what these people did but why and how they did it. You need to give your audience a real sense of who these people are. To meet this goal, your speech should include anecdotes, quotes, and stories that show the motivations behind their actions. Chapter 12 offers help in adding these speech supports.

EVALUATING**COMMUNICATION**ETHICS

THINK ABOUT THIS

Ulterior Motives

As captain of the school swim team, you've been asked to deliver an informative speech to the school's alumni during homecoming week detailing the team's past three seasons and hopes for the future. You've outlined a short, simple speech that notes individual members' personal bests, team achievements, and the coach's laudable efforts to recruit promising high school athletes. When your coach reviews your speech outline, she asks you to include more about the many scholarships that the school makes available to athletes.

You know that the coach has many motives for asking you to include more information about scholarship money. She's hoping, first and foremost, to convince alumni to support the team financially, in order to entice more financially strapped but talented swimmers to choose your school. But you're feeling torn: you know that most of the money that goes to your school's sports programs is devoted to the larger and more popular basketball program. You're also feeling annoyed because four years ago, the coach recruited you as a high school scholar-athlete with a partial scholarship that she promised would grow to a full scholarship the following year. The full scholarship never materialized, and now you're about to graduate with huge student loans that you had thought you'd be able to avoid when you chose to attend this school over others that courted you.

As team captain, you're proud of your team's record and eager to inform the alumni about it. But you also don't want to give them information that you feel is somewhat misleading. What should you do?

① What are the ethical obligations of a speaker in preparing informative presentations? Can you ignore the coach's request and just say what you want to say?

② Is the coach's request really an attempt to inform alumni of what the swim program needs in order to persuade them to donate money?

③ Are your motivations really ethical? Do you want to avoid talking about scholarship money because you think it will never materialize or because you're angry that the coach misled you?

Places

Like people, places can be interesting and compelling topics for an informative speech. You might focus on an inspired description of a real but perhaps unfamiliar place (the surface of Mars, the Arctic tundra) or even a fictional one (the fires of Mount Doom in *The Lord of the Rings*). Even a very familiar place offers opportunities to provide audiences with some new information. For example, you might investigate the oldest building on your campus or in your town and detail some of its history in your speech. This will allow you not only to describe the place but also to talk about the people who designed and built it and how the building has been changed over the years.

Objects and Phenomena

A third source of ideas for informative speeches consists of objects or phenomena. These speeches explore anything that isn't human, such as living things (like animals, plants, even entire ecosystems), as well as inanimate objects, such as your first car, an iPad, or the *Mona Lisa*. Objects can also be imaginary things (light sabers) or hypothetical ones (a perpetual motion machine) or even entire phenomena (the El Niño wind patterns in the western United States).

Events

Noteworthy occurrences (past and present) are good topics for informative speeches. Our understanding of history is shaped by events—the Civil War, the assassination of Martin Luther King Jr., the breakup of the former Soviet Union, the 2011 earthquake and tsunami in Japan. At a more intimate level, events of personal significance can also make interesting and compelling topics for speeches.

You might build an informative speech around important, tragic, funny, or instructive events in your personal life—the day you went skydiving, your bar mitzvah, the death of a close friend, or the birth of your first child. Just remember that these stories of personal events must be ethical and truthful! Another

● **YOUR SPEECH** doesn't necessarily have to be about a historical event. The first time you went skydiving can be just as compelling a topic as the first time man walked on the moon.

helpful reviewer of this textbook told us that one of her students lied about having cancer (and her "last day of chemotherapy") in order to infuse some personal spark into her informative speech. This is never OK—exaggeration or fabrication is never ethical! This student would have been better off finding quotes from real cancer survivors on important events in their treatment: the end of radiation treatment or the surgery that saved a life.

In addition to helping an audience understand the meaning of personal and historical single events, a speaker can also explore the social significance of *collections* of events. A speaker might, for example, talk about the significance of dances for Native American tribes, high school football games in a small town, or the role of weddings and funerals in his or her family.

Processes

A process is a series of actions, changes, or functions that bring about a particular result. Informative speeches about processes therefore explain how something is done, how something is made, or how something works. Process speeches help an audience understand the stages or steps through which a particular outcome is produced and usually fall into one of two categories. The first is speeches that explain how something works or develops. For example, you might give a speech detailing how a hybrid car works, how the human brain system processes sound, or how lightening forms. The second type of process speech teaches how to do something: how to knit, for example, or how to use a new MP3 player. For this type of speech, it is often helpful to incorporate props, visuals, or hands-on demonstrations into your presentation.

Concepts

What images come to mind when you encounter concepts like "art," "patriotism," "artificial intelligence," and "free speech"? Whereas people, places, objects, events, and processes are concrete things that we can readily visualize, concepts are abstract or complex ideas or even theories, which are much more difficult for us to understand. The challenge of a concept speech, then, is to take a general idea, theory, or thought and make it concrete and meaningful for your audience.

Although the challenge is great, many worthwhile informative speeches focus on the explanation of a concept. The idea of ethnocentrism, the belief that one's cultural ways are superior to those of other cultures, would be an informative speech about a concept (Armstrong & Kaplowitz, 2001). You could then make reference to important historical events that were influenced by ethnocentrism: the Holocaust, ethnic cleansing in Bosnia, or the 9/11 terrorist attacks. Other examples of concepts include feminism, schadenfreude (taking pleasure in the misfortune of others), and nanotechnology.

Issues

An issue is a problem or matter of dispute that people hope to resolve. Informative speeches about issues provide an overview or a report of problems in order to increase understanding and awareness. Issues include social and personal

● **DO YOU THINK** you could be objective about abortion? If not, it's probably a good idea to stay away from this topic for your informative speech.

problems (such as racial profiling, obesity, health care, outsourcing of jobs, or unemployment) as well as ideas, activities, and circumstances over which opinions vary widely (such as birth control or affirmative action).

Because of the controversial nature of many issues, giving an informative presentation on one can be a challenge, as it can be difficult to keep your own opinions from influencing the speech. But if you keep your focus on delivering a speech that is truly one of discovery, inquiry, and objectivity, then even controversial topics often break down into more manageable components that you can look at objectively. For example, if you were to give an informative speech on the nature of stem cell research, you could break all of your information down into groups of basic facts related to the research: what the current laws concerning stem cell research are, how it is done, where the stem cells come from, what happens to them, and why such research is being conducted. You should also address the controversy over the issue itself by presenting differing opinions from both within and outside the scientific community. If, however, you take a look at the research and plot your speech points but still doubt your ability to describe an issue objectively, you probably should save the topic for a persuasive speech.

Plans and Policies

Allen and McKerrow's final category for informative speeches concerns plans and policies. In such speeches, the speaker tries to help an audience understand the important dimensions of potential courses of action (for example, raising fares on commuter trains in your city or eliminating work-study scholarships at your college). Such speeches do not argue for a particular plan or policy; they simply lay out the facts. Like issue speeches, plan and policy speeches can easily evolve into persuasive addresses, so you must be very careful to focus on objective facts; if you find yourself unable to keep your opinion from influencing your speech, consider a different topic.

AND YOU?

Would you find it hard to speak in a purely informative manner on certain subjects? Would you be able to speak, for example, in a nonpersuasive way about your religious beliefs? Your favorite film? A musical act that you just can't stand?

At this point, you may have many good topics for an informative speech. But if you need more ideas, remember the advice we offer in Chapter 12 on searching for topics. Try *brainstorming* or *clustering*, soliciting ideas from others, or using the Internet to identify possible topics. Always ask yourself: Is this topic interesting to me? Do I know enough about it? Is it a good topic for an informative speech?

Approaches to Conveying Information

Once you have selected a topic for an informative speech, you can develop it in a variety of ways. Here we will briefly describe the four major approaches to informative speeches: description, demonstration, definition, and explanation.

Description

Description is a way of verbally expressing things you have experienced with your senses. While most speeches use some type of description to add drama or clarity, some focus on this task more closely than others. The primary task of a **descriptive presentation** is to paint a mental picture for your audience; this type of speech allows the speaker to portray places, events, persons, objects, or processes clearly and vividly.

An effective descriptive speech begins with a well-structured idea of what you want to describe and why. As you move through the development process, you emphasize important details and eliminate unimportant ones, all the while carefully considering your audience as you think of ways to make your details more vivid. Descriptive speeches are most effective when the topic is personally connected to the speaker. Consider the following excerpt from President Barack Obama's January 2011 speech at the "Together We Thrive: Tucson and America" memorial held at the University of Arizona to honor those killed and wounded in the Tucson shootings. Many people found Obama's description of the youngest victim, Christina Taylor Green, to be particularly moving:

> And then there is nine-year-old Christina Taylor Green. Christina was an A student; she was a dancer; she was a gymnast; she was a swimmer. She decided that she wanted to be the first woman to play in the Major Leagues, and as the only girl on her Little League team, no one put it past her.
>
> She showed an appreciation for life uncommon in a girl her age. She'd remind her mother, "We are so blessed. We have the best life." And she'd pay those blessings back by participating in a charity that helped children who were less fortunate (White House, 2011).

From these few vivid lines, audience members learn who Christina was and they can imagine who she might have become.

Demonstration

New York City resident Peggy Paul was offered the opportunity to appear on *The Rachael Ray Show* after informing the celebrity host that she could prepare a four-course gourmet dinner in her tiny apartment with just a toaster oven, a microwave, and a hot plate (Annino, 2007). Sound impossible? But what if she showed you? Rachael Ray (and Peggy Paul) caught on to an important truth: often the best way to explain how something works is to demonstrate it. **Demonstration speeches** answer "how" questions—how to use a smartphone, how to bake a pie crust, how to salsa dance—by showing an audience the way something works. In this case,

Peggy used a combination of explanatory narration and physical demonstration to show how she whips up baked apple pork chops, pear and gorgonzola salad, and chocolate hazelnut quesadillas as easily as we make peanut butter and jelly sandwiches, all the while making use of props, models, and other visual aids.

The key to delivering an effective demonstration speech is to begin with a clear statement of purpose and to follow a very straightforward organizational pattern. In most cases, a chronological pattern works best for a demonstration, with the process broken down into a number of steps that are presented in order of completion. Even with a strict chronological format, however, it can be helpful to introduce the completed end product first before going through the process of creating or completing it from the first step. The following outline of the steps in the process of decorative painting techniques illustrates a demonstration speech in chronological order. You can imagine the speaker showing each of the three methods.

● **PEGGY PAUL** demonstrates her resourceful culinary abilities.

> To demonstrate how to liven up a room with faux paint, you can use three popular types of decorative wall painting: color washing, sponging on, and ragging off.
>
> Color washing hides flaws in the wall and gives it a textured look. First, paint your wall a base color. Next, with short strokes, brush one or more glaze colors loosely over the contrasting base color (show photographs).
>
> The sponging-on technique gives the wall depth and texture with a variable pattern. Apply two or more coats of paint—satin, flat, semigloss, or gloss—on your wall. After the base coat dries, apply a glaze coat using a sea sponge (show sea sponge and photograph).
>
> Ragging off gives the wall a delicate, evenly textured appearance. Apply two base coats of two colors. While the second color is still wet, use a clean, dry rag (such as an old T-shirt) wrapped around a paint roller, and roll it across the wall (demonstrate this technique). Replace the rag after it becomes soaked with glaze mix.[1]

Definition

Informative speaking often involves defining information; when you define something, you identify its essential qualities and meaning. Most informative speeches require that the speaker define a term or an idea. For example, in a speech about the work of a training and development consultant, you would define the term *benchmarking* for your listeners: the process of comparing your

When offering definitions, competent speakers remember that words have *connotative meanings*—emotional meanings—for people (Chapter 4). Consider the words *marriage* and *torture*. Even if you offer clear dictionary definitions of these terms, your audience may have strong attitudes about them that are influenced by their cultural backgrounds. As an informative speaker, you should be aware of the power of connotative meanings while not trying to persuade people to feel differently about terms.

---

[1]We thank Daniel Bernard and Cory Cunningham and their students for contributing the examples featured in this discussion.

technique, program, or organization against the best in the field in order to aspire to the highest standards. By answering the question "What is benchmarking?" you elevate your entire audience to a certain level of knowledge that enables them to understand your presentation.

Although we typically think of definitions as short entries in a dictionary, in fact a great many speeches (as well as books, journal articles, and Supreme Court decisions) are focused entirely on definitions. The main goal of **definitional speeches** is to provide answers to "what" questions. Such questions as "What is torture?" and "What is marriage?" have prompted heated debate in the halls of Congress (and elsewhere) in recent years, making it clear that defining terms is neither simple nor unimportant. As a speaker, you can approach a definitional speech in a variety of ways. A definition in a speech might use one of these approaches; a definitional speech might incorporate more or even all of them.

▶ An **operational definition** defines something by explaining what it is or what it does. For example, a salsa can be defined by what it is: "A salsa is a condiment, usually made of tomatoes, onions, and peppers, common in Spanish and Latin American cuisine." Alternatively, it can be defined by what it does: "Salsas are most commonly used as dipping sauces for fried tortilla chips, but they also work well alongside grilled fish."

▶ **Definition by negation** defines something by telling what it is not. For example, "A salsa is not the same as taco or piquante sauce."

▶ **Definition by example** defines something by offering concrete examples of what it is. For example, "Salsas include the basic tomato version you get at your local Mexican restaurant, as well as variants made from mangoes, pineapples, or tomatillos."

▶ **Definition by synonym** defines something by using words that closely mean the same thing. For example, "A salsa is basically just a chunky sauce, similar to a chutney in Indian cuisine."

▶ **Definition by etymology** defines something by using the origin of a word or phrase. For example, "Salsa is the Spanish and Italian word for sauce, derived from the Latin word for 'salty.'"

As noted, definitional speeches can take one or more of these approaches to defining a specific term. In the following speech excerpt, for example, the speaker's goal is to define the concept of "nanotechnology." Note that the speaker's explanation is primarily operational.

Nanotechnology is a term often used but seldom described. According to Merriam-Webster's online dictionary, *nanotechnology* is "the art of manipulating materials on an atomic or molecular scale, especially to build microscopic devices." The main unifying theme is the control of matter on a scale, smaller than 1 micrometer, normally between 1 and 100 nanometers, as well as the fabrication of devices on this same length scale. The most difficult part of understanding nanotechnology is its size in relation to things we can see. Just take comfort in the fact that you will never have to visually observe nanotechnology.

Explanation

The basic purpose of most informative speeches is to create awareness or understanding; **explanatory speeches** answer the question "Why?" or "What does that mean?" For example, a speech demonstrating how to upload a video to YouTube creates awareness of the process, whereas a speech explaining how YouTube works deepens understanding. Explanatory presentations delve into more complexity by providing reasons or causes and demonstrating relationships. To make your points in an explanatory speech, you must use interpretation and analysis. To this end, you should keep three main goals in mind: clarifying concepts, explaining the "big picture," and challenging intuition.

Clarifying Concepts

If an audience's chief difficulty rests with understanding the meaning and use of a certain term, the speaker should provide **elucidating explanations**—details that illuminate the concept's meaning and use. Good elucidating explanations do three things. First, they define a concept by listing each of its critical features. For example, notice in the following sentence how the speaker provides succinct illustrations for the concept of rhetoric: "Aristotle described the canons of rhetoric as consisting of *pathos* (appeal to emotions), *logos* (appeal to logic), and *ethos* (appeal to character)."

Second, elucidating explanations contrast examples of the concept. For instance, a speaker might suggest that the difference between gun control and partial gun control is as distinct as night and day. Finally, elucidating examples present opportunities for audiences to distinguish examples from contrasting examples by looking for a concept's critical features—for instance, demonstrating that the most important features of a golf swing are keeping the left arm straight and keeping the head still.

One of our students opened an informative speech with an effective elucidating example that explained what "science" means. The student began:

> We all know what science is. It's what Carl Sagan and Mr. Wizard do, right? Since we know, we should agree on some basic ideas. How many people think biology is a science? [Nearly all hands rise.] How many think psychology is? [A few hands rise.] How about astrology? [A few hands rise.]

This speech was effective because after establishing that science is hard to explain, the speaker offered a definitional listing of the concept's critical features, gave an array of examples and nonexamples of science, and offered the audience opportunities to distinguish examples from contrasting examples with a short oral quiz.

Explaining the Big Picture

If an idea is difficult chiefly because its complexity makes its main points—the "big picture"—hard to grasp, speakers should use a quasi-scientific explanation. Just as scientists try to develop models of the world, **quasi-scientific explanations** model or picture the key dimensions of some phenomenon for a typical audience. Speakers presenting complex topics to laypeople—how microchips work, the similarities and differences between levees and dams, or how DNA

● **DOCTORS ESSENTIALLY** give explanatory speeches to their patients, describing the causes of a medical condition and how it may be treated.

molecules pass along genetic information—should try to use quasi-scientific explanations. For example, we heard a particularly good quasi-scientific speech explanation for how radar works. The speaker made use of a simple comparison, noting that radar works essentially the way an echo does, except that it involves radio waves rather than sound waves. The presentation was effective because consistent references to this analogy clarified the speaker's main points.

Effective quasi-scientific explanations highlight the main points with such features as titles, organizing analogies, presentation aids, and signposts ("The first key point is . . ."). Good quasi-scientific explanations also connect key points by using transitional phrases (such as "for example"), connectives ("because"), and diagrams depicting relationships among parts.

Challenging Intuition

Sometimes the chief source of difficulty is that the idea is contrary to what intuition tells us. Consider the polio vaccine, which was tested in 1952 and used an injected dose of an inactive (essentially, dead) polio virus. The notion of using

---

COMMUNICATIONACROSSCULTURES

Let's Talk About Sex

Few subjects can make an audience as uncomfortable as sex. Religious beliefs, age, experience, and even politics inform not only people's views about sex but also the degree to which they are willing to discuss sexual matters publicly. In many cases, for example, it is unthinkable for Muslims to discuss sexual practices, especially with strangers or in public (El Ahl & Steinvorth, 2006). And in many villages in South Africa, sex is a taboo many women do not—or are told they should not—discuss (le Roux, 2006). And even in cultures without such restrictions, talking about sex is often considered impolite and can make listeners feel embarrassed or uneasy. In diverse populations like the United States, speakers—including health care providers, educators, social workers, and policymakers—must be responsive to the sensitive nature of sexual openness when they speak to audiences.

Some people are already learning how. One of these individuals is Heba Kotb (El-Magd, 2005), whose weekly television program offers information on sex to women throughout the Middle East. Kotb remains respectful of her audience's—and her own—religious beliefs by framing her discussion in a religious context, accompanying scientific information about the body with explanations of how Islamic texts address the subject at hand. Indeed, both medical experts and Islamic clerics participate in her show. She also pays careful attention to nonverbal communication: she wears the traditional Muslim headscarf and speaks in a serious tone and uses serious facial expressions. Kotb's sensitive approach, taking cultural taboos, norms, and beliefs into account, seems to allow her to talk more freely about this once forbidden topic.

THINK ABOUT THIS

❶ Kotb's approach to informing women about sex is a far cry from the often lighthearted and humorous approaches used by talk show hosts in the United States. How might her approach to informative speaking be perceived in the United States?

❷ Imagine that you have to give an informative speech about a sexual topic in front of your nursing class. How would you approach the subject? Would you handle it differently if you were speaking in front of your parents? Your religious community?

❸ Does gender play a role in public speaking as well? Would Kotb's message be as well received by her audience if she were a man?

something that makes people sick to prevent people from getting sick is, to all appearances, counterintuitive. Imagine how difficult this must have been to explain to patients and worried parents at the time.

If you are giving an informative speech on how vaccines work, you might want to design your talk around transformative explanations. **Transformative explanations**, which help people understand ideas that are counterintuitive, are designed to help speakers transform "theories" about phenomena into more accepted notions. For your speech on vaccines, you might start by talking about how the body learns to fight diseases through exposure. Then you could discuss how the most dangerous viruses tend to be the ones that are the most novel—that is, those that the body has not yet been exposed to and has not yet learned to fight off. You could simplify your description further by describing how, by exposing the body to a similar but benign virus (like the dead polio virus), a vaccine essentially teaches the body to defend itself against a specific disease.

Guidelines for Informative Speeches

In Chapters 12 through 14, we provided the basics for developing, preparing, writing, and delivering effective presentations. In this section, we'll take a look at how you can tailor those basic strategies to the needs of an informative speech. Your first goal as a speaker is to get your audience interested in your topic. After all, if you can't demonstrate to your listeners that the subject is important or relevant, they are unlikely to give you their attention. But you'll also want to make sure that your speech is easy to listen to. It's hard to inform people who are struggling to keep up with you—or wishing they were somewhere else!

Create Information Hunger

You want to make your audience hungry for the information you are going to present—get them excited about, or at least interested in, your topic. As you consider a topic for your informative speech, ask yourself, "How will this audience benefit from this information?" If you can't come up with a compelling reason for each person to pay attention to what you say, you need to rethink your topic. Several strategies help you create information hunger, including arousing curiosity and working your topic.

Arouse People's Curiosity

A few years ago, we watched a student inform the audience about kimonos. A kimono is a long, loose Japanese robe with wide sleeves traditionally worn with a broad sash as an outer garment. The speaker defined a kimono, contrasted different types of kimonos, and then demonstrated how to get into one and wear it properly. Although her speech was interesting and her demonstration was effective, in the end we had no idea why we had listened to it! The

● **KIMONOS** are beautiful, but you'll still need to make them relevant to your audience if you really want to draw them in.

problem was that although she competently explained the historical and cultural significance of the kimono and gave a detailed demonstration of the process of designing and wearing one, she did little to make the audience interested in the subject as a whole. She might have fared better had she offered some sort of connection between the kimono and the daily lives of the audience. For example:

> Think of your favorite article or ensemble of clothing—that one perfect item or outfit that you just hope you have the occasion to wear. Would you have worn it ten years ago? Will it still be stylish ten years from now? Magazine editors and clothing designers like to throw the word *timeless* around, claiming that some things—the Armani suit, the little black dress—will never go out of fashion. But the truth is that style is a fickle thing, and lapels, hemlines, colors, and waistbands change with the tides. Today, I'm going to talk about an article of clothing that truly is timeless, one that is worn by both men and women and has remained largely unchanged in shape and form for over one thousand years. I'm speaking, of course, about the traditional garment of Japan, the kimono.

Here we've piqued people's interest by asking them first to think about their own experience—about something they own or wish to own. We then draw them into our subject, the kimono, by contrasting it with what Westerners tend to consider "classic" fashion. Such comparisons and personalization of the subject can help keep the audience interested. We might, for example, go on to show ways in which the kimono has influenced Western fashion or compare the time involved in getting into a kimono to that of modern Western clothing.

Work Your Topic

But what if you can't change the topic? Sometimes, as in a speech class or at a convention, you may have the luxury of choosing a topic that you find interesting and engaging. But in many real-world situations, you may be asked to explain, define, describe, or demonstrate something that strikes you as boring or irrelevant. A CEO will frequently need to address shareholders with reports of profits and losses, for example, and spokespersons for government agencies are often required to make statements about public policies or current events.

In every one of these cases, the speaker must find the relevance of the subject and establish it for the audience quickly and assertively. If your topic seems somehow disconnected from your audience, it's your job to find the relevance. For example, can you save the audience money or time? Can you help people do something better (such as make higher grades) or improve quality (such as increasing the worth of a stamp collection)? Even if the benefit is not for the short term, will listening to your speech help them in some way in the future, once they become parents or graduate students or homeowners? Unless you present a clear benefit that people can derive from listening to you, you will not get or keep their attention.

● **PEOPLE USUALLY** groan at the thought of sitting through a boring software presentation, but if the speaker makes it relevant to their needs, they might change their minds.

For example, imagine that you are an office manager and need to deliver a presentation to your colleagues explaining how to fill out the company's new expense reports. Your first job, then, is to get them interested in what they might initially perceive as an unnecessary and time-consuming presentation about a

real communicator

NAME: Nick Hengen
HOMETOWN: Rapid City, South Dakota
OCCUPATION: Graduate instructor at the University of Minnesota
FUN FACT: I played in punk rock bands in high school.

I'm a teaching assistant at the University of Minnesota. I've been doing this for a couple of years now, but I still remember—with perfect clarity—the first time I led a discussion section. I was standing at the front of the classroom, wearing the one tie I own.

"So what did everyone think about the Robert Frost poems?" I asked.

Silence.

"Were they good?"

Silence.

"Bad?"

Silence. Only forty-eight minutes left in the class period. I loosened my tie, getting chalk all over it. Forty-seven minutes to go.

I thought we'd all just sit around in a circle and discuss poetry. But before we could get to that point, I needed—as the teacher—to provide my students with some information; in other words, I needed to deliver an informational presentation. OK, not too scary. I took a class on public speaking in college. Step one is creating information hunger. Why do my students want to hear about Robert Frost's poems? I decided I'd start with Robert Frost the person.

People love hearing about people. In creating information hunger, I've found that biography is a good starting point. I like to balance the big accomplishments (Frost's four Pulitzer Prizes) with the wackier, more human facts. For instance, Frost married his high school sweetheart, was consistently late to his college classes (I advise

against this), joined a fraternity, dropped out of college (I also advise against this), was a failure as a chicken farmer, read his work at John F. Kennedy's presidential inauguration, visited the USSR as a goodwill ambassador, and was born in California and not New England as one might expect. I also bring supplementary material into class when going over Frost's biography. I play audio of him reading his work. I show the episode of *The Simpsons* in which Krusty the Clown dumps a bucket of snow on Frost's head. My intent with all this is to get my students curious and to create some information hunger about Frost and his work.

However, I still need to make the information *relevant* to each student's life. The easiest way for me to do this is to get my audience involved. I have the class members write poems of their own. In order to think about creative works, it helps to write creative works. I let my students know that these poems won't be graded; therefore, the stakes are low, and no one has anything to lose. And I tie this assignment specifically to Frost's work, asking students to write poems that tackle some of his more frequent themes: love, loss, war, death, destructive relationships, violent emotions. Everyone has some kind of experience with these things. Articulating these ideas through writing allows students to access Frost's poems on a more personal level.

Suddenly, the silence is gone. People are talking. The informational presentation becomes interactive. Just as I'd hoped, we are sitting around in a circle and discussing poetry.

AND YOU?

What techniques can you use to look at a subject and find its relevance to you or to your audience? How can these tactics help you create more interesting informative speeches?

As you learn in Chapter 6, there are many challenges to competent listening. Your audience members have an obligation to overcome these barriers, but you (as the speaker) must help them. If you've analyzed your audience (Chapter 12), you've likely chosen a topic and support material that our audience will care about. And don't forget that your nonverbal and verbal communication should also be appropriate when speaking (Chapter 14).

● **IF YOUR SPEECH** is on punk rock, you might organize it chronologically, moving from the Ramones to Green Day.

boring and mundane task. One way to do this is to show them that learning how to do this task will benefit them in some way:

> I know it's hard to get excited about something as mundane as filing expense reports. But the good news is that our new electronic transmittal system will get your reimbursements to you faster and more reliably. As you know, it typically takes four to six weeks for an expense report to be routed, approved, and transmitted to accounts payable and another two weeks for accounts payable to cut the check. With this new system, we'll be able to have funds deposited directly to your bank account in as little as ten business days. So with that in mind, let's take a look at how the new system works.

By clearly connecting the subject with the lives and needs of your listeners, you're more likely to have their attention as you demonstrate the less interesting aspects of the process. If you cannot find the subject's relevance, you may need to refine or revise the topic.

Make It Easy

Creating a good informative speech is hard work; listening to one should not be. Your job as speaker is to find and distill a lot of information in a way that is easy for your audience to listen to, absorb, and learn. In short, you need to do your listeners' work for them. To this end, there are a number of objectives to bear in mind as you prepare your speech, which we will now discuss.

Choose a Clear Organization and Structure

People have orderly minds. When they are presented with new information, they need to organize it in a way that makes sense to them. You can help them in this endeavor by organizing your speech around a clear and logical structure. Recall from Chapter 13 that there are a number of arrangements for presentations, including chronological, topical, and spatial organizations; problem-solution, cause-effect, and narrative patterns; and arrangements based on motivated sequences. Your choice of organizational pattern will depend on your topic, and every speech will have several organizational options.

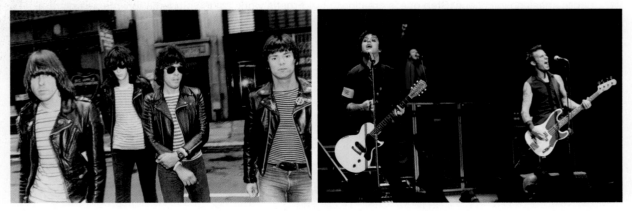

For example, if you're planning to deliver a speech on the history of punk rock, you might choose a chronological organization, beginning with mid-1960s garage bands and following through the 1970s peak with bands like the Sex Pistols and the Ramones, through the post-punk era, and ending with modern punk-influenced bands like Green Day and the Libertines. But you might find it more interesting to approach the topic spatially, noting differences between American and British punk, or even causally, demonstrating how the form arose as a reaction to the popular music that preceded it as well as to the economic and political climate of the times. Table 15.2 on page 454 offers some ideas for using organizational approaches to different informative topics, in addition to considering the approaches we discussed earlier (definition, description, demonstration, and explanation).

Emphasize Important Points

Another way to make it easier for your audience to follow and absorb your speech is to clarify what the important parts are. As you learned in Chapter 13, one of the best means to achieve this is by using a preview device and a concluding summary. The preview device tells the audience what you are going to cover ("First, I will discuss X, second, Y, and third, Z"). A concluding summary reviews what the audience heard during the speech ("Today, I talked about X, then showed you Y, and finally, discussed Z").

Careful and deliberate use of phrases like "The key issue here is . . ." and "I have three main points regarding this piece of legislation" can also signal to your audience that you're about to say something important. In some cases, you might actually highlight what is important by saying so. You may choose to be even more direct, saying, "This is what I really want you to remember," or "The most important thing I want you to take away from this presentation is this." When you use phrases like these, you're not only supporting the organization of your speech but also giving people useful tools for organizing the information as they listen. It's important to make certain, however, that you don't contradict yourself. If you say, "I have one key point to make," and you then list four points of equal importance, you will likely confuse (and annoy) your audience.

Don't Overwhelm Your Audience

Have you ever sat through a lecture or a presentation where the speaker seemed to give far too much information? Ironically, too many points can make a speech seem pointless, and an overabundance of facts and statistics can make it difficult to follow and impossible to retain. Research shows that message receivers' attention and interest levels drop significantly due to information overload. Simply put, too much information overwhelms the audience (Van Zandt, 2004).

Your goal, then, is to keep your presentation as simple as possible so that audiences will find it easy to follow. As you review and rehearse your speech, critically evaluate each and every fact, point, example—indeed, every word—to make certain that it makes a real contribution to your speech. Eliminate anything that is redundant or goes off on a tangent. You want to strike a perfect balance by telling your listeners just what they need to know to understand your topic—nothing more, nothing less.

TYPES OF INFORMATIVE SPEECHES, SAMPLE TOPICS, INFORMATIONAL STRATEGIES, AND ORGANIZATIONAL PATTERNS

Subject Matter	Sample Topics	Informational Strategy (*definition, description, demonstration, explanation*)	Suggested Organizational Patterns
Speeches about objects or phenomena	• Personal digital assistants • Dialects • Comparison of weight-loss diets • El Niño wind patterns in the western United States	*Define* and *describe* the object or phenomenon in question. Depending on your specific speech purpose, either conclude at that point or continue with an in-depth *explanation* or a *demonstration* of the object or phenomenon.	You might use a *spatial* pattern if you are explaining how a geographic positioning system (GPS) works in cars. Other patterns that could be used for speeches about objects include *topical*, *problem-solution*, and *cause-effect*.
Speeches about people	• Authors • Humanitarians • Inventors • Athletes • Unsung heroes • British royalty	Paint a vivid picture of your subject using *description*. Use *explanation* to address the person's or group's significance.	*Narrative* patterns could be useful for speeches about people since stories can include rich details about a person's life. Other patterns that could be used for speeches about people include *motivated sequence* and *chronological*.
Speeches about events	• MTV Awards • Democratic or Republican National Convention • Battle of the Bulge • Iraq War • Olympic Games	Use *description* to paint a vivid picture. Use *explanation* to analyze the meaning of the event.	You might use a *chronological* pattern for a topic focusing on events if time or sequence is relevant to your purpose. Other patterns that could be used for speeches about events include *motivated sequence*, *problem-solution*, and *spatial*.
Speeches about processes	• How tsunamis form • How the thyroid regulates metabolism • How to practice "power yoga" • Using visualization in sports	If physically showing a process, rely on *demonstration*. If explaining a process, vary strategies as needed.	*Cause-effect* patterns of speech organization are helpful in explaining processes of various kinds. Additional patterns of organization could include *spatial*, *problem-solution*, or *chronological*.
Speeches about issues	• Police brutality • Political issues in the Middle East • Climate change	Focus on *description* and *explanation*.	*Problem-solution* is a strong choice for organizing speeches about issues. Other helpful patterns for issues include *topical*, *spatial*, and *cause-effect*.
Speeches about concepts	• Artificial intelligence • Chaos theory • Nanotechnology • Free speech • Time travel	Focus on clear *definitions* and *explanations*; the more difficult a concept is, the more ways you will want to define and explain it. Vivid *description* can also be useful.	Consider *topical* organizational patterns for speeches about concepts, as well as the *narrative* pattern. Other patterns that might work well include *spatial* and *problem-solution*.

Source: O'Hair, Stewart, & Rubenstein (2007), p. 23. Adapted with permission.

Build on Prior Knowledge

Another way to make your speech easier to listen to and retain is to relate old ideas to new ones. In other words, introduce concepts that are new by relating them to familiar ideas. People are more open to new ideas when they understand how they relate to things they already know about. In an informative speech about successful Internet fashion businesses, you might discuss the concept of the "virtual model image." Instead of trying on clothes in a store (a familiar idea), shoppers can see how certain garments would look on their particular body types. By supplying your measurements online, you can visualize what you would look like in outfits by using the virtual model image (new idea).

Define Your Terms

Defining your terms is not just for definitional speeches. As we've emphasized throughout this book, words are symbols that carry meaning, and it's important to use terms in a way that all parties understand if communication is to be competent. When delivering a speech, that means choosing terms that your audience will know and understand—and providing clear definitions for any words they might not. If at any point in your speech, audience members find themselves wondering what or who you are talking about, you will begin to lose their attention. When a term comes up that requires definition, you must explain it clearly and succinctly before moving on; for example, "For those of you who are unfamiliar with the term, *rhinoplasty* is the technical name for cosmetic or reconstructive surgery on a person's nose." If you think an audience is familiar with a word but you just want to be sure, you can simply allude to a more common synonym: "People tend to think of rhinoplasties—commonly referred to as 'nose jobs'—as cosmetic in nature, but in fact many are performed to help improve nasal functioning."

Note that definitions are often necessary for proper nouns as well. Audiences may not have a strong background in geography, politics, or world events, so it can be useful to identify organizations and individuals in the same way that you would define a term: "People for the Ethical Treatment of Animals, or PETA, is the largest animal rights organization in the world," or "Colin Powell, a former U.S. Army general and secretary of state under President George W. Bush, noted that. . . ." If you can define words and identify people, places, and things in a way that is smooth and diplomatic, you will enable audience members who are unfamiliar with them to continue to participate in your presentation. At the same time, you'll gain the confidence of audience members who do know the terms when you explain them accurately.

Use Interesting and Appropriate Supporting Material

Select examples that are interesting, exciting, and clear, and use them to reinforce your main ideas. Examples not only support your key points but also provide interesting ways for your audience to visualize what you are talking about. If you are giving a speech about the movie career of Clint Eastwood, you would provide examples of some of his most popular films (*Dirty Harry*, *In the Line of Fire*), his early western films (*Fistful of Dollars*, *Hang 'Em High*), his lesser-known

● **AN ENGAGING SPEECH** on Clint Eastwood's career would include examples that span his many films, from the classic *The Good, the Bad, and the Ugly* to the more recent and highly acclaimed *Gran Torino*.

films (*The First Traveling Saleslady, Honkytonk Man*), and his directorial efforts (*Gran Torino, Mystic River, Hereafter*). You might also provide quotes from reviews of his films to show the way Eastwood has been perceived at different points in his career.

When you are offering examples to explain a concept, it's important to choose examples that your audience will understand. Some examples may be familiar enough to your audience that you can make quick references to them with little explanation. If you are giving a speech on city planning and rebuilding after disasters today, you could probably mention New Orleans after Hurricane Katrina or Haiti after the 2010 earthquake, and almost any adult member of your audience will get it. But other examples or audiences might require more detail and explanation. For example, if you are giving a speech about conformity, you might wish to use as an example the incident in Jonestown, Guyana, in 1978, when more than nine hundred members of a religious cult committed mass suicide by drinking cyanide-laced punch. As with many aspects of delivering a speech, audience analysis is crucial: if you are speaking to an audience of people in their late teens and early twenties, you'll need to offer a good deal of explanation to make this example work. However, an audience consisting mainly of baby boomers, historians, or social psychologists would require little more than a brief reference to "Jonestown" to get the point of the example.

Use Appropriate Presentation Aids

Presentation aids help audiences follow and understand the information you present in your speech. As you will recall from Chapter 14, the value that effective presentation aids add to your speech can be immense (Mayer, 2001). Such aids can be especially helpful in informative speeches. For example, in an informative speech about the importance of a person's credit score, the speaker might show (via slides or handouts) sample credit reports from the three main credit bureaus: TransUnion, Experian, and Equifax. Seeing this information in addition to hearing about it will underscore the importance of your message: everyone has a credit report and a credit score. By viewing the information while hearing the oral message, audience members will understand what to look for in their own credit reports and how to go about correcting any mistakes.

AND YOU?

Consider your specific speech purpose—what are your objectives for your informative speech? Now consider what types of presentation aids might help you achieve your purpose. How might you use aids to drive home the point you are trying to make or the central idea that you wish to convey to your audience?

Informative speeches also benefit greatly from the use of graphic presentation aids. In a speech describing a process, for example, a flowchart outlining the steps you describe in your speech can help audiences visualize how the process works. Since many informative speeches include a wealth of numerical or statistical information, graphs can be very helpful presentation aids. If you take time to think of the best ways to enhance your speech and put forth the effort to create professional, imaginative presentation aids, your speech will be a success. Furthermore, the combination of hearing your message (the speech content) and seeing your message (through presentation aids) helps the audience retain the information in your informative speech.

Let's take a look at an informative speech that undergraduate Zachary Dominque gave for his communication course at St. Edward's University. Zachary chose to inform

 **PRESENTATION AIDS** are especially appropriate in informative speaking because they enable the audience to not only hear about but also visualize a new topic.

WIREDFORCOMMUNICATION

Learning via Podcast

In 2004, Duke University made news by giving each first-year student an iPod. Students may have been happy to have an additional tool for carrying portable music, but the university's intention was academic. Instructors at the university would be recording their lectures, as well as additional supplementary material, and making them available as podcasts, which students could easily download and play back on their computers, iPods, or other MP3 players. And while students and instructors are not entirely in agreement over the experiment—some have argued that it is more marketing than education—the program has continued, and other schools are following suit (Read, 2005).

Of course, audio recordings of lectures and presentations are nothing new. For decades, speakers have made their presentations available on audiocassette or, more recently, CD. And corporations and consultants have long offered audio training seminars on cassette so that employees could learn on the road. Podcasting makes producing and distributing audio files cheaper and more convenient than ever before. So what's all the fuss about?

In fact, recordings of informative presentations have proved valuable in a number of ways. For auditory learners—learners who prefer to take in information through the aural channel—listening to a playback of a presentation is an effective strategy for retaining information. Any student who may have missed something while taking notes or may not have understood something in the lecture can play back the troublesome parts; this is an especially helpful tool for nonnative speakers of English. And podcasts allow all students to compare their notes to the speech to see if they missed anything or to make up a missed class (Kaplan-Leiserson, 2005).

THINK ABOUT THIS

❶ What are the benefits of having an audio file available? Why is podcasting more effective than old-fashioned analog recordings?

❷ Are downloaded presentations as effective as live ones? Can they replace live presentations, or should they just supplement them?

❸ What kinds of presentations do you think would work best as podcasts? What kinds would not work well? Are podcasts useful outside academia?

his audience of fellow students about the history and sport of mountain biking, offering them new and interesting information. Zachary himself is a championship cyclist, and his personal experiences and enthusiasm for the topic help him to deliver his message effectively.

Zachary organizes the speech in a topical pattern: each of his main points is a subtopic or category of the overall speech topic of mountain biking. This is one of the most frequently used patterns for informative speeches. Zachary's speaking outline and references are included here as well.

what about you?

○ Assessing Your Informative Speech

As you prepare and rehearse your informative speech, you will do well to remember the main points we developed in this chapter. They will guide you and help you approach your audience competently. Use the following questions to assess your speech honestly. You may also ask your friends, family, or roommates to assess your speech using these questions if you are rehearsing in front of them.

_____ 1. Have you selected an informative topic that will teach your audience members something new?

_____ 2. Are you certain that you can be objective when delivering a speech on this topic, rather than subjective as in a persuasive speech?

_____ 3. Did you select an appropriate approach for your informative speech? Will your audience be able to clearly identify your approach?

_____ 4. Have you presented a clear benefit to learning the information that you are sharing in your speech?

_____ 5. Have you stressed the topic's relevance to your audience?

_____ 6. Does your speech have a clear and logical structure?

_____ 7. Have you defined your terms clearly and related unfamiliar terms to familiar ideas?

_____ 8. Have you selected the most interesting, vivid examples you found in your research?

_____ 9. Are your presentation aids solid, and do they back up your main points (without overwhelming your speech)?

If you cannot answer "yes" to these questions, then you will likely benefit from additional research and rehearsal time. Remember, the more you employ these tips and guidelines, the more successful you will be at informing your audience—and hopefully teaching them something that they will use and apply in their own lives.

Sample Student Informative Speech 15.1

ZACHARY DOMINQUE
St. Edward's University

The History and Sport of Mountain Biking

To help his listeners recognize their familiarity with his topic, Zachary informally polls them.

Before I begin, if you'd like, close your eyes for a moment and picture this. You're on a bike, plunging down a steep, rock-strewn mountain, yet fully in control. Adrenaline courses through your body as you hurtle through the air, touch down on pebbled creeks and tangled grasses, and rocket upward again at breakneck speed. You should be scared, but you're not. In fact, you're having the time of your life. •

How many of you like to bike? Perhaps you ride to campus, bike for fitness, or cycle just for fun. Some of you might own bikes with lightweight frames and thin wheels, and use them to log some serious mileage. Or possibly you ride a comfort bike with a cushy seat and bigger tires.

Good morning, ladies and gentlemen. My name is Zachary Dominique, and I'm a mountain biker. Today, I'm going to take you on a tour of this exciting sport with a rich history. Our stops along the way will include an overview of mountain biking, followed by a brief history of the sport. We'll also investigate the forms and functions of mountain bikes (as compared to road bikes), the different types of mountain biking, and some noteworthy bike courses. • I've been racing since I was eight years old and won the state championship three years ago, so this topic is close to my heart. •

To start, let me briefly define mountain biking. •

A simple but powerful image accompanies a definition.

Mountain biking is a sport that can be extreme, recreational, or somewhere in between. The ABC-of-Mountain Biking Web site offers a good basic definition: "Mountain biking is a form of cycling on off-road or unpaved surfaces such as mountain trails and dirt roads; the biker uses a bicycle with a sturdy frame and fat tires." •

Mountain bikes are built to tackle rough ground. They feature wide tires with tough tread, straight and wide handlebars, rugged but light frames, and eighteen to twenty-four or more specialized gears. The idea behind mountain biking is to go where other bikes can't take you because they aren't equipped to handle rough terrain. This might mean riding on backcountry roads or on single-track trails winding through fields or forest. It can involve climbing steep hills and racing down them. The focus is on self-reliance because mountain bikers often venture miles from help.

• By asking the audience to visualize racing down a mountain, Zachary effectively captures listeners' attention.

• Zachary previews his main points.

• Pointing to his personal experience with the sport lends Zachary credibility to address the topic.

• Zachary transitions into the speech body.

• Zachary clearly defines his topic for the audience.

• Zachary uses a reputable source and informs the audience of where the information is located.

• Zachary uses a transition to signal a change in focus.

• To add interest and involvement, Zachary supplements his description with photographs.

• To help foster understanding, Zachary compares and contrasts the mountain bike with the more familiar road bike.

According to the Web site of the National Bicycle Dealer's Association, mountain bikes accounted for 28 percent of all bikes sold in the United States in 2009. If you factor in sales of the comfort bike, which is actually a modified mountain bike for purely recreational riders, sales jump to nearly 40 percent of all bikes sold. •

So, you see, mountain biking is popular with a lot of people. But the sport itself is fairly new. •

The man in this picture is Gary Fisher, one of the founders of mountain biking. According to *The Original Mountain Biking Book*, written by pioneering mountain bikers Rob Van der Plas and Charles Kelly, they, along with Fischer and others from the Marin County, California, area, founded the modern sport of mountain biking in the early 1970s.

A photo of one of the sport's founders. Zachary could trim the text for better legibility.

Early on, these guys decided to take on the adventure of racing down the slopes of Mount Tamalpais, or "Mount Tam," in Corte Madera, California. Back then, they didn't have mountain bikes as we know them, so as you can see, Fisher is riding a modified one-speed Schwinn Cruiser. • Cruisers aren't made for off-road use at all; they're just supposed to ferry people around town on their so-called "balloon tires." They have hard shocks, and the brakes aren't remotely equipped to handle stops on steep descents. But this is how Fisher and others started out.

Very quickly, however, Kelly, Fisher, and other cyclists like Charles Cunningham began to adapt the bikes to their needs. By the mid-1970s, growing numbers of bikers in California were racing one another down the rough slopes of mountains on "fat tire" bikes. This activity led to the famed Repack Downhill Race on Mount Tam, which took place between 1976 and 1979. According to a brief history of mountain biking on the London 2012 Olympics Web site, the race attracted many participants and contributed to putting the sport on the map. Bit by bit, Fisher, Cunningham, Kelly, and others modified their bikes, adding gears, drum brakes, and suspension systems to the frames. As Van der Plas and Kelly noted in *The Original Mountain Biking Book*, it wasn't until 1982, however, that standardized production of these machines began.

To get a better sense of what the mountain bike can and cannot do, consider how they compare to road bikes, the class of bikes that such cyclists as Tour de France winners Alberto Contador and Lance Armstrong use. •

Whereas mountain bikes are built to tackle rough ground, road bikes stay on paved, smooth surfaces. And while mountain bikes feature wide tires with tough tread, road bike tires are very thin and the frames are extremely lightweight, letting the cyclist race hard and fast on a road course. This is fine for them, because they're all about productivity. If you take the road bike off-road, however, chances are you'll destroy it.

Zachary contrasts his own mountain bike (an object) with a photograph of a road bike (onscreen). On his bike, he can also point out important elements such as gears and shocks.

The thinner tires can't provide the stability required, and without the knobby tires found on mountain bikes, road bike tires can't grip the rocks, roots, and other obstacles that cover off-road courses.

The seats—or saddles as we call them—on road and mountain bikes also differ, as do the gears, suspension systems, and handlebar configurations.

Road bike seats are thin and hard to sit on. This suits road cyclists well because they tackle flat, relatively smooth courses. We mountain bikers need a bit more cushion, and as you can see our seats have a split in the middle so they bend with our gluteus maximus. •

Road bikes are geared to go faster than mountain bikes, with higher or harder gears than those on mountain bikes. With mountain bikes, riders can rapidly adjust the gears to match conditions, using lower gears to overcome higher resistance (such as when climbing hills) and higher gears when the cycling is easier. The big gear on a road bike is probably twice the size of my big gear on this mountain bike.

The suspension systems on the two bikes also differ. Many mountain bikes have at least a great front shock-absorbing suspension system; some have rear-suspension systems, and some other bikes have dual suspension systems. Road bikes generally don't have shock absorbers because they're not supposed to hit anything.

A final feature distinguishing mountain from road bikes is the handlebars. Mountain bikes have flat handlebars. These promote an upright stance, so that cyclists don't flip over when they hit something. The drop handlebars on road bikes require the cyclist to lean far forward to hold onto them. This position suits this type of cycling, which prizes speed.

I hope by now you have a sense of the form and functions of the mountain bike. The exact configurations of these bikes vary according to the type of riding they're designed to handle—downhill, trails, and cross-country. Let's begin with downhill. •

Downhill biking is a daredevil sport. These bikers slide down hills at top speeds, and they go off jumps. As described on the Trails.com Web site, downhill racers catch a shuttle going

• Zachary again supplements his verbal description with a visual.

• Zachary internally summarizes the speech points he's covered thus far and signals a shift in gears.

As he discusses each type of mountain biking, Zachary displays a photo of that type.

up the mountain, then speed downhill while "chewing up" obstacles. Downhill racing has been compared to skiing with a bike, and in fact in the summer many downhill racers do race on ski slopes.

As far as bikes go, downhill racers need a special downhill bike—one with fewer gears and that is heavier than other types of mountain bikes.

Revealing one photo at a time keeps the audience focused on the subject at hand.

• In any speech, transitions serve as critical "traffic signals" that alert audience members to where they've been and where they will go next.

Now let's ride over to Trails biking. •

Trails bikers hop and jump their bikes over obstacles such as cars, rocks, and large logs. Their goal is not to put their foot down on the ground. In trail biking, the course is set right there in front of you. This is one of the few types of biking where you can watch the entire race, and it's done by time, not all a mass start.

Trails bikes look quite different from other types of mountain bikes. They have very small wheels, measuring either twenty, twenty-four, or twenty-six inches, and they have smaller frames.

A third type of mountain biking, cross-country, is my sport.

Cross-country biking—also called "XC cycling"—is the most common type of mountain biking. It's also the type of mountain biking sponsored by the Olympics. That's right. In 1996, mountain biking became an Olympic sport—just two decades after its inception.

With cross-country biking, you get the best of all worlds. The courses are creative, incorporating hills and valleys and rough to not-so-rough terrain. If done competitively, cross-country biking is like competing in a marathon. Done recreationally, it offers you the chance to see the great outdoors while getting, or staying, in great shape.

The photos clearly represent each type of mountain biking, aiding audience comprehension and retention.

Cross-country bikes come in two forms: XC bikes are very lightweight, with either full or partial suspension, whereas trail/marathon XC bikes are a bit heavier, with full suspension. These latter bikes are designed for the seriously long ride.

Now that you're familiar with the main types of mountain biking, let's cruise through some notable cross-country courses. •

• Here Zachary uses the "cast-recast" form of transition, in which he states what he has just discussed and previews what he will describe next.

There are many great cross-country courses throughout the United States, some designed for entry-level cyclists and others for the pros. Depending on what state you're in, you may find very technical or very rocky courses. The McKenzie River Trail in Eugene, Oregon, goes on for hours through gorgeous, old-growth forest. In Utah you'll find awesome biking meccas among the incredible canyons and mesas of Moab.

Our own state of Texas draws a lot of riders, with courses running through the desert in the south and flats and mountains in the west and north. My personal favorite is in Colorado. Breckenridge, a ski town in the Rockies, has some of the best courses I've ever ridden. Although I haven't been to Fruita in Colorado, its courses are legendary.

You can find great courses in New York, Vermont, North Carolina, and Puerto Rico; in Ketchum, Idaho, and Downieville, California; and in many other areas nationwide. Trails.com is a good resource for exploring the variety of trails available.

Well, it has been quite a tour. Our course began with an overview of mountain biking and a brief history of the sport. •

• Using metaphoric language, in which the speech becomes a tour of a biking course, Zachary signals the close of the speech.

We also learned about the forms and functions of mountain bikes compared to road bikes, the different types of mountain biking, and noteworthy mountain biking courses around the country.

To me, mountain biking is the perfect sport—fulfilling physical, spiritual, and social needs. It's a great sport to take up recreationally. And if you decide to mountain bike competitively, just remember: ride fast, drive hard, and leave your blood on every trail. •

• Zachary's use of vivid language makes the conclusion memorable and leaves the audience with something to think about.

References

Cycling—Mountain bike. (n.d.). *London 2012 Olympics*. Retrieved from http://www.london 2012.com/games/Olympic-sports/cycling -mountain-bike.php

National Bicycle Dealer's Association. (2009). *Industry overview 2009: A look at the bicycle industry's vital statistics*. Retrieved from http://nbda.com/articles/industry-overview-2009-pg34.htm

Van der Plas, R., & Kelly, C. (1998). *The original mountain biking book*. Menasha, WI: Motorbooks International.

Weiss, C. (n.d.). Types of mountain bikes. Retrieved from http://www.trails.com/list_3232_types-mountain-bikes.html

What is mountain biking? (n.d.). ABC-of-mountain biking. Retrieved from http://www.abc-of-mountainbiking.com/mountain-biking -basics/whatis-mountain-biking.asp

Speaking Outline

ZACHARY DOMINQUE
St. Edward's University

The History and Sport of Mountain Biking

General Purpose: To inform
Specific Purpose: To inform my audience members about mountain biking to increase their knowledge about this sport.
Thesis Statement: Today, I'm going to take you on a tour of mountain biking, an exciting sport with a rich history.

Introduction

I. **Attention Getter:** Draw mental picture of mountain biking (MB) for audience.
II. Ask listeners about their biking experience.
III. Introduce self and personal experience with MB.
IV. I will discuss MB: overview, history, bikes, types, courses.

Transition: Define MB.

Body

I. Overview of MB = extreme, recreational, in between.

    A. "Mountain biking is a form of cycling on off-road or unpaved surfaces such as mountain trails and dirt roads; the biker uses a bicycle with a sturdy frame and fat tires." (ABC-of-Mountain Biking)

    B. Bikes = wide tires, tough tread, straight/wide handlebars, rugged/light frames, 18 to 24+ gears.

        1. Go where other bikes won't (backcountry roads, fields, forests, hills).
        2. In 2009, MB bikes = 28 percent of bikes sold in United States. Factor in comfort bikes and sales jump to 40 percent of all bikes. (National Bicycle Dealer's Association)

Transition: Popular sport, but fairly new.

II. History of MB

    A. **[Show photo of GF]** Gary Fisher, one of the founders of MB
    B. *The Original Mountain Bike Book* authors Rob Van der Plas and Charles Kelly (with Fisher) founded MB in Marin County, CA, in early 1970s.

        1. Adventure of racing down Mount Tamalpais [*Tam*el*pie*us*] in Corte Madera, CA.

      2.   **[Show photo]** No special bikes; used modified one-speed Schwinn Cruiser.

  C. Sport grows in popularity

      1.   Mid-1970s: more bikers racing downhill on "fat tire" bikes.

      2.   Repack Downhill Race on Mt. Tam (1976–1979) attracted many participants and put sport on map. (London 2012 Olympics Web site)

      3.   Standardized production of bikes begins in 1982. (*The Original Mountain Biking Book*)

Transition: Understand mountain bikes and compare to familiar road bikes (like ones Alberto Contador and Lance Armstrong use).

III. Form and function of mountain bikes (compare to road bikes) **[Show photos]**

  A. Mountain bikes tackle rough ground. Road bikes stay on smooth surfaces.

  B. Mountain bikes have wide tires/tough tread. Road bikes have thin tires and lightweight frames.

  C. Mountain bikes have cushioned seats. Road bikes have hard seats.

  D. Mountain bikes have versatile gears. Road bikes have higher gears.

  E. Mountain bikes have great front shock-absorbing suspension systems. Road bikes don't need this.

  F. Mountain bikes have flat handlebars for safety. Road bikes have drop handle bars.

Transition/Internal Summary: You should understand form and functions of mountain bikes. Exact configurations depend on the type of riding—downhill, trails, and cross-country.

IV. Types of MB **[Show photos]**

  A. Downhill

      1.   Daredevil sport (slide down hills, top speeds, jumps)

      2.   Shuttle up the mountain, then speed down "chewing up" obstacles. (Trails.com)

      3.   Compare to skiing

      4.   Special bike: heavy with fewer gears

  B. Trails

      1.   Hop and jump over obstacles (cars, rocks, logs).

      2.   Object: don't put foot on ground

      3.   Done by time

      4.   Special bike: small wheels and smaller frame

    C.   Cross-country (my sport)

        1.   Most common type
        2.   Became Olympic sport in 1996
        3.   Creative courses: hills, valleys, rough terrain, easy terrain
        4.   Competition like marathon; recreational for health and enjoyment
        5.   Special bikes: XC (lightweight, full or partial suspension) and trail/marathon XC (heavier, full suspension)

Transition: Now you know the main types of MB. Let's look at cross-country courses.

V.   Courses

    A.   McKenzie River Trail, Eugene, OR: old-growth forest
    B.   UT: canyons and mesas of Moab
    C.   TX: desert courses in south and flats/mountains in west/north
    D.   CO: Breckenridge and Fruita
    E.   Also great courses in NY; VT; NC; PR; Ketchum, ID; Downieville, CA

Conclusion

I.   Quite a tour!
II.   Looked at overview of MB and history of sport. Learned about forms and functions of bikes, types of mountain biking, various courses.
III. To me, MB is perfect sport: physical, spiritual, social.
IV. If you bike, ride fast, drive hard, leave blood on trails!

BACK TO Neil deGrasse Tyson

At the beginning of this chapter, we read about astrophysicist Neil deGrasse Tyson, who is widely respected not only as one of the foremost researchers on space, but also as one of science's most competent and enthusiastic communicators. Let's consider how his informative presentations measure up to the concepts outlined in this chapter:

▶ Tyson knows his listeners. He understands that while they are not well versed in astrophysics, they are curious about it. He makes abstract topics tangible by using familiar metaphors and examples. When speaking to an audience of fellow astrophysicists, he would not have to take such measures.

▶ Tyson uses effective nonverbal communication in his presentations. He uses appropriate gestures, laughs heartily at his own jokes, moves around the stage rather than gluing himself to a podium, and uses a tone of voice that generates a casual atmosphere. His trademark vests—embroidered with images of the cosmos—indicate his enthusiasm for the subject.

▶ Like everyone, Tyson has personal opinions and beliefs. But when he is speaking informatively, he limits his discussions to facts. In his discussion of the universe noted at the beginning of this chapter, for example, Tyson explains, "None of this is about 'belief.' It's about 'what does the evidence show'?" (Tyson, 2009).

THINGS TO TRY Activities

1. Review Zachary's speech on mountain biking in this chapter. What category does the topic of this speech fall into? Which approaches (description, demonstration, definition, explanation) did the speaker use, and was he successful in using those approaches? Did the speaker prove himself to be reliable and well informed? In what ways did he attempt to create information hunger and make the speech easy to listen to? Was he successful?

2. Informative speeches are everywhere—in your classroom, on the news, and in your community. Watch an informative speech (or read a transcript, available at the Web sites of many government agencies and officials). Look to apply the concepts you have learned in this chapter to these informative presentations. For example, is the presentation well organized and well delivered? Does the speaker or author present information objectively? At any point in the speech, do you feel as though the speaker is trying to persuade you to do or believe something? It's important to be a critical listener in order to catch the often subtle differences between informing and persuading.

3. Locate a persuasive speech that you found particularly compelling. Print it out and edit it, removing any and all of the material that you feel is persuasive in nature (for example, the speaker's opinions, any notably biased statements, any evidence that you feel is subjective rather than objective). Does the remainder of the speech hold up as an informative speech? How could you change it to make it a purely informative presentation?

4. Think of a topic that you find excruciatingly dull (for example, balancing your checkbook, studying for a required course you don't like, or taking a summer or part-time job doing something utterly mind-numbing). What would you do if you had to give an informative presentation on such a subject? Based on the information presented in this chapter, can you think of ways to build a presentation on the topic that is informative and interesting? As strange as this task may sound, it is likely that you will have to do something like this at times in your career. (Recall the example from this chapter on informing employees about a new electronic reimbursement system.)

5. Imagine a process you do every day, such as driving a car. Think about how you would explain the process to someone who's never done it or even seen it done before. Consider different ways you could make the level of the presentation appropriate for different audiences. Talking to a child, for example, you might simply say that pressing on the gas pedal makes the car go; you might offer more detail when speaking to adults, explaining how the car works.

Now that you have finished reading this chapter, you can

Describe the goals of informative speaking:

▶ Use **informative speaking** to teach the audience something new (p. 436).

▶ Gauge what the audience already knows to determine where to begin (p. 436).

▶ Find an approach that will engage the audience (pp. 436–437).

▶ Explain the subject's relevance to the audience (p. 437).

▶ Present facts and information in an **objective**, even-handed way, unlike in a persuasive speech, which is **subjective**, presenting a point of view (p. 437).

▶ Speak ethically (pp. 437–438).

List and describe each of the eight categories of informative speeches:

▶ People: focus on human qualities as well as achievements (pp. 439–440).

▶ Places: find new aspects of known places, or describe the unfamiliar (p. 441).

▶ Objects and phenomena: focus on any nonhuman topic (p. 441).

▶ Events: describe noteworthy events in history, or relate a personal experience (p. 441).

▶ Processes: show how something works, or teach how to do something (p. 442).

▶ Concepts: explain an abstract idea (p. 442).

▶ Issues: remain objective to report on a social or personal problem (pp. 442–443).

▶ Plans and policies: describe the important dimensions of potential courses of action (p. 443).

Outline the four major approaches to informative speeches:

▶ The **descriptive presentation** paints a mental picture, portraying places, events, persons, objects, or processes (p. 444).

▶ **Demonstration speeches** combine explanatory narration and physical demonstration (p. 444).

▶ There are five categories of **definitional speeches:** an **operational definition** defines something by explaining what it is or what it does; **definition by negation** defines something by telling what it is not; **definition by example** offers concrete examples; **definition by synonym** defines something with closely related words; **definition by etymology** explains the origin of a word or phrase (pp. 445–446).

▶ **Explanatory speeches** answer the question "Why?" with **elucidating explanations**, with **quasi-scientific explanations** or models, or with **transformative explanations** that change preconceptions (pp. 447–449).

Employ strategies to make your audience hungry for information:

▶ Make listeners curious by personalizing the topic and contrasting it to what they know (pp. 449–450).

▶ Present a clear benefit to learning about the topic (p. 450).

▶ Stress the topic's relevance (p. 450).

Structure your speech to make it easy to listen to:

▶ Devise a clear, logical structure (p. 452).

▶ Signal your audience when you're about to say something important (p. 453).

▶ Keep it simple (p. 453).

▶ Relate new ideas to familiar ideas (p. 455).

▶ Define terms your audience may not know (p. 455).

▶ Select interesting examples (pp. 455–456).

▶ Use strong presentation aids (pp. 456–457).

Jamie Oliver accepted his TED prize with a persuasive address on obesity and food education, in which he explained causes, identified solutions, and ended with a personal appeal.

chapter 16

Persuasive Speaking

Suppose you have found a magic lamp with a genie inside. The genie will grant you one wish, but there's a catch: you need to convince him that your wish is worthwhile and that it will have a positive impact on the world. Each year, TED (short for Technology, Entertainment, and Design), an organization devoted to "ideas worth spreading," plays the role of this magic genie. Winners receive $100,000—in addition to the organization's considerable talent and resources—to turn a beneficial and world-changing idea into reality. After months of preparation, TED Prize winners then unveil their wishes and plans at the annual TED conference (TED Prize, 2011).

TED Prize winner and celebrity chef Jamie Oliver presented his wish ("To teach every child about food") at the 2010 conference in Long Beach, California. He opened his speech with a simple statement identifying an important social and medical problem: "In the next 18 minutes when I do our chat, four Americans that are alive will be dead from the food that they eat" (Oliver, 2010, para. 1). Oliver went on to discuss the realities of obesity in the United States and elsewhere, noting the personal health costs as well as the financial costs of caring for people suffering from preventable, diet-related diseases. He then discussed his experiences educating Americans in Huntington, West Virginia, as part of his *Food Revolution* television program, sharing stories of real people whose lives have been shaped by a lack of simple knowledge about food.

Oliver openly considered the causes for the problem he was addressing: a lack of education about healthy food choices at home and in schools; school lunch programs focused on economics rather than on nutrition; a food industry that promotes highly processed, unhealthy foods rather than more costly, healthy options; and confusing or misleading labeling on the foods we buy. But he also proposed solutions, pointing to successful (and nutritious) school lunch programs that could be easily rolled out on a larger scale for a relatively small influx of cash. He also considered and explained how food businesses can—and, indeed, must—be an integral part of the solution.

Oliver ended his speech by reminding his listeners of his personal wish and his goal for speaking that day: to form "a strong sustainable movement to educate every child about food, to inspire families to cook again, and to empower people everywhere to fight obesity" (Oliver, 2010, para. 39).

After you have finished
reading this chapter,
you will be able to

◦ Define the goals of
persuasive speaking

◦ Develop a persuasive
topic and thesis

◦ Evaluate your listeners
and tailor your speech
to them

◦ Explain three forms of
rhetorical proof: ethos,
logos, and pathos

◦ Identify the logical
fallacies, deceptive
forms of reasoning

◦ Choose an appropriate
organizational strategy
for your speech

What do you think of when you hear the word *persuasion*? We often ask our students this question—and their answers are telling. They think of sneaky used-car salespeople and dishonest politicians. They also point to *Inception*'s Dom Cobb, a spy who attempts to persuade his targets by manipulating their subconscious minds. The first two examples might involve people attempting to be persuasive, but they certainly involve unethical communication. The final example is a clear-cut description of **coercion**, the act of using manipulation, threats, intimidation, or violence to gain compliance.

Persuasion is none of these things. It is, quite simply, the process of influencing (often changing or reinforcing) others' attitudes, beliefs, and behaviors on a given topic. When done properly and respectfully, it is also an ethical practice. Think of all of the important accomplishments that can come from a competent use of persuasion, such as petitioning for money to support victims of natural disasters or, like Jamie Oliver, lobbying for changes in behaviors and policies that could save millions of lives. What's more, persuasion is not just a tool for people driven by a particular vision for society. It's a tool that you use every day, whether you are persuading your roommates to switch from a cable TV subscription to Hulu Plus or convincing your four-year-old to eat his peas. In this chapter, we will examine the nature and goals of persuasive speaking while helping you consider your audience, the support for your speech, and helpful organizational patterns.

The Goals of Persuasive Speaking

Persuasive speaking is speech that is intended to influence the attitudes, beliefs, and behavior of your audience. Although these three terms may be familiar to you, let's take a moment to examine them in light of how we will think about them in this chapter.

▶ **Attitudes** are our general evaluations of people, ideas, objects, or events (Stiff & Mongeau, 2003). When you evaluate something, you judge it as good or bad, important or unimportant, boring or interesting, and so on. For example, you might have a positive attitude toward sports and exercise: "Exercising regularly is good."

▶ **Beliefs** are the ways in which people perceive reality (Stiff & Mongeau, 2003). They are our feelings about what is true and real and refer to how confident we are about the existence or validity of something: "I believe that exercise is an important component of a healthy lifestyle."

▶ **Behavior** is the manner in which we act or function. It refers to what we do in response to our attitudes and beliefs (Homer, 2006). For example, if your attitude about exercise is really positive and you believe that it is an important component of a healthy lifestyle, you'll probably be motivated to get out there and walk or jog or lift weights.

In many ways, speaking to persuade your listeners is similar to speaking for informative purposes. Just look at any presidential campaign. The candidates all want to inform you about their plans and goals for the nation, but they also use organized and well-developed presentations to influence their audience's attitudes and beliefs about their suitability for the presidency (for example, "I really like Candidate X—what a nice person!" or "I believe that Candidate Y is the most competent person for the job"). And, of course, they want to influence your behavior by getting you to vote for them.

Influencing your audience's attitudes, beliefs, or behavior does not necessarily mean changing them. It can also mean reinforcing attitudes, beliefs, or behavior that already exists. For example, when a political party attempts to rally its base, it will usually focus its candidates' speeches on issues on which the party faithful already agree. To do this, they must first correctly identify an existing attitude or belief among listeners. The key to determining your audience's attitudes—as well as whether your goal is to change or reinforce those attitudes—lies with audience analysis (discussed in Chapter 12).

● **IN THE FILM** *Inception,* spy Dom Cobb takes coercion to the next level by manipulating his targets' subconscious minds to extract valuable information.

Developing a Persuasive Topic and Thesis

An effective topic for a persuasive speech must share characteristics with an informative one: it should be something that you're interested in, that you know something about, and that is specific enough that you can find a variety of appropriate sources on the topic but not so specific that you can't possibly develop it. When your general purpose is to persuade, however, you must keep a few other points in mind.

First, your topic should be somewhat controversial—that is, a topic that people could have reasonable disagreement about or resistance to. Issues such as stem cell research, campaign finance reform, and mandatory year-round schooling lend themselves to a persuasive purpose because people hold strongly differing opinions about them. Second, the topic must allow the speaker to develop a message intended to cause some degree of change in the audience. For example, the topic of mandatory smoking bans could seek changes from different audiences who hold very different views: encouraging action (a change in behavior) from people who already agree that smoking should be banned in public or seeking a change in the attitudes of smokers who currently see no problem with smoking in public places.

Once you have determined that a particular topic interests you and can be persuasive, it's time to think about developing your thesis statement. In a persuasive speech, thesis statements are often given as a proposition, or a statement about your viewpoint or position on an issue. There are three types of propositions that we will examine: propositions of fact, propositions of value, and propositions of policy.

As you consider your audience's attitudes, beliefs, and behavior, don't forget the cultural context (Chapter 1) and their group affiliations (Chapter 3). Your listeners' gender, religious beliefs, socioeconomic status, and ethnicity—as well as their personal experiences— inform their attitudes, beliefs, and behavior. If you fail to respect these factors, you may fail to persuade your audience.

Propositions of Fact

If you've ever argued on behalf of something you believed to be true, you've made a **proposition of fact**—a claim of what is or what is not. Persuasive speeches built on propositions of fact commonly involve issues that are open to some interpretation and on which there are conflicting beliefs or evidence. The truth of the statement may be debatable, but the goal of the speech is clear: you want to align the audience's perception or opinion of the fact with your own.

Now, it may seem simple to give a speech on a proposition of fact: state your belief, back up your points with research that persuades your audience, and you're done! However, it can actually be quite challenging. Propositions of fact get at the heart of how you view the world, and your viewpoints may be quite different from how members of your audience perceive reality (beliefs about religion, family, marriage, friendship, education, money, and so on). Consider the following proposition-of-fact thesis statements:

- ▶ "Single people are as capable of raising happy, healthy, well-adjusted children as married couples."

- ▶ "Your auto dealership will lose money on its sales of compact cars if your inventory is too small."

- ▶ "HMOs are a sensible choice for less expensive health care coverage."

Each statement is presented as a fact, yet audiences realize that they are really the beliefs of the speaker, presented for the listeners' consideration.

Take a closer look at the sample thesis regarding single people raising children. At the heart of this proposition is your definition of *family*—that a family need not contain two parents. However, members of your audience may very well believe—and feel strongly—that *family* refers to a married couple and children. It's important to be tolerant and understanding of people's deeply held beliefs, especially if you hope to get others to see your point of view.

Propositions of Value

Some speeches go beyond discussing what is or what is not and make claims about something's worth. Such evaluative claims are called **propositions of value**. In speeches of this type, you seek to convince an audience that something meets or does not meet a specific standard of goodness or quality or right or wrong. For example:

- ▶ "Torturing prisoners of war is immoral."

- ▶ "The Olympics are becoming less relevant as a sporting event."

- ▶ "Organized religion has done a great deal of good for the world."

Each statement offers a judgment about the overall value of the person, event, object, way of life, condition, or action discussed. Like propositions of fact, it's clear to the audience that these statements of value are not absolute truths but rather the opinion of the speaker. And as with propositions of fact, the speaker must present arguments and evidence that will persuade listeners to align their beliefs and attitudes with the speaker's.

Propositions of Policy

The third type of proposition is concerned with what *should* happen. In **propositions of policy**, the speaker makes claims about what goal, policy, or course of action should be pursued. For example:

▶ "Gays and lesbians should have the same rights as all other Americans."

▶ "Colleges and universities should not consider race when making admission decisions."

▶ "Any vehicle that gets poor gas mileage (say, less than 25 miles per gallon) should be banned in the United States."

In advocating for any of these statements, your task as the speaker would be to persuade the audience that a current policy is not working or that a new policy is needed. Propositions of policy are common during election campaigns as candidates—especially challengers—offer their ideas and plans for what the government should do and how they would do it.

No matter what your topic, and no matter which type of proposition you are advocating, you'll need to know as much as possible about your listeners in order to persuade them effectively. This is the topic of the next section.

● **FROM PROPOSING** to improve the quality of campus dining to championing for more money for student events, propositions of policy are common in student government elections.

Persuading Your Audience

A student once told us an interesting story about audience analysis. At a church service the Sunday after Thanksgiving, her pastor preached on the religious meaning of Christmas (likely in response to the shopping binges known to take place the weekend after many of us eat a little too much turkey, stuffing, and pie). He was hoping to persuade his audience to remember the religious meaning of the holiday and to avoid getting caught up in commercialism, present swapping, and credit card debt. "He was passionate about the topic, and his points were right on," the student said, "but the congregation already agreed with him. It almost felt like he was angry with us or something. It was uncomfortable."

As this story shows, it is crucial to know your audience before developing your speech, as this knowledge will help you tailor your organization, research, and supporting points. It will even help you determine your specific purpose—whether to try to change or to reaffirm the audience's attitudes, beliefs, and behavior. This was the mistake of our student's pastor. He would have benefited from thoroughly understanding his listeners' disposition and needs as well as what is most relevant to them.

Understanding Your Audience's Disposition

According to **social judgment theory** (often called *ego involvement*), your ability to successfully persuade your audience depends on the audience's current attitudes or disposition toward your topic (Sherif, Sherif, & Nebergall, 1965). As such, you might think about your audience members as belonging to one of three different categories: the receptive audience, the neutral audience, or the hostile audience.

● **CORETTA SCOTT KING** found a receptive audience when she spoke to other like-minded individuals at a press conference on ending the Vietnam War.

▶ A **receptive audience** is an audience that already agrees with your viewpoints and your message and is likely to respond favorably to your speech.

▶ A **hostile audience** is one that opposes your message (and perhaps you personally); this is the hardest type of audience to persuade, particularly if you are trying to change people's behavior.

▶ A **neutral audience** falls between the receptive audience and the hostile audience: its members neither support you nor oppose you. Their neutrality can be based on several causes: perhaps they are simply uninterested in your topic, or they don't see how the topic affects them personally. Or they may know very little about the topic and are therefore unable to take a stance until they learn more.

Consider the importance of your audience's disposition in light of the following example. Imagine that you are the student government president at a residential school in a small state where it is easy for students to get home on weekends. While this may be a benefit for some students, your school has gained a reputation of being a "suitcase" school, making for dull weekends for those students who do remain on campus. To address this problem, you propose that the school ban first- and second-year students from having cars on campus so that they remain on campus and invest more in life at the school. To garner support for your position, you speak to three different groups of first- and second-year students:

▶ Residential students who wish that there were more to do on campus every weekend and that there were more people to hang out with (the receptive audience)

▶ Nonresidential commuting students who are typically off campus on the weekends anyway (the neutral audience)

▶ Residential students who regularly leave campus on weekends (the hostile audience)

When you address the receptive audience, you probably don't need to do too much to get your listeners to like what you're saying—they already agree with you. You're reaffirming what they believe and strengthening your case.

Your neutral audience may need some more information about the issue: What percentage of students leave campus each weekend? How exactly does that affect campus life? Most important, you'll need to tell your listeners why they should care. Perhaps, for example, if there were more to do on campus on the weekends (and more students to interact with), commuting students would be more interested in getting involved in weekend cultural and social events, helping them feel more connected to the community.

Your hostile audience will, of course, need some very special consideration. You will want the members of this audience to find you trustworthy and full of goodwill. You also want to avoid making them feel as though you are trying to force them to accept your viewpoint; research shows that such behavior will backfire and make your audience less likely to engage with you (Brehm, 1966). Instead, you want to acknowledge their point of view, look for ways to bridge the gap between your beliefs and their beliefs—perhaps encouraging them to get friends and family involved on campus (rather than going home as frequently) or even making allowances for students who need cars for medical reasons or to get to off-campus jobs.

You must also consider what you want your audience to do at the end of your speech. A lot of what listeners will be willing to do is related to their **latitude of acceptance and rejection**, which is the range of positions on a topic that are acceptable or unacceptable to them based on their **anchor position**—or their position on the topic at the outset of the speech (Sherif & Sherif, 1967). In the case of our example, you can probably get members of your receptive audience to do quite a bit, including change their behavior. They might, for example, be very willing to help you collect names for a petition or pass out flyers. Members of your neutral audience might be willing to sign a petition or to discuss the topic with friends, but they're not going to go out of their way to help you. When it comes to your hostile audience, it's unlikely that you'll see much behavior change. But you might be able to affect some level of belief and attitude change, helping them at least see your point of view and thus not actively oppose your plan.

Understanding Your Audience's Needs

If you feel that your child isn't getting sufficient or proper instruction in mathematics, you probably aren't going to be too interested in hearing a speech on the importance of raising money for new school football uniforms. And if you're working two jobs to pay for college, you probably aren't going to want to hear anyone speak on the great value of buying a particular $40,000 luxury car. That's because these speech topics don't address your personal *needs*, or deficits that create tension. Helpful in understanding audience needs is the work of Abraham Maslow (1954). Maslow argues that an individual's motivations, priorities, and behavior are influenced primarily by that person's needs. He identifies needs in a hierarchical structure of five categories (see Figure 16.1 on p. 478), from low (immature) to high (mature), known as the **hierarchy of needs**.[1]

The theory is that the most basic needs must be met before an individual can become concerned with needs farther up in the hierarchy.

1. *Physiological/survival needs:* These are the things you need for basic survival, such as air, water, food, shelter, sleep, clothing, and so on. Even in the short term, if you listen to a speech while you are very hungry, your mind is likely not on the message but rather on getting food.

---

[1]While Maslow's heirarchy of needs has been recently revised (see Kenrick, Griskevicius, Neuberg, Schaller, 2010), we have elected to offer the original model as advanced by Maslow given its utility and application to public speaking.

CONNECT

Maslow's famous *hierarchy of needs* matters in organizations as well. As you learn in Chapter 11, the *human resources approach* to management helps managers to better understand the higher-level needs of their employees— things like self-esteem and personal development. This helps employees feel more *self-actualized* in their communication (Chapter 2) and motivated to achieve on the job.

FIGURE 16.1

MASLOW'S HIERARCHY
OF NEEDS

2. *Safety needs:* These are needs for security, orderliness, protective rules, and avoidance of risk. They include not only actual physical safety but safety from emotional injury as well. When people in a community are concerned with violence and crime, for example, they are less likely to listen to persuasive appeals to increase local arts funding.

3. *Belongingness/social needs:* These needs center around your interactions with others. They include the desire to be accepted and liked by other people and the need for love, affection, and affiliation. These needs are normally met by family ties, friendships, and membership in work and social groups.

4. *Esteem/ego-status needs:* These needs involve validation—being accepted by some group and being recognized for achievement, mastery, competence, and so on. They can be satisfied by special recognition, promotions, power, and achievement. Unlike the previous three categories, esteem needs are not satisfied internally; they require praise and acknowledgment from others.

5. *Self-actualizing needs:* Needs at the highest level focus on personal development and self-fulfillment—becoming what you can become. Instead of looking for recognition of your worth from others, you seek to measure up to your own criteria for personal success.

The implications of Maslow's hierarchy for persuasive speaking are straightforward: understanding your audience's needs will help you determine your strategy for persuading your listeners. The message must target the unfulfilled need of the audience. A need that is already met will not move an audience, nor will one that seems too far out of reach in the hierarchy. A speech persuading audience members to plant more flowers on an already beautiful college campus is unlikely to have much effect; the same appeal to plant flowers on a campus where buildings are in serious disrepair is also unlikely to get a response, as the audience may be more concerned with those basic infrastructure issues.

Understanding What Is Relevant to Your Audience

Along with appealing to audience needs, you can also work to persuade listeners—especially neutral listeners—by anticipating their question, "How is this relevant to me?" The **Elaboration Likelihood Model (ELM)**, developed by

● **MASLOW'S HIERARCHY** of needs is helpful in understanding your audience's needs. For example, it might be hard to convince a group of low-income single mothers to enroll their kids in various costly extracurricular activities.

Richard Petty, John Cacioppo, and their associates, highlights the importance of relevance to persuasion. ELM is based on the belief that listeners process persuasive messages by one of two routes, depending on how important the message is to them (Petty & Cacioppo, 1986; Petty & Wegener, 1998; see also Kruglanski et al., 2006). When they are motivated and personally involved in the content of a message, they engage in **central processing**—they think critically about the speaker's message, question it, and may seriously consider acting on it. When listeners lack motivation to listen critically or are unable to do so, they engage in **peripheral processing** of information, giving little thought to the message or even dismissing it as irrelevant, too complex to follow, or simply unimportant.

Whenever possible, you want your audience to engage in central processing, as it produces deeper, more long-lasting changes in audience perspective than peripheral processing does. Audience members who engage peripherally can certainly be influenced, but they tend to pay attention to things other than the central message, such as the speaker's appearance or reputation or any slogans or emotional manipulation used in the speech (Petty & Cacioppo, 1986). Such shallow acceptance of a speaker's message is unlikely to lead to meaningful long-term changes in attitudes or behavior.

To put the principles of the ELM model of persuasion into practice, consider the following points:

▶ *Make certain that your message is relevant.* Use language and examples to connect your message to your listeners' lives.

▶ *Be sure to present your message at an appropriate level of understanding.* You can't persuade your audience members if they don't understand the message.

It will be hard to get your audience to engage in *central processing* if you can't get them to listen to your speech. As you learn in Chapter 6, you need to encourage thoughtful *active listening*. While your audience certainly bears some of the responsibility, you can help by making sure that you offer relevant, effective supporting material (Chapter 12) and ensuring that your delivery is easy to listen to (Chapter 14).

▶ *Establish credibility with the audience.* Show your research, cite experts, and (if relevant) clearly explain your own credentials and experience.

▶ *Establish a common bond with your listeners.* Ensure that they see you as trustworthy. Clearly explain why you support this specific message; if you have a specific interest in it, let them know.

These steps will increase the odds that your persuasive appeal will produce lasting, rather than fleeting, changes in the audience's attitudes and behavior. (O'Hair, Stewart, & Rubenstein, 2007).

WIREDFORCOMMUNICATION

THINK ABOUT THIS

Interactive Advertising: Persuasion for a Millennial Audience

If you were born between 1980 and 2000, advertisers want you, even if they aren't quite sure what to do with you. They call you the Millennials or the Bridgers or by a variety of generational initials: Generation Y (because you follow Generation X), Generation D (for Digital), Generation M (for Multitaskers). Your Generation X predecessors (born between 1964 and 1979) were challenging enough, with their tendency to videotape television programs and speed through commercials. But you're even trickier with your TV and video downloads and customized, commercial-free programming. This presents a challenge for advertisers, as well as a wealth of opportunities. They want to reach you, they want to persuade you, and they're just starting to figure out how.

One strategy they are employing is viral marketing—marketing that takes advantage of preexisting social networks. While viral marketing exists offline (where it is better known as a word-of-mouth campaign), it really blossoms online. Advertisers can produce an advertisement and get it in front of millions of potential customers, provided that you find it funny or compelling enough to forward a link to your friends (Elliott, 2010).

Marketers have also tapped into your generation's unprecedented technological know-how to get you involved in the advertising process. User-generated content is persuasive on several levels. Contests for user-generated advertisements can boost interest in a product or service, and the ads themselves can potentially go viral. They also lend an edgy, young image to the product being advertised. Converse sneakers, for example, posted user-generated videos on its Web site, which became an online hit, and MasterCard solicits users to create copy for its ongoing "Priceless" campaign (Bosman, 2006). More recently, advertisers have started trolling through public feeds on Facebook and Twitter, looking for posts related to their products or services. A mobile team responds to such posts, delivering palettes of crunchy goodness to cracker-loving Tweeters (Elliott, 2010). Whether these new tricks of the advertising trade will lure in your Millennial dollars is yet to be determined. But until Generation Z comes along, they'll keep trying.

❶ How many advertisements do you think you encounter in a day? How persuasive do you think they are?

❷ Do you think user-generated content is more persuasive to people in their twenties than traditional advertisements? Do you think it is more persuasive to people in other age groups as well?

❸ When advertisements appear on a Web page, are you annoyed? What kind of Web ad would prompt you to click it?

Strategies for Persuasive Speaking

> When the conduct of men is designed to be influenced, persuasion, kind unassuming persuasion, should ever be adopted. It is an old and true maxim that "a drop of honey catches more flies than a gallon of gall." So with men, if you would win a man to your cause, first convince him that you are his sincere friend. Therein is a drop of honey that catches his heart, which, say what he will, is the great highroad to his reason, and which, once gained, you will find but little trouble in convincing him of the justice of your cause. . . . (Lincoln, 1842, para. 6)

This quote from President Abraham Lincoln truly touches on the important strategies you will need to keep in mind as you persuade your audience, though it was Aristotle who first named these three means of persuasion or **forms of rhetorical proof**. The first, appeals to ethos, concerns the qualifications and personality of the speaker; the second, appeals to logos, concerns the nature of the message in a speech; the third, appeals to pathos, concerns the nature of the audience's feelings. According to Aristotle—and generations of theorists and practitioners who followed him—you can build an effective persuasive speech by incorporating a combination of these factors. We will examine each of these appeals in turn in addition to considering examples of problematic reasoning that undermine your effective use of ethos, logos, and pathos.

Ethos

If audience members have little or no regard for the speaker, they will not respond positively to his or her persuasive appeals. In fact, attitude change in your audience is related to the extent to which you, as the speaker, are perceived to be credible (McCroskey & Teven, 1999; Priester & Petty, 1995). Aristotle believed that speechmaking should emphasize the quality and impact of ideas, but he recognized that the speaker's character and personality also play an important role in how well the audience listens to and accepts the message. He referred to this effect of the speaker as **ethos**, or moral character.

Exactly which elements of a persuasive appeal are based on ethos? The first element is *credibility* or the speaker's knowledge and experience with the subject matter. You can evoke this quality by skillfully preparing the speech at all stages (from research to delivery), by demonstrating personal acquaintance with the topic, by revealing familiarity with the work of experts on your topic, and by ensuring that your speech is well organized.

Another element of an ethos-based appeal is the speaker's *character*; the speaker's own ethical standards are central to this element. Research suggests, for example, that a brief disclosure of personal moral standards relevant to the speech or the occasion made in the introduction of a speech will boost audience regard for the speaker (Stewart, 1994). Indeed, you should prepare and present every aspect of your speech with the utmost integrity so that your audience will regard you as *trustworthy*.

CONNECT

Part of revealing *ethos* to your audience is offering an accurate, ethical presentation of yourself. As you learn in Chapter 2, *self-presentation* is often strategic—you reveal or hide particular things about yourself to achieve a goal. But if you're giving a speech on the importance of safe driving and you fail to mention that you've been issued five tickets for speeding, you aren't being ethical. Your ethos would be increased if you shared your story and the lesson you've learned from it.

● **AS HE DEFENDS** criminals in the courtroom, *Lincoln Lawyer* Mick Haller's credibility and character play a critical role in whether he can persuade the jury in his favor.

A third element of ethos is communicating *goodwill*, the degree to which an audience perceives the speaker caring for them and having their best interests at heart (Teven & McCroskey, 1997). To show goodwill, you must remember that one of your responsibilities is to help your audience make informed choices. By giving listeners all the information they need to make a decision, you show that you have their best interests at heart. Furthermore, you can show your goodwill by demonstrating an interest in and a concern for the welfare of your listeners and by addressing their needs and expectations relative to the speech.

Research does indicate additional ways in which a speaker can effectively create credibility. For example, audiences tend to be more easily persuaded by speakers who they perceive as being similar to them in background, attitudes, interests, and goals, a concept known as *homophily* (Wrench, McCroskey, & Richmond, 2008). Indeed, we tend to find other communicators (whether in public, group, or interpersonal contexts) with whom we have much in common to be more likeable. And research clearly reveals that we trust (and are more easily persuaded by) speakers we like (Teven, 2008). However, if a speaker is similar to us and very likeable but unprepared, uninformed, or disorganized, we probably won't find him or her to be particularly credible. And, as Frymier and Nadler (2010) explain, when liking and credibility come into conflict (for example, when we like a source who has low credibility), credibility outweighs liking and we're unlikely to be moved by the speaker's message.

Logos

Many persuasive speeches focus on issues that require considerable thought. Should the United States adopt a national health care plan? Are certain television programs too violent for children? When an audience needs to make an important decision or reach a conclusion regarding a complicated issue, appeals to reason and logic are necessary. Aristotle used the term **logos** to refer to persuasive appeals directed at the audience's reasoning on a topic.

Reasoning is the line of thought we use to make judgments based on facts and inferences from the world around us. This basic human capability lies at the heart of logical proof: when we offer our evidence to our audience in hopes that our listeners will reach the same logical conclusions as we have, we are appealing to their reason. There are two types of reasoning: inductive and deductive.

Inductive reasoning occurs when you draw general conclusions based on specific evidence. When you reason inductively, you essentially find and draw in specific examples, incidents, cases, or statistics into a conclusion that ties them all together. For example, if you work at an animal shelter and have been bitten or snapped at several times by small dogs but never by a large dog, you might conclude inductively that small dogs are more vicious than large dogs. If you were trying to persuade an audience to come to the same conclusion, you would do well to highlight your extensive experience with animals (revealing your credibility), but also point to specific research about particular dog breeds or particular stories in which small dogs have attacked children or other pets.

Deductive reasoning, by contrast, proceeds from the general to the specific. You begin with a general argument and then apply it to specific cases, incidents, and locations. The most popular way to argue deductively is with a **syllogism**, a three-line deductive argument that draws a specific conclusion from two general premises (a major and a minor premise). Consider this syllogism:

Major premise: All cats are mammals.
Minor premise: Fluffy is a cat.
Conclusion: Therefore, Fluffy is mammal.

The speaker starts with a proposed conclusion or argument and then tests that argument by gathering facts and observations and evidence. Applied to a speech, you might use a syllogism in the following ways:

Major premise: Regular cleanings and visits to the dentist will help keep your teeth in excellent condition and reduce your chances of developing costly medical complications.
Minor premise: The proposed student dental insurance plan is affordable and provides for two free cleanings per year and additional coverage on orthodontics and dental procedures.
Conclusion: Therefore, adopting the proposed student dental insurance plan will keep your teeth in excellent condition and help you avoid costly medical complications.

The extent to which your syllogism is persuasive depends on how well the audience accepts the major premise of your case. If the people in your audience do accept your major premise that regular cleanings and visits to the dentist will help keep your teeth in excellent condition and prevent medical complications, then they may believe that the student dental insurance plan that you're advocating is worthwhile and may be inclined to sign up. Hence, your conclusion may be acceptable to them.

Pathos

Another means of persuasion is appealing to the listeners' emotions. The term Aristotle used for this is **pathos**. It requires "creating a certain disposition in the audience." Speakers often evoke such dispositions through vivid description and emotionally charged words. For example, consider this statement: "The vivid picture of cold, emotionless fishermen slashing and slicing baby seals should send chills through even the numbest and most stoic capitalists on earth." Makes your skin crawl, doesn't it?

Although emotion is a powerful means of moving an audience, emotional appeals should not be used in isolation—particularly if the emotion you arouse

CONNECT

Your word choices have a powerful impact on your audience, as words have different meanings for different people (Chapter 4). Let's say you're persuading your audience to adopt a healthy diet. Some people define healthy as low fat and high fiber, whereas others perceive healthy as an organic, vegan diet. To make sure your audience is on the same page, define how *you* are using the term.

is fear (Rothman, Salovey, Turvey, & Fishkin, 1993; Sutton, 1982). In fact, fear appeals are typically only effective if the speaker can get the audience to see that the threat is serious, that it is likely to happen to them, and that there is a specific action they can take to avoid the threat (Boster & Mongeau, 1984).

Pathos is typically most effective when used alongside logos and ethos, which offer ways of dealing with and addressing the emotions. For example, consider the Montana Meth Project (2007), a research-based marketing campaign that "realistically and graphically communicates the risks of methamphetamine to the youth of Montana." Devised to address that state's growing meth use problem, the ads and commercials are indeed emotional, graphic, and frightening, playing into viewers' love of family and friends, fear of poor health and degenerating appearance, and sense of shame and horror. A particularly moving print ad depicts a mother crumpled in front of a kitchen sink, bloodied and bruised by her meth-addicted son or daughter. It reads, "My mom knows I'd never hurt her. Then she got in the way" (Montana Meth Project, 2007). The logical appeal is sound—teenagers who become addicted to methamphetamines will destroy

EVALUATINGCOMMUNICATIONETHICS

THINK ABOUT THIS

Pathos and Persuasive Accounts

Adding personal accounts to your speech can appeal to your audience's emotions and also lend you credibility as a speaker. But what if you don't have any firsthand experiences to share? Some of the most persuasive pieces of writing—Upton Sinclair's book *The Jungle,* Harriet Beecher Stowe's *Uncle Tom's Cabin,* and John Steinbeck's *The Grapes of Wrath,* to name just a few—are works of fiction. The stories are not real, even if the experiences and the people described in them were inspired by real people and events.

But is it ethical to fabricate details in order to persuade an audience about an issue? Imagine this scenario. You are an anti–death penalty activist, and your organization successfully delivered a series of speeches that persuaded your city council to sign a resolution condemning the state government for reinstating the death penalty.

You were particularly impressed with your group's leader, Anthony, who delivered a powerful speech in front of the council in which he detailed his experience watching the execution of a young convict in a Texas prison. At dinner with other group members that night, you say to Anthony: "That must have been just terrible for you, as a young reporter, to watch a man die such a horrible death!" He replies with a funny smile on his face, "Not really. You see, I kind of took a few liberties there. I never witnessed any executions. But I had read a really moving firsthand account in a book while I was researching. It was such a good illustration, so much better than any thirdhand description I could have prepared. I think," he grins and continues, "that might have been the very thing that won them over! There's nothing like a 'personal account' to get your audience in your corner!"

You and your other group members sit in an uncomfortable silence that your leader doesn't appear to notice. What do you think you should do?

❶ Is it ethical for Anthony to make up a "personal account" to use as an illustration in his persuasive appeal, even if it's based on a true story? Is there a difference between lying "for a good cause" and lying for any other reason?

❷ How do Anthony's actions differ from those of the three writers mentioned? Does it matter that Tom Joad, the hero of *The Grapes of Wrath,* never existed?

❸ If you were a member of the city council, would you have reacted to the story differently if the speaker had presented it as a thirdhand account? Why or why not?

❹ How will your group react to this revelation? What will you do or say to Anthony about this issue?

themselves, their futures, and their loved ones—and the ring of truth enhances the persuasiveness of the emotional appeal. The project's follow-up research reveals that the ads have had a significant effect on teens' attitudes toward meth, showing that the ads' credibility is solid as well. The campaign tagline leaves viewers and readers with a practical suggestion to avoid the fearful images of

COMMUNICATIONACROSSCULTURES

Persuading Across Borders

Actress and activist Angelina Jolie, a goodwill ambassador for the United Nations Refugee Agency, speaks frequently with the desire to raise awareness of and influence policies related to the plight of refugees worldwide. This can be a particular challenge culturally, as some groups in wealthy and stable nations are rather removed from the experiences of refugees and cannot fathom what it would be like to be robbed not merely of one's home, but of one's country by political turmoil or natural disaster.

In a speech marking World Refugee Day in 2009 in Washington, D.C., Jolie explained:

> I'm here today to say that refugees are not numbers. They are not even just refugees. They are mothers, and daughters, and fathers, and sons. They are farmers, teachers, doctors, engineers. They're individuals, all. And most of all they are survivors, each one with a remarkable story that tells of resilience in the face of great loss. They are the most impressive people I have ever met. And they are also some of the world's most vulnerable. Stripped of home and country, refugees are buffeted from every ill wind that blows across this planet. (Jolie, 2009).

By evoking American values like family, individualism, and hard work in her appeal for assistance for refugees worldwide, Jolie establishes that helping refugees is an ethical goal that her American audience should commit to. By noting that refugees are mothers, daughters, doctors, teachers, and so on, she engages her audience members' emotions and reminds them that victims are *just like the rest of us*—people with families, professions, and lives that matter.

Jolie follows up by detailing the kindness, generosity, and character she has seen in the refugees she has met during her charitable work. In this way, she puts a human face on the plight of refugees while also establishing her own credibility, showing she is not merely a movie star lending her face to a cause: she is on the ground working for the change she is advocating.

As a global superstar (as well as a spokesperson for an international organization), Jolie must also bear in mind that her audience is *rarely* culturally homogenous. Even when speaking to a large crowd in the United States, she is aware that her message will be viewed by people all over the world— some of them involved in international efforts for change and awareness; others simply interested in what she says because she is, after all, a famous actress. Among those stargazers, her example is an inspiration: she effectively combines the important elements of persuasion to shed light on a co-culture that listeners might otherwise have ignored.

THINK ABOUT THIS

❶ Many celebrities (including Ricky Martin, Selena Gomez, Laurence Fishburne, and Edward Norton) work with the United Nations as goodwill ambassadors for a variety of specific causes. Why do you think that the United Nations seeks their help? Why would a famous actor or singer be more persuasive than, say, a journalist or a medical doctor?

❷ What kinds of cultural values speak to you in a persuasive speech? Do you think that Jolie's focus on resilience and individuals would be as crucial in a more collectivist culture?

❸ Do many Americans dismiss the plight of refugees as something that is not a problem? Does putting a human face on displaced people make them seem more real? How else might Jolie make her largely American audience feel more connected to refugees?

● **THE MONTANA METH** Project persuades with appeals to reason, emotion, and credibility.

meth addiction: "Meth, not even once" (Montana Meth Project, 2007). The message is clear: don't try meth even once, and this won't happen to you.

Logical Fallacies

In a predictable scene from just about any coming-of-age television drama or film—or from real life—a teenager argues with her parents: "Why can't I go to the party? All of my friends are going!" she cries. The exasperated parents roll their eyes and counter, "If your friends were all jumping off a bridge, would you jump too?" In their attempts to persuade the other, both the parents and the child fail miserably. In the eyes of the parents, "All of my friends are going" is simply not a valid reason why the child should go to the party as well, and comparing attending a party to jumping off a bridge makes absolutely no sense to the teenager (and perhaps anyone reading this example).

Logical fallacies are invalid or deceptive forms of reasoning. While they may, at times, be effective in persuading uncritical listeners, active audience members will reject you as a speaker as well as your argument when they hear a fallacy creep into your speech (Hansen, 2002). So be on the lookout for several types of logical fallacies as you listen to a speaker's arguments.

● **ON THE SITCOM** *Are We There Yet?*, teenager Lindsay could be expected to pull the "But all of my friends are going" argument on her parents, but they would know better than to fall for the bandwagon fallacy.

Bandwagoning

When our teenager uses "All of my friends are going" as an argument, she's guilty of what the Greeks called *argumentum ad populum* (literally, an "appeal to the people"), more commonly referred to as the **bandwagon fallacy**—accepting a statement as true because it is popular. Unfortunately, bandwagoning can sometimes persuade passive audience members who assume that an argument must be correct if others accept it (Hansen, 2002). But credible speakers and critical audience members must be careful not to confuse consensus with fact. A large number of people believing in ghosts is not proof that ghosts exist.

Reduction to the Absurd

When parents counter their daughter's request to go to a party with her friends by comparing it to following them off a bridge, they are doing little to persuade her. That's because they have extended their argument to the level of absurdity, a fallacy the Greeks referred to as *reductio ad absurdum* and we know as **reduction to the absurd**. Pushing an argument beyond its logical limits in this manner can cause it to unravel: the teenager sees no connection between going to a party (which is fun) and jumping off a bridge (which is committing suicide).

Red Herring

According to popular myth, a red herring—a particularly pungent smelling fish—can throw hounds off track when they are pursuing a scent. When a speaker relies on irrelevant information for his or her argument, thereby diverting the direction of the argument, he is guilty of the **red herring fallacy**. If you say, for example, "I can't believe that police officer gave me a ticket for going 70 in a 55-mile-per-hour zone! Yesterday, I saw a crazy driver cut across three lanes of traffic without signaling while going at least 80. Why are the cops bugging people like me instead of chasing down these dangerous drivers?" you would be using a red herring. There may well be worse drivers than you, but that doesn't change the fact that you broke the law.

● **POLITICAL RACES** take a turn for the worse and run on logical fallacies when candidates campaign against their opponents with personal attacks.

Personal Attacks

A speaker who criticizes a person rather than the issue at hand is guilty of the ***ad hominem* fallacy**—an attack on the person instead of on the person's arguments. From the Latin meaning "to the man," the *ad hominem* fallacy is a common feature of political campaigns. For example, if a speaker says, "Terry Malone is the better candidate for district court judge because she is happily married, whereas her opponent just kicked his wife out of their house," the argument is focused on the individual and not the person's particular qualifications for the job.

Begging the Question

Speakers who use the fallacy of **begging the question** present arguments that no one can verify because they're not accompanied by valid evidence. For example, if Amanda notes, "People only watch *The Vampire Diaries* because *Twilight* is so awesome," she's basing her argument on an unprovable premise (the notion that *Twilight* is awesome—which is a subjective opinion, rather than a verifiable fact). If you accept Amanda's premise, you must accept her conclusion. For this reason, this fallacy is often referred to as a *circular argument*.

Either-Or Fallacy

Speakers might try to persuade by using the **either-or fallacy** (sometimes called the *false dilemma fallacy*), presenting only two alternatives on a subject and failing to acknowledge other alternatives. For example, in a speech about local sports teams, Charlie notes, "In this town, you're either a Bears fan or a Packers fan." He fails to acknowledge that there might be fans of other football teams living in the city, or individuals who don't care about football at all.

real communicator

NAME: Bryan Au
HOMETOWN: Los Angeles, California
OCCUPATION: Raw organic chef, cookbook author, and spokesperson
FUN FACT: I honestly believe that raw organic desserts are the best desserts you will ever try, and they're a great way to get into raw and organic eating.

Cheeseburger combo meals. Frozen pizzas. Drive-thru fried chicken and microwaveable fried chicken. Get a burrito at the convenience store. Tear off the plastic wrapper. Throw the burrito in the microwave. Press 3. This isn't how college students eat. This is how many people eat. It's SAD—the Standard American Diet.

I advocate the benefits of raw organic food. I recently published a cookbook, *Raw in Ten Minutes,* and I pitch my ideas to agents, publishers, businesses, and TV executives. I deliver persuasive presentations over the Internet, on television shows, in conference rooms, one on one, and in front of thousands of people. I talk about vegan food, and I promote wheat-, gluten-, and dairy-free food. And as you may have already guessed—*what? no cheese? no burgers? no cheeseburgers?*—I run into some very hostile audiences.

Fortunately, I have a background in communication. As an undergraduate, I took a number of communication classes, and the principles and concepts I learned in those classes have been especially valuable to me as a persuasive speaker. For example, as a persuasive speaker, I seek to influence my audience's preexisting attitudes and beliefs toward raw organic food. Those attitudes and beliefs include, but are not limited to, raw food = gross. I try to counteract those beliefs and attitudes, and by doing so, I hope to influence my audience's *behavior*. In other words, I hope to change people's eating habits.

The proposition-of-fact part is easy. Through stories, slides, examples, and statistics, I can persuade my audience that organic food is healthier than overprocessed food. There is, for example, a great bonus feature on the *Super Size Me* DVD that shows a plate of french fries from a certain fast-food restaurant. Those fries have been left out on a counter, unrefrigerated, for a number of months. At the end of those months, the fries look exactly the same. Images like that bolster my propositions of fact.

Because I deal with hostile audiences, it's particularly important that I make appeals to ethos. I need to come across as trustworthy and full of goodwill. I start my presentation with an informal question-and-answer session. People ask me questions, and I ask them questions. *Has anyone eaten any raw food this week? What about a salad?* Through this informal Q&A, I try to demonstrate to my listeners that I'm not trying to force a particular diet on them. I acknowledge their point of view (*hey, I like fast food too!*), and I look for ways to bridge the gap between us. I also appeal to their senses. My raw organic food recipes don't look like lumpy white tofu on a bed of wheatgrass. My recipes look and taste like comfort food.

Finally, with a bridge established between me and my audience, I make a quick little pathos appeal. I dare everyone to give raw organic food a try. Just as I'm daring you.

Appeal to Tradition

A local community board informs a merchant group that existing "blue laws" preventing them from doing business on Sundays will continue because they have been on the books since the town's founding. This kind of argument is a fallacy known as an **appeal to tradition**—an argument that uses tradition as proof. When speakers appeal to tradition, they are suggesting that listeners should agree with their point because "that's the way it has always been."

The Slippery Slope

The **slippery slope fallacy** is employed when a speaker attests that some event must clearly occur as a result of another event without showing any proof that the second event is caused by the first. For example, "Video surveillance cameras should not be installed in major metropolitan areas. The next thing you know, the government will be listening in on our cell phone conversations and reading our personal e-mail."

Avoiding these logical fallacies goes a long way toward building ethos with your audience—particularly if the audience is hostile toward your speech topic. You want to rely on facts, research, honest emotion, and your own well-rehearsed presentation to persuade your audience. If you're finding yourself slipping into any logical fallacy to persuade your listeners, you are lacking solid, compelling evidence in that area of your speech.

AND YOU?

What kinds of logical fallacies do you regularly see used in the media? What is your reaction when advertisers, political campaigns, or pundits try to persuade you using faulty logic?

Organizing Patterns in Persuasive Speaking

You've got everything you need to get going on your persuasive speech. You've picked a topic that you're excited about, you've done some research on your audience, and you've thought about how to deal with logic, emotion, and competence in your presentation. Now what? It's time to organize all of the information you've compiled. As you will recall from Chapter 13, there are a number of organizational strategies available for your speech; the choice you make depends on your objective, your audience, and your available time. When it comes to persuasive speeches, certain organizational strategies can be particularly helpful.

Problem-Solution Pattern

As discussed in Chapter 13, when you use a *problem-solution pattern* for your speech, you establish and prove the existence of a problem and then present a solution. When your objective is to persuade, you also need to add a set of arguments for your proposed solution. This format is valuable because it allows you to establish common ground with your audience about the existence of a problem before moving to more delicate matters (your solution). Although audience members may disagree with the evidence and reasoning you use to build your case, your presentation allows for the possibility that they will find the information interesting and plausible. In some cases, an audience may reject a solution that you present but at least leave convinced that "something has to be done."

For example, note in the following outline that the first two main points consider the problem and the third main point offers a solution:

Thesis: Present methods for recycling in our community are inadequate.

Main point 1: The current system for recycling generates low participation by citizens.

Main point 2: Each community in our area has its own recycling plan and system.

Main point 3: Recycling should be a regional, not local, responsibility.

Some speakers like to use a problem-cause-solution format, making the second point the cause of the problem. This format is often useful because getting your listeners to understand the cause helps them reflect on the problem—and makes your solution seem plausible or even inevitable. In the following example, the first main point proves the problem, the second main point proves the cause, and the third main point offers a solution:

Thesis: United States presidents should be able to serve more than two terms.

Main point 1: Acceptance of foreign and domestic politics is harmed by changes in administrations.

Main point 2: Historically, our country's greatest periods of weakness have occurred with changes in the presidency.

Main point 3: The American people should choose whether a president is worthy of serving up to four consecutive terms.

● **WHEN SPEAKING ABOUT** recycling, you might use the problem-solution pattern to clearly establish the problem before persuading your audience with a solution.

This type of format tends to work particularly well when you are presenting a proposition of policy because it often proposes a course of action or a series of steps to achieve resolution.

Refutational Organizational Pattern

If people in your audience have strong objections to a position you are promoting, you will be wise to present, and then refute, their arguments against your main point. Organizing your speech around those counterpoints can be an effective way to engage, if not entirely persuade, an audience (Allen, 1991; O'Keefe, 1999). In the **refutational organizational pattern**, speakers begin by presenting main points that are opposed to their own position and then follow them with main points that support their own position. You would likely select this organizational pattern when the opposing side has weak arguments that you can easily attack.

Having said that, however, it is to your advantage to select—and then disprove—the strongest points that support the opposing position (DiSanza & Legge, 2002). Your purpose is to win over audience members who initially disagree with your stance or who may feel uncertain about their own position on the issue.

In your first main point, you should present the opposing position. Describe that claim and identify at least one key piece of evidence that supports it. In the second main point, you should present the possible effects or implications of that claim. Your third main point should present arguments and evidence for your own position. The final main point should contrast your position with the one that you started with and leave no doubt in the listeners' minds of the superiority of your viewpoint. For example:

> *Thesis:* Universities are justified in distributing condoms to students free of charge or at reduced prices.
>
> *Main point 1:* Some parents claim that providing condoms is immoral and encourages casual sex among students.
>
> *Main point 2:* Making condoms difficult to obtain will result in unwanted pregnancies and sexually transmitted diseases.
>
> *Main point 3:* Sexual relations do occur among students in a college atmosphere.
>
> *Main point 4:* If students will engage in sexual relations regardless of whether condoms are available, it is to everyone's advantage that they do so safely.

The use of this format with a hostile audience can actually help you build credibility with the audience. If you were presenting this speech to a group of concerned parents, for example, you could explain in your first main point that you understand parents' concerns. If you are a parent yourself, you can draw further connections with the feelings of your audience members. Having established that respect and goodwill between speaker and audience, you can then move on to explain the reasons why you believe, nonetheless, that your thesis is true.

Comparative Advantage Pattern

Another way to organize speech points is to show that your viewpoint is superior to other viewpoints on the topic. This arrangement, called the **comparative advantage pattern**, is most effective when your audience is already aware of the issue or problem and agrees that a solution is needed. Because listeners are aware of the issue, you don't have to spend time establishing its existence. Instead, you can move directly to favorably comparing your position with the alternatives. With this strategy, you are assuming that your audience is open to various alternative solutions.

To maintain your credibility, it is important that you identify alternatives that your audience is familiar with as well as those that are supported by

AND YOU?

Have you ever sat through a lecture or a class where the instructor offered a lesson that affirmed a point of view different from your own? Did the instructor acknowledge differing viewpoints? If so, what was your reaction to hearing the instructor's argument against your belief? Did you respect the speaker more or less for addressing your counterpoints?

opposing interests. If you omit familiar alternatives, your listeners will wonder if you are fully informed on the topic and become skeptical of your comparative alternative as well as your credibility. The final step in a comparative advantage speech is to drive home the unique advantages of your option relative to competing options with brief but compelling evidence.

> *Thesis:* New members of our hospital's board of directors must be conflict-free.
> *Main point 1:* Justin Davis is an officer in two other organizations.
> *Main point 2:* Vivian Alvarez will spend six months next year in London.
> *Main point 3:* Lillian Rosenthal's husband served as our director two years ago.
> *Main point 4:* Sam Dhatri has no potential conflicts for service.

Monroe's Motivated Sequence

In Chapter 13, we gave you a brief introduction to Alan Monroe's *motivated sequence pattern* for organizing your speech. It is a time-tested variant of the problem-solution pattern and has proved quite effective for persuasive speaking, particularly when you want your audience to do something—buy a product or donate time or money to a cause, for example. We'll elaborate on Monroe's five-step sequence here:

Step 1: Attention. The attention step gets the audience interested in listening to your speech. It often highlights how the speech will be relevant to them.

> It's two in the morning and you're staring at a blank screen on your computer. You've got a term paper for your history class and a lab report to finish, but these aren't what have you worried right now. It's figuring out your résumé—how to take your work, personal, and educational experiences and cram them all onto one page.

Step 2: Need. This step allows you to identify a need or problem that matters to your audience. You want to show that this issue should be addressed.

> Each person in this room will be applying for internships and jobs; such positions are highly competitive. Your résumé, for better or worse, will make a first impression on your potential employer.

Step 3: Satisfaction. The satisfaction step allows you to show your audience the solution that you have identified to meet the problem or need addressed in step 2. This step is crucial as you are offering the audience members a proposal to reinforce or change their attitudes, beliefs, or behavior regarding the problem or need at hand.

> Visiting our college's Office of Career Services is a great way to get help and direction for your résumé. The professionals employed there will be able to help make your job application materials stand out while making the process seem less overwhelming.

Step 4: Visualization. As its name implies, the visualization step helps your audience see how your proposed solution might play out. It helps people imagine how they'll benefit from your solution.

> Instead of sitting up at your computer at 2 A.M., you could be sitting with Tamela, a career counselor, at 2 P.M. as she makes suggestions for formatting your résumé or asks you questions about your past work experiences in order to highlight achievements that you had never even thought to mention.

Step 5: Action. The final step, the action step, clarifies what you want your audience members to do. This may involve reconsidering their attitudes or beliefs or even influencing a particular behavior.

> Make an appointment with a career counselor today. Don't wait—you need those early-morning hours for that history term paper, not your résumé!

Now that you've considered organizational patterns and you have a solid grasp on how to handle persuasive speaking, let's take a look at a sample speech by Una Chua from Tufts University (see p. 495). In this speech, Una is persuading her audience to recognize the problem of cyberbullying and explaining how

● **WHEN PERSUADING STUDENTS** to utilize their college's career center, use the visualization step in Monroe's motivated sequence to help your audience members picture themselves discussing how to improve their résumés with a college counselor.

listeners can address and prevent it. Organizationally, the speech is arranged along the lines of the problem-cause-solution pattern. Note that Una uses a variety of sources—from books and scholarly articles to publications posted on reputable Web sites—to support her arguments. Be sure to check out Una's reference list as well as her speaking outline, both of which follow the speech sample.

what about you?

Assessing Your Persuasive Speech

As you prepare and rehearse your persuasive speech, you will do well to remember the main points we developed in this chapter. They will guide you and help you approach your audience competently. Use the following questions to assess your speech honestly. You may also ask your friends, family, or roommates to assess your speech using these questions if you are rehearsing in front of them.

1. Have you selected a topic about which audience members can have a reasonable disagreement? Is it a topic that allows you to influence attitudes, beliefs, or behaviors?

2. Have you developed your thesis statement as a proposition of fact, value, or policy?

3. Have you assessed your audience's disposition and needs? Have you considered what is most relevant to them?

4. Have you worked to ensure that your speech—and your delivery—will help the audience to engage in central processing?

5. Do you demonstrate credibility to your audience? Have you effectively worked goodwill, trustworthiness, homophily, and likeability into your delivery?

6. Have you used solid reasoning in your argument?

7. Have you effectively made use of emotion in your speech? Is it appropriately supported by logic and credibility?

8. Have you checked (and rechecked) your speech for logical fallacies? Have you addressed and removed any that you've identified?

9. Have you selected an appropriate organizational pattern for your persuasive speech? Is the organization clear and understandable to your listeners during practice sessions?

10. Do you make effective use of presentation aids throughout your speech? Do the aids help you to achieve your persuasive goals?

If you cannot answer "yes" to these questions, then you will likely benefit from additional research and rehearsal time. Remember, the more you employ these tips and guidelines, the more successful you will be at persuading your audience—and hopefully teaching them something that they will use and apply in their own lives.

Sample Student Persuasive Speech 16.1

UNA CHUA
Tufts University

Preventing Cyberbullying

Appropriate attire and a sincere facial expression suit Una's serious topic.

On the evening of September 22, 2010, Rutgers University freshman Tyler Clementi updated his Facebook status: "Jumping off the gw [George Washington] Bridge sorry." A few hours later, he did just that. But what would cause Clementi, recognized as a bright student and talented musician with a promising future, to take his own life? The answer, unhappily, involves two bullies and a webcam.

According to a *New York Times* report, Clementi's roommate and a female acquaintance stand accused of invasion of privacy. The charge? Using a webcam to view and transmit private images of Clementi in an intimate encounter with another young man. Tyler Clementi's story is tragic, but it's not an isolated event. You may recall an *ABC News* report on March 29, 2010, regarding the January 2010 suicide of Phoebe Prince. She was a fifteen-year-old high school student from Massachusetts who hanged herself after months of torment from other teens via text messages and social networking sites. •

What is going on here? • In a word—it's cyberbullying.

My name is Una Chua, and I'm here today to confront the growing problem of electronic harassment and to persuade you to fight cyberbullying so that you don't have to endure the kind of pain and humiliation experienced by Tyler Clementi. • I'll start with a look at the various forms cyberbullying takes and describe the scope of the problem. • Next, I'll consider what causes cyberbullies to act as they do and explore the conditions that make this alarming crime so easy to commit. I will also show you how you and your loved ones can stay safe—both by carefully guarding your personal information and by actively thwarting cyberbullies and taking a stand against them. Finally, should you or someone you know become a victim, I want you to be able to respond constructively. All of these steps will make the Internet a safer place for all members of your community to enjoy.

As you can imagine from the heartbreaking stories I've shared about Tyler Clementi and Phoebe Prince, cyberbullying poses serious mental health risks to the nation's children, teens, and young adults. The Cyberbullying Research Center, a leading resource on the topic, • defines *cyberbullying* as "willful and repeated harm inflicted through the use of computers, cell phones, and other electronic devices." • Cyberbullying can take many forms, including the following: posting or sending harassing messages via Web sites, blogs, or text messages; posting embarrassing or private photos of someone without their permission;

• Una begins her speech with several dramatic examples that capture the audience's attention.

• Una introduces her topic with a rhetorical question.

• Una sets up the organizational pattern of the speech, indicating that she will describe a problem, review its causes, and offer solutions.

• She previews her main points.

• Una qualifies her source and demonstrates its credibility.

• Una begins the body of her speech by ensuring that her audience knows what *cyberbullying* means.

recording or videotaping someone and sharing it without permission; and creating fake Web sites or social networking profiles in someone else's name to humiliate them. Often these acts are done anonymously. School psychologists Ted Feinberg and Nicole Robey, writing in *Education Digest*, further explain that cyberbullying can involve stalking, threats, harassment, impersonation, humiliation, trickery, and exclusion.

• This transition effectively alerts the audience to what's coming next.

Cyberbullying is a fairly recent social problem, but a substantial body of research has already formed around it. • The research paints a chilling picture. According to the Cyberbullying Research Center, about 20 percent of the over 4,400 randomly selected eleven- to eighteen-year-old students surveyed in 2010 said that they were repeatedly picked on by another person or persons online, via e-mail, or through text messages. About 10 percent said that in addition to being victims, they had been cyberbullies themselves. Similarly, a 2010 study published in the *American Journal of Orthopsychiatry* found that of the more than two thousand teenagers questioned, 49.5 percent indicated that they had been the victims of cyberbullying, and 33.7 percent confessed to bullying others online.

A brief glance at her notes helps Una present these statistics accurately.

Whether as victims, victimizers, or both, we see that many young people are touched by the problem of cyberbullying. What does the research say about the causes of cyberbullying? What motivates the cyberbully, and under what conditions is cyberbullying most likely to occur? •

• Una now moves from describing the problem to exploring its causes.

Sadly enough, one explanation for the motivation behind cyberbullying is that the bully wishes merely to "joke around." The National Crime Prevention Council, a leading anticrime public service organization, • reports on its Web site that 81 percent of a nationally representative sample of youths said that others cyberbully because they think it's "funny." In other words, despite the potentially disastrous consequences for victims, the cyberbully's harassing text messages and cruel Facebook wall postings are meant simply as a "joke."

• Note how Una lends credibility and context to this source by noting that it is a "leading anticrime public service organization."

In a lot of cases, underlying this drive to amuse oneself at another's expense is an insecure sense of self. Insecurity, combined with a tendency toward aggressiveness, appears to characterize many cyberbullies, according to researchers Sameer Hinduja and Justin Patchin of the Cyberbullying Research Center. For the bullies, the act of harassing other people serves as an outlet for their aggression and makes them feel at least momentarily powerful.

• This transition summarizes the previous point and previews the next one.

For many bullies, then, wanting to feel powerful and superior to someone else appears to be a prime motivation to bully. But what are the conditions that allow cyberbullies to act on this drive? •

According to the research, a lack of parental supervision and the ability to be anonymous provide especially fertile ground. As television talk show host Dr. Phil McGraw notes in his June 24, 2010, congressional

Eye contact and natural movement around the presentation area sustain audience interest.

testimony—and as many of us have experienced in our own lives—children and teens often know more about texting and social networking than parents and adult guardians. This makes their Internet and cell phone activities difficult for parents to regulate. One study by the National Crime Prevention Council found that a nationally representative sample of 80 percent of youths in the United States do not have enforced rules about Internet use at home, or the rules are easy to get around.

A second, particularly powerful condition enabling cyberbullying is anonymity. Cyberbullies feel emboldened by their ability to do nasty things with impunity because they believe no one will know they are the culprits. In his book *Girls on the Edge: The Four Factors Driving the New Crisis for Girls*, psychologist and pediatrician Leonard Sax describes it this way:

> Twenty years ago, if a girl wanted to spread rumors about another girl, everybody would know who was doing it. That knowledge constrained what the bully might say. If you got too nasty, your nastiness could reflect badly on you. But now, you can pretend to be a boy who's just received sexual services from Leeanne, then post something about Leeanne online, and nobody will ever know that you are actually a girl who invented the whole story to make Leeanne look bad.

A simple but effective sequence of gestures highlights the speech content.

In essence, the anonymity of the Internet makes cyberbullying easy and, in many circumstances, difficult to catch and stop.

By now, you may be feeling that we Internet users are doomed to be victims of cruel torment at the hands of anonymous bullies who will never suffer the consequences of their actions. This is hardly the case, however. You can take steps to protect yourself. ●

For one, you can be vigilant about safeguarding your personal information. Our school's information technology office lists the following advice on its Web site. First, never, ever leave your laptops unattended. Second, keep your account passwords and social security numbers totally private. Third, use the highest privacy settings on your social networking sites. Finally, think carefully about the types of pictures of yourself and your friends that you post online, and restrict views of them to "friends" only. Each of these steps can dissuade bullies from having the ability to pose as you in order to harm or embarrass you in some way.

● Una moves on to the solution part of the organizational pattern.

In addition to zealously guarding your personal information, you can help combat cyberbullying by being a voice against it whenever you see it happening.

Don't Stand By, Stand Up! is a student-led organization that was formed soon after Tyler Clementi's suicide and is featured on Facebook. The group urges Internet users to take a stand against cyberbullying by recognizing that bullies—in all forms—rarely succeed in their harassment without the support and attention of bystanders. The National Crime Prevention Council site gives more specific tips on how to thwart a bully's attempts. One is to refuse to pass bullying messages along to others— whether via text or photo messaging, social networking, or e-mailing— and another is to let the original sender know that you find the message offensive or stupid. Remember, if bullies bully because they think their behavior is harmless and funny, then it makes sense to tell them that you find their messages to be quite the opposite.

Una reveals her visual aid at the right moment.

Despite your best efforts to keep your personal information private and speak out against cyberbullying, you may still become a victim. I don't say this to scare you, but rather to advise you on what to do if it does happen to you or to someone you know. In this event, consider the "stop, block, and tell" method of combating cyberbullying.

Online safety expert Parry Aflab, in a July 28, 2009, interview for PBS's *Frontline*, advises victims to use the "stop, block, and tell" method to respond to bullying behaviors directed against them. While often directed at younger children, this method proves to be useful for victims of any age, as explained on the Don't Stand By, Stand Up! Web site. They advise that after receiving a bullying message you should first "stop." In other words, do nothing. Take five minutes to cool down, take a walk, breathe deeply, or do whatever helps to calm down the understandable anger you are feeling. Then "block": prevent the cyberbully from having any future communication with you. This may mean anything from removing the person from your social networking sites' friend lists to having your cell phone service provider block the bully from being able to call or text you. The third step is to "tell" someone about the abuse without embarrassment or shame. For example, you might call campus security or confide in a counselor at the health center. Similarly, parents should encourage their children to report bullying to a trusted adult, whether a parent, teacher, principal, or guidance counselor.

Una gestures toward a clear presentation aid designed to help the audience remember an important part of her speech.

Today, we've ventured into the very real—and very dangerous—world of cyberbullying. • We've seen cyberbullying's negative impact on children, teens, and young adults. We've analyzed the insecure and aggressive personality traits that characterize cyberbullies and looked at two key conditions that make it easier for the cyberbully to operate: lack of parental supervision and the ability to be anonymous. We've also seen how you can counter this potentially deadly problem.

Panning to all corners of the room helps Una's conclusion hit home.

Be vigilant about protecting your personal information.

Speak out against cyberbullying.

And if you or someone you know experiences cyberbullying, react constructively with the "stop, block, and tell" method.

Cyberbullying isn't just someone else's problem. It's very likely something you need to guard against, now or in the future. I urge each of you to make a personal commitment to do your part to combat the problem. Refuse to stay silent in the face of cyberbullying. Resolve that you will never send or pass along cyberbullying messages of any kind, no matter how harmless they might seem. This act alone can make a world of difference in the life of an intended victim. After all, wouldn't you want someone to take this simple step for you? • In addition, voice your concerns at the campus and community levels. For example, a student group from our university recently organized a candlelight vigil to remember those who fell victim to bullying and discrimination. Even if you're not interested in becoming a member, you can support events that bring cyberbullying—and its serious consequences—to light.

We must never forget Tyler Clementi, Phoebe Prince, and the other young lives cut short by unnecessary bullying. Who knows? Your best friend, your younger brother, or your son could just have easily been on that bridge that fateful September evening. •

Annotations (right margin):

• Una signals the conclusion of her speech with a summary of her main points.

• Una issues a call to action.

• By stressing the personal relevance of her topic to her audience, Una leaves her listeners with something to think about.

References

Ensuring Student Cyber Safety: Hearing before the U.S. House Education Subcommittee to Examine Cyber Safety for Students of the U.S. House of Representatives Education and Labor Committee. (2010, June 24). (Testimony of Dr. Phillip C. McGraw, Ph.D.). Retrieved from http://republicans.edlabor.house.gov/UploadedFiles/06.24.10_mcgraw.pdf

Feinberg, T., & Robey, N. (2009). Cyberbullying. *Education Digest, 74*(7), 26–31.

Foderaro, L. W. (2010, September 29). Private moment made public, then a fatal jump. *The New York Times.* Retrieved from http://www.nytimes.com/2010/09/30/nyregion/30suicide.html

Goldman, R. (2010, March 29). Teens indicted after allegedly taunting girl who hanged herself. *ABC News*. Retrieved from http://abcnews.go.com /Technology/TheLaw/teens-charged-bullying-mass-girl-kill /story?id=10231357

Hinduja, S. & Patchin, J. W. (2010a). Cyberbullying: Identification, prevention, and response. Cyberbullying Research Center Fact Sheet. Retrieved from http://www.cyberbullying.us/Cyberbullying_Identification _Prevention_Response_Fact_Sheet.pdf

Hinduja, S., & Patchin, J. W. (2010b). *Cyberbullying research summary: Cyberbullying and self-esteem.* Cyberbullying Research Center Fact Sheet. Retrieved from http://www.cyberbullying.us/cyberbullying_and_self _esteem_research_fact_sheet.pdf

Mishna, F., Cook, C., Gadella, T., Daciuk, J., & Solomon, S. (2010). Cyberbullying behaviors among middle and high school students. *American Journal of Orthopsychiatry, 80*(3), 362–74.

Sax, L. (2010). *Girls on the edge: The four factors driving the new crisis for girls.* New York: Basic Books.

Stop, block, and tell. (2009, July 28). *Relationships: Predators and bullies.* Video retrieved from http://www.pbs.org/wgbh/pages/frontline/digitalnation/ relationships/predators-bullies/s top-block-and-tell.html?play

Stop cyberbullying. (n.d.). Retrieved from http://www.stopcyberbullying.org/ take_action/stop_block_and_tell.html

Stop cyberbullying before it starts. (n.d.). National Crime Prevention Council. Retrieved from http://www.ncpc.org/resources/files/pdf/bullying/ cyberbullying.pdf

Speaking Outline

UNA CHUA
Tufts University

Preventing Cyberbullying

General Purpose: To persuade
Specific Purpose: To persuade my audience to understand and confront the growing problem of electronic harassment.
Thesis Statement: I'm here today to confront the growing problem of electronic harassment and to persuade you to fight cyberbullying.

Introduction

I. **Attention Getter:** Relate tragic stories of cyberbullying.

   A. 9/22/10: Rutgers U freshman Tyler Clementi (TC) updates Facebook (FB) "Jumping off gw [George Washington] Bridge sorry." He does.

   B. TC's roommate and female friend accused of invasion of privacy. Used webcam to transmit private images. (Forderaro, *NYT*, Sept. 29, 2010)

    C.   15-year-old high school student from MA, Phoebe Prince (PP), commits suicide after text/social networking torment. (Goldman, *ABC News*, March 29, 2010)

II. Here to confront electronic harassment and fight cyberbullying (CB)

III. Introduce self.

IV. Will discuss forms, scope, and causes of CB; conditions allowing it; staying safe from and responding to CB.

Body

I. Forms of CB

    A.   "Willful and repeated harm inflicted through the use of computers, cell phones, and other electronic devices" (CB Research Center)

    B.   Posting/sending harassing messages via Web sites, blogs, texts

    C.   Posting embarrassing photos w/o permission

    D.   Recording/videotaping someone and sharing w/o permission

    E.   Creating fake Web sites/profiles to humiliate

    F.   CB involves stalking, threats, harassment, impersonation, humiliation, trickery, exclusion. (Feinberg & Robey, *Education Digest*)

Transition: CB = recent problem with a substantial body of research.

II. Scope of CB

    A.   CB Research Center's 2010 study

        1. 20% of 4,400 11–18-year-old students experienced CB.

        2. 10% initiated CB

    B.   *American Journal of Orthopsychiatry* (2010) study

        1. 49.5% of 2,000 teens experienced CB.

        2. 33.7% initiated CB.

Transition: Many lives are touched by CB. But why? What are its causes?

III. Causes of CB

    A.   Joking around

        1. 81% of youths said CB is funny. (National Crime Prevention Council)

        2. FB postings and texts are meant as a joke.

    B.   Bully insecurity

        1. Insecurity and aggressiveness = CB behavior. (Hinduja & Patchin, CB Research Center)

        2. CB makes bullies feel powerful.

Transition: What conditions allow CB to happen?

IV. Conditions allowing CB

    A. Lack of supervision

        1. Kids know more about texting and social networking than adults. (McGraw, congressional testimony, June 24, 2010)

        2. Difficult to track kids' Internet and cell phone activities

        3. 80% of youths don't have rules for home Internet use. (National Crime Prevention Council)

    B. Anonymity

        1. Psychologist/pediatrician Leonard Sax: *Girls on the Edge: The Four Factors Driving the New Crisis for Girls* [**Read extended quote from transparency.**]

        2. Makes CB difficult to catch/stop

Transition: Are we doomed to suffer? No. Take steps to protect yourself.

V. Steps for staying safe from CB

    A. Safeguard personal information (school IT office).

        1. Never leave laptop unattended.

        2. Keep passwords and SSN private.

        3. Use privacy settings.

        4. Post photos with caution.

    B. Be a voice against CB.

        1. Don't Stand By, Stand Up! (formed in honor of TC on FB): bullies don't succeed without help.

        2. Don't pass on CB messages and inform the senders that their messages are offensive/stupid. (National Crime Prevention Council)

Transition: You may still become a CB victim.

VI. [**Show poster board.**] Responding to CB: use "stop, block, tell." (Parry Afrlab, July 28, 2009, *Frontline* interview)

    A. Stop: take 5, cool down, walk, breathe deeply.

    B. Block: prevent communication—remove bully from social networking lists and block cell #.

    C. Tell: campus security, counselor, etc. Children tell parent, teacher, principal.

Transition/Internal Summary: We've seen CB's negative impact, analyzed causes/conditions, discussed countering CB (privacy, speak out, "stop, block, tell").

Conclusion

I. CB is not someone else's problem.

II.   Call to action: make a personal commitment to combat CB.

        A.   Refuse to be silent.

        B.   Never pass along CB messages.

        C.   Voice your concerns at the campus and community levels.

   III.   Don't forget CT, PP, and other CB victims. Your loved one could be next.

BACK TO → Jamie Oliver's TED Prize-Winning Wish

At the beginning of this chapter, we discussed celebrity chef Jamie Oliver's TED speech, in which he presented his wish to educate children about food (Oliver, 2010). Let's consider his speech in light of what we've learned in this chapter.

▶ Oliver has done his share of informative speaking: as a celebrity chef and star of *Food Revolution*, he gives regular cooking demonstrations that are designed to teach techniques and provide information about food. But this speech, and much of the speaking he does as an activist, is persuasive in nature—he wants to teach people to use the information he provides to change their lives and improve their health, as well as the health of the public at large.

▶ Oliver organizes his speech with a problem-cause-solution pattern. First, he identifies the problem, offering startling statistics and compelling personal stories. He then details the causes behind the problem before moving on to solutions, such as giving people the proper information and tools to change their eating behavior and take charge of their lives. He ends with his "wish," his purpose for speaking, hoping to motivate his audience to make it a reality.

▶ Oliver successfully uses presentation aids during his speech. He shares a few clips and photos of people who are dying from obesity-related diseases. He shows a graph detailing deaths from diet-related illnesses like type 2 diabetes and heart disease. For maximum impact, he dumps a wheelbarrow filled with sugar cubes on the stage to demonstrate the amount of sugar an average child consumes in five years by drinking just two containers of chocolate milk per day.

▶ Oliver considers his audience when he speaks. He knows that the crowd at his TED speech is receptive to his message; they gave him the award, after all. His message is therefore directed at broad solutions at the institutional level—changes he knows the TED audience can help enact. When speaking to individuals who are less educated about or interested in food and nutrition, he would likely focus on change at the personal level.

THINGS TO TRY ▶ Activities

1. Check out a persuasive speech video. You can view one of the persuasive speeches available on VideoCentral at this book's accompanying Web site (if you have access), or you can check one out on YouTube. Listen to and watch the speech critically in light of what you have learned about persuasion. Does the speaker use a clear proposition of fact, value, or policy as a thesis statement? What do you feel the speaker is aiming at—influencing your beliefs, attitudes, or behavior? Maybe all three? Is the speaker's use of rhetorical proofs effective? Consider the elements we have discussed: ethos (character), logos (reasoning), and pathos (emotion).

2. On your next grocery store trip or wait in a doctor's office, look through some magazine advertisements (bridal magazines are particularly interesting to search). Page through the advertisements, looking for examples of appeals to ethos, logos, and pathos. Consider the following questions:

   ▶ What magazine and ads did you choose to examine?

   ▶ Which form of proof do you find most persuasive? Why?

   ▶ Which form of proof do you find least persuasive? Why?

   ▶ Is there a form of proof used consistently in the ads of the particular magazine you looked at? Why do you think that is?

3. At one point in this chapter, we asked you to think of a time when an instructor presented a viewpoint that went against one of your deeply held beliefs. Now it's time for you to be the speaker.

   ▶ Choose a topic that you feel very passionate about (a controversial topic would work best here).

   ▶ Now imagine that you are presenting the topic to a receptive audience, a neutral audience, and a hostile audience. What do you as a speaker need to do in order to prepare to present your topic to each type of audience? What do you know about your listeners' beliefs, attitudes, and behavior? What do you know about their needs? What is most relevant to them?

   ▶ Particularly when dealing with your neutral and hostile audiences, what are some ways that you can bridge the gap between your beliefs and those of your audience members? How can you generate goodwill and understanding?

   ▶ Is there a particular organizational pattern that would best suit you, your topic, or your audience? For example, are you comfortable with and knowledgeable enough about your hostile audience's counterpoints that you are comfortable refuting them using the refutational organizational pattern?

Now that you have finished reading this chapter, you can

Define the goals of persuasive speaking:

▶ **Coercion** involves threats, intimidation, or violence (p. 472).

▶ **Persuasive speaking** uses the process of **persuasion** to influence **attitudes**, **beliefs**, and **behavior** (p. 472).

Develop a persuasive topic and thesis:

▶ Choose a topic that is controversial, and aim to create change in the audience (p. 473).

▶ Thesis statements are often given as a proposition, a statement of your viewpoint on an issue (p. 473).

▶ A **proposition of fact** is a claim of what is or what is not and addresses how people perceive reality (p. 473).

▶ A **proposition of value** makes claims about something's worth (p. 474).

▶ A **proposition of policy** concerns what should happen and makes claims about what goal, policy, or course of action should be pursued (p. 474).

Evaluate your listeners and tailor your speech to them:

▶ **Social judgement theory** holds that your ability to persuade depends on audience members' attitudes toward your topic (p. 475).

▶ A **receptive audience** agrees with you (p. 476).

▶ A **hostile audience** opposes your message (p. 476).

▶ A **neutral audience** neither supports nor opposes you (p. 476).

▶ **Latitude of acceptance and rejection** refers to the range of positions on a topic that are acceptable or unacceptable to your audience, influenced by their original or **anchor position** (p. 477).

▶ Maslow's **hierarchy of needs** holds that our most basic needs must be met before we can worry about needs farther up the hierarchy (p. 477).

▶ The **Elaboration Likelihood Model (ELM)** highlights the importance of relevance to persuasion and holds that listeners will process persuasive messages by one of two routes: **central processing** (deep, motivated thinking) or **peripheral processing** (unmotivated, less critical thought) (pp. 478–479).

Explain three **forms of rhetorical proof**:

▶ The speaker's moral character, or **ethos**, influences the audience's reaction to the message (p. 481).

▶ **Logos** refers to appeals to the audience's **reasoning**, judgments based on facts and inferences (p. 482).

▶ **Inductive reasoning** involves drawing general conclusions from specific evidence; **deductive reasoning** applies general arguments to specific cases (pp. 482–483).

▶ A **syllogism** is a three-line deductive argument, drawing a conclusion from two general premises (p. 483).

▶ **Pathos** appeals to the listeners' emotions (p. 483).

Identify the **logical fallacies**, deceptive forms of reasoning:

▶ The **bandwagon fallacy**: a statement is considered true because it is popular (p. 486).

▶ **Reduction to the absurd**: an argument is pushed beyond its logical limits (p. 487).

▶ The **red herring fallacy**: irrelevant information is used to divert the direction of the argument (p. 487).

▶ The *ad hominem* **fallacy**: a personal attack; the focus is on a person rather than on the issue (p. 487).

▶ **Begging the question**: advancing an argument that cannot be proved because there is no valid evidence (p. 487).

▶ **Either-or fallacy**: only two alternatives are presented, omitting other alternatives (p. 487).

▶ **Appeal to tradition**: "that's the way it has always been" is the only reason given (p. 489).

▶ The **slippery slope fallacy**: one event is presented as the result of another, without showing proof (p. 489).

Choose an appropriate organizational strategy for your speech:

▶ The *problem-solution pattern* proves the existence of a problem and then presents a solution (p. 489).

▶ The **refutational organizational pattern** presents the main points of the opposition to an argument and then refutes them. This works well when the opposing argument is weak (p. 490).

▶ The **comparative advantage pattern** tells why your viewpoint is superior to other viewpoints on the issue (p. 491).

▶ Monroe's *motivated sequence pattern* is a five-step process that begins with arousing listeners' attention and ends with calling for action (pp. 492–493).

Although their spin on the news is anything but serious, *The Daily Show*'s correspondents conduct journalistic interviews with (measured) professionalism and purpose.

appendix

Competent Interviewing

Jon Stewart has interviewed countless celebrities, politicians, and authors on *The Daily Show*. But not every guest on the show gets to sit down with Stewart. A good many interviews are conducted by the show's correspondents, who travel the country to cover absurd stories—or to cover real and important stories in an absurd way. For example, in the wake of a series of business scandals in 2009, *Daily Show* correspondent John Oliver reported on the teaching of ethics in American business schools. He interviewed a Columbia University School of Business professor as well as MBA candidates at Harvard and MIT. Specifically, he wanted to know what future MBAs were learning about ethics, and whether they would be willing to commit to a new business ethics oath being circulated by students from the Harvard Business School.

It was a serious subject, and the interviews were presented in the familiar tone of a nightly newscast. But the content was anything but serious. The interviewees were forced to respond to a series of inane questions designed to cast them in an unflattering light: For example, after the professor described the ethics program at Columbia, noting that they've been teaching ethics for decades, Oliver responded with sarcasm: "Would you say you're good at your job?" (*The Daily Show*, 2009).

In the early days of *The Daily Show*, interviewees were sometimes taken by surprise when the correspondent pieced together clips that made them, or their cause, look foolish. But today, most interviewees are in on the joke. The MBA students Oliver interviewed were all *Daily Show* fans and were well aware of how their refusal to take the ethics oath might come off after the footage got through the show's editors and producers. "We all knew what we were going into and had fun with it," said one participant, Roy Ben-Ami. "Despite the fact that this is indeed a fake news show, it does talk about real issues and makes a point about them. . . ." (Marcott, 2009).

chapter outcomes

After you have finished reading this Appendix, you will be able to

- Define the nature of interviews

- Outline the different types of interviews

- Describe the three parts of an interview: opening, questions, and conclusion

- Devise an interview strategy from the interviewer's point of view

- Prepare for the role of interviewee

- Secure job interviews and manage them with confidence

Although *The Daily Show*'s correspondent "reports" are not serious, they do follow many important rules for interviews. From John Oliver and company, for example, we can learn about the roles of the interviewer and interviewee and the effects of questions and answers. In this Appendix, we examine interviews from a communication standpoint—how they relate to other forms of communication, what kinds of factors are at work in an interview situation, and how all people, from recent college graduates to newscasters, can improve their interviewing skills.

The Nature of Interviews

Although interviewing is not exactly like grabbing a Big Mac with one of your friends, the same principles that apply to all forms of communication are also at work in an interview, with some important differences.

An **interview** is an interaction between two parties that is deliberate and purposeful for at least one of the parties involved. By nature, interviews are more structured and goal-driven than other forms of communication, and they are a form of discourse that is planned, dyadic, and interactive (O'Hair, Friedrich, & Dixon, 2007).

- *Interviews are planned.* Interviews have a purpose that goes beyond the establishment and development of a relationship. At least one of the parties has a predetermined reason for initiating the interview (for example, to gather information).

- *Interviews are goal-driven.* Because a goal exists in advance of the interaction, at least one of the participants plans a strategy for initiating, conducting, and concluding the interview. For example, if you want to obtain a family history from a relative, you plan questions that focus on places and people and still give your interviewee the freedom to add things you may not have thought about.

- *Interviews are structured.* The primary goal of an interview is almost always defined at the beginning of the meeting, something that's rarely true of a conversation with a friend. Interview relationships are more formally structured, and clear status differences often exist. One party usually expects to exert more control than the other.

- *Interviews are dyadic.* Like other forms of interpersonal communication, the interview is dyadic, meaning that it involves two parties. In some instances, a "party" consists of more than one person, as when survey researchers conduct group interviews or when job applicants appear before a panel of interviewers. In such situations, even though a number of individuals are involved, there are only two parties (interviewers and interviewees), each with a role to play.

- *Interviews are interactive.* Interviews involve two-way interactions in which both parties take turns in speaking and listening roles, with a heavy dependence on questions and answers. Although most interviews occur face to face, interactions over the phone or via a videoconference are also considered interactive discourse.

● **ALL INTERVIEWS,** whether a question-and-answer session with *E!* on the red carpet or a serious job interview, are goal-driven, as well as dyadic and interactive in nature.

Think back to Jon Stewart and company. The correspondents' interviews are not only dyadic and interactive but also highly planned. They write questions ahead of time, based on the interviewee's views and background, and they structure their interviews in a way that helps Stewart and company achieve their goal: a hilarious spoof on key topics.

Types of Interviews

What type of scene plays out in your mind when you think of the word *interview?* Maybe you start sweating thinking about an upcoming job interview for a position that you really want. Or maybe you even laugh, thinking about scenes from *The Office,* in which nervous new parents Jim and Pam worry about perfecting the interview to get their daughter into the right day-care center. But interviewing encompasses much more than just getting a job or getting into the right school. In this section, we look at the different types of interviews that play a role in most of our lives (Stewart & Cash, 2011).

The Information-Gathering Interview

In the film *Juno,* sixteen-year-old Juno MacGuff sits in the expensively furnished living room of Mark and Vanessa Loring, a couple interested in adopting Juno's unborn child. Vanessa and her adoption lawyer pepper Juno with questions like "How far along are you?" and "You really think you're going to go ahead with this?" They're trying to obtain *information* from Juno by collecting attitudes, opinions, facts, data, and experiences through an **information-gathering interview**. We take part in, or are exposed to, the results of such interviews every day; we complete telephone surveys on political or cultural topics or read interviews with musicians in *Rolling Stone.* Perhaps you've compiled a survey about

AND YOU?

Have you ever imagined interviewing a particular celebrity, political leader, or historical figure? If you were given such an opportunity, what would your goals be for the interview? What kinds of questions would you ask?

experiences with campus parking, or maybe you've initiated information gathering when you asked your communication professor about career possibilities. In all these instances, the information-gathering interview serves to transfer knowledge from one party to the other.

The Appraisal Interview

In just about every career—including your academic career—**performance appraisals** are a regular part of reviewing your accomplishments and developing goals for the future. In most corporate environments, a performance appraisal is a highly structured routine dictated by company policies, involving a written appraisal and a one-on-one interview between a supervisor and an employee. But in other less structured performance appraisals, you might meet with your professor to discuss a project or paper or lobby for a change in your grade. Although being evaluated can be stressful, the appraisal can offer insight into strengths as well as weaknesses. In other words, if the appraisal interview offers reassurance about what you're doing well and gives some guidance for improvement or growth, it is less threatening and more useful (Culbert, 2010).

AND YOU?

Do you think of a problem-solving interview as a reprimand or as an opportunity to create needed changes? How can you change the nature of a negative-toned interview into a more positive experience?

The Problem-Solving Interview

Of course, not every appraisal interview is positive. Sometimes a **problem-solving interview** is needed to deal with problems, tensions, or conflicts. If you've ever seen an episode of A&E's *Intervention* or *Hoarders*, you've seen this type of interview in action. Typically, friends and family contact a counselor to help them deal with a loved one's addictive behavior, whether it's drug abuse, video game addiction, or an inability to discard personal items. The counselor works with the family, asking questions, gathering information, and formulating a plan or solution before the official intervention, when the counselor, friends, and family all confront the loved one.

Problem-solving interviews can also occur in the workplace (typically when there are performance issues) and even in medical situations. For example, your primary care physician interviews you about problems or concerns in your life that may affect your physical health; in the interview, you should also prepare ahead of time and ask questions that will help you and the doctor understand your health better (Dwamena, Mavis, Holmes-Rovner, Walsh, & Loyson, 2009). Of course, during the interviewing, you should always volunteer information to help solve the problem (Coulehan & Block, 2006).

● **ON THE POPULAR A&E** documentary series, counselors work with compulsive hoarders to assess the case and devise a treatment plan.

The Exit Interview

Hiring and training new people is an expensive process in terms of both time and money, so most organizations want to keep good employees. By conducting **exit interviews** with employees who opt to leave the company, employers can identify organizational problems—such as poor management style, noncompetitive salary, or weak employee benefits—that might affect employee retention. College professors (us included) often conduct similar exit interviews with students who are moving on in their education or embarking on a career. We use the information to help them clarify their goals and help us build a stronger program.

The Persuasive Interview

At times the goal of an interview is not merely to inform or gather information. In a **persuasive interview**, questions are designed to elicit some change in the

---

EVALUATINGCOMMUNICATIONETHICS

Surveys: Interviewing at Large

Imagine that you are an officer in your college's alumni association, and you have been asked to interview other alumni in order to produce marketing materials that will help increase the number and quality of students applying to your school. Your association wants to show how much graduates enjoyed their school experience and how well they have succeeded in their careers.

You produce a simple one-page survey that asks alumni to rate their school and their postgraduate experience from poor to excellent, which you plan to mail to everyone listed in the alumni register. You are hoping that once all the responses have been tallied, you'll be able to make declarative statements in your marketing materials noting the high percentage of graduates who rate their experience as "excellent." But when you submit your plan and a draft of the survey to the alumni association, you are shot down. "We don't want to hear from everyone," says the alumni president. "We only want to hear from successful graduates who are working at *Fortune* 500 companies or who have made big names for themselves in the sciences."

You are asked instead to create an in-depth survey and conduct it by phone with graduates who have donated more than $1,000 to the school in the past five years. You know that this will skew the results of your survey toward former students who love the school and who have been financially successful since graduating. The association is asking you to present this information as though these students are representative of all students. But you know that although the alumni association depends on successful and wealthy graduates for support, such graduates represent a minority of the students who have attended your school. You know that many students have gone on to successful and fulfilling, if less lucrative, careers in education and the arts. You are concerned that the skewed survey you are being asked to conduct will not paint an accurate picture of the school for prospective students. What are the ethical implications here?

THINK ABOUT THIS

❶ Does your plan for a survey of graduates present a more accurate picture of the school than a telephone survey with only the wealthiest graduates?

❷ What about students who attended the school but did not graduate or who are not in the alumni rolls? Would leaving them out skew the results of your survey as well?

❸ Does it really matter? Remember, this survey is for material to be used in marketing. Do you think students will infer that quotes from very successful graduates mean that every student at the school goes on to a high-profile, six-figure-salary career?

Ethical considerations are important when planning a persuasive interview. As you learn in Chapter 16, there is a difference between persuading people and coercing them with threats. If you're going door-to-door to support a political candidate, remember that your job is to give people information—not to intimidate or belittle them into supporting your candidate. That is clearly unethical communication.

interviewee's behavior or opinions. Some political surveys, for example, are aimed at securing your support for (or against) a particular candidate or cause. After you graduate, your alma mater may call to ask you questions about your college experience (hoping to remind you of the good times you had) and then ask you to contribute to a scholarship fund or an annual financial drive. You might also do some persuasive interviewing to convince others to give blood during a campus campaign or to vote for your candidate in a campus, local, or national election.

The Service-Oriented Interview

Did your computer freak out and delete all of your programs? Do you have a roach problem? Have you ever found unauthorized charges on your credit card bill? If any of these things have ever happened to you, you are probably intimately familiar with "help desks" or customer service lines. Representatives contacted at these organizations will conduct **service-oriented interviews** or helping interviews designed to cull information and provide advice, service, or support based on that information. Such interviews are crucial in many contexts—consider what kind of work you'd get from a lawyer, a health care provider, or a landscaper if the person didn't talk to you about your case, ideas, or desires first.

The Selection Interview

● **PARODYING THE FORMAT** of shows like *The Bachelor*, Cartman and the gang question and screen various secondary characters on the show, hoping to uncover the new Kenny.

If you're a fan of *South Park,* you might remember the episode in which Stan, Kyle, and Cartman hold a series of interviews and competitions to fill the open slot in their group left void by Kenny's demise. Silly as it may be, it's an example of a **selection interview**, the primary goal of which is to secure or fill a position within an organization. Selection interviews usually involve recruiting, screening, hiring, and placing new candidates (Baker & Spier, 1990; Joyce, 2008). Members of an organization (such as a university, company, sorority, fraternity, or volunteer organization) and candidates evaluate one another by exchanging information to determine if they'd make a good match. Usually both parties want to make a good impression: the interviewer wants to persuade the interviewee about the value of the position or organization, while the interviewee wants to sell his or her unique qualities and abilities.

The **job interview** is one of the most common types of selection interviews in business, government, and military organizations, with the end goal of filling a position of employment (DiSanza & Legge, 2002). Since job interviewing is usually very important to college students, we devote much of this chapter to helping you become more competent in this context.

The Format of an Interview

For the premiere season of Donald Trump's reality TV show *The Apprentice*, more than two hundred thousand people applied for sixteen slots (Naughton & Peyser, 2004); sixteen lucky winners were thrown into a lengthy employment interview in front of approximately eighteen million weekly fans. Drama, tears, yelling, and backstabbing ensued. This is certainly not a typical interview format (and doesn't sound like much fun to us), but *The Apprentice* illustrates the goal orientation of all interviews. Whether you are interviewing for a job or answering questions for a news reporter, you will note the same basic pattern: an opening, the questions, and a conclusion.

The Opening

Jay Leno's interviewees are always welcomed with a grand entrance and audience clapping and cheering (Babad & Peer, 2010). Even Jerry Springer's guests are ushered in with some fanfare (unfortunately, most of it involves cursing, booing, and attempts at violence). But if you're not planning to star in an Oscar-nominated film or find out the paternity of a child on national television, you probably won't have to worry about this. Your interviews will begin in a calmer manner, setting the tone for the discourse to follow. Before or just as the interview begins, you should always think about three interrelated issues:

▶ The *task:* the nature of this interview and how it will proceed

▶ The *relationship:* whether you like or trust the other party

▶ *Motivation:* what you hope to gain by participating in the interview

For example, Eva is doing a telephone survey on student attitudes about parking on campus. The students she calls want to know about the topic of the interview and how long it will take (the task). They want to know something about her and how the information she gathers will be used (the relationship). They want to know how they (or someone else) will benefit from participating in the interview (the motivation). Eva needs to plan what she can say or do at the *start* of the interview that is responsive to these needs (see Table A.1).

The Questions

Once you have set the stage for the interview with an appropriate opening, you need to develop the organizational plan for the body of the interview. Questions and answers are the core of the interview. They accomplish the goals of the interview through structuring, soliciting, responding, and reacting. The interviewer sets up the structure of the interview (identifying the purpose of the interview)

CONNECT

The opening of an interview is much like the introduction to a speech. As we discuss in Chapter 13, speech introductions help you achieve four goals: capturing your audience's attention, introducing your purpose, previewing your main points, and connecting with your audience. Openings in both contexts establish the interaction that follows, so your success in engaging your listeners depends on your competency from the start.

● **AFTER EVERY CHALLENGE** on *The Apprentice*, the losing team is subjected to lengthy questioning by "The Donald" and his advisers to try to figure out what went awry.

Goal	Description	Example
Clarify the *task*	Orient the interviewee, who may not be well informed about the reason for the interview.	"As you may know, we're looking for ways to increase productivity among our sales associates. I'm hoping you will give me information to jump-start this initiative."
Define the *relationship*	Make a connection to a third party respected by the interviewee if the interviewee doesn't know you and you want to put him or her at ease.	"I was referred to you by Liam Fitzpatrick, who told me that you've done great work for him in the past."
Determine the *motivation*	Request the interviewee's advice or assistance with regard to a problem.	"I'm hoping that you can help me get insight into the way things work between your division and marketing."

and then solicits a response from the interviewee. This response then prompts reactions from the interviewer, and it just keeps building from there. To have the most effective and most successful interview possible, whether you're the interviewer or interviewee, you need to consider question type, impact, and sequence.

Types of Questions

The path of the interview is largely determined by the types of questions asked. Questions vary in two distinct ways: the amount of freedom the respondent has and how the questions relate to what has happened in the course of the interview.

First, questions vary in terms of how much leeway the interviewee has in generating responses. An **open question** gives the interviewee great freedom in terms of how to respond. Questions like "What's it like being a student here?" and "What issues will influence your decision to vote for one of the presidential candidates?" allow the interviewee to determine the amount and depth of information provided. Interviewers often ask open questions when the interviewee knows more about a topic than the interviewer does or to help the interviewee relax (there is no "correct" answer, so no answer is wrong).

In other situations, the interviewer will want a more direct answer. **Closed questions** give less freedom to the interviewee by restricting answer choices. For example, an interviewer conducting a survey of student attitudes toward parking on campus might ask more closed questions ("When do you arrive on campus?" "Where do you park?" "How long do you stay?"). The most closed form of a question is the

● **PROSPECTIVE STUDENTS** on a campus tour should ask their student guides open questions ("What's the social scene like?") and closed questions ("Is the dining hall open on the weekends?") to figure out what student life is *really* like.

bipolar question, for which there are only two possible responses, "yes" and "no" ("Do you normally eat breakfast?" "Do you own a car?" "Did you vote in the last election?"). Another possibility is to ask interviewees to respond to a scale, as with the question "How would you rate parking availability on campus?"

1	2	3	4	5
Very poor	Poor	Adequate	Good	Excellent

Questions also vary in terms of how they relate to what has happened so far in the interview. **Primary questions** introduce new topics; **secondary questions** seek clarification or elaboration of responses to primary questions. Thus, if you were interviewing an older family member, you might open an area of questioning by asking, "What can you tell me about my family history?" This primary question might then be followed by a number of secondary questions, such as "How did my grandparents meet?" and "How did they deal with the fact that their parents disapproved of their marriage?" Secondary questions can take a variety of forms. Some of the more common forms are illustrated in Table A.2.

TABLE A.2

SECONDARY QUESTIONS

Behavior	Definition	Example
Clarification	Directly requests more information about a response	"Could you tell me a little more about the reasons you chose to join the military after high school?"
Elaboration	Directly requests an extension of a response	"Are there any other specific features that you consider important in your search for a new house?"
Paraphrasing	Puts the response in the questioner's language in an attempt to establish understanding	"So, you're saying that the type of people you work with is more important to you than location?"
Encouragement	Uses brief sounds and phrases that indicate attentiveness to and interest in what the respondent is saying	"Uh-huh," "I see," "That's interesting," "Good," "Yes, I understand."
Summarizing	Summarizes several previous responses and seeks confirmation of the correctness of the summary	"Let's see if I've got it: your ideal job involves an appreciative boss, supportive colleagues, interesting work, and living in a large metropolitan area?"
Clearinghouse	Asks if you have elicited all the important or available information	"Have I asked everything that I should have asked?"

Source: Labels and definitions from O'Hair, Friedrich, & Dixon (2007).

Question Impact

In addition to considering question type, interviewers must also consider the likely impact of a question on the interviewee. The way in which a question is constructed can directly influence the information received in response. A good question is clear, relevant, and unbiased. To create clear questions, consider the criteria on the next page.

real communicator

NAME: Cynthia Guadalupe Inda
HOMETOWN: Santa Barbara, California
OCCUPATION: Trial attorney
FUN FACT: I'm a foster parent for abandoned dogs and cats (while they are waiting to find permanent homes).

When I mention that I'm a lawyer, many people are surprised to learn that I spend a great deal of time interviewing people. In fact, I like to think of my job as asking questions and culling information in ways similar to talk show hosts, counselors, and reporters. But before I confuse you, allow me to explain these aspects of my career.

When I was with a district attorney's office for a number of years, my biggest challenge was interviewing many witnesses for the dozens of cases I was assigned in a limited amount of time. In order to do my job effectively, I needed to interview all the witnesses quickly and efficiently—but not make them feel rushed.

The talk show host aspect of my job is putting people at ease during an interview. People are often intimidated by lawyers, so I look people in the eye, smile, and try to be as down-to-earth as possible. (I think I'm this way in real life, so I just have to remember to treat my interviewees as I would my friends and family.) When dealing with Spanish-speaking witnesses, I always conduct interviews in Spanish. This helps to put people at ease because the law doesn't seem as terrifying in one's own language.

The counselor aspect of my job is having empathy for people's situations. I often tell people who are afraid to bring charges or get involved in any way that I understand their fear and reticence. I'll say something like, "I know that there are other things you'd rather be doing; just tell the judge exactly what you are telling me." If an interviewee is very upset, I'll often switch the subject away from the task at hand; I get them talking about themselves instead of the law. They usually relax and it makes it easier to get back to the interview questions.

The reporter aspect of my job is in culling information from my interviewees to focus on what is essential to the case. Preparation really matters here. When I have witnesses on the stand, my questions are targeted toward the achievement of a goal. I ask open-ended questions, but I also have a series of background and clarifying questions to help make my point. When I'm cross-examining a witness, however, my questions are much more closed: I try to ask only questions that call for "yes" or "no" responses. The facts established by the "yes" or "no" answers I'm searching for give less credibility to the opposition's case.

Effective interviewing skills are crucial to my professional success and the well-being of my clients. Interviewing is not all work—I have fun getting to know people and helping them achieve justice.

- Make questions understandable. Ask the classic and simple news reporter's questions of who, what, when, where, why, and how before you proceed to more complex ones (Payne, 1951).

- Ensure that the wording of the questions is as direct and simple as possible. For example, asking "For whom did you vote in the last mayoral election?" will get you a more precise answer than asking "How do you vote?"

- Keep the questions short and to the point.

- Phrase questions positively and remain civil (Ben-Porath, 2010). For example, asking "Have you ever voted in campus student government elections?" is clear and objective; using negative phrasing ("You haven't ever voted in the campus student government elections, have you?") can be confusing and in some cases, may be unethical and biased (Doris, 1991).

Speaking of ethics, a question that suggests or implies the answer that is expected is called a **directed question**. Some directed questions are subtle in the direction they provide ("Wouldn't it be so much fun if we all got together to paint my apartment this weekend?"). These subtle directed questions are **leading questions**. Other directed questions are bolder in their biasing effect and are called **loaded questions** ("When was the last time you cheated on an exam?" which assumes, of course, that you *have* cheated). Questions that provide no hint to the interviewee concerning the expected response are **neutral questions**—for example, "What, if anything, is your attitude toward the fraternities and sororities on this campus?" Additional examples are given in Table A.3.

Question Sequence

The order in which the interviewer asks questions can have a big impact on the interview; it can affect both the accomplishment of goals and the comfort level of the interviewee. There are three main "shapes" that guide the ordering of questions: the funnel, inverted funnel, and tunnel sequences.

CONNECT

Even neutral questions can become leading questions if you fail to consider nonverbal communication (Chapter 5). If you grimace, roll your eyes, or change your tone of voice when you ask the neutral question "What, if anything, is your attitude toward fraternities and sororities on this campus?" you are actually asking a leading question (and letting others know your attitude toward the Greek system on campus).

TABLE A.3

LEADING, LOADED, AND NEUTRAL QUESTIONS

Question Behavior	Definition	Example
Leading	Questions that subtly direct interviewees to the correct or desired answer	"Do you take home office supplies like most employees?"
Loaded	Extremely leading questions that almost dictate the correct answer; to be avoided in most cases	"When was the last time you took home supplies from the office?"
Neutral	Questions that allow respondents to choose their answers without pressure from the interviewer's wording	"Do you think the office should provide you with supplies to work at home?"

In the **funnel sequence**, the interviewer starts with broad, open-ended questions (picture the big end of a funnel) and moves to narrower, more closed questions. The questions become more personal or more tightly focused as the interview progresses, giving the interviewee a chance to get comfortable with the topic and open up. The funnel sequence works best with respondents who feel comfortable with the topic and the interviewer.

▶ "What do you think about children playing competitive sports?" (general)

▶ "So what disadvantages have you witnessed?" (specific)

▶ "What constraints would you advocate for young players?" (very specific)

The **inverted funnel sequence** starts with narrow, closed questions and moves to more open-ended questions. The inverted funnel works best with interviewees who are emotional, are reticent, or need help "warming up."

▶ "Did you perform a Mozart piece for your piano recital in junior high school?" (very specific)

▶ "What other classical compositions are you comfortable playing?" (specific)

▶ "How did you feel about taking piano lessons as a child?" (general)

In the **tunnel sequence**, all of the questions are at one level. The tunnel sequence works particularly well in polls and surveys. A large tunnel would involve a series of broad, open-ended questions. A small tunnel (the more common form) would ask a series of narrow, closed questions, as in the following example:

▶ "Have you attended any multicultural events on campus?" (specific)

  ▶ "Have you attended sports games or matches?" (specific)

  ▶ "Have you attended any guest lecturer series on campus?" (specific)

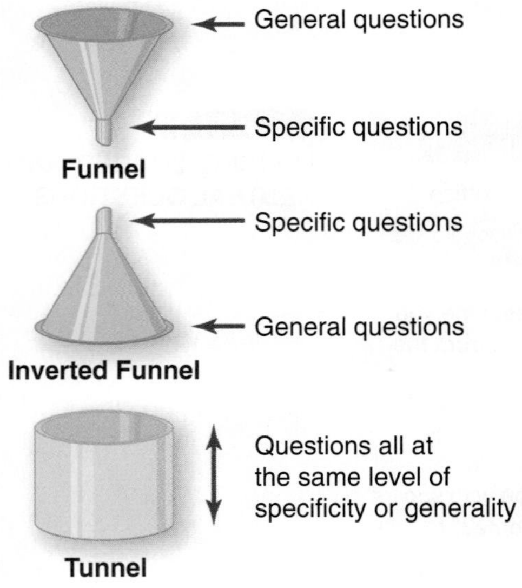

The three sequences are depicted visually in Figure A.1.

Interviewers can put together the three sequences in various combinations over the course of an interview based on the goals for the interview, the direction the interview takes, and the comfort level of both parties involved.

FIGURE A.1

FUNNEL, INVERTED FUNNEL, AND TUNNEL SEQUENCES

◀— General questions

◀— Specific questions

Funnel

◀— Specific questions

◀— General questions

Inverted Funnel

↕ Questions all at the same level of specificity or generality

Tunnel

The Conclusion

When *CSI: Miami*'s Horatio Caine is finished interviewing a suspect or gathering information at the scene of the crime, he often delivers a killer punch line (frequently pausing somewhere in the middle to put on his trademark sunglasses). While Caine's tactics are quite amusing—inspiring countless YouTube tributes—we can promise that most interviews will end on a far less dramatic note. Once the purpose of the interview has been achieved, the interaction should come to a comfortable and satisfying close. This closing phase of the interview is especially important because it is likely to determine the impression the interviewee retains of the interview as a whole.

There are important norms involved when individuals take leave of each other (Knapp, Hart, Friedrich, & Shulman, 1973), so in closing the interview, the interviewer needs to employ both verbal and nonverbal strategies to serve three important functions (Von Raffler-Engel, 1983):

▶ To *conclude,* or signal the end of the interview

▶ To *summarize,* or review the substantive conclusions produced by the interview

▶ To *support,* or express satisfaction with the interaction and project what will happen next

Table A.4 illustrates closing strategies that may help you conclude, summarize, and support. As these sample statements indicate, bringing the interview to a close is largely the responsibility of the interviewer. In the next section, look at how this and other responsibilities and roles are filled in a variety of interviewing situations.

Understanding Roles and Responsibilities in Interviews

Jan, a thirty-five-year-old high school biology teacher, is on the hunt for a new career. She can approach this job hunt in two ways. First, she could simply answer advertisements for open positions and hope to be called in for an interview. Alternatively, she can identify people or organizations that she thinks she'd like to work for and arrange for information-gathering interviews with them. In the first approach, Jan, the job hunter, fills the role of *interviewee*—she answers questions posed by the interviewer. In the second example, Jan acts as the *interviewer,* asking people in various positions for information about potential career paths in their industry. So how are these roles different? How are they similar? Let's find out.

Roles and Responsibilities of the Interviewer

In any interview situation, there are specific behaviors that competent interviewers share. Specifically, they must identify potential barriers, make the interviewee comfortable, ask ethical and appropriate questions, and effectively listen and respond to the interviewee. In addition, interviewers must be culturally sensitive. (You'll read more about this issue in the "Communication Across Cultures" box on p. 522.)

● **HORATIO CAINE'S** suave move indicates that he's finished interviewing a suspect or surveying the crime scene. Your job interview will have a simple, comfortable conclusion.

TABLE A.4

CLOSING STRATEGIES

Behavior	Definition	Example
Declare the completion of the purpose or task.	The word *well* probably signals a close more than any other phrase; people automatically assume the end is near and prepare to take their leave.	"Well, I think we've covered a lot of territory today."
Signal that time for the meeting is up.	This is most effective when a time limit has been announced or agreed on in the opening of the interview. Be tactful; avoid being too abrupt or giving the impression that you're moving the interviewee along an assembly line.	"We have just a few minutes left, so . . ."
Explain the reason for the closing.	Be sure the reasons are real; if an interviewee thinks you're giving phony excuses, future interactions will be strained.	"Unfortunately, I've got another meeting in twenty minutes, so we'll have to start wrapping things up."
Express appreciation or satisfaction.	This is a common closing because interviewers have usually received something from the interview (information, help, a sale, a story, a new employee).	"Thank you for your interest in our cause."
Plan for the next meeting.	This reveals what will happen next (date, time, place, topic, content, purpose) or arranges for the next interview.	"I think we should follow up on this next week; my assistant will call you to arrange a time."
Summarize the interview.	This common closing for informational, appraisal, counseling, and sales interviews may repeat important information, stages, or agreements or verify accuracy or agreement.	"We've come to three major agreements here today." (List them briefly.)

Source: Labels from Stewart & Cash (2006).

Identify Potential Barriers

Before heading into an interview situation, interviewers should take some time to reflect on potential barriers that might disrupt the interview. For example, is the space where the interview will take place quiet, private, and fairly neat and organized? True story: Val is an academic counselor at a prestigious university who is unfortunate enough to have an office next door to the copy room. The old Xerox machine causes her wall to shake whenever one of her colleagues makes a photocopy; on top of this, her university recently installed "see-through" blinds that don't actually keep the sunlight out. Every afternoon, she must take students to a private conference room when interviewing them about their coursework or their career plans in order to avoid distractions.

Make the Interviewee Comfortable

Interviewees, particularly job applicants and medical patients, are often very nervous in interview situations—and understandably so. A good interviewer should adapt to the situational and relational contexts to help the interviewee feel at ease (Ralston, Kirkwood, & Burant, 2003). It would be effective and appropriate, for example, for an interviewer to smile, make eye contact, and offer a handshake. But imagine if your doctor entered the examining room and gave you a big hug or if a job interviewer told you about his problems with his partner's parents. Be sure to keep verbal and nonverbal behaviors appropriate to the context.

Ask Ethical and Appropriate Questions

We've already discussed types of questions and question sequences that you can use to guide productive, competent interviews that achieve your goals. But beyond knowing how to use open and closed questions or funnel or inverted funnel sequences, it's important to remember that good questions are also ethical and appropriate questions. For example, if Erik is a representative from his school newspaper interviewing a biology professor about her recent grant from the National Institutes of Health (NIH), his questions should stick to her research and her plans to implement a new lab on campus. It would be inappropriate and unethical for him to ask how much money she will be receiving from the NIH or whether she expects to receive a promotion and salary increase from the university after receiving the award.

On a job interview, certain unethical and inappropriate questions are also illegal. We illustrate these later in this chapter.

Listen and Respond Effectively

The role of the interviewer is not limited to structuring an interview and asking questions. After all, an effective interviewer needs to listen, respond, and evaluate the information that those questions reveal. Throughout the interview, the interviewer should keep both immediate and future goals in mind by making notes (written or mental) during the interview. A medical doctor might take notes about your family history and ask follow-up questions or order tests regarding your health based on this discussion.

Roles and Responsibilities of the Interviewee

True, the interviewer is responsible for quite a bit of work in an interview situation, but that doesn't mean that the interviewee is off the hook. If you are the interviewee, you will benefit greatly by clarifying your personal goals, being prepared, listening and responding effectively, and adapting to the interviewer and the situation.

Clarify and Fulfill Personal Goals

One of the most important things that an interviewee can bring to the interview is a clear sense of personal goals. That is, you should have a clear idea of what *you* want to achieve in the interview. This insight allows you to look for and seek out opportunities to advance your aims, such as looking for specific openings in the conversation (Waldron & Applegate, 1998). A job interviewee—whose goal it might be to impress a hiring manager—can

AND YOU?

Have you ever been in an interview where you felt that the interviewer neglected his or her responsibilities? In what ways did the interviewer fail? How would you have handled things differently?

seek out appropriate places to give examples of his or her energy, drive, and willingness to be a team player. An informational interviewee may advance the public relations goals of her organization by selecting information to be shared with the press ("Our office has always been supportive of student groups; last year alone, we gave over $5,000 to the Intercultural Student Union at XYZ Community College").

COMMUNICATIONACROSSCULTURES

THINK ABOUT THIS

Doctors, Patients, and Cultural Considerations

The ways we perceive others, our expectations of certain communication events, and how we express ourselves always carry some cultural component. For medical professionals, who must interview patients every day, cultural differences can have major consequences.

Consider Su. Su has suffered from allergies and asthma for most of her life, but her attacks have recently become more frequent and severe. Her doctor is busy with other patients and is frustrated to see Su in his office yet again with the same complaints. He has already advised her to remove her carpeting and replace her old drapes, invest in a top-quality air filter for her bedroom, and take her medication regularly. In the doctor's estimation, Su is back in the office because she has not followed orders because she is either lazy or noncompliant.

But the doctor is overlooking several important cultural clues that offer tremendous insight into Su's health situation. First, Su is seventy-two years old. Like many older individuals, she wants her doctor to sit down and explain factors that trigger her condition; she wants to understand what the medication will do and why she needs to take pills that cost her $60 a month. But her doctor rarely has the opportunity to give Su such attention because he is slotted to see two other patients at the same time. In addition, Su is a widow who lives on a very small fixed income, her deceased husband's pension. It is entirely impractical for her to replace all the drapes in her home, have her carpet replaced with hardwood floors, or spend $300 on an air filter for her room.

Would it make a difference to know that Su and her family immigrated to the United States from China fifty years ago? According to research, yes, it would. Direct questions requiring yes or no answers are often seen as invasive and pushy by people from high-context cultures like China, so the physician should avoid putting Su on the spot. Questions like "Did you purchase that air filter I mentioned?" might be more disconcerting to Su than asking, "What questions might you have about the cleaning suggestions we discussed at your last visit?" (Stewart & Cash, 2006). Su's gender plays a role as well. Women are more likely to use questions ("Do you really think this regimen will help?") that may seem hesitant to men, and women's hedges ("I guess I could try this medication") may be their way of maintaining relational harmony even if they are unsure or unconvinced (Mulac, 1998).

1 Is it really possible for Su's doctor to pay attention to all of the cultural factors that play into her health care simultaneously? Is it enough for him to consider her financial constraints but not her needs as an older woman?

2 How might Su's doctor be able to improve his competence in these health interviews?

3 Would your assessment of Su's doctor's competence be different if you knew that, for instance, most of his patients shared Su's cultural and socioeconomic background? Would you feel differently about his reactions to her if he worked at a large public clinic or if she were visiting him at a small, private practice specializing in geriatric health care?

4 Should Su be responsible for making any changes in her communication with her doctor?

Prepare Yourself Responsibly

Your school's career services office and your previous employment situations have likely prepared you for the fact that you'll need to draft a résumé and a cover letter in advance of a job interview. But all interviews, from job interviews to legal interviews, benefit from some advance planning.

For one thing, you'll want to be well rested and physically and mentally alert for the interview. From personal experience, we urge you not to skip meals—more than a few of our students have had growling stomachs during interviews! You'll also want to be dressed appropriately for the occasion. Now, this can mean different things to different people—the key is to think about the context. If you are having an information-gathering interview with your neighbor in your backyard because he's interested in learning about your vegetable and herb garden, you can certainly wear jeans and a favorite football team T-shirt. But if you have an official job interview at a large financial firm that has a conservative dress policy, it would be best to wear a dark-colored professional suit or dress.

Another point to keep in mind is to plan what you should bring with you to the interview. If you're going to a medical interview with a new doctor, you should bring your medical history (perhaps your file from your previous physician), a list of the medications you take, your family's medical history, and a list of any symptoms you are experiencing (Gosselin, 2007).

Listen and Respond Effectively

Just as interviewers must listen and respond effectively, so must the interviewee. For example, you should listen carefully to your doctor's specific questions about your sprained, swollen knee and offer clear and concise responses—don't go off on tangents about the hiking trip where you hurt yourself. In a performance appraisal, carefully consider your answers to your boss's questions. If she asks you to assess what you have accomplished and excelled at, honestly highlight your individual achievements or your contributions to the team you work with—without exaggerating.

Adapt to the Interviewer and the Situation

It is the interviewee's responsibility to adapt to the interviewer and the interview situation appropriately—particularly with verbal and nonverbal communication. If a professor in your department is interviewing you to see if you would be a good fit for your college's honors program, you should plan on looking at the interview quite formally. For example, you would use professional, formal address when speaking to the professor ("Professor Arisetty" or "Dr. Edmunds"). But if you have known this professor for three years, you babysit her children, and she insists that you call her Emilia, you can adapt, feeling free to use her first name and a less strict, more personal style of conversation.

As we've mentioned, culture plays a profound role in interviewing situations, and job interviews are no exception (Gardner, Reithel, Foley, Cogliser, & Walumbwa, 2009). As an interviewee or as an interviewer, you should expect to adapt to the culture of your communication partner. For example, many people from various ethnic and religious backgrounds find it difficult to brag about their accomplishments at a job interview, either because their

● **THE KIND** of job you're interviewing for dictates your dress. For an interview in the typically more conservative finance industry, you will need a suit. For an interview at an art gallery, you *might* wear a more casual outfit.

Consider the relational context in competent communication (Chapter 1). It is effective and appropriate to respond differently to the same question posed by your doctor and your mother, or by your boss and your romantic partner. How intimate you are with the person, your relational history, what you know about them, and status differences between you have a profound effect on the interview situation.

● **NOT ALL** bosses are like Miranda Priestly, and not all offices are like *Runway*'s. So don't worry that your interviewer will make fun of your cerulean polyester-blend sweater!

culture frowns on such boastful behavior or because it violates their personal moral code. Research shows that rather than clearly state a strength ("I have extremely strong organizational skills"), African American interviewees often tell stories about themselves to illustrate their strengths (Hecht, Jackson, & Ribeau, 2003). But how might such storytelling be perceived if the interviewer is from a different background? Researchers note that European American interviewers often miss the point of African American interviewees' stories and judge the candidates to be "unfocused." Thus African Americans who adapt by directly listing their strengths for a job are perceived more positively in interviews (Hecht, Jackson, & Ribeau, 2003). Conversely, a European American interviewer who looks for the message behind the story an interviewee tells has competently adapted.

The Job Interview

In the film *The Devil Wears Prada*, young Andy (Anne Hathaway) arrives for her interview at *Runway*, a fictional fashion magazine. She is dressed in a plain and simple yet respectable outfit suitable for an aspiring young journalist on the hunt for her first job out of college. Yet when she arrives at *Runway*, she encounters an office full of sleek, stylish people dressed in expensive designer clothes. They feel quite free to laugh at her outfit and remind her that for this job, "an interest in fashion is crucial." And when she finally has the opportunity to interview with editor-in-chief Miranda Priestly (Meryl Streep), Priestly insults her for not reading *Runway*, not being familiar with the editor's reputation, and having no interest in fashion.

While such scenes make for great entertainment, in truth, most job interviews are polite and diplomatic affairs. In the remaining pages of this chapter, we describe how job interviews usually occur and offer solid advice on how to prepare for, engage in, and follow up on the process (Muir, 2008).

Getting the Interview

The first step involves actually getting the interview. This important phase involves three interrelated tasks: locating jobs and doing homework on the organizations, preparing materials to be used in the process (the résumé and cover letter), and building realistic expectations about the interviewing process.

The Job Search

The first element of preinterview preparation involves identifying potential jobs and then researching the field and the organizations. Although there are many strategies for locating jobs, your three best sources are likely to be people you know or manage to meet, placement centers, and discipline-specific job sites.

A great place to start is with family, friends, professors, former employers, and individuals working in your field of interest. In fact, personal referrals account for over 27 percent of new employees hired from outside an organization (Crispin & Mehler, 2011). You should also plan to network (Brazeel, 2009). **Networking** is the process of using interconnected groups or associations of persons you know to develop relationships with their connections that you don't know. Human resources executive and consultant John O'Loughlin (2010) notes that many job searches involve some degree of networking. So contact everyone you know who works in your field or who might know someone who does. Let these individuals know the kind of job you are looking for, and ask for suggestions. You can also make new contacts via social networking services like Facebook and LinkedIn or through an organization for professionals in your chosen field (many offer student memberships).

Placement centers are another source of jobs. Most college campuses have a centralized placement center where recruiters from major companies come to interview potential employees.

Finally, start looking for specific job openings. While general employment Web sites (like Monster.com) can be starting places, they may not yield significant results simply because they attract a large number of applicants (O'Loughlin, 2010). A more productive search uses sites that cater to specific industries or even an organization's site (Pearce & Tuten, 2001; Young & Foot, 2005). For example, mediabistro.com and entertainmentcareers.net focus on jobs in the media and entertainment industries. You can also find job postings on the Web sites for most major companies and organizations (look for links to "Careers" or "Employment"). Consider using job information and posting aggregators (such as LexisNexis) that will let you set criteria or parameters for

CONNECT

Preparing for a job interview is similar to preparing for a speech. In Chapter 12, we suggest studying your audience to know how to present information they'll find useful and interesting; in a job interview, you must do the same. Your goal is to learn about the organization's culture (Chapter 11). Is it a formal or informal place? What does the organization value? This information helps you adapt your communication competently and impress a hiring manager.

● **THERE ARE** many different avenues that you can explore when you begin your job hunt. Industry-specific magazines like *Variety*, job placement centers, and employment Web sites are all good places to start.

what you want—for example, Human Resources/Full-time/Regular. Doing so will put you in touch with sites that have less traffic and give you a better chance of being noticed. (You can even limit your search geographically.)

WIREDFORCOMMUNICATION

Presenting Yourself: Your Online Persona

Savvy job applicants will always prepare for a job interview by doing a little armchair research. A few quick Internet searches can yield a wealth of information on a company's history, status, and corporate culture and even some insights into its future. A curious applicant might go even further, checking local and industry sources to see what has been written on, about, or by the person who will be conducting the interview.

But often, inexperienced job hunters fail to realize that those searches can go both ways. As easily as you can Google a company name, a potential employer can also do a search on your name or e-mail address. You might put forth a fantastic résumé and buy the most professional suit for your first interview, but what you've posted on online chats, blogs, Web pages, and MySpace or Facebook pages might very well be the most important factor in shaping the first impression you make on a potential employer.

Consider Brad Karsh, the president of a small company in Chicago, who was looking to hire a summer intern. When he came across a promising candidate, he did a quick online background check, taking a peek at his Facebook page. There the candidate described his interests as including marijuana use, shooting people, and obsessive sex. That the student was clearly exaggerating didn't matter. His lack of judgment regarding what to say about himself publicly, Karsh says, took him out of the running for the position (Finder, 2006). Karsh and many other potential employers are increasingly using the Web to do background checks on potential candidates. They're looking for red flags: personal information that candidates have chosen to announce to the world that makes the employer reconsider their adequacy for the position.

And so posting information about yourself on a public or semipublic-electronic forum is a risky endeavor for a job hunter—or anyone else trying to make a good impression. While photos of you and your best friends being crazy at a sorority toga party might be fun to share with fellow students, such images create an immature and unprofessional impression that can be hard to shake. Likewise, postings to blogs and Web pages can reveal insights into your political leanings, religious beliefs, opinions, habits, or personal history that you might not want employers to know about. One student reported that he was having a hard time landing an interview. Upon Googling himself, he found an essay he'd posted on a student Web site a few years ago, titled "Lying Your Way to the Top." Only after he had it removed did he begin getting calls (Finder, 2006).

THINK ABOUT THIS

❶ Take a moment to Google yourself. Search not only for your name but also your e-mail address. What comes up?

❷ Do you have a page on Facebook, MySpace, or some other social networking site? Think objectively about the impression of you that the page conveys. Would you hire you?

❸ Do you consider the material you post on various Web sites private? Do you think it's ethical for employers to be looking at your postings?

❹ How can you create a better online image for yourself?

Prepare Your Materials

Once you've identified potential jobs, you'll need to make contact with the people in a position to hire you. As you know, first impressions are important. And as a job applicant, the first impression you will make on a potential employer will likely be via your written materials—a formal cover letter and résumé. In this section, we show you how to prepare these materials so that they communicate the right message about you.

But first, a cautionary note: *before* you send off these written materials, make sure you have cleaned up any searchable information that does not portray you in a favorable light (Brandenburg, 2008; Holson, 2010). If you use social networking sites, adjust your privacy settings to ensure that you have not been, and cannot be, tagged in any photographs that you wouldn't want a potential employer to see and that your wall is not visible to anyone other than your approved friends. Perform searches for your name and e-mail address to make sure that any comments you've left on public forums or chat rooms don't come back to haunt you (see the accompanying Wired for Communication box).

The résumé.   Begin by pulling together a **résumé**—a printed summary of your education, work experiences, and accomplishments. It is a vehicle for making a positive first impression on potential employers. An effective résumé tells just enough about you to make employers believe they may need your skills and experience.

No two résumés look exactly alike, but most résumés should contain the following general information:

▶ *Contact information.* Include both campus and home addresses if necessary, phone numbers, and your e-mail address. Make sure that your voice mail greets callers with a clear, professional message, and check it often. If you have an odd or cute address for your regular e-mail (partygirl@provider .com, numberonedad@provider.net), consider opening another account with a more serious name for all of your professional communication.

▶ *Employment objective.* Be concise and specific about what you're looking for in a position and your career goals. If you are applying for several types of jobs, you should create multiple résumés tailored to specific positions.

▶ *Education.* List the institutions you have attended, their locations, and the dates of attendance. List degrees received (or dates to be received), academic majors, and areas of concentration. Awards and GPA can be listed if they enhance your marketability.

▶ *Work experience.* If your work experiences are all in the same area, list them in reverse chronological order, focusing on concrete examples of achievement or skills that you have mastered. Explain job functions as well as titles. If, like many students, you have had a variety of jobs (for example, waiting tables and being a camp counselor), reverse chronological order may not be very practical. Consider grouping actual employment and volunteer activities together in a way that best matches the job responsibilities you are seeking. Remember that prospective employers read this section carefully to discover how your experience, abilities, and achievements relate to their organization's needs.

▶ *Activities.* For employers, participation in a variety of academic, extra-curricular, or social activities indicates that you are motivated and get involved. Include activities that are relevant to your career objective, emphasizing accomplishments and leadership roles—and link them clearly together.

▶ *Special skills.* Do you speak fluent Spanish? Are you skilled in a particular programming language? Did you climb Mount Everest? Don't be shy—let potential employers know this information. Your skills may be useful to the organization, and your accomplishments show dedication and determination.

▶ *References.* Your references are typically professors, previous supervisors, or anyone else who can confirm your employment history and attest to your work ethic and character. You are not necessarily required to include your references as part of your résumé, but be sure to have their current contact information handy in case a hiring manager requests them. Be sure to include only people who have agreed to serve as references for you.

A sample résumé appears in Figure A.2.

Once your résumé is complete, take some time to prepare it for electronic submission. You can avoid translation issues by saving it as a PDF document, so that employers can read it regardless of what type of computer they have. You should also name the file carefully, so that employers will be able to identify it easily. Include your name (or just your last name) in the file title, along with the word *resume* and perhaps a date. For example, *MartinezResumeJan2012.pdf* is a title preferable to *MyResume.pdf*.

The cover letter. Whenever you send your résumé to a potential employer, it should be accompanied by a formal **cover letter**, a one-page letter indicating your interest in a specific position. The cover letter gives you the opportunity to express how you learned of the position and the organization, how your skills and interests can benefit the organization, and why you are interested in applying for this particular job. The cover letter also serves as a means by which you can demonstrate your written communication skills, so make sure that you use correct grammar, punctuation, and spelling—and proofread carefully! Figure A.3 shows a strong cover letter.

In many cases, prospective employers accept e-mails as cover letters. So when you e-mail a hiring manager or a human resource representative at an organization, your e-mail should contain the same information as your cover letter. If you are unsure of the protocol, it's always best to be more formal and include an official cover letter with your e-mail. Be sure to include a subject line and to proofread your e-mail carefully before you press Send.

AND YOU?

Do you have your résumé ready all the time, in preparation for any unexpected opportunities? How might pulling together a solid résumé be beneficial even when you are not on the job hunt?

SAMPLE RESUME

Ellen Ng

111 A Street, Apt. 2C, San Marcos, TX 78666

(555) 375-7111 • ellen.ng@serviceprovider.com

OBJECTIVE

To obtain an entry-level editorial position where I can use my strong writing and editing skills while expanding my knowledge of the publishing process.

EDUCATION

Texas State University, *San Marcos, TX*   *2009–2011*
    Bachelor of Arts, English, May 2011   GPA: 3.7/4.0
    Honors: Recipient of the Lorin D. Parkin scholarship (2010); Member of the Sigma Tau Delta honor society.

Northwest Vista College, *San Antonio, TX*   *2007–2009*
    Associate of Arts, Liberal and Media Arts (General), May 2009

RELATED WORK EXPERIENCE

Intern, Chronicle Books, *San Francisco, CA*   *Summer 2010*
    Wrote reports on the marketability and publication potential of cookbook proposals and manuscripts submitted to publisher. Drafted rejection letters, letters to authors, and letters requesting outstanding permissions fees. Created cost and sales figure spreadsheets. Prepared manuscripts and artwork for production.

Writing Counselor, Writing Center, *Texas State University*   *Fall 2009–Spring 2011*
    Aided students with their academic research papers, résumés, and cover letters. Developed exercises and writing samples to aid with college-level writing.

Writer/Editor, MyWay in Education, *Hong Kong*   *Summer 2009*
    Created and edited reading comprehension articles and over 300 grammar questions per week for ten different grade levels in accordance with Hong Kong public school standards for company's Web site.

Volunteer, San Antonio Public Library, *San Antonio, TX*   *Fall 2005–Spring 2009*
    Created themed book displays for special events, such as Hispanic Heritage Month and various national and international holidays. Read to children ages 3–5 weekly and created arts-and-crafts activities or games structured around the stories.

OTHER WORK EXPERIENCE AND ACTIVITIES

Waitress/Hostess, Applebee's, *San Marcos, TX*   *Fall 2009–Present*
    Waited tables three nights a week. Took food orders, brought meals to tables, and cleared tables. Promoted to hostess in 2010. Take names at host station, greet guests, and show them to their tables.

Cheerleader, Texas State Spirit Program, *Texas State University*   *Fall 2009–Spring 2011*

Cashier, Home Depot, *San Antonio, TX*   *Fall 2007–Fall 2008*
    Rang up customer purchases three nights a week. Assisted in closing up store at the end of each shift.

SKILLS AND INTERESTS

Languages: Fluent in English, proficient in written and conversational Mandarin and Cantonese, conversational Spanish

Computer: Word, Excel, PowerPoint, FileMaker Pro, Internet research

SAMPLE COVER LETTER

111 A Street, Apt. 2C
San Marcos, TX 78666

September 6, 2011

Jane Smith
Director of Human Resources
Roaring Brook Press
A Division of Macmillan
175 Fifth Avenue
New York, NY 10010

Dear Director Smith:

I was extremely excited to see a posting for an editorial assistant position with Roaring Brook Press. I greatly admire your organization's dedication to children and youth, and I would be honored to interview for a position that would allow me to develop my interests in publishing while working on the creative editorial projects that Roaring Brook Press supports.

My publishing experience coupled with my understanding of children's education make me well suited for an editorial assistant position with your company. I worked as an editorial intern at Chronicle Books in San Francisco, where I maintained author and permissions databases and collated manuscripts and artwork for review and production. I also honed my writing skills through critiquing cookbook proposals and manuscripts based on analysis of the cookbook market.

I have also worked with children in an educational setting. As a volunteer at the San Antonio Public Library, I organized and created various informational displays aimed at getting children interested in subjects or cultures unfamiliar to them. I also created games and activities for children based on the books I read to them during story hour. Through this position, I learned to communicate with children in a creative yet educational way.

I have included my résumé as requested in the job posting, and I can provide references as required. I look forward to discussing my experiences and perspectives with you in person. I can be contacted at ellen.ng@serviceprovider.com or by phone at (555) 375-7111. Thank you for your kind consideration.

Sincerely,

Ellen Ng

Ellen Ng

Build Realistic Expectations

The final component of job hunting involves developing realistic expectations about the process. It is important to remember that only a few résumés will make it through the screening process and that you will not be the only candidate that gets called for an interview. Therefore, you will likely face rejection at least once during the course of a job search, either because there was a better-qualified applicant or because an equally qualified candidate had some advantage (such as a personal contact in the company). You should therefore constantly remember that rejection is not uncommon and that it is the inevitable result of a tight job market and a less-than-perfect selection process (Fisk, 2010; Hershatter & Epstein, 2010; Lebo, 2009; Luo, 2010). Persistence pays. If you approach the job search intelligently and persistently, you will eventually get a job.

During the Interview

After a diligent job search, you've finally been called for an interview. Now what? Well, now you impress the socks off your interviewer by making your best first impression, preparing for and anticipating different types of questions, preparing questions of your own, and following up after your interview.

Making a Good First Impression

Salina, who works in the nonprofit world, interviewed a candidate who came forty-five minutes late to the interview. To make matters worse, he explained his tardiness by noting that he had to "run home" to get his mom to help him with his tie. Later, Salina had a phone interview with a young woman who didn't bother to ensure that she had adequate cell phone reception, meaning that the question "What did you say?" dominated the conversation. What these candidates forgot is that the interview begins with the very first impression, even before the questions are asked.

In any interview, both verbal and nonverbal behaviors contribute to a good first impression. Thus, control the things you can at the outset. Give yourself plenty of extra time to get there, so that if something comes up (traffic, a stalled train) you'll still make it on time. Have your clothing ready ahead of time. If it's a phone interview, find a quiet place where you can talk undisturbed.

During the interview, do your best to control your nervousness so that you don't appear hesitant, halting, unsure, or jittery (Ayers, Keereetaweep, Chen, & Edwards, 1998; Tsa, Chen, & Chiu, 2005). As with all competent communication, you should adapt your behavior to be both effective and appropriate. Specifically, sit or stand as the other person directs; lower or raise your voice tone, rate, and pitch to fit in with the tone and pacing of the other person (DeGroot & Gooty, 2009). Also limit gestures so that you don't distract the interviewer from your words—and relax enough to express genuine smiles (Krumhuber, Manstead, Cosker, Marshall, & Rosin, 2009; Woodzicka, 2008). If you practice with an understanding friend (or even record yourself), you can

In Chapter 14, you learn that communication apprehension is a general fear of real or anticipated communication with a person or persons. Speaking before an audience causes anxiety for many people—but so does speaking with a hiring manager. To make sure that anxiety doesn't adversely affect your communication, try some of our suggestions for building confidence (Chapter 14, p. 410), such as performance visualization and preparing for the unexpected.

● **SOME FIRST IMPRESSIONS** may be memorable, but that probably didn't help this *American Idol* hopeful!

identify your positive behaviors and minimize any distracting behavior before you go into the interview situation.

If you are still feeling nervous about your first impression, take a look at Box A.1, "What *Not* to Do at an Interview." Even if you wind up failing to make eye contact once or twice or you feel your voice shaking a few times, you can at least say that you weren't the candidate who brought her pet snake to the interview!

Anticipating Common Questions

To discover whether there is a potential match between an applicant and a position, an interviewer typically explores five areas of information as they relate to the specific job:

▶ *Ability.* First, based on the résumé and the interview, questions will assess your experience, education, training, intelligence, and ability to do what the job requires.

▶ *Desire.* Second, questions will focus on your desire or motivation to use your abilities to do a good job by exploring such things as your record of changes in jobs, schools, and majors; reasons for wanting this job; knowledge of the company; and concrete examples of prior success that indicate your drive to achieve.

▶ *Personality.* The third area involves an assessment of your personality and how well you are likely to fit into the position and the organization. Questions are designed to discover your personal goals, degree of independence and self-reliance, imagination and creativity, and ability to manage or lead.

BOX A.1

WHAT *NOT* TO DO AT AN INTERVIEW

The following are real stories about job applicants shared by hiring managers. Needless to say, they didn't get the positions. . . .

▶ "Said if he was hired, he'd teach me ballroom dancing at no charge, and started demonstrating."

▶ "Took three cellular phone calls. Said she had a similar business on the side."

▶ "Man brought in his five children and cat."

▶ "Arrived with a snake around her neck. Said she took her pet everywhere."

▶ "Left his dry cleaner tag on his jacket and said he wanted to show he was a clean individual."

▶ "When asked about loyalty, showed a tattoo of his girlfriend's name."

▶ "After a very long interview, he casually said he had already accepted another position."

▶ "After a difficult question, she wanted to leave the room for a moment to meditate."

Source: Miller (1991). Used with permission.

▶ *Character.* A fourth area of judgment is that of character, learning about your personal behavior, honesty, responsibility, and accuracy and objectivity in reports.

▶ *Health.* This is a sensitive topic in interviews; certain questions about your health and medical background are illegal. But if a health issue directly affects your ability to do the job in question, the interviewer may ask. For example, if you are applying for a position at a candy factory, the interviewer may ask if you have a peanut allergy because you would be unable to work in a plant where peanuts are processed.

Some examples of frequently asked interview questions are offered in Table A.5.

Dealing with Difficult or Unethical Questions

"What fictional character most clearly reflects your outlook on life?" This is an actual question that an interviewer asked a colleague of ours some years

---

TABLE A.5

COMMON INTERVIEW QUESTIONS

▶ Tell me about yourself. What led you to choose your particular field (or your academic major)? Describe your level of satisfaction with your choice.

▶ Describe what you understand is required in the position you are applying for. Summarize your qualifications in light of this description.

▶ Why do you want to leave your current employer? *or* Why did you leave your last employer?

▶ Describe the place/city/surroundings that would be your ideal working environment.

▶ Tell me what you know about our organization that led you to be interested in us.

▶ Give me a specific example of something you learned from a previous work experience.

▶ Describe your ideal working day.

▶ Describe the job you'd like to be doing five years from now.

▶ Describe a time when you demonstrated initiative in your employment (or volunteer) position.

▶ Tell me about a time when your willingness to work was demonstrated to your supervisors.

▶ Describe your strongest attribute with an example of how it paid off.

▶ Tell me about a recent project that didn't turn out the way you wanted. What did you do to try to make it work?

▶ Describe a time when you worked through a difficult coworker situation.

▶ If I gave you this job, what would you accomplish in the first three months?

▶ Are there any questions that you want to ask?

Source: Greco (1977). Used with permission.

ago when she was applying to college. To this day, she remembers the question because she panicked. It wasn't that she lacked an answer; she simply wasn't *expecting* the question. An interviewer might use such unexpected questions to seek insights into the way candidates view themselves or to judge how well they think on their feet. Some questions are simply tricky—they offer a challenge to the interviewee but also a great opportunity to show one's strengths.

Other questions are more than just difficult; they are unethical and sometimes even illegal. Questions that have no direct bearing on job performance and have the potential to lead to discrimination on the basis of race, color, religion, national origin, sex, age, disability, and marital or family status are illegal in the United States. Although an organization whose employees ask illegal questions during employment interviews can be subject to a variety of penalties imposed by the federal government's Equal Employment Opportunity Commission (EEOC), such questions continue to be asked, and applicants must consider how to answer them. Stewart and Cash (2011) suggest five tactics you can use to respond to illegal questions. By answering briefly but directly, tactfully refusing to answer, or neutralizing the question, you respond without giving too much information or inviting further inquiry. You can also consider posing a tactful inquiry—that is, asking another question in response—or using the question as an opportunity to present some positive information about yourself. These five strategies are outlined in Table A.6.

TABLE A.6

TACTICS FOR RESPONDING TO ILLEGAL QUESTIONS

Tactic	Sample Illegal Question	Sample Answer
Answer directly but briefly	"Do you attend church regularly?"	"Yes, I do."
Pose a tactful inquiry	"What does your husband do?"	"Why do you ask?" (in a nondefensive tone of voice)
Tactfully refuse to answer the question	"Do you have children?"	"My family plans will not interfere with my ability to perform in this position."
Neutralize	"What happens if your partner needs to relocate?"	"My partner and I would discuss locational moves that either of us might have to consider in the future."
Take advantage of the question	"Where were you born?"	"I am quite proud that my background is Egyptian because it has helped me deal effectively with people of various ethnic backgrounds."

Source: Stewart & Cash (2011). Used with permission.

what about you?

○ Your Career Preparation

Use the following grid as a starting point to assess your career strengths and goals as you prepare for job interviews. Write three descriptions of your skills, career goals, and life goals. Next, score the organizations that you plan on applying to from 1 to 5 (5 being the highest) as to how they match up with your skills and goals.

MY SKILLS	Organization A	Organization B	Organization C
(Examples: strong writing skills, foreign-language proficiency, computer programming skills)			
1.			
2.			
3.			
MY CAREER GOALS			
(Examples: become marketing executive, work in the Dallas area, have a job with little mandatory travel)			
1.			
2.			
3.			
MY LIFE GOALS			
(Examples: have children, live near siblings, retire at age sixty)			
1.			
2.			
3.			

Now assess your results. Is there one organization that best supports your goals and skills? If not, consider which goals and skills are *most* important to you. Which organization might be the best fit?

Asking Questions of Your Own

Of course, the interviewer should not be the only person asking questions in a job interview. A candidate for any job should arrive at an interview prepared to ask thoughtful questions about the position itself and related career paths within the organization, as well as about the organization itself (Johnson, 2010). These questions should indicate that the applicant has done solid homework (your preinterview research and preparation can shine here) and is able and willing to do a good job for the company.

Avoid saying things like "I really don't have any questions right now" (even if you don't have any questions), which might imply disinterest. Likewise, try not to focus on questions about your own compensation and benefits, such as "How much vacation will I get?"—at least not at the first interview. Instead, try to pose thoughtful questions that show your interest while enhancing your understanding of the position and the potential for your future. Be prepared to ask such questions as "I noticed in your annual report that you are developing a new training program. If I were hired, would I be in it?" and "If you were sitting on my side of this desk, what would you say are the most attractive features of the job?" And when the interview is ending, be sure to ask what to expect next, such as "What is your time frame for filling this position?"

Following Up After the Interview

You should continue to demonstrate good manners once the interview is over. Thank the interviewer, as well as anyone else you have met within the organization, as you leave. Follow up immediately with a written or e-mailed note of appreciation. Thank the interviewer not only for the interview but also for the chance to expand your knowledge of the organization and the industry. Put in writing how excited you are about the chance to work with such a dynamic organization. Send along any support materials that you discussed during the interview (perhaps a writing sample). Since few interviewees remember to send additional materials and thank yous, you will certainly stand out.

AND YOU?

Have you ever gone through an interview process to secure a job or admission to college? How prepared did you feel for your first interview? If you could do it again, what would you do differently?

BACK TO ▷ The *Daily Show* Interview

At the beginning of this Appendix, we talked about the special "reports" filed by *Daily Show* correspondents. Let's examine the nature of those interviews in the context of what we've discussed throughout this chapter.

▶ Like all interviews, these *Daily Show* interviews are planned, but the process of editing them down to a few minutes makes them less interactive than a real-time interview. Comments and reaction shots are taken out of context, and during editing, the correspondent is able to integrate alternative footage that was not part of the actual interview. This gives the correspondent an unusual amount of control at the expense of the interviewee.

▶ John Oliver makes comic use of questioning, offering the Columbia University professor a loaded question. It's clear that Oliver doesn't want or expect an answer—the question itself is the joke.

▶ The format and structure of the interview are also clear to both parties: interviewees are familiar with the show and are essentially in on the joke. Participants are well aware that their comments can and will be heavily edited and that much of what they say will be taken out of context.

▶ The goals of the interviewee and interviewer are at once similar and quite different. As satire, *The Daily Show* seeks to illuminate real issues by poking fun at them. The students who participated appreciated that goal: "I am extremely happy with the clip in the sense that it did what it's supposed to do—make people laugh and give them a little something to think about," said Samantha Joseph. "Did it fully express our opinions? No. Were our words twisted? Yes . . . but again, anyone who goes on *The Daily Show* would be nuts to think that wouldn't happen!" (Marcott, 2009).

THINGS TO TRY   Activities

1. Observe a press conference on television. Who is being interviewed? Who is conducting the interview? What is the goal of the press conference? How is control distributed? List five questions that are asked, and label them according to the types listed in this chapter (open, closed, bipolar, primary, secondary). Did the questioning involve a particular sequence (funnel, inverted funnel, tunnel)? What did you learn about this interview format by answering these questions?

2. A good source for seeing the subtle differences between legal and illegal job interview questions is at this job Web site: www.jobweb.com/Interview/help .aspx?id=1343&terms=illegal+questions. Use this site to organize a discussion with your classmates about how you would respond to illegal questions in a job interview. Practice and compare your responses.

3. Assess your goals for employment, and then design (or revise) a résumé for the job you are most interested in. Use the guidelines in this chapter to make it clear and action-oriented. Prepare additional résumés for other positions, keeping in mind that your résumé should highlight the aspects of your training and experience most relevant to each particular position. Discuss your résumé with other students in the class; ask them if your goals are clear. Can they tell what job you are seeking based on the different résumés you show them? Compare your résumé to theirs; while the format may be similar, the content should be unique to you.

4. Create a questionnaire that you will use the next time you visit a physician. Focus your questions on what is already known about your condition, and what you want to know about possible treatment. You also may want to ask questions about the training and experience of the physician in a way that will give you the information you want without you seeming contentious. If you have no

medical issues, perhaps your questionnaire can be designed for someone else (a child you have, or a friend or relative who could benefit from your help).

5. Conduct an in-depth information-gathering interview, and write a report (no more than five typed pages) in which you summarize the information you received and comment on what you learned about the interview process. The interview must last at least one hour; the interviewee must be a close acquaintance who is older than you and who must have children (consider interviewing one of your parents). The interview must cover at least two of the following topics:

   a. The person's philosophy of raising children (discipline, finances, making friends, respect for authority, character formation)

   b. The person's political beliefs (political affiliation and commitment, involvement in civic affairs, involvement in government)

   c. The person's religious beliefs, their effect on the person's life, and how these beliefs relate to family life

   d. The person's goals in life and how the person is working to achieve these goals

   e. The person's philosophy of leisure time (ideally how one should spend leisure time versus how this person actually spends it)

Now that you have finished reading this Appendix, you can

Define the nature of interviews:

➤ An **interview** is an interaction between two parties that is deliberate and purposeful (p. 508).

➤ Interviews are planned, goal-driven, structured, dyadic (involving two parties), and interactive (p. 508).

Outline the different types of interviews:

➤ The **information-gathering interview** serves to transfer knowledge from one party to the other (p. 509).

➤ **Performance appraisals** allow you to review your accomplishments and plan your goals (p. 510).

➤ A **problem-solving interview** deals with problems, tensions, or conflicts (p. 510).

➤ In **exit interviews**, employers seek to identify organizational problems that might affect employee retention (pp. 510–511).

➤ In a **persuasive interview**, questions are designed to change the interviewee's behavior or opinions (pp. 511–512).

➤ **Service-oriented interviews** are designed to cull information and provide advice or support (p. 512).

➤ In a **selection interview**, the primary goal is to fill a position in an organization (p. 512).

Describe the three parts of an interview: opening, questions, and conclusion:

➤ An interview should open with the three things interviewees will want to know: the topic and length (the task), something about the interviewer and how the information will be used (the relationship), and who will benefit (the motivation) (p. 513).

➤ Questions and answers accomplish the goals of the interview (p. 513).

➤ An **open question** gives the interviewee freedom in how to respond (p. 514).

➤ **Closed questions** restrict answer choices; **bipolar questions** can be answered with only "yes" or "no" (pp. 514–515).

➤ **Primary questions** introduce new topics; **secondary questions** seek clarification (p. 515).

➤ **Neutral questions** do not hint at a preferred answer, whereas **directed questions**, **leading questions**, or **loaded questions** may subtly or even blatantly influence the answer (p. 517).

➤ There are three main structures for ordering interview questions: the **funnel sequence**, **inverted funnel sequence**, or **tunnel sequence**, each varying in its level of specificity (pp. 517–518).

➤ Interviewers use verbal and nonverbal strategies to conclude and summarize the interview (p. 519).

Devise an interview strategy from the interviewer's point of view:

➤ Consider potential barriers that might be disruptive (p. 520).

➤ Find ways to put the interviewee at ease (p. 520).

➤ Make sure the questions are ethical and appropriate (p. 521).

➤ Remember to listen well and take notes (p. 521).

Prepare for the role of interviewee:

➤ Have a clear idea of your personal goals, what you want to achieve in the interview (pp. 521–522).

➤ Don't arrive tired or hungry. Dress appropriately, and bring any documents you may need (p. 523).

➤ Listen and respond effectively (p. 523).

➤ Adapt to the situation, being particularly sensitive to cultural differences (pp. 523–524).

Secure **job interviews** and manage them with confidence:

➤ The three best sources for finding jobs are networking connections, placement centers, and job-specific sites (p. 524).

➤ **Networking** involves meeting new people through people you already know (p. 525).

➤ Write an effective **cover letter** and **résumé** (pp. 527–528).

➤ Remember that rejection is not uncommon (p. 531).

➤ Nonverbal cues are as important as what you say to make a good first impression (p. 531).

➤ Come prepared to answer standard questions about your abilities, desire, personality, character, and health (pp. 532–533).

➤ Answer difficult questions honestly to show that you know how to evaluate your own weaknesses and improve on them, but be brief; decline to answer a question that is unethical (pp. 533–534).

➤ Ask thoughtful questions about the position and the organization (p. 536).

➤ Follow up with a note of thanks (p. 536).

glossary

abstraction ladder: A model that ranks communication from specific, which ensures clarity, to general and vague.

accent: A pattern of pronunciation that is specific to a certain upbringing, geographical region, or culture.

accenting: Nonverbal behavior that clarifies and emphasizes specific information in a verbal message.

accommodation: Adapting and adjusting one's language and nonverbal behaviors for other people or cultures.

achievement-oriented leader: A leader who sets challenging goals and communicates high expectations and standards to members.

action-oriented listeners: Communicators who are usually focused on tasks; they tend to keep the discourse on track and are often valuable in meetings.

active listening: Being an active participant in making choices about selecting, attending, and the other steps in the listening process.

active strategies: In relationship management, strategies that allow one to obtain information about a person more directly, by seeking information from a third party.

adaptability: An organization's ability to adjust to changing times and circumstances.

adaptors: Body movements that satisfy some physical or psychological need, such as rubbing your eyes when you're tired or twisting your hair when you're nervous or bored.

ad hominem fallacy: A logical fallacy that entails attacking a person instead of the person's arguments.

adjourning: The stage of group development in which members reflect on their accomplishments and failures as well as determine whether the group will disassemble or take on another project.

affect displays: Body movements that convey feelings, moods, and reactions; they are often unintentional, reflecting the sender's emotions.

affiliation: The affect, or feelings, we have for others.

agenda: A plan for a meeting that details the subject and goal, logistics, and a schedule.

all-channel network: A network in which all members are an equal distance from one another and all members interact with each other.

anchor position: An audience's position on a topic at the outset of the speech.

anecdotes: Brief, personal stories that have a point or punch line.

antigroup roles: Roles that create problems because they serve individual members' priorities at the expense of overall group needs.

appeal to tradition: A logical fallacy in which the speaker uses tradition as proof, suggesting that listeners should agree with his or her point because "that's the way it has always been."

appreciative listening: Listening with the simple goal of taking pleasure in the sounds that one receives.

articulation: The clarity and forcefulness with which sounds are made, regardless of whether they are pronounced correctly.

artifacts: Accessories carried or used on the body for decoration or identification.

attending: The step in the listening process of focusing attention on both the presence and communication of someone else.

attitudes: Our general evaluations of people, ideas, objects, or events.

attraction-similarity hypothesis: The belief that the extent to which we project ourselves onto another person is the direct result of the attraction we feel for that person.

attributions: Personal characteristics that are used to explain other people's behavior.

audience analysis: A highly systematic process of getting to know one's listeners relative to the topic and speech occasion.

back-channel cues: Vocalizations that signal when we want to talk versus when we are just encouraging others to continue their talking.

bandwagon fallacy: Accepting a statement as true because it is popular.

bar graph: A presentation aid that shows the relationship of two or more sets of figures.

begging the question: A logical fallacy in which the speaker presents arguments that no one can verify because they are not accompanied by valid evidence.

behavior: Observable communication, including both verbal and nonverbal messages; the manner in which we act or function in response to our attitudes and beliefs.

behavioral affirmation: Seeing or hearing what one wants to see or hear in the communication of assorted group members.

behavioral confirmation: Acting in a way that makes one's expectations about a group come true.

behavioral flexibility: The ability to have a number of communication behaviors at one's disposal and the willingness to use different behaviors in different situations.

beliefs: The ways in which people perceive reality; our feelings about what is true and real and how confident we are about the existence or validity of something.

biased language: Words that are infused with subtle meanings that influence our perceptions about the subject.

bipolar question: The most closed form of a question, for which there are only two possible responses, "yes" and "no."

bonding: The process of relational partners sharing formal symbolic messages with the world that their relationship is important and cherished.

boundary turbulence: Readjusting the need for privacy against the need for self-disclosure and connection when there is a threat to one's privacy boundaries.

brainstorming: A process that entails focusing on a general area of interest, amassing information, thinking creatively, and considering problems and solutions related to the topic.

bullying: Behaviors such as harsh criticism, name-calling, gossip, slander, personal attacks, or threats to safety or job security, used to try to acquire and keep control over an entire group or individual members within a group.

burnout: A sense of apathy or exhaustion that results from long-term stress or frustration.

call to action: In a persuasive speech, a challenge to listeners to act in response to the speech, see the problem in a new way, or change their beliefs, actions, and behavior.

cause-effect pattern: A pattern of speech arrangement that organizes the message around cause-to-effect or effect-to-cause relationships.

central processing: Thinking critically about the speaker's message, questioning it, and seriously considering acting on it; occurs when listeners are motivated and personally involved in the content of a message.

chain network: A network in which information is passed from one member to the next rather than shared among members.

challenging strategies: Strategies that promote the objectives of the individual who uses them, rather than the desires of the other person or the relationship.

channel: The method through which communication occurs.

channel discrepancy: When one set of behaviors says one thing, and another set says something different.

chronemics: The study of how people perceive the use of time.

chronological pattern: A pattern of speech arrangement that presents the main points of a message forward (or backward) in a systematic, time-related fashion.

civility: The social norm for appropriate behavior.

classical management approach: An approach to organizational communication that likens organizations to machines, with a focus on maximizing efficiency.

clique: A small subgroup of individuals who have bonded together within a group; also called *coalitions.*

closed question: A type of interview question that gives less freedom to the interviewee by restricting answer choices.

clustering: A technique for identifying potential speech topics whereby the writer begins with a core idea and branches out into a web of related thoughts and ideas.

co-culture: A smaller group of people within a culture who are distinguished by features such as race, religion, age, generation, political affiliation, gender, sexual orientation, economic status, educational level, occupation, and a host of other factors.

code: A set of symbols that are joined to create a meaningful message.

code switching: A type of accommodation in which communicators change their regular language and slang to fit into a particular group.

coercion: The act of using manipulation, threats, intimidation, or violence to gain compliance.

coercive power: Power that stems from a person's ability to threaten or harm others.

cognitions: Thoughts that communicators have about themselves and others.

cognitive forces: Group members' thoughts and beliefs, which affect how members perceive, interpret, evaluate, store, and retrieve information and, in turn, influence the group's decisions.

cognitive language: The specific system of symbols that one uses to describe people, things, and situations in one's mind.

cohesion: The degree to which group members have bonded, like each other, and consider themselves to be one entity.

collectivistic culture: A culture in which individuals perceive themselves first and foremost as members of a group and communicate from that perspective.

communication: The process by which individuals use symbols, signs, and behaviors to exchange information.

communication acquisition: The process of learning individual words in a language and learning to use that language appropriately and effectively in the context of the situation.

communication apprehension (CA): Fear or anxiety associated with communication, which is often a common barrier to effective delivery.

communication boundary management: Reluctance to discuss certain topics with particular people.

communication climate: The dominant temper, attitudes, and outlook of relational partners.

Communication Privacy Management theory (CPM): An explanation of how people perceive the information they hold about themselves and whether they will disclose or protect it.

communication processing: The means by which we gather, organize, and evaluate the information we receive.

communication skills: Behaviors based on social understandings that help communicators achieve their goals.

comparative advantage pattern: An organizing pattern for persuasive speaking in which the speaker shows that his or her viewpoint is superior to other viewpoints on the topic.

competent communication: Communication that is effective and appropriate for a given situation, in which the communicators continually evaluate and reassess their own communication process.

competent communication model: A transactional model of communication in which communicators send and receive messages simultaneously within a relational, situational, and cultural context.

complementing: Nonverbal behavior that matches (without actually mirroring) the verbal message it accompanies.

compromise: A way to resolve conflict in which both parties must give up something to gain something.

conflict: A negative interaction between two or more interdependent people, rooted in some actual or perceived disagreement.

conflict management: The way we engage in conflict and address disagreements with relational partners.

connotative meaning: The emotional or attitudinal response people have to a word.

contact cultures: Cultures that depend on touch as an important form of communication.

content-oriented listeners: Critical listeners who carefully evaluate what they hear; they prefer to listen to information from sources they feel are credible and critically examine the information they receive from a variety of angles.

contradicting: Nonverbal behavior that conveys meaning opposite of the verbal message.

control: The ability of one person, group, or organization to influence others, and the manner in which their relationships are conducted.

convergence: When speakers shift their language or nonverbal behaviors toward each other's way of communicating.

cooperative strategies: Strategies that benefit a relationship, serve mutual rather than individual goals, and strive to produce solutions that benefit both parties.

costs: The negative elements of a relationship.

countercoalitions: Subgroups that are positioned against other subgroups.

cover letter: A one-page letter indicating interest in a specific position.

credibility: The quality, authority, and reliability of a source of information.

critical listening: Evaluating or analyzing information, evidence, ideas, or opinions; also known as *evaluative listening.*

cultural myopia: A form of cultural nearsightedness grounded in the belief that one's own culture is appropriate and relevant in all situations and to all people.

culture: A learned system of thought and behavior that belongs to and typifies a relatively large group of people; the composite of their shared beliefs, values, and practices.

cyberbullying: Multiple abusive attacks on individual targets conducted through electronic channels.

deception: The attempt to convince others of something that is false.

declining stage: The stage at which a relationship begins to come apart.

decoding: The process of receiving a message by interpreting and assigning meaning to it.

deductive reasoning: The line of thought that occurs when one draws specific conclusions from a general argument.

defensive climate: A communication climate in which the people involved feel threatened.

defensive listening: Responding with aggression and arguing with the speaker without fully listening to the message.

definitional speech: A presentation whose main goal is to provide answers to "what" questions by explaining to an audience what something is.

definition by etymology: Defining something by using the origin of a word or phrase.

definition by example: Defining something by offering concrete examples of what it is.

definition by negation: Defining something by telling what it is not.

definition by synonym: Defining something by using words that closely mean the same thing.

delivery cues: In a speech outline, brief reminders about important information related to the delivery of the speech.

demographics: The systematic study of the quantifiable characteristics of a large group.

demonstration speech: A speech that answers "how" questions by showing an audience the way something works.

denotative meaning: The basic, consistently accepted definition of a word.

descriptive presentation: An approach to conveying information that involves painting a mental picture for the audience.

devil's advocate: A role that involves pointing out worst-case scenarios.

dialectical tensions: Tensions that arise when opposing or conflicting goals exist in a relationship; can be external or internal.

directed question: A type of interview question that suggests or implies the answer that is expected.

directive leader: A leader who controls the group's communication by conveying specific instructions to members.

directory: A type of secondary resource that is created and maintained by people rather than automatically by computers; guides visitors to the main page of a Web site organized within a wider subject category.

discrimination: Behavior toward a person or group based solely on their membership in a particular group, class, or category.

division of labor: An aspect of the classical management approach that assumes each part of an organization (and each person involved) must carry out a specialized task for the organization to run smoothly.

dyad: A pair of people.

either-or fallacy: A fallacy in which the speaker presents only two alternatives on a subject and fails to acknowledge other alternatives; also known as the *false dilemma fallacy.*

Elaboration Likelihood Model (ELM): A model that highlights the importance of relevance to persuasion and holds that listeners process persuasive messages by one of two routes, depending on how important the message is to them.

elucidating explanation: An explanation that illuminates a concept's meaning and use.

emblems: Movements and gestures that have a direct verbal translation in a particular group or culture.

empathic listening: Listening to people with openness, sensitivity, and caring; attempting to know how another person feels.

encoding: The process of mentally constructing a message for production.

equivocation: Using words that have unclear or misleading definitions.

escapist strategies: Strategies that people use to try to prevent or avoid direct conflict.

ethics: The study of morals, specifically the moral choices individuals make in their relationships with others.

ethnocentrism: A belief in the superiority of one's own culture or group and a tendency to view other cultures through the lens of one's own.

ethos: A form of rhetorical proof that appeals to ethics and concerns the qualifications and personality of the speaker.

euphemism: An inoffensive word or phrase that substitutes for terms that might be perceived as upsetting.

evasion: Intentionally failing to provide specific details.

exit interview: An interview that employers hold with employees who opt to leave the company, to identify organizational problems that might affect future employee retention.

expert power: Power that comes from the information or knowledge that a leader possesses.

expert testimony: The opinion or judgment of an expert, a professional in his or her field.

explanatory speech: A speech that answers the question "Why" or "What does that mean?" by offering thorough explanations of meaning.

exploratory stage: The stage of a relationship in which one seeks relatively superficial information from one's partner.

extemporaneous speaking: A style of public speaking that involves delivery with little or no notes, but for which the speaker carefully prepares in advance.

family: A small social group bound by ties of blood, civil contract (such as marriage, civil union, or adoption), and a commitment to care for and be responsible for one another, usually in a shared household.

feedback: A message from the receiver to the sender that illustrates responses that naturally occur when two or more people communicate.

feeling: The use of language to express emotion; one of the five functional communication competencies.

feminine culture: A culture that places value on relationships and quality of life; sometimes referred to as a *nurturing culture.*

flaming: The posting of online messages that are deliberately hostile or insulting toward a particular individual.

focus group: A set of individuals asked by a researcher to come together to give their opinions on a specific issue.

forming: The stage of group development in which group members try to negotiate who will be in charge and what the group's goals will be.

forms of rhetorical proof: Means of persuasion that include *ethos, logos,* and *pathos;* first named by Aristotle.

friendship: A close and caring relationship between two people that is perceived as mutually satisfying and beneficial.

functional perspective: An examination of how communication behaviors work to accomplish goals in personal, group, organizational, or public situations.

fundamental attribution error: The tendency to overemphasize the internal and underestimate the external causes of behaviors we observe in others.

funnel sequence: A pattern of questioning that progresses from broad, open-ended questions to narrower, more closed questions.

gender: The behavioral and cultural traits assigned to one's sex; determined by the way members of a particular culture define notions of masculinity and femininity.

generation: A group of people who were born into a specific time frame, along with its events and social changes that shape attitudes and behavior.

genetic-similarity hypothesis: The theory that two individuals who hail from the same ethnic group are more genetically similar than two individuals from different ethnic groups.

globalization: The growing interdependence and connectivity of societies and economies around the world.

goal achievement: Relying on communication to accomplish particular objectives.

grammar of media: For each form of media, a set of rules and conventions that dictates how it operates.

group: A collection of more than two people who share some kind of relationship, communicate in an interdependent fashion, and collaborate toward some shared purpose.

Group Decision Support Systems (GDSS): Computer programs specifically designed to help groups, whether face-to-face or long distance, collaborate and make more effective decisions.

groupthink: A situation in which group members strive to maintain cohesiveness and minimize conflict by refusing to critically examine ideas, analyze proposals, or test solutions.

haptics: The study of touch as a form of communication.

harassment: Communication that hurts, offends, or embarrasses another person, creating a hostile environment.

hearing: The physiological process of perceiving sound; the process through which sound waves are picked up by the ears and transmitted to the brain.

hierarchy: The layers of power and authority in an organization.

hierarchy of needs: A hierarchical structure that identifies needs in five categories, from low (immature) to high (mature).

high-context culture: A culture that relies on contextual cues—such as time, place, relationship, and situation—to both interpret meaning and send subtle messages.

high language: A more formal, polite, or "mainstream" language, used in business contexts, in the classroom, and at formal social gatherings.

homogeny: Sameness, as applied to a public speaker and his or her audience.

hostile audience: An audience that opposes the speaker's message and perhaps the speaker personally; the hardest type of audience to persuade.

human relations approach: An approach to management that considers the human needs of organizational members—enjoying interpersonal relationships, sharing ideas with others, feeling like a member of a group, and so on.

human resources approach: An approach to management that considers organizational productivity from workers' perspectives and considers them assets who can contribute their useful ideas to improve the organization.

human trafficking: The recruitment of people for exploitative purposes.

hyperbole: Vivid, colorful language with great emotional intensity and often exaggeration.

hyperpersonal communication: A phenomenon surrounding online communication in which a lack of proximity, visual contact, and nonverbal cues result in exaggerated perceptions.

illustrators: Body movements that reinforce verbal messages and help to visually explain what is being said.

imagining: The ability to think, play, and be creative in communication; one of the five functional communication competencies.

immediacy: The feeling of closeness, involvement, and warmth between people as communicated by nonverbal behavior.

impromptu speaking: A style of public speaking that is spontaneous, without any warning or preparation.

inclusion: To involve others in our lives and to be involved in the lives of others.

individualist culture: A culture whose members place value on autonomy and privacy, with relatively little attention to status and hierarchy based on age or family connections.

inductive reasoning: The line of thought that occurs when one draws general conclusions based on specific evidence.

informal-formal dimension: A psychological aspect of the situational context of communication, dealing with our perceptions of personal versus impersonal situations.

informational listening: Processing and accurately understanding a message; also known as *comprehensive listening.*

information-gathering interview: An interview that serves to transfer knowledge from one party to another by collecting attitudes, opinions, facts, data, and experiences.

informative speaking: A form of public speaking intended to increase the audience's understanding or knowledge.

informing: The use of language to both give and receive information; one of the five functional communication competencies.

ingroup: The group with which one identifies and to which one feels one belongs.

initiating stage: The stage of a relationship in which one makes contact with another person.

insensitive listening: Listening that occurs when we fail to pay attention to the emotional content of someone's message, instead taking it at face value.

integrating: The process of relational partners "becoming one."

intensification stage: The stage of a relationship in which relational partners become increasingly intimate and move their communication toward more personal self-disclosures.

interaction appearance theory: The argument that people change their attributions of someone, particularly their physical attractiveness, the more they interact.

interaction model: Communication between a sender and a receiver that incorporates feedback.

interactive strategies: Speaking directly with a relational partner rather than observing them passively or asking others for information.

intercultural communication: The communication between people from different cultures who have different worldviews.

intercultural sensitivity: Mindfulness of behaviors that may offend others.

interdependence: Mutual dependence where the actions of each partner affect the other(s).

intergroup communication: A branch of the communication discipline that focuses on how communication within and between groups affects relationships.

intergroup contact theory: The argument that interaction between members of different social groups generates a possibility for more positive attitudes to emerge.

internal preview: In public speaking, an extended transition that primes the audience for the content immediately ahead.

internal summary: An extended transition that allows the speaker to crystallize the points made in one section of a speech before moving to the next section.

interpersonal communication: The exchange of verbal and nonverbal messages between two people who have a relationship and are influenced by the partner's messages.

interpersonal relationships: The interconnections and interdependence between two individuals.

interview: An interaction between two parties that is deliberate and purposeful for at least one of the parties involved.

intimacy: Closeness and understanding of a relational partner.

inverted funnel sequence: A pattern of questioning that progresses from narrow, closed questions to more open-ended questions.

jargon: Technical language that is specific to members of a particular profession, interest group, or hobby.

job interview: A type of selection interview, with the end goal of filling a position of employment.

key-word outline: The briefest type of outline, consisting of specific "key words" from the sentence outline to jog the speaker's memory.

kinesics: The way gestures and body movements communicate meaning.

language: The system of symbols (words) that we use to think about and communicate experiences and feelings.

latitude of acceptance and rejection: The range of positions on a topic that are acceptable or unacceptable to an audience based on their *anchor position.*

lay testimony: The opinion of a nonexpert who has personal experience of or has witnessed an event related to the speaker's topic.

leadership: The ability to direct or influence others' behaviors and thoughts toward a productive end.

leading question: A type of directed question that subtly suggests or implies the answer that is expected.

legitimate power: Power that comes from an individual's role or title.

library gateway: A collection of databases and information sites arranged by subject, generally reviewed and recommended by experts (usually librarians).

linear model (of communication): Communication in which a sender originates a message, which is carried through a channel—perhaps interfered with by noise—to the receiver.

linguistic determinism: The idea that language influences how we see the world around us.

linguistic relativity: The belief that speakers of different languages have different views of the world.

listening: The process of recognizing, understanding, accurately interpreting, and responding effectively to the messages communicated by others.

listening apprehension: A state of uneasiness, anxiety, fear, or dread associated with a listening opportunity; also known as *receiver apprehension.*

listening barrier: A factor that interferes with the ability to accurately comprehend information and respond appropriately.

listening fidelity: The degree to which the thoughts of the listener and the thoughts and intentions of the message producer match following their communication.

loaded question: A type of directed question that boldly suggests the answer that is expected.

logical fallacy: An invalid or deceptive form of reasoning.

logos: A form of rhetorical proof that appeals to logic and is directed at the audience's reasoning on a topic.

love: A deep affection for and attachment to another person involving emotional ties, with varying degrees of passion, commitment, and intimacy.

low-context culture: A culture that uses very direct language and relies less on situational factors to communicate.

low language: A more informal, easy-going language, used in informal and comfortable environments.

main points: In public speaking, the central claims that support the specific speech purpose and thesis statement.

masculine culture: A culture that places value on assertiveness, achievement, ambition, and competitiveness; sometimes referred to as an *achievement culture.*

masking: A facial management technique in which an expression that shows true feeling is replaced with an expression that shows appropriate feeling for a given interaction.

matching hypothesis: The theory that we seek relationships with others who have comparable levels of attractiveness.

media richness: The degree to which a particular channel is communicative.

mentor: A seasoned, respected member of an organization who serves as a role model for a less experienced individual.

message: The words or actions originated by a sender.

metasearch engine: A search engine that scans multiple search engines simultaneously.

mimicry: The synchronized and usually unconscious pattern of imitating or matching gestures, body position, tone, and facial expressions to create social connections between people.

mindfulness: The process of being focused on the task at hand; necessary for competent communication.

mindlessness: A passive state in which the communicator is a less critical processor of information, characterized by reduced cognitive activity, inaccurate recall, and uncritical evaluation.

model: A presentation aid—an appropriately scaled object.

monochronic culture: A culture that treats time as a limited resource, as a commodity that can be saved or wasted.

monopolistic listening: Listening in order to control the communication interaction.

monotone: A way of speaking in which the speaker does not vary his or her vocal pitch.

motivated sequence pattern: A pattern of speech arrangement that entails five phases based on the psychological elements of advertising: attention, need, satisfaction, visualization, and action.

multitasking: Attending to several things at once.

mumbling: Omitting certain sounds in a word, running words together, or speaking so softly that listeners can hardly hear.

narrative pattern: A pattern of speech arrangement that ties points together in a way that presents a vivid story, complete with characters, settings, plot, and imagery.

network: A pattern of interaction that governs who speaks with whom in a group and about what.

networking: The process of using interconnected groups or associations of persons one knows to develop relationships with their connections that one does not know.

neutral audience: An audience that falls between the receptive audience and the hostile audience; neither supports nor opposes the speaker.

neutral question: A type of interview question that provides no hint to the interviewee concerning the expected response.

noise: Interference with a message that makes its final form different from the original.

nonbinding straw poll: An informal vote on a decision that can help a group move forward when time is an issue.

noncontact culture: A culture that is less touch-sensitive or even tends to avoid touch.

nonverbal codes: Symbols we use to send messages without, or in addition to, words.

nonverbal communication: The process of intentionally or unintentionally signaling meaning through behavior other than words.

norming: The stage of group development in which members establish agreed-upon norms that govern expected behavior.

norms: Recurring patterns of behavior or thinking that come to be accepted in a group as the "usual" way of doing things.

objectivity: Presenting facts and information in a straightforward and evenhanded way, free of influence from the speaker's personal thoughts and opinions.

oculesics: The study of the use of eyes to communicate.

openness: An organization's awareness of its own imbalances and problems.

open question: A type of interview question that gives the interviewee great freedom in terms of how to respond.

operational definition: Defining something by explaining what it is or what it does.

oral citation: A reference to source materials that the speaker mentions in the narrative of a speech.

oratory: A form of public speaking in which a speech is committed to memory.

organization: A group with a formal governance and structure.

organizational assimilation: The process by which newcomers learn the nuances of the organization and determine if they fit in.

organizational communication: The interaction necessary to direct a group toward multiple sets of goals.

organizational culture: An organization's unique set of beliefs, values, norms, and ways of doing things.

organizational hero: An individual who achieves great things for an organization through persistence and commitment, often in the face of great risk.

organizational storytelling: The communication of the company's values through stories and accounts, both externally (to an outside audience) and internally (within the company).

outcome: The product of an interchange.

outgroups: Those groups one defines as "others."

outline: A structured form of a speech's content.

overaccommodation: Going too far in changing one's language or nonverbal behavior, based on an incorrect or stereotypical notion of another group.

paralanguage: The vocalized sounds that accompany words.

paraphrasing: A part of listening empathetically that involves guessing at feelings and rephrasing what one thinks the speaker has said.

participative leader: A leader who views group members as equals, welcomes their opinions, summarizes points that have been raised, and identifies problems that need discussion rather than dictating solutions.

passive listening: Failing to make active choices in the listening process.

passive strategies: Observing others in communication situations without actually interacting with them.

pathos: A form of rhetorical proof that concerns the nature of the audience's feelings and appeals to their emotions.

peer communication: Communication between individuals at the same level of authority in an organization.

peer relationships: The friendships that form between colleagues at an organization as a result of *peer communication.*

people-oriented listeners: Communicators who listen with relationships in mind; they tend be most concerned with others' feelings.

perception: A cognitive process through which one interprets one's experiences and comes to one's own unique understandings.

performance appraisal: An interview designed to review an individual or party's accomplishments and develop goals for the future; used in corporate and academic environments.

performance visualization: Spending time imagining positive scenarios and personal success in order to reduce negative thoughts and their accompanying anxiety.

performing: The stage of group development in which members combine their skills and knowledge to work toward the group's goals and overcome hurdles.

peripheral processing: Giving little thought to a message or even dismissing it as irrelevant, too complex to follow, or simply unimportant; occurs when listeners lack motivation to listen critically or are unable to do so.

persuasion: The process of influencing others' attitudes, beliefs, and behaviors on a given topic.

persuasive interview: An interview in which questions are designed to illicit some change in the interviewee's behavior or opinions.

persuasive speaking: Speech that is intended to influence the attitudes, beliefs, and behaviors of an audience.

phrase outline: A type of outline that takes parts of sentences and uses those phrases as instant reminders of what the point or subpoint means.

pie chart: A presentation aid that shows percentages of a circle divided proportionately.

pitch: Variations in the voice that give prominence to certain words or syllables.

plagiarism: The crime of presenting someone else's words, ideas, or intellectual property as one's own, intentionally or unintentionally.

planting: A technique for limiting and controlling body movements during speech delivery by keeping the legs firmly set apart at a shoulder-width distance.

politically correct language: Language that replaces exclusive or negative words with more neutral terms.

polychronic culture: A culture whose members are comfortable dealing with multiple people and tasks at the same time.

posture: The position of one's arms and legs and how one carries the body.

power distance: The way in which a culture accepts and expects the division of power among individuals.

pragmatics: The ability to use the symbol systems of a culture appropriately.

prejudice: A deep-seated feeling of unkindness and ill will toward particular groups, usually based on negative stereotypes and feelings of superiority over those groups.

preparation outline: A draft outline the speaker will use, and probably revisit and revise continually, throughout the preparation for a speech; also known as a *working outline.*

primacy-recency effect: In public speaking, the tendency for audiences to remember points the speaker raises at the very beginning, or at the very end, of a message.

primary group: A long-lasting group that forms around the relationships that mean the most to its members.

primary question: A type of interview question that introduces new topics.

probing: Asking questions that encourage specific and precise answers.

problem-solution pattern: A pattern of speech arrangement that involves dramatizing an obstacle and then narrowing alternative remedies down to the one the speaker wants to recommend.

problem-solving group: A group with a specific mission.

problem-solving interview: An interview that is used to deal with problems, tensions, or conflicts.

process: The methods by which an outcome is accomplished.

productive conflict: Conflict that is managed effectively.

profanity: Words or expressions considered insulting, rude, vulgar, or disrespectful.

pronunciation: The correct formation of word sounds.

prop: A presentation aid—an object that removes the burden from the audience of having to imagine what something looks like as the speaker is presenting.

proposition of fact: A claim of what is or what is not.

proposition of policy: A claim about what goal, policy, or course of action should be pursued.

proposition of value: A claim about something's worth.

protégé: A new or inexperienced member of an organization who is trained or mentored by a more seasoned member.

provocation: The intentional instigation of conflict.

proxemics: The study of the way we use and communicate with space.

proximity: A state of physical nearness.

pseudolistening: Pretending to listen when one is actually not paying attention at all.

psychological forces: Group members' personal motives, emotions, attitudes, and values.

public-private dimension: An aspect of the situational context of communication dealing with the physical space that affects our nonverbal communication.

public speaking: A powerful form of communication that includes a speaker who has a reason for speaking, an audience that gives the speaker attention, and a message that is meant to accomplish a specific purpose.

public speaking anxiety (PSA): The nervousness one experiences when one knows one has to communicate publicly to an audience.

quasi-scientific explanation: An explanation that models or pictures the key dimensions of some phenomenon for a typical audience.

random selection: A way to reach compromise that entails choosing one of two options at random, such as by a coin toss.

reasoning: The line of thought we use to make judgments based on facts and inferences from the world around us.

receiver: The target of a message.

receptive audience: An audience that already agrees with the speaker's viewpoints and message and is likely to respond favorably to the speech.

reconciliation: A repair strategy for rekindling an extinguished relationship.

red herring fallacy: A fallacy in which the speaker relies on irrelevant information for his or her argument, thereby diverting the direction of the argument.

reduction to the absurd: A logical fallacy that entails extending an argument beyond its logical limits to the level of absurdity; also known as *reductio ad absurdum.*

referent power: Power that stems from the admiration, respect, or affection that followers have for a leader.

refutational organizational pattern: An organizing pattern for persuasive speaking in which the speaker begins by presenting main points that are opposed to his or her own position and then follows them with main points that support his or her own position.

regulating: Using nonverbal cues to aid in the coordination of verbal interaction.

regulators: Body movements that help us to manage our interactions.

relational dialectics theory: The theory that *dialectical tensions* are contradictory feelings that tug at us in every relationship.

relational network: A web of relationships that connects individuals to one another.

relationships: The interconnection or interdependence between two or more people required to achieve goals.

remembering: The step in the listening process of recalling information.

repair tactics: Ways to save or repair a relationship.

repeating: Nonverbal behavior that offers a clear nonverbal cue that repeats and mirrors the verbal message.

responding: The step in the listening process of generating some kind of feedback or reaction that confirms to others that one has received and understood their messages.

résumé: A printed summary of one's education, work experiences, and accomplishments.

reward power: Power that derives from an individual's capacity to provide rewards.

rewards: The beneficial elements of a relationship.

ritualizing: Learning the rules for managing conversations and relationships; one of the five functional communication competencies.

role conflict: A situation that arises in a group whenever expectations for members' behavior are incompatible.

running bibliography: A list of resources the speaker has consulted, to which he or she can refer on note cards.

salient: Brought to mind in the moment; one's social identity and communication shift depending on which of one's multiple group memberships is salient in a given moment.

Sapir-Whorf hypothesis: The claim that the words a culture uses or doesn't use influence its members' thinking.

scanning: A technique for making brief eye contact with almost everyone in an audience by moving one's eyes from one person or section of people to another.

schema: A mental structure that puts together individual but related bits of information.

scientific research findings: Hard numbers and facts that are particularly useful for public speeches on medicine, health, media, or the environment.

search engine: A program that indexes Web content and searches all over the Web for documents containing specific keywords that the researcher has chosen.

secondary questions: A type of interview question that seeks clarification or an elaboration of responses to primary questions.

selecting: The step in the listening process of choosing one sound over another when faced with competing stimuli.

selection interview: An interview whose primary goal is to secure or fill a position within an organization.

selective listening: Listening that involves zeroing in only on bits of information that interest the listener, disregarding other messages or parts of messages.

selective perception: Active, critical thought resulting in a communicator succumbing to the biased nature of perception.

self-actualization: The feelings and thoughts one experiences when one knows that one has negotiated a communication situation as well as possible.

self-adequacy: The feelings one experiences when one assesses one's own communication competence as sufficient or acceptable; less positive than *self-actualization.*

self-concept: One's awareness and understanding of who one is, as interpreted and influenced by one's thoughts, actions, abilities, values, goals, and ideals.

self-denigration: A negative assessment about a communication experience that involves criticizing or attacking oneself.

self-directed work team: A group of skilled workers who take responsibility for producing high-quality finished work.

self-disclosure: Revealing oneself to others by sharing information about oneself.

self-efficacy: The ability to predict, based on self-concept and self-esteem, one's effectiveness in a communication situation.

self-esteem: How one feels about oneself, usually in a particular situation.

self-fulfilling prophecy: A prediction that causes an individual to alter his or her behavior in a way that makes the prediction more likely to occur.

self-monitoring: The ability to watch one's environment and others in it for cues as to how to present oneself in particular situations.

self-presentation: Intentional communication designed to show elements of self for strategic purposes; how one lets others know about oneself.

self-serving bias: The idea that we usually attribute our own successes to internal factors while explaining our failures by attributing them to situational or external effects.

semantics: The study of the relationship among symbols, objects, people, and concepts; refers to the meaning that words have for people, either because of their definitions or because of their placement in a sentence's structure (syntax).

sender: The individual who originates communication, with words or action.

sentence outline: A type of outline that offers the full text of a speech, often the exact words that the speaker wants to say to the audience.

separation: Removing oneself from a conflicted situation or relationship.

service-oriented interview: An interview that is designed to cull information and provide advice, service, or support based on that information; used, for example, by customer service representatives.

sexual harassment: "Unwelcome sexual advances, requests for sexual favors, and other verbal or physical harassment of a sexual nature . . . when it is so frequent or severe that it creates a hostile or offensive work environment or when it results in an adverse employment decision (such as the victim being fired or demoted)" (from the U.S. Equal Employment Opportunity Commission, 2011).

signposts: Key words or phrases within sentences that signify transitions between main points.

slang: Language that is informal, nonstandard, and usually particular to a specific group.

slippery slope fallacy: A logical fallacy that is employed when a speaker attests that some event must clearly occur as a result of another event without showing any proof that the second event is caused by the first.

social comparison theory: A theory that explains our tendency to compare ourselves to others, be they friends and acquaintances or popular figures in the media, as we develop our ideas about ourselves.

social exchange theory: A theory that explains the process of balancing the advantages and disadvantages of a relationship.

social forces: Group standards for behavior that influence decision making.

social group: A group in which membership offers opportunities to form relationships with others.

social identity theory: The theory that we each have a *personal identity*, which is our sense of our unique individual personality, and a *social identity*, the part of our self-concept that comes from group memberships.

social information processing theory: The theory that communicators use unique language and stylistic cues in their online messages to develop relationships that are just as close as those that grow from face-to-face content; because using text takes time, it takes longer to become intimate.

social judgment theory: The theory that a speaker's ability to successfully persuade an audience depends on the audience's current attitudes or disposition toward the topic.

social loafing: Failure to invest the same level of effort in the group that people would put in if they were working alone or with one other person.

Social Penetration Theory (SPT): The theory that partners move from superficial levels to greater intimacy.

social roles: Group roles that evolve to reflect individual members' personality traits and interests.

spatial pattern: A pattern of speech arrangement that arranges main points in terms of their physical proximity or position in relation to each other (north to south, east to west, bottom to top, left to right, outside to inside, and so on).

speaking outline: The final speech plan, complete with details, delivery tips, and important notes about presentational aids; also known as the *delivery outline.*

speaking rate: How fast or slow one speaks.

specific purpose statement: A statement that expresses both the topic and general speech purpose in action form and in terms of the specific objectives the speaker hopes to achieve with his or her presentation.

speech repertoire: A set of complex language behaviors or language possibilities that one calls on to most effectively and appropriately meet the demands of a given relationship, situation, or cultural environment.

stable stage: The stage of a relationship in which it is no longer volatile or temporary; both partners have a great deal of knowledge about one another, their expectations are accurate and realistic, and they feel comfortable with their motives for being in the relationship.

statistics: Information provided in numerical form.

stereotyping: The act of organizing information about groups of people into categories so that we can generalize about their attitudes, behaviors, skills, morals, and habits.

storming: The stage of group development in which members inevitably begin experiencing conflicts over issues such as who will lead the group and what roles members will play.

strategic topic avoidance: When one or both relational partners maneuver the conversation away from undesirable topics because of the potential for embarrassment, vulnerability, or relational decline.

study groups: Groups that are formed for the specific purpose of helping students prepare for exams.

style switching: A type of accommodation in which communicators change their tonality, pitch, rhythm, and inflection to fit into a particular group.

subjectivity: Presenting facts and information from a particular point of view.

subpoints: In public speaking, points that provide support for the main points.

substituting: Replacing words with nonverbal cues.

support group: A set of individuals who come together to address personal problems while benefiting from the support of others with similar issues.

supportive climate: A communication climate that offers communicators a chance to honestly and considerately explore the issues involved in the conflict situation.

supportive leader: A leader who attends to group members' emotional needs.

surveillance: Monitoring employees to see how they use technology.

survey: To solicit answers to a question or series of questions related to one's speech topic from a broad range of individuals.

syllogism: A three-line deductive argument that draws a specific conclusion from two general premises (a major and a minor premise).

symbols: Arbitrary constructions (usually in the form of language or behaviors) that refer to people, things, and concepts.

systems approach: An approach to management that views an organization as a unique whole consisting of important members who have interdependent relationships in their particular environment.

task roles: Roles that are concerned with the accomplishment of the group's goals.

team: A group that works together to carry out a project or specific endeavor or to compete against other teams.

termination stage: The end of a relationship; may come about by passing away or sudden death.

territoriality: The claiming of an area, with or without legal basis, through continuous occupation of that area.

thesis statement: A statement that conveys the central idea or core assumption about the speaker's topic.

time orientation: The way cultures communicate about and with time.

time-oriented listeners: Communicators who are most concerned with efficiency; they prefer information that is clear and to the point.

tone: A modulation of the voice, usually expressing a particular feeling or mood.

topical pattern: A pattern of speech arrangement that is based on organization into categories, such as persons, places, things, or processes.

trading: A way to reach compromise whereby one partner offers something of equal value in return for something he or she wants.

transactional: Involving two or more people acting in both sender and receiver roles whose messages are dependent on and influenced by those of their communication partner.

transformative explanation: An explanation that helps people understand ideas that are counterintuitive and is designed to help speakers transform "theories" about phenomena into more accepted notions.

transitions: Sentences that connect different points, thoughts, and details in a way that allows them to flow naturally from one to the next.

trolling: The posting of provocative or offensive messages to whole forums or discussion boards to elicit some type of general reaction.

tunnel sequence: A pattern of questioning in which all questions are at the same level, either broad and open-ended or narrow and closed; commonly used in polls and surveys.

uncertain climate: A communication climate in which at least one of the people involved is unclear, vague, tentative, and awkward about the goals, expectations, and potential outcomes of the conflict situation.

uncertainty avoidance: The process of adapting behaviors to reduce uncertainty and risk.

uncertainty event: An event or behavioral pattern that causes uncertainty in a relationship.

uncertainty reduction theory: The theory that when two people meet, their main focus is on decreasing the uncertainty about each other.

understanding: The step in the listening process of interpreting and making sense of messages.

understatement: Language that downplays the emotional intensity or importance of events, often with euphemisms.

undue influence: Giving greater credibility or importance to something shown or said than should be the case.

unproductive conflict: Conflict that is managed poorly and has a negative impact on the individuals and relationships involved.

verbal aggressiveness: Attacks on individuals, rather than on issues.

vocalizations: Paralinguistic cues that give information about the speaker's emotional or physical state, for example, laughing, crying, or sighing.

volume: How loud or soft the voice is.

wheel network: A network in which all group members share their information with one central individual, who then shares the information with the rest of the group.

work-life balance: Achieving success in one's personal and professional life.

worldview: The framework through which one interprets the world and the people in it.

references

Aakhus, M., & Rumsey, E. (2010). Crafting supportive communication online: A communication design analysis of conflict in an online support group. *Journal of Applied Communication Research, 38*(1), 65–84.

Adkins, M., & Brashers, D. E. (1995). The power of language in computer-mediated groups. *Management Communication Quarterly, 8,* 289–322.

Afifi, T. D., McManus, T., Hutchinson, S., & Baker, B. (2007). Parental divorce disclosures, the factors that prompt them, and their impact on parents' and adolescents' well-being. *Communication Monographs, 74,* 78–103.

Afifi, T. D., McManus, T., Steuber, K., & Coho, A. (2009). Verbal avoidance and dissatisfaction in intimate conflict situations. *Human Communication Research, 35*(3), 357–383.

Ahlfeldt, S. L. (2009). Serving our communities with public speaking skills. *Communication Teacher, 23*(4), 158–161.

Albada, K. F., Knapp, M. L., & Theune, K. E. (2002). Interaction appearance theory: Changing perceptions of physical attractiveness through social interaction. *Communication Theory, 12,* 8–40.

Alexander, A. L. (2008). Relationship resources for coping with unfulfilled standards in dating relationships: Commitment, satisfaction, and closeness. *Journal of Social & Personal Relationships, 25*(5), 725–747.

Alge, B. J., Wiethoff, C., & Klein, H. J. (2003). When does the medium matter? Knowledge-building experiences and opportunities in decision-making teams. *Organizational Behavior and Human Decision Processes, 91,* 26–37.

Allen, M. (1991). Comparing the persuasiveness of one-sided and two-sided messages using meta-analysis. *Western Journal of Speech Communication, 55,* 390–404.

Allen, R. R., & McKerrow, R. E. (1985). *The pragmatics of public communication* (3rd ed.). Dubuque, IA: Kendall/Hunt.

Allport, G. W. (1954). *The nature of prejudice.* Cambridge, MA: Addison-Wesley.

Altman, I., & Taylor, D. A. (1973). *Social penetration: The development of interpersonal relationships.* New York: Holt, Rinehart & Winston.

Amodio, D. M., & Showers, C. J. (2005). "Similarity breeds liking" revisited: The moderating role of commitment. *Journal of Social and Personal Relationships, 22,* 817–836.

Andersen, P. A., & Blackburn, T. R. (2004). An experimental study of language intensity and response rate in e-mail surveys. *Communication Reports, 17,* 73–84.

Anderson, C. M., & Martin, M. M. (1999). The relationship of argumentativeness and verbal aggressiveness to cohesion, consensus, and satisfaction in small groups. *Communication Reports, 12,* 21–31.

Anderson, C. M., Riddle, B. L., & Martin, M. M. (1999). Socialization in groups. In L. Frey, D. Gouran, & M. Poole (Eds.), *Handbook of group communication theory and research* (pp. 139–163). Thousand Oaks, CA: Sage Publications.

Anderson, T., & Emmers-Sommer, T. (2006). Predictors of relationship satisfaction in online romantic relationships. *Communication Studies, 57*(2), 153–172.

Annino, J. (Executive producer). (2007, July 5). Cooking in cramped quarters [Television series episode]. In *The Rachael Ray Show.* Video retrieved from http://www.rachaelrayshow.com/show/segments/view/cooking-in-cramped-quarters

Antheunis, M. L., Valkenburg, P. M., & Peter, J. (2010). Getting acquainted through social network sites: Testing a model of online uncertainty reduction and social attraction. *Computers in Human Behavior, 26*(1), 100–109.

Antonijevic, S. (2008). From text to gesture online: A microethnographic analysis of nonverbal communication in the *Second Life* virtual environment. *Information, Communication & Society, 11*(2), 221–238.

Appleby, C. (1996, December). Getting doctors to listen to patients. *Managed Care Magazine.* Retrieved from http://www.managedcaremag.com/archives/9612/MC9612.listening.shtml

Arasaratnam, L. (2007). Research in intercultural communication competence. *Journal of International Communication, 13,* 66–73.

Araton, H. (2010, April 26). The understated elegance of the Yankees' Rivera. *The New York Times,* p. D1.

Armstrong, B., & Kaplowitz, S. A. (2001). Sociolinguistic interference and intercultural coordination: A Bayesian model of communication competence in intercultural communication. *Human Communication Research, 27,* 350–381.

Atkinson, J., & Dougherty, D. S. (2006). Alternative media and social justice movements: The development of a resistance performance paradigm of audience analysis. *Journal of Western Communication, 70,* 64–89.

Aust, P. J. (2004). Communicated values as indicators of organizational identity: A method for organizational assessment and its application in a case study. *Communication Studies, 55,* 515–535.

Avtgis, T. A., & Rancer, A. S. (2003). Comparing touch apprehension and affective orientation between Asian-American and European-American siblings. *Journal of Intercultural Communication Research, 32*(2), 67–74.

Avtgis, T. A., West, D. V., & Anderson, T. L. (1998). Relationship stages: An inductive analysis identifying cognitive, affective, and behavioral dimensions of Knapp's relational stages model. *Communication Research Reports, 15,* 280–287.

Axtell, R. E. (1991). *Gestures: The do's and taboos of body language around the world.* New York: Wiley.

Ayres, J. (2005). Performance visualization and behavioral disruption: A clarification. *Communication Reports, 18,* 55–63.

Ayres, J., & Hopf, T. (1993). *Coping with speech anxiety.* Norwood, NJ: Ablex.

Ayres, J., Keereetaweep, T., Chen, P., & Edwards, P. (1998). Communication apprehension and employment interviews. *Communication Education, 47,* 1–17.

Ayres, J., Wilcox, A. K., & Ayres, D. M. (1995). Receiver apprehension: An explanatory model and accompanying research. *Communication Education, 44,* 223–235.

Babad, E., & Peer, E. (2010). Media bias in interviewers' nonverbal behavior: Potential remedies, attitude similarity and meta-analysis. *Journal of Nonverbal Behavior, 34*(1), 57–78.

Bailenson, J. N., Beall, A. C., Loomis, J., Blascovich, J., & Turk, M. (2005). Transformed social interaction, augmented gaze, and social influence in immersive virtual environments. *Human Communication Research, 31,* 511–537.

Baird, J. E., Jr. (1986). Sex differences in group communication: A review of relevant research. *Quarterly Journal of Speech, 62,* 179–192.

Baker, H. G., & Spier, M. S. (1990). The employment interview: Guaranteed improvement in reliability. *Public Personnel Management, 19,* 85–90.

Bakke, E. (2010). A model and measure of mobile communication competence. *Human Communication Research, 36*(3), 348–371.

Balaji, M., & Worawongs, T. (2010). The new Suzie Wong: Normative assumptions of white male and Asian female relationships. *Communication, Culture & Critique, 3*(2), 224–241.

Baldwin, M. W., & Keelan, J. P. R. (1999). Interpersonal expectations as a function of self-esteem and sex. *Journal of Social and Personal Relationships, 16,* 822–833.

Ball, K. (2010). Workplace surveillance: An overview. *Labor History, 51*(1), 87–106.

Balz, D., & Fears, D. (2005, July 21). Some disappointed nominee won't add diversity to court. *The Washington Post.* Retrieved from http://www.washingtonpost.com/wp-dyn/content/article/2005/07/20/AR2005072002381.html

Bandura, A. (1982). Self-efficacy mechanism in human agency. *American Psychologist, 37,* 122.

Barker, L. L., & Watson, K. W. (2000). *Listen up: How to improve relationships, reduce stress, and be more productive by using the power of listening.* New York: St. Martin's Press.

Barry, D. (1996, November 7). L.I. widow's story: Next stop, Washington. *The New York Times.* Retrieved from http://www.nytimes.com

Barstow, D., Dodd, L., Glanz, J., Saul, S., & Urbina, I. (2010, June 21). Regulators failed to address risks in oil rig fail-safe device. *The New York Times,* p. A1.

Bates, B. (1988). *Communication and the sexes.* New York: Harper & Row.

Bavelous, A. (1950). Communication patterns in task-oriented groups. *Journal of the Acoustical Society of America, 22,* 725–730.

Baxter, L. A., Braithwaite, D. O., Bryant, L., & Wagner, A. (2004). Stepchildren's perceptions of the contradictions in communication with stepparents. *Journal of Social and Personal Relationships, 21,* 447–467.

Baxter, L. A., & Erbert, L. (1999). Perceptions of dialectical contradictions in turning points of development in heterosexual romantic relationships. *Journal of Social and Personal Relationships, 16,* 547–569.

Baxter, L. A., Foley, M., & Thatcher, M. (2008). Marginalizing difference in personal relationships: How partners talk about their differences. *Journal of Communication Studies, 1*(1), 33–55.

Baxter, L. A., & Simon, E. P. (1993). Relationship maintenance strategies and dialectical contradictions in personal relationships. *Journal of Social and Personal Relationships, 10,* 225–242.

Baxter, L. A., & Wilmot, W. W. (1985). Taboo topics in close relationships. *Journal of Social and Personal Relationships, 2,* 253–269.

Bayly, S. (1999). Caste, society and politics in India from the eighteenth century to the modern age. Cambridge: Cambridge University Press.

Beall, M. L. (2006). Contributions of a listening legend. *International Journal of Listening, 20,* 27–28.

Bearak, B. (2010, September 6). Dead join the living in a family celebration. *The New York Times,* p. A7.

Beard, D. (2009). A broader understanding of the ethics of listening: Philosophy, cultural studies, media studies and the ethical listening subject. *International Journal of Listening, 23*(1), 7–20.

Beatty, M. J., & Payne, S. K. (1984). Effects of social facilitation on listening comprehension. *Communication Quarterly, 32,* 37–40.

Behnke, R. R., & Sawyer, C. R. (1999). Milestones of anticipatory public speaking anxiety. *Communication Education, 48,* 164–172.

Bellis, T. J., & Wilber, L. A. (2001). Effects of aging and gender on interhemispheric function. *Journal of Speech, Language, and Hearing Research, 44,* 246–264.

Benne, K. D., & Sheats, P. (1948). Functional roles in group members. *Journal of Social Issues, 4,* 41–49.

Bennett, J. M., & Bennett, M. J. (2004). Developing intercultural sensitivity: An integrative approach to global and domestic diversity. In D. Landis, J. M. Bennett, & M. J. Bennett (Eds.), *Handbook of intercultural training,* 3rd ed. (pp. 147–165). Thousand Oaks, CA: Sage Publications.

Ben-Porath, E. (2010). Interview effects: Theory and evidence for the impact of televised political interviews on viewer attitudes. *Communication Theory, 20*(3), 323–347.

Bentley, S. C. (2000). Listening in the twenty-first century. *International Journal of Listening, 14,* 129–142.

Bergen, K. M. (2010). Accounting for difference: Commuter wives and the master narrative of marriage. *Journal of Applied Communication Research, 38*(1), 47–64.

Berger, C., & Calabrese, R. (1975). Some explorations in initial interaction and beyond: Toward a developmental theory of interpersonal communication. *Human Communication Research, 1,* 99–112.

Berrisford, S. (2006). How will you respond to the information crisis? *Strategic Communication Management, 10,* 26–29.

Berryman-Fink, C. (1993). Preventing sexual harassment through male-female communication training. In G. Kreps (Ed.), *Sexual harassment: Communication implications* (pp. 267–280). Cresskill, NJ: Hampton Press.

Berscheid, E. (1985). Interpersonal attraction. In G. Lindzey & E. Aronson (Eds.), *Handbook of social psychology: Vol. 2. Special fields and applications* (3rd ed., pp. 413–484). New York: Random House.

Beyerlein, M. M. (2001). The parallel growth of team practices and the center for the study of work teams. *Team Performance Management, 7,* 93–98.

Biever, C. (2004, August). Language may shape human thought. *New Scientist.* Retrieved from http://www.newscientist.com

Bippus, A. M., & Daly, J. A. (1999). What do people think causes stage fright? Native attributions about the reasons for public speaking anxiety. *Communication Education, 48,* 63–72.

Bishop, G. (2010, February 20). On and off the ice, Ohno is positioned for success. *The New York Times,* p. D3.

Bishop, R. (2000). More than meets the eye: An explanation of literature related to the mass media's role in encouraging changes in body image. In M. E. Roloff (Ed.), *Communication yearbook* (Vol. 23, pp. 271–304). Thousand Oaks, CA: SAGE PUBLICATIONS.

Biskupic, J. (2009, October 5). Ginsburg: Court needs another woman. *USA Today.* Retrieved from http://www.usatoday.com/news/washington/judicial/2009-05-05-ruthginsburg_N.htm

Blumstein, P., & Schwartz, P. (1983). *American couples: Money, work, sex.* New York: Morrow.

Bodie, G. D. (2010). A racing heart, rattling knees, and ruminative thoughts: Defining, explaining, and treating public speaking anxiety. *Communication Education, 59*(1), 70–105.

Boje, D. M. (1991). The storytelling organization: A study of story performance in an office-supply firm. *Administrative Science Quarterly, 36,* 106–126.

Bommelje, R., Houston, J. M., & Smither, R. (2003). Personality characteristics of effective listeners: A five factor perspective. *International Journal of Listening, 17,* 32–46.

Boonzaier, F. (2008). "If the man says you must sit, then you must sit": The relational construction of woman abuse: Gender, subjectivity and violence. *Feminism & Psychology, 18*(2), 183–206.

Bosman, J. (2011, January 4). Publisher tinkers with Twain. *The New York Times.* Retrieved from http://www.nytimes.com/2011/01/05/books/05huck.html

Boster, F. J., & Mongeau, P. (1984). Fear-arousing persuasive messages. In R. N. Bostrom (Ed.), *Communication yearbook 8* (pp. 330–375). Beverly Hills, CA: Sage Publications.

Botta, R., & Dumlao, R. (2002). How do conflict and communication patterns between fathers and daughters contribute to or offset eating disorders? *Health Communication, 14,* 199–219.

Bourhis, R. Y. (1985). The sequential nature of language choice in cross-cultural communication. In R. L. Street Jr. & J. N. Cappella (Eds.), *Sequence and pattern in communicative behaviour* (pp. 120–141). London: Arnold.

boyd, d. (2010). Social network sites as networked publics: Affordances, dynamics, and implications. In Z. Papacharissi (Ed.), *A networked self: Identity, community, and culture on social network sites* (pp. 39–58). New York: Routledge.

Bradac, J. J. (1983). The language of lovers, flovers, and friends: Communicating in social and personal relationships. *Journal of Language and Social Psychology, 2,* 234.

Bradac, J. J., & Giles, H. (2005). Language and social psychology: Conceptual niceties, complexities, curiosities, monstrosities, and how it all works. In K. L. Fitch & R. E. Sanders (Eds.), *The new handbook of language and social psychology* (pp. 201–230). Mahwah, NJ: Erlbaum.

Brandau-Brown, F. E., & Ragsdale, J. D.(2008). Personal, moral, and structural commitment and the repair of marital relationships. *Southern Communication Journal, 73*(1), 68–83.

Brandenburg, C. (2008). The newest way to screen job applicants: A social networker's nightmare. *Federal Communications Law Journal, 60*(3), 597–626.

Brazeel, S. (2009). Networking to top talent or networking your way to top talent. *POWERGRID International, 14*(10), 2.

Brehm, J. W. (1966). *A theory of psychological reactance.* New York: Academic Press.

Brenneis, D. (1990). Shared and solitary sentiments: The discourse of friendship, play, and anger in Bhatgaon. In C. A. Lutz & L. Abu-Lughod (Eds.), *Language and the politics of emotion* (pp. 113–125). Cambridge: Cambridge University Press.

Brilhart, J. K., & Galanes, G. J. (1992). *Effective group discussion* (7th ed.). Dubuque, IA: Brown.

Brock, C. (2010, March 17). Padres breaking down language barrier. Retrieved from mlb.com

Brody, L. R. (2000). The socialization of gender differences in emotional expression: Display rules, infant temperament, and differentiation. In A. H. Fischer (Ed.), *Gender and emotion: Social psychological perspectives* (pp. 24–47). Cambridge: Cambridge University Press.

Brooks, J., & Groening, M. (Producers). (2006, April 30). Girls just want to have sums. [Television series episode]. In *The Simpsons*. Culver City, CA: Gracie Films.

Brown, S. L. (2000). The effect of union type on psychological well-being: Depression among cohabitors versus marrieds. *Journal of Health and Social Behavior, 41,* 241–255.

Buck, R. (1988). Emotional education and mass media: A new view of the global village. In R. P. Hawkins, J. M. Wiemann, & S. Pingree (Eds.), *Advancing communication science: Merging mass and interpersonal processes* (pp. 44–76). Beverly Hills, CA: Sage Publications.

Buckley, R. (1999). *Strictly speaking.* New York: McGraw-Hill.

Burgoon, J. K., & Bacue, A. E. (2003). Nonverbal communication skills. In J. O. Greene & B. R. Burleson (Eds.), *Handbook of communication and social interaction skills* (pp. 179–219). Mahwah, NJ: Erlbaum.

Burgoon, J. K., Buller, D. B., & Woodall, W. G. (1989). *Nonverbal communication: The unspoken dialogue.* New York: Harper & Row.

Burgoon, J. K., & Hoobler, G. D. (2002). Nonverbal signals. In M. L. Knapp & J. A. Daly (Eds.), *Handbook of interpersonal communication* (pp. 240–299). Thousand Oaks, CA: Sage Publications.

Burleson, B. R. (1994). Comforting messages: Features, functions, and outcomes. In J. A. Daly & J. M. Wiemann (Eds.), *Strategic interpersonal communication* (pp. 135–161). Hillsdale, NJ: Erlbaum.

Burleson, B. R., Holmstrom, A. J., & Gilstrap, C. M. (2005). "Guys can't say that to guys": Four experiments assessing the normative motivation account for deficiencies in the emotional support provided by men. *Communication Monographs, 72,* 468–501.

Busch, D. (2009). What kind of intercultural competence will contribute to students' future job employability? *Intercultural Education, 20*(5), 429–438.

Byrd, D. (2010, January 16). *Neil deGrasse Tyson: "Learning how to think is empowerment."* Retrieved from http://earthsky.org/human-world/neil-degrasse-tyson

Byrne, D. (1971). *The attraction paradigm.* New York: Academic Press.

Calhoun, B. (Producer). (2010, September 12). Right to remain silent [Show 414] [Audio podcast]. In *This American Life.* Retrieved from http://www.thisamericanlife.org/radio-archives/episode/414/right-to-remain-silent

Cambria, E., Chandra, P., Sharma, A., & Hussain, A. (2010, November 8). Do not feed the trolls. Paper presented at the 3rd international workshop Social Data on the Web, co-located with the 9th International Semantic Web Conference, Shanghai, China. Retrieved from http://sdow.semanticweb.org/2010/pub/sdow2010_paper_1.pdf

Campbell, J. D. (1990). Self-esteem and clarity of the self-concept. *Journal of Personality and Social Psychology, 59,* 538–549.

Canary, D. J. (2003). Managing interpersonal conflict: A model of events related to strategic choices. In J. O. Greene & B. R. Burleson (Eds.), *Handbook of communication and social interaction skills* (pp. 515–550). Mahwah, NJ: Erlbaum.

Canary, D. J., & Cody, M. J. (1993). *Interpersonal communication: A goals-based approach.* New York: St. Martin's Press.

Canary, D. J., Cody, M. J., & Manusov, V. (2003). *Interpersonal communication: A goals-based approach* (3rd ed.). New York: Bedford/St. Martin's.

Canary, D. J., Cody, M. J., & Manusov, V. (2008). *Interpersonal communication: A goals-based approach* (4th ed.). New York: Bedford/St. Martin's.

Canary, D. J., Cody, M. J., & Smith, S. (1994). Compliance-gaining goals: An inductive analysis of actors' goal types, strategies, and successes. In J. A. Daly & J. M. Wiemann (Eds.), *Strategic interpersonal communication* (pp. 33–90). Hillsdale, NJ: Erlbaum.

Canary, D. J., Cunningham, E. M., & Cody, M. J. (1988). Goal types, gender, and locus of control in managing interpersonal conflict. *Communication Research, 15,* 426–446.

Canary, D. J., & Dainton, M. (Eds.). (2003). *Maintaining relationships through communication: Relational, contextual, and cultural variations.* Mahwah, NJ: Lawrence Erlbaum Associates.

Canary, D. J., & Spitzberg, B. H. (1993). Loneliness and media gratifications. *Communication Research, 20,* 800–821.

Caplan, S. (2001). Challenging the mass-interpersonal communication dichotomy: Are we witnessing the emergence of an entirely new communication system? *Electronic Journal of Communication, 11.* Retrieved March 24, 2003, from http://www.cios.org/getfile/CAPLAN_v11n101

Capozzoli, T. (2002). How to succeed with self-directed work teams. *SuperVision, 63,* 25–26.

Carey, B. (2008, February 12). You remind me of me. *The New York Times.* Retrieved from http://www.nytimes.com/2008/02/12/health/12mimic.html

Carey, B. (2010, April 6). Seeking emotional clues without facial cues. *The New York Times,* p. D1.

Cargile, A. C., & Giles, H. (1996). Intercultural communication training: Review, critique, and a new theoretical framework. In B. R. Burleson (Ed.), *Communication yearbook 19* (pp. 3835–3423). Newbury Park, CA: Sage Publications.

Carless, S. A., & DePaola, C. (2000). The measurement of cohesion in work teams. *Small Group Research, 31,* 71–88.

Caruso, P. (1996, September). Individuality vs. conformity: The issue behind school uniforms. *National Association of Secondary School Principals Bulletin, 83*–88.

Casmir, F. L. (Ed.). (1997). *Ethics in intercultural and international communication.* Mahwah, NJ: Erlbaum.

Cassell, J., Huffaker, D., Tversky, D., & Ferriman, K. (2006). The language of online leadership: Gender and youth engagement on the Internet. *Developmental Psychology, 42*(3), 436–449.

Caughlin, J. (2003). Family communication standards: What counts as excellent family communication, and how are such standards associated with family satisfaction? *Human Communication Research, 29,* 5–40.

CBS News. (2010a, January 5). Survey: More Americans unhappy at work. Retrieved from http://www.cbsnews.com

CBS News. (2010b, November 28). Colin Firth on playing King George VI: Katie Couric talks with *The King's Speech* star about the monarch's battle against a debilitating stutter. Retrieved from http://www.cbsnews.com/stories/2010/11/28/sunday/main7096682.shtml

Cegala, D. (1981). Interaction involvement: A cognitive dimension of communicative competence. *Communication Education, 30,* 109–121.

Census seen lax on diversity. (2010, February 25). *The Washington Times.* Retrieved from http://www.washingtontimes.com/news/2010/feb/25/census-seen-lax-on-diversity/

Centers for Disease Control and Prevention. (2010). *Childhood obesity.* Retrieved from http://www.cdc.gov/healthyyouth/obesity

Chaiken, S. (1979). Communicator physical attractiveness and persuasion. *Journal of Personality and Social Psychology, 37,* 1387–1397.

Chen, G., & Starosta, W. J. (1996). Intercultural communication competence: A synthesis. In B. R. Burleson (Ed.), *Communication yearbook* (Vol. 19, pp. 353–383). Thousand Oaks, CA: Sage Publications.

Chen, Y., & Nakazawa, M. (2009). Influences of culture on self-disclosure as relationally situated in intercultural and interracial friendships from a social penetration perspective. *Journal of Intercultural Communication Research, 38*(2), 77–98.

Childs, C. (2009). Perfect quiet. *Miller-McCune, 2*(4), 58–67.

Christenson, P. (1994). Childhood patterns of music uses and preferences. *Communication Reports, 7,* 136–144.

Christians, C., & Traber, C. (Eds.). (1997). *Communication ethics and universal values.* Thousand Oaks, CA: Sage Publications.

Christophel, D. M. (1990). The relationships among teacher immediacy behaviors, student motivation, and learning. *Communication Education, 39,* 323–340.

Cialdini, R. (2008). *Influence: Science and practice* (5th ed.). Englewood Cliffs, NJ: Prentice Hall.

Clark, A. J. (1989). Communication confidence and listening competence: An investigation of the relationships of willingness to communicate, communication apprehension, and receiver apprehension to comprehension of content and emotional meaning in spoken messages. *Communication Education, 38,* 237–248.

Clarke, I., Flaherty, T. B., Wright, N. D., & McMillen, R. M. (2009). Student intercultural proficiency from study abroad programs. *Journal of Marketing Education, 31*(2), 173–181.

Classroom clickers make the grade. (2005, July 4). *Wired.* Retrieved from http://www.wired.com/science/discoveries/news/2005/07/68086

CNN.com. (2006, October 5). Amish grandfather: "We must not think evil of this man." *Cable News Network.* Retrieved from http://www.cnn.com/2006/US/10/04/amish.shooting/index.html

CNN.com. (2007, April 18). Massacre at Virginia Tech. *Cable News Network.* Retrieved from http://www.cnn.com/2007/US/04/17/cho.profile/index.html

CNN.com/living. (2008). *Having it all: Quiz: Are you off balance?* Retrieved May 27, 2008, from http://www.cnn.com

Cohen, J. (2010, March 2). Want a better listener? Protect those ears. *The New York Times,* p. D6.

Cohen, M., & Avanzino, S. (2010). We are people first: Framing organizational assimilation experiences of the physically disabled using co-cultural theory. *Communication Studies, 61*(3), 272–303.

Comer, D. R. (1998). A model of social loafing in real work groups. *Human Relations, 48,* 647–667.

Conlin, M. (2006, December 11). Online extra: How to kill meetings. *Business Week.* Retrieved from http://www.businessweek.com

Connelly, S. (2009, December 3). Rupert Everett: Coming out of the closet ruined my career in Hollywood. *Daily News.* Retrieved from http://articles.nydailynews.com/2009-12-03/gossip/17940844_1_gay-best-friend-closet-major-stars

Conville, R. L. (1991). *Relational transitions: The evolution of personal relationships.* Westport, CT: Praeger.

Cook, G. (2002, February 14). Debate opens anew on language and its effect on cognition. *The Boston Globe,* p. A10.

Cook, K. S. (1987). *Social exchange theory.* Beverly Hills, CA: Sage Publications.

Cooper, L. O. (1997). Listening competency in the workplace: A model for training. *Business Communication Quarterly, 60*(4), 74–84.

Cornwell, B., & Lundgren, D. C. (2001). Love on the Internet: Involvement and misrepresentation in romantic relationships in cyberspace vs. realspace. *Computers in Human Behavior, 17*(2), 197–211.

Costa, M. (2010). Interpersonal distances in group walking. *Journal of Nonverbal Behavior, 34*(1), 15–26.

Coulehan, J. L., & Block, M. L. (2006). *The medical interview: Mastering skills for clinical practice.* Philadelphia: Davis.

Covel, S. (2008, June 9). The benefits of a "feminine" leadership style. *The Wall Street Journal.* Retrieved from http://www.wsj.com

Cox, A. (2005, August 15). Custom made fit for school: Dress codes, student uniforms back in style. *Cable News Network.* Retrieved from http://www.cnn.com/2005/US/08/12/style.rules

Crane, D. (2000). *Fashion and its social agendas: Class, gender, and identity in clothing.* Chicago: University of Chicago Press.

Crawford, M. (1995). *Talking difference: On gender and language.* Thousand Oaks, CA: Sage Publications.

Crispin, G., & Mehler, M. (2011). CareerXroads tenth annual source of hire report: By the numbers. Retrieved from www.careerxroads.com/news/sourcesofhire11.pdf

Cuda, G. (2006, April 11). Troops learn to not offend. *Wired.* Retrieved from http://www.wired.com/science/discoveries/news/2006/04/70576

Culbert, S. A. (2010). *Get rid of the performance review! How companies can stop intimidating, start managing—and focus on what really matters.* New York: Business Plus/Hachette Book Group.

Cupach, W. R., & Spitzberg, B. H. (Eds.) (2011). *The dark side of close relationships II.* New York: Routledge.

Daft, R. L., & Lengel, R. H. (1984). Informational richness: A new approach to managerial behavior and organizational design. In B. M. Staw & L. L. Cummings (Eds.), *Research in organizational behavior* (Vol. 6, pp. 191–233). Greenwich, CT: JAI.

Daft, R. L., & Lengel, R. H. (1986). Organizational information requirements, media richness, and structural design. *Management Science, 32,* 554–571.

Dailey, R. M., & Palomares, N. A. (2004). Strategic topic avoidance: An investigation of topic avoidance frequency, strategies used, and relational correlates. *Communication Monographs, 71,* 471–496.

Dainton, M., & Gross, J. (2008). The use of negative behaviors to maintain relationships. *Communication Research Reports, 25,* 179–191.

Danet, B., & Herring, S. C. (Eds.) (2007). *The multilingual Internet: Language, culture, and communication online.* New York: Oxford University Press.

Daniel, E. (2008). *Stealth germs in your body.* New York: Union Square Press.

Davies, P. T., Sturge-Apple, M. L., Cicchetti, D., & Cummings, E. M. (2008). Adrenocortical underpinnings of children's psychological reactivity to interparental conflict. *Child Development, 79,* 1693–1706.

Davis, M. S. (1973). *Intimate relations.* New York: Free Press.

Davis, S., & Mares, M. (1998). Effects of talk show viewing on adolescents. *Journal of Communication, 48,* 69–86.

Day, L. A. (2007). *Ethics in media communications: Cases and controversies* (2nd ed.). Belmont, CA: Wadsworth.

DeGroot, T., & Gooty, J. (2009). Can nonverbal cues be used to make meaningful personality attributions in employment interviews? *Journal of Business and Psychology, 24*(2), 179–192.

DeKay, S. H. (2009). The communication functions of business attire. *Business Communication Quarterly, 72*(3), 349–350.

Derks, D., Box, A. E. R., & von Grumbkow, J. (2008). Emoticons and online message interpretation. *Social Science Computer Review, 26*(3), 379–388.

Derlega, V. J., Winstead, B. A., Mathews, A., & Braitman, A. L. (2008). Why does someone reveal highly personal information? Attributions for and against self-disclosure in close relationships. *Communication Research Reports, 25*(2), 115–130.

DeSanctis, G., Poole, M. S., Zigurs, I., DeSharnais, G., D'Onofrio, M., Gallupe, B., Holmes, M., Jackson, B., Jackson, M., Lewis, H., Limayem, M., Lee-Partridge, J. E., Niederman, F., Sambamurthy, V., Vician, C., Watson, R., Billingsley, J., Kirsch, L., Lind, R., Shannon, D. (2008). The Minnesota GDSS research project: Group support systems, group processes, and outcomes. *Journal of the Association for Information Systems, 9*(10/11), 551–608.

Dewan, S. (2006, October 5). Amish school survivors struggle after killings. *The New York Times.* Retrieved from http://www.nytimes.com

Dewey, J. (1933). *How we think.* Lexington, MA: Heath.

Diehl, W. C., & Prins, E. (2008). Unintended outcomes in Second Life: Intercultural literacy and cultural identity in a virtual world. *Language & Intercultural Communication, 8*(2), 101–118.

Diener, E., & Diener, M. (1995). Cross-cultural correlates of life satisfaction and self-esteem. *Journal of Personality and Social Psychology, 68,* 653–663.

Dillard, J. P., Solomon, D. H., & Palmer, M. T. (1999). Structuring the concept of relational communication. *Communication Monographs, 66,* 49–65.

Dillon, R. K., & McKenzie, N. J. (1998). The influence of ethnicity on listening, communication competence, approach, and avoidance. *International Journal of Listening, 12,* 106–121.

Dindi, K., & Timmerman, L. (2003). Accomplishing romantic relationships. In J. O. Greene & B. R. Burleson (Eds.), *Handbook of communication and social interaction skills* (pp. 685–722). Mahwah, NJ: Erlbaum.

Dipper, L., Black, M., & Bryan, K. (2005). Thinking for speaking and thinking for listening: The interaction of thought and language in typical and non-fluent comprehension and production. *Language and Cognitive Processes, 20,* 417–441.

Dirksen Bauman, H. (2003, Fall). Redesigning literature: Toward a cinematic poetics of ASL poetry. *Sign Language Studies, 4*(1), 34–47.

DiSanza, J. R., & Legge, N. J. (2002). *Business and professional communication: Plans, processes, and performance* (2nd ed.). Boston: Allyn & Bacon.

Dixon, J. A., & Foster, D. H. (1998). Gender, social context, and backchannel responses. *Journal of Social Psychology, 138,* 134–136.

Docter, P., & Peterson, B. (Directors). (2009). *Up* [motion picture]. United States: Pixar Walt Disney Studios.

Doll, B. (1996). Children without friends: Implications for practice and policy. *School Psychology Review, 25,* 165–183.

Döring, N., & Pöschl, P. (2009). Nonverbal cues in mobile phone text messages: The effects of chronemics and proxemics. In Ling, R., & Campbell, S. W. (Eds.), *The reconstruction of space and time: Mobile phone practices.* New Brunswick, NJ: Transaction Publishers.

Doris, J. (Ed.). (1991). *The suggestibility of children's recollections.* Washington, DC: American Psychological Association.

Doshi, A. (with Drvaid, S., Giri, R., & David, S.). (2005, June 20). Sweep stake: Technology, television and the fast pace of modern life have dramatically altered the rules of the dating game. *India Today.* Retrieved from http://proquest/umi.com

Douglas, C. (2002). The effects of managerial influence behavior on the transition to self-directed work teams. *Journal of Managerial Psychology, 17,* 628–635.

Douglass, J., Jr. (2005, January 23). Some Norwegians thought Bush was saluting Satan. *The Standard-Times,* p. B3.

Drummond, K. (2010, February 26). New Pentagon sim teaches troops to play nice. *Wired* Danger Room blog. Retrieved from http://www.wired.com/dangerroom/2010/02/new-pentagon-sim-teaches-troops-to-play-nice/

Ducharme, J., Doyle, A., & Markiewicz, D. (2002). Attachment security with mother and father: Associations with adolescents' reports of interpersonal behavior with parents and peers. *Journal of Social and Personal Relationships, 19,* 203–231.

Duck, S. W. (1984). A perspective on the repair of personal relationships: Repair of what, when? In S. W. Duck (Ed.), *Personal relationships: Vol. 5. Repairing personal relationships.* New York: Macmillan.

Dues, M., & Brown, M. (2004). *Boxing Plato's shadow: An introduction to the study of human communication.* New York: McGraw-Hill.

DuFrene, D., & Lehman, C. (2004). Concept, content, construction and contingencies: Getting the horse before the PowerPoint cart. *Business Communication Quarterly, 67*(1), 84–88.

Dunbar, N. E., & Burgoon, J. K. (2005). Perceptions of power and interactional dominance in interpersonal relationships. *Journal of Social & Personal Relationships, 22*(2), 207–233.

Duncan, S., & Fiske, D. (1977). *Face-to-face interaction.* Hillsdale, NJ: Erlbaum.

Dunleavy, V., & Millette, D. (2007). Measuring mentor roles and protégé initiation strategies: Validating instruments in academic mentoring. *Conference Papers—National Communication Association,* 1. Retrieved from http://www.allacademic.com/meta/p194103_index.html

Dunning, D. A., & Kruger, J. (1999). Unskilled and unaware of it: How difficulties in recognizing one's own incompetence lead to inflated self-assessments. *Journal of Personality and Social Psychology, 77,* 1121–1134.

Dwamena, F., Mavis, B., Holmes-Rovner, M., Walsh, K., & Loyson, A. (2009). Teaching medical interviewing to patients: The other side of the encounter. *Patient Education and Counseling, 76*(3), 380–384.

Dwyer, K. M., Fredstrom, B. K., Rubin, K. H., Booth-LaForce, C., Rose-Krasnor, L., & Burgess, K. B. (2010). Attachment, social information processing, and friendship quality of early adolescent girls and boys. *Journal of Social & Personal Relationships, 27*(1), 91–116.

Eckholm, E. (2010, May 10). What's in a name? A lot, as it turns out. *The New York Times,* p. A12.

Edwards, C., & Edwards, A. (2009). Communication skills training for elementary school students. *Communication Currents, 4*(4), 1–2.

Edwards, R. (1990). Sensitivity to feedback and the development of self. *Communication Quarterly, 28,* 101–111.

Efran, M. G. (1974). The effect of physical appearance on the judgment of guilt, interpersonal attraction, and severity of recommended punishment in a simulated jury task. *Journal of Research in Personality, 8,* 45–54.

Eibl-Eibesfeldt, I. (1973). The expressive behavior of the deaf-and-blind-born. In M. von Cranach & I. Vine (Eds.), *Social communication and movement: Studies of interaction and expression in man and chimpanzee* (pp. 163–194). New York: Academic Press.

Eisenberg, E., Goodall, H. L., Jr., & Trethewey, A. (2010). *Organizational Communication: Balancing creativity and constraint* (6th ed.). Boston: Bedford/St. Martin's.

Ekman, P., & Friesen, W. V. (1969). The repertoire of nonverbal behavior: Categories, origins, usage, and coding. *Semiotica, 1,* 49–98.

Ekman, P., & Friesen, W. V. (1971). Constants across cultures in the face and emotion. *Journal of Personality and Social Psychology, 17,* 124–129.

Ekman, P., Friesen, W. V., & Ellsworth, P. (1972). *Emotion in the human face: Guidelines for research and an integration of findings.* New York: Pergamon Press.

El Ahl, A., and Steinvorth, D. (2006, October 20). Sex and taboos in the Islamic world. *Spiegel Online International.* Retrieved March 12, 2008, from http://www.spiegel.de/international/spiegel/0,1518,443678,00.html

Elliott, S. (2010, June 30). Food brands get sociable on Facebook and Twitter. *The New York Times.* Retrieved from http://mediadecoder.blogs.nytimes.com/2010/06/30/food-brands-get-sociable-on-facebook-and-twitter

El-Magd, N. A. (2006, December 3). Muslim woman gives sex advice on Arab TV. *The Washington Post.* Retrieved from http://www.washingtonpost.com

Endo, Y., Heine, S. J., & Lehman, D. R. (2000). Culture and positive illusions in close relationships: How my relationships are better than yours. *Personality and Social Psychology Bulletin, 26,* 1571–1586.

Entertainment Software Association (2009). Essential facts about the computer and video game industry. Retrieved from http://www.theesa.com/facts/pdfs/ESA_EF_2009.pdf

Erdur-Baker, O. (2010). Cyberbullying and its correlation to traditional bullying, gender and frequent and risky usage of Internet-mediated communication tools. *New Media and Society, 12,* 109–125.

Etcoff, N. (1999). *Survival of the prettiest: The science of beauty.* New York: Anchor Books.

Ewald, J. (2010). "Do you know where X is?": Direction-giving and male/female direction-givers. *Journal of Pragmatics, 42*(9), 2549–2561.

Ewalt, D. (2005, September 17). Jane Goodall on why words hurt. *Forbes.* Retrieved from http://www.forbes.com

Faiola, A. (2005, September 22). Men in land of samurai find their feminine side. *Washington Post Foreign Service.* Retrieved from http://www.washingtonpost.com/wp-dyn/content/article/2005/09/21/AR2005092102434.html

Farley, S. D. (2008). Attaining status at the expense of likeability: Pilfering power through conversational interruption. *Journal of Nonverbal Behavior, 32*(4), 241–260.

Farroni, T., Csibra, G., Simion, F., & Johnson, M. (2002, July 9). Eye contact detection in humans from birth. *Proceedings of the National Academy of Sciences of the United States of America, 99,* 9602–9605. Retrieved from http://www.pnas.org/cgi/doi/10.1073/pnas.152159999

Federal Communications Commission. (2008, January 8). *Understanding workplace harassment.* Retrieved September 3, 2008, from http://www.fcc.gov/owd/understanding harassment.html

Fehr, B. (2001). The life cycle of friendship. In C. Hendrick & S. S. Hendrick (Eds.), *Close relationships: A sourcebook* (pp. 71–82). Thousand Oaks, CA: Sage Publications.

Feldman, C., & Ridley, C. (2000). The role of conflict-based communication responses and outcomes in male domestic violence toward female partners. *Journal of Social and Personal Relationships, 17,* 552–573.

Fent, B., & MacGeorge, E. L. (2006). Predicting receptiveness to advice: Characteristics of the problem, the advice-giver, and the recipient. *Southern Communication Journal, 71,* 67–85.

Festinger, L. (1954). A theory of social comparison processes. *Human Relations, 7,* 117–140.

Fey, T., Hubbard, M., (Writers) & Riggi, J. (Director). (2011). "¡Que Sorpresa!" [Television series episode]. In T. Fey, R. Carlock, M. Klein, D. Miner, J. Richmond, & J. Riggi (Producers), *30 Rock.* New York: NBC Universal.

Finder, A. (2006, June 11). For some, online persona undermines a résumé. *The New York Times.* Retrieved from http://www.nytimes.com

Fisk, G. M. (2010). "I want it all and I want it now!" An examination of the etiology, expression, and escalation of excessive employee entitlement. *Human Resource Management Review, 20*(2), 102–114.

Fiske, S. T., & Taylor, S. E. (1991). *Social cognition.* New York: McGraw-Hill.

Fitch-Hauser, M., Powers, W. G., O'Brien, K., & Hanson, S. (2007). Extending the conceptualization of listening fidelity. *International Journal of Listening, 21*(2), 81–91.

Flecha-García, M. (2010). Eyebrow raises in dialogue and their relation to discourse structure, utterance function and pitch accents in English. *Speech Communication, 52*(6), 542–554.

Fletcher, C. (1999). Listening to narratives: The dynamics of capturing police experience. *International Journal of Listening, 13,* 46–61.

Floyd, J. J. (2006). Ralph G. Nichols: Prophet, pioneer, and visionary. *International Journal of Listening, 20,* 18–19.

Foels, R., Driskell, J. E., Mullen, B., & Salas, E. (2000). The effects of democratic leadership on group member satisfaction. *Small Group Research, 31,* 676–701.

Folger, J. P., Poole, M. S., & Stutman, R. K. (1997). *Working through conflict* (3rd ed.). New York: Longman.

Folger, J. P., Poole, M. S., & Stutman, R. K. (2001). *Working through conflict: Strategies for relationships, groups, and organizations* (4th ed.). New York: Longman.

Ford, W. S. Z. (1999). Communication and customer service. In M. E. Roloff (Ed.), *Communication yearbook* (Vol. 22, pp. 341–375). Thousand Oaks, CA: Sage Publications.

Fowers, B. J., Fışıloğlu, H., & Procacci, E. K. (2008). Positive marital illusions and culture: American and Turkish spouses' perceptions of their marriages. *Journal of Social & Personal Relationships, 25*(2), 267–285.

Fox, M. J. (2002). In His own words. In *Lucky man* (chap. 8). Retrieved from The Michael J. Fox Foundation for Parkinson's Research, http://www.michaeljfox.org/about_aboutMichael_inHisOwnWords_excerpt.cfm

Fraleigh, D. M. & Tuman, J. S. (2011). *Speak up! An illustrated guide to public speaking* (2nd ed.). New York: Bedford/St. Martin's.

Frantz, R. (2007). Groups continue to meet: Independent reviewers assess practice delineation. *Communications Magazine, 45,* 16.

French, J. R. P., & Raven, B. (1959). The bases for power. In D. Cartwright (Ed.), *Studies in social power* (pp. 150–167). Ann Arbor, MI: Institute for Social Research.

Friedman, T. L. (2007). *The world is flat: A brief history of the twenty-first century.* New York: Farrar, Straus & Giroux.

Frum, D. (2000). *How we got here: The '70s.* New York, NY: Basic Books.

Frymier, A. B. (1994). A model of immediacy in the classroom. *Communication Quarterly, 42,* 133–144.

Frymier, A. B., & Nadler, M. K. (2010). *Persuasion: Integrating theory, research, and practice.* Dubuque, IA: Kendall Hunt.

Gabriel, T. (2010, November 4). Learning in dorm, because class is on the Web. *The New York Times.* Retrieved from http://www.nytimes.com/2010/11/05/us/05college.html

Gagnon, M., Gosselin, P., Hudon-Ven Der Buhs, I., Larocque, K., & Milliard, K. (2010). Children's recognition and discrimination of fear and disgust facial expressions. *Journal of Nonverbal Behavior, 34*(1), 27–42.

Gallois, C., Franklyn-Stokes, A., Giles, H., & Coupland, N. (1988). Communication accommodation in intercultural encounters. In Y. Y. Kim & W. B. Gudykunst (Eds.), *Theories in intercultural communication* (pp. 157–85). Newbury Park, CA: Sage Publications.

Gardner, W. L., Reithel, B. J., Foley, R. T., Cogliser, C. C., & Walumbwa, F. O. (2009). Attraction to organizational culture profiles: Effects of realistic recruitment and vertical and horizontal individualism–collectivism. *Management Communication Quarterly, 22*(3), 437–472.

Garner, J. T., & Poole, M. S. (2009). Opposites attract: Leadership endorsement as a function of interaction between a leader and a foil. *Western Journal of Communication, 73*(3), 227–247.

Gates, B. (2009, February). TED Talks: Bill Gates on Mosquitoes, Malaria, and Education. Retrieved from http://www.ted.com/talks/lang/eng/bill_gates_unplugged.html

Gawande, A. (2009). *The checklist manifesto: How to get things right.* New York: Metropolitan Books.

Geffner, M. B. (2005, April 17). Voices behind the stars. *Times Herald-Record.* Retrieved from http://www.recordonline.com/apps/pbcs.dll/article?AID=/20050417/SPORTS/304179972

Gettleman, J. (2008, October 18). Rape victims' words help jolt Congo into change. *The New York Times,* p. A1.

Gibb, J. (1961). Defensive communication. *Journal of Communication, 2,* 141–148.

Gilbert, A. (2005, March 28). Why can't you pay attention anymore? *CNET News.* Retrieved from http://www.news.com/Why-cant-you-pay-attention-anymore/2008-1022_3-5637632.html?tag=item

Gilbertson, J., Dindi, K., & Allen, M. (1998). Relational continuity constructional units and the maintenance of relationships. *Journal of Social and Personal Relationships, 15,* 774–790.

Giles, H., Fortman, J., Dailey, R. M., Barker, V., Hajek, C., Anderson, M. C., & Rule, N. O. (2006). Communication accommodation: Law enforcement and the public. In R. M. Dailey and B. A. LePoire (Eds.), *Applied interpersonal communication matters: Family, health, and community relations* (pp. 241–269). New York: Peter Lang Publishing, Inc.

Giles, H., Reid, S., & Harwood, J. (Eds.) (2010). *The dymanics of intergroup communication.* New York: Peter Lang.

Giles, H., & Smith, P. M. (1979). Accommodation theory: Optimal levels of convergence. In H. Giles & R. N. Saint Clair (Eds.), *Language and social psychology* (pp. 45–65). Oxford: Blackwell.

Giles, H., & Wiemann, J. M. (1987). Language, social comparison, and power. In C. R. Berger & S. H. Chaffee (Eds.), *Handbook of communication science* (pp. 350–384). Newbury Park, CA: Sage Publications.

Gillath, O., McCall, C. Shaver, P. R., & Blascovich, J. (2008). What can virtual reality teach us about prosocial tendencies in real and virtual environments? *Media Psychology, 11*(2), 259–282.

Gitlow v. New York, 268 U.S. 652 (1925).

Goffman, E. (1967). *Interaction ritual: Essays on face-to-face behavior.* Garden City, NY: Doubleday.

Goffman, E. (1971). *Relations in public: Microstudies of the public order.* New York: Harper & Row.

Golish, T., & Caughlin, J. (2002). "I'd rather not talk about it": Adolescents' and young adults' use of topic avoidance in stepfamilies. *Journal of Applied Communication Research, 30,* 78–106.

Gonzaga, G. C., Campos, B., & Bradbury, T. (2007). Similarity, convergence, and relationship satisfaction in dating and married couples. *Journal of Personality & Social Psychology, 93*(1), 34–48.

Goodrich, A. (2007, March 28). Anxiety about study abroad. *The Georgetown Independent.* Retrieved from http://travel.georgetown.edu/51469.html

Goodstein, L. (2006, October 4). Strong faith and community may help Amish cope with loss. *The New York Times.* Retrieved from http://www.nytimes.com

Goodwin, D. K. (2002, January 27). How I caused that story. *Time.* Retrieved from http://www.time.com/time/nation/article/0,8599,197614,00.html#ixzz1FMvG5yK9

Google, Inc. (2009). Our philosophy. Retrieved from http://www.google.com/corporate/tenthings.html

Google, Inc. (2011a). The Google culture. Retrieved from http://www.google.com/corporate/culture.html

Google, Inc. (2011b). Life at Google: Benefits. Retrieved from http://www.google.com/jobs/lifeatgoogle/benefits.html

Google, Inc. (2011c). Life at Google: The engineer's life at Google. Retrieved from http://www.google.com/intl/en/jobs/lifeatgoogle/englife/index.html

Gordon, P. (2004, October 15). Numerical cognition without words: Evidence from Amazonia [Supplementary online materials]. *Science Online.* Retrieved March 25, 2008, from http://www.sciencemag.org/cgi/content/full/sci;1094492/DC1

Gore, J. (2009). The interaction of sex, verbal, and nonverbal cues in same-sex first encounters. *Journal of Nonverbal Behavior, 33*(4), 279–299.

Goss, B., & O'Hair, D. (1988). *Communicating in interpersonal relationships.* New York: Macmillan.

Gosselin, D. K. (2007). *Smart talk: Contemporary interviewing and interrogation.* Upper Saddle River, NJ: Prentice Hall.

Gottman, J. M. (1994). *What predicts divorce? The relationship between marital processes and marital outcomes.* Hillsdale, NJ: Erlbaum.

Gottman, J. M., & Silver, N. (1999). *The seven principles for making marriages work: A practical guide from the country's foremost relationship expert.* New York: Three Rivers Press.

Gouran, D. S. (2003). Communication skills for group decision making. In J. O. Greene & B. R. Burleson (Eds.), *Handbook of communication and social interaction skills* (pp. 835–870). Mahwah, NJ: Erlbaum.

Grahe, J. E., & Bernieri, F. J. (1999). The importance of nonverbal cues in judging rapport. *Journal of Nonverbal Behavior, 23,* 253–269.

Gray, F. E. (2010). Specific oral communication skills desired in new accountancy graduates. *Business Communication Quarterly, 73*(1), 40–67.

Greco, B. (1977). Recruiting and retaining high achievers. *Journal of College Placement, 37* (2), 34–40.

Greenhouse, S. (2006, September 3). Now bringing home the leaner bacon: Borrowers we be. *The New York Times.* Retrieved from http://www.nytimes.com

Greenwalk, A. G., Bellezza, F. S., & Banaji, M. R. (1988). Is self-esteem a central ingredient of self-concept? *Personality and Social Psychology Bulletin, 14,* 34–45.

Greulich, M. (2005, Fall). Are you a feminist? *E-Quality.* Retrieved March 25, 2008, from http://www.cbeinternational.org/new/E-Journal/2005/05fall/05fallsurvey.html

Grieves, R. (1984, January 30). Telecommuting from a flexiplace: Fans and foes take second looks at work-at-home programs. *Time.* Retrieved from http://www.time.com

Grossman, R. B., & Kegl, J. (2007). Moving faces: Categorization of dynamic facial expressions in American Sign Language by deaf and hearing participants. *Journal of Nonverbal Behavior, 31,* 23–28.

Gudykunst, W. B. (1993). Toward a theory of effective interpersonal and intergroup communication: An anxiety/uncertainty management (AUM) perspective. In R. L. Wiseman & J. Koester (Eds.), *Intercultural communication competence* (pp. 33–71). Newbury Park, CA: Sage Publications.

Gudykunst, W. B. (2004). *Bridging differences: Effective intergroup communication* (4th ed.) Thousand Oaks, CA: Sage Publications.

Gudykunst, W. B., & Ting-Toomey, S. (1988). *Culture and interpersonal communication.* Newbury Park, CA: Sage Publications.

Gudykunst, W. B., Ting-Toomey, S., Sudweeks, S., & Stewart, L. P. (1995) *Building bridges: Interpersonal skills for a changing world.* Boston: Houghton Mifflin Company.

Guerrero, L. K., & Afifi, W. A. (1995). Some things are better left unsaid: Topic avoidance in family relationships. *Communication Quarterly, 43,* 276–296.

Guerrero, L. K., Andersen, P. A., & Afifi, W. A. (2007). *Close encounters: Communication in relationships.* Los Angeles, CA: Sage Publications.

Guerrero, L. K., Farinelli, L., & McEwan, B. (2009). Attachment and relational satisfaction: The mediating effect of emotional communication. *Communication Monographs, 76*(4), 487–514.

Guerrero, L. K., & Floyd, K. (2006). *Nonverbal communication in close relationships.* Mahwah, NJ: Lawrence Erlbaum Associates.

Guerrero, L. K., La Valley, A. G., & Farinelli, L. (2008). The experience and expression of anger, guilt, and sadness in marriage: An equity theory explanation. *Journal of Social & Personal Relationships, 25*(5), 699–724.

Hall, E. T. (1959). *The silent language.* New York: Doubleday.

Hall, E. T. (1976). *Beyond culture.* New York: Anchor/Doubleday.

Hall, E. T., & Hall, M. R. (1990). *Understanding cultural differences: Germans, French, and Americans.* Yarmouth, Maine: Intercultural Press, Inc.

Hall, J. A. (1998). How big are nonverbal sex differences? The case of smiling and sensitivity to nonverbal cues. In D. J. Canary & K. Dindia (Eds.), *Sex differences and similarities in communication: Critical essays and empirical investigations of sex and gender in interaction* (pp. 155–178). Mahwah, NJ: Erlbaum.

Hall, J. A., Carter, J. D., & Hogan, T. G. (2000). Gender differences in nonverbal communication of emotion. In A. H. Fischer (Ed.), *Gender and emotion: Social psychological perspectives* (pp. 97–117). Cambridge: Cambridge University Press, 2000.

Hallsten, L., Voss, M., Stark, S., & Josephson, M. (2011). Job burnout and job wornout as risk factors for long-term sickness absence. *Work, 38*(2), 181–192.

Hample, D. (1987). Communication and the unconscious. In B. Dervin & M. J. Voight (Eds.), *Progress in communication sciences* (Vol. 8, pp. 83–121). Norwood, NJ: Ablex.

Han, B., & Cai, D. (2010). Face goals in apology: A cross-cultural comparison of Chinese and U.S. Americans. *Journal of Asian Pacific Communication, 20*(1), 101–123.

Hansen, H. V. (2002). The straw thing of fallacy theory: The standard definition of "fallacy." *Argumentation, 16,* 133–155.

Hardaker, C. (2010). Trolling in asynchronous computer-mediated communication: From user discussions to academic definitions. *Journal of Politeness Research: Language, Behaviour, Culture, 6*(2), 215–242.

Hare, B. (2010, March 2). Roger Ebert debuts his "new voice" on "Oprah." *CNN.com.* Retrieved from http://articles.cnn.com/2010-03-02/entertainment/roger.ebert.oprah_1_roger-ebert-text-to-speech-software-voice?_s=PM:SHOWBIZ

Harford, T. (2007, February 3). If telecommuting is so easy, why do we travel for work more than ever? *Slate.* Retrieved from http://www.slate.com/id/2158571

Harmon, A. H., Metaxas, P. T. (2010). *How to create a smart mob: Understanding a social network capital.* Unpublished manuscript, Wellesley College. Retrieved from http://cs.wellesley.edu/~pmetaxas/How-to-create-Smart-Mobs%20eDem2010.pdf

Harrigan, J. A., & Taing, K. T. (1997). Fooled by a smile: Detecting anxiety in others. *Journal of Nonverbal Behavior, 21,* 203–221.

Harris, T. E. (2002). *Applied organizational communication: Principles and pragmatics for future practice* (2nd ed.). Mahwah, NJ: Erlbaum.

Hartnett, S. J. (2010). Communication, social justice, and joyful commitment. *Western Journal of Communication, 74*(1), 68–93.

Hartup, W. W., & Stevens, N. (1997). Friendships and adaptation in the life course. *Psychological Bulletin, 121,* 355–370.

Harvey, J. H., Weber, A. L., & Orbuch, T. L. (1990). *Interpersonal accounts: A social psychological perspective.* Cambridge, MA: Blackwell.

Harwood, J. (2000). Communication media use in the grandparent-grandchild relationship. *Journal of Communication, 50*(4), 56–78.

Harwood, J., & Giles, H. (Eds.) (2005). *Intergroup communication: Multiple perspectives.* New York: Peter Lang.

Hauser, C., & O'Connor, A. (2007, April 16). Virginia Tech shooting leaves thirty-three dead. *The New York Times.* Retrieved from http://www.nytimes.com

Hayakawa, S. I. (1964). *Language in thought and action.* New York: Harcourt Brace Jovanovich.

Hazel, M., Wongprasert, T. K., & Ayres, J. (2006). Twins: How similar are fraternal and identical twins across four communication variables? *Journal of the Northwest Communication Association, 35,* 46–59.

Hebdige, D. (1999). The function of subculture. In S. During (Ed.), *The cultural studies reader* (2nd ed., pp. 441–450). New York: Routledge.

Hecht, M. L., Jackson, R. L., II, & Ribeau, S. A. (2003). *African American communication: Exploring identity and culture.* Mahwah, NJ: Erlbaum.

Helgesen, S. (1990). *The female advantage: Women's ways of leadership.* Garden City, NY: Doubleday.

Hemphill, J. K., & Coons, A. E. (1957). Development of the leader behavior description questionnaire. In R. M. Stogdill & A. E. Coons (Eds.), *Leader behavior: Its description and measurement* (pp. 6–38). Columbus: Bureau of Business Research, Ohio State University.

Hendrick, S. S., & Hendrick, C. (1992). *Liking, loving, and relating.* Pacific Grove, CA: Brooks/Cole.

Hendriks, A. (2002). Examining the effects of hegemonic depictions of female bodies on television: A call for theory and programmatic research. *Critical Studies in Media Communication, 19,* 106–123.

Hershatter, A., & Epstein, M. (2010). Millennials and the world of work: An organization and management perspective. *Journal of Business and Psychology, 25*(2), 211–223.

Heslin, R. (1974). *Steps toward a taxonomy of touching.* Paper presented at the Western Psychological Association Convention, Chicago.

Hinckley, D. (2010, March 14). The price of beauty. *NYDailyNews.com.* Retrieved from http://www.nydailynews.com/entertainment/tv/2010/03/14/2010-03-14_vh1s_price_of_beauty_hosted_by_jessica_simpson_is_ditzy_look_at_international_be.html

Hinkle, L. L. (1999). Nonverbal immediacy communication behaviors and liking in marital relationships. *Communication Research Reports, 16,* 81–90.

Hirokawa, R. Y., Gouran, D. S., & Martz, A. E. (1988). Understanding the sources of faulty group decision-making: A lesson from the *Challenger* disaster. *Small Group Behavior, 19,* 411–433.

Hockenbury, D. H., & Hockenbury, S. E. (2002). *Psychology* (3rd ed.). New York: Worth.

Hoeken, H., Van den Brandt, C., Crijns, R., Domínguez, N., Hendriks, B., Planken, B., & Starren, M. (2003). International advertising in Western Europe: Should differences in uncertainty avoidance be considered when advertising in Belgium, France, the Netherlands and Spain? *Journal of Business Communication, 40*(3), 195–218.

Hoffman, L. R., & Maier, N. R. F. (1964). Valence in the adoption of solutions by problem-solving groups: Concept, method, and results. *Journal of Abnormal and Social Psychology, 69,* 264–271.

Hofstede, G. (1984). *Culture's consequences: International differences in work-related values.* Beverly Hills, CA: Sage Publications.

Hofstede, G. (2001). *Culture's consequences: Comparing values, behaviors, institutions, and organizations across nations.* Thousand Oaks, CA: Sage Publications.

Holland, K. (2006, December 3). Under new management: When work time isn't face time. *The New York Times.* Retrieved from http://www.nytimes.com

Holson, L. M. (2008, March 9). Text generation gap: U r 2 old (jk). *The New York Times.* Retrieved from http://www.nytimes.com/2008/03/09/business/09cell.html

Holson, L. M. (2010, May 8). Tell-all generation learns to keep things offline. *The New York Times,* p. A1.

Homer, P. M. (2006). Relationships among ad-induced affect, beliefs, and attitudes: Another look. *Journal of Advertising, 35,* 35–51.

Hoover, K. (2006, February). Alumni to know: He brought Trader Joe's to Main Street. *Stanford Business Magazine.* Retrieved from http://www.gsb.stanford/edu

Horn, J. (2010, October 31). The production: How *The King's Speech* found its voice. *Los Angeles Times.* Retrieved from http://articles.latimes.com/2010/oct/31/entertainment/la-ca-sneaks-kings-speech-20101031

Horwitz, A. V., & White, H. R. (1998). The relationship of cohabitation and mental health: A study of a young adult cohort. *Journal of Marriage and the Family, 60,* 505–514.

Hott, L., & Garey, D. (2007, March). *Through deaf eyes* [Television documentary]. Washington, DC: WETA.

Howard, D. L. (2004, August 2). Silencing Huck Finn. *The Chronicle of Higher Education.* Retrieved from http://chronicle.com/jobs/2004/08/2004080201c.htm

Howe, N. & Strauss, W. (1992). *Generations: The history of America's future, 1584 to 2069.* New York: Quill.

Husband, C. (2009). Between listening and understanding. *Continuum: Journal of Media & Cultural Studies, 23*(4), 441–443.

Huston, A., & Wright, J. C. (1998). Television and the informational and educational needs of children. *The Annals of the American Academy of Political and Social Science, 557*(1), 9–23.

Iedema, R., Jorm, C., Wakefield, J., Ryan, C., & Sorensen, R. (2009). A new structure of attention? Open disclosure of adverse events to patients and their families. *Journal of Language & Social Psychology, 28*(2), 139–157.

Infante, D. A. (1988). *Arguing constructively.* Prospect Heights, IL: Waveland Press.

Ivy, D., & Backlund, P. (2004). *Gender speak: Personal effectiveness in gender communication* (3rd ed.). New York: McGraw-Hill.

Jablin, F. M. (2001). Organizational entry, assimilation, and disengagement/exit. In F. M. Jablin & L. L. Putnam (Eds.), *The new handbook of organizational communication: Advances in theory, research, and methods* (pp. 732–818). Thousand Oaks, CA: Sage Publications.

Jackson, D. (2006, January 29). State of the Union address: A meshing of many ideas. *USA Today.* Retrieved from http://www.usatoday.com/news/washington/2006-01-29-sotu-speech_x.htm?POE=click-refer

Jacobs, C. D., and Heracleous, L. (2006). Constructing shared understanding: The role of embodied metaphors in organization development. *Journal of Applied Behavioral Science, 42,* 207–227.

Jacobs, T. O. (1970). *Leadership and exchange in formal organizations.* Alexandria, VA: Human Resources Research Organization.

James, C. H., and Minnis, W. C. (2004, July–August). Organizational storytelling: It makes sense. *Business Horizons,* 23–32.

Janis, I. L. (1982). *Groupthink: Psychological studies of policy decisions and fiascoes* (2nd ed.). Boston: Houghton Mifflin.

Janusik, L. (2005). Conversational listening span: A proposed measure of conversational listening. *International Journal of Listening, 19,* 12–28.

Janusik, L. A., & Wolvin, A. D. (2009). 24 hours in a day: A listening update to the time studies. *International Journal of Listening, 23*(2), 104–120.

Jay, T., & Janschewitz, K. (2008). The pragmatics of swearing. *Journal of Politeness Research: Language, Behavior, Culture, 4*(2), 267–288.

Jin, B., & Oh, S. (2010). Cultural differences of social network influence on romantic relationships: A comparison of the United States and South Korea. *Communication Studies, 61*(2), 156–171.

Johannesen, R. L. (1996). *Ethics in human communication.* Prospect Heights, IL: Waveland Press.

Johnson, A., Williams, P., Jansing, C., & Stewart, A. (2007, April 17). Worst U.S. shooting ever kills 33 on Va. campus. *MSNBC News.* Retrieved from http://www.msnbc.msn.com/id/18134671

Johnson, I. W., Pearce, C. G., Tuten, T. L., & Sinclair, L. (2003). Self-imposed silence and perceived listening effectiveness. *Business Communication Quarterly, 66*(2), 23–45.

Johnson, S., Bettenhausen, K., & Gibbons, E. (2009). Realities of working in virtual teams: Affective and attitudinal outcomes of using computer-mediated communication. *Small Group Research, 40*(6), 623–649.

Johnson, T. (2010, April 19). Land that job: What interviewers really want you to ask them. *Good Morning America.* Retrieved from http://abcnews.go.com/GMA/JobClub/questions-job-interview/story?id=10409243

John-Steiner, V. (1997). *Notebooks of the mind: Explorations of thinking.* New York: Oxford University Press.

Johnston, M. K., Weaver, J. B., Watson, K. W., & Barker, L. B. (2000). Listening styles: Biological or psychological differences? *International Journal of Listening, 14,* 32–46.

Jolie, A. (2009, June 18). Angelina Jolie speaks on World Refugee Day. Video retrieved from http://www.youtube.com/user/AngelinaJolieUNHCR#p/u/87/qtt1Vs9Lcp0. Quote begins at 0:20 and ends at 1:00.

Jones, C. (2005, May 16). Gay marriage debate still fierce one year later. *USA Today.* Retrieved from http://www.usatoday.com/news/nation/2005-05-16-gay-marriage_x.htm

Jones, D. (2004, November 30). Best friends good for business. *USA Today.* Retrieved May 10, 2008, from http://www.usatoday.com/money/workplace/2004=/=30=best=friends_x.htm

Jones, E. E. (1990). *Interpersonal perception.* New York: Freeman.

Joyce, M. P. (2008). Interviewing techniques used in selected organizations today. *Business Communication Quarterly, 71*(3), 376–380.

Kalbfleisch, P. J. (2002). Communicating in mentoring relationships: A theory for enactment. *Communication Theory, 12,* 63–69.

Kanter, R. M. (2009). *Supercorp: How vanguard companies create innovation, profits, growth, and social good.* New York: Crown Business.

Kaplan-Leiserson, E. (2005, June). Trend: Podcasting in academic and corporate learning. *Learning Circuits.* Retrieved from http://www.learningcircuits.org/2005/jun2005/0506_trends

Kato, S., Kato, Y., & Scott, D. (2009). Relationships between emotional states and emoticons in mobile phone email communication in Japan. *International Journal on E-Learning, 8*(3), 385–401.

Katzenbach, J. R., & Smith, D. K. (1993). *The wisdom of teams.* Boston: Harvard Business School Press.

Keaten, J. A., & Kelly, L. (2008). "Re: We really need to talk": Affect for communication channels, competence, and fear of negative evaluation. *Communication Quarterly, 56*(4), 407–426.

Kennedy, R. (2003). *Nigger: The strange career of a troublesome word.* New York: Vintage Books.

Kenrick, D. T., Griskevicius, V., Neuberg, S. L., & Schaller, M. (2010). Renovating the pyramid of needs: Contemporary extensions built upon ancient foundations. *Perspectives on Psychological Science, 5*(3), 292–314.

Keyton, J., Ferguson, P., & Rhodes, S. C. (2001). Cultural indicators of sexual harassment. *Southern Communication Journal, 67,* 33–50.

Kiesling, S. F. (1998). Men's identities and sociolinguistic variation: The case of fraternity men. *Journal of Sociolinguistics, 2*(1), 69–99.

Kline, S., Horton, B., & Zhang, S. (2005). *How we think, feel, and express love: A cross-cultural comparison between American and East Asian cultures.* Paper presented at the annual meeting of the International Communication Association, New York.

Klocke, U. (2007). How to improve decision making in small groups: Effects of dissent and training interventions. *Small Group Research, 38,* 437–468.

Knapp, M. L., & Hall, J. A. (2010). *Nonverbal communication in human interaction.* Boston, MA: Wadsworth, Cengage Learning.

Knapp, M. L., Hart, R. P., Friedrich, G. W., & Shulman, G. M. (1973). The rhetoric of goodbye: Verbal and nonverbal correlates of human leave-taking. *Communication Monographs, 40,* 182–198.

Knapp, M. L., & Vangelisti, A. (2000). *Interpersonal communication and human relationships* (4th ed.). Newton, MA: Allyn & Bacon.

Knapp, M. L., & Vangelisti, A. L. (2008). *Interpersonal communication and human relationships.* Boston: Allyn and Bacon.

Knobloch, L. K., & Solomon, D. H. (2002). Information seeking beyond initial interaction: Negotiating relational uncertainty within close relationships. *Human Communication Research, 28,* 243–257.

Kohut, A. (2007, May 9). Are Americans ready to elect a female president? *Pew Research Center Publications.* Retrieved from http://pewresearch.org/pubs/474/female-president

Kotlowitz, A. (2008, May 4). Blocking the transmission of violence. *The New York Times Magazine.* Retrieved from http://www.nytimes.com

Kowitz, A. C., & Knutson, T. J. (1980). *Decision making in small groups: The search for alternatives.* Needham Heights, MA: Allyn & Bacon.

Kram, K. E. (1983). Phases of the mentor relationship. *Academy of Management Journal, 12,* 608–625.

Kramer, M. W., & Pier, P. M. (1999). Students' perceptions of effective and ineffective communication by college teachers. *Southern Communication Journal, 65,* 16–33.

Kraybill, D. B. (2007, October 6). Shunning: It's tough love for the Amish. *Winston-Salem Journal.* Retrieved from http://www.journalnow.com

Krayer, K. (2010). *Influencing skills for effective leadership.* Dallas: University of Dallas College of Business.

Krcmar, M., & Greene, K. (1999). Predicting exposure to and uses of television violence. *Journal of Communication, 49,* 24–46.

Kruglanski, A. W., Chen, X., Pierro, A., Mannetti, L., Erb, H.-P., & Spiegel, S. (2006). Persuasion according to the unimodel: Implications for cancer communication. *Journal of Communication, 56,* 105–122.

Krumhuber, E., Manstead, A., Cosker, D., Marshall, D., & Rosin, P. (2009). Effects of dynamic attributes of smiles in human and synthetic faces: A simulated job interview setting. *Journal of Nonverbal Behavior, 33*(1), 1–15.

Kuhn, T., & Poole, M. S. (2000). Do conflict management styles affect group decision making? Evidence from a longitudinal field study. *Human Communication Research, 26,* 558–590.

Kuo, F., & Yu, C. (2009). An exploratory study of trust dynamics in work-oriented virtual teams. *Journal of Computer-Mediated Communication, 14*(4), 823–854.

Kurdek, L. (1989). Relationship quality of gay and lesbian cohabiting couples. *Journal of Homosexuality, 15*(3–4), 93–118.

Kutcher, A. (2010, December 8). Has texting killed romance? *Harper's Bazaar.* Retrieved from http://www.harpersbazaar.com/magazine/feature-articles/ashton-kutcher-relationships-interview-0111

La Ferla, R. (2009, August 6). An everywoman as beauty queen. *The New York Times,* p. E1.

Landau, D. (2003, September). Changing the blame game: Attributional retraining as a conflict intervention. *Mediate.com.* Retrieved from http://www.mediate.com/articles/landauD.cfm

Landis, D., Bennett, J. M., and Bennett, M. J. (Eds.). (2004). *Handbook of intercultural training.* Thousand Oaks, CA: Sage Publications.

Landsford, J. E., Antonucci, T. C., Akiyama, H., & Takahashi, K. (2005). A quantitative and qualitative approach to social relationships and well-being in the United States and Japan. *Journal of Comparative Family Studies, 36,* 1–22.

Larkey, L., & Hecht, M. (2010). A model of effects of narrative as culture-centric health promotion. *Journal of Health Communication, 15*(2), 114–135.

Lawson, A. E., & Daniel, E. S. (2010). Inferences of clinical diagnostic reasoning and diagnostic error. *Journal of Biomedical Informatics, 43*(5), 563–574.

le Roux, M. (2006, November 27). Let's talk about sex: Cult South African director shatters taboos. *Namibian.* Retrieved from http://www.namibian.com.na/2006/November/africa/065E8B0EB5.html

Leal, S., & Vrij, A. (2008). Blinking during and after lying. *Journal of Nonverbal Behavior, 32*(4), 187–194.

Leathers, D. (1986). *Successful nonverbal communication: Principles and applications.* New York: Macmillan.

Leavitt, H. J. (1951). Some effects of certain communication patterns on group performance. *Journal of Abnormal and Social Psychology, 46,* 38–50.

Lebo, B. (2009). Employing millennials: Challenges and opportunities. *New Hampshire Business Review, 31*(26), 21.

Ledbetter, A. M. (2008). Chronemic cues and sex differences in relational e-mail: Perceiving immediacy and supportive message quality. *Social Science Computer Review, 26*(4), 486–482.

Lee, E-J. (2007). Effects of gendered language on gender stereotyping in computer-mediated communication: The moderating role of depersonalization and gender-role orientation. *Human Communication Research, 33*(4), 515–535.

Lee, J. A. (1973). *The colors of love: An exploration of the ways of loving.* Don Mills, Ontario, Canada: New Press.

Leland, J. (2008, October 7). In "sweetie" and "dear," a hurt for the elderly. *The New York Times,* p. A1.

Lemonick, M. (2007, May 3). The *Time* 100: Neil deGrasse Tyson. *Time.* Retrieved from www.time.com/time/specials/2007/time100

Lenhart, A. (2010, Sept. 2). Cell phones and American adults. Pew Internet and American Life Project. Retrieved from http://www.pewinternet.org

Lewis, L. (2005). Foster a loyal workforce. In *Trader Joe's adventure: Turning a unique approach to business into a retail and cultural phenomenon* (pp. 137–152). New York: Dearborn/Kaplan.

Lewis, L. F. (2010). Group support systems: Overview and guided tour. *Handbook of Group Decision and Negotiation: Advances in Group Decision and Negotiation, 4*(3), 249–268.

Lewis, T., & Manusov, V. (2009). Listening to another's distress in everyday relationships. *Communication Quarterly, 57*(3), 282–301.

Ligos, M. (2001, June 20). Getting over the fear-of-speaking hump. *The New York Times.* Retrieved from http://www.nytimes.com

Lim, G. Y., & Roloff, M. E. (1999). Attributing sexual consent. *Journal of Applied Communication Research, 27,* 1–23.

Lincoln, A. (1842, February 22). Temperance address. *Repeat After Us.* Retrieved August 14, 2007, from http://www.repeatafterus.com/title.php?i=9700

Lindsley, S. L. (1999). Communication and "the Mexican way": Stability and trust as core symbols in *maquiladoras. Western Journal of Communication, 63,* 1–31.

Lipari, L. (2009). Listening otherwise: The voice of ethics. *International Journal of Listening, 23*(1), 44–59.

Lipman, A. (1986). Homosexual relationships. *Generations, 10* (4), 51–54.

Lira, E., Ripoll, P., Peiró, J., & Orengo, V. (2008). How do different types of intragroup conflict affect group potency in virtual compared with face-to-face teams? A longitudinal study. *Behaviour & Information Technology, 27*(2), 107–114.

Lithwick, D. (2009, April 21). Search me: The Supreme Court is neither hot nor bothered by strip searches. *Slate.* Retrieved from http://www.slate.com/id/2216608

Loden, M., & Rosener, J. B. (1991). *Workforce America! Managing employee diversity as a vital resource.* Chicago: Business One Irwin.

Lohr, S. (2007, October 31). Hello, India? I need help with my math. *The New York Times.* Retrieved from http://www.nytimes.com

Longley, R. (2007). From time to time: The State of the Union. *About.com: U.S. government info.* Retrieved December 31, 2007, from http://usgovinfo.about.com/od/thepresidentandcabinet/a/souhistory.htm

Longman, J. (2010, June 15). World Cup's incessant drone will stay for now. *The New York Times,* p. B12.

Lubell, S. (2004, February 19). On the therapist's couch, a jolt of virtual reality. *The New York Times.* Retrieved from http://www.nytimes.com

Luo, M. (2010, March 29). Overqualified? Yes, but happy to have a job. *The New York Times,* p. A1.

Lustig, M. W., & Koester, J. (1993). *Intercultural competence: Interpersonal communication across cultures.* New York: HarperCollins.

Lustig, M. W., & Koester, J. (2006). *Intercultural competence: Interpersonal communication across cultures* (5th ed.). Boston: Allyn & Bacon.

Lutz, C. A. (1996). Engendered emotion: Gender, power, and the rhetoric of emotional control in American discourse. In R. Harre & W. G. Parrott (Eds.), *The emotions: Social, cultural and biological dimensions* (pp. 132–150). Thousand Oaks, CA: Sage Publications.

Lyall, S. (2009, April 17). Unlikely singer is YouTube sensation. *The New York Times.* Retrieved from http://www.nytimes.com/2009/04/18/arts/television/18boyle.html

Maag, C. (2007a, November 28). A hoax turned fatal draws anger but no charges. *The New York Times.* Retrieved from http://www.nytimes.com

Maag, C. (2007b, December 16). When the bullies turned faceless. *The New York Times.* Retrieved from http://www.nytimes.com

Madden, M., & Smith, A. (2010, May 26). Reputation management and social media. *Pew Internet & American Life Project.* Retrieved from http://www.pewinternet.org/Reports/2010/Reputation-Management.aspx

Madlock, P. E., & Kennedy-Lightsey, C. (2010). The effects of supervisors' verbal aggressiveness and mentoring on their subordinates. *Journal of Business Communication, 47*(1), 42–62.

Maguire, K. C. (2007). "Will it ever end?": A (re)examination of uncertainty in college student long-distance dating relationships. *Communication Quarterly, 55*(4), 415–432.

Maguire, K. C., & Kinney, T. A. (2010). When distance is problematic: Communication, coping, and relational satisfaction in female college students' long-distance dating relationships. *Journal of Applied Communication Research, 38*(1), 27–46.

Mansson, D. H., Myers, S. A., & Turner, L. H. (2010). Relational maintenance behaviors in the grandchild-grandparent relationship. *Communication Research Reports, 27*(1), 68–79.

Manusov, V. & Patterson, M. L. (2006). *The Sage handbook of nonverbal communication.* Thousand Oaks, CA: Sage Publications, Inc.

Marcott, A. (2009, August 14). Four Sloanies take on a *Daily Show* correspondent. *Slice of M.I.T.* Retrieved from http://alum.mit.edu/pages/sliceofmit/2009/08/14/sloanies-on-daily-show/

Martinez, E. (2010, March 26). Alexis Pilkington brutally cyber bullied, even after her suicide. *CBS News.* Retrieved from http://www.cbsnews.com/8301-504083_162-20001181-504083.html

Maslach, C. (1982). *Burnout: The cost of caring.* Englewood Cliffs, NJ: Prentice Hall.

Maslow, A. *Motivation and personality.* New York: Harper & Row, 1954.

Mast, M. S. (2002). Dominance as expressed and inferred through speaking time. *Human Communication Research, 28,* 420–450.

Matsumoto, D. (1989). Cultural influences on the perception of emotion. *Journal of Cross-Cultural Psychology, 20*(1), 92–105.

Mayer, R. E. (2001). *Multimedia learning.* New York: Cambridge University Press.

Mayo Clinic. (2006, June 1). Work-life balance: Ways to restore harmony and reduce stress. Retrieved May 10, 2008, from http://www.mayoclinic.com/health/work-life-balance/WL00056

McCain, J. S. (2008, January 28). John McCain, prisoner of war: A first person account. *U.S. News & World Report.* Retrieved from http://politics.usnews.com/news/articles/2008/01/28/john-mccain-prisoner-of-war-a-first-person-account.html

McClanahan, A. (2006, March 9). What does a feminist "look" like? *Pocono Record.* Retrieved April 8, 2008, from http://www.poconorecord.com

McClintock, E. A. (2010). When does race matter? Race, sex, and dating at an elite university. *Journal of Marriage & Family, 72*(1), 45–72.

McConnell, M. (1987). *Challenger: A major malfunction.* Garden City, NY: Doubleday.

McCroskey, J. C. (1977). Oral communication apprehension: A summary of recent theory and research. *Human Communication Research, 4,* 78–96.

McCroskey, J. C. (1982). *An introduction to rhetorical communication* (4th ed.). Englewood Cliffs, NJ: Prentice Hall.

McCroskey, J. C. (1997). The communication apprehension perspective. In J. A. Daly & J. C. McCroskey (Eds.), *Avoiding communication: Shyness, reticence, and communication apprehension* (pp. 13–38). Cresskill, NJ: Hampton Press.

McCroskey, J. C., & Teven, J. J. (1999). Goodwill: A reexamination of the construct and its measurement. *Communication Monographs, 66,* 90–103.

McDaniel, E., & Andersen, P. A. (1998). International patterns of interpersonal tactile communication: A field study. *Journal of Nonverbal Behavior, 22,* 59–75.

McGinn, M. M., McFarland, P. T., & Christensen, A. (2009). Antecedents and consequences of demand/withdraw. *Journal of Family Psychology, 23*(5), 749–757.

McGroarty, P. (2011, March 1). German minister resigns over plagiarism scandal. *The Wall Street Journal Online.* Retrieved from http://online.wsj.com/article/SB100014240527487045060045761739707650 20528.html

McLean, C. (2011, January 24). *Glee*: The making of a musical phenomenon. *The Telegraph.* Retrieved from http://www.telegraph.co.uk/culture/8271318/Glee-the-making-of-a-musical-phenomenon.html

McLeod, D. N., Detenber, B. H., & Eveland, W. P., Jr. (2001). Behind the third-person effect: Differentiating perceptual processes for self and other. *Journal of Communication, 51,* 678–695.

Mehrabian, A. (1971). *Silent messages.* Belmont, CA: Wadsworth.

Mello, B. (2009). For k-12 educators: Speaking, listening, and media literacy standards. *Spectra, 45*(3), 11.

Memmot, C. (2006, April 24). *Opal Mehta* author apologizes. *USA Today.* Retrieved from http://www.usatoday.com

Men's secret language. (2010). Retrieved from http://www.allstocks.com/fun/html/men_s_secret_language.html

Merkin, R. S. (2009). Cross-cultural communication patterns—Korean and American communication. *Journal of Intercultural Communication, 20,* 5.

Merolla, A. J. (2010a). Relational maintenance and noncopresence reconsidered: Conceptualizing geographic separation in close relationships. *Communication Theory, 20*(2), 169–193.

Merolla, A. J. (2010b). Relational maintenance during military deployment: Perspectives of wives of deployed U.S. soldiers. *Journal of Applied Communication Research, 38*(1), 4–26.

Meyer, J. C. (1995). Tell me a story: Eliciting organizational values from narratives. *Communication Quarterly, 43,* 210–224.

Microsoft, Inc. (2005, March 15). Survey finds workers average only three productive days per week [Press release]. Retrieved April 30, 2008, from http://www.microsoft.com

Miczo, N. (2008). Dependence and independence power, conflict tactics and appraisals in romantic relationships. *Journal of Communication Studies, 1*(1), 56–82.

Mignerey, J. T., Rubin, R. B., & Gorden, W. I. (1995). Organizational entry: An investigation of newcomer communication behavior and uncertainty. *Communication Research, 22,* 54–85.

Miller, C. W., & Roloff, M. E. (2007). The effect of face loss on willingness to confront hurtful messages from romantic partners. *Southern Communication Journal, 72*(3), 247–263.

Miller, D. T., & Morrison, K. R. (2009). Expressing deviant opinions: Believing you are in the majority helps. *Journal of Experimental Social Psychology, 45*(4), 740–747.

Miller, K. (2009). *Organizational communication: Approaches and processes* (5th ed.). Boston: Wadsworth.

Miller, L. C., Cooke, K. K., Tsang, J., & Morgan, F. (1992). Should I brag? Nature and impact of positive boastful disclosures for women and men. *Human Communication Research, 18,* 364–399.

Miller, R. (1991, January 31). Personnel execs reveal the truth about job applicants. *Dallas Morning News,* p. 2D.

Moeller, S., Crocker, J., & Bushman, B. J. (2009). Creating hostility and conflict: Effects of entitlement and self-image goals. *Journal of Experimental Social Psychology, 45*(2), 448–452.

Molloy, J. T. (1983). *Molloy's live for success.* New York: Bantam Books.

Money is the top subject for marital spats. (2006, March 20). *Webindia123.com.* Retrieved May 1, 2006, from http://news.webindia123.com/news/ar_showdetails.asp?id=603200038&cat=&n_date=20060320

Monge, P. (1977). The systems perspective as a theoretical basis for the study of human communication. *Communication Quarterly, 25,* 19–29.

Montana Meth Project. (2007). Retrieved August 1, 2007, from http://www.montanameth.com

Montepare, J., Koff, E., Zaitchik, D., & Alberet, M. (1999). The use of body movements and gestures as cues to emotions in younger and older adults. *Journal of Nonverbal Behavior, 23,* 133–152.

Montoya, M., Massey, A., Hung, Y., & Crisp, C. (2009). Can you hear me now? Communication in virtual product development teams. *Journal of Product Innovation Management, 26*(2), 139–155.

Moran, B. (2003, November 18). She explores the world of language and thought. *The Boston Globe,* p. C2.

Moreland, R. L., & Levine, J. M., (1994). *Understanding small groups.* Boston: Allyn & Bacon.

Morris, D. (1977). *Manwatching.* New York: Abrams.

Morry, M. M. (2005). Relationship satisfaction as a predictor of similarity ratings: A test of the attraction-similarity hypothesis. *Journal of Social and Personal Relationships, 22,* 561–584.

Morzy, M. (2009). On mining and social role discovery in Internet forums. *Social Informatics,* 74–79. Retrieved from http://www.cs.put.poznan.pl/mmorzy/papers/socinfo09.pdf

Motley, M. T. (1990). On whether one can(not) communicate: An examination via traditional communication postulates. *Western Journal of Speech Communication, 56,* 1–20.

Motley, M. T., & Reeder, H. M. (1995). Unwanted escalation of sexual intimacy: Male and female perceptions of connotations and relational consequences of resistance messages. *Communication Monographs, 62,* 355–382.

Mouawad, J., & Krauss, C. (2010, June 4). Another torrent BP works to stem: Its CEO. *The New York Times,* p. A1.

Moutot, M. (2010, October 4). Lessons beamed from Afghanistan for future U.S. officers. *AFP.* Retrieved from http://www.google.com/hostednews/afp/article/ALeqM5hKxe8qqw2FvZs7IHNtyIjo4amCVw?docId=CNG.b5ed066c5c7b913aee54b25ac349f1b0.621

Muir, C. (2008). Job interviewing. *Business Communication Quarterly, 71*(3), 374–376.

Mulac, A. (1998). The gender-linked language effect: Do language differences really make a difference? In D. J. Canary & K. Dindia (Eds.), *Sex differences and similarities in communication: Critical essays and empirical investigations of sex and gender in interaction* (pp. 127–153). Mahwah, NJ: Erlbaum.

Mulac, A. J., Wiemann, J. M., Widenmann, S. J., & Gibson, T. W. (1988). Male-female language differences and effects in same-sex and mixed-sex dyads: The gender-linked language effect. *Communication Monographs, 55,* 315–335.

Mulanax, A., & Powers, W. (2001). Listening fidelity development and relationship to receiver apprehension and locus of control. *International Journal of Listening, 15,* 69–78.

Mumby, D. (2000). Communication, organization, and the public sphere: A feminist perspective. In P. Buzzanell (Ed.), *Rethinking organizational and managerial communication from feminist perspectives* (pp. 3–23). Thousand Oaks, CA: Sage Publications.

Mungazi, F.(2009, June 19). In defense of the vuvuzela. *BBC Sport.* Retrieved from http://news.bbc.co.uk/sport2/hi/football/africa/8108691.stm

Muntigl, P., & Choi, K. T. (2010). Not remembering as a practical epistemic resource in couples therapy. *Discourse Studies, 12*(3), 331–356.

Murphy, D. R., Daneman, M., & Schneider, B. A. (2006). Do older adults have difficulty following conversations? *Psychology and Aging, 21,* 49–61.

Nagel, L., Blignaut, A. S., & Cronje, J. C. (2009). Read-only participants: A case for student communication in online classes. *Interactive Learning Environments, 17*(1), 37–51.

National Organization for Women. (2006, March 2). *Sexual harassment remains serious problem on campus.* Retrieved May 14, 2008, from http://www.now.org/issues/harass/030206aauwreport.html

Naughton, K., & Peyser, M. (2004, March 1). The world according to Trump. *Newsweek,* pp. 48–57.

Nelson, B. (2002). Making teamwork work. *ABA Bank Marketing, 34,* 10.

Nelson, J. (2011, January 5). Do word changes alter "Huckleberry Finn"? *The New York Times.* Retrieved from http://www.nytimes.com/roomfordebate/2011/01/05/does-one-word-change-huckleberry-finn

Nelson, K. (2009, November 8). Hideki Matsui's most valuable translator gets key to the city. *New York*

Daily News. Retrieved from http://articles.nydailynews. com/2009-11-08/local/17938517_1_roger-kahlon-hideki-matsui-japan

Newcomb, A. F., & Bagwell, C. L. (1995). Children's friendship relations: A metaanalytic review. *Psychological Bulletin, 117,* 306–347.

Newman, M. L., Groom, C. J., Handelman, L. D., & Pennebaker, J. W. (2008). Gender differences in language use: An analysis of 14,000 text samples. *Discourse Processes, 45*(3), 211–236.

Nicholas, S. (2009). "I live Hopi, I just don't speak it"—The critical intersection of language, culture, and identity in the lives of contemporary Hopi youth. *Journal of Language, Identity & Education, 8*(5), 321–334.

Nichols, R. G. (2006). The struggle to be human: Keynote address to first International Listening Association convention, February 17, 1980. *International Journal of Listening, 20,* 4–12.

Nichols, R. G., Brown, J. I., & Keller, R. J. (2006). Measurement of communication skills. *International Journal of Listening, 20,* 13–17.

Nicotera, A. M. (1997). Managing conflict communication groups. In L. R. Frey & J. K. Barge (Eds.), *Managing group life: Communicating in decision-making groups* (pp. 104–130). Boston: Houghton Mifflin.

Nierenberg, R. (2009). *Maestro: A surprising story about leadership by listening.* New York: Portfolio.

No wrong answer: Click it. (2005, May 14). *Wired.* Retrieved from http://www.wired.com/culture/lifestyle/news/2005/05/67530

Nomani, A. Q. (2005, December 14). Tapping Islam's feminist roots. *The Washington Post.* Retrieved March 7, 2008, from http://www.seattletimes.nwsource.com

O'Brian, L. (2010, September 30). Facebook fakery: The alternate reality of Aaron Sorkin's *The Social Network.* Retrieved from http://www.slate.com

O'Hair, D., & Cody, M. (1994). Deception. In W. R. Cupach & B. H. Spitzberg (Eds.), *The dark side of interpersonal communication* (pp. 181–213). Hillsdale, NJ: Erlbaum.

O'Hair, D., Friedrich, G. W., & Dixon, L. D. (2002). *Strategic communication in business and the professions* (4th ed.). Boston: Houghton Mifflin.

O'Hair, D., Friedrich, G. W., & Dixon, L. D. (2007). *Strategic communication in business and the professions* (6th ed.). Boston: Houghton Mifflin.

O'Hair, D., & Krayer, K. (1987). *A conversational analysis of reconciliation strategies.* Paper presented at the Western Speech Communication Association, Salt Lake City.

O'Hair, D., O'Rourke, J., & O'Hair, M. J. (2000). *Business communication: A framework for success.* Cincinnati, OH: South-Western.

O'Hair, D., & Stewart, R. (1998). *Public speaking: Challenges and choices.* New York: Bedford/St. Martin's.

O'Hair, D., Stewart, R., & Rubenstein, H. (2007). *A speaker's guidebook* (3rd ed.). New York: Bedford/St. Martin's.

O'Hair, D., Stewart, R., & Rubenstein, H. (2010). *A speaker's guidebook: Text and reference* (4th ed.). New York: Bedford/St. Martin's.

O'Keefe, D. J. (1999). How to handle opposing arguments in persuasive messages: A meta-analytic review of the effects of one-sided and two-sided messages. In M. E. Roloff (Ed.), *Communication yearbook 22* (pp. 209–249). Thousand Oaks, CA: Sage Publications.

O'Loughlin, J. P. (2010, July 23). Senior HR executive, HR Capital Partners. Personal interview.

100 best companies to work for (2011, February 7). *Fortune.* Retrieved from http://money.cnn.com/magazines/fortune/bestcompanies/2011/index.html

O'Sullivan, P. B. (2000). What you don't know won't hurt me: Impression management functions of communication channels in relationships. *Human Communication Research, 26,* 403–431.

O'Sullivan, P. B., Hunt, S. K., & Lippert, L. R. (2004). Mediated immediacy: A language of affiliation in a technological age. *Journal of Language and Social Psychology, 23,* 464–490.

Oetzel, J. G., & Ting-Toomey, S. (Eds.). (2006). *The Sage handbook of conflict communication: Integrating theory, research, and practice.* Thousand Oaks, CA: Sage Publications.

Office friends: Who needs them? (2005). *Management Today.* Retrieved May 14, 2008, via LexisNexis.

Oliver, J. (2010, February). Jamie Oliver's TED Prize wish: Teach every child about food. Video retrieved from http://www.ted.com/talks/jamie_oliver.html

Olsen, L., & Golish, T. (2002). Topics of conflict and patterns of aggression in romantic relationships. *Southern Communication Journal, 67,* 180–200.

Olson, L. (2004). The role of voice in the (re)construction of a battered woman's identity: An authethnography of one woman's experiences of abuse. *Women's Studies in Communication, 27*(1), 1–33.

Oprah.com. (2008). *Oprah's debt diet.* Retrieved from http://www.oprah.com/packages/oprahs-debt-diet.html

Pagotto, L., Voci, A., & Maculan, V. (2010). The effectiveness of intergroup contact at work: Mediators and moderators of hospital workers' prejudice towards immigrants. *Journal of Community & Applied Social Psychology, 20*(4), 317–330.

Palomares, N. A. (2008). Explaining gender-based language use: Effects of gender identity salience on references to emotion and tentative language in intra- and intergroup contexts. *Human Communication Research, 34*(2), 263–286.

Palomares, N. A. (2009). Women are sort of more tentative than men, aren't they?: How men and women use tentative language differently, similarly, and counterstereotypically as a function of gender salience. *Communication Research, 36*(4), 538–560.

Palomares, N. A., & Lee, E-J. (2010). Virtual gender identity: The linguistic assimilation to gendered avatars in computer-mediated communication. *Journal of Language & Social Psychology, 29*(1), 5–23.

Paolini, S., Harwood, J., & Rubin, M. (2010). Negative intergroup contact makes group members salient: Explaining why intergroup conflict endures. *Personality and Social Psychology Bulletin, 36,* 1723–1738.

Park, C. (2003). In other (people's) words: Plagiarism by university students—literature and lessons. *Assessment and Evaluation in Higher Education, 28,* 471–488.

Park, W. (2000). A comprehensive empirical investigation of the relationships among variables of the groupthink model. *Journal of Organizational Behavior, 21,* 874–887.

Parker-Pope, T. (2010a, April 18). Is marriage good for your health? *The New York Times,* p. MM46.

Parker-Pope, T. (2010b, May 11). The science of a happy marriage. *The New York Times,* p. D1.

Parks, M., & Roberts, L. (1998). "Making MOOsic": The development of personal relationships on line and a comparison of their off-line counterparts. *Journal of Social and Personal Relationships, 15,* 517–537.

Patry, M. W. (2008). Attractive but guilty: Deliberation and the physical attractiveness bias. *Psychological Reports, 102*(3), 727–733.

Patterson, B. R., & O'Hair, D. (1992). Relational reconciliation: Toward a more comprehensive model of relational development. *Communication Research Reports, 9,* 119–127.

Pauley, P. M., & Emmers-Sommer, T. M. (2007). The impact of Internet technologies on primary and secondary romantic relationship development. *Communication Studies, 58*(4), 411–427.

Pavitt, C. (1999). Theorizing about the group communication-leadership relationship. In L. R. Frey, D. S. Gouran, & M. Poole (Eds.), *Handbook of group communication theory and research* (pp. 313–334). Thousand Oaks, CA: Sage Publications.

Pawlowski, D. (1998). Dialectical tensions in marital partners' accounts of their relationships. *Communication Quarterly, 46,* 396–416.

Payne, S. L. (1951). *The art of asking questions.* Princeton, NJ: Princeton University Press.

Pearce, C., & Tuten, T. (2001). Internet recruiting in the banking industry. *Business Communication Quarterly, 64*(1), 9–18.

Pearson, J. C., & Spitzberg, B. H. (1990). *Interpersonal communication: Concepts, components, and contexts* (2nd ed.). Dubuque, IA: Brown.

Pearson, J. C., Turner, L. H., & Todd-Mancillas, W. R. (1991). *Gender and communication* (2nd ed.). Dubuque, IA: Brown.

Peck, J. (2007, December 29). *Top 7 tips for conquering public speaking fear.* Retrieved January 9, 2008, from http://ezinearticles.com/?expert=Jason_Peck

Perception of IT professionals. (2003, April 8). User comment. Retrieved from http://www.geek.com/articles/rants/perception-of-it-professionals-2003048

Perrin, C. (2007, February 27). Jargon good. Buzzwords bad. *Tech Republic.* Retrieved from http://techrepublic.com/blog/geekend/jargon-good-buzzwords-bad/555

Petronio, S. (2000). The boundaries of privacy: Praxis of everyday life. In S. Petronio (Ed.), *Balancing the secrets of private disclosures* (pp. 37–50). Mahwah, NJ: Erlbaum.

Petronio, S. (2002). *The boundaries of privacy: Dialectics of disclosure.* Albany: State University of New York Press.

Petronio, S. (2004). Road to developing communication privacy management theory: Narrative in progress, please stand by. *Journal of Family Communication, 4,* 193–207.

Pettigrew, T. F., & Tropp, L. R. (2006). A meta-analytical test of the intergroup contact theory. *Journal of Personality and Social Psychology, 90,* 751–783.

Petty, R. E., & Cacioppo, J. T. (1986). The Elaboration Likelihood Model of persuasion. In L. Berkowitz (Ed.), *Advances in experimental social psychology* (Vol. 19, pp. 123–205). San Diego, CA: Academic Press.

Petty, R. E., & Wegner, D. T. (1998). Matching versus mismatching attitude functions: Implications for scrutiny of persuasive messages. *Personality and Social Psychology Bulletin, 24*(3), 227–240.

Phanor-Faury, A. (2010, June 24). "Nude" doesn't translate in fashion. *Essence.* Retrieved from http://www.essence.com/fashion_beauty/fashion/nude_dresses_racial_bias_fashion_world.php

Pines, M. (1997). The civilizing of Genie. In L. F. Kasper (Ed.), *Teaching English through the disciplines: Psychology* (2nd ed.). New York: Whittier.

Planalp, S., & Honeycutt, J. (1985). Events that increase uncertainty in personal relationships. *Human Communication Research, 11,* 593–604.

Prager, K. J. (2000). Intimacy in personal relationships. In C. Hendrick & S. S. Hendrick (Eds.), *Close relationships: A sourcebook* (pp. 229–242). Thousand Oaks, CA: Sage Publications.

Pratkanis, A. R., & Aronson, E. (2001). *Age of propaganda: The everyday use and abuse of persuasion.* New York: W. H. Freeman.

Preston, D. R. (1998). Language myth #17: They speak really bad English Down South and in New York City. In L. Bauer & P. Trudgill (Eds.), *Language myths* (pp. 139–149). New York: Penguin Putnam.

Priester, J. R., & Petty, R. E. (1995). Source attributions and persuasion: Perceived honesty as a determinant of message scrutiny. *Personality and Social Psychology Bulletin, 21,* 637–654.

Public speaking. (n.d.). *Compton's online encyclopedia.* Retrieved June 10, 2000, from http://www.comptons.com/encyclopedia

Punyanunt-Carter, N. M. (2005). Father and daughter motives and satisfaction. *Communication Research Reports, 22,* 293–301.

Purdy, M. (2006). Ralph Nichols: A leader in and of his time. *International Journal of Listening, 20,* 20–21.

Quenqua, D. (2007, September 24). Survey finds women own more game consoles than men. *Online Media Daily.* Retrieved from http://www.mediapost.com/publications/?fa=Articles.showArticle&art_aid=67924

Quenqua, D. (2010, March 18). I need to vent. Hello, Facebook. *The New York Times,* p. E1.

Quinn, A. (2008, July 18). Review: *WALL-E:* Out of this world. *The Independent.* Retrieved from http://www.independent.co.uk/arts-entertainment/films/reviews/walle-u-870497.html

Rabinowitz, J. (1995, July 25). *Huckleberry Finn* without fear: Teachers gather to learn how to teach an American classic, in context. *The New York Times.* Retrieved from http://www.query.nytimes.com

Rains, S. A. (2007). The impact of anonymity on perceptions of source credibility and influence in computer-mediated group communication: A test of two competing hypotheses. *Communication Research, 34*(1), 100–125.

Ralston, S. M., Kirkwood, W. G., & Burant, P. A. (2003). Helping interviewees tell their stories. *Business Communication Quarterly, 66,* 8–22.

Ramirez, A., Sunnafrank, M., & Goei, R. (2010). Predicted outcome value theory in ongoing relationships. *Communication Monographs, 77*(1), 27–50.

Rappaport, S. D. (2010). Putting listening to work: The essentials of listening. *Journal of Advertising Research, 50*(1), 30–41.

Rawlins, W. K. (1992). *Friendship matters: Communication, dialectics, and the life course.* Piscataway, NJ: Aldine Transaction.

Rawlins, W. K. (1994). Being there and growing apart: Sustaining friendships during adulthood. In D. J. Canary & L. Stafford (Eds.), *Communication and relational maintenance* (pp. 275–294). New York: Academic Press.

Rawlins, W. K. (2008). *The compass of friendship: Narratives, identities, and dialogues.* Thousand Oaks, CA: Sage Publications.

Ray, R., & Schmitt, J. (2007, May). No-vacation nation. Washington, DC: Center for Economic and Policy Research. Retrieved from http://www.cepr.net

Reaction to the president's speech. (2009, September 9). *CNN Larry King Live.* [Television program]. Retrieved from http://transcripts.cnn.com/TRANSCRIPTS/0909/09/lkl.01.htm

Read, B. (2005, March 18). Seriously, iPods are educational. *The Chronicle of Higher Education.* Retrieved from http://www.chronicle.com

Rehling, D. L. (2008). Compassionate listening: A framework for listening to the seriously ill. *International Journal of Listening, 22*(1), 83–89.

Reis, H. T. (1998). Gender differences in intimacy and related behaviors: Context and process. In D. J. Canary & K. Dindia (Eds.), *Sex differences and similarities in communication: Critical essays and empirical investigations of sex and gender in interaction* (pp. 203–231). Hillsdale, NJ: Erlbaum.

Rempel, J., Holmes, J., & Zanna, M. (1985). Trust in close relationships. *Journal of Personality and Social Psychology, 49,* 95–112.

Rheingold, H. (2002). *Smart mobs: The next social revolution.* New York: Basic Books.

Richmond, V. P., McCroskey, J. C., & Payne, S. K. (1991). *Nonverbal behavior in interpersonal relations.* Englewood Cliffs, NJ: Prentice Hall.

Richmond, V. P., Smith, R. S., Jr., Heisel, A. D., & McCroskey, J. C. (2001). Nonverbal immediacy in the physician-patient relationship. *Communication Research Reports, 18,* 211–216.

Richmond, V., & McCroskey, J. C. (1998). *Communication apprehension, avoidance, and effectiveness* (5th ed.). Boston: Allyn & Bacon.

Richtel, M. (2010, June 6). Attached to technology and paying a price. *The New York Times,* p. A1.

Ridge, S. B. (2007). Balance: The new workplace perk. *Forbes.* Retrieved May 14, 2008, from http://www.forbes.com

Rill, L., Baiocchi, E., Hopper, M., Denker, K., & Olson, L. N. (2009). Exploration of the relationship between self-esteem, commitment, and verbal aggressiveness in romantic dating relationships. *Communication Reports, 22*(2), 102–113.

Riordan, M. A., & Kreuz, R. J. (2010). Cues in computer-mediated communication: A corpus analysis. *Computers in Human Behavior, 26,* 1806–1817.

Robbins, L. (2010, June 20). BP chief draws outrage for attending yacht race. *The New York Times,* p. A20.

Roberto, A., Carlyle, K. E., Goodall, C. E., & Castle, J. D. (2009). The relationship between parents' verbal aggressiveness and responsiveness and young adult children's attachment style and relational satisfaction with parents. *Journal of Family Communication, 9*(2), 90–106.

Roberts, S. (2010, November 19). Unlearning to tawk like a New Yorker. *The New York Times.* Retrieved from http://www.nytimes.com/2010/11/21/nyregion/21accent.html

Rogers Commission. (1986, June 6). *Report of the presidential commission on the space shuttle* Challenger *accident.* Retrieved from http://science.ksc.nasa.gov/shuttle/missions/51-l/docs/rogers-commission/Chapter-5.txt

Roloff, M. E. (1980). Self-awareness and the persuasion process: Do we really know what we are doing? In M. E. Roloff & G. Miller (Eds.), *Persuasion: New directions in theory and research* (pp. 29–66). Beverly Hills, CA: Sage Publications.

Rose, G., Evaristo, R., & Staub, D. (2003). Culture and consumer responses to Web download time: A four-continent stoudy of mono and polychronism. *IEEE Transaction on Engineering Management, 50*(1), 31–44.

Rosen, M. (2004, February). Can you truly trust an office friend? When to share and when to shy away—a guide to getting along with your workplace pals (on the job). *Good Housekeeping,* 56.

Rosenbloom, S. (2006, August 10). Please don't make me go on vacation. *The New York Times.* Retrieved from http://www.nytimes.com

Rosener, J. (1990). Ways women lead. *Harvard Business Review, 68,* 119–125.

Rosenthal, M. J. (2001). High-performance teams. *Executive Excellence, 18,* 6.

Ross, L., & Nisbett, R. E. (1991). *The person and the situation: Perspectives of social psychology.* Philadelphia: Temple University Press.

Rothman, A. J., Salovey, P., Turvey, C., & Fishkin, S. A. (1993). Attributions or responsibility and persuasion: Increasing mammography utilization among women over 40 with an internally oriented message. *Health Psychology, 12,* 39–47.

Roup, C. M., & Chiasson, K. E. (2010). Effect of dichotic listening on self-reported state anxiety. *International Journal of Audiology, 49*(2), 88–94.

Ruben, B. D. (2005). Linking communication scholarship and professional practice in colleges and universities. *Journal of Applied Communication Research, 33,* 294–304.

Rubin, A. M., Perse, E. M., & Powell, R. A. (1985). Loneliness, parasocial interaction, and local television news viewing. *Human Communication Research, 12,* 155–180.

Rubin, D. L., Hafer, T., & Arata, K. (2000). Reading and listening to oral-based versus literate-based discourse. *Communication Education, 49,* 121–133.

Rushton, J. P. (1980). *Altruism, socializiation, and society.* Englewood Cliffs, NJ: Prentice Hall.

Rushton, J. P. (1990). Sir Francis Galton, epigenetic rules, genetic similarity theory, and human life-history analysis. *Journal of Personality, 58,* 117–140.

Russell, J. E., & Adams, D. M. (1997). The changing nature of mentoring in organizations: An introduction to the special issue on mentoring in organizations. *Journal of Vocational Behavior, 51,* 1–14.

Rutherford, S. (2001). Any difference? An analysis of gender and divisional management styles in a large airline. *Gender, Work and Organization, 8*(3), 326–345.

Sahlstein, E., Maguire, K. C., & Timmerman, L. (2009). Contradictions and praxis contextualized by wartime deployment: Wives' perspectives revealed through relational dialectics. *Communication Monographs, 76*(4), 421–442.

Salazar, A. J. (1996). An analysis of the development and evolution of roles in the small group. *Small Group Research, 27,* 475–503.

Salkever, A. (2003, April 24). Home truths about meetings. *Business Week.* Retrieved from http://www.businessweek.com

Samovar, L. A., Porter, R. E., & McDaniel, E. R. (Eds.). (2009). *Intercultural communication: A reader.* Belmont, CA: Wadsworth Cengage Learning.

Samovar, L. A., Porter, R. E., & Stefani, L. A. (1998). *Communication between cultures.* Belmont, CA: Wadsworth.

Samter, W. (2003). Friendship interaction skills across the life span. In J. O. Greene & B. R. Burleson (Eds.), *Handbook of communication and social interaction skills* (pp. 637–684). Mahwah, NJ: Erlbaum.

Sanford, K. (2010). Perceived threat and perceived neglect: Couples' underlying concerns during conflict. *Psychological Assessment, 22,* 288–297.

Sapir, E., & Whorf, B. L. (1956). The relation of habitual thought and behavior to language. In J. B. Carroll (Ed.), *Language, thought, and reality: Selected writings of Benjamin Lee Whorf* (pp. 134–159). Cambridge, MA: MIT Press.

Sarich, V., & Miele, F. (2004). *Race: The reality of human differences.* Boulder, CO: Westview Press.

Savage, D. (2010, September 23). Give 'em hope. *The Stranger.* Retrieved from http://www.thestranger.com/seattle/SavageLove?oid=4940874

Sawyer, C., & Behnke, R. (1990). The role of self-monitoring in the communication of public speaking anxiety. *Communication Reports, 3,* 70–74.

Sawyer, C., & Behnke, R. (1996). Public speaking anxiety and the communication of emotion. *World Communication, 25,* 21–30.

Sawyer, C., & Behnke, R. (2002). Behavioral inhibition and communication of public speaking state anxiety. *Western Journal of Communication, 66,* 412–422.

Scheerhorn, D., & Geist, P. (1997). Social dynamics in groups. In L. R. Frey & J. K. Barge (Eds.), *Managing group life: Communicating in decision-making groups* (pp. 81–103). Boston: Houghton Mifflin.

Schelbert, L. (2009). Pathways of human understanding: An inquiry into Western and North American Indian worldview structures. In L. A. Samovar, R. E. Porter, & E. R. McDaniel (Eds.), *Intercultural communication: A reader* (pp. 48–58). Belmont, CA: Wadsworth Cengage Learning.

Schenck v. United States, 249 U.S. 47 (1919).

Schofield, H. (2003, October). Jewish dad backs headscarf daughters. *BBC News.* Retrieved from http://news.bbc.co.uk/2/low/europe/3149588.stm

Schofield, T., Parke, R., Castañeda, E., & Coltrane, S. (2008). Patterns of gaze between parents and children in European American and Mexican American families. *Journal of Nonverbal Behavior, 32*(3), 171–186.

Schrodt, P. (2009). Family strength and satisfaction as functions of family communication. *Communication Quarterly, 57*(2), 171–186.

Schrodt, P., & Wheeless, L. R. (2001). Aggressive communication and informational reception apprehension: The influence of listening anxiety and intellectual inflexibility on trait argumentativeness and verbal aggressiveness. *Communication Quarterly, 49,* 53–69.

Schrodt, P., Wheeless, L. R., & Ptacek, K. M. (2000). Informational reception apprehension, educational motivation, and achievement. *Communication Quarterly, 48,* 60–73.

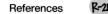

Schroeder, L. (2002). The effects of skills training on communication satisfaction and communication anxiety in the basic speech course. *Communication Research Reports, 19,* 380–388.

Schullery, N. M., & Gibson, M. K. (2001). Working in groups: Identification and treatment of students' perceived weaknesses. *Business Communication Quarterly, 64,* 9–30.

Schulman, P. R. (1996). Heroes, organizations, and high reliability. *Journal of Contingencies and Crisis Management, 4,* 72–82.

Schweitzer, T. (2007). *Seven out of 10 employees admit to abusing office computers, phones.* Retrieved May 13, 2008, from http://www.inc.com

Scott, W. R. (1981). *Organizations: Rational, natural, and open systems.* Englewood Cliffs, NJ: Prentice Hall.

Scully, M. (2005, February 2). Building a better State of the Union address. *The New York Times.* Retrieved from http://www.nytimes.com

Secret of the wild child [Transcript]. (1997, March 4). *Nova.* Public Broadcasting System. Retrieved March 25, 2008, from http://www.pbs.org/wgbh/nova/transcripts/2112gchild.html

Segrin, C., Hanzal, A., & Domschke, T. J. (2009). Accuracy and bias in newlywed couples' perceptions of conflict styles and the association with marital satisfaction. *Communication Monographs, 76,* 207–233.

Segrin, C., & Passalacqua, S. A. (2010). Functions of loneliness, social support, health behaviors, and stress in association with poor health. *Health Communication, 25*(4), 312–322.

Seidler, D. (2011, February 27). Acceptance speech presented at the 83rd Annual Academy of Motion Picture Arts and Sciences Awards, Hollywood, CA.

Shachaf, P., & Hara, N. (2010). Beyond vandalism: Wikipedia trolls. *Journal of Information Science, 36*(3), 357–370.

Shannon, C. E., & Weaver, W. (1949). *The mathematical theory of communication.* Urbana: University of Illinois Press.

Shannon, M., & Stark, C. (2003). The influence of physical appearance on personnel selection. *Social Behavior & Personality: An International Journal, 31*(6), 613.

Sherif, C. W., Sherif, M. S., & Nebergall, R. E. (1965). *Attitude and attitude change.* Philadelphia: W. B. Saunders.

Sherif, M., & Sherif, C. W. (1967). Attitude as the individual's own categories: The social judgment-involvement approach to attitude and attitude change. In C. W. Sherif & M. Sherif (Eds.), *Attitude, ego-involvement, and change* (pp. 105–139). New York: Wiley.

Shotter, J. (2009). Listening in a way that recognizes/realizes the world of "the other." *International Journal of Listening, 23*(1), 21–43.

Shuangyue, Z., & Merolla, A. J. (2006). Communicating dislike of close friends' romantic partners. *Communication Research Reports, 23*(3), 179–186.

Shultz, B. G. (1999). Improving group communication performance: An overview of diagnosis and intervention. In L. Frey, D. Gouran, & M. Poole (Eds.), *Handbook of group communication theory and research* (pp. 371–394). Thousand Oaks, CA: Sage Publications.

Sides, C. H. (2000). Ethics and technical communication: The past quarter century. *Journal of Technical Writing and Communication, 30,* 27–30.

Siegler, M. G. (2010, August 4). Schmidt talks Wave's death: "We celebrate our failures." *Tech Crunch.* Retrieved from http://techcrunch.com/2010/08/04/google-wave-eric-schmidt

Sinickas, A. (2000). How many focus groups do you need? *Total Communication Measurement, 2,* 11.

Siple, L. (2003). American Sign Language communication. *Signing Resources.* Retrieved April 26, 2007, from http://www.signingresources.net/deaf_connect_understanding_culture.html

Slutkin, G. (2011, February 9). The homicide that didn't happen. *The Chicago Tribune.* Retrieved from http://articles.chicagotribune.com/2011-02-09/news/ct-oped-0209-violence-20110209_1_murder-rate-violence-interrupters-homicide.

Smith, A. (2010a, August 11). *Home broadband 2010.* Pew Research Center Internet & American Life Project Report. Retrieved from http://www.pewinternet.org/Reports/2010/Home-Broadband-2010.aspx.

Smith, A. (2010b, July 7). *Mobile access 2010.* Pew Research Center Internet & American Life Project Report. Retrieved from http://www.pewinternet.org/Reports/2010/Mobile-Access-2010.aspx

Smith, P. (2005, February 11). Bullies incorporated. *Sydney Morning Herald.* Retrieved from http://www.smh.com.au

Smith, R. E. (1993). Clustering: A way to discover speech topics. *The Speech Teacher, 7*(2), 6–7.

Smith, R., Jr. (2004). Recruit the student: Adapting persuasion to audiences. *Communication Teacher, 18,* 53–56.

Smith, T. E., & Frymier, A. B. (2006). Get "real": Does practicing speeches before an audience improve performance? *Communication Quarterly, 54,* 111–125.

Snyder, B. (2003, May). Teams that span time zones face new work rules. *Stanford Business Magazine.* Retrieved from http://www.gsb.stanford.edu

Snyder, M. (1974). Self-monitoring of expressive behavior. *Journal of Personality and Social Psychology, 30,* 526–537.

Snyder, M. (1979). Self-monitoring processes. In L. Berkowitz (Ed.), *Advances in social psychology* (Vol. 12, pp. 86–128). New York: Academic Press.

Snyder, M., & Klein, O. (2005). Construing and constructing others: On the reality and the generality of the behavioral confirmation scenario. *Interaction Studies, 6,* 53–67.

Sobkowicz, P., & Sobkowicz, A. (2010). Dynamics of hate based networks. *The European Physical Journal B—Condensed Matter and Complex Systems, 73*(4), 633–643.

Sokol, R. I., Webster, K. L., Thompson, N. S., & Stevens, D. A. (2005). Whining as mother-directed speech. *Infant and Child Development, 14,* 478–486.

Sonnenfeld, J. (2011, January 23). The genius dilemma. *Newsweek.* Retrieved from http://www.newsweek.com/2011/01/23/the-genius-dilemma.html

Stafford, L. (2003). Summarizing and questioning Canary and Stafford's model of relational maintenance. In D. Danary & M. Dainton (Eds.), *Maintaining relationships through communication* (pp. 51–77). Mahwah, NJ: Erlbaum.

Stafford, L. (2005). *Maintaining long-distance and cross-residential relationships.* Mahway, NJ: Laurence Erlbaum Associates.

Stafford, L. (2010). Geographic distance and communication during courtship. *Communication Research, 37*(2), 275–297.

Standage, T. (2005). *A history of the world in six glasses.* New York: Walker.

Stearns, P. N., & Knapp, M. (1996). Historical perspectives on grief. In R. Harre & W. G. Parrott (Eds.), *The emotions: Social, cultural and biological dimensions* (pp. 151–170). Thousand Oaks, CA: Sage Publications.

Steil, L. K., Barker, L. L., & Watson, K. W. (1983). *Effective listening: Key to success.* Reading, MA: Addison-Wesley.

Steil, L. K., Summerfield, J., & de Mare, G. (1983). *Listening: It can change your life.* New York: Wiley.

Steinberg, B. (2010). Swearing during family hour? Who gives a $#*! *Advertising Age, 81*(22), 2–20.

Steinberg, J. (2010a, November 15). How clickers work. *The New York Times.* Retrieved from http://www.nytimes.com/2010/11/16/education/16clickerside.html

Steinberg, J. (2010b, November 15). More professors give out hand-held devices to monitor students and engage them. *The New York Times.* Retrieved from http://www.nytimes.com/2010/11/16/education/16clickers.html?ref=education

Stephens, K. K., & Davis, J. (2009). The social influences on electronic multitasking in organizational meetings. *Management Communication Quarterly, 23*(1), 63–83.

Steptoe, S. (2006, January 8). Q&A: Defining a new deficit disorder. *Time.com.* Retrieved from http://www.time.com/time/health/article/0,8599,1147207,00.html

Sternberg, R. J. (1988). *The triangle of love: Intimacy, passion, commitment.* New York: Basic Books.

Stevens, D. (2007, March 23). Television without pity: Will corporate ownership ruin a cult Web site? *Slate.* Retrieved from http://www.slate.com/id/2162470

Stewart, C. J., & Cash, W. B., Jr. (2006). *Interviewing: Principles and practices* (11th ed.). New York: McGraw-Hill.

Stewart, C. J., & Cash, W. B., Jr. (2011). *Interviewing: Principles and practices* (12th ed.). New York: McGraw-Hill.

Stewart, L. P., Cooper, P. J., & Steward, A. D. (2003). *Communication and gender.* Boston: Pearson Education.

Stewart, R. A. (1994). Perceptions of a speaker's initial credibility as a function of religious involvement and religious disclosiveness. *Communication Research Reports, 11,* 169–176.

Stiff, J. B., & Mongeau, P. (2003). *Persuasive communication.* New York: Guilford Press.

Stillion Southard, B. F., & Wolvin, A. D. (2009). Jimmy Carter: A case study in listening leadership. *International Journal of Listening, 23*(2), 141–152.

Stollen, J., & White, C. (2004). The link between labels and experience in romantic relationships among young adults. Paper presented at the International Communication Association, New Orleans Sheraton, New Orleans, LA, LA Online.

Stommel, W., & Koole, T. (2010). The online support group as a community: A micro-analysis of the interaction with a new member. *Discourse Studies, 12*(3), 357–378.

Sugihara, Y., & Katsurada, E. (2002). Gender role development in Japanese culture: Diminishing gender role differences in a contemporary society. *Sex Roles, 47*(9/10), 443–52.

Sugitani, Y. (2007). Why is it easier to communicate by e-mail? CMC contributes to the self-presentation efficacy. *The Japanese Journal of Social Psychology, 22*(3), 234–244.

Suler, J. (2007). The psychology of cyberspace. Retrieved December 26, 2007, from http://www-usr.rider.edu/~suler/psycyber/psycyber.html (Original work published 1996)

Sullivan, L. (2006, July 26). In U.S. prisons, thousands spend years in isolation [Audio podcast]. In *All Things Considered.* Retrieved from http://www.npr.org/templates/story/story.php?storyId=5582144

Susan G. Komen 3-Day for the Cure (2011a). *Thank you* [Informational video]. Retrieved from http://www.the3day.org

Susan G. Komen 3-Day for the Cure (2011b). *Why walk 60 miles?* [Informational video]. Retrieved from http://www.the3day.org

Sutton, S. R. (1982). Fear arousal and communication: A critical examination of theories and research. In J. Eiser (Ed.), *Social psychology and behavioral medicine* (pp. 303–337). Chichester, UK: Wiley.

Suzuki, B. H. (2002). Revisiting the model minority stereotype: Implications for student affairs practice and higher education. *New Directions for Student Services, 97,* 21.

Sybers, R., & Roach, M. E. (1962). Clothing and human behavior. *Journal of Home Economics, 54,* 184–187.

Tajfel, H., & Turner, J. C. (1986). An integrative theory of intergroup conflict. In S. Worchel & W. Austin (Eds.), *Psychology of intergroup relations* (pp. 2–24). Chicago: Nelson-Hall.

Tannen, D. (1992). *You just don't understand: Women and men in conversation.* London: Virago Press.

Tannen, D. (2009). Framing and face: The relevance of the presentation of self to linguistic discourse analysis. *Social Psychology Quarterly, 72*(4), 300–305.

Tannen, D. (2010). Abduction and identity in family interaction: Ventriloquizing as indirectness. *Journal of Pragmatics, 42*(2), 307–316.

Tannen, D., Kendall, S., & Gorgon, C. (Eds.) (2007). *Family talk: Discourse and identity in four American families.* New York: Oxford University Press.

Tannenbaum, R., Weschler, I. R., & Massarik, F. (1961). *Leadership and organization.* New York: McGraw-Hill.

Tao, T. (2000, March 7). Caring for new mothers. *Shanghai Star.* Retrieved December 26, 2007, from http://app1.chinadaily.com.cn/star/history/00-03-07/l01-care.html

Taylor, P., & Keeter, S. (Eds.). (2010). Millennials: A portrait of generation next. Confident, connected, open to change. *PewResearch.* Retrieved from http://pewresearch.org/millennials/

Taylor, P., Morin, R., Cohn, D., & Wang, W. (2008, December 29). Who moves? Who stays put? Where's home? *PewResearch.* Retrieved from http://pewresearch.org/movers-and-stayers.pdf

TEDPrize. (2011). About the TED Prize. *TEDPrize: Wishes big enough to change the world.* Retrieved from http://www.tedprize.org/about-tedprize/

Teven, J. J. (2007a). Effects of supervisor social influence, nonverbal immediacy, and biological sex on employees' perceptions of satisfaction, liking, and supervisor credibility. *Communication Quarterly, 55,* 155–177.

Teven, J. J. (2007b). Teacher caring and classroom behavior: Relationships with student affect, teacher evaluation, teacher competence, and trustworthiness. *Communication Quarterly, 55,* 433–450.

Teven, J. J. (2008). An examination of perceived credibility of the 2008 presidential candidates: Relationships with believability, likeability, and deceptiveness. *Human Communication, 11,* 383–400.

Teven, J. J. (2010). The effects of supervisor nonverbal immediacy and power use on employees' ratings of credibility and affect for the supervisor. *Human Communication, 13,* 69–85.

Teven, J. J., & Hanson, T. L. (2004). The impact of teacher immediacy and perceived caring on teacher competence and trustworthiness. *Communication Quarterly, 52,* 39–53.

Teven, J. J., & McCroskey, J. C. (1997). The relationship of perceived teacher caring with student learning and teacher evaluation. *Communication Education, 46,* 1–9.

The Daily Show with Jon Stewart. (2009, August 12). Oliver-MBA ethics oath. Video retrieved from http://www.thedailyshow.com/watch/wed-august-12-2009/mba-ethics-oath

Theiss, J. A., Knobloch, L. K., Checton, M. G., & Magsamen-Conrad, K. (2009). Relationship characteristics associated with the experience of hurt in romantic relationships: A test of the relational turbulence model. *Human Communication Research, 35*(4), 588–615.

Thomas, A. P. (2006, January 31). The CSI effect: Fact or fiction. *The Yale Law Journal Online.* Retrieved from http://www.yalelawjournal.org/the-yale-law-journal-pocket-part/criminal-law-and-sentencing/the-csi-effect:-fact-or-fiction

Thomas, L. T., & Levine, T. R. (1994). Disentangling listening and verbal recall: Related but separate constructs? *Human Communication Research, 21,* 103–127.

Tidwell, L. C., & Walther, J. B. (2002). Computer-mediated communication effects on disclosure, impressions, and interpersonal evaluations: Getting to know one another a bit at a time. *Human Communication Research, 28*(3), 317–348.

Tierney, J. (2007, July 31). The whys of mating: 237 reasons and counting. *The New York Times,* p. F1.

Todd, T. L., & Levine, T. R. (1996). Further thoughts on recall, memory, and the measurement of listening: A rejoinder to Bostrom. *Human Communication Research, 23,* 306–308.

Tong, S. T. , Van Der Heide, B., Langwell, L., & Walther, J. B. (2008). Too much of a good thing? The relationship between number of friends and interpersonal impressions on Facebook. *Journal of Computer-Mediated Communication, 13*(3), 531–549.

Toobin, J. (2007, May 7). The CSI effect. *The New Yorker.* Retrieved from http://www.newyorker.com/reporting/2007/05/07/070507fa_fact_toobin

Torregrosa, L. L. (2010, August 31). Palin woos women and stirs up foes. *The New York Times.* Retrieved from http://www.nytimes.com/2010/09/01/us/01iht-letter.html

Tracy, J. L., & Robins, R. W. (2008). The nonverbal expression of pride: Evidence for cross-cultural recognition. *Journal of Personality & Social Psychology, 94*(3), 516–530.

Tracy, K. (2008). "Reasonable hostility": Situation-appropriate face-attack. *Journal of Politeness Research: Language, Behavior, Culture, 4*(2), 169–191.

Treaster, J. B. (2002, March 30). Home insurers frown on many dogs. *The New York Times.* Retrieved from http://www.nytimes.com

Triandis, H. C. (1986). Collectivism vs. individualism: A reconceptualization of a basic concept in cross-cultural psychology. In C. Bagley & G. Verma (Eds.), *Personality, cognition, and values: Cross-cultural perspectives of childhood and adolescence.* London: Macmillan.

Triandis, H. C. (1988). Collectivism vs. individualism. In G. Verma & C. Bagley (Eds.), *Cross-cultural studies of personality, attitudes, and cognition.* London: Macmillan.

Triandis, H. C. (2000). Culture and conflict. *The International Journal of Psychology, 35*(2), 1435–1452.

Triandis, H. C., Brislin, R., & Hul, C. H. (1988). Cross-cultural training across the individualism-collectivism divide. *International Journal of Intercultural Relations, 12,* 269–289.

Tripathy, J. (2010). How gendered is gender and development? Culture, masculinity, and gender difference. *Development in Practice, 20*(1), 113–121.

Troester, R. L., & Mester, C. S. (2007). *Civility in business and professional communication.* New York: Peter Lang Publishing.

Tsa, W. C., Chen, C. C., & Chiu, S. F. (2005). Exploring boundaries of the effects of applicant impression management tactics in job interviews. *Journal of Management, 31*(1), 108–125.

Tuckman, B. (1965). Developmental sequences in small groups. *Psychological Bulletin, 63,* 384–399.

Tufte, E. (2003, September). PowerPoint is evil: Power corrupts; PowerPoint corrupts absolutely. *Wired.* Retrieved from http://www.wired.com/wired/archive/11.09/ppt2.html

Tyson, N. D. (2009, February 17). *Is the universe infinite?* Speech presented at the University of Texas, Arlington. Retrieved from http://www.youtube.com/watch?v=yD1qA Eeyets&feature=related

U.S. Department of Health & Human Services, Office of the Surgeon General. (2007). *Overweight in children and adolescents.* Retrieved from http://www.surgeongeneral.gov/topics/obesity/calltoaction/fact_adolescents.htm

U.S. Department of Justice, Federal Bureau of Investigation. (2010, September). *Crime in the United States, 2009.* Retrieved from http://www2.fbi.gov/ucr/clus2009/index.html

U.S. Equal Employment Opportunity Commission. (2011). Sexual harassment charges. Retrieved from http://www.eeoc.gov/eeoc/statistics/enforcement/sexual_harassment.cfm

Van Zandt, T. (2004). Information overload and a network of targeted communication. *RAND Journal of Economics, 35,* 542–561.

Vangelisti, A., & Banski, M. (1993). Couples' debriefing conversations: The impact of gender, occupation, and demographic characteristics. In *Family relations* (Vol. 42, pp. 149–157).

Victor, D. A. (1992). *International business communication.* New York: HarperCollins.

Vijayasiri, G. (2008). Reporting sexual harassment: The importance of organizational culture and trust. *Gender Issues, 25*(1), 43–61.

Villaume, W. A., & Brown, M. H. (1999). The development and validation of the vocalic sensitivity test. *International Journal of Listening, 13,* 24–45.

Vogel, D. R., Dickson, G. W., & Lehman, J. A. (1986). Persuasion and the role of visual presentation support: The UM/3M study (MISRC-WP-86-11), Minneapolis, MN: University of Minnesota, Management Information Systems Research Center.

Von Raffler-Engel, W. (1983). *The perception of nonverbal behavior in the career interview.* Philadelphia: Benjamin.

Voss, B. (2010, December 22). Sibling revelry. *TheAdvocate.com.* Retrieved from http://www.advocate.com/Arts_and_Entertainment/Television/Sibling_Revelry/

Wade, N. (2010, January 12). Deciphering the chatter of monkeys and chimps. *The New York Times,* p. D1.

Wailgum, T. (2008, June 8). How Steve Jobs beats presentation panic. *CIO.com.* Retrieved from http://www.cio.com/article/596271/How_Steve_Jobs_Beats_Presentation_Panic

Waldron, V. R., & Applegate, J. A. (1998). Effects of tactic similarity on social attraction and persuasiveness in dyadic verbal disagreements. *Communication Reports, 11,* 155–166.

Walker, A. (1982). *The color purple.* New York: Harcourt Brace Jovanovich.

Wallace, A., Wallace, I., & Wallechinsky, D. (2004). *The book of lists.* New York: Bantam Books.

Wallis, C. (2006, March 27). The multitasking generation. *Time,* 48–55.

Walther, J. B. (1996). Computer-mediated communication: Impersonal, interpersonal, and hyperpersonal interaction. *Communication Research, 23,* 3–43.

Walther, J. B. (2004). Language and communication technology: Introduction to the special issue. *Journal of Language and Social Psychology, 23,* 384–396.

Walther, J. B., & Parks, M. R. (2002). Cues filtered out, cues filtered in: Computer-mediated communication and relationships. In M. L. Knapp & J. A. Daly (Eds.), *Handbook of interpersonal communication* (pp. 529–563). Thousand Oaks, CA: Sage Publications.

Walther, J. B., & Ramirez Jr., A. (2009). New technologies and new directions in online relating. In S. W. Smith & S. R. Wilson (Eds.), *New directions in interpersonal communication research* (pp. 264–284). Newbury Park, CA: Sage Publications.

Walther, J. B., Van Der Heide, B., Kim, S-Y., Westerman, D., & Tong, S. T. (2008). The role of friends' appearance and behavior on evaluations of individuals on Facebook: Are we known by the company we keep? *Human Communication Research, 34*(1), 28–49.

Walther, J. B., Van Der Heide, B., Tong, S. T., Carr, C. T., & Atkin, C. K. (2010). Effects of interpersonal goals on inadvertent intrapersonal influence in computer-mediated communication. *Human Communication Research, 36*(3), 323–347.

Wang, G., & Liu, Z. (2010). What collective? Collectivism and relationalism from a Chinese perspective. *Chinese Journal of Communication, 3*(1), 42–63.

Wasserman, B., & Weseley, A. (2009). ¿Qué? Quoi? Do languages with grammatical gender promote sexist attitudes? *Sex Roles, 61*(9/10), 634–643.

Watson, K. W., & Barker, L. L. (1984). Listening behavior: Definition and measurement. In R. N. Bostrom (Ed.), *Communication yearbook 8.* Beverly Hills, CA: Sage Publications.

Watson, K., Barker, L., & Weaver, J. (1995). The listening styles profile (LSP-16): Development and validation of an instrument to assess four listening styles. *International Journal of Listening, 9,* 1–13.

Weger, H., Jr., Castle, G. R., & Emmett, M. C. (2010). Active listening in peer interviews: The influence of message paraphrasing on perceptions of listening skill. *International Journal of Listening, 24*(1), 34–49.

Weisz, C., & Wood, L. F. (2005). Social identity support and friendship outcomes: A longitudinal study predicting who will be friends and best friends 4 years later. *Journal of Social and Personal Relationships, 22,* 416–432.

Werner, J. (2011, February 16). Bucks County teacher suspended for "lazy whiners" comments defends herself in new blog. *The Trentonian*. Retrieved from http://www.trentonian.com

West, A. (2007, August 20). Facebook labeled a $5b waste of time. *Sydney Morning Herald*. Retrieved May 13, 2008, from http://www.smh.com.au

Westmyer, S., DiCioccio, R., & Rubin, R. (1998). Appropriateness and effectiveness of communication channels in competent interpersonal communication. *Journal of Communication, 48,* 27–48.

Wheelan, S. (1994). *Group process: A developmental perspective.* Boston: Allyn & Bacon.

Wheeless, L. R. (1975). An investigation of receiver apprehension and social context dimensions of communication apprehension. *Speech Teacher, 24*(3), 261–268.

Wherfritz, G., Kinetz, E., & Kent, J. (2008, April 21). Lured into bondage: A growing back channel of global trade tricks millions into forced labor. *Newsweek*. Retrieved from http://www.newsweek.com/id/131707

White House, Office of the Press Secretary. (2011, January 12). Remarks by the president at a memorial service for the victims of the shooting in Tucson, Arizona [Press release]. Retrieved from http://www.whitehouse.gov/the-press-office/2011/01/12/remarks-president-barack-obama-memorial-service-victims-shooting-tucson

Why most meetings stink. (2005, October 31). *Business Week*. Retrieved from http://www.businessweek.com

Wiemann, J. M. (1977). Explication and test of a model of communication competence. *Human Communication Research, 3,* 195–213.

Wiemann, J. M., & Backlund, P. M. (1980). Current theory and research in communication competence. *Review of Educational Research, 50,* 185–189.

Wiemann, J. M., & Knapp, M. L. (1999). Turn-taking in conversations. In L. K. Guerrero, J. A. DeVito, & M. L. Hecht (Eds.), *The nonverbal communication reader: Classic and contemporary readings* (pp. 406–414). Prospect Heights, IL: Waveland Press.

Wiemann, J. M., & Krueger, D. L. (1980). The language of relationships. In H. Giles, W. P. Robinson, & P. M. Smith (Eds.), *Language: Social psychological perspectives* (pp. 55–62). Oxford: Pergamon Press.

Wiemann, J. M., Takai, J., Ota, H., & Wiemann, M. O. (1997). A relational model of communication competence. In B. Kovčaić (Ed.), *Emerging theories of human communication* (pp. 25–44). Albany, NY: State University of New York Press.

Wiemann, J. M., & Wiemann, M. O. (1992). *Interpersonal communicative competence: Listening and perceiving.* Unpublished manuscript, University of California–Santa Barbara.

Wiemann, M. O. (2009). *Love you/hate you: Negotiating intimate relationships.* Barcelona, Spain: Editorial Aresta.

Wierzbicka, A. (2006). *English: Meaning and culture.* New York: Oxford.

Wiesenfeld, D., Bush, K., & Sikdar, R. (2010). The value of listening: Heeding the call of the Snuggie. *Journal of Advertising Research, 50*(1), 16–20.

Wilde, M. (2008, January). Do uniforms make schools better? *GreatSchools*. Retrieved April 16, 2008, from http://www.greatschools.net/cgi-bin/showarticle/ga/361

Willard, G., & Gramzow, R. (2008). Exaggeration in memory: Systematic distortion of self-evaluative information under reduced accessibility. *Journal of Experimental Social Psychology, 44*(2), 246–259.

Williams, A. (2005, Summer). "Doing the month": Ancient tradition meets modern motherhood. *Urban Baby and Toddler*. Retrieved December 26, 2007, from http://www.urbanbaby.ca/postpartum.htm#Doing

Williams, D., Consalvo, M., Caplan, S., & Yee, N. (2009). Looking for gender: Gender roles and behaviors among online gamers. *Journal of Communication, 59*(4), 700–725.

Williams, K. N., Herman, R., Gajewski, B., & Wilson, K. (2009). Elderspeak communication: Impact on dementia care. *American Journal of Alzheimer's Disease & Other Dementias, 24*(1), 11–20.

Williams, D. E., & Hughes, P. C. (2005). Nonverbal communication in Italy: An analysis of interpersonal touch, body position, eye contact, and seating behaviors. *North Dakota Journal of Speech & Theatre, 18,* 17–24.

Williams, P. (1993). Surveillance hurts productivity, deprives employees of rights. *Advertising Age, 64,* 14.

Wilmot, W. W. (1987). *Dyadic communication* (3rd ed.). New York: Random House.

Winston, C. (2002, January 28). State of the Union stew. *The Christian Science Monitor*. Retrieved from http://www.csmonitor.com

Winter, J., & Pauwels, A. (2006). Men staying at home looking after their children: Feminist linguistic reform and social change. *International Journal of Applied Linguistics, 16*(1), 16–36.

Witteman, H. (1993). The interface between sexual harassment and organizational romance. In G. Kreps (Ed.), *Sexual harassment: Communication implications* (pp. 27–62). Cresskill, NJ: Hampton Press.

Wolvin, A. D. (2006). Modeling listening scholarship: Ralph G. Nichols. *International Journal of Listening, 20,* 22–26.

Wolvin, A. D., & Coakley, C. G. (1991). A survey of the status of listening training in some *Fortune* 500 corporations. *Communication Education, 40,* 151–164.

Woo, E. (2011, March 13). Sam Chwat dies at 57; actors lost, and learned, accents under dialect coach's tutelage. *Los Angeles Times*. Retrieved from http://articles.latimes.com/2011/mar/13/local/la-me-sam-chwat-20110313

Wood, B. (1982). *Children and communication: Verbal and nonverbal language development* (2nd ed.). Englewood Cliffs, NJ: Prentice Hall.

Wood, J. T. (2008). Gender, communication, and culture. In L. A. Samovar, R. E. Porter, and E. R. McDaniel (Eds.), *Intercultural communication: A reader* (pp. 170–180). Belmont, CA: Wadsworth Cengage.

Wood, J. T. (2009). *Gendered lives: Communication, gender, and culture* (8th ed.). Boston, MA: Wadsworth Publishing.

Wood, J. T. (2011). *Gendered lives: Communication, gender, and culture* (9th ed.). Boston, MA: Wadsworth Publishing.

Woodzicka, J. (2008). Sex differences in self-awareness of smiling during a mock job interview. *Journal of Nonverbal Behavior, 32*(2), 109–121.

Wrench, J. S., McCroskey, J. C., & Richmond, V. P. (2008). *Human communication in everyday life: Explanations and applications.* Boston: Allyn & Bacon.

Wright, C. N., Holloway, A., & Roloff, M. E. (2007). The dark side of self-monitoring: How high self-monitors view their romantic relationships. *Communication Reports, 20*(2), 101–114.

Wright, J. W., & Ross, S. (1997). Trial by media? Media reliance, knowledge of crime and perception of criminal defendants. *Communication Law & Policy, 2*(4), 397–416.

Wyatt, E. (2009, November 14). More than ever, you can say that on television. *The New York Times,* p. A1.

Yaguchi, M., Iyeiri, Y., & Baba, Y. (2010). Speech style and gender distinctions in the use of *very* and *real/really.* An analysis of the Corpus of Spoken Professional American English. *Journal of Pragmatics, 42*(3), 585–597.

Yandrick, R. M. (2001). A team effort. *HR Magazine, 46,* 136–141.

Yasui, E. (2009, May). Collaborative idea construction: The repetition of gestures and talk during brainstorming. *A paper presented at the 59th meeting of the International Communication Association,* Chicago, IL.

Yee, N., & Bailenson, J. (2007). The Proteus effect: The effect of transformed self-representation on behavior. *Human Communication Research, 33*(3), 271–290.

Yoo, C. Y. (2007). Implicit memory measures for Web advertising effectiveness. *Journalism & Mass Communication Quarterly, 84*(1), 7–23.

Yook, E. (2004). Any questions? Knowing the audience through question types. *Communication Teacher, 18,* 91–93.

York, M. (2006, December 25). A place where sign language is far from foreign. *The New York Times,* p. B1.

Young, J., & Foot, K. (2005). Corporate e-cruiting: The construction of work in Fortune 500 recruiting Web sites. *Journal of Computer-Mediated Communication, 11*(1), 44–71.

Zacchilli, T. L., Hendrick, C., & Hendrick, S. S. (2009). The romantic partner conflict scale: A new scale to measure relationship conflict. *Journal of Social and Personal Relationships, 26*(8), 1073–1096.

Zeller, T., Jr. (2010, June 18). Drill ban means hard time for rig workers. *The New York Times,* p. B1.

Zimbushka (2008, May 27). *Mike Caro's 10 ultimate poker cues.* Retrieved from http://www.youtube.com/watch?v=QqF8m12JSDE

acknowledgments

Text Credits

Box 1.2: National Communication Association, "Credo for Ethical Communication." Copyright © 1999 by the National Communication Association. Reprinted with permission.

Figure 2.4: "Assessing Our Perceptions of Self." Adapted from Dan O'Hair et al., *Competent Communication*, second edition. Copyright © 1997 by Bedford/St. Martin's. Adapted with the permission of Bedford/St. Martin's.

Page 57: M. Snyder, "Self-Monitoring Test." Adapted from M. Snyder, "Self-monitoring and expressive behavior" in *Journal of Personality and Social Psychology* 30 (1974): 526–537. Copyright © 1974 by the American Psychological Association. Adapted with permission. The use of APA information does not imply endorsement by the APA.

Figure 4.1: "The Abstraction Ladder." Adapted from Dan O'Hair et al., *Competent Communication*, second edition. Copyright © 1997 by Bedford/St. Martin's. Adapted with the permission of Bedford/St. Martin's.

Table 5.1: "The Power of Eye Contact." Adapted from Dale G. Leathers, *Successful Verbal Communication: Principles and Applications*, third edition. Published by Allyn and Bacon, Boston, MA. Copyright © 1997 by Pearson Education. Adapted with the permission of the publisher.

Figure 5.2: "Four Zones of Personal Space." From Dan O'Hair et al., *Competent Communication*, second edition. Copyright © 1997 by Bedford/St. Martin's. Adapted with the permission of Bedford/St. Martin's.

Table 6.1: "Listening Goals." From Dan O'Hair et al., *Competent Communication*, second edition. Copyright © 1997 by Bedford/St. Martin's. Adapted with the permission of Bedford/St. Martin's.

Page 174: Lawrence R. Wheeless, "An Investigation of Receiver Apprehension and Social Context Dimensions of Communication Apprehension." *Communication Education*, January 9, 1975: 261–268. Copyright © 1975. Adapted with permission of Taylor & Francis, Ltd., www.informaworld.com.

Table 7.1: "Family Communication Qualities." From John Caughlin, "Family Communication Standards: What Counts as Excellent Family Communication, and How Are Such Standards Associated with Family Satisfaction?" from *Human Communication Research* 29 (2003): 5–40. Reprinted with the permission of John Wiley and Sons.

Table 7.4: "Termination Strategies for Romantic Relationships." Adapted from D. J. Canary and Michael J. Cody, *Interpersonal Communication: A Goals-Based Approach*. Copyright © 1994 by Bedford/St. Martin's. Adapted with the permission of Bedford/St. Martin's.

Page 239: "Self-Assessment: Hitting Above and Below the Belt." Dominic A. Infante. Reprinted with the permission of Waveland Press, Inc., from Dominic A. Infante, *Arguing Constructively* (Long Grove, IL: Waveland Press, 1988). All rights reserved.

Figure 9.1: "Complexity of Group Relationships." From Dan O'Hair et al., *Competent Communication*, second edition. Copyright © 1997 by Bedford/St. Martin's. Adapted with the permission of Bedford/St. Martin's.

Figure 9.2: "Group Communication Networks." From W. Richard Scott, *Organizations: Rational, Natural, and Open Systems*. Copyright © 1981 by Pearson Education. Reprinted with the permission of Pearson Education, Upper Saddle River, NJ.

Page 276: "How Well Do You Interact in a Group Setting?" Adapted from J. C. McCroskey (1982), *An Introduction to Rhetorical Communication* (4th ed., Englewood Cliffs, NJ: Prentice Hall). Reprinted with permission.

Figure 11.1: "A College or University System." From Dan O'Hair et al., *Competent Communication*, second edition. Copyright © 1997 by Bedford/St. Martin's. Adapted with the permission of Bedford/St. Martin's.

Figure 11.2: "Employee Survey of Appropriate Communication Channels for Organizational Tasks." From Deborah Fallows, "E-mail at Work." Pew Internet and American Life Project (April–May 2002). http://pewinternet.org/Reports/2002/Email-at-work.aspx. Reprinted with permission of Pew Research Center.

Page 331: "Are You Off Balance?" From "Having It All: Work/Life Balance" (August 1, 2007), © 2007. www.cnn.com/2007/LIVING/personal/07/30/wlb.quiz.balance/index.html. All rights reserved. Used by permission and protected by the Copyright Laws of the United States. The printing, copying, redistribution, or retransmission of this Content without express written permission is prohibited.

Page 344: Sample Speech 12.2: Ricky Martin. Speech presented at the Vienna Forum. Ricky Martin—President and Founder of Ricky Martin Foundation. Used with permission of Ricky Martin.

Page 345: Sample Speech 12.3: Excerpts from "Bruce Springsteen inducts U2 into the Rock and Roll Hall of Fame," March 17, 2005. www.u2station.com/news/archives/2005/03/transcript_bruc.php. Used with permission of Bruce Springsteen.

Table 12.1: "Personal Interests Topics." Adapted from D. O'Hair, R. Stewart, and H. Rubenstein, *A Speaker's Guidebook*, third edition. Copyright © 2007 by Bedford/St. Martin's. Adapted with the permission of Bedford/St. Martin's.

Figure 12.1: "Example of a Web of Associations Produced by Clustering." Adapted from Dan O'Hair et al., *Competent Communication*, second edition. Copyright © 1997 by Bedford/St. Martin's. Adapted with the permission of Bedford/St. Martin's.

Table 13.1: "Useful Signposts." From D. O'Hair, R. Stewart, and H. Rubenstein, *A Speaker's Guidebook*, third edition. Copyright © 2007 by Bedford/St. Martin's. Reprinted with the permission of Bedford/St. Martin's.

Table 13.3: "Useful Delivery Cues." Adapted from D. O'Hair, R. Stewart, and H. Rubenstein, *A Speaker's Guidebook*, third edition. Copyright © 2007 by Bedford/St. Martin's Press. Adapted with the permission of Bedford/St. Martin's Press.

Table 15.2: "Types of Informative Speeches, Sample Topics, Informational Strategies, and Organizational Patterns." From D. O'Hair, R. Stewart, and H. Rubenstein, *A Speaker's Guidebook*, third edition. Copyright © 2007 by Bedford/St. Martin's. Adapted with the permission of Bedford/St. Martin's.

Photo Credits

Cover photos: A portrait, © Francesca Durbano/Getty Images; Mother's Day, © Hulton Collections/Getty Images; Young boy with cap, © Thomas Grass/Getty Images; Woman leaning on headrest in convertible, © Thomas Barwick/Getty Images; Young man with afro standing on city sidewalk, © Shannon Fagan/Getty Images; Young man eating pizza in restaurant, © Aaron Farley/Getty Images; Street portrait of two friends holding hands, © Peter Boel Nielsen/Getty Images; Senior man with beard talking on the telephone, © Mary Hockenbery/Getty Images; Group portrait of firemen, © Smith Collection/Getty Images; Lincoln, Nebraska. An infant boy is lifted by his parents, © Joel Sartore/Getty Images; Couple posing, © MASSIVE/Getty Images; Businessman sitting in chair at desk smiling, © Thomas Barwick/Getty Images; Blond boy with arms crossed, © Marcus Lyon/Getty Images; Woman on snow-covered street wearing winter clothing, © Johner/Getty Images; Generations of women on cushion outdoors, © Century/Getty Images; Group of teenagers smiling, portrait, © Philip Lee Harvey/Getty Images; Businesswoman sitting at desk in office, © Thomas Barwick/Getty Images; Senior couple sitting on sofa listening to MP3 player, portrait, © Erin Patrice O'Brien/Getty Images; Businessman looking at camera, headshot, © Tony Metaxas/Getty Images; Man in baseball cap, © Tim Chumley/

Getty Images; Chef making notes on clipboard, © Smith Collection/Getty Images; Happy biker, © Jamel Toppin/Getty Images; Great Hall Market, Budapest, © Ian Spanier/Getty Images; An impromptu photo dance. Close up of happy mother and daughter, © Anita Anand/Getty Images; Skateboarder, blurred motion, © Michael Wong/Getty Images. **Page 2:** John Moore/Getty Images; **6:** (grid, L-R) © JoeFoxNewYork/Alamy, Carin Baer/© AMC/Courtesy Everett Collection, © Focus Features/Courtesy Everett Collection, Kevin Mazur/WireImage/Getty Images; **7:** Fox Film Corporation/Photofest; **9:** © David Grossman/The Image Works; **10:** Brian Bahr/Allsport/Getty Images; **12:** Jeff Kravitz/FilmMagic/Getty Images; **14:** (top) © 20th Century Fox Film Corp/Courtesy Everett Collection. All rights reserved, (bot) Chip Somodevilla/Getty Images; **16:** (top) Greg Gayne/© FOX/Courtesy Everett Collection, (bot) Chip Somodevilla/Getty Images; **25:** (L) © Mango Productions/Corbis, (R) © Robert Fried/Alamy; **27:** (L) Kablonk!/Photolibrary, (R) © Bonnie Kamin/PhotoEdit; **34:** Photo by Ken McKay/Rex USA, Courtesy Everett Collection; **37:** Chris Hondros/Getty Images; **38:** David Young-Wolff/PhotoEdit; **42:** (grid, L-R) Digital Vision/Getty Images, Michael Williamson/The Washington Post/Getty Images, PATRICK ANDRADE/Landov, Tom Shaw/Getty Images; **44:** AP Photo/Eric Gay; **45:** Skip Bolen/© HBO/Courtesy Everett Collection; **47:** (top) AP Photo/Pablo Martinez Monsivais, (bot) Paul Drinkwater/NBCU Photo Bank/AP Photo; **48:** Neilson Barnard/WireImage for New York Magazine/Getty Images; **49:** Patrick McElhenney/© FX/Courtesy Everett Collection; **51:** Kyodo via AP Images; **56:** Wathiq Khuzaie/Getty Images; **64:** Matthias Clamer/© Fox Television/Courtesy Everett Collection; **67:** (L) © Design Pics Inc./Alamy, (R) Knauer/Johnston/Getty Images; **68:** © NBC Universal, Inc./Photofest; **73:** Yellow Dog Productions/Getty Images; **75:** © BBC. Courtesy Everett Collection; **76:** © Gideon Mendel/Corbis; **79:** Kevin Mazur/WireImage/Getty Images; **83:** KEVIN DIETSCH/UPI/Landov; **85:** Ryan Sensenig/Photo Agora; **86:** Brendan Smialowski/Getty Images; **91:** Bob Daemmerich/The Image Works; **92:** (L) PhotoAlto/Eric Audras/Getty Images, (R) Clarissa Leahy/Getty Images; **96:** (grid, L-R) Getty Images, ABC/Photofest, Getty Images, © Martin Norris/Alamy, © Photofusion Picture Library/Alamy, Stockbyte/Getty Images; **99:** (L) Charles Shoffner/Index Stock/Jupiter Images, (R) Comstock/Jupiter Images; **101:** Rubberball/Jupiter Images; **102:** © Ian Middleton/Alamy; **104:** Phil Bray/© Screen Gems/Courtesy Everett Collection; **106:** Michael Sharkey/Getty Images; **111:** (L) © Beathan/Corbis, (R) © Stephanie Sinclair/Corbis; **114:** Adam Taylor/© CBS/Courtesy Everett Collection; **116:** Ronnie Kaufman/Larry Hirshowitz/Blend Images/Getty Images; **120:** © Foodcollection.com/Alamy; **122:** © Amit Bhargava/Corbis; **126:** © Walt Disney Co./courtesy Everett Collection; **129:** (L) Simon Baker/Getty Images, (R) AP Photo/Al Behrman; **130:** © Getty Images; **131:** © Sandy Felsenthal/Corbis; **134:** Hiroko Masuike/Getty Images; **136:** © Paramount. Courtesy Everett Collection; **138:** (top-bot) © ACE

STOCK LIMITED/Alamy, John Henley/Getty Images, Vladimir Godnik/Getty Images, © Image Source/Alamy, ColorBlind Images/Getty Images, © Image Source/Alamy; **139:** Patrick Jube/Getty Images; **140:** TLC/Photofest; **144:** MIKE ANSELL/CBS/Landov; **147:** Matt Campbell-Pool/Getty Images; **149:** AP Photo/The Advocate Messenger, Clay Jackson; **156:** Blend Images/Punchstock; **159:** Blend Images/Punchstock; **162:** ABC/Photofest; **165:** Photo by Michael Ochs Archives/Getty Images; **166:** Jeffrey R Staab/CBS via Getty Images; **167:** Juice Images/Punchstock; **169:** © vikki martin/Alamy; **171:** Imagestate/Photolibrary; **175:** © Warner Brothers/Courtesy Everett Collection; **178:** Fox/Photofest; **179:** Jetta Productions/Getty Images; **180:** © 20th Century Fox Film Corp. All rights reserved/Courtesy The Everett Collection; **186:** Harry How/Getty Images; **189:** TLC/Photofest; **191:** Frazer Harrison/Getty Images for AFI; **193:** (grid, L-R) Mike Powell/Getty Images, © John Birdsall/The Image Works, ZHAO YINGQUAN/Xinhua/Landov, Hola Images/Getty Images; **196:** © Bettmann/Corbis; **197:** Jonathan Wenk/© Columbia Pictures/Courtesy Everett Collection; **201:** CBS/Photofest; **204:** Myles Aronowitz/TM and copyright © 20th Century Fox Film Corp. All rights reserved/Courtesy Everett Collection; **207:** Byron J. Cohen/© NBC/Courtesy Everett Collection; **209:** BENOIT TESSIER/Reuters/Landov; **218:** Merrick Morton/© Columbia Pictures/Courtesy Everett Collection; **221:** DK Stock/Donn Thompson; **222:** © Warner Bros. Pictures/Courtesy Everett Collection; **224:** (top) ABC/Photofest, (bot) JIM RUYMEN/UPI/Landov; **227:** © NBC Photographer: Mitchell Haaseth/Photofest; **229:** © American Movie Classics/Courtesy Everett Collection; **232:** MANDALAY/SAINT AIRE/10TH HOLE/ANTIDOTE/THE KOBAL COLLECTION; **233:** © Rick Friedman/Corbis; **235:** Jennifer Durham/Jupiter Images; **237:** Creatas/Jupiter Images; **244:** John Lund/Drew Kelly/Getty Images; **251:** AP Photo/J. Scott Applewhite; **253:** © David Atlas/Retna; **255:** (grid, L-R) David Furst/AFP/Getty Images, © 20th Century Fox Film Corp. All rights reserved. Courtesy Everett Collection, AP Photo/Vail Daily, Shane Macomber, ABC/Photofest; **257:** Monty Brinton/CBS via Getty Images; **259:** (L) © Bob Mahoney/The Image Works, (R) AP Photo/Damian Dovarganes; **261:** ROBERT VOETS/CBS/Landov; **264:** AP Photo/Herbert Knosowski; **266:** ABC via Getty Images; **269:** © Hill Street Studios/Blend Images/age fotostock; **271:** © Bettmann/Corbis; **275:** Fox/Photofest; **277:** © Buena Vista Pictures/Courtesy Everett Collection; **280:** Mitchell Haaseth/© NBC/Photofest; **283:** © Universal Pictures/courtesy Everett Collection; **286:** © NBC/Photofest; **288:** Carin Baer/© FOX/Courtesy Everett Collection; **289:** © 20th Century Fox Film Corp. All rights reserved, Courtesy Everett Collection; **291:** (L) Image 100/Punchstock, (R) Blend Images/Punchstock; **294:** Punchstock; **295:** © 2007 Getty Images; **297:** © Warner Bros./Courtesy Everett Collection; **300:** © FOX/Photofest; **303:** Busco/Getty Images; **304:** Jon Feingersh/Getty Images; **308:** © Getty Images; **311:** (grid, L-R) Elena Rooraid/PhotoEdit, Inc.,

© Yuriko Nakao/Reuters/Corbis, © Jim Young/Reuters/Corbis, © Bob Rowan; Progressive Image/Corbis; **312:** © Warner Brothers/Courtesy Everett Collection; **313:** Tim Klein/Photodisc/Getty Images; **316:** Andy Kropa/Redux; **318:** © NBC Photographer: Mitchell Haaseth/Photofest; **320:** © Marty Heitner/The Image Works; **322:** © ABC/Photofest; **325:** (L) Image Source/Punchstock, (R) GoGo Images/Punchstock; **327:** © Jens Büttner/epa/Corbis; **328:** Tom Grill/Getty Images; **338:** Justin Sullivan/Getty Images; **342:** Marie Hansen/Time Life Pictures/Getty Images; **345:** © Michael Goulding/Orange County Register/Corbis; **347:** © Jeff Greenberg/Alamy; **350:** (L) ROGER L. WOLLENBERG/UPI/Landov, (R) AP Photo/Boris Heger, UNHCR; **352:** © Radius Images/Alamy; **358:** SMIRNOV VLADIMIR/ITAR-TASS/Landov; **360:** (L) www.bing.com, (R) Courtesy of Google; **367:** ©NMPFT/DHA/SSPL/The Image Works; **370:** Photo by Pete Souza/The White House via Getty Images; **373:** Comstock/Jupiter Images; **374:** © Caro/Alamy; **377:** THE KOBAL COLLECTION/DAVIS FILMS/BOLAND, JASIN; **379:** Jonathan Larsen/Veer; **381:** © ilbusca/istockphoto.com; **382:** © Bettmann/Corbis; **386:** Digital Vision/Getty Images; **387:** THE KOBAL COLLECTION/UNIVERSAL TV/WOLF FILM; **392:** © 20th Century Fox/Photofest; **394:** Michael Newman/PhotoEdit Inc.; **406:** © The Weinstein Company/Courtesy Everett Collection; **409:** Blend Images/Veer; **410:** © Blend Images/Alamy; **412:** BILL GREENBLATT/UPI/Landov; **413:** AP Photo/Robert F. Bukaty; **414:** Dreamworks/Photofest; **415:** (grid, L-R) Streeter Lecka/Getty Images, JJ/Getty Images, © Jeff Morgan education/Alamy, © Chris Kleponis/Zuma/Corbis; **416:** © ABC/Photofest; **421:** © Wally McNamee/Corbis; **424:** Fernando Castillo/LatinContent/Getty Images; **425:** Susana Gonzalez/AFP/Getty Images; **434:** Bryan Bedder/Getty Images; **437:** © Roger Ressmeyer/Corbis; **439:** (grid, L-R) Getty Images, © Buena Vista Pictures/Courtesy Everett Collection, TOSHIFUMI KITAMURA/AFP/Getty Images, imago stock&people/Newscom; **441:** (L) Digital Vision/Photolibrary, (R) NASA-KSC; **443:** (L) AP Photo/Nati Harnik, (R) AP Photo/Bill Haber; **445:** Courtesy Peggy Paul; **447:** Image Source/Getty Images; **449:** Claude Estebe/OnAsia.com; **450:** © factoria singular/Alamy; **452:** (L) Sire Records/Getty Images, (R) Kevin Winter/Getty Images; **456:** (L) Courtesy Everett Collection, (R) © Warner Bros./Courtesy Everett Collection; **457:** Justin Sullivan/Getty Images; **470:** Gustavo Caballero/Getty Images; **473:** Stephen Vaughan/© Warner Bros./Courtesy Everett Collection; **475:** © Bob Daemmrich/The Image Works; **476:** © Bettmann/Corbis; **479:** (grid, L-R) AP Photo/Jose Luis Magana, Getty Images, Josephine Soughan & Simon Pentleton/PYMCA/Jupiter Images, David Emmite/Getty Images, AFP/Getty Images; **482:** Saeed Adyani/© Lions Gate/Courtesy Everett Collection; **486:** (top) © The Meth Project, (bot) Eric Liebowitz/© TBS/Courtesy: Everett Collection; **487:** © Mark Makela/In Pictures/Corbis; **490:** RL Productions/Getty Images; **493:** Photodisc/Punchstock; **506:** © Comedy Central/courtesy Everett Collection; **509:** (grid, L-R) Roth

index